Knowledge and Power
in Muslim Societies

New Series at Gerlach Press

Studies in Islamic Intellectual History

ISSN: 2941-1491 (Print)

General Editors:
Elizabeth R. Alexandrin
University of Manitoba, alexandr@cc.umanitoba.ca
Kazuo Morimoto
University of Tokyo, morikazu@ioc.u-tokyo.ac.jp
Sajjad Rizvi
University of Exeter, S.H.Rizvi@exeter.ac.uk

As intellectual history emerges as a dominant paradigm across research in the humanities, and in order to draw new attention in the field of the study of Islam, this new series engages critically with issues of method, theory, and approach. Our vision is to continue to develop Islamic studies in this direction by presenting the most exciting recent studies in intellectual history across the fields of philosophy, history and historiography, mysticism, legal theory, theology, the study of the Qurʾan and hadith, exegesis, and the study of religion, in short all aspects of the intellectual activity and production by Muslims and in Islamicate contexts. These studies will interrogate questions that cut across social, political, spiritual, and cultural phenomena with a focus on ideas as the critical dynamic of historical analysis. We seek to inform broader debates on the study of Islam and religion, across cultural contexts and diachronically across periods and epochs.

We particularly welcome studies that bring intellectual history into conversation with other fields in the spirit of multi-disciplinarity. The series includes multi-authored collections of studies united by theme, purpose, and method as well as learned individual monographs that examine an idea, a personality, or a tendency in a thick description.

Already Published:

Volume 1 (2023)
Knowledge and Power in Muslim Societies: Approaches in Intellectual History
Edited by Kazuo Morimoto and Sajjad Rizvi
ISBN: 978-3-95994-164-8 (HC)
ISBN: 978-3-95994-165-5 (eBook)

Knowledge and Power in Muslim Societies: Approaches in Intellectual History

Edited by Kazuo Morimoto and Sajjad Rizvi

GerlachPress

First published 2023
by Gerlach Press
Berlin, Germany
www.gerlachpress.com

Cover Design: Frauke Schön, Hamburg
Set by Anne Jeschke, Gerlach Press
Printed and bound in Germany

British Library Cataloguing in Publication Data.
A catalogue record for this book is available from the British Library.

Bibliographic data available from Deutsche Nationalbibliothek
http://d-nb.info/128103228X

Volume 1
Studies in Islamic Intellectual History
ISSN: 2941-1491
ISBN: 978-3-95994-164-8 (HC)
ISBN: 978-3-95994-165-5 (eBook)

Contents

Foreword vii
Ian Richard Netton

Introduction:
Diversifying the Intellectual History of Islam and Muslim Cultures 1
Sajjad Rizvi and Kazuo Morimoto

PHILOSOPHY

1 Three Portraits of a Philosopher in Islamic Cultures 15
Sajjad Rizvi

2 Philosophy for Politics: Ancient Greek Philosophy Echoed in Ibn al-Muqaffaʿ's Writings 53
István T. Kristó-Nagy

3 The Sorcerer Scholar: Sirāj al-Dīn al-Sakkākī between Grammar and Grimoire 95
Emily Selove and Mohammed Sanad

4 Knowledge for All: Zayn al-Dīn al-Kaššī (d. before 1228) on Philosophical Writing 121
Hisashi Obuchi

5 Cancelling the Apocalypse: Refracted Anticipation for the Awaited Mahdī in Sayyid Muḥammad al-Mushaʿshaʿ's Discourse 147
Tetsuro Sumida

SCHOLARLY PRODUCTION

6 Didactic Discourse and Sarcastic Expressions in the Context of Abū Hilāl al-ʿAskarī's Literary Criticism 175
Mohammed Sanad

7 Writing the Imams' Virtues under the Interconfessional Policy of al-Nāṣir li-Dīn Allāh: Ibn al-Biṭrīq al-Ḥillī and His *Faḍā'il* Works 193
Ryo Mizukami

8 A Jaʿfarid-Zaynabid Genealogy from Thirteenth-Century Egypt: *ʿUrbān* Uprising, Najafi Connection, and the Representation of the Twelve Imams 221
Kazuo Morimoto

9 *ʿIlm al-Siyāq* and Bureaucrats in Safavid Iran 261
Nobuaki Kondo

10 Ma Dexin's Criticism of Saint Veneration: "Chinese"-Flavored Islam Formed by a Denominational Conflict 289
Tatsuya Nakanishi

THE MAKING OF THE MODERN

11 The Politics of the *Bayʿa* Ceremony in Modern Morocco 317
Nozomi Shiratani

12 The *Tawḥīd* of the Painting of God the Mother 337
William Gallois

13 Teaching Iranian History: Narrative Style and Messages 367
Keiko Sakurai

14 Inscribing "God's Words" in Japan: Connecting the Past to the Present through the Translations of the Qur'an 391
Emi Goto

Postscript 415
Shigeru Kamada

About the Contributors 419

Foreword

Ian Richard Netton

"Knowledge is concerned with what exists [. . .]."[1]
"Seek knowledge even as far as China."[2]

Knowledge and power. Power and knowledge. Plato in his famous cave image in *The Republic* recognised the power that would ultimately ensue from a proper perception and knowledge of reality.[3] Paul in his *Epistle to the Corinthians* stressed that our present knowledge is imperfect knowledge, but to be rectified in the future.[4]

A popular hadith counsels that one should seek knowledge even as far as China. We will not investigate here the authenticity of this particular hadith but rather note its epistemological sentiments, sentiments echoed in the Qur'an itself: "And say: 'Oh, my Lord, grant me an increase in knowledge!'" (*Wa-qul, rabbī, zidnī 'ilm).*[5] It is clear that we need such knowledge and wisdom, especially if we are to explore any aspects of the past. The past for L. P. Hartley was famously a foreign country,[6] while for Margaret Atwood "the past is a great darkness, and filled with echoes."[7]

It was therefore a huge pleasure to join with colleagues from universities in China's near neighbour, Japan, and attempt via a major seminar to explore the past, (with some genuflection to the present), to illuminate that darkness of which Atwood spoke, as it concerns our knowledge of the Near and Middle East. It is a truism that Islam's past has multivalent echoes in the present and knowledge speaks to power in Islamic societies today as yesterday.

The joint Exeter-Japanese Universities Seminar on the subject of *Inscribing Knowledge and Power in Islamic Societies: A Diachronic Study,* held on zoom between 9th–12th March 2021, brought together distinguished colleagues from two continents. It acted as a follow up to the earlier in person All-Japan–Exeter Joint Workshop / Tobunken Symposium *Knowledge as Power: Production, Control, and Manipulation of Knowledge in Muslim Societies* that was held at the University of Tokyo on 27th–28th April 2019. The Seminar was jointly supported by the JSPS Bilateral Joint Research Projects (Joint Seminars) and the Global Engagement Fund of the Institute of Arab and Islamic Studies (IAIS) in the College of Social Sciences and International Studies at the University of Exeter in the United Kingdom.

The impressive essays collected in this volume are the happy fruit of that Seminar. They are varied in content, eclectic in style and erudite in their scholarship. They provide a corrective, if ever any were needed, to any idea that Arabic, Islamic and Middle Eastern Studies have been mainly the preserve of Universities in the West. The contribution of the great Japanese scholar Toshihiko Izutsu (1914–93) to the study of Islam, and especially Qurʾanic semantics,[8] is very well-known to all of us. In this volume we have the joy of meeting other distinguished Japanese scholars of the Middle East in company and dialogue with their Western counterparts.

In addition, the essays collected here emphasise the major global contribution to the field that scholars from the University of Exeter's Institute of Arab and Islamic Studies have made – and continue to make – to the Social Sciences and Humanities study of the Middle East. This contribution was publicly acknowledged in the outstanding success of the IAIS in the recent UK Research Excellence Framework (REF) of 2021, where we consolidated our position as the leading unit in the study of Islam and the Middle East in the country.

In this volume, scholars present essays within a variety of sub-disciplines of the Middle Eastern field: they cover philosophy, language and literary criticism, Qurʾānic Studies, history, Sufism, theology and art, politics, literature, poetry, and intellectual history.

This was a Seminar to remember: it is to be hoped that those who read the essays collected in this volume will gain the same pleasure that those of us who participated in the original Seminar enjoyed. We hope that this will be the first of a number of important collaborations in the study of Islam and the Middle East between colleagues at Exeter and at Japanese universities.

Notes

1 Plato, *Republic, Books 1–5,* Loeb Classical Library, ed. and transl. by Chris Emlyn-Jones and William Preddy (Cambridge, Mass. and London: Harvard University Press, 2013), Bk. V, 477 a, b, p. 552 (Gk.), 553 (Eng.).
2 Popular hadith.
3 Plato, *Republic, Books 6–10,* Loeb Classical Library, ed. and transl. by Chris Emlyn-Jones and William Preddy (Cambridge, Mass. and London: Harvard University Press, 2013), Bk.V11, 514ff, pp. 106ff (Gk. & Eng.).
4 1 Corinthians 13: 12.
5 Q. 20: 114.
6 L. P. Hartley, *The Go-Between,* Penguin Modern Classics, London, 1953, repr. (London: Penguin Books, 2000).
7 Margaret Atwood, *The Handmaid's Tale*, 1985, repr. (London: Folio Society, 2017), 318.
8 See, for example, Toshihiko Izutsu, *Ethico-Religious Concepts in the Qurʾān* (Montreal: McGill-Queen's University Press, 2002).

Introduction: Diversifying the Intellectual History of Islam and Muslim Cultures

Sajjad Rizvi and Kazuo Morimoto

A concern with the present and one's position, with the need to diversify and globalise, and a turn towards more careful consideration of texts, ideas, and their contexts seem to animate academic history in recent times.[1] Even in more popular works one finds these emphases, trying to make sense of our current ideological and cultural impasses as well as environmental and socio-economic challenges. Why does religion continue to hold significance in our times?[2] Are humans better off, adaptable, less violent, consistently unpredictable?[3] How can we understand the course of our political history and the seeming dominance of democracy and its discontents, not least the legacies of coloniality and empire? While nationalist historiographies prevail in many contexts as well as Marxist and other approaches, the trend seems to be towards connected histories, the transnational and the global. Much of this constitutes intellectual history, which as one leading expert puts it, "seeks to restore a lost world, to recover perspectives and ideas from the ruins, to pull back the veil, and explain why the ideas resonated in the past and convinced their advocates."[4] Ideas are expressive of cultures and norms, practices and dispositions, of actions and events that lie at the very core of human experience such as sovereignty and power, mind and matter, profanity and spirituality.

Ideas require us to make sense of their bearers, their transmitters, the discourses, epistemic and conceptual frameworks in which they are debated, and the apparatuses that they evince and produce. Of course, that brings with it raging debates on questions of method, assumptions about the nature of the agency of individuals, as well as the desire to go beyond ideas as the domain of intellectual elites and those privileged to inscribe their prejudices into history.[5] The key question for historians is what sort of academic practice best fits our connected, globalised times in which different positions vie for dominance but in which we also have arrived at broad consensuses on the nature of the good of diversity and difference that enrichens our understanding and experience.

The study of Islam and of Islamic history similarly is enjoying something of a revival with an emphasis on intellectual history and a greater concern with the 'subaltern' with that. While there are those interested in discerning normative structures and even looking for sociological norms, increasingly specialists who work on texts and relate them to different contexts and study them diachronically often self-designate their work as Islamic intellectual history.[6] Perhaps of the most enduring histories of Islam contested but widely used in the classroom is an intellectual history: Marshall Hodgson's *The Venture of Islam*.[7] Similarly, Shahab Ahmed's very influential and posthumous musing on the importance of being Islamic locates itself in the broad contours of the intellectual history of the 'Bengal-to-Balkans' complex.[8] Another alternative grand theory of Islam locates the key in the culture of ambiguity expressed in literary and intellectual production.[9] Two further interventions in method are also predicated on the practice of intellectual history: Lawrence's discernment of Islamicate cosmopolitan spirit as a trilogy of themes that permeate the study of Islam, and Reinhart's deployment of notions from socio-linguistics to argue for dialectical and cosmopolitan aspects of Islamic cultures throughout history and in the present.[10] Other studies focus their attention on one or another generic tradition. Irfan Ahmed studies the phenomenon of critique in Islamic cultures bringing together an anthropological focus on South Asia alongside an intellectual historical analysis of a neglected feature of Islamic thought.[11] Zahra Ayubi's major contribution is on the development of ethics and the gendered subject, which is of critical importance to both the intellectual history of Islam in the middle period as well as making sense of the roots of contemporary debates.[12] SherAli Tareen's masterful study of Muslim subjectivities under the colonial state and their understanding of sovereignty illuminates for us an intellectual history of a critical aspect of the current debate on *shariʿa* in the public sphere and the intersection of the transcendent and the immanent in history.[13] Alex Dika Seggerman's creative intervention on the 'Islam' debate alongside a broader concern with art history, modernism, and orientalism says much of the ways in which we can insert the study of Muslim cultures into our contemporary global concerns.[14] Oludamini Ogunnaike's pioneering comparative study of Sufism and Ifa in West Africa within and alongside the increasingly prominent 'philosophy as a way of life' paradigm constitutes a strikingly original re-orientation of the study of Islamic thought.[15] All of these are recognisable works of intellectual history that provide insights into method and approach in the study of Islam.[16]

So, in that sense, justifying a volume that has its focus on intellectual history is not particularly an arduous task. This is the broader area in which we are locating our individual and quite distinct efforts. Some years ago, first on email and then in Tokyo, we discussed the possibility of collaborating on a workshop, possible research projects, and at least one publication stemming from that. The volume before you is the fruit of the discussions that we enjoyed, and the time spent together in Tokyo (April 2019) and online (March 2021; unfortunately the lockdown and the global Covid-19 pandemic obviated the convening of a follow-up workshop in Exeter). There were noticeable differences of approach in the various chapters presented but what brought them together was a careful study of texts, not in a reductively philological manner derided quite often these days but in the way in which we recognise that texts are forms of speech acts and lie alongside other forms of self-expression that can elucidate and illuminate as well as occlude.

One figure that was often evoked – and Professor Kamada again returns to him in his Postscript – was the late Toshihiko Izutsu (1914–93), a giant in the field of Islamic studies in Japan but also in many ways a pioneer in the study of anglophone Islamic intellectual history as well. As Goto mentions in her chapter, he was the first to translate the Qur'an into Japanese and one of the first to write a history of Islamic thought in Japanese. Izutsu's own conception of 'Oriental Philosophy' and the idea of Asia was critical as a way of connecting his growing interests in Islamic philosophy but also accounted later perhaps for his return to the study of Buddhism as well as forms of Indian thought. His desire to elucidate 'Oriental Philosophy' and the structures of being and consciousness in Islamic, Indian, Chinese, and Japanese thought was with a clear desire to insert it into the global intellectual activity of the contemporary world.[17] He recognised that any postulation of a tradition of thought of 'Oriental Philosophy' involves a form of construction, "artificially creating an organic space of thought, which could include all these traditions structurally, by taking off the philosophical traditions of the Orient from the axis of time and by recombining them paradigmatically."[18] It was in fact this work, *Ishiki to honshitsu: Seishinteki Toyo wo motomete [Conciousness and Essence: A Quest for the Spiritual Orient]*, written in 1983 that he drew on the whole range of his research including Islamic philosophy, and especially his interest in the Safavid sage Mullā Ṣadrā (d. 1636), whose *Kitāb al-mashāʿir* he translated in Japanese and published in 1978.[19] What is important for his work were the many years he spent teaching in Tehran and also at McGill.

Two further examples of Izutsu's contribution to Islamic intellectual history and the study of the history of philosophy might be apposite here. The first is his major comparative work that studies Sufism – in this case the school of Ibn ʿArabī (d. 1240) and in particular his *Bezels of Wisdom* (*Fuṣūṣ al-ḥikam*) and its commentaries – and Taoism – in particular the thought of Lao-Tzu and Chaung-Tzu. This was first published in two volumes in Japan in 1967 and then scheduled to be published in English in Tehran but then the revolution happened and so it appeared in Berkeley in 1984. This work is a serious reflection on the major philosophical concepts in both systems – and interesting in that one might argue that neither properly constitutes a system. Applying the term 'philosophy' to them requires at least some element of a more expansive sense of philosophy and a violation of dominant 'analytic' approaches to philosophy. As such this was very much against the grain of what constituted Arabic and Islamic philosophy in anglophone academia either in the 1960s or even in the 1980s. Each of the two sections on Sufism and Taoism may be read fruitfully independently of each other. But the tantalising final concluding comparison is instructive. For Izutsu, comparative philosophy is not merely an act of translation or even finding common conceptual or philological ground. Rather, it requires a reconceptualization of structures. In that Izutsu focuses on two themes: the self-transformation of the human through philosophical inquiry and the dynamic of existence, and that the totality of what exists lies in the broad process of becoming stemming from the True One (*al-ḥaqq*) or the Tao to the manifold contingent entities that we phenomenally experience in the cosmos. His own ontological commitments are clear in the end with a hint of mysticism:

> It is remarkable that neither in Sufism nor in Taoism is the ontological Descent – from the Mystery of Mysteries down to the stage of phenomenal things – made to represent the final completion of the activity of Existence. The Descent is followed by its reversal. That is, Ascent. The ten thousand things flourish exuberantly at the last stage of the descending course, and then take an ascending course toward their ultimate source until they disappear in the original Darkness and find their resting place in the cosmic pre-phenomenological Stillness. Thus, the whole process of creation forms a huge ontological circle in which there is in reality neither an initial point nor a final point. The movement from one stage to another, considered in itself, is surely a temporal phenomenon. But the whole circle, having neither an initial point nor a final point, is a trans-temporal or a-temporal phenomenon. It is, in other words, a metaphysical process. Everything is an occurrence in an Eternal Now.[20]

Thus, he concludes the study. Not surprisingly it makes one think of his friend and interlocutor Henry Corbin as well as Martin Heidegger among others.

The second piece to mention is Izutsu's magisterial study of the metaphysics of the Qajar period thinker Mullā Hādī Sabzawārī (d. 1873), the person who did most to establish the hegemony of Mullā Ṣadrā's school in the Iranian Shiʿi seminary system. This study was published in 1969 as part of his edition – along with his colleague in Tehran, Mehdi Mohaghegh – of the metaphysics section of Sabzawārī's major philosophical work *Sharḥ Ghurar al-farāʾid*.[21] The significance of this piece is multiple. It was written at a time when the prevailing assumptions were arguably to deny philosophical activity in Islamic contexts after Averroes and it represented an important attempt to demonstrate the analytic, argumentative, and philosophical value of Sabzawārī's work. Second, he presented Sabzawārī as a philosopher *and* a Sufi and mystic and asserted that one could profitably read him in both ways, indicating the later philosophical or *ḥikmat* tradition in Iran was one that combined these two approaches to the ultimate reality and was highly inflected with the metaphysics of Ibn ʿArabī. Third, he retained a critical comparative framework citing Aristotle and Maritain, Taoism and Zen Buddhism – while demonstrating the differences: for example, the vision of existence in Sabzawārī, drawing upon Mullā Ṣadrā, was quite distinct from modern existentialism as well as Martin Heidegger's 'existence in an open clearing' (*Lichtung*). Thus, Sabzawārī was useful as a comparative foil but also deserved to be studied in his own right. Fourth, as a more traditional form of intellectual history, it is impressive, drawing upon the influences and criticisms as well as modifications that emerge in the work of Sabzawārī with respect to pivotal earlier thinkers like Suhrawardī (d. 1191), al-Rāzī (d. 1210), and al-Ṭūsī (d. 1274) among others. Overall, he described his approach as a mix of analytical and historical to "bring to light the relevance of this kind of philosophy in the contemporary situation of world philosophy."[22]

Izutsu thus represents a model and an influential approach that brings together two aspects that we did find across our workshops and in the chapters of this volume: a careful consideration of the text especially in its intellectual historical context, as well as a desire to make it speak to broader intellectual and disciplinary concerns. While the volume does not have a singular theme, we have divided the chapters into three broad sections on philosophy, on knowledge production, and on the encounter with the modern (with a recognition that terms such as modern and modernism bear their own genealogy and trajectory).

The philosophy section opens with Rizvi on portraits of a philosopher. This chapter falls within a series that he is currently writing that attempts to make sense of decoloniality applied to the study of Islamic thought. The chapter thus comprises a long methodological consideration of why we should want to study Islamic philosophy in history, followed by three case studies. Deliberately – in order to open up the question of what we mean by philosophy and the borders of the discipline in a decolonised contemporary academic context – Rizvi has selected three 'minor figures' who are probably unknown to most specialists in Islamic intellectual history. And alongside that, the selection includes those who would not normally be considered to be philosophers and who do not self-identity and designate their work as *ḥikma*. This is followed by a valuable contribution by Kristó-Nagy on the origins of philosophy in Arabic. The translation movement from Greek (and Syriac) into Arabic is a well-trodden path of inquiry. What is perhaps less well known is the Persian into Arabic translations. Focusing on the case study of the administrative official and intellectual Ibn al-Muqaffaʿ he demonstrates that the first examples of philosophy in Arabic – in particular political philosophy – is mediated by Pahlavi texts in the ʿAbbasid milieu of Baghdad.

Selove and Sanad's chapter that follows raises the important question of the scope of philosophy. What is clear is that thinkers in the occult sciences had a clear conception of the hierarchy of the sciences and knowledge in which philosophy had the privileged position – and then within philosophy it was the occult whether in the form of theoretic astral and Hermetic magic and lettrism (*ʿilm al-ḥurūf*) or the practical skills of geomancy and other magical arts that mirrored the Aristotelian dichotomy of theoretical philosophy and practical philosophy. More intriguing is the implication for the relationship between language (and even poetry) and philosophy. By selecting the case study of Sirāj al-Dīn al-Sakkākī, perhaps one of the leading linguist-rhetoricians of the Islamic traditions, Selove and Sanad show how the use of language itself can be magical and efficacious as the practice of the occult sciences.

Obuchi's chapter continues the meditation upon the meaning and practice of philosophy by examining the work of a much neglected but influential student of Fakhr al-Dīn al-Rāzī, Zayn al-Dīn al-Kashshī. This is a model of a careful textual study in intellectual history that locates al-Kashshī in his historical context and raises critical questions about the relationship between logic, metaphysics, and the tradition of philosophical theology (*kalām*) as well as the perennial problem of logocentrism, the relation between spoken and written tokens of language and their philosophical import.

The final chapter in this section by Sumida brings us again to the fundamental question of the scope of philosophy. Another study of manuscripts – and given the riches of the Islamic intellectual traditions, we know that the vast majority of the scholarly output remains unedited in manuscripts – he ventures into a growing field on the messianic and millenarian borders of the Timurid period and the intellectual foment of Sufis, mystics, Shiʿi charismatic leaders, and philosophers. While the theological presentation of the arguments is paramount, the mode of argumentation draws upon paradigms from logic and philosophy. Furthermore, it alerts us to one element of what is sometimes for convenience called the post-classical traditions of Islamic philosophy, namely the significance of eschatology and the apocalypse. While many of a more 'analytic' training might baulk at that, the messianic and the apocalyptic has been a feature of much modern French and German philosophy. A next step might be to bring the studies of the messianic and the apocalyptic in Islamic thought through the ages with these developments.

The next section is described as scholarly production. In a sense every chapter of this collection could fit in this section. What we want to suggest here is that these contributions each represent a distinct genre and tradition of scholarly production: accounting, hagiographical literature, genealogy, literary criticism, and reformist Sufism. Sanad looks at the work of the ʿAbbasid literary critic and litterateur Abū Hilāl al-ʿAskarī and the way in which one could argue that he formed the literary tradition by evaluating poetry, distinguishing the good from the bad and ugly. Furthermore, Sanad indicates how al-ʿAskarī's work fits within a broad debate in the tenth and eleventh centuries CE on the nature of meaning or cognitive content (*maʿnā*) that is conveyed by terms. Mizukami's work picks up one of the themes earlier in Sumida's chapter, namely the question of 'confessional ambiguity' or rather how some scholarly production was deliberately interconfessional. The case study is a prominent Shiʿi scholar of the late ʿAbbasid period who wrote hagiographies and works on the excellences and virtues of the Shiʿi Imams that were designed to appeal to readers who did not identify exclusively as Shiʿi while subtly defending normative Shiʿi positions.

Morimoto also takes up the question of how to discern Shiʿi identity through the examination of a thirteenth century genealogy. Just like *faḍāʾil* literature was written by Shiʿi and non-Shiʿi alike, similarly genealogies were. Once again, we have here a careful textual study based on manuscripts. Thus, we have a few articles that address the key growing literature on 'Imamophilism' or 'confessional ambiguity,' the process of elite interconfessionality in scholarly circles in the period from the fall of the ʿAbbasids (or from even before, as Mizukami's and Morimoto's contributions indicate) to the rise of the Safavids. Certainly, the notion that our modern exclusive identities of Sunni and Shiʿi owe much to the Ottoman-Safavid conflict seems to hold not least in the light of what came before it (without denying that exclusive affiliations and theologies were present in that earlier period).

Kondo's contribution lies in Safavid studies but also is of critical importance for anyone working on archives and administrative texts in the 'Gunpowder Empires.' The development of the accounting genre known as *ʿilm al-siyāq* is particularly useful in the quest of archival documents that tell us about the functioning of empire and administration not least given the dearth of documentary material in the Safavid context in contrast to the Ottoman and the Mughal. The final chapter in this section is Nakanishi's study of Ma Dexin. One of the features of recent developments in Islamic intellectual history is the growth of work on China. One thinks, when it comes to anglophone scholarship, of Kristian Petersen's study of the Han Kitab tradition, as well as Atwill on the interactions across Asia of the Tibetan Muslim communities.[23] Nakanishi shows us that the ways in which scholars makes sense of what is Islamic depends on their contexts and their intellectual requirements. While this is very much a study of reformist thinking in Muslim contexts that people have been studying for decades from their South Asian, North and West African and Arab speaking contexts, this is a good example of understanding that Ma Dexin's thought is not just a Wahhābī intervention in a Chinese Hui context but rather a negotiation of Sufi practices in which an adherence to the Sufi metaphysics of the school of Ibn ʿArabī is balanced with a critique of saint veneration and the seeming excesses of the master-disciple relationship in Sufi orders.

The final section brings us to the encounter with modernity. Shiratani's study of the *bayʿa* ceremony in Morocco could be classified as an exemplum of the 'invention of tradition'. She shows how the post-colonial Moroccan monarchy's desire to bolster its legitimacy requires both a traditional emphasis on their claims to descent from the Prophet and a new deployment of a traditional Arab nomadic ritual of pledging allegiance to the leader in order to enact their investiture. What she demonstrates is that it is not just the theory of the investiture and its proclamation, but the language used and the location selected that tell us much about the development of politics in Morocco. Gallois continues the North African theme by looking at Tunisia. His work is a major intervention on the debate on what constitutes Islamic art and what is Islamic about Islamic art, with an ironically iconoclastic approach to the question of aniconism in Islamic art. By looking at colonial period features of resistance in which locals defended this monotheistic Islamic faith by invoking images of a pre-Islamic divine mother, he problematises the way in which the colonialist episteme objectifies what is Islamic, what is theologically normative and what is artistic.

Sakurai's chapter takes us to Iran and the educational policy that is central to the formation of the nation-state. The histories that people narrate and that they teach in state schools tell us much about the nature of identity and becoming in the contemporary. The textbooks that she studies – which are often the result of the work of serious historians – do not just present a narrative; they represent and express a culture and a people. The final chapter brings us to Japan – and in many ways it is fitting that the volume ends with Islam and Japan. Goto looks at the process and examples of translation of the Qur'an into Japanese from Izutsu and early academic efforts through to the emergence of a Japanese Muslim community and its self-narration and self-image in the Qur'an.

It has been a pleasure bringing together this volume to publication not least because of the number of early career researchers who represent the future of the field of Islamic intellectual history and intellectual history in Muslim contexts both in anglophone British academia as well as Japan. We hope that this will be the first of a series of such volumes and in future we look forward to collaborating on more thematic volumes as well as those which subject the study of Islam in these two contexts to the approach of intellectual history.

Lastly but not least, we would like to gratefully acknowledge the financial support by the Japan Society for the Promotion of Science (JSPS Bilateral Open Partnership Joint Research Projects [Joint Seminars]), Institute of Arab and Islamic Studies (IAIS) in the College of Social Sciences and International Studies at the University of Exeter (Global Engagement Fund), and the Institute for Advanced Studies on Asia, University of Tokyo for their financial supports throughout the process of our joint-venture.

Notes

1 Sebastian Conrad, *What Is Global History?* (Princeton: Princeton University Press, 2016); Samuel Moyn and Andrews Sartori, eds., *Global Intellectual History* (New York: Columbia University Press, 2015).
2 Robin Dunbar, *How Religion Evolved; and How It Endures* (London: Pelican, 2022).
3 Jared Diamond, *Collapse: How Nations Cope with Crisis and Change* (London: Penguin, 2020); Steven Pinker, *The Better Angels of Our Nature: A History of Violence and Humanity* (London: Penguin, 2012); Nassim Nicholas Taleb, *The Black Swan: The Impact of the Highly Improbable* (London: Penguin, 2010).
4 Richard Whatmore, *What Is Intellectual History?* (Cambridge: Polity Press, 2015), 5.
5 Richard Rorty, J. B. Schneewind, and Quentin Skinner, eds., *Philosophy in History* (Cambridge: Cambridge University Press, 1984); Quentin Skinner, *Visions of Politics 1: Regarding Method* (Cambridge: Cambridge University Press, 2002); Mogens Laerke, Justin E. H. Smith, and Eric Schliesser, eds., *Philosophy and Its History* (New York: Oxford University Press, 2013); but also Walter Mignolo and Catherine Walsh, *On Decoloniality: Concepts, Analytics, Praxis* (Durham, NC: Duke University Press, 2018); Achille Mbembe, *Necropolitics* (Durham, NC: Duke University Press, 2019); Sven Lindqvist, *Exterminate All the Brutes* (London: Granta, 2018); Roxanne Dunbar-Ortiz, *Not a Nation of Immigrants: Settler Colonialism, White Supremacy, and a History of Erasure and Exclusion* (New York: Beacon Press, 2022); and Satnam Sanghera, *Empireland: How Imperialism Has Shaped Modern Britain* (London: Viking, 2021).
6 Even the work of one individual can demonstrate this development: from Mohammed Bamyeh, *Social Origins of Islam: Mind, Economy, Discourse* (Minneapolis: University of Minnesota Press, 1999) to idem, *Lifeworlds of Islam: The Pragmatics of a Religion* (New York: Oxford University Press, 2019).
7 Marshall Hodgson, *The Venture of Islam: Conscience and History in a World Civilization*, 3 vols. (Chicago: University of Chicago Press, 1974).
8 Shahab Ahmed, *What Is Islam? The Importance of Being Islamic* (Princeton: Princeton University Press, 2016).
9 Thomas Bauer, *A Culture of Ambiguity: An Alternative History of Islam*, transl. by Hinrich Biesterfeldt and Tricia Tunstall (New York: Columbia University Press, 2021).
10 Bruce Lawrence, *Islamicate Cosmopolitan Spirit* (New York: Wiley Blackwell, 2021); and A. Kevin Reinhart, *Lived Islam: Colloquial Religion in a Cosmopolitan Tradition* (Cambridge: Cambridge University Press, 2020).
11 Irfan Ahmed, *Religion as Critique: Islamic Critical Thinking from Mecca to the Marketplace* (Chapel Hill, NC: University of North Carolina Press, 2017).
12 Zahra Ayubi, *Gendered Morality: Classical Islamic Ethics of Family, Self, and Society* (New York: Columbia University Press, 2019).
13 SherAli Tareen, *Defending Muhammad in Modernity* (Notre Dame: Notre Dame University Press, 2019).
14 Alex Dika Seggerman, *Modernism on the Nile: Art in Egypt between the Islamic and the Contemporary* (Chapel Hill, NC: University of North Carolina Press, 2019).
15 Oludamini Ogunnaike, *Deep Knowledge: Ways of Knowing in Sufism and Ifa, Two West African Intellectual Traditions* (University Park, PA: The Pennsylvania State University Press, 2020).
16 There are other examples of intellectual history that take Islamic cultures as their case studies that are more ambitious in scope in their critique of the humanities. Two cases in point: Wael Hallaq, *Restating Orientalism: A Critique of Modern Knowledge* (New York: Columbia University Press, 2018); and Talal Asad, *Secular Translations: Nation-State, Modern Self, and Calculative Reason* (New York: Columbia University Press, 2019).
17 Toshihiko Izutsu, *Kosumosu to anchikosumosu: Tōyō-tetsugaku no tameni [Cosmos and Anti-cosmos: Toward an Oriental Philosophy]* (Tokyo: Iwanami Shoten, 1989), 3, cited in Yoshitsugu

Sawai, "Izutsu's Creative 'Reading' of Oriental Thought and Its Development," in Toshihiko Izutsu, *The Structure of Oriental Philosophy: Collected Papers of the Eranos Conference*, 2 vols., The Izutsu Library Series on Oriental Philosophy, 4 (Tokyo: Keio University Press, 2008), vol. 2, 216.,

18 Toshihiko Izutsu, *Ishiki to honshitsu [Consciousness and Essence]* (Tokyo: Iwanami Shoten, 1983), 429, cited in Sawai, "Izutsu's Creative 'Reading'," 221.

19 Shigeru Kamada discusses Mullā Ṣadrā and Izutsu's conception of philosophy and mysticism in his article, "The Place of Mullā Ṣadrā's *Kitāb al-Mashāʿir* in Izutsu's Philosophy," in *Japanese Contributions to Islamic Studies: The Legacy of Toshihiko Izutsu*, ed. by Anis Thoha (Kuala Lumpur: Japan Foundation in association with IIUM Press, 2010), 41–51.

20 Toshihiko Izutsu, *Sufism and Taoism: A Comparative Study of Key Philosophical Concepts* (Berkeley: University of California Press, 1984), 493.

21 Toshihiko Izutsu, "The Fundamental Structure of Sabzawari's Metaphysics," in Mullā Hādī Sabzawārī, *Sharḥ-i Ghurar al-farāʾid or Sharḥ-i manẓūmah, Part One Metaphysics*, ed. by Mehdi Mohaghegh and Toshihiko Izutsu (Tehran: McGill Institute of Islamic Studies Tehran Branch, 1969), 1–152.

22 Izutsu, "The Fundamental Structure of Sabzawari's Metaphysics," 151.

23 Kristian Petersen, *Interpreting Islam in China: Pilgrimage, Scripture, and Language in the Han Kitab* (New York: Oxford University Press, 2017); and David G. Atwill, *Islamic Shangri-La: Inter-Asian Relations and Lhasa's Muslim Communities* (Berkeley: University of California Press, 2018).

Bibliography

Ahmed, Irfan. *Religion as Critique: Islamic Critical Thinking from Mecca to the Marketplace*. Chapel Hill, NC: University of North Carolina Press, 2017.

Ahmed, Shahab. *What Is Islam? The Importance of Being Islamic*. Princeton: Princeton University Press, 2016.

Asad, Talal. *Secular Translations: Nation-State, Modern Self, and Calculative Reason*. New York: Columbia University Press, 2019.

Atwill, David G. *Islamic Shangri-La: Inter-Asian Relations and Lhasa's Muslim Communities*. Berkeley: University of California Press, 2018.

Ayubi, Zahra. *Gendered Morality: Classical Islamic Ethics of Family, Self, and Society*. New York: Columbia University Press, 2019.

Bamyeh, Mohammed. *Social Origins of Islam: Mind, Economy, Discourse*. Minneapolis: University of Minnesota Press, 1999.

Bamyeh, Mohammed. *Lifeworlds of Islam: The Pragmatics of a Religion*. New York: Oxford University Press, 2019.

Bauer, Thomas. *A Culture of Ambiguity: An Alternative History of Islam*. Transl. by Hinrich Biesterfeldt and Tricia Tunstall. New York: Columbia University Press, 2021.

Conrad, Sebastian. *What Is Global History?* Princeton: Princeton University Press, 2016.

Diamond, Jared. *Collapse: How Nations Cope with Crisis and Change*. London: Penguin, 2020.

Dunbar, Robin. *How Religion Evolved; and How It Endures*. London: Pelican, 2022.
Dunbar-Ortiz, Roxanne. *Not a Nation of Immigrants: Settler Colonialism, White Supremacy, and a History of Erasure and Exclusion*. New York: Beacon Press, 2022.
Hallaq, Wael. *Restating Orientalism: A Critique of Modern Knowledge*. New York: Columbia University Press, 2018.
Hodgson, Marshall. *The Venture of Islam: Conscience and History in a World Civilization*. 3 vols. Chicago: University of Chicago Press, 1974.
Izutsu, Toshihiko. "The Fundamental Structure of Sabzawari's Metaphysics." In Mullā Hādī Sabzawārī. *Sharḥ-i Ghurar al-farāʾid or Sharḥ-i manẓūmah, Part One Metaphysics*. Ed. by Mehdi Mohaghegh and Toshihiko Izutsu. Tehran: McGill Institute of Islamic Studies Tehran Branch, 1969, 1–152.
Izutsu, Toshihiko. *Ishiki to honshitsu [Consciousness and Essence]*. Tokyo: Iwanami Shoten, 1983.
Izutsu, Toshihiko. *Sufism and Taoism: A Comparative Study of Key Philosophical Concepts*. Berkeley: University of California Press, 1984.
Izutsu, Toshihiko. *Kosumosu to anchikosumosu: Tōyō-tetsugaku no tameni [Cosmos and Anti-cosmos: Toward an Oriental Philosophy]*. Tokyo: Iwanami Shoten, 1989.
Kamada, Shigeru. "The Place of Mullā Ṣadrā's *Kitāb al-Mashāʿir* in Izutsu's Philosophy." In *Japanese Contributions to Islamic Studies: The Legacy of Toshihiko Izutsu*. Ed. by Anis Thoha. Kuala Lumpur: Japan Foundation in association with IIUM Press, 2010, 41–51.
Laerke, Mogens, Justin E. H. Smith, and Eric Schliesser, eds. *Philosophy and Its History*. New York: Oxford University Press, 2013.
Lawrence, Bruce. *Islamicate Cosmopolitan Spirit*. New York: Wiley Blackwell, 2021.
Lindqvist, Sven. *Exterminate All the Brutes*. London: Granta, 2018.
Mbembe, Achille. *Necropolitics*. Durham, NC: Duke University Press, 2019.
Mignolo, Walter and Catherine Walsh. *On Decoloniality: Concepts, Analytics, Praxis*. Durham, NC: Duke University Press, 2018.
Moyn, Samuel and Andrews Sartori, eds. *Global Intellectual History*. New York: Columbia University Press, 2015.
Ogunnaike, Oludamini. *Deep Knowledge: Ways of Knowing in Sufism and Ifa, Two West African Intellectual Traditions*. University Park, PA: The Pennsylvania State University Press, 2020.
Petersen, Kristian. *Interpreting Islam in China: Pilgrimage, Scripture, and Language in the Han Kitab*. New York: Oxford University Press, 2017.
Pinker, Steven. *The Better Angels of Our Nature: A History of Violence and Humanity*. London: Penguin, 2012.
Reinhart, A. Kevin. *Lived Islam: Colloquial Religion in a Cosmopolitan Tradition*. Cambridge: Cambridge University Press, 2020.

Rorty, Richard, J. B. Schneewind, and Quentin Skinner, eds. *Philosophy in History.* Cambridge: Cambridge University Press, 1984.

Sanghera, Satnam. *Empireland: How Imperialism Has Shaped Modern Britain.* London: Viking, 2021.

Sawai, Yoshitsugu. "Izutsu's Creative 'Reading' of Oriental Thought and Its Development." In Toshihiko Izutsu. *The Structure of Oriental Philosophy: Collected Papers of the Eranos Conference.* 2 vols. The Izutsu Library Series on Oriental Philosophy, 4. Tokyo: Keio University Press, 2008, vol. 2, 215–23.

Seggerman, Alex Dika. *Modernism on the Nile: Art in Egypt between the Islamic and the Contemporary.* Chapel Hill, NC: University of North Carolina Press, 2019.

Skinner, Quentin. *Visions of Politics 1: Regarding Method.* Cambridge: Cambridge University Press, 2002.

Taleb, Nassim Nicholas. *The Black Swan: The Impact of the Highly Improbable.* London: Penguin, 2010.

Tareen, SherAli. *Defending Muhammad in Modernity.* Notre Dame: Notre Dame University Press, 2019.

Whatmore, Richard. *What Is Intellectual History?* Cambridge: Polity Press, 2015.

PHILOSOPHY

1

Three Portraits of a Philosopher in Islamic Cultures

Sajjad Rizvi

Without a taste for composition, this life is death.
In the fashioning of our selves lies godlikeness.
Muḥammad Iqbāl

As thinkers from ancient times have noted, humans have a desire to express themselves, to project and assert their selfhood and their dominion over their environment, to understand, grasp and master their reality. Plato famously wondered about the human capacity and insatiable desire to know oneself and one's environment, to express oneself as a quintessential human, even to portray oneself as a philosopher (*Republic* V, 475c). In doing so, humans construct self-portraits for others to appreciate, understand, and to contest.[1] The possibility of a global philosophy is at least partially predicated on this insight that humans feel the need to compose, fashion, create, project, inscribe and express their selfhood in thought and the arts, though one needs to investigate further epistemologies and praxes of the south to find philosophising everywhere, *without* attempting to universalise a particular European trajectory of it. This desire for self-expression stems directly from the desire to know, to uncover truth, and to arrive at some certainty. It seems that we want to think that we are not tricked or deluded in our understanding of the world; in this endeavour, the very self, as the ancient Indian sages note, can act as the agent of concealment but also as the instrument of revelation.[2] Philosophy then as an expression of the self and as the discovery of reality holds within itself both the ability to reveal and occlude. Definitions, expressions, and features of philosophy vary across cultures – even the very terms that capture 'philosophy' may not exist or map well[3] – but at the very least what seems to unite those conceptions might be a 'family resemblances' approach to philosophy; indeed, portraits themselves are a classic example of a term united by family resemblances.[4]

Portraits attempt to capture a reality or even to mirror it, or they may occlude in their representation what they claim to capture, or they present traces and vestiges of the person or thing depicted. They might even sketch out key features of the subject so that someone who experiences the portrait might be able to pick out the subject when they encounter it. This is portrait is map or guide to extra-mental reality. Alternatively, portraits might present a mandala or a talisman that encodes the homologies of the worlds and the key to the intersection of the esoteric with the exoteric. This is portrait as microcosm or a homologous token that decodes extra-mental reality. All these elements, the revelatory, the aesthetic, the essential, and the self-fashioning, the occult even, are present in the use of the notion of portrait, of the *naqsh* to use an appropriate Arabo-Persian-Urdu term, that I wish to present in this analysis of what philosophy was and might be in Islamic cultures.

A good parable for the multivalence, and even one might say trickery or the irony of the portrait or *naqsh* is the famous story of the competition between the Chinese and the Greeks to be adjudicated by Alexander recounted in Neẓāmī Gangavī (d. 1209) and Rūmī (d. 1273) and which has become a commonplace in Persianate literature.[5] In Neẓāmī, a sage or philosopher is asked to adjudicate and discern who is the winner, to seek within the portraits their truth and reality and the extent to which the portrait captures and represents reality. His function is to discern reality, to decode the mandala, between the exceptional realism of the Chinese and the exquisitely polished mirror of the Greeks. Thus, the function of the philosopher in this sense becomes the work of the hermeneut attempting to seek the hidden in the manifest portrait. In Rūmī, the parable becomes one in which the portrait or the mirror stands in for the heart of the Sufi or the seeker whose purity and transparency reveal truth.[6] The perfect portrait in that sense becomes a complete theophany, like the burning bush on Mount Sinai, or the sign of Moses' glowing hand, or indeed the very throne of God and the heart of the believer (the latter two conflated in the wider homology). True seekers transcend the confines of exoteric learning, inculcating within themselves the divine theophanies and realising the very essence of divine certainty (*ḥaqq al-yaqīn*); that is a true portrait – and that person is the true *imago dei* (*ṣūrat al-Raḥmān* in Islamic discourse). Portraits thus reveal and occlude, with reference to, and in correspondence with, extra-mental reality and the nature of God; at one level, that is the onto-theological affirmation of philosophy in the Islamic idiom.

This chapter examines the nature of philosophy in Islam and the guises, portraits, and masks of the philosopher by turning to three rather different case studies. These studies demonstrate the very idea of the portrait, the ambiguity of representation and reproduction in art, and the method for studying the history of Islamic philosophy in Islamic cultures and sketches in the period just before the onset of colonial modernity. There is a sense that this later epoch makes the portraits more difficult to effect and appreciate; schizophrenia and an absurdist attitude make the mandala increasingly arduous to decipher – potentially a surrealist reading of the portrait would leave the door open to the esoteric, but this is not a study in surrealism, or a nod to Borges' Pierre Menard. Perhaps Menard would find in the vestiges and traces of these philosophical portraits the palimpsestic structure of Islamic philosophy (or perhaps a collage) and a key to what unites the body of text.[7] But before we consider the case studies, I want to interject two preliminary discussions: the first explains my decolonial strategy in the study of Islamic philosophy, while the second outlines a method for studying texts in search of philosophy beyond the simple colonialist binaries of reason versus revelation, logic versus poesis, and inscription versus logocentrism.

A Decolonial Strategy

How can we understand philosophy in a global context and read Islamic philosophy to be something more than a relic of ethno-cultural chauvinism and nativism? Can it act as a space for conversations about the nature of inquiry, of lived experience, and a way of life, the very meaning of what it is to be human? Can our portraits contribute to a growing global conversation on philosophy? Global philosophy is motivated by a cosmopolitan ethos of networks of exchange based on dialogue, overlapping reason and moral disagreement, as well as a desire to sustain and perpetuate a dialogue of rationalities and hermeneutics within a truly multicultural context through a fusion of the horizons of meaning and understanding (with a nod to Gadamer).[8] Philosophy, understood within such a context, needs to be more than *philosophia*, that is, it needs to go beyond a particular Greek heritage of rationality that has structured the history of European philosophy (and not just European philosophy – the Greek ancients need to be rescued from their modern European appropriation).[9] We also need to reject framing non-Western traditions, especially where philosophical reasoning might be more oral than written (or rather where the oral and the written are mutually constitutive, and the relation between the two is crucially at stake in philosophy), as wisdom traditions (which is how these other traditions have been framed in the West). One reason for doing so is that this idea continues to exclude global philosophical traditions, since metropolitan academia does not have departments of wisdom traditions or of 'paraphilosophy.'[10] We need to recognise the history of the term 'philosophy' and its privilege but also its historicity and the rich traditions that it needs to exclude for its disciplinary cohesion.[11] One objection might be to consider that traditions like *falsafa* in the Arabo-Islamic context tended to see philosophy arising from the Greeks as well – after all they valorised the work of the 'divine Plato' (*Aflāṭūn al-ilāhī*) and Aristotle 'the philosopher' (*al-ḥakīm*). To this objection, I would say that Islamic philosophers had a more connected genealogy of the origins of philosophy and thinking in which Greece does not have a privileged place. For example, the Safavid sage Mullā Ṣadrā

(d. 1045/1636) put it thus (drawing on the very ancient narrative that dates back at least to the tenth century CE):

> Know that philosophy first issued from Adam, the chosen one of God and from his progeny Seth and Hermes – I mean Idrīs – and from Noah, because the world can never be free of a person who establishes knowledge of the unity of God and of the return [to God]. The great Hermes disseminated it [philosophy] in the climes and in the countries and explained it and gave benefit of it to the people. He is the father of philosophers and the most learned of the knowledgeable.
>
> As for Rome and Greece, philosophy is not ancient in those places as their original sciences were rhetoric, epistolatory, astrology, and poetry [. . .] until Abraham became a prophet, and he taught them the science of divine unity. It is mentioned in history that the first to philosophise from among them [the Greeks] was Thales of Miletus and he named it philosophy. He first philosophised in Egypt and then proceeded to Miletus when he was an old man and disseminated his philosophy. After him came Anaxagoras and Anaximenes of Miletus. After them emerged Empedocles, Pythagoras, Socrates and Plato.[12]

He then goes on to trace another trajectory that connects philosophy, poetics, and mathematics as an inheritance to Pythagoras and Plato from Solomon. This account neither pits Athens against Jerusalem nor does it oppose poets like Rainer Maria Rilke to philosophers like A.J. Ayer. Not only is Greece provincialized, the assumptions of a desacralized cosmos without either creator or providence that tends to animate our discussions today are noticeably absent.

Therefore, in this sense philosophy began as globally connected enterprise (and should return to the pristine situation). The move towards a global philosophy is integral to the attempt to decolonise knowledge and especially the humanities within the academy. One of the best cases for a properly global and cosmopolitan philosophy is made by the eminent philosopher and specialist of Indian philosophy, Jonardon Ganeri who argues that we are living in a new age of the re-emergence of competing reasons based on four observations.[13] First, cultural forms of reason predicated on lived experience and self-reflection are finding authentic voices – the very fact that Peter Adamson's well known podcast is moving in this way and academic departments from institutions such as SOAS and Leiden are establishing degree programmes in global philosophy suggests as much. The task is the (re)discovery of philosophical ideas and the creation of spaces in which we might engage non-Western traditions of philosophy and study their own 'ways or forms of life' on their own terms.[14] Second, academic philosophy – much like metropolitan academia accepting the post-colonial and multicultural critique – is becoming more polycentric and embracing plural and diverse forms of intellectual production. Third, colonial powers and epistemologies are being provincialized; Westerners are no longer accepted as privileged interlocutors in a global dialogue. Fourth, Anglophone philosophy in particular is becoming more self-reflective about its obligations to consider an international context and cognisant that its role is less a result of intellectual superiority and more a legacy of colonialism and empire; hence, it needs to facilitate space and open participation for all. What is thus needed is a new map of philosophy and forms of pluralist realisms in the academic and even popular philosophical circles. Julian Baggini – perhaps one of our more prominent philosopher public intellectuals – has reflected this turn in his recent work *How the World Thinks*.[15]

At the same time, to decolonise philosophy does not mean that global philosophy should be motivated by white guilt and a compensatory inclusion, nor should it be a vehicle for the dissemination of essentialised ethnic chauvinism. Nor is the call for global philosophy a manifesto for (cultural and epistemological) relativism: van Norden, Ganeri and others are very much committed to forms of realism and highly critical of relativism. Rather, as I contend, non-European traditions of philosophy, including Islamic ones, have something to offer by way of argument, thought experiment, ontology, hermeneutics, narrative, mimesis, and even poetics.[16] Islamic philosophy requires a double movement of decolonisation; not just overcoming the Western condescending gaze that restricts philosophy to a marginal Aristotelianism in the cultures of Islam or even concerning an Arabic proleptic Lockeanism (à la Gutas), but also to look beyond the narrowly ratiocinative and the generic boundaries of *falsafa* and even *ḥikma* in search of persuasive discourse and argumentation. Recognising the extent of the coloniality of philosophy is critical to effect an emancipatory and reparative decolonial turn against the ethnocentrism, commodification, and solipsistic complacence of metropolitan academic (Anglophone) philosophy.[17]

Decoloniality, much more than the narrowly political and historical process of decolonisation, concerns ontology, epistemology, and praxis – how we are and how we think and act authentically, with a clear critical notion of history itself, without falling back on essentialist notions of cultural traditions and ways of being, or even reverting to nativism.[18] It can present 'local' definitions of the human.[19] Coloniality "used in recent scholarship indicates the epistemic dominance of western and Eurocentric modernity, including its suppression of methodological critiques and alternate modes of thought."[20] It is a regime of power that survives formal historical and colonial governance and continues to reproduce Eurocentrism, an idea of Europe, and privileged notions of race.[21] Decoloniality, by contrast, is a non-linear movement towards possibilities of modes of being, thinking, knowing, sensing, and living in the plural that are other than those complicit (without necessarily entirely overcoming) coloniality.[22] As such, it proposes forms of relationality and interdependence that contest the totalising, epistemic claims and power of modernity and its abstract universals that set up hierarchical binaries: mind and matter, science and magic, reason and superstition, orality and literacy, male and female, and modernity and tradition, among other major concepts. Significantly, it is a process and an endeavour – much like philosophy in this conception.

Such a conceptual approach is not without its critics. Here I consider another objection. Decolonisation remains a Eurocentric and hierarchical pursuit of the Western academy. As a form of identity politics, it suffers from 'elite capture,' furthering the interests of metropolitan elites and fails to live up to Marx's call for philosophy to change the world and not merely interpret it (in the eleventh of his "Theses on Feuerbach").[23] From another perspective within Africana thought, decolonialisation denies history and agency and fails to deal with incommensurabilities of language.[24] These are reasonable criticisms and one cannot fail to notice that there is a 'decolonial bandwagon.'[25] However, there are different modes of decoloniality that do not need to valorise native knowledge systems in an uncritical manner, nor do they need to ignore the question of agency and choice among intellectuals in the global south. A historical approach to the study of those systems will reveal internal critiques and contestations as well as the emergence of major traditions alongside minor ones. To reiterate, decoloniality as understood here entails a praxis as well as an ontology and epistemology. Put simply, how we do philosophy should change us and the world around us.

Global philosophy dislodges us from our parochial and highly specialised, perhaps trivial, concerns, and reorients us towards the notion that the pressing task of philosophy is to consider, debate, and keep alive the major, fundamental, urgent problems that we face as embodied and self-reflective beings, to examine attempts to make sense and even solve problems, and finally, to evaluate the success of those possible solutions. The study of the humanities in Muslim cultures is precisely concerned with what it means to be human and that cuts across different modes of expression – poetry, prose, plastic arts, music, calligraphy – as well different genres from Sufism to philosophical theology to law and legal theory. Sometimes the most philosophically profound work that changes our assumptions about knowing, being, and doing arises from compositions that do not self-identity as philosophy. Furthermore, an approach to philosophy as a way of life, following Pierre Hadot, may well be a better comparative framework for some traditions.[26] Philosophy in pursuit of wisdom needs to embrace the affective and the broad sense of our cognitive, embodied lives that cannot be ratiocinatively reductionist. It needs to be more than what can be inscribed in Greek, or German, or Arabic.

How to Study Islamic Texts in 'Philosophy'

The study of philosophy today seems to be animated by two related inquiries. The first concerns how and to what end should we study the history of philosophy? Should it be concerned with the processes of canon formation and the 'making of the western mind' or should it instead seek a more connected and holistic inter-cultural approach to broader, and more pressing, questions located within modes of rationality? To what extent, should philosophy be engaged in a process of decolonisation and 'provincialization' of Europe?[27] Furthermore, should it focus on discerning contexts or discovering philosophical problems (though this latter concept is not so transparent)? Is the history of philosophy itself primarily a philosophical endeavour of appropriation, mining past sources for own contemporary concerns, or is it an historical process of contextualising?[28] Certainly, anglophone analytic philosophers often take pride in being negligent of history, dismissing the continental tradition for its enthusiastic embrace of exegesis of past philosophers and the history of concepts and arguments.[29] But as Tom Sorrell, who cites this view, notes: while it might be true that philosophy has merely been the logical reconstruction of certain objects, the history of philosophy, even in an analytic mode, can shed light on arguments and problems – especially as all history proceeds from some present location.[30] That explains not only why Heidegger engaged with Aristotle and Kant, and why Brandom recently wrote an extensive commentary on Hegel's *Phenomenology of the Spirit*, but also why Mullā Ṣadrā's *al-Ḥikma al-mutaʿāliya* is a *tour de force* engagement with practically every major thinker in the Islamic traditions before him.[31]

The second inquiry relevant here concerns the very universality of philosophy: are we speaking about a universal pursuit and practice with different cultural expressions or are there distinct traditions of thinking that might overlap but remain irreconcilable with each other due to their substantial differences? An important corollary question here is what does it meant to identify a particular cultural tradition as philosophical? For example, what mode of reasoning and rationality is indexed in the name "Islamic philosophy"? Are we interested in finding philosophical truths or meaning? These questions indicate that we need a more connected approach to traditions of thinking in our globalising times: we need "connected histories" that challenge nationalist historiographies and other modes of historical research that search for cosmopolitanisms or rationalities or knowledge networks or commonalities of vernacular traditions. The objective of these alternative histories would be to seek connections that interrogate the common concepts involved in world-making.[32] Of course, there might be a reason for questioning the humanistic assumption of such globalised philosophical inquiry: is it reasonable to expect philosophical cultures to forgo their ethical, cultural, and religious commitments in order to find a place at the table of philosophical conversation?

As William Edelglass and Jay Garfield put it:

> Philosophy – the aim [. . .] to understand how things, in the broadest sense of the term, hang together, in the broadest sense of that term – has been a significant activity in many cultures for several millennia at least, even when we restrict that mode of understanding to something like, *rational*, *analytic*

> understanding. It seems to be a natural development in all literate societies, and in many nonliterate societies as well, to ask difficult questions about the fundamental nature of reality, about what it is to be human, about what constitutes the good life, about the nature of beauty, and about how we can know any of these things.[33]

It is indeed one of the legacies of colonialism to consider philosophy as compartmentalised into cultural traditions – a point to which we will return shortly. But let us start with the universal before going to the particular. The late Richard Rorty, in an influential article on philosophy in history, put forward four paradigms for considering why we should study the history of philosophy.[34] The first is rational and historical reconstruction, which sometimes takes the form, among analytic philosopher, of treating past thinkers as contemporaries since a mere historical approach would render them little more than doxographers. However, the more successful and dominant form of reconstruction is modelled by the Cambridge school of contextualism, which eschews prolepsis and is predicated on the axiom of rationality as articulated by Quentin Skinner: "No agent can eventually be said to have meant or done something which he could never be brought to accept as a correct description of what he had meant or done."[35] Similarly, being aware of other intellectual contexts forces us to face up to the contingency of our own situation and choices that we argue.[36] But the problem with this is how to determine? Is it Eurocentric? Or too focused on political thought? What is the nature of the historical contingency? Can we know the context? A number of commentators have critiqued Skinner, not least Jonardon Ganeri, who points out the shortcomings of applying this method to the study of Indian philosophy.[37] Islamic traditions of philosophy arguably also have the same challenges of determining the context, that of the original utterance seeking the illocutionary (within the context of Skinner's application of speech act theory) and of the evaluation, made more complicated by the layers of commentary and hence of many further contexts.

Rorty's second paradigm concerns how we may wish to engage in Whiggish canon-formation; but beyond collecting the classics in the history of reason, how does this constitute philosophy? If philosophy plays a critical role in the questions of our assumptions and frames of reference, if it involves as Rorty put it in a famous earlier volume, a critique of the optimistic vision of philosophy as the science of mapping reality onto the mind, then should we not be deconstructing canons instead of forming them?[38] His third paradigm is about doxography that constitutes a way of understanding doctrine, and while this is not the study of philosophy as such, it is often indispensable. Certainly in the classical Islamic period, doxographies played a major role in inspiring philosophical argument, even when they significantly distorted the thought that they presented – but then as Pierre Hadot famously held, it is often the creative but mistaken reading that is the dynamic impetus for the charge of philosophy.[39]

Rorty's final point allows us to grapple with intellectual history. This is critical to see the intellectual life interacting in society, the importance of addressing minor figures who have been minoritized, and richness of the sense of philosophy and seeking new materials for the history of philosophy. It further involves taking philosophy back into culture and connecting it with other literary disciplines. Perhaps like Rorty we should just cast our net wide, and not guard the borders between philosophy and non-philosophy.[40] Moreover, texts related to a range of contexts must be considered: the immediate historical context, the generic context, the longer intellectual context, and levels of reception within the commentary tradition, culminating with our own attempt to make sense of the text. Our logic of selection should avoid rubrics such as "good" or "bad" philosophy; rather we should see how things 'once hung together' and how we can understand philosophy in its particular place and time.[41] The particular and the historical can also be a means to retain memory; the decolonial uncovering of epistemicide is critical in the case of phenomena such as slavery, for example.[42]

One of the more famous recent attempts to define philosophy begins with the classical distinction between wisdom (*sophia*) and philosophy as love of wisdom (*philosophia*) – as such we should engage in the latter as a process of concept formation across time. Deleuze and Guattari critique the Platonic ideal – philosophy for them is not about contemplation (of the ideas) or reflection or even communication (following Wittgenstein) which they consider to be based not on concepts but on consensus: "the idea of a Western democratic conversation between friends has never produced a single concept."[43] They continue their critique of the Greek ideas by arguing that the universal explains nothing, philosophy is not about knowing oneself or learning to think, or even questioning what is or is not self-evident.[44] The tradition we call today "philosophy" may have arisen in Greece but the cultural context is a pre-philosophical given and does not necessarily obstruct the process of concept formation.[45]

Nevertheless, they remain naively optimistic:

> The philosopher is expert in concepts and in the lack of them. He knows which of them are not viable, which are arbitrary or inconsistent, which ones do not hold up for an instant. On the other hand, he also knows which are well formed and attest to a creation, however disturbing or dangerous it may be.[46]

This, of course, begs the question of how the philosopher does these things. Based on rational discernment? Mystical intuition? Taste and prejudice?

> The philosopher is the friend of concepts and of the ultimate concept of wisdom; but that friendship brings with it a claim upon the object as well as rivalry and distrust recognising the elusive nature of the transcendental given.[47]

This type of philosophy, as a critical – even sceptical – endeavour, can lead to a rather narrow sense of philosophy as a particular heritage of argumentation, dismissing more intuitive, mystical, and even narratological modes of presenting rationales. We tend to think that philosophy – or what Smith calls *philosophia* – originates with the Greeks and constitutes a cultural specific mode of philosophising that we have universalised because of the European tradition, but which remained rooted in the particularity of Eurocentrism. Our analytic tradition has no doubt been misled by Hegel's dismissal of the non-European in his famous *Philosophy of World History* in which, somewhat ironically, Chinese and Indian philosophy were dismissed as tending to mysticism; philosophy properly "begins in Greece" as Hegel put it.[48] By locating Africa and Asia at the end of the introduction to the History of Philosophy, he sought to clarify that the idea of philosophy was absolute but exclusive and did not embrace 'barbarisms'; even Jewish and Islamic philosophy did not constitute 'philosophy proper' tainted by those barbarisms despite sharing the common heritage of European thought and indeed influencing it.[49]

Hegel's neglect of the East was coupled with a political dismissal; philosophy, for Hegel, could only arise in the *polis* and be articulated by a citizen bearing political freedoms.[50] The development of our modern conception of philosophy and its teleology of the Greeks to Kant and Hegel owes much to the colonial and racist contexts whence it emerged. If we use the history of philosophy to re-affirm a canon, then in effect through our selection and exclusions, we are perpetuating the notion of philosophy as a peculiarly European phenomenon.[51] It is this history of philosophy, which requires de-colonising, and the recent trends towards global and comparative philosophies are playing a major role in doing so – and as Richard Rorty once said, canon formation is not the main reason why we might wish to do the history of philosophy. This is also precisely why some prefer the notion of cross-cultural instead of comparative philosophy, rejecting the mere juxtaposition of texts in which there is an assumed dominance of the conceptual framework of the analytic tradition, in favour of conversation and not interrogation of texts, communication with a recognition of equal distance, a conversation of peers.[52] This conversation needs to work across traditions and embedded in tradition so that one is not applying an analytic reading of Mādhyāmaka but bringing the latter tradition in conversation with the former. As Jay Garfield puts it,

> Traditions make understanding possible. But this possibility is achieved through occlusion. When we understand a text, we exploit its anaphoric relation to its predecessors, as well as our background of cultural prejudices. These considerations apply mutatis mutandis to conversational interactions. Locating a text as an object of analysis involves making salient particular features of that text while suppressing others, privileging certain intertextual relationships

> over others, and selecting among commentarial traditions. Interrogating a text is always interrogation with interest. A decontextualized text is impossible to read; a decontextualized interchange is impossible to follow, just because of the essentially intertextual character of any text. But all of this means that in *selecting*, and in *foregrounding*, we unavoidably select *against*, and *background*. Understanding hence involves, as part of its very structure, blindness.[53]

Of necessity, this requires not just philological skills but also a recognition that in different contexts the relationships between philosophy, religion, and literature may not be the same in those traditions as we have now in the analytic tradition (in a post-Enlightenment, desacralized and secularized world). Again Garfield: "Ignoring the philosophical traditions of other cultures in fact, whether we like it or not, continues the colonial project of subordinating those cultures to our own."[54] And this at a time when pragmatists and other post-structuralists have exploded the simple generic boundaries between narratives, literature, philosophy, religion, and the arts.[55]

Philosophy has a practical and artistic aspect to it; it may even constitute a way of life as articulated by Pierre Hadot, a concept that especially recently has been extended to modern philosophy and the wider notion of a non-religious or even religious sets of spiritual practices and therapies of the soul.[56] In the work of Jean Greisch, philosophy does not arise *ex nihilo* from an act of revelation or of closeted learning but accrues from the experience of life and living philosophically.[57] It is the very nature of the human condition and its suffering – and in this sense faithful to the notion of *theosis* (*taʾalluh* in the Arabic tradition) as a 'fleeing from the vicissitudes' of this material world and acquiring virtue articulated in Plato's *Theaetetus* and *Timaeus*.[58] As Porphyry wrote to his wife Marcella (Letter to Marcella 31):

> Vain is the word of that philosopher who can ease no mortal trouble. As there is no profit in the physician's art unless it cure the diseases of the body, so there is none in philosophy, unless it expel the troubles of the soul.[59]

In this sense can philosophy be a practical pursuit – and alongside that one ought to consider a more expansive sense of philosophy by considering the nature of the problems and questions posed and not whether the subject matter overlaps with theology, mysticism or literature.[60] Thus includes *ʿilm al-kalām* and mysticisms as well as elements of linguistic analysis and exegesis. This does not mean that philosophy is everything but rather that one may find approaches to philosophical reasoning in texts that do not signpost themselves as such. The blurring of – or perhaps bleeding across – the boundaries of the ratiocinative and contemplative with the intuitive and praxis-oriented is akin to the ways in which the analytic-continental divide and even the Eastern and Western philosophy divides are increasingly obsolete and uninformative.

So what might be the features of philosophy in Islamic contexts that may speak to these cross-cultural concerns while remaining faithful to their origins?[61] The first is that it constitutes a tradition of rationality, following both Garfield on the need for authenticity and MacIntyre's (and to an extent Seyyed Hossein Nasr's) notion of a rational tradition.[62] As Aristotle would put it, humans desire to know – or as the Qur'an might, "will you not then reflect?" One ought to pay attention to the text, to its levels of contexts, avoid an appropriation that is proleptic, recognise the historical contingency of the object of study and of ourselves, and make full sense of that tradition including, following Rorty, engaging with the minor figures that for their time defined the philosophical pursuit.

Second, philosophy is a way of life, an *askesis* including the textual study of scripture, a therapy of the soul and a lived experience in which, in concert with and in allegiance to, one seeks to become a sage. It is an art of living – and of dying, a path of perfection. As Hadot put it, speaking of ancient philosophy:

> Each school, then, represents a form of life defined by an ideal of wisdom. The result is that each one has its corresponding fundamental inner attitude [. . .] but above all every school practises exercises designed to ensure spiritual progress towards the ideal state of wisdom, exercises of reason that will be, for the soul, analogous to the athlete's training or to the application of a medical cure [. . .].
>
> It seems to me, indeed, that in order to understand the works of the philosophers of antiquity we must take account of all the concrete conditions in which they wrote, all the constraints that weighted upon them: the context of the school, the very nature of *philosophia*, literary genres, rhetorical rules, dogmatic imperatives, and traditional modes of reasoning. One cannot read an ancient author the way one does a contemporary author [. . .] in fact, the works of antiquity are produced under entirely different conditions than those of their modern counterparts.[63]

Thus, we return to the theme of distance. The notion of spiritual exercises takes us to the third feature of philosophy as a religious commitment, a spiritual practice, and especially a soteriology. We need to take religion seriously and pay attention to what thinkers claim for themselves; language and rhetoric – and the totality of the illocutionary – are part and parcel of the message. There is an element of a Wittgensteinian emphasis of language as a means for the bewitchment of our minds. If a thinker uses scriptural texts or poetry as part of his argumentation, we need to examine why he is doing so.[64]

Fourth, both a process of rationality and a way or form of life require a discerning, contemplative and reflective subject. While not all forms and traditions of Islamic philosophy are necessarily so foundationalist, most do have a notion of selfhood and of subjectivity that is located in our deepest intuitions. That is, after all the function of Avicenna's famous thought experiment of the suspended person (or perhaps merely being) that is presented in the context of his definition of the rational soul in the opening chapter of his *De Anima*. Practices and ideas about selfhood tend to bind together various notions of philosophy even in those traditions that either espouse selfhood as a bundle of experiences or those that are more radically sceptical about any substantial form of the self or the person.[65]

Now we can take these features of philosophising in Islamic contexts and find one popular exemplum, namely the definition that the Safavid thinker Mullā Ṣadrā Šīrāzī gives in the introduction to his magnum opus the *Four Journeys*:

> Know that philosophy is the perfecting of the human soul through cognition of the realities of existents as they truly are, and through judgements about their being ascertained through demonstrations and not understood through conjecture or adherence to authority, to the measure of human capacity. You might say that philosophy ascribes to the world a rational order understood according to human capacity so that one may attain a resemblance to the creator.
>
> The human emerges as a mixture of two: a spiritual form from the world of command, and sensible matter from the world of creation, and thus he possesses in his soul both attachment to the physical and detachment from it. Philosophy is sharpened through the honing of two faculties relating to two practices: one theoretical and abstract, and the other practical, attached to creation [. . .].
>
> The theoretical art [metaphysics] is the wisdom sought by the Lord of the messengers – peace be with him – when he sought in his supplication to his lord, saying, "O my Lord, show me things as they truly are!"[66]

Given our desire for deploying Islamic philosophy for cross-cultural purposes, one can discern a number of instructive themes in these features and in this key definition of philosophy a number of instructive themes. First, philosophy in history must go beyond a Eurocentric canon and transcend exclusionary practices. Second, one needs to pay attention to more holistic forms of discourse, desire to seek meaning and understanding, alongside ethical commitments. Third, by opening up to Islamic philosophy, we can further the process of decolonising philosophy, and enrich if not discard the old notion of a Eurocentric liberal education and replace it with a wider pedagogy of modes of contemplative living and being. Times change – what was Islamic philosophy in the Safavid period should be something more contextual today. We do not have the systems of patronage that sustained it and our notion of the humanities is both similar and distinct from the notion of science in the middle period (given a particular trajectory of Western history). Nevertheless, it would, one suspects, remain a dialogical, cumulative, critical, and rational enterprise predicated on the individuality of thought of the philosopher and ideally independent of the seats of power.[67] Our desire that philosophy decolonises hegemonies and speaks truth to power would be rather consistent with a vision of Islam that is spiritually, intellectually, and ethically oppositional. Such a vision puts forward a portrait and a picture of what has been and what might be. Islamic philosophical futures may construct those portraits profitably by considering those from the history of Islamic intellectual traditions from which we now present three examples.

Abū l-ʿAbbās Aḥmad Bābā of Timbuktu: Legal Activist as Philosopher

Our first portrait – and a figure who rarely if ever reckons in any intellectual history of philosophy in Islam is the Ṣanḥāğa Berber and legal scholar Aḥmad Bābā (963/1556–1063/1627) of Timbuktu who lived in the turbulence of the Moroccan invasion of Timbuktu and the developing slave trade in West Africa that transforms into the North Atlantic slave trade. Primarily a jurist, he also wrote an important biographical dictionary of Mālikī jurists, entitled *Nayl al-ibtiḥāğ*, that placed the tradition of Timbuktu at the heart even if he said little of the role of black scholars in the exposition of the tradition. The significance of this history of knowledge production, scholars, and their transmission lies in his quest to make sense of and take seriously not just learning for its sake but the lived experience that arises from a way of life.[68] His own experience of being taken as a prisoner (as a slave?) to Marrakech and living there for years in confinement might have something to do with his own understanding of the question of slavery. It is unlikely that Aḥmad Bābā considered himself to be black and it is not clear whether the Moroccans did.

Aḥmad Bābā did not define himself as a philosopher but his name remains ever linked to the intellectual history of Islam not least because of the library in Timbuktu named after him. But as a legal scholar, he was perfectly aware that legal language was both an attempt to make sense of the ethics of the moral obligation humans undertook as a step towards rational faith, and as a means to make the world and understand commitments. This of course required expertise in logic and language, the principles of the law and textual hermeneutics; the intimate link of legal reasoning and philosophy is quite clear. He wrote extensively in these areas, manuscripts of which a number survive in his library. In the question of legal selfhood and understanding the legal subjectivity of others, his work makes an important contribution not least because it engages with issues of race and social justice that a critical history of slavery needs to address.

Here, I want to present *Miʿrāğ al-ṣuʿūd ilā nayl muğallab al-sūd* on his critique of racial slavery as undignified for humans, on the trade of black Africans to North Africa.[69] The question of race in the premodern Sahel is not a simple one to unpack; notions of blackness were complicated by Arabness, being Berber, and of course by religion.[70] Earlier in exile in Marrakech, he responded with rulings on two questions.[71] The first concerned ontology and identity: who can and who cannot be enslaved. Here his response was based on religious distinction, but he also recognised that in West Africa the situation of conversion was fluid. The second question was whether there could be slaves in a Muslim context if one did not know of their origins and provenance. Here the reply was simple: if someone claims to be free, that claim should be respected, and one ought to be cautious not to buy free people. To an extent this also seems to accord to a well-known principle in legal theory that one should presume the continuation of a *status quo ante* (*al-istiṣḥāb*) with respect to one's original status (*al-wuğūd al-aṣlī*).[72] The main work was written later in 1616 back in Timbuktu. This argued that the only justification for slavery was someone's status as an unbeliever, and that one could not enslave Muslims, and indeed that colour was not a factor.[73] As people were constantly coming to the faith, the basic humanity of the people of West Africa was affirmed. He went further and showed how a jurist needs to reflect upon rational and even philosophical norms and social experience; the basic prejudice that associated being black with being a slave as a result of the 'curse of Ham' was strongly rejected by him as being baseless. He even drew upon his experience as a slave and argued that one ought to demonstrate some empathy as slavery was a devastating indignity that Muslims ought not to support.[74]

The main contribution of Aḥmad Bābā was to decouple blackness from slavery and focus on dignity and religious confession; race was a construction whether following notion of geographical determination or other forms of social consideration. The true distinction between peoples (following Ibn Ḫaldūn) was religious confession. Nevertheless, he did not seem immune from essentialising race; all races were equal on the path to salvation, just as they were all equally capable of being enslaved.[75] While there is evidence for a more nuanced way in which law can allow us to apply a more decolonial understanding of the enslaved/free binary, his work did not constitute an emancipatory shift.

Three important issues might arise here. The first concerns the ethics of the human subject both the person investigating as well as the subjects of his inquiry. Alongside this is the positionality of our philosopher as a jurist seeking the legal self and personality entailed in the consideration. There is evidence that Aḥmad Bābā saw the slave other as one worthy of empathy and dignity. He was clear about his scholarship and his pride in his hometown, but he did not necessarily champion it as a black space even if it was primarily thus. His assertion of his selfhood and those in Timbuktu ought to be read in the wider context of how we see the emergence of selfhood in different contexts.

Second, while his works and others are recorded – and many works remain unread and barely known in the study of Islam and of philosophy more broadly – there was much that was not. In Aḥmad Bābā's own critique of essentialism, perhaps we ought to extend that to the way in which philosophy in Africa is often conceived. Philosophy in Africa needs to be considered critically beyond colonialist borrowings from French trained thinkers as well as reducing all premodern thought to a privileged set of oral tales over the written archive and argumentation.[76] The challenge is to find the philosophical in the mythical and in the narrative. The arguments are there for those seeking them – and even in a legal judgement the recourse to social conventions and metaphysics seems to be clear. How might we find philosophy in all literary spaces? Does it matter for the portrait of Aḥmad Bābā whether he was black?

Third, a philosophical reflection on language as well as selfhood is clear here and the potential to speak truth to power and critique that is often associated with the act of philosophising. But one should also recognise the limits of the scope of such an approach in the same way as when we look at other historical accounts. The rejection of essentialist language as well as an essential approach to the question of race is still a useful indicator that can inform some of the current debates in philosophical contexts in West Africa.

Umm Salama Bēgum Nayrīzī: Lover and Mystic as Philosopher

Our second case is that of the 18th century Sufi and daughter of the Ẕahabī pīr Sayyid Quṭb al-Dīn Muḥammad Nayrīzī (d. 1173/1760), Umm Salama Bēgum Nayrīzī (b. 1143/1731). We know very little about her beyond the composition date of the work as 1173/1761. We know from the recent work of Ata Anzali that the Ẕahabī order emerged in the 18th century around the city of Shiraz as a Shiʿi development claiming roots in the Central Asian Kubravī tradition aligned to the metaphysics of the school of Ibn ʿArabī as well as a spiritual lineage in the golden chain (*silsilat al-ḏahab*) of the Shiʿi Imams to ʿAlī al-Riḍā.[77] The emergence of the order is associated with three figures: Nağīb al-Dīn Rižā Zargar Tabrīzī (d. c. 1108/1697), his successor ʿAlī-Naqī Isṭahbānātī (d. 1129/1717) and then his successor Quṭb al-Dīn Nayrīzī – each chain of succession was also strengthened by filiation as the successor married the daughter of his spiritual master. Thus, Umm Salama's mother was the daughter of Isṭahbānātī and her maternal grandmother was the daughter of Nağīb al-Dīn Rižā; she herself in turn married Muḥammad Hāšim Darvīsh-i Šīrāzī (d. 1199/1785) who was her father's successor. In that sense she came from a female lineage at the very heart of the order and its teachings. The milieu of her father's students also included her brothers Sayyid ʿAlī and Sayyid Ḥasan, some prominent Sufi-inclined jurists in the shrine cities of Iraq such as Sayyid Muḥammad Mahdī Baḥr al-ʿulūm (d. 1212/1797), and prominent philosophers of the school of Mullā Ṣadrā in the post-Safavid period such as Mullā Miḥrāb Gīlānī (d. 1217/1802) and Āqā Muḥammad Bīdābādī (d. 1197/1783).[78] Born in Shiraz, she grew up on Karbala and Najaf, the Shiʿi shrine cities in Iraq that were centres for the study of philosophy and mysticism in the middle of the 18th century.

Ǧāmiʿ al-kulliyyāt is a summary of her father's metaphysics (based on the monism of the school of Ibn ʿArabī) and demonstrates her own understanding and learning. As is often the case, the author presents her portrait as an imitation of the prior precursor of her father; she claims no originality and regards her work as a Persian and hence accessible summary of her father's Arabic poem *Faṣl al-ḫiṭāb*. The work itself was completed when her father died – and she was thirty years old:

> This is a mere book that this lowly servant and descendant of the family of the prophet, servitor of the Sufis, whose pen-name is Supplicant (*duʿā'*), but whose name is Umm Salama Bēgum, has gleaned from the lights of the suns of philosophy and mysticism; I have gathered together here issues of divine philosophy that express arcana in few words of profound meaning and hence have named this work Compendium of Universal Topics (*Ǧāmiʿ al-kullīyāt*). No work can bring quicker comprehension of the problems of philosophy and knowledge of God than *Faṣl al-ḫiṭāb*, known as *Philosophy of the Mystics* that my late, blessed father the cream of mystics and pillar of leaders, wrote [. . .]. The problems of philosophy are clearly and precisely presented, and the pearls of wisdom gathered in one vessel, as well as the teachings of the Imams on these issues, in the order that most efficaciously explains [. . .].
>
> However, the work *Faṣl al-ḫiṭāb* is in Arabic verse and many students on the path to God are Persian speakers and do not have sufficient Arabic. There I compiled this work over a fifteen-year period from the age of fifteen until the passing of my father from this ephemeral world, attending the classes of my father in which he explained philosophy, and I attended each one of these sessions collecting the gems of wisdom, and of these fifteen years, five were in Fars [Shiraz], then ten in Najaf [. . .].
>
> This work is a mere sample of that larger work such that when one reads *Faṣl al-ḫiṭāb*, having acquired Arabic, one will understand it better.[79]

The work – for a Shiʿi author – is significantly structured into fourteen chapters on the model of the procession and then reversion of being, beginning with discussions of the divine presences and the modes of the manifestation of being and its becoming in the cosmos followed by the stages of the development of the human soul, its recollection of its true abode, and return to the presence of the divine. This is classic onto-theology, cosmogony, soteriology, psychology, and epistemology all presented in a holistic image. The final sections as one often finds in such texts discuss the ethical modalities of the Sufi path and the role of exemplars and narrative and portraiture in that process.

In terms of her method, Nayrīzī, like her father, extensively cites her own poetry along with her prose discussion of the issues; the poetry is the vehicle for philosophical ideas. Not all of the poetry is hers; she also cites the classics of the tradition such as ʿIrāqī, Rūmī, and ʿAṭṭār.[80] This mixture of styles of inscription coalesces with her reflective philosophical commentary which is 'exegesis as philosophy' based on homologies of the three books or inscribed texts of the cosmos (scripture, macrocosm and microcosm). In doing so she demonstrates her knowledge of Arabic and her skill at rendering celebrated supplications of the Shiʿi tradition into Persian such as the famous dawn supplication (*duʿāʾ al-ṣabāḥ*).[81] Similar to the Safavid philosophical tradition, we see her intersperse argument with commentary on certain key sayings of the Shiʿi Imams: for example, citing ʿAlī from the well-known first sermon of *Nahǧ al-balāġa* on divine simplicity and how the existence and essence of God, and indeed her essence, attributes and names might have different senses but a singular referent in extra-mental reality, and the equally famed exchange between the eighth Imam ʿAlī al-Riḍā at the court of al-Maʾmūn with ʿImrān the Sabean on the critical existential link between God and the cosmos and what the true referent of existence is.[82] Metaphysics as exegesis indeed – and even as reflection upon ritual performance.

The school of Mullā Ṣadrā was emerging as the most significant in the 18th century and while she demonstrates a sense of that tradition but – unlike Nayrīzī – she does not explicitly cite his work (though at times it seems that she cites the same texts that Mullā Ṣadrā does). On one point, the eschatological production by the soul of a body of the afterlife, she seems to be aware of this in terms of the 'corporealisation' of the soul.[83] Consistent with her father, she seems to support an unconditioned monism or unity of existence and not a modulated sense of existence or its reality that one finds in Mullā Ṣadrā. Similarly, she shares the desire to use scriptural terms such as *rūḥ* for the soul as opposed to *nafs* which commonplace in the philosophical tradition: the levels and stages of the soul are not associated with Avicennian psychology of the faculties and the inner senses but the Qurʾanic idea of the moral psychology of the soul as inclining to evil, self-blaming, and contented with God and self.[84]

Is this a sufficient recovery of a voice and the representation of a significant portrait? If one extends one's sense of the role of Sufi metaphysics, then it certainly constitutes philosophy in the Islamic traditions. The work constitutes a cycle of teachings on the nature of metaphysics, on philosophical anthropology, on the nature of the human soul, its knowledge and its agency, and on the culmination of existence and human life in eschatology. This is philosophy with clear theological commitments. And, while the claim to be derivative is there throughout along with the claims to divine inspiration, these lies easily alongside the pride in her own work and expression – and one finds that in the concluding lines starting with a poem and then her final words:

> Praise to God and with your grace, God,
> For bestowing a book in response to my prayer.
> A book that captures the completion that is attached
> To this very world, itself a [divine] inscription.
> Inscribed in hand, now one thousand and
> One hundred and seventy-three after the migration [year 1173/1761].
> Lord, be merciful to each three,
> The compiler, the writer and the reader.
> Each person who seeks and desire its explanation
> May they find and achieve it.
> May the cooling of the eye of the sun be achieved [of her father]
> A rising sun that emerges from the water's edge.
>
> Know, seekers of the path to God, that this lowly one is a mote of the dust of the threshold of the Sufis of the Ẕahabī Kubravī order. This order, passes from hand to hand from the leader of the path, the master of the order and the Pole of the people of mysticism Shaykh Muḥammad ʿAlī Muʾaḏḏin Ḫurāsānī, and from him to the father of the mother of the mother this lowly author, namely, the person who manifests divine attraction and is the result of the infinite grace and revealer of the mysteries of the Qurʾan and the manifestation of the secrets of the Seven oft-repeated (*Sabʿ-i maṯānī*), Shaykh Naǧīb al-Dīn Riżā Tabrīzī, may his secret be sanctified, and from him to the treasure trove of the arcana of the divine and the rising point of the lights of the divine realm and the leader of the people of realization and the caravan leader of true knowledge and precision understanding Shaykh ʿAlī Naqī Iṣṭahbānātī and from him to my blessed late father the master of those on the path, the Pole of mystics, and the one who establishes the order of the people of intimacy and certainty and carries the legacy of the perfect masters of old, and author of fourteen works including *Faṣl al-ḫiṭāb*, known as *Philosophy of the Mystics*, Sayyid Quṭb al-Dīn Muḥammad Šīrāzī, may God bless his soul and elevate his rank, who is buried in Najaf in Wādī al-Salām.[85]

This is then followed by a final whispered prayer in verse. She has established her credentials and as one expects in the patriarchy of Sufism connected to her paternal line but also mentioned how that spiritual lineage is carried through marriage and the maternal line.

ʿAbd al-ʿAlī Muḥammad b. Niẓām al-Din [Baḥr al-ʿulūm]: Sunni Metaphysician and Court Philosopher

Our final example is definitely someone who does figure in histories of philosophy in the world of Islam and for the later period from 1750 he is arguably one of the most successful portraits of a philosopher in the Islamic East. The history of Islamic philosophy in India still awaits a serious monograph or sustained critical and textual study.[86] The embarrassment of riches available in manuscript form has attracted little attention beyond scholars attempting to cull materials from Indian libraries for research in earlier periods of thought whether in Islamic Neoplatonisms or the transmission of the Hellenic texts themselves.[87] However, the field is not entirely devoid of its devotees. While the history of Islamic thought in India has yet to be properly written, the learned culture of the high Mughal period has increasingly attracted attention, focusing on the role of texts in the *Dars-i Niẓāmī* curriculum, devised in the 18th century to produce cohorts of capable imperial administrators, and on the intellectual life of Delhi, Lucknow and the Doab in the middle to late Mughal period.[88] If indeed, as Dimitri Gutas indicated in a famous article twenty years ago, the post-Avicennian period is the golden age of Arabic-Islamic philosophy, then the multiplicity of texts, authors and interest in the Islamic East of India that were marked by the influence of that period and the Safavid renaissance surely deserves some consideration, not least because it provides further evidence of the sustained influence of Avicennism.[89] ʿAbd al-ʿAlī Muḥammad was born in Lucknow 1144/1731, the son of Mullā Niẓām al-Dīn the famous founder of the so-called *Dars-i Niẓāmī* with its strong emphasis on the study of the rational arts, especially logic and philosophy.[90] He studied with his father and with his father's leading student (and his cousin) Mullā Kamāl al-Dīn Fateḥpurī (d. 1175/1761). The well-known biographical dictionary *Nuzhat al-ḫawāṭir* refers to him as a leader in law and jurisprudence, an itinerant Imam in philosophy, logic and rational theology. His fame as a learned person and a consummate teacher was such that he built a large network of students as he travelled around in response to patronage, first after some disputes leaving Lucknow for Shāhjahānpūr and the court of the Rohilla ruler Ḥāfiẓ Raḥmat Khān (d. 1774), then after his defeat in the wars against the British and their allies to the court of the Rohilla Nawāb of Rampur Fayżullāh Ḫān (d. 1794) where he taught at the Madrasa-yi ʿĀliya, moving briefly to Burdhwan in Bengal to teach at the madrasa of Būhār established in 1178/1764 by the notable Munšī Sayyid Ṣadr al-Dīn Mūsawī on a princely stipend of 400 rupees, and finally to Arcot to the court of Nawāb Vālāğāh Muḥammad ʿAlī Ḫān (d. 1795) in Madras, where a madrasa was built for him, he was given the title of *Malik al-ʿulamāʾ* (perhaps we could consider this to be the philosopher's version of a poet laureate) and *Baḥr al-ʿulūm* (Sea of Knowledge), and where he died in 1225/1810. In each of these places, his philosophical traces are present not least in the manuscripts in these collections that became known for their holdings in the subject, in the margins and para-texts, commentaries and glosses, and in the copies of codices.

He was both a court asset and a prolific glossator. Two major works of his were glosses on the work of Muḥibb Allāh Bihārī (d. 1119/1707) on the *Sullam al-ʿulūm* in logic and his extensive commentary *Fawātiḥ al-Raḥamūt on Musallam al-ṯubūt* on legal theory in which he defended a Ḥanafī method alongside Māturīdī theology.[91] Beyond that he was best known for writing on four major glosses and commentaries: the so-called *Ṣadrā* or the *Šarḥ al-hidāya* of Mullā Ṣadrā Šīrāzī, focusing on the definition of philosophy and the sciences, as well as on the natural philosophy, alongside the three glosses of Mīr Zāhid Hirawī (d. c. 1061/1651) on the section on general ontology in the text of rational theology *Šarḥ al-mawāqif* of al-Šarīf ʿAlī al-Ǧurǧānī (d. 816/1413), and on his gloss on the logic text *Tahḏīb al-manṭiq* of Taftazānī (d. 791/1390). His commitment to the Sufism of the school of Ibn ʿArabī was clear in his commentary on the *Masnavī* of Rūmī, and in a short treatise he wrote on the unity of existence and monism. Apart from these works, he wrote one independent treatise on metaphysics entitled *al-ʿUǧāla al-nāfiʿa.*

In his work, one discerns a focus on logic and precision of expression that locates logic as a supreme art within philosophy whose role it is to excavate a proper understanding of the problemata, to expound on the significance of semantics and the proper understanding of subject terms, and to see in general ontology or *umūr ʿāmma* the key to the links between things, terms and concepts that connects human language to minds and to the extra-mental. In *al-ʿUǧāla,* he makes it clear that the scope of metaphysics depends on the ambiguous nature of the term existence: it denotes the concept that is primary in our minds or it can refer to an extra-mental reality (ultimately God), or it can refer to a cause of effects or it can refer to the effects themselves.[92] Furthermore there is a basic distinction between the fact of being an existent and the general sense of existing for which he draws upon the Persian distinction between the verb to be and the substantive 'existence' (*hastī*). He seems to want to parse existence into a set of semantic markers while retaining the reality of existence for God alone consistent. Such an approach of denying the independent reality of existence to contingents is consistent with the school of Ibn ʿArabī.

His conception of metaphysics further brings together Avicennian cosmology and essentialism alongside the insights of the school of Ibn ʿArabī on the singular reality of existence lying with God and that all other than God are mere manifestations and theophanies with no independent reality of their own. Within 18th century debates and ever since the middle period and especially the attack on monism by the Naqshbandī Šayḫ Aḥmad Sirhindī (d. 1034/1624) through the supposedly alternative of *waḥdat al-šuhūd* (testifying to the singular vision of existence while adhering the metaphysical pluralism), Sufis were caught between the unconditioned monism of the classic school of Ibn ʿArabī and the metaphysical pluralism of *waḥdat al-šuhūd*.[93] On this, he wrote *Waḥdat al-wuǧūd wa-šuhūd al-ḥaqq fī kull mawǧūd* completed in the lifetime of Navvāb Vālāǧāh on his request in Persian to help disseminate it, although he had written an earlier version in Arabic.[94] The only true reality and reference of existence is God; in fact wading into the debate on the meaning of absolute or unconditioned existence (*wuǧūd muṭlaq*), he sides with the school of Ibn ʿArabī to assert that this can only be God and not the mere mentally posited concept of existence as such (or what Aristotelian tradition called being *qua* being).[95] Everything apart from God is a manifestation and sign; God's being flows in the phenomenal multiplicity that we experience but it neither inheres in them or is substantially identical to them.[96] God's perfection, his transcendence and his immanence means that God's existence cannot be associated with the notion of existence in general ontology: he cannot be made universal or particular, general and specific, cause and effect. He defends the doctrine of the unity of existence against the theological and philosophical contention that it is rationally absurd but stresses the limitations of human reason; mystical intuition asserts that it is true.[97] As it is common in Sufi works on existence, he extensively cites notions from the school of Ibn ʿArabī such as the divine presences whereby existence descends in grades of manifestation culminating in the perfect human, exemplified by the Prophet, who manifests the totality of God's existence and qualities. He says:

> The most sublime God has directed: "Truly those who pledge allegiance to you, O Muḥammad, do no less than pledge their allegiance to God; the hand of God is above their hands" (Q. 48: 10). This noble verse clearly informs us that the messenger of God was in fact the very essence of God. At the time of pledging allegiance to him, the companions were perfectly aware of the truth. At that moment, he was the manifestation of God [. . .]. There are numerous prophetic reports that corroborate the meaning that God is singular through his theophanies in the realm of the contingent, even if they are too numerous to recount.[98]

The human soul itself is the ultimate manifestation of divine existence – and within that category the soul of the prophets and the saints as perfect beings have a primary rank. One feature of this metaphysics of the prophet as the perfect human that is common with cognate accounts in Naqshbandī Sufi Šāh Walīullāh (d. 1176/1762) and Nāṣir ʿAlī ʿAndalīb (d. 1172/1759) is the stress upon the Sunni context of the Muḥammadan presence and reality; Baḥr al-ʿulūm extensively cites the spiritual and metaphysical authority of Abū Bakr and ʿUmar and rejects the Shiʿi notion of the perfect human as a sustaining cause and warrant for the cosmos.[99] This is very much the portrait of the philosopher as a Sunni metaphysician. Or rather the Sunni Sufi metaphysician as he asserts that only the Sufi in the guise of his own is the true sage, the *ḥakīm*: he can discern the rational order in the cosmos and see the links between the contingents and does possesses the ability to manifest the divine attributes, to affect godlikeness (in the mode of the demiurgic intellect of Plato's *Timaeus*).[100] He says:

> The real Sufis are those who protect and preserve the divine virtues throughout the creaturely realm, which would be impossible for those who have not attained this degree of perfection. In the real Sufi the truth becomes apparent that among the creation of God not every individual is in the position to cultivate inner contention because what causes the contentment of one individual may be the discontent of another. Since it is impossible to transmit divine virtue equally to all creatures these excellent authorities have instilled divine virtues into the inner states of those who are worthy of it [. . .]. These excellent ones have become the recipients of the divine virtues, of the most sublime God, the angels, the messengers, the prophets and the saints. Through their intervention the divine virtues permeate the world.[101]

Metaphysics as a speculative science thus becomes marginalised in his work by setting aside the two dominant Avicennian readings of Mīr Dāmād and Mullā Ṣadrā especially the latter with his modulated reality of existence, along with a stress upon Avicennian natural philosophy that explains the motions of the heart, the reality of scientific inquiry based on empirical observations, and a critique of atomism and other elements of the speculative occasionalism and cosmology of the Ashʿarī school. On the first of these, he critiques both the modulated reality of existence of Mullā Ṣadrā as well as the monism of Mīr Dāmād in which only God exists and we use the term to apportion parts of the derivative universal term of existence to things that we denote as existing outside of our minds – positions that he considers to be philosophically unsound.[102] In fact, the entirety of his relatively short *al-ʿUǧāla al-nāfiʿa* is designed to take down the positions of these two major Safavid thinkers.

Finally, it is worth mentioning his work in legal theory and theology that demonstrates his adherence to Māturīdī thought, *Fawātiḥ al-Raḥamūt* commenting on the *Musallam al-ṯubūt* of Bihārī, a push-back against the supposed reformism of the 18th century as well as a critical assessment of Ashʿarism. He begins in the sermon with a strong affirmation of Sunni identity: the companions and especially the caliphs are the source of true knowledge and understanding (*al-ʿirfān*), indeed of sanctity and intimacy with the divine (*al-walāya*).[103] He considers the science of legal theory and jurisprudence to represent the rational perfection of the human both in terms of the pure reason that pertains the metaphysics and practice of faith and practical reasons that considers actual precepts in our world. This science is thus like kohl that sharpens the ability of the eye to discern veracity and see the world as it is (in metaphysical terms).[104] The principles of deriving the law and understanding the moral obligations of humans constitutes for Baḥr al-ʿulūm the ultimate confluence of the scriptural and the rational arts, philosophy and revelation works in tandem.[105] He then again lays out his confessional colours by cleaving to the school of Abū Ḥanīfa and his central Asian followers: Ḥanafī and Māturīdī.[106] On the definitions of the science, he makes it clear that while *uṣūl al-fiqh* is not to the positive law what logic is to philosophy, nevertheless there are important logical structures and argumentation to legal precepts and their derivation; ever the consummate logician.[107] The text itself is divided into problemata, the second half of which deals with the classic four sources of the law; but the first half begins with the metaphysics and epistemology – what is speech and the nature of a divine command and prohibition that involves extensive discussions on the nature of onto-theology, and a discussion on the nature of language and primary terms and their signification. This is a classic example of how an expansive sense of philosophy can bring a portrait of the philosopher into focus in which philosophy of language and linguistics is present alongside metaphysics in a text that is about the principles of the law.

Concluding Remarks

These portraits invite us to think creatively about the meaning and scope of philosophy. We have seen how those considered minor to us now – perhaps a smidgen in a wider canvas of philosophy – were significant to their time, as well as considered the importance of the organic lived experience whence the portrait arose that allows us to project an expansive sense of philosophy in engaging with thinkers who neither defined themselves as such nor necessarily were considered as being so; who frames and composes remains an important determinant. Similarly, our choices were inspired by the exigency of a new epistemology of the south, a decolonial reading of philosophy in Muslim cultures, breaking down the boundaries whereby we determine and project onto our materials what is philosophy as opposed to what is poetry, what is rational versus what is emotional in a colonialist epistemicide of the composers of earlier portraits.[108]

But for these to be effective and for us to make sense of philosophy in a broader, intersectional, and even more dynamic sense, do we need those portraits to be metaphysically real in the sense that their referents existed and exist in extra-mental reality? They can indeed be truthful without such a requirement, truthful in the sense of corresponding to a mentally constructed portrait or image as well as an idealised one in the realm of facticity (*nafs al-amr*). Such a line of inquiry is too broad to initiate here and should be left for a future endeavour. Perhaps, we can draw once again on literature and the classical Arabic *maqāma* as an imposture or a mode of fictive portraiture; whilst recognising with Abdelfattah Kilito (and Hayden White) the overlap between the fictive and non-fictive depictive and narrative mechanisms.[109] The portrait in this genre of impostures is that of a self-identifying person of letters, a scholar, but also a vagabond and a trickster. It is easy to see in the history of portraits of philosophers plenty of such tricksters, not least if one cleaves rather piously to Aristotelian notions of rationality and philosophical inquiry. But just as poesis constitutes an argument (recognisably even in the theory of al-Fārābī and Avicenna) alongside apodictic demonstration, so too does the fictive imposture of the *maqāma* tell us something about the course of philosophy; in fact, by choosing figures who are so minor to not have 'existed,' they tell us much of the portrayal and presence of philosophies in the arts, in literature, in vagabondage: al-Ḥarīrī's Abū Zayd as the archetypal figure of the philosopher, the thinker as gadfly and picaresque imposter, a tragi-comic figures presenting and re-presenting themselves in their linguistic sketches.[110] That performative portrait of the self is after all what the philosopher wishes to present, embedded within a culture and expressive of it – the deep texture of the role of philosophy that one seeks in intellectual history. As one finds in the song of Abū Zayd in the ninth *maqāma*:

> My tale is tragi-comical and when it's done you'll realize
> That though I dress the truth a bit I never stoop to real lies.
> Although I come from noble stock, I live by arts rhetorical,
> For which the going rate is less than what you'd pay an oracle.
> I trade in verses panegyrical and confrontational,
> And all the texts you need to preach at prayers congregational.
> In metaphor, metathesis, ellipsis, and metonymy,
> In simile and syncricis, why [. . .] you can ask a ton o' me![111]

Notes

* I am grateful to the participants of our Exeter-Japan workshops for their discussion of this chapter as well as audiences in Syracuse, Karachi, and Istanbul who have heard and engaged with elements of the larger project on decolonizing the study of Islamic philosophy. I am particularly grateful to Ali Altaf Mian for his careful and judicious reading and his suggestions which have saved me from many an infelicitous phrase.

1 This point seems to hold true for differential phenomena from the Renaissance's *fare bella figura* to the contemporary anthropologist's observations of *tafannas* in Lebanon and the Mediterranean in the 20th century. On the former, see the classic work of Stephen Greenblatt, *Renaissance Self-Fashioning: From More to Shakespeare* (Chicago: University of Chicago Press, 1980), and on the latter, Michael Gilsenan, *Lords of the Lebanese Marches: Violence and Narrative in an Arab Society* (London: I.B. Tauris, 1996). On the integrity of the ontological and the aesthetic in the pursuing of realising one's humanity in ancient India, see Sheldon Pollock, *A Rasa Reader: Classical Indian Aesthetics* (New York: Columbia University Press, 2016), especially 5–16.

2 Jonardon Ganeri, *The Concealed Art of the Soul: Theories of Self and Practices of Truth in Indian Ethics and Epistemology* (Oxford: Oxford University Press, 2012), especially 23–60.

3 One thinks here of the debate on the term *anvīkṣiki* and 'philosophy' within the attempt to globalise philosophy; see Hanna Hnatovska, "The Image of Philosophy in Indian Culture:

Etymology and Untranslateability of Terms," *Future Human Image* 13 (2020): 14–23 https://doi.org/10.29202/fhi/13/2 (accessed September 12, 2022).

4 For a popularising attempt to communicate this 'family resemblances' unity of philosophising across the world, see Julian Baggini, *How the World Thinks: A Global History of Philosophy* (London: Granta Books, 2018).

5 For a discussion, see Christine van Ruymbeke, "L'histoire du concours des peintres Rūmīs et chīnīs chez Niẓāmī et chez Rūmī: Deux aspects du miroir," in *Miroir et savoir: La transmission d'une thème platonicien des Alexandrins à la philosophie arabo-musulmane*, ed. by Daniel de Smet, Meryem Sebti and Godfroid de Callataÿ (Leuven: Leuven University Press, 2008), 273–91.

6 Jalāl al-Dīn Rūmī, *The Masnavi Book One*, tr. by Jawid Mojaddedi (Oxford: Oxford University Press, 2004), 212–4 (ll. 3482–513).

7 See Jorge Luis Borges, "Pierre Menard, the Author of Quixote," in Idem, *Labyrinths* (London: Penguin, 2015), 70–1.

8 On cognitive elements of cosmopolitan reason, see Carol A. Breckenridge et al., eds., *Cosmopolitanism* (Durham, NC: Duke University Press, 2002); Kwame Appiah, *Cosmopolitanism: Ethics in a World of Strangers* (London: Penguin, 2007); and Jonardon Ganeri, *Identity as Reasoned Choice: The Reach and Resources of Public and Practical Reason* (London: Bloomsbury, 2014). On the fusion of horizons, see Hans-Georg Gadamer, *Wahrheit und Methode*, transl. by Joel Weinsheimer and Donald G. Marshall as *Truth and Method*, 2nd ed., repr. (London: Continuum, 2004).

9 For a good reconsideration of this issue, see Maria Michela Sassi, *The Beginnings of Philosophy in Greece* (Princeton: Princeton University Press, 2020); Marc van der Mieroop, *Philosophy before the Greeks: The Pursuit of Truth in Ancient Babylonia* (Princeton: Princeton University Press, 2017), and from a Marxist perspective, Kōjin Karatani, *Isonomia and the Origins of Philosophy*, transl. by Joseph A. Murphy (Durham, NC: Duke University Press, 2017). For a traditional account of the origins of philosophy in the West, see Bernard Williams, "Plato: The Invention of Philosophy," in idem, *The Sense of the Past: Essays in the History of Philosophy* (Princeton: Princeton University Press, 2006), 148–86. For an important alternative trajectory in Arabo-Islamic thought, see the classic Marxist study of Ḥusayn Muruwwa (d. 1987), *al-Nazaʿāt al-māddiyya fī l-falsafa al-ʿArabiyya al-Islāmiyya*, 5 vols. (Beirut: Dār al-Fārābī, 1978) and, in a similar vein but earlier, Ernst Bloch (d. 1959), *Avicenna and the Aristotelian Left*, transl. by Loren Goldman (New York: Columbia University Press, 2019).

10 Justin E. Smith, *The Philosopher: A History in Six Types* (Princeton: Princeton University Press, 2016), 2–9. A good example of a scholar whose beginning point has been *philosophia* but, who has been engaged in the comparative study of science and philosophy (ancient Greece and China in particular) is Sir Geoffrey Lloyd in works such as "'Philosophy': What Did the Greeks Invent and Is It relevant to China?" *Extrême-orient, Extrême-occident* 27 (2005): 149–59. Paraphilosophy is, of course, the dismissive term for the non-Aristotelian 'pseudo-philosophy' that has strong theological commitments deployed by Dimitri Gutas, "Avicenna and After: The Development of Paraphilosophy: A History of Science Approach," in *Islamic Philosophy from the 12th to the 14th Century*, ed. by Abdelkader Al-Ghouz (Bonn: V&RUnipress for Bonn University Press, 2018), 19–71.

11 On its 'other,' see the classic study of V.Y Mudimbe, *The Invention of Africa: Gnosis, Philosophy, and the Order of Knowledge* (Bloomington, IN: Indiana University Press, 1988), and Richard King, *Indian Philosophy: An Introduction to Hindu and Buddhist Thought* (Edinburgh: Edinburgh University Press, 1999), especially 21–41.

12 Mullā Ṣadrā Šīrāzī, *Risālat al-ḥudūṯ*, ed. by Sayyid Ḥusayn Mūsawiyān (Tehran: Sadra Islamic Philosophy Research Institute, 1378 AHS/1999), 153–4.

13 Jonardon Ganeri, "Why Philosophy Must Go Global: A Manifesto," *Confluence* 4 (2016): 134–86. It might seem strange to consider our age to be one of reason and not irrationality given the post-truth nature of much of the public domain of reason – but see Julian Baggini, *A*

Short History of Truth: Consolations for a Post-Truth World (London: Querus, 2017). For an interesting postmodernist reading that retains the utility of truth (or perhaps truthfulness), see John D. Caputo, *Truth: The Search for Wisdom in the Postmodern Age* (London: Penguin, 2013).

14 To an extent, one finds this even in the Eurocentric approach of Peter Sloterdijk in his *Philosophical Temperaments: From Plato to Foucault*, transl. by Thomas Dunlap (New York: Columbia University Press, 2013), and *The Art of Philosophy: Wisdom as Practice*, transl. by Karen Margolis (New York: Columbia University Press, 2012).

15 Baggini, *How the World Thinks*.

16 If pushed to enumerate these, I would point to the following (just from Avicenna): the proof for the existence of God by radical contingency, the suspended person thought experiment, the argument about the eternal now, and the allegory of the soul as a bird.

17 Lewis R. Gordon, "Decolonizing Philosophy," *The Southern Journal of Philosophy* 57 Spindel Supplement (2019): 16–36.

18 For a critique of the colonialist notion of history, see Priya Satia, *Time's Monster: History, Conscience, and Britain's Empire* (Cambridge, MA: Harvard University Press, 2020), and on the myth of progress, Amy Allen, *The End of Progress: Decolonizing the Normative Foundations of Critical Theory* (New York: Columbia University Press, 2016). For a more venerable critique of the modern and the quantitative norms of progress, see René Guénon, *La règne de la quantité et les signes des temps* (Paris: Gallimard, 1945).

19 Mayra Rivera, "Embodied Counterpoetics: Sylvia Wynter on Religion and Race," in *Beyond Man: Race, Coloniality, and Philosophy of Religion*, ed. by An Yountae and Eleanor Craig (Durham, NC: Duke University Press, 2021), 57–85, and Sylvia Wynter, "Unsettling the Coloniality of Being/Power/Truth/Freedom," *The New Centennial Review* 3 (2003): 257–337.

20 Eleanor Craig and An Yountae, "Introduction," in *Beyond Man*, ed. by Yountae and Craig, 3.

21 Idid., 4.

22 Walter Mignolo and Catherine Walsh, *On Decoloniality: Concepts, Analytics, Praxis* (Durham, NC: Duke University Press, 2018), 81.

23 Olúfémi O. Táíwò, *Elite Capture: How the Powerful Took Over Identity Politics (and Everything Else)* (London: Pluto Press, 2022).

24 Olúfémi Táíwò, *Against Decolonisation: Taking African Agency Seriously* (London: Hurst & Co., 2022).

25 Leon Moosavi, "The Decolonial Bandwagon and the Dangers of Intellectual Decolonisation," *International Review of Sociology* 30.2 (2020): 332–54.

26 Oludamini Ogunnaike, "African Philosophy Reconsidered: Africa, Religion, Race, and Philosophy," *Journal of Africana Religions* 5.2 (2017): 181–216.

27 One of the ironies of such decolonisation is that, of necessity, it uses Eurocentric resources such as the invocation of Heidegger and other postmodernist thinkers, for example, in Dipesh Chakrabarty, *Provincializing Europe: Postcolonial Thought and Historical Difference* (Princeton: Princeton University Press, 2000). But decoloniality as a strategic is neither identitarian nor nativist and hence extensively draws on the 'minority reports' of the European traditions that question the hegemony of colonialist ontology and epistemology.

28 Mogens Laerke, Justin Smith and Eric Schliesser, "Introduction," in *Philosophy and Its History: Aims and Methods in the Study of Early Modern Philosophy*, ed. by Mogens Laerke, Justin Smith and Eric Schliesser (New York: Oxford University Press, 2013), 1–6.

29 Tom Sorrell, "Introduction," in *Analytic Philosophy and History of Philosophy*, ed. by Tom Sorrell and G.A.J. Rogers (Oxford: Clarendon Press, 2005), 1–2.

30 Tom Sorrell, "On Saying No to the History of Philosophy," in *Analytic Philosophy and History of Philosophy*, ed. by Sorrell and Rogers, 44–5.

31 Martin Heidegger, *Basic Concepts of Aristotelian Philosophy*, transl. by Robert D. Metcalf and Mark B. Tanzer (Bloomington, IN: Indiana University Press, 2009), and idem, *Kant and the Problem of Metaphysics*, transl. by Richard Taft (Bloomington, IN: Indiana University Press,

1997); Robert Brandom, *A Spirit of Trust: A Reading of Hegel's Phenomenology* (Cambridge, MA: Harvard University Press, 2019); Mullā Ṣadrā Šīrāzī, *al-Ḥikma al-muta ʿāliya fī l-asfār al-ʿaqliyya al-arba ʿa*, ed. by Ġulām-Riḍā Aʿwānī et al. (Tehran: Sadra Islamic Philosophy Research Institute, 2004).

32 Sanjay Subrahmanyam, "Par-delà l'incommensurabilité: Pour une histoire connectée des empire aux temps modernes," *Revue d'histoire moderne et contemporain* 54.4 (2007): 34–53, and idem, "A Tale of Three Empires: Mughals, Ottomans and Habsburgs in a Comparative Context," *Common Knowledge* 12.1 (2006): 66–92; Ben-Ami Scharfstein, *A Comparative History of World Philosophy* (Albany, NY: State University of New York Press, 1998); Sheldon Pollock, ed., *Forms of Knowledge in Early Modern Asia* (Durham, NC: Duke University Press, 2011).

33 William Edelglass and Jay Garfield, "Introduction," in *The Oxford Handbook of World Philosophy*, ed. by William Edelglass and Jay Garfield (Oxford: Oxford University Press, 2011), 3.

34 Richard Rorty, "The Historiography of Philosophy: Four Genres," in *Philosophy in History*, ed. by Richard Rorty, J. B. Schneewind and Quentin Skinner (Cambridge: Cambridge University Press, 1984), 49–76.

35 Quentin Skinner, "Meaning and Understanding in the History of Ideas," *History and Theory* 8 (1969), 28.

36 Skinner, "Meaning and Understanding in the History of Ideas," 52–3.

37 Jonardon Ganeri, *The Lost Age of Reason: Philosophy in Early Modern India 1450–1700* (Oxford: Oxford University Press, 2011), 63–73.

38 Richard Rorty, *Philosophy and the Mirror of Nature* (Princeton: Princeton University Press, 1978).

39 Pierre Hadot, *Philosophy as a Way of Life*, transl. by Michael Chase (Oxford: Blackwells, 1995), 71–6.

40 Most post-structuralist thinkers have rejected policing the borders of the philosophy in favour of the literary; for example, Jacques Derrida, *Acts of Literature*, ed. by Derek Attridge (London: Routledge, 1992), or even earlier Walter Benjamin, *The Writer of Modern Life: Essays on Charles Baudelaire*, ed. by Michael W. Jennings, transl. by Howard Eiland (Cambridge, MA: Harvard University Press, 2006).

41 Rorty, "The Historiography of Philosophy," 73, and Justin Smith, "The History of Philosophy as Past and Process," in *Philosophy and Its History*, ed. by Laerke, Smith and Schliesser, 41.

42 Mogobe Ramose, "A Philosophy without Memory Cannot Abolish Slavery: On Epistemic Justice in South Africa," in *Debating African Philosophy: Perspectives on Identity, Decolonial Ethics and Comparative Philosophy*, ed. by George Hull (London: Routledge, 2019), 60–72.

43 Gilles Deleuze and Félix Guattari, *What Is Philosophy?* transl. by Graham Burchell and Hugh Tomlinson (New York: Continuum, 1994), 6.

44 Ibid., 7.

45 Ibid., 43, 92–5.

46 Ibid., 3.

47 Ibid., 4–5.

48 Hegel, *Lectures in Philosophy of World History 1829/30*, 26a, cited in Peter K. J. Park, *Africa, Asia and the History of Philosophy: Racism in the Formation of the Philosophical Canon, 1780–1830* (Albany, NY: State University of New York Press, 2013), 113; Wilhelm Halbfass, *India and Europe: An Essay in Understanding* (Albany, NY: State University of New York Press, 1988), 84–99.

49 Park, *Africa, Asia and the History of Philosophy*, 113–25.

50 Ibid., 123.

51 Ibid., 1.

52 Jay Garfield, *Empty Words: Buddhist Philosophy and Cross-Cultural Interpretation* (New York: Oxford University Press, 2002), 231–5.

53 Ibid., 238.

54 Ibid., 260.
55 For example, Stanley Cavell, *The Claim of Reason* (New York: Oxford University Press, 1979).
56 Hadot, *Philosophy as a Way of Life*, and Michael Chase, Stephen R. L. Clark and Michael McGhee, eds., *Philosophy as a Way of Life Ancients and Moderns: Essays in Honor of Pierre Hadot* (Chichester: Wiley, 2013), but also see John Cooper, *Pursuits of Wisdom: Six Ways of Life in Ancient Philosophy from Socrates to Plotinus* (Princeton: Princeton University Press, 2012), who is sceptical about the claim that *all* philosophy in the ancient world was necessarily a way of life.
57 Jean Greisch, *Vivre en philosophant: Expérience philosophique, exercices spirituels et théraphies de l'âme* (Paris: Cerf, 2015).
58 John M. Armstrong, "After the Ascent: Plato on Becoming like God," *Oxford Studies in Ancient Philosophy* 26 (2004): 171–83; Dirk Baltzly, "The Virtues and 'Becoming like God': Alcinous to Proclus," *Oxford Studies in Ancient Philosophy* 26 (2004): 297–321; David Sedley, "The Idea of Godlikeness," in *Plato 2: Ethics, Politics, Religion*, ed. by Gail Fine (Oxford: Oxford University Press, 1999), 309–28.
59 Porphyry, *Letter to Marcella*, transl. by Alice Zimmern (Oxford: Clarendon Press, 1910), 149–50.
60 An advocate of this expansive sense is Peter Adamson, *Philosophy in the Islamic World: A History of Philosophy without Any Gaps Volume III* (Oxford: Oxford University Press, 2016).
61 On the debate between the universal and the cultural in Chinese philosophy that is instructive, see Carine Defoort, "Is There Such a Thing as Chinese Philosophy? Arguments of an Implicit Debate," *Philosophy East & West* 51 (2001): 393–413, and Rein Raud, "Philosophies versus Philosophy: In Defence of a Flexible Definition," *Philosophy East & West* 56 (2006): 618–25, and the follow ups in Carine Defoort, "Is 'Chinese Philosophy' a Proper Name? A Response to Rein Raud," *Philosophy East & West* 56 (2006): 625–60, and Rein Raud, "Traditions and Tendencies: A Reply to Carine Defoort," *Philosophy East & West* 56 (2006): 661–4.
62 Alisdair MacIntyre, *Whose Justice? Whose Rationality?* (Notre Dame, IN: Notre Dame University Press, 1988). Nasr's is rooted in the conception of a 'prophetic' philosophy: see his *Islamic Philosophy from Its Origins to the Present: Philosophy in the Land of Prophecy* (Albany, NY: State University of New York Press, 2006).
63 Hadot, *Philosophy as a Way of Life*, 59–61.
64 It might be useful to consider the uses of Wittgenstein applied to the Islamic traditions in Talal Asad, "Thinking about Religion through Wittgenstein", *Critical Times* 3.3 (2020): 403–42.
65 Mark Siderits et al., eds., *Self, No Self? Perspectives from the Analytic, Phenomenological and Indian Traditions* (Oxford: Oxford University Press, 2010). Jonardon Ganeri, *Attention, Not Self* (Oxford: Oxford University Press, 2017) is perhaps the best global approach to selfhood available.
66 Mullā Ṣadrā Šīrāzī, *al-Ḥikma al-mutaʿāliya fī l-asfār al-ʿaqliyya al-arbaʿa*, vol. 1, 23–4.
67 Drawing on Raud, "Philosophies vs Philosophy."
68 Aḥmad Bābā al-Tinbuktī, *Nayl al-ibtihāğ bi-taṭrīz al-dībāğ*, ed. by ʿAbd al-Ḥamīd al-Harrāma (Tripoli: Dār al-kātib, 2000), 27–8. On the approach of philosophy as a way of life lying in ethical and embodied commitments to knowledge and understanding in a cognate West African context, see Oludamini Ogunnaike, *Deep Knowledge: Ways of Knowing in Sufism in Ifa, Two West African Intellectual Traditions* (University Park: Pennsylvania State University Pres, 2020).
69 John O. Hunwick, "Aḥmad Bābā on Slavery," *Sudanic Africa* 11 (2000): 131–9; Timothy Cleveland, "Ahmad Baba al-Timbukti and His Islamic Critique of Racial Slavery in the Maghreb," *Journal of North African Studies* 20 (2015): 42–64; Chris Gratien, "Race, Slavery, and Islamic Law in the Early Modern Atlantic," *Journal of North African Studies* 18 (2013): 454–68; Ousmane Oumar Kane, *Beyond Timbuktu: An Intellectual History of Muslim West Africa* (Cambridge: Harvard University Press, 2016), 98–105.
70 See, for example, Bruce Hall, "The Question of 'Race' in the Precolonial Southern Sahara," *Journal of North African Studies* 10 (2005): 339–67.
71 Gratien, "Race, Slavery, and Islamic Law," 462–3.

72 See the discussion in the work of the Mālikī jurist Šihāb al-Dīn al-Qarāfī (d. 684/1285), *Šarḥ Tanqīḥ al-fuṣūl fī iḫtiṣār al-maḥṣūl*, ed. by Ṭāhā ʿAbd al-Raʾūf (Cairo: Maktabat al-Kulliyya al-Azhariyya, 1983), 447.

73 Gratien, "Race, Slavery, and Islamic Law," 464.

74 Ibid., 465.

75 Cleveland, "Ahmad Baba al-Timbukti and His Islamic Critique of Racial Slavery," 51–3.

76 Ogunnaike, *Deep Knowledge*, 1–18, 379–96.

77 Ata Anzali, "The Emergence of the Ẕahabiyya in Safavid Iran," *Journal of Sufi Studies* 2 (2013): 149–75.

78 Maʿṣūm ʿAlī Šāh Šīrāzī, *Ṭarāyiq al-ḥaqāyiq*, ed. by M. J. Maḥǧūb (Tehran: Kitābḫāna-yi Sanāʾī, 1339 AHS/1960), vol. 3, 216–9; Ġulām-Ḥusayn Ḫudrī, *Taʾammulī bar sayr-i taṭavvur-i ḥukamāʾ va ḥikmat-i mutaʿāliya* (Tehran: Pažūhišgāh-i ʿulūm-i insānī va muṭālaʿāt-i farhangī, 1391 AHS/2012), 270–3; Manūčihr Ṣadūqī Suhā, *Taḥrīr-i s̱ānī-yi Tārīḫ-i ḥukamāʾ va ʿurafāʾ-yi mutaʾaḫḫir az Ṣadr al-mutaʾallihīn* (Tehran: Intišārāt-i ḥikmat, 1383 AHS/2004), 211–3; Abū l-Qāsim Amīn al-Šarīʿa Ḫūyī, *Mīzān al-ṣavāb dar šarḥ-i Faṣl al-ḫiṭāb*, ed. by Muḥammad Ḫvāǧavī (Tehran: Intišārāt-i Mawlā, 1383 AHS/2004), vol. 1, vi–xviii; Richard Gramlich, *Die schiitischen Derwischorden Persiens* (Wiesbaden: Franz Steiner Verlag, 1965), vol. 1, 17–8, vol. 3, 78; Ata Anzali, *"Mysticism in Iran": The Safavid Roots of a Modern Concept* (Columbia, SC: University of South Carolina Press, 2017), 141–66.

79 Umm Salama Bēgum Nayrīzī, *Ǧāmiʿ al-kulliyyāt*, ed. by Mahdī Iftiḫār (Qum: Kitābsarā-yi išrāq, 1386 AHS/2007), 18–9.

80 Ibid., 35–6.

81 Ibid., 34.

82 Ibid., 28, 38, 31, 34.

83 Ibid., 154–5.

84 Ibid., 157–76.

85 Ibid., 195–6.

86 General surveys that include some elements on thought and transmission are Sayyid ʿAbd al-Ḥayy al-Ḥasanī, *al-Ṯaqāfa al-Islāmiyya fī l-Hind* (Damascus: Maǧmaʿ al-luġa al-ʿArabiyya, 1983), 253–68; M. Zubaid Ahmad, *The Contribution of Indo-Pakistan to Arabic Literature* (Lahore: Sh. Muhammad Ashraf, 1946), 129–56.

87 Hans Daiber, "New Manuscript Findings from Indian Libraries," *Manuscripts of the Middle East* 1 (1986): 26–48; Rudiger Arnzen, "Mapping Philosophy and Science in Ṣafawid Iran and Mughal India: The Case of Niẓāmaddīn Aḥmad Gīlānī and Ms. Khudā Bakhsh 2641," *Mélanges de l'Université de Saint-Joseph* 56 (1999–2003): 107–60.

88 Jamal Malik, *Islamische Gelehrtenkultur in Nordindien: Entwicklungsgeschichte und Tendenzen am Beispiel von Lucknow* (Leiden: E.J. Brill, 1997); Francis Robinson, *The ʿUlama of Farangi Mahall and Islamic Culture in South Asia* (Delhi: Permanent Black, 2001).

89 Dimitri Gutas, "The Heritage of Avicenna: The Golden Age of Arabic Philosophy, 1000–ca. 1350," in *Avicenna and His Heritage*, ed. by Jules Janssens and Daniel de Smet (Leuven: Peeters, 2002), 81–97.

90 Maulvī Raḥmān ʿAlī, *Taẕkira-yi ʿulamāʾ-yi Hind*, ed. by Yūsuf Bēg Bābāpūr (Qum: Maǧmaʿ-i ẕaḫāʾir-i Islāmī, 1391 AHS/2012), 154–5; Sayyid ʿAbd al-Ḥayy al-Ḥāsanī, *Nuzhat al-ḫawāṭir wa-bahǧat al-masāmiʿ wa-l-nawāẓir* (Beirut: Dār Ibn Ḥazm, 1999), part 7, 1021–3. Maulvī ʿInāyatullāh, *Taẕkira-yi ʿulamāʾ-yi Farangī Maḥall* (Lucknow: Niẓāmī Press, 1930), 137–42; Alṭāf al-Raḥmān, *Aḥvāl-i ʿulamāʾ-yi Farangī Maḥall* (Lucknow: Newal Kishore, 1907), 64–5; M. Hidayat Husain, "The Life and Works of Baḥr al-ʿulūm," *Journal of the Asiatic Society of Bengal* new series 7 (1911): 6935; Asad Q. Ahmed, "Baḥr al-ʿulūm," in *The Encyclopaedia of Islam Three*, ed. by Kate Fleet et al. (http://dx.doi.org.uoelibrary.idm.oclc.org/10.1163/1573-3912_ei3_COM_25153 [accessed September 14, 2022]).

91 For an excellent study of the *Sullam* and its layers, see Asad Ahmed, *Palimpsests of Themselves: Logic and Commentary in Postclassical Muslim South Asia* (Berkeley: University of California Press, 2022).

92 Baḥr al-ʿulūm, *al-ʿUǧāla al-nāfiʿa*, MS British Library Delhi Arabic 1653, 1v.

93 Khaled el-Rouayheb, *Islamic Intellectual History in the Seventeenth Century: Scholarly Currents in the Ottoman Empire and the Maghreb* (Cambridge: Cambridge University Press, 2015), 235–71, 312–62.

94 Thomas Dahnhardt, "The Doctrine of the Unicity of Existence in the Light of an Eighteenth Century Indian Ṣūfī Treatise: The *Waḥdat al-wuǧud* by Baḥr al-ʿulūm," *Oriente Moderno* 92.2 (2012): 323–60, based on the Persian version edited and translated in Urdu by Abū l-Ḥasan Zayd Fārūqī (Delhi, 1971).

95 Dahnhardt, "The Doctrine of the Unicity of Existence," 329. For a useful introduction to this philosophical theological problem, see Rosabel Ansari, "Al-Taftazānī's Refutation of Akbarian Metaphysics and the Identification of Absolute Being with the Necessary Being," *Oriens* 50.3-4 (2022): 207–43.

96 Dahnhardt, "The Doctrine of the Unicity of Existence," 330.

97 Ibid., 335.

98 Ibid., 339, translation modified.

99 Ibid., 356–7. One finds this in the introductions of his works such as *al-ʿUǧāla al-nāfiʿa* as well.

100 Dahnhardt, "The Doctrine of the Unicity of Existence," 358–60.

101 Ibid., 359–60.

102 Baḥr al-ʿulūm, *al-ʿUǧāla al-nāfiʿa*, 2r, 8v–9v.

103 Baḥr al-ʿulūm, *Fawātiḥ al-Raḥamūt fī šarḥ Musallam al-ṯubūt* (Beirut: Dār al-kutub al-ʿilmiyya, 2002), vol. 1, 5.

104 Baḥr al-ʿulūm, *Fawātiḥ al-Raḥamūt*, vol. 1, 5.

105 Ibid., vol. 1, 6.

106 Ibid., vol. 1, 7.

107 Ibid., vol. 1, 10.

108 Boaventura de Sousa Santos, *Epistemologies of the South: Justice against Epistemicide* (Boulder, CO: Paradigm, 2014), and idem, *The End of the Cognitive Empire: The Coming of Age of Epistemologies of the South* (Durham, NC: Duke University Press, 2018).

109 For example, on philosophy and the *maqāma*, see Philip Kennedy, "Reason and Revelation or the Philosopher's Squib (The Sixth Maqāma of Ibn al-Nāqiyā)," *Journal of Arabic and Islamic Studies* 3 (2000): 84–113; Abdelfattah Kilito, *L'auteur et ses doubles: Essai sur la culture arabe classique* (Paris: Éditions du Seuil, 1985); Hayden White, *Metahistory: The Historical Imagination in Nineteenth-Century Europe* (Baltimore: Johns Hopkins University Press, 1973).

110 Abū Muḥammad al-Ḥarīrī, *Impostures by al-Ḥarīrī. A Groundbreaking Translation by Michael Cooperson*, Library of Arabic Literature (New York: New York University Press, 2020).

111 Ibid., 77.

Bibliography

Adamson, Peter. *Philosophy in the Islamic World: A History of Philosophy without Any Gaps Volume III*. Oxford: Oxford University Press, 2016.

Ahmad, M. Zubaid. *The Contribution of Indo-Pakistan to Arabic Literature*. Lahore: Sh. Muhammad Ashraf, 1946.

Ahmed, Asad Q. *Palimpsests of Themselves: Logic and Commentary in Postclassical Muslim South Asia*. Berkeley: University of California Press, 2022.

Ahmed, Asad Q. "Baḥr al-ʿulūm," in *The Encyclopaedia of Islam Three*. Ed. by Kate Fleet et al. http://dx.doi.org.uoelibrary.idm.oclc.org/10.1163/1573-3912_ei3_COM_25153. Accessed September 14, 2022.

ʿAlī, Maulvī Raḥmān. *Taẕkira-yi ʿulamāʾ-yi Hind*. Ed. by Yūsuf Bēg Bābāpūr. Qum: Mağmaʿ-i ẕaḫāʾir-i Islāmī, 1391 AHS/2012.

Allen, Amy. *The End of Progress: Decolonizing the Normative Foundations of Critical Theory*. New York: Columbia University Press, 2016.

Alṭāf al-Raḥmān. *Aḥvāl-i ʿulamāʾ-yi Farangī Maḥall*. Lucknow: Newal Kishore, 1907.

Ansari, Rosabel. "Al-Taftazānī's Refutation of Akbarian Metaphysics and the Identification of Absolute Being with the Necessary Being." *Oriens* 50.3-4 (2022): 207–43.

Anzali, Ata. "The Emergence of the Ẕahabiyya in Safavid Iran." *Journal of Sufi Studies* 2 (2013): 149–75.

Anzali, Ata. *"Mysticism in Iran": The Safavid Roots of a Modern Concept* (Columbia, SC: University of South Carolina Press, 2017.

Appiah, Kwame Anthony. *Cosmopolitanism: Ethics in a World of Strangers*. London: Penguin, 2007.

Armstrong, John M. "After the Ascent: Plato on Becoming like God." *Oxford Studies in Ancient Philosophy* 26 (2004): 171–83.

Arnzen, Rudiger. "Mapping Philosophy and Science in Ṣafawid Iran and Mughal India: The Case of Niẓāmaddīn Aḥmad Gīlānī and Ms. Khudā Bakhsh 2641." *Mélanges de l'Université de Saint-Joseph* 56 (1999–2003): 107–60.

Asad, Talal. "Thinking about Religion through Wittgenstein." *Critical Times* 3.3 (2020): 403–42.

Baggini, Julian. *A Short History of Truth: Consolations for a Post-Truth World*. London: Querus, 2017.

Baggini, Julian. *How the World Thinks: A Global History of Philosophy*. London: Granta Books, 2018.

Baḥr al-ʿulūm. *Al-ʿUğāla al-nāfiʿa*. MS British Library Delhi Arabic 1653.

Baḥr al-ʿulūm. *Fawātiḥ al-Raḥamūt fī šarḥ Musallam al-ṯubūt*. Beirut: Dār al-kutub al-ʿilmiyya, 2002.

Baltzly, Dirk. "The Virtues and 'Becoming like God': Alcinous to Proclus." *Oxford Studies in Ancient Philosophy* 26 (2004): 297–321.

Benjamin, Walter. *The Writer of Modern Life: Essays on Charles Baudelaire*. Ed. by Michael W. Jennings. Transl. by Howard Eiland. Cambridge, MA: Harvard University Press, 2006.

Bloch, Ernst. *Avicenna and the Aristotelian Left*. Transl. by Loren Goldman. New York: Columbia University Press, 2019.

Borges, Jorge Luis. "Pierre Menard, the Author of Quixote." In idem, *Labyrinths*. Repr. London: Penguin, 2015.

Brandom, Robert. *A Spirit of Trust: A Reading of Hegel's Phenomenology*. Cambridge, MA: Harvard University Press, 2019.

Breckenridge, Carol A. et al., eds. *Cosmopolitanism*. Durham, NC: Duke University Press, 2002.

Caputo, John D. *Truth: The Search for Wisdom in the Postmodern Age*. London: Penguin, 2013.

Cavell, Stanley. *The Claim of Reason*. New York: Oxford University Press, 1979.

Chakrabarty, Dipesh. *Provincializing Europe: Postcolonial Thought and Historical Difference*. Princeton: Princeton University Press, 2000.

Chase, Michael, Stephen R. L. Clark and Michael McGhee, eds. *Philosophy as a Way of Life Ancients and Moderns: Essays in Honor of Pierre Hadot*. Chichester: Wiley, 2013.

Cleveland, Timothy. "Ahmad Baba al-Timbukti and His Islamic Critique of Racial Slavery in the Maghreb." *Journal of North African Studies* 20 (2015): 42–64.

Cooper, John. *Pursuits of Wisdom: Six Ways of Life in Ancient Philosophy from Socrates to Plotinus*. Princeton: Princeton University Press, 2012.

Dahnhardt, Thomas. "The Doctrine of the Unicity of Existence in the Light of an Eighteenth Century Indian Ṣūfī Treatise: The *Waḥdat al-wuǧud* by Baḥr al-ʿulūm." *Oriente Moderno* 92.2 (2012): 323–60.

Daiber, Hans. "New Manuscript Findings from Indian Libraries." *Manuscripts of the Middle East* 1 (1986): 26–48.

Defoort, Carine. "Is There Such a Thing as Chinese Philosophy? Arguments of an Implicit Debate." *Philosophy East & West* 51 (2001): 393–413.

Defoort, Carine. "Is 'Chinese Philosophy' a Proper Name? A Response to Rein Raud." *Philosophy East & West* 56 (2006): 625–60.

Deleuze, Gilles and Félix Guattari. *What Is Philosophy?* Transl. by Graham Burchell and Hugh Tomlinson. New York: Continuum, 1994.

Derrida, Jacques. *Acts of Literature*. Ed. by Derek Attridge. London: Routledge, 1992.

Edelglass, William and Jay Garfield, eds. *The Oxford Handbook of World Philosophy*. Oxford: Oxford University Press, 2011.

El-Rouayheb, Khaled. *Islamic Intellectual History in the Seventeenth Century: Scholarly Currents in the Ottoman Empire and the Maghreb*. Cambridge: Cambridge University Press, 2015.

Gadamer, Hans-Georg. *Wahrheit und Methode*. Transl. by Joel Weinsheimer and Donald G. Marshall, *Truth and Method*. 2nd ed. Repr. London: Continuum, 2004.

Ganeri, Jonardon. *The Lost Age of Reason: Philosophy in Early Modern India 1450–1700*. Oxford: Oxford University Press, 2011.

Ganeri, Jonardon. *The Concealed Art of the Soul: Theories of Self and Practices of Truth in Indian Ethics and Epistemology*. Oxford: Oxford University Press, 2012.

Ganeri, Jonardon. *Identity as Reasoned Choice: The Reach and Resources of Public and Practical Reason*. London: Bloomsbury, 2014.

Ganeri, Jonardon. "Why Philosophy Must Go Global: A Manifesto." *Confluence* 4 (2016): 134–86.

Ganeri, Jonardon. *Attention, Not Self*. Oxford: Oxford University Press, 2017.

Garfield, Jay. *Empty Words: Buddhist Philosophy and Cross-Cultural Interpretation*. New York: Oxford University Press, 2002.

Gilsenan, Michael. *Lords of the Lebanese Marches: Violence and Narrative in an Arab Society*. London: I.B. Tauris, 1996.

Gordon, Lewis R. "Decolonizing Philosophy." *The Southern Journal of Philosophy* 57 Spindel Supplement (2019): 16–36.

Gramlich, Richard. *Die schiitischen Derwischorden Persiens*. 3 vols. Wiesbaden: Franz Steiner Verlag, 1965.

Gratien, Chris. "Race, Slavery, and Islamic Law in the Early Modern Atlantic." *Journal of North African Studies* 18 (2013): 454–68.

Greenblatt, Stephen. *Renaissance Self-Fashioning: From More to Shakespeare*. Chicago: University of Chicago Press, 1980.

Greisch, Jean. *Vivre en philosophant: Expérience philosophique, exercices spirituels et théraphies de l'âme*. Paris: Cerf, 2015.

Guénon, René. *La règne de la quantité et les signes des temps*. Paris: Gallimard, 1945.

Gutas, Dimitri. "The Heritage of Avicenna: The Golden Age of Arabic Philosophy, 1000–ca. 1350." In *Avicenna and His Heritage*. Ed. by Jules Janssens and Daniel de Smet. Leuven: Peeters, 2002, 81–97.

Gutas, Dimitri. "Avicenna and After: The Development of Paraphilosophy: A History of Science Approach." In *Islamic Philosophy from the 12th to the 14th Century*. Ed. by Abdelkader Al-Ghouz. Bonn: V&RUnipress for Bonn University Press, 2018, 19–71.

Hadot, Pierre. *Philosophy as a Way of Life*. Transl. by Michael Chase. Oxford: Blackwells, 1995.

Halbfass, Wilhelm. *India and Europe: An Essay in Understanding*. Albany, NY: State University of New York Press, 1988.

Hall, Bruce. "The Question of 'Race' in the Precolonial Southern Sahara." *Journal of North African Studies* 10 (2005): 339–67.

Al-Ḥarīrī, Abū Muḥammad. *Impostures by al-Ḥarīrī. A Groundbreaking Translation by Michael Cooperson*. Library of Arabic Literature. New York: New York University Press, 2020.

Al-Ḥasanī, Sayyid ʿAbd al-Ḥayy. *Al-Ṯaqāfa al-Islāmiyya fī l-Hind*. Damascus: Maǧmaʿ al-luġa al-ʿArabiyya, 1983.

Al-Ḥasanī, Sayyid ʿAbd al-Ḥayy. *Nuzhat al-ḫawāṭir wa-bahǧat al-masāmiʿ wa-l-nawāẓir*. Beirut: Dār Ibn Ḥazm, 1999.

Heidegger, Martin. *Kant and the Problem of Metaphysics*. Transl. Richard Taft. Bloomington, IN: Indiana University Press, 1997.

Heidegger, Martin. *Basic Concepts of Aristotelian Philosophy*. Transl. by Robert D. Metcalf and Mark B. Tanzer. Bloomington, IN: Indiana University Press, 2009.

Hnatovska, Hanna. "The Image of Philosophy in Indian Culture: Etymology and Untranslateability of Terms." *Future Human Image* 13 (2020): 14–23. https://doi. org/10.29202/fhi/13/2. Accessed September 12, 2022.

Ḫudrī, Ġulām-Ḥusayn. *Taʾammulī bar sayr-i taṭavvur-i ḥukamāʾ va ḥikmat-i mutaʿāliya*. Tehran: Pažūhišgāh-i ʿulūm-i insānī va muṭālaʿāt-i farhangī, 1391 AHS/2012.

Hunwick, John O. "Aḥmad Bābā on Slavery." *Sudanic Africa* 11 (2000): 131–9.

Ḫūyī, Abū l-Qāsim Amīn al-Šarīʿa. *Mīzān al-ṣavāb dar sharḥ-i Faṣl al-ḫiṭāb*. Ed. by Muḥammad Ḫvāǧavī. 3 vols. Tehran: Intišārāt-i Mawlā, 1383 AHS/2004.

Husain, M. Hidayat. "The Life and Works of Baḥr al-ʿulūm." *Journal of the Asiatic Society of Bengal* new series 7 (1911): 693–5.

ʿInāyatullāh, Maulvī. *Tazkira-yi ʿulamāʾ-yi Farangī Maḥall*. Lucknow: Niẓāmī Press, 1930.

Kane, Ousmane Oumar. *Beyond Timbuktu: An Intellectual History of Muslim West Africa*. Cambridge: Harvard University Press, 2016.

Karatani, Kōjin. *Isonomia and the Origins of Philosophy*. Transl. by Joseph A. Murphy. Durham, NC: Duke University Press, 2017.

Kennedy, Philip. "Reason and Revelation or the Philosopher's Squib (The Sixth Maqāma of Ibn al-Nāqiyā)." *Journal of Arabic and Islamic Studies* 3 (2000): 84–113.

Kilito, Abdelfattah. *L'auteur et ses doubles: Essai sur la culture arabe classique*. Paris: Éditions du Seuil, 1985.

King, Richard. *Indian Philosophy: An Introduction to Hindu and Buddhist Thought*. Edinburgh: Edinburgh University Press, 1999.

Laerke, Mogens, Justin E. Smith and Eric Schliesser, eds. *Philosophy and Its History: Aims and Methods in the Study of Early Modern Philosophy*. New York: Oxford University Press, 2013.

Lloyd, Geoffrey E.R. "'Philosophy': What Did the Greeks Invent and Is It Relevant to China?" *Extrême-orient, Extrême-occident* 27 (2005): 149–59.

MacIntyre, Alasdair. *Whose Justice? Whose Rationality?* Notre Dame, IN: Notre Dame University Press, 1988.

Malik, Jamal. *Islamische Gelehrtenkultur in Nordindien: Entwicklungsgeschichte und Tendenzen am Beispiel von Lucknow*. Leiden: E.J. Brill, 1997.

Mignolo, Walter and Catherine Walsh. *On Decoloniality: Concepts, Analytics, Praxis*. Durham, NC: Duke University Press, 2018.

Moosavi, Leon. "The Decolonial Bandwagon and the Dangers of Intellectual Decolonisation." *International Review of Sociology* 30.2 (2020): 332–54.

Mudimbe, V.Y. *The Invention of Africa: Gnosis, Philosophy, and the Order of Knowledge*. Bloomington, IN: Indiana University Press, 1988.

Muruwwa, Ḥusayn. *Al-Nazaʿāt al-māddiyya fī l-falsafa al-ʿArabiyya al-Islāmiyya*. 4 vols. Beirut: Dār al-Fārābī, 1978.

Nasr, Seyyed Hossein. *Islamic Philosophy from Its Origins to the Present: Philosophy in the Land of Prophecy*. Albany, NY: State University of New York Press, 2006.

Nayrīzī, Umm Salama Bēgum. *Ǧāmiʿ al-kulliyyāt*. Ed. by Mahdī Iftiḫār. Qum: Kitābsarā-yi išrāq, 1386 AHS/2007.

Ogunnaike, Oludamini. "African Philosophy Reconsidered: Africa, Religion, Race, and Philosophy." *Journal of Africana Religions* 5.2 (2017): 181–216.

Ogunnaike, Oludamini. *Deep Knowledge: Ways of Knowing in Sufism in Ifa, Two West African Intellectual Traditions*. University Park: Pennsylvania State University Press, 2020.

Park, Peter K. J. *Africa, Asia and the History of Philosophy: Racism in the Formation of the Philosophical Canon, 1780–1830*. Albany, NY: State University of New York Press, 2013.

Pollock, Sheldon, ed. *Forms of Knowledge in Early Modern Asia*. Durham, NC: Duke University Press, 2011.

Pollock, Sheldon. *A Rasa Reader: Classical Indian Aesthetics*. New York: Columbia University Press, 2016.

Porphyry. *Letter to Marcella*. Transl. by Alice Zimmern. Oxford: Clarendon Press, 1910.

Al-Qarāfī, Šihāb al-Dīn. *Šarḥ Tanqīḥ al-fuṣūl fī iḫtiṣār al-maḥṣūl*. Ed. by Ṭāhā ʿAbd al-Raʾūf. Cairo: Maktabat al-Kulliyya al-Azhariyya, 1983.

Ramose, Mogobe. "A Philosophy without Memory Cannot Abolish Slavery: On Epistemic Justice in South Africa." In *Debating African Philosophy: Perspectives on Identity, Decolonial Ethics and Comparative Philosophy*. Ed. by George Hull. London: Routledge, 2019, 60–72.

Raud, Rein. "Philosophies versus Philosophy: In Defence of a Flexible Definition." *Philosophy East & West* 56 (2006): 618–25.

Raud, Rein. "Traditions and Tendencies: A Reply to Carine Defoort." *Philosophy East & West* 56 (2006): 661–4.

Robinson, Francis. *The 'Ulama of Farangi Mahall and Islamic Culture in South Asia*. Delhi: Permanent Black, 2001.

Rorty, Richard. *Philosophy and the Mirror of Nature*. Princeton: Princeton University Press, 1978.

Rorty, Richard. "The Historiography of Philosophy: Four Genres." In *Philosophy in History*. Ed. by Richard Rorty, J.B. Schneewind and Quentin Skinner. Cambridge: Cambridge University Press, 1984, 49–76.

Rūmī, Jalāl al-Dīn. *The Masnavi Book One*. Transl. by Jawid Mojaddedi. Oxford: Oxford University Press, 2004.

Sassi, Maria Michela. *The Beginnings of Philosophy in Greece*. Princeton: Princeton University Press, 2020.

Satia, Priya. *Time's Monster: History, Conscience, and Britain's Empire*. Cambridge, MA: Harvard University Press, 2020.

Scharfstein, Ben-Ami. *A Comparative History of World Philosophy*. Albany, NY: State University of New York Press, 1998.

Sedley, David. "The Idea of Godlikeness." In *Plato 2: Ethics, Politics, Religion*. Ed. by Gail Fine. Oxford: Oxford University Press, 1999, 309–28.

Siderits, Mark et al, eds. *Self, No Self? Perspectives from the Analytic, Phenomenological and Indian Traditions*. Oxford: Oxford University Press, 2010.

Šīrāzī, Ma'ṣūm 'Alī Šāh. *Ṭarāyiq al-ḥaqāyiq*. Ed. by M. J. Maḥǧūb. 3 vols. Tehran: Kitābḫāna-yi Sanā'ī, 1339 AHS/1960.

Šīrāzī, Mullā Ṣadrā. *Risālat al-ḥudūṯ*. Ed. by Sayyid Ḥusayn Mūsawiyān. Tehran: Sadra Islamic Philosophy Research Institute, 1378 AHS/1999.

Šīrāzī, Mullā Ṣadrā. *Al-Ḥikma al-muta'āliya fī l-asfār al-'aqliyya al-arba'a*. Ed. by Ġulām-Riḍā A'wānī et al. 9 vols. Tehran: Sadra Islamic Philosophy Research Institute, 1380–83 AHS/2001–04.

Skinner, Quentin. "Meaning and Understanding in the History of Ideas." *History and Theory* 8.1 (1969): 3–53.

Sloterdijk, Peter. *The Art of Philosophy: Wisdom as Practice*. Transl. by Karen Margolis. New York: Columbia University Press, 2012.

Sloterdijk, Peter. *Philosophical Temperaments: From Plato to Foucault*. Transl. by Thomas Dunlap. New York: Columbia University Press, 2013.

Smith, Justin E. *The Philosopher: A History in Six Types*. Princeton: Princeton University Press, 2016.

Sorrell, Tom and G.A.J. Rogers, eds. *Analytic Philosophy and History of Philosophy*. Oxford: Clarendon Press, 2005.

de Sousa Santos, Boaventura. *Epistemologies of the South: Justice against Epistemicide*. Boulder, CO: Paradigm, 2014.

de Sousa Santos, Boaventura. *The End of the Cognitive Empire: The Coming of Age of Epistemologies of the South*. Durham, NC: Duke University Press, 2018.

Subrahmanyam, Sanjay. "A Tale of Three Empires: Mughals, Ottomans and Habsburgs in a Comparative Context." *Common Knowledge* 12.1 (2006): 66–92.

Subrahmanyam, Sanjay. "Par-delà l'incommensurabilité: Pour une histoire connectée des empire aux temps modernes." *Revue d'histoire moderne et contemporain* 54.4 (2007): 34–53.

Suhā, Manūčihr Ṣadūqī. *Taḥrīr-i s̲ānī-yi Tārīḫ-i ḥukamāʾ va ʿurafāʾ-yi mutaʾaḫḫir az Ṣadr al-mutaʾallihīn*. Tehran: Intišārāt-i ḥikmat, 1383 AHS/2004.

Táíwò, Olúfémi. *Against Decolonisation: Taking African Agency Seriously*. London: Hurst & Co., 2022.

Táíwò, Olúfémi. *Elite Capture: How the Powerful Took Over Identity Politics (and Everything Else)*. London: Pluto Press, 2022.

Al-Tinbuktī, Aḥmad Bābā. *Nayl al-ibtihāǧ bi-taṭrīz al-dībāǧ*. Ed. by ʿAbd al-Ḥamīd al-Harrāma. Tripoli: Dār al-kātib, 2000.

van der Mieroop, Marc. *Philosophy before the Greeks: The Pursuit of Truth in Ancient Babylonia*. Princeton: Princeton University Press, 2017.

van Ruymbeke, Christine. "L'histoire du concours des peintres Rūmīs et chīnīs chez Niẓāmī et chez Rūmī: Deux aspects du miroir." In *Miroir et savoir: La transmission d'une thème platonicien des Alexandrins à la philosophie arabo-musulmane*. Ed. by Daniel de Smet, Meryem Sebti and Godfroid de Callataÿ. Leuven: Leuven University Press, 2008, 273–91.

White, Hayden. *Metahistory: The Historical Imagination in Nineteenth-Century Europe*. Baltimore: Johns Hopkins University Press, 1973.

Williams, Bernard. "Plato: The Invention of Philosophy." In Idem, *The Sense of the Past: Essays in the History of Philosophy*. Princeton: Princeton University Press, 2006, 148–86.

Wynter, Sylvia. "Unsettling the Coloniality of Being/Power/Truth/Freedom." *The New Centennial Review* 3 (2003): 257–337.

Yountae, An and Eleanor Craig, eds. *Beyond Man: Race, Coloniality, and Philosophy of Religion*. Durham, NC: Duke University Press, 2021.

2

Philosophy for Politics: Ancient Greek Philosophy Echoed in Ibn al-Muqaffaʿ's Writings

István T. Kristó-Nagy

Introduction

It is widely recognised among scholars of Arabic literature and Islamic studies that Ibn al-Muqaffaʿ's (d. in 757 or 758)[1] writings are amongst the earliest and foundational pieces of Arabic belles-lettres and fiction as well as of Islamic *naṣīḥa* (political and ethical advice)[2] literature.[3] However, belonging to the realm of *adab* (educative and entertaining prose) and conveying political agendas, the works attributed to Ibn al-Muqaffaʿ have been scarcely studied as pertaining to the sphere of philosophy and remain little explored from the aspect of the integration of ancient Greek philosophy into Islamic thought.[4]

We need to reflect briefly on some key terms used. Both ancient Greek philosophy and Islamic advice literature are fluid terms.[5] In the case of *ancient Greek* philosophy, *ancient* refers to an era and *Greek* refers to a language. However, due to the distance in space and time between ancient Greek philosophy and Islamic advice literature, the impact of the former on the latter was in most cases mediated through late antique texts[6] that were written by authors of diverse ethnicities, and composed in various languages (including Greek, Syriac[7] and Persian[8]). Most of what was integrated into Islamic civilization from ancient Greek philosophy reached it through the filters of late antique commentators. Their work had both a catalysing and restricting effect on the Islamic reception of ancient Greek philosophy. The social habitat and niche, and thus the concerns and interests of the late antique imperial elites were similar to those of the elites linked to the court of the Islamic empire. The latter were receptive to the former's monotheism, monarchy, and hierarchy-favouring take of Greek philosophy; hence the predominance of Neoplatonism[9] and Neoplatonising Aristotelianism that marked Christendom also characterized Islamic philosophy. In the case of *Islamic* political advice literature, the term *Islamic* refers to a religious adherence and needs to be qualified. In the sense used here, Islamic simply means that the text was written in a time and place that was dominated by Muslims, for a (non-exclusively) Muslim readership, regardless of the actual religion of the author and the religiosity of the text.[10] Regarding *philosophy* and *advice (or wisdom) literature*, the reconsideration of the rigid distinction between the two is one of the major objectives of this study.

As modern scholars of philosophy tended to disregard advice literature, its importance, as a living carrier of philosophical ideas and as philosophy in application, escaped most of them. Authors of advice literature were, however, not by definition less deep and original thinkers than the philosophers, and they were often considerably more influential. Furthermore, the two fields were not necessarily as distinct in the view of the authors of either philosophical or advice literature texts as it has been too often in modern academia. The first to write a treatise titled *Peri basileias* (*On Kingship*) was probably Aristotle, to his disciple, Alexander.[11] Advice literature, and especially political advice literature, could be both theoretical and practical, advising about general principles as well as actual political situations; presenting and producing political philosophy applied in action.

Does the distinction between philosophy and advice literature need revision? Can early Islamic advice literature texts shed new light on when, how, and why the integration of ancient Greek philosophy into Islamic thought originated? What was regarded as philosophy and wisdom, and why was it seen as important? By investigating the presence and application of elements of ancient Greek philosophy in writings attributed to Ibn al-Muqaffaʿ, as well as the aim these texts proclaim, the goal of this present study is twofold. It seeks to fill the conceptual gap between philosophy and advice/wisdom literature, as well as to shed light on their use in the formative period of Islamic political thought.

Discussing the movement of translation into Arabic, Dimitri Gutas suggests that "the initial translations of Greek works were made from Middle Persian intermediaries or compilations [. . .], and they were preponderantly of astrological character."[12] Gutas also points out that the "exigencies of the religio-political confrontation played a major role" in the translation movement.[13]

The hypothesis proposed in this present chapter consists in the following. One of the first means of bringing ancient Greek philosophical ideas and structures into Islamic civilization was the emerging Islamic political advice literature, including writings translated from or influenced by Middle Persian texts. These Middle Persian texts probably comprehended translations of Greek works, but the bulk of this literature, which was not translated from Greek, also absorbed Greek ideas and structures.[14] Rhetoric, logic and political theories were at least as important for supporting the powerful as astrology, while medical knowledge – which will be tangentially treated in this chapter – was as vital for them as for anyone.[15] Political advice literature played a crucial part in the assimilation of these elements of ancient Greek philosophy – through late antique filters – into Islamic civilization. This process was underway possibly already during the rule of the Umayyad caliph Hishām b. ʿAbd al-Malik (r. 105–25/724–43),[16] and at the latest by the time of the immediate aftermath of the revolution that brought the ʿAbbasids to power as evidenced by Ibn al-Muqaffaʿ's oeuvre. The fact that these elements of Greek thought had been already absorbed by late antique civilizations facilitated their early integration into Islamic civilization, which rose and formed in interaction with, and building on, the cultural and human resources of its late antique – preceding and contemporary – counterparts.[17]

Ibn al-Muqaffaʿ and the Political Advice Texts Attributed to Him

The Persian Ibn al-Muqaffaʿ was a representative par excellence of a segment of society that played a crucial part in the integration of the antique political theories and practices into Islamic civilisation. He belonged to the *kuttāb* (pl. for *kātib*), scribes or secretaries, who served the military elite, up to the rulers, as advisers and administrators.[18] Ibn al-Muqaffaʿ started his career under the Umayyads, and his expertise in Sāsānian political know-how, combined with his eloquence in Arabic, allowed him to rise to the highest sphere of the political elite. After the downfall of the Umayyads, he advised, as secretary, members of the new ruling dynasty, and lost his life in a power struggle within the ʿAbbasid family.

In tandem with his political career, Ibn al-Muqaffaʿ played a key role in translating Middle Persian political advice texts (*andarz*) into Arabic *adab* and in transmitting both their form and content into Islamic civilization. Furthermore, he also applied late antique theories that are present in these texts to pertinent political agendas of his time, as manifested in both of his surviving political epistles. In this present study, three *adab* works and the two political epistles attributed to Ibn al-Muqaffaʿ will be discussed. The *adab* works are his translation of *Kalīla wa-Dimna* (*Kalīla and Dimna*), as well as the *Kitāb al-Ādāb al-kabīr* (*The Great Book of* Adabs) and the *Kitāb al-Adab al-ṣaghīr* (*The Small Book of* Adab). The epistles are the *Risāla fī l-ṣaḥāba* (*Epistle on the Companions [of the Caliph]*) and *al-Yatīma* (*The Peerless Pearl*).

Al-Manṭiq

Before turning to the above texts attributed to Ibn al-Muqaffaʿ, it is important to mention that an Arabic version of the most influential work of logic of antiquity, the Aristotelian *Organon*, with Porphyry's introduction, the *Isagoge*, survives under the title *al-Manṭiq* (*The Logic*) and Ibn al-Muqaffaʿ or his son's name.[19] This may be the first known extant Arabic translation of a Greek philosophical text.[20] According to Dimitri Gutas's recent study assessing the authorship of the text based on the colophons of the manuscripts, Ibn al-Muqaffaʿ, or his son, might have worked together with an otherwise unknown translator, Hīlyā the Melkite, and their text was possibly reworked by two further translators, who are known to have worked for the caliphs al-Mahdī (r. 158–69/775–85) and Hārūn al-Rashīd (r. 170–93/786–809).[21] Another recent study, by Erik Hermans, summarizes the previous scholarship on the text, and argues for the attribution to Ibn al-Muqaffaʿ, or his son, gathering also the circumstantial evidences that it was translated from Middle Persian.[22] Whether the text was translated by Ibn al-Muqaffaʿ, or his son, and whether it was translated directly from Greek (by Hīlyā), or from Middle Persian, does not change the fact that its translation fits well in the context of Ibn al-Muqaffaʿ's oeuvre and politico-literary agenda.[23]

We read in a satirical attack on the *kuttāb* attributed to al-Jāḥiẓ (d. 869) that translations of Middle Persian political advice literature, including *Kalīla wa-Dimna*, "Ibn al-Muqaffaʿ's *adab*," as well as *al-Manṭiq*, belonged to the core of the *kuttāb*'s learning.[24] It is well possible that this *al-Manṭiq*, mentioned among the *kuttāb*'s favourites, is *The Logic* attributed to Ibn al-Muqaffaʿ. A book on logic could be a valuable asset for the learning of *kuttāb*, secretaries-advisors-administrators of Ibn al-Muqaffaʿ's ilk. In addition to their familiarity with the political traditions of the past they claimed to be authoritative, their social status depended on their intellectual capital comprising reasoning and rhetoric, astute action and argumentation. The analysis of *al-Manṭiq* awaits further studies, including a comparison of its style and content with other texts attributed Ibn al-Muqaffaʿ, which cannot be covered in this chapter.[25]

Kalīla wa-Dimna

Ibn al-Muqaffaʿ's works had an instrumental role in the Islamization of late antique political and ethical thought, including Greek and Indian logic and rhetoric, as it had been distilled into Middle Persian advice literature. He authored the Arabic version of the quintessential book of advice for princes and courtiers, *Kalīla wa-Dimna* (*Kalīla and Dimna*), which consists of a collection of edifying fables and tales featuring both animal and human characters. It includes versions of all the five chapters of the Sanskrit *Pañcatantra*, three that are part of the *Mahābhārata*, as well as further chapters and a series of introductions.[26] The introductions of *Kalīla wa-Dimna* present the text as having originated in India, translated into Pahlavi (Middle Persian) by Burzawayh/Burzōy,[27] and then into Arabic by Ibn al-Muqaffaʿ.[28] Ibn al-Muqaffaʿ's "original" Arabic version does not subsists, but it has been the source of a multitude of variants in Arabic and a number of other languages. It is one of the most global texts in history and new versions and translations still proliferate.[29]

Kalīla wa-Dimna is a prime example for the conflation between philosophy and advice literature. The Arabic versions are presented in the literary form of a narrative dialogue between a king and a philosopher that frames each chapter after the introductory ones.[30] Strikingly, in the Arabic versions, the wise man advising the ruler is consistently termed *faylasūf*, philosopher, using the Arabicised Greek word, probably introduced by Ibn al-Muqaffaʿ, as it is not included in the old Syriac text, which is considered to be a translation of the Middle Persian version independent from that of Ibn al-Muqaffaʿ.[31] In the old Syriac version, the advisor of the frame story is always mentioned by name.[32]

In using the term *faylasūf*, Ibn al-Muqaffaʿ may have followed the text published under the title *The Correspondence between Aristotle and Alexander the Great*, which is possibly an even earlier specimen of Islamic political advice literature. The authorship of the Arabic version of this text is attributed to Sālim Abū l-ʿAlāʾ (alone or with others), secretary of the Umayyad caliph Hishām b. ʿAbd al-Malik. The complexity of genesis of this text is similar to that of *Kalīla wa-Dimna*. Rooted in Greek advice literature, its transmission through Middle Persian, the origin of its different parts and the role of Sālim Abū l-ʿAlāʾ in its composition remains debated.[33] The text evolved into the *Sirr al-asrār* (*Secret of Secrets*), different versions of which impacted both Islamic and Western Medieval political thought. Similar to *Kalīla wa-Dimna*, it is also structured as a dialogue between two parties – in the form of written correspondence –[34] and uses the term *faylasūf*.[35]

It is quite possible that Ibn al-Muqaffaʿ knew Sālim Abū l-ʿAlāʾ. They belonged to the same scribal elite working at the peaks of power in the Islamic empire. Sālim Abū l-ʿAlāʾ married his daughter or sister to ʿAbd al-Ḥamīd b. Yaḥyā al-Kātib (d. 132/750), who also wrote letters for the caliph Hishām b. ʿAbd al-Malik, and was the secretary of the last Umayyad caliph, Marwān II (r. 127–32/744–50), when he was killed. ʿAbd al-Ḥamīd b. Yaḥyā was "a third-generation Muslim of non-Arab, probably Persian, extraction"[36] and preceded his younger friend, Ibn al-Muqaffaʿ,[37] as the first celebrated author of Arabic prose.

This consistent use of the term *faylasūf* throughout the text, corroborated by the guidance given in the preface under Ibn al-Muqaffaʿ's name, demonstrates that he presented this most prominent text of advice literature as a book of philosophy enveloped into entertaining examples. The following sentences conclude some versions of Ibn al-Muqaffaʿ's preface to *Kalīla wa-Dimna*:

> The one who considers the substance of this book ought to know that it is divided into four aims. The first of these is that which is intended by placing it on the tongues of non-speaking animals so that youths given to jest (*hazl*) would rush to read it and their hearts might be won over by it because the aim is delightful anecdotes (*nawādir*) about the stratagems of animals. The second

> [aim] is to display depictions (*khayālāt*) of animals in various hues and colors so that it might delight the hearts of kings and that their desire for it might be stronger by virtue of its entertaining quality. The third [aim] is that, for this reason, kings and commoners will take it up and thus it will increasingly be copied and not fall into disuse and become shabby over the course of time, thus benefiting the illustrators and copyists in perpetuity. The fourth aim is the most remote and that is reserved especially for the philosophers.

This translation is provided by Matthew L. Keegan, who rightly points out that this section may well be a later interpolation into the text.[38] Keegan's studies lead us to think about how *Kalīla wa-Dimna*'s reception is interconnected with its continuous rewriting and re-creation by its translators and copyists. He compares the passage quoted above to al-Ḥarīrī's (d. 516/1122) "typology of readers," which may have been influenced by the above passage, *or*, may have inspired an anonymous copyist to insert this passage into the preface attributed to Ibn al-Muqaffaʿ.[39]

In another paper, Keegan analyses the multifarious reception of *Kalīla wa-Dimna* in classical Arabic and Persian literature. We can observe that this reception follows broadly the typology provided in the passage above as some later authors regarded the text as frivolous fiction, advice for rules, or philosophy. The philosophical interpretation of *Kalīla wa-Dimna* is especially salient in the reception of the "Chapter of the Ring Dove." Keegan presents the interpretation of this chapter by the eminent theologian and exegete Fakhr al-Dīn al-Rāzī (d. 606/1209) as "an allegory for the soul's descent into the material world and its eventual extrication from it"[40] and links the story also to the *Risālat al-Ṭayr* (*The Epistle of the Bird*) by the illustrious physician and philosopher Ibn Sīnā (Avicenna, d. 428/1037) and to the "The Ode of the Soul" attributed to him,[41] as well as to the *Manṭiq al-Ṭayr* (*Conference of the Birds*) by the Persian Sufi master Farīd al-Dīn al-ʿAṭṭār (d. 1221).[42] Keegan points out that "it seems that the tradition of using animal allegories and particularly allegories involving birds as a way of imagining the soul's descent to the material realm inflected a certain strand of interpretation of 'The Chapter of the Ring Dove'."[43] He also indicates that the chapter and others in *Kalīla wa-Dimna* discuss indeed philosophical problems such as the question of fate or agency, intelligence and choice.[44] Indeed this is one of the most fundamental themes of *Kalīla wa-Dimna*.[45]

Keegan also refers to the fact that the self-designation of the "philosophically-inclined" authors of the collection of texts known as the epistles of the *Ikhwān al-Ṣafāʾ* (Brethren of Purity) derives probably from the introduction of the "Chapter of the Ring Dove."[46] We can add that the choice of their name was not the only instance when the *Ikhwān al-Ṣafāʾ* referred to *Kalīla wa-Dimna* as a source of inspiration. Their epistle *The Case of the Animals versus Man before the King of the Jinn* clearly follows the precedent set by *Kalīla wa-Dimna*.[47] The collection translated into Arabic by Ibn al-Muqaffaʿ established the model of embedding philosophy in fables and also includes a chapter reporting about a trial featuring animals at the royal court of a lion. This is the "Chapter of the Investigation of Dimna's Conduct," which was interpolated into the text probably by Ibn al-Muqaffaʿ.[48] It ends with the death of the supremely intelligent but completely immoral jackal, Dimna. Before him, his brother, Kalīla also dies. He is resurrected, however, in the *Ikhwān al-Ṣafā*'s epistle to be the spokesperson of one group of the animals, namely the carnivores. He is sent by the lion, the predators' king, and represent them in the animals' trial against men castigating the much more predatory nature of humans.[49] According to Johann Christoph Bürgel, this choice of Kalīla by the *Ikhwān al-Ṣafā*ʾ presents "an interesting allusion to the older text, by which the Brethren, I think very consciously, place their text in that tradition of – almost heretic – rationalism."[50]

A similar suspicion is expressed in an insightful note by the translators of the *Ikhwān al-Ṣafā*'s epistle:

> The Ikhwān tip their hats to Ibn al-Muqaffaʿ as their predecessor in Aesopian satire. Part of what they owe to him is their tone, and the conceit of a court of animals and their kings and courtiers. They take their pen name form an epithet given to a body of animals mentioned in the 'Tale of the Ring-Dove'. Ibn al-Muqaffaʿ was a disciple of the Umayyad author of the earliest Arabic prose works. He himself set the patterns of the Persian mode in court literature for Arabic writers, fusing the two senses of *adab*, courtesy and literary urbanity in a single medium of polite letters, the literature of the 'secretarial school'. It is doubtful that Ibn al-Muqaffaʿ was a whole-hearted Muslim. The fact that he was executed make the tribute to him by the Ikhwān, by casting Kalīla as a paragon of urbanity, all the more telling.[51]

Doubts about the compatibility of *Kalīla wa-Dimna* with Islam were also raised by Muslim authors. Keegan discusses classical texts perceiving *Kalīla wa-Dimna* as a "scriptural alternative to or competitor with the Quran."[52] We can add to his insightful discussion of this topic that while this "rivalry," to which the above mentioned satire on the *kuttāb* attributed to al-Jāḥiẓ also alludes,[53] is due partly to the Persian *kuttāb*'s quest for authority, claiming the superiority of their cultural tradition.[54] Ibn al-Muqaffaʿ was a key figure and a symbol of this trend,[55] which was resisted by pro-Arab scholars, for instance Abū ʿAbd Allāh al-Yamanī (d. c. 400/1009–10), who, in his commentary of *Kalīla wa-Dimna*, claimed that its real author was Ibn al-Muqaffaʿ, who took the wise sayings (*ḥikam*) from the poetry of the ancient Arabs, turned them into prose, and composed on this basis *Kalīla wa-Dimna*.[56]

In addition to being an emblem of Persian prestige, the fact that *Kalīla wa-Dimna* touches ultimate questions of philosophy and religion was another core factor that made the text suspicious. Ibn al-Muqaffaʿ is described in classical sources as the author of a *Muʿāraḍat al-Qurʾān*, i.e. of a text imitating the Qurʾan, taking up the challenge of inimitability launched by the Qurʾan. Fragments of such a text attributed to Ibn al-Muqaffaʿ still survive in a refutation against them. In another refutation "against the the damned Zindīq Ibn al-Muqaffaʿ," we also find the fragments of another text attributed to him launching a rationalist, philosophical criticism of the Qurʾan, Islam and monotheism in general.[57] The argumentation of this latter text has been long linked to one of the most important sceptical texts[58] that was widely read in the Islamic world, the intellectual autobiography of Burzawayh/Burzōy, the physician who authored the Middle Persian version of *Kalīla wa-Dimna*.[59] This autobiography became one of the introductory chapters of the book. It exhibits Burzawayh/Burzōy's quest for a meaningful life, resulting in deep religious scepticism and transreligious morality. This scepticism did not remain unnoticed and both the outstanding Muʿtazilī theologian, the *qāḍī* ʿAbd al-Jabbār (b. ca. 325/936–37, d. 415/1025) and the otherwise supremely open-minded genius al-Bīrūnī (b. 362/973, d. 440/1046) accused Ibn al-Muqaffaʿ of adding Burzawayh's chapter to the text in order to spread religious doubt and propagate Manicheism.[60] Both ʿAbd al-Jabbār and al-Bīrūnī were, like Ibn al-Muqaffaʿ, high profile Iranian intellectuals. However, they did not look any more on Islam as a religion of the conquerors of their land, but rather as their own religion. They represent a later phase of mutual integration and assimilation between conquerors and the vanquished. They were still able to detect but did not share any more Ibn al-Muqaffaʿ's ambiguous attitudes and intentions.[61]

It is noteworthy that the profoundly philosophical (in the most general sense of the word) and religious (sceptical and trans-religious), ethical and existential preoccupations of Burzawayh/Burzōy were translated because they were included in a collection that primarily aimed at offering political advice. *Kalīla wa-Dimna* was translated from an old imperial language (Middle Persian) to a new one (Arabic) in an effort to satisfy the need of the new imperial elites for imperial political literature. Ibn al-Muqaffaʿ lived before the book producing boom that was facilitated by the introduction of paper. Around the time of the ʿAbbasid (or rather Hāshimite) revolution, the primary interest of the members of the political elite, who ruled the Islamic empire and were able to sponsor the translation and production of books, lied in established and applicable imperial literature advising them about the practice and theory of power including its ideological (and rhetorical) support.[62] *Kalīla wa-Dimna* teaches philosophy – politics, rhetoric and ethic – in application, packed into the literary framework of fables and tales, which provides both amusement for its audience and a shield for its authors.

While *Kalīla wa-Dimna* and the entire oeuvre of Ibn al-Muqaffaʿ shows continuity in the usage of philosophy between late antique civilizations and Islam, it also allows us to inquire about the changes in the role played by philosophers and other "wise men." Although the ancient Greek ideal of *parrhēsia* "telling all" and the image of the philosopher confronting the tyrant and legitimising the just monarch[63] is present in *Kalīla wa-Dimna*,[64] its advice for rulers is usually indirect and wrapped into several layers of tales referring to past and/or fictitious authorities.[65] This indirectness allows rulers to take the advice without losing their supremacy and allows advisors to advise them without losing their position or life. The text does not only advise rulers, but also those in their entourage who provide advice to them. Furthermore, writing in a time of religious, ethnical and social tensions, Ibn al-Muqaffaʿ may well have used "Aesopian language," i.e. coding for covert messages, intended to be understood by some readers and to be hidden from others.[66]

Before turning to other texts attributed to Ibn al-Muqaffaʿ, let us conclude our section on *Kalīla wa-Dimna* by looking at some passages of the text that provide examples of how another field of ancient Greek thought related to philosophy, namely medical ideas, started to permeate Islamic civilization before the translation of Greek works dedicated to the field. The autobiography of Burzawayh/Burzōy concludes with a parable of Indian provenance, that of "The man in the well."[67] The version in *Kalīla wa-Dimna* refers to the theory of the four humours, which does not appear in the Indian versions.[68] As this theory was a commonplace in Greek medicine, it is possible that its presence in the autobiography of the author of the Middle Persian version of *Kalīla wa-Dimna* points to Greek influences on Sāsānian culture. On the other hand, historians of science identified the influence of Indian medicine in Persia and Baghdad in the eighth century.[69]

Kalīla wa-Dimna features other medical metaphors. In the conclusion of the chapter of "The Lion and the Ox/Bull," when the lion/king regrets having killed the ox, who was his best friend, Dimna, the crafty jackal/courtier, consoles him with the following examples:

> A prudent person may sometimes detest someone, yet take him as a close companion for his great competence and shrewd judgment. It is just like the painful medicine that one must swallow to be cured. Similarly, one may love a person very dearly, yet shun him or even kill him if he suspects possible harm from him. It is just like a person who cuts off the finger that was bitten by a snake, to save himself from the deadly venom.[70]

The medical similes of this passage bear parallels to the following section of Aristotle's *Nicomachean Ethics*:

> Also those processes which are thought to be bad will in some cases, though bad absolutely, be not bad relatively, but in fact desirable for a particular person, or in other cases, though not even desirable generally for the particular person,

> nevertheless desirable for him in particular circumstances and for a short time, although not really desirable. And some such processes are not really pleasures at all, but only seem to be so: I mean the painful processes that are undergone for their curative effects, for instance, treatment applied to the sick.[71]

According to Edgerton's reconstructed version of the Sanskrit text, the image of the unpleasant, but useful medicine was not part of "original" Sanskrit version, and while the image of cutting off one's own arm was possibly already included, it was not of medical character:

> Cut off your very arm if it offends you.[72]

Both similes are included, however, in the old Syriac version,[73] just like the variants of Ibn al-Muqaffaʿ's Arabic translation. Thus, they were most likely part of the Middle Persian text.[74] Bitter medicine and its use in similes were both widespread in antiquity. It is included for instance in *The Beatitudes* of Gregory of Nyssa (d. c. 395).[75] Amputation, as "sad but solitary remedy to secure the safety of the rest of the body," is described in ancient Greek medical literature.[76] It also appears in the *Discourses* of Epictetus (d. c. 135):

> For I will assert of the foot as such that it is natural for it to be clean, but if you take it as a foot, and not as a thing detached, it will be appropriate for it to step into mud and trample on thorns and sometimes to be cut off for the sake of the whole body; otherwise it will no longer be a foot.[77]

The image of a necessary amputation is used in a simile by Clement of Alexandria (d. c. 215), in his *Exhortation to the Greeks*:

> [. . .] just as a good doctor, in dealing with diseased bodies, uses poulticing for some, rubbing for others, and bathing for others; some he cuts with a knife, others he cauterizes, and in some cases he even amputates, if by any means he can restore the patient to health by removing some part or limb. So the Saviour uses many tones and many devices in working for the salvation of men.[78]

Though these parallels can be coincidental, we can still discern that the medical images concluding the chapter of "The Lion and the Ox/Bull" in *Kalīla wa-Dimna* were probably not included in the Sanskrit text, but appeared plausibly in the Middle Persian version, and have distant parallels in Greek texts. As we saw above, this was also the case of the medical reference in the parable of "The Man in the Well" at the conclusion of autobiography of Burzawayh/Burzōy. These medical examples provide a further possible case when elements of Greek thought, fused with Indian ideas and images, reached Islamic political advice literature through Sāsānian political advice literature.

The *Kitāb al-Ādāb al-kabīr*

Ibn al-Muqaffaʿ's *Kitāb al-Ādāb al-kabīr*[79] (*The Great Book of* Adab*s*) is also an excellent example of the integration of Sāsānian cultural patrimony into Arabic advice literature.[80] It includes different sections of *adab*, educative advice, for the ruler and his entourage, which are preceded by carefully constructed introductory sections.[81]

The first[82] of these introductions refers to the common antique myth of a past in which men were superior to the contemporaries of the author in every respect, and the second[83] echoes the notion of the four virtues reflecting a strong influence of ancient Greek philosophy through Sāsānian advice literature, shaped to fit into an Islamic framework. As Andras Hamori notes:

> I doubt that it is a mere coincidence that Ibn al-Muqaffaʿ starts off with the three moral virtues of Antiquity: what the Greeks called *sôphrosunê*, *andreia*, and *dikaiosunê*. Although the Greeks and their Hellenistic followers had no monopoly on thinking about the mean, it is also worth noting that the statement on courage has an entirely Aristotelian look, establishing not only a lower limit for that virtue (not running away when others advance) but, in the clause "without forsaking caution," also an upper limit, beyond which virtue turns to vice.[84]

It is noteworthy that the first of the virtues, which is wisdom or prudence, is replaced in the text by religion.[85]

This idea of the four virtues is also echoed in the introduction to *Kalīla wa-Dimna* attributed to Bahnūd b. Saḥwān and/or ʿAlī b. al-Shāh al-Fārisī:[86]

> I found that the things which distinguish man from other animals are four and they comprise everything in the World. They are wisdom, chastity, reason, and justice. Knowledge, education, and thoughtfulness are within wisdom. Magnanimity, patience, and dignity are within reason. Modesty, generosity, protection, and self-respect are within chastity. Sincerity, charity, self-control, and good disposition are included in justice.[87]

The conclusion of the *Kitāb al-Ādāb al-kabīr* includes an account of the perfect man,[88] reflecting the Greek ideal of *kalokagathia*.[89]

Writing about the style of Ibn al-Muqaffaʿ's *Kitāb al-Ādāb al-kabīr*, J. D. Latham rightly points out that:

> To point his contrasts and enforce his parallels, he makes full use of a range of devices that could have been drawn straight out of the teachings of the ancient schools of classical rhetoric: alliteration, assonance, antithetical isocola, interlocking antithetical phrases, anaphoras, epistrophes, rhetorical repetitions of phrases and structures, rhythmic balance, measured terminations, and so on.[90]

Rhetoric is a part of Greek philosophy, mediated through late antique texts, that appears already in the first works of Arabic and Islamic advice literature including Ibn al-Muqaffaʿ's compositions, which display an extensive use of rhetorical devices.

The *Kitāb al-Adab al-ṣaghīr*

The *Kitāb al-Adab al-ṣaghīr*, attributed to Ibn al-Muqaffaʿ,[91] addresses the intelligent/reasonable man (*ʿāqil*) and discusses similar topics as his other *adab* works based on Middle Persian advice literature. As compared to *Kitāb al-Ādāb al-kabīr*, the extant version of the *Kitāb al-Adab al-ṣaghīr* does not have a conclusion, but its introduction also follows a strict logical structure. Its first sentence presents the use of anadiplosis, repeating the last element of the previous clause at the start of the new one:

> All creatures have a need, and all needs have an aim and all aims have a way.[92]

This opening continues with a reference to a Qurʾanic verse,[93] and develops the argument further:

> And God fixed to the things their time limits, set up to the aims their ways and prepared to the needs their means. And the aim of the people and their need is the rightness of this life and of the afterlife,[94] and the way to reach them is the sound intellect. And the sign of the soundness of intellect is the choice of things by discernment and the implementation of the discernment by determination.[95]

The following sentences explain that the intellects (*ʿuqūl*) need education/manners (*adab*); the major part of the education/manners relies on logic/speech (*manṭiq*); there is nothing in the learning and terminology of logic/speech that would not originate from a primary authority/preceding guide (*imām sābiq*), orally transmitted or in a book; and this is a proof that men did not invent its principles but the science/knowledge (*ʿilm*) of its principles came to them from the Omniscient, the Wise

(God).[96] What we see here is an ingenious use of Greek rhetoric blended with Islamic formulas and concepts in an attempt to "Islamize" the science/knowledge (*ʿilm*) of logic/speech (*manṭiq*), by integrating it into an Islamic framework and matching it to the Islamic criteria regarding respectable knowledge.[97] This presentation of the roots of the science/knowledge of logic/speech mirrors the structure of hadith transmission and the general concept that all valuable knowledge has to emanate from a divinely inspired past authority. It was in a similar pattern that grammarians in the eighth and ninth century sanctified the science of speech.[98]

It is tempting to see the following three facts as linked to one another. First, texts attributed to Ibn al-Muqaffaʿ, such as the *Kitāb al-Adab al-ṣaghīr*, follow clear logical and rhetorical structures. Second, the same *Kitāb al-Adab al-ṣaghīr* vindicates the importance of logic (*manṭiq*). Third, an extant translation of Aristotelian logic titled *al-Manṭiq* is ascribed to Ibn al-Muqaffaʿ or his son. There is, however, an important caveat to make. Due to the fact that the *Kitāb al-Adab al-ṣaghīr* blends Sāsānian and Islamic elements, while a polemical text against Islam (which also manifests logical reasoning) is also attributed to Ibn al-Muqaffaʿ (as mentioned above, the fragments of this polemical text subsist as quoted in a refutation, which ascribes the refuted text to him),[99] the authenticity of both have been questioned. I have argued elsewhere that rather than being mutually exclusive they are interrelated and reflect, together with other writings attributed to him, the social and intellectual struggles of the period around the ʿAbbasid/Hāshimite revolution.[100] Nevertheless, both the authenticity of the texts attributed to Ibn al-Muqaffaʿ, as well as the meaning of the terms used in them remain open to debate. Such is the case of the term *manṭiq*, which, similarly to the term *logic*, is related to speech, and while one meaning of *manṭiq* is logic, it can also mean speech, manner of speaking, diction, or eloquence.

With regard to knowledge, action, right and wrong, passion, religion and intellect, all common themes in Ibn al-Muqaffaʿ's writings deriving from the stock of late antique wisdom, the *Kitāb al-Adab al-ṣaghīr* includes an aphorism that provides another example of anadiplosis, and logical structure:

> It used to be said: If a man does what he knows it is erroneous, that is passion, and passion is a flaw of decency; and if he abandons doing what he knows it is right, that is neglect, and neglect is a flaw of religion, and if he ventures in what he does not know whether it is right or erroneous, that is recklessness, and recklessness is flaw of the intellect.[101]

The contrast between reason and passion is commonplace in Greek philosophy, as well as use of the rhetorical device of anadiplosis, however, the following passage, parallel to the one quoted above, is not from a Greek philosophical text but the *Dēnkard VI*, the most important Zoroastrian compendium of the gnomic *andarz* literature in Middle Persian:

> One who knows something to be a good deed and does not do it, that is contempt. Contempt is the opponent of character. One who knows something to be a sin and does it, that is lustfulness. Lustfulness is the opponent of wisdom. One who knows not a thing to be either a good deed or a sin, and before he comes to knowledge he performs it, that is self-love. Self-love is the opponent of religion.[102]

Although the *Dēnkard* was composed roughly two centuries after the Islamic conquest (when the translation movement into Arabic was at its peak), it draws on Sāsānian sources.[103] The fact that Middle Persian advice literature is one of the most fundamental sources of Islamic advice literature is often clearly stressed by Islamic texts themselves (such as the above mentioned translation of the *Kalīla wa-Dimna* and this is also the case of his translation of the *Letter of Tansar*).[104]

The "teach yourself, before teaching the others" motif, which had been present already in Paul's *Letter to the Romans* 2: 21, is also included in the *Kitāb al-Adab al-ṣaghīr*:

> And who establishes himself as a religious guide of people, he should start by teaching and rectifying himself, in what pertains to conduct, food, opinion, speech, and companionship. Then, his teaching by the way of his own conduct would be more eloquent than the one he delivers through speech. As speaking wisdom pleases the ears, doing wisdom delights the eyes and the hearts; he whoever teaches and educates himself is more deserving glorification and predilection than the one who teaches and educates the others.[105]

In the *Dēnkard*, we read:

> No person is taught or becomes better by a man except by one who disciplines himself and who arouses other people by the goodness which he possesses.[106]

Another passage of the *Kitāb al-Adab al-ṣaghīr* insists on the importance of the application of knowledge:

> By education (*adab*) the hearts live, and by knowledge (*ʿilm*) the judgments are judiciously made (*tustaḥkamu al-aḥkām*). The pure reason that is not effective is like the good land that is wasted.[107]

Ibn al-Muqaffaʿ' introduction to *Kalīla wa-Dimna* encapsulates ideas that are similar to all those cited above from the *Kitāb al-Adab al-ṣaghīr*.[108] This last one, on knowledge and action, might point to Aristotle's distinction between theoretical and practical wisdom in the *Book VI* of his *Nicomachean Ethics*, but it is also related to the Zoroastrian (and Buddhist) principle of "good thought, good speech, good deed."[109] The formulation by Ibn al-Muqaffaʿ, especially the version in his introduction to *Kalīla wa-Dimna*, is echoed in the *Ayyuhā al-walad* ("*Letter to a Disciple*"), a text attributed to al-Ghazālī. Intriguingly, in the *Ayyuhā al-walad*, this idea is applied specifically against the philosophers, attributing to them the belief that bare knowledge without action would suffice for salvation.[110] This anti-philosophical stance provides an example that philosophy was not always praised in Islamic advice literature.[111]

Regarding the limits of one's knowledge, the *Kitāb al-Adab al-ṣaghīr* includes an aphorism related to the Socratic paradox:

> It belongs to knowledge that you know that you do not know what you do not know.[112]

This aphorism is very similar to the formulation of the idea in Plato's *Charmides*:

> [. . .] temperance is the knowledge of what one knows and does not know [. . .].[113]

But while the Greek version of the *Charmides* and the Arabic version of the *Kitāb al-Adab al-ṣaghīr* are slightly different, the latter is nearly identical with a Middle Persian version that is included into the *Dēnkard*:

> [. . .] sagacity is best, one who knows: "I do not know" with regard to a thing which he does not know.[114]

It is noteworthy that a variant of this idea appears also in the Confucian *Analects*:

> The Master said, "You [Zilu], keep in mind (zhi 知) what I am about to teach you. If you know then hold it as you know, and if you do not know then hold it as you don't. That is wisdom (zhi 知)." [115]

Political Epistles: The *Risāla fī l-ṣaḥāba* and *al-Yatīma*

Ibn al-Muqaffaʿ used late antique political theories and logical and rhetorical devices in both of his surviving political epistles; the *Risāla fī l-ṣaḥāba*[116] written to, and *al-Yatīma*,[117] written on behalf of the caliph, shortly after the victory of the ʿAbbasid/Hāshimite revolution over the Umayyads. These epistles are an integral part of this foundational layer of Islamic advice literature, as the *Risāla fī l-ṣaḥāba* advises the caliph on how to consolidate his rule and *al-Yatīma* advises his subjects on why to obey him. While the importance of the *Risāla fī l-ṣaḥāba* has been recognized by modern scholarship,[118] *al-Yatīma* remains as neglected in modern scholarship as it was celebrated in classical Arabic literature.[119]

Both the *Risāla fī l-ṣaḥāba* and *al-Yatīma* are characterized by an elaborate and sophisticated use of logical and rhetorical structures as well as theories drown from Sāsānian advice literature[120] (which had been already in interaction with Greek thought, and had been using such structures, as we saw earlier in the case of the *Dēnkard* and of *Kalīla wa-Dimna*). These antique elements are carefully combined with Qur'anic references, adapted to an Islamic framework, and used to solidify the rule of the new dynasty, the ʿAbbasids. The extant fragments of *al-Yatīma* show conscientious composition, and the entire text of the *Risāla fī l-ṣaḥāba* is structured according to the theory of the *circle of justice* that formulate the interdependence of the ruler, the military, the peasants and the administrators, and was attributed in Islamic texts both to Sāsānian authorities and Aristotle.[121] The *Risāla fī l-ṣaḥāba* also contains another important idea of uncertain origin that became widespread in Islamic political thought: Ibn al-Muqaffaʿ writes that God provides prosperity through an *Imām* (that is the ruler) who leads the elite (*khāṣṣa*) and through them the common people (*ʿāmma*).[122] This conception might be related to the hierarchy of power and knowledge – composed of the philosopher-lawgiver, the guardians, and the workers – in Plato. Instead of this tripartite structure, in *al-Yatīma*, Ibn al-Muqaffaʿ systematically uses the binary image of the shepherd (*rāʿī*) and his flock (*raʿiyya*),[123] which is not Qur'anic,[124] but had been a commonplace in ancient literature, including Sumerian texts,[125] the Bible,[126] and Greek philosophy,[127] and became similarly ubiquitous in Islamic political thought.

The *Risāla fī l-ṣaḥāba* contains a thick layer of logic in its argumentation. Ibn al-Muqaffaʿ uses several times the word *ḥujja* (proof), in evidencing the righteousness of the present ruler as compared to the previous evil rulers. He describes the addressee of the epistle as a sovereign who firmly acquires knowledge by proof when he examines the affairs of his flock.[128] While in Islamic judicial literature, evidence-based investigation on behalf of the judge is the norm, in Islamic political thought, evidence-based governance is a rare motif.[129] Ibn al-Muqaffaʿ also uses it in his *al-Yatīma* in the context of his argumentation supporting the legitimacy of the ruler.[130] In the *Risāla fī l-ṣaḥāba* again, he encourages the ruler to persuade the soldiers of Khurāsān by means of proof.[131] In his discussion of juristic analogy, *qiyās*, Ibn al-Muqaffaʿ displays acquaintance with logical criticism of juristic analogy.[132]

In the *Risāla fī l-ṣaḥāba*, the treatment of the question of the obedience to the caliph is also constructed following a clear logical structure and connected to the question of reason and religion.[133] The extant fragments of *al-Yatīma* display a similar argumentation.[134] Intriguingly, in this section of the *Risāla fī l-ṣaḥāba*, Ibn al-Muqaffaʿ's objective is not to measure the absolute truth of the contrasted arguments, but to advise the ruler to embrace the doctrine that can ensure the largest possible support for his rule.[135] This attitude is in perfect harmony with Ibn al-Muqaffaʿ's advice in the *Kitāb al-Ādāb al-kabīr* where he articulates the pragmatic role of religion as political tool.[136] In Ibn al-Muqaffaʿ's oeuvre, religious rhetoric is a powerful element of political rhetoric, and political rhetoric is a key instrument of politics.

Conclusions

Ibn al-Muqaffaʿ's oeuvre includes ample evidence of the fact that constituents of the diverse cultures of Antiquity were already in fusion at the formative stage of Islamic civilization in general, and of Islamic advice literature in particular. The texts attributed to Ibn al-Muqaffaʿ show that elements of Greek (and Indian) philosophy, including political and ethical thought, as well as logic and rhetoric, were organically integrated into Middle Persian advice literature. His writings also reflect the broader tendencies of how components of Greek philosophy – as part of the late antique heritage nurturing Islamic thought – were used in Islamic political, ethical, and religious literature in support of specific interests and values.

In Islamic advice literature, since its first appearance, ancient Greek elements are commonly mixed with Persian and Indian as well as Arabic and Islamic influences. This calls for caution in reading Islamic advice literature with an exclusivist eye. The fact that concepts and formulations that had characterised Greek philosophy abound in early works of Islamic advice literature that were translated from or influenced by Middle Persian texts – such as *Kalīla wa-Dimna* and Ibn al-Muqaffaʿ's entire oeuvre – demonstrates that these Greek elements had been already incorporated into Middle Persian advice literature. Early Islamic literature complements the evidence of late antique texts, in providing indirect but strong evidence for an advanced level of coalescence between Greek, Iranian and Indian thought preceding already the rise of Islam and allowing for further fusion and elaboration within its new civilization.

The Arabic *adab* works of Ibn al-Muqaffaʿ are a continuation of the Greek *paideia* through the Middle Persian *andarz*, which was influenced also by the Indian tradition. They present practical philosophy; ethics and politics; advice for the elites. It does not mean, however, that in Ibn al-Muqaffaʿ's thought, ethics and politics would not have been based on ontological and epistemological foundations. We saw that both religious and epistemological scepticism appeared in his *adab* works. But, further than that, according to reports about him as well as some texts attributed to him, he was a *Zindīq* thinker, an heir and prominent author of the tradition of dualist criticism against monotheism. Working for the elites of the Islamic empire, he was very able to use the Islamic idiom as a tool, when necessary, such as in his political epistles, nevertheless, his ethical and political advice is deeply trans-religious. His

Kitāb al-Ādāb al-kabīr advises the reader about both the pragmatic political use, and the privacy of religion.[137] The close reading of Ibn al-Muqaffaʿ's oeuvre gives us insights into the context of their creation and the tensions of his time, ʿAbbasid (or rather Hāshimite) revolution, which was a crucial period in the formation of Islamic civilisation. They also provide an outstanding example of the constant need to balance between morality and pragmatism that is a universal feature of politics. In order to promote moral goals, some degree of pragmatism and compromises are necessary, while even purely amoral ambitions require some moral coating in order to make them acceptable.[138] Ibn al-Muqaffaʿ was a key participant in a collective project providing politics a moral purpose and making of philosophy practical (ethical and political) use. His contribution to the introduction of philosophy into Islamic civilisation is even more significant considering that Ibn al-Muqaffaʿ was murdered approximately a century before the death of al-Kindī, labelled "the first Arab philosopher."

Forms and content derived from ancient Greek philosophy (as mediated by late antique sources) appeared in Islamic political advice literature *before* interest in philosophy as a system of theoretical worldview emerged in Islamic civilization. The political – and religious – utility of Greek rhetoric, as well as the benefits of Greek science, had been recognized already by the elites of late antiquity, who blended them with the heritage of other civilizations. Translations of late antique political advice literature into Arabic and the creation of Islamic political literature had an instrumental role in the initiation of the translation of Greek philosophical works into Arabic, leading to the creation of what is commonly designated as "Islamic philosophy."

Greek philosophical influences did not reach only the philosophical circles (and the often overlapping medical sphere) or philosophizing theological milieus, but also affected the realms of secretaries and jurists, already at an early stage of the formation of Islamic civilization (eighth–ninth centuries CE). The first extant translations into Arabic belong to political advice literature. These texts included already important components of Greek philosophy, namely rhetorical and logical devices as well as political and ethical ideas and patterns (such as the relationship between the ruler and the philosopher-advisor). All these elements provided powerful ammunition in political struggles. The Islamization of them immediately began, in order to allow their acceptance by Muslim audiences and their use in religious arguments, which themselves underpinned political claims.

The influence of Greek philosophy shaped both the methods and the contents of Islamic advice literature. Authors of advice literature were among the first to appropriate Greek rhetorical devices, logic and theories, and adapt them into Islamic frameworks. Meanwhile, they integrated into their works the ideas they deemed relevant for their times and concerns, reshaping them accordingly. An analysis of how they maintained and modified the late antique legacy provides significant insights into their agendas. Their fields of interest include the entire realm of power: good, mediocre and bad government, rulers, and courtiers (advisers), as well as the relationships between the ruler and his adviser, the ruler and the elite, between members of this elite, and between the ruler, the elite and the common subjects. They deal with individual traits of character and the know-how (*adab*) required in different roles, as well as with institutions and social strata. Their views express political and ethical ideals and reflect social realities. Producing or commissioning advice literature presented a subtle means for negotiations for power, authority and resources, and for claiming or consolidating status. While often regarded, or disregarded, as tiresomely platitudinous, works of Islamic advice literature, if contextualized and studied with a comparative approach, offer rich and exciting material for intellectual and social history.

Notes

* I wish to express my gratitude to Abdessamad Belhaj, Vasileios Syros, Sajjad Rizvi, Kazuo Morimoto, Erik Hermans, Jonathan Lee, Ammarah Fattani and Andrew Wiles for their beneficial comments on earlier versions of this chapter.

1 For these dates, see István T. Kristó-Nagy, *La pensée d'Ibn al-Muqaffaʿ: Un «agent double» dans le monde persan et arabe* (Versailles: Éditions de Paris, 2013), 57 and 62. Most other dates in this chapter are taken from *The Encyclopaedia of Islam, New Edition*; *The Encyclopaedia of Islam Three* or *Encyclopædia Iranica.*

2 The term advice, *naṣīḥa*, has a deep-rooted religious connotation in Islam, from hadith literature until today. In Western scholarship such works are often labelled as *mirror for princes*. This term is European and has its own conceptual history, nevertheless, it is commonly used for non-European works of political advice literature as well. Its generalised use is due, however, more to convenience than accuracy. Even in the case of European works, see the criticism, especially concerning its usage for antique texts, of Matthias Haake, "Writing to a Ruler, Speaking to a Ruler, Negotiating the Figure of the Ruler: Thoughts on 'Monocratological' Texts and Their Contexts in Greco-Roman Antiquity," in *Global Medieval: Mirrors for Princes Reconsidered*, ed. by Regula Forster and Neguin Yavari (Boston: Ilex Foundation, 2015), 58–82; and idem, "Across All Boundaries of Genre? On the Uses and Disadvantages of the Term Mirror for Princes in Graeco-Roman Antiquity: Critical Remarks and Unorthodox Reflections," in *Concepts of Ideal Rulership from Antiquity to the Renaissance*, ed. by Geert Roskam and Stefan Schorn (Turnhout: Brepols, 2018), 293–327. The term *mirror for courtiers* is rarely used, but I find it helpful in the context of Ibn al-Muqaffaʿ's oeuvre, for his texts provided advice not only for rulers, but also for their entourages.

For studies on Islamic advice literature, see Clifford E. Bosworth, "Naṣīḥat al-Mulūk," in *The Encyclopaedia of Islam, New Edition*, ed. by H. A. R. Gibb et al., available online at https://referenceworks.brillonline.com/entries/encyclopaedia-of-islam-2/*-COM_0850 (accessed September 21, 2022); Ann K. S. Lambton, "Islamic Mirrors for Princes," in *Atti del convegno internazionale sul tema: La Persia nel medioevo (Roma, 31 marzo–5 aprile 1970)* (Rome: Accademia Nazionale dei Lincei, 1971), 419–42, reprinted in eadem, *Theory and Practice in Medieval Persian Government* (London: Variorum reprints, 1980); Dimitri Gutas, "Classical Arabic Wisdom Literature: Nature and Scope," *Journal of the American Oriental Society* 101 (1981): 49–86; Patricia Crone, *God's Rule: Government and Islam* (New York, Columbia University Press, 2004), 148–64, 193, and 195; Louise Marlow, "Advice and Advice Literature," in *The Encyclopaedia of Islam Three*, ed. by Kate Fleet et al., available online at https://referenceworks.brillonline.com/entries/encyclopaedia-of-islam-3/advice-and-advice-literature-COM_0026 (accessed September 21, 2022); eadem, "Surveying Recent Literature on the Arabic and Persian Mirrors for Princes

Genre," *History Compass* 7 (2009): 528–38; Deborah G. Tor, "The Islamisation of Iranian Kingly Ideals in the Persianate Fürstenspiegel," *Iran* 49 (2011): 115–22; Neguin Yavari, *Advice for the Sultan: Prophetic Voices and Secular Politics in Medieval Islam* (London: Hurst & Company, 2014); and Forster and Yavari, eds., *Global Medieval*. The studies relevant for specific texts of Islamic political advice literature are too numerous to be listed here. I will reference such studies whenever they pertain to texts that are discussed in this chapter.

3 On Ibn al-Muqaffaʿ's oeuvre (including his religious thought), see Kristó-Nagy, *La pensée d'Ibn al-Muqaffaʿ* and idem, "Marriage after Rape: The Ambiguous Relationship between Arab Lords and Iranian Intellectuals as Reflected in Ibn al-Muqaffaʿ's Oeuvre," in *Tradition and Reception in Arabic Literature: Essays Dedicated to Andras Hamori*, ed. by Margaret Larkin and Jocelyn Sharlet (Wiesbaden: Harrassowitz Verlag, 2019), 161–88.

4 The few but highly valuable studies dedicated to this topic are focused on *al-Manṭiq* (*The Logic*) attributed to Ibn al-Muqaffaʿ, see below, 53–54, and his *Kitāb al-Ādāb al-kabīr* (*The Great Book of* Adab*s*), see below, 61–62.

5 For a general introduction on the influence of ancient Greek philosophy on Islamic thought, see Cristina D'Ancona, "Greek Sources in Arabic and Islamic Philosophy," in *The Stanford Encyclopedia of Philosophy*, ed. by Edward N. Zalta, available online at https://plato.stanford.edu/entries/arabic-islamic-greek/ (accessed September 21, 2022). For some of the most influential works on the field, see F.E. Peters, *Aristoteles Arabus: The Oriental Translations and Commentaries on the Aristotelian Corpus* (Leiden: Brill, 1968); Gerhard Endress and Remke Kruk, eds., *The Ancient Tradition in Christian and Islamic Hellenism: Studies on the Transmission of Greek Philosophy and Sciences Dedicated to H.J. Drossaart Lulofs on His Ninetieth Birthday* (Leiden: Research School CNWS, 1997); Dimitri Gutas, *Greek Thought, Arabic Culture: The Graeco-Arabic Translation Movement in Baghdad and Early ʿAbbasid Society (2nd–4th/8th–10th Centuries)* (London and New York: Routledge, 1998); and Ulrich Rudolph, Rotraud Hansberger and Peter Adamson, eds., *Philosophy in the Islamic World*, Volume 1, *8th–9th Centuries*, transl. by Rotraud Hansberger (Leiden and Boston: Brill, 2017).

6 See Ulrich Rudolph, "The Late Ancient Background," in *Philosophy in the Islamic World*, ed. by Rudolph, Hansberger and Adamson, 29–73.

7 For a recent survey, see Hans Daiber, "The Syriac Tradition in the Early Islamic Era," in *Philosophy in the Islamic World*, ed. by Rudolph, Hansberger and Adamson, 74–94; Rudolph, "The Late Ancient Background," 54–60.

8 For a summary (and references to the relevant studies) of the way how Greek philosophy was appropriated by and integrated into Sāsānian and then into ʿAbbasid ideology, see 98 and 100–3 of Dimitri Gutas, "The Rebirth of Philosophy and the Translations into Arabic," in *Philosophy in the Islamic World*, ed. by Rudolph, Hansberger and Adamson, 95–142. See also Rudolph, "The Late Ancient Background," 59–60.

9 For a recent overview, see Christian Wildberg, "Neoplatonism," in *The Stanford Encyclopedia of Philosophy*, ed. by Zalta, available online at https://plato.stanford.edu/entries/neoplatonism/ (accessed September 21, 2022). See also Rudolph, "The Late Ancient Background."

10 The term *Islamicate* coined by Marshall G. S. Hodgson – see his *The Venture of Islam* (Chicago and London: The University of Chicago Press, 1973), vol. 1, 57–60 – could be used here. It has not, however, become a generally accepted term. Due to this reason and to the fact that the distinction between Islamic and Islamicate is often difficult to make, I decided to use the term Islamic throughout this chapter.

11 See Haake, Matthias. "Writing down the King: The Communicative Function of Treatises *On Kingship* in the Hellenistic Period," in *The Splendors and Miseries of Ruling Alone: Encounters with Monarchy from Archaic Greece to the Hellenistic Mediterranean*, ed. by Nino Luraghi (Stuttgart: Franz Steiner Verlag, 2013), 168 and 172. See also below, 55.

12 Gutas, "The Rebirth of Philosophy," 101. He also lists the most relevant studies regarding the translations from Middle Persian to Arabic (see also above n. 8). Referring to Manfred Ullman,

"Ḫālid ibn Yazīd und die Alchemie: Eine Legende," *Der Islam* 55 (1978): 181–218, Gutas states: "The report that the Umayyad prince Ḫālid b. Yazīd had had Greek books on alchemy, astrology, and other sciences translated into Arabic has been demonstrated to a later fabrication [. . .]" ("The Rebirth of Philosophy," 99).

13 Ibid., 101.

14 The source language of some of the early translations into Arabic remain debated. This is the case of the "*The Correspondence between Aristotle and Alexander the Great*," see n. 33 below, and of *The Logic* attributed to Ibn al-Muqaffaʿ, see n. 22 below.

15 See also Gutas, "The Rebirth of Philosophy," 99.

16 See below, 55.

17 See n. 97 below.

18 István T. Kristó-Nagy, "Conflict and Cooperation between Arab Rulers and Persian Administrators in the Formative Period of Islamdom, c. 600–c. 950 ce," in *Empires and Bureaucracy in World History: From Late Antiquity to the Twentieth Century*, ed. by Peter Crooks and Timothy Parsons (Cambridge: Cambridge University Press, 2016), 54–80.

19 The text is published in Muḥammad Taqī Dānishpazhūh, ed., *al-Manṭiq (Logic) by Ibn al-Muqaffaʿ, Ḥudūd al-Manṭiq (Definitions of Logic) by Ibn Bihrīz*, Tehran: Anjuman-i shāhanshāhī-i falsafah-i Īrān, 1978, reprinted Tehran: Muʾassasah-i pazhūhishī-i ḥikmat va falsafah-i Īrān, 1381 AHS/2002–03.

20 Preceded possibly by the "*The Correspondence between Aristotle and Alexander the Great*," see n. 33 below.

21 See Gutas, "The Rebirth of Philosophy," 95–142.

22 See Erik Hermans, "A Persian Origin of the Arabic Aristotle? The Debate on the Circumstantial Evidence of the Manteq Revisited," *Journal of Persianate Studies* 11 (2018): 72–88. See also the section "1.1 The Early Translations" of Tony Street, "Arabic and Islamic Philosophy of Language and Logic," in *The Stanford Encyclopedia of Philosophy*, ed. by Zalta, available online at https://plato.stanford.edu/entries/arabic-islamic-language/ (accessed September 21, 2022).

23 On Ibn al-Muqaffaʿ's oeuvre and politico-literary agenda, see Kristó-Nagy, *La pensée d'Ibn al-Muqaffaʿ*, and Kristó-Nagy, "Marriage after Rape."

24 See (Pseudo-?)al-Jāḥiẓ, "*Akhlāq al-kuttāb*," in *Three Essays of Abu ʿOthman ʿAmr Ibn Baḥr al-Jaḥiẓ (D. 869)*, ed. by Joshua Finkel, Cairo: The Salafyah Press, 1344/1926, reprinted 1382/1962–63, 42–3. For an English translation of this section, see Charles Pellat, *The Life and Works of Jāḥiẓ: Translation of Selected Texts*, transl. from the French by D.M. Hawke (Berkeley and Los Angeles: University of California Press, 1969), 273–5. See also Kristó-Nagy, *La pensée d'Ibn al-Muqaffaʿ*, 101.

25 An example of research in this spirit can be found in Hans Daiber, "*De praedicamento relationis in philosophia arabica et islamica*: The Category of Relation in Arabic-Islamic Philosophy (Extended Version)," *Enrahonar* 61 Supplement Issue (2018): 431–90, available online at https://ddd.uab.cat/pub/enrahonar/enrahonar_a2018nsupissue/enrahonar_a2018nSupplp431.pdf (accessed September 21, 2022), reprinted in idem, *From the Greeks to the Arabs and Beyond*, Volume 2, *Islamic Philosophy* (Leiden and Boston: Brill, 2021), 153–223. In his chapter on *al-Manṭiq* attributed to Ibn al-Muqaffaʿ 437–40, Daiber provides a translation of a section of the text (the chapter on the relative) and points out that it contains examples for homonyms that are not found in the text by Aristotle and his other commentators but can be linked to the conceptual word of the texts attributed to Ibn al-Muqaffaʿ. I suggest that this also applies to the examples given for heteronyms in the same section and it would be worthy to analyse the whole text in a similar way. See also n. 92 below.

26 On the different chapters of the book and their origin, see François de Blois, *Burzōy's Voyage to India and the Origin of the Book of Kalīlah wa Dimnah* (London: Royal Asiatic Society, 1990), 12–7.

27 The name برزويه found in the Arabic text is vocalised and transliterated in various ways:

Burzawayh, Burzuwayh, Barzuwayh, Barzawayh, Burzūyah, Barzūyah and so on. Its reconstructed Pahlavi form is transcribed Burzōē, Burzōy or Borzūya. The historicity and the memory (within the collection itself) of Burzōy's figure and mission is the main topic of de Blois, *Burzōy's Voyage to India*. See also Djalal Khaleghi-Motlagh, "Borzūya," in *Encyclopædia Iranica Online*, available at http://dx.doi.org/10.1163/2330-4804_EIRO_COM_7095 (accessed September 21, 2022); and Ibn al-Muqaffaʿ, *Kalīla wa-Dimna*, ed. by ʿAbd al-Wahhāb ʿAzzām, 2nd revised ed. (Algiers: al-Sharika al-waṭaniyya li-l-nashr wa-l-tawzīʿ and Beirut: Dār al-shurūq, 1973), 19, with n. 4 (the text of the note is on p. 320).

28 The Middle Persian version has not survived, but the comparison between the existing Indian versions and those deriving from the Middle Persian version indicates that the Middle Persian version was significantly different from the Sanskrit text of which a reconstructed version and English translation was published: Franklin Edgerton, ed. and transl., *The Pancatantra Reconstructed: An Attempt to Establish the Lost Original Sanskrit Text of the Most Famous of Indian Story-Collections on the Basis of the Principal Extant Versions*, Vol. 1, *Text and Critical Apparatus*, Vol. 2, *Introduction and Translation*, New Haven: American Oriental Society and London: Oxford University Press, 1924, reprinted New York: Kraus Reprint Corporation, 1967. Ibn al-Muqaffaʿ's version is also lost in its original form but survives in a multitude of different variants. A collation of these copies with an Old Syriac translation (made independently from Ibn al-Muqaffaʿ's Arabic translation) of the Middle Persian version reveals how Ibn al-Muqaffaʿ's Arabic translation differed from the latter. See François de Blois, *Burzōy's Voyage to India* and István T. Kristó-Nagy, "Wild Lions and Wise Jackals: Killer Kings and Clever Counsellors in *Kalīla wa-Dimna*," in *Prophets, Viziers, and Philosophers: Wisdom and Authority in Early Arabic Literature*, ed. by Emily J. Cottrell (Groningen: Barkhuis & Groningen University Library, 2020), 147–209. For an edition and German translation of the old Syriac version, see Friedrich Schulthess, ed. and transl., *Kalīla und Dimna: Syrisch und deutsch*, 2 vols. (Berlin: Georg Reimer, 1911). For a recent description of "the Syriac manuscript situation," see Beatrice Gruendler et al., "An Interim Report on the Editorial and Analytical Work of the Anonym Classic Project," *Medieval Worlds* 11 (2020): 245–7 (by Jan J. van Ginkel), available online at https://medievalworlds.net/0xc1aa5576_0x003ba1d6.pdf (accessed September 21, 2022).

29 Two of the oldest manuscripts of the Arabic text of *Kalīla wa-Dimna* were published. ʿAbd al-Wahhāb ʿAzzām published a manuscript of the Ayasofya library, Istanbul, dated 618/122. Its edition referred to hereinafter as ʿAzzām, is the 2nd revised ed. Algiers: al-Sharika al-waṭaniyya li-l-nashr wa-l-tawzīʿ and Beirut: Dār al-shurūq, 1973. The Jesuit Father Louis Cheikho published a manuscript found in the Dayr al-Shīr monastery, Lebanon, dated 739/1339: *La version arabe de Kalîlah et Dimnah d'après le plus ancien manuscrit arabe daté,* ed. by Louis Cheikho (Beirut: Imprimerie catholique, 1905), hereinafter Cheikho. I agree with the following statement by de Blois (*Burzōy's Voyage to India*, 4): "On the whole, one gains the impression that ʿAzzām's manuscript represents a rather drastically abridged version of *Kalīlah wa Dimnah*, and that in Shaykhū's more extended version a smaller amount of authentic material has been omitted. In general, students are best advised to use the two editions side by side." For a French translation of ʿAzzām, see Ibn al-Muqaffaᶜ, *Le livre de Kalila et Dimna*, transl. by André Miquel, 2nd ed. (Paris: Klincksieck, 1980). The edition by M. Silvestre de Sacy, *Calila et Dimna, ou Fables de Bidpai, en arabe* (Paris: Imprimerie Royal, 1816), hereinafter de Sacy, is the first modern edition of the text, based principally on the manuscript of the Bibliothèque Nationale de France, Paris, Arabe 3465, available online at https://gallica.bnf.fr/ark:/12148/btv1b84229611/f11.image.r=Arabe%203465 (accessed September, 21 2022), complemented by six other manuscripts (see de Sacy's introduction, 57–64). De Sacy's edition was used for the English translation by the A. M. Wyndham Knatchbull, *Kalila and Dimna: Or, The Fables of Bidpai: Translated from the Arabic* (Oxford: W. Baxter, 1819). For a critique of de Sacy's edition, see de Blois, *Burzōy's*, 3.
For a newer English translation, see Saleh Saʿadeh Jallad, transl., *The Fables of Kalilah and Dimnah: Adapted and Translated from the Sanskrit through the Pahlavi into Arabic by ᶜAbdullah*

ibn al-Muqaffaʿ AD 750, London: Melisende, 2002, reprinted 2004, hereinafter Jallad. In his foreword, 23–4, Jallad writes about the "Bulaq imprint" of 1817 as derived from de Sacy's edition, and, on the same page, he indicates "the popular Bulaq edition" as the main source of his translation (with the exception of the chapter "Mehrize, King of the Rats" or "The King of the Mice," which he translated from ʿAzzām's edition). I could not access the "Bulaq imprint" of 1817, but Jallad's translation considerably differs from de Sacy's text. His translation does not seem to correspond to any of the editions I could check.
A new edition and translation has recently been published in the Library of Arabic Literature series: Ibn al-Muqaffaʿ, *Kalīlah and Dimnah: Fables of Virtue and Vice*, ed. by Michael Fishbein and transl. by Michael Fishbein and James E. Montgomery (New York and London: New York University Press, 2021). It is based mainly on the undated manuscript British Library Or. 4044 (produced possibly in the ninth/fifteenth century).
For the different versions of the Arabic text (and its translations), see Beatrice Gruendler, "Les versions arabes de *Kalīla wa-Dimna*: Une transmission et une circulation mouvantes," in *Enoncés sapientiels en Méditerranée: Aliento, vol. 3 = Enoncés sapientiels et littérature exemplaire: Une intertextualité complexe*, ed. by Marie-Sol Ortola (Nancy: Presses Universitaires de Nancy, 2013), 387–418 (regarding the extant Arabic manuscripts, especially 396–401). See also eadem, "*Kalīla wa-Dimna*: A Unique Work of World Literature," in *Arab and German Tales: Transcending Cultures*, ed. by Verena M. Lepper in collaboration with Sara Aisha Sabea (Berlin: Kadmos, 2018), 67–8, which offers a short summary also about the importance of the book. Regarding the Syriac and Arabic manuscripts and the reception of *Kalīla wa-Dimna*, see the research and synoptic digital edition in progress in the framework of the project *Kalīla and Dimna – AnonymClassic* also led by Beatrice Gründler, available online at https://www.geschkult.fu-berlin.de/en/e/kalila-wa-dimna/index.html (accessed September 21, 2022), as well as Gruendler et al., "An Interim Report."

30 The *Kitāb Bilawhar wa-Būdhāsf* (*The Book of Bilawhar and Būdhāsf*), another important early text of advice literature, also features tales and dialogues, but it uses the term *nāsiq*, hermit, rather than philosopher, *faylasūf*. See Daniel Gimaret, ed., *Kitāb Bilawhar wa-Būḏāsf* (Beirut: Dār al-mashriq, 1972), 10, 33 etc. and idem, transl., *Le livre de Bilawhar et Būḏāsf selon la version arabe ismaélienne* (Geneva and Paris: Droz, 1971). The figure of the advising wise hermit is also prominent in *Kalīla wa-Dimna*, for instance in the chapter *The Hermit and His Guest,* which was interpolated into the text by Ibn al-Muqaffaʿ. On this chapter see István T. Kristó-Nagy, "The Crow Who Aped the Partridge: Ibn al-Muqaffaʿ's Aesopian Language in a Fable of *Kalīla wa-Dimna*," in *L'Adab toujours recommencé: Origines, transmission et métamorphoses*, ed. by Catherine Mayeur-Jaouen, Francesca Bellino and Luca Patrizi (Leiden and Boston: Brill, forthcoming).

31 See n. 28 above.

32 The expression "the head of the philosophers" in the translation by Schulthess, 1, occurs in the section missing from the Syriac text and reconstructed on the basis of Cheikho, 53 (رأس الفلاسفة), see Schulthess, 171, n. 1. It also appears (in the form رأس فلاسفته "the head of his [the king's] philosophers") in ʿAzzām, 49.

33 For the edition of the text with an introductory study, see Miklós Maróth, ed., *The Correspondence between Aristotle and Alexander the Great: An Anonymous Greek Novel in Letters in Arabic Translation* (Piliscsaba: The Avicenna Institute of Middle Eastern Studies, 2006). See also Dimitri Gutas's review article, "On Graeco-Arabic Epistolary 'Novels'," *Middle Eastern Literatures* 12.1 (2009): 59–70, as well as n. 11 above.

34 In that it is different from *Kalīla wa-Dimna*, but similar to *The Letter of Tansar*, of which the by now lost Arabic translation is also attributed to Ibn al-Muqaffaʿ. This letter was, according to the text itself, written by a Persian high priest advising a local ruler why to accept the authority of the founder of the new, Sāsānian, dynasty. The epistle survives only in a New Persian translation of Ibn al-Muqaffaʿ's Arabic translation of the Middle Persian text. For an English translation, see Mary Boyce, transl., *The Letter of Tansar* (Rome: Istituto italiano per il Medio ed Estremo Oriente, 1968).

35 See for instance Maróth, *The Correspondence*, 3 (of the Arabic text).

36 See Wadād al-Qāḍī, "ʿAbd al-Ḥamīd al-Kātib," in *The Encyclopaedia of Islam Three*, ed. by Kate Fleet et al., available online at https://referenceworks.brillonline.com/entries/encyclopaedia-of-islam-3/*-COM_22586 (accessed September 22, 2022). According to the introduction of Maróth, *The Correspondence*, 8, following Mario Grignaschi, "Les Rasā'il 'Arisṭāṭālīsa 'ilā-l-Iskandar de Sālim Abū-l-ʿAlāʾ et l'activité culturelle à l'époque omayyade," *Bulletin d'Études Orientales* 19 (1965–66), 12, Sālim Abū l-ʿAlāʾ was Syriac Christian. Gutas, "On Graeco-Arabic Epistolary 'Novels'," 65, states: "Sālim, just like his protégé, ʿAbd al-Ḥamīd b. Yaḥyā, was of Persian descent, and he and ʿAbd al-Ḥamīd introduced Persian stylistic and other elements in the Arabic epistolary style they were developing."

37 For an account on Ibn al-Muqaffaʿ risking his life trying to save ʿAbd al-Ḥamīd b. Yaḥyā from being captured, see al-Jahshiyārī, *Kitāb al-Wuzarāʾ wa-l-kuttāb*, ed. by M. Muṣṭafā al-Saqqā, Ibrāhīm al-Abyārī and ʿAbd al-Ḥafīẓ Shalabī (Cairo: Maṭbaʿat Muṣṭafā al-Bābī al-Ḥalabī wa-awlādihi, 1357/1938), 80, ll. 1–6; al-Jahshiyārī (a-Ǧahšiyārī), *Das Kitāb al-Wuzarāʾ wa-l-kuttāb des Abū ʿAbdallāh Muḥāmmad Ibn ʿAbdūs al-Ǧahšiyārī*, ed. by Hans von Mžik (Leipzig: Otto Harrassowitz, 1926), fol. 40a/79, ll. 8–14, as well as Kristó-Nagy, *La pensée d'Ibn al-Muqaffaʿ*, 247.

38 Matthew L. Keegan, "Before and after *Kalīla wa-Dimna*: An Introduction to the Special Issue on Animals, *Adab*, and Fictivity," *Journal of Abbasid Studies* 8 (2021): 3–5. Keegan also presents the Arabic text, based on the manuscript Arabe 3465 of the Bibliothèque nationale de France, 33v. On this passage, as a possible later interpolation, see also Kristó-Nagy, "Wild Lions and Wise Jackals," 197, n. 263.

39 See Keegan, "Before and after *Kalīla wa-Dimna*," 1–5 and idem, "'Elsewhere Lies Its Meaning': The Vagaries of *Kalīla and Dimna*'s Reception," *Poetica* 52 (2021): 13–40.

40 Keegan, "'Elsewhere Lies Its Meaning'," 30–1 et passim.

41 Ibid., 31–2.

42 Ibid., 33.

43 Ibid., 33.

44 Ibid., 33–4.

45 See Kristó-Nagy, *La pensée d'Ibn al-Muqaffaʿ*, 136 (with n. 371), and 324, as well as idem, "Wild Lions and Wise Jackals," 166–9.

46 ʿAzzām, 127, l. 2; Cheikho 125, l. 4. Keegan, "'Elsewhere Lies Its Meaning'," 31. The first to notice this link was Ignác Goldziher. See Carmela Baffioni, "Ikhwân al-Safâ'," in *The Stanford Encyclopedia of Philosophy*, ed. by Zalta, available at http://plato.stanford.edu/entries/ikhwan-al-safa/ (accessed September 14, 2022).

47 Lenn Goodman, "Introduction", in *The Case of the Animals versus Man before the King of the Jinn: A Translation from the Epistles of the Brethren of Purity*, transl. by Lenn E. Goodman and Richard McGregor (Oxford: Oxford University Press in association with The Institute of Ismaili Studies, 2012), 10.

48 On this chapter and the concerning studies, see Kristó-Nagy, "Wild Lions and Wise Jackals," 169–72.

49 Goodman and McGregor, transl., *The Case of the Animals versus Man*, 156–62 and 259–68.

50 Johann Christoph Bürgel, "Language on Trial, Religion at Stake? Trial Scenes in Some Classical Arabic Texts and the Hermeneutic Problems Involved," in *Myths, Historical Archetypes and Symbolic Figures in Arabic Literature: Towards a New Hermeneutic Approach: Proceedings of the International Symposium in Beirut, June 25th–June 30th, 1996*, ed. by Angelika Neuwirth et al. (Stuttgart: Franz Steiner Verlag, 1999), 198. See also the insightful note 163 in Goodman and McGregor, transl., *The Case of the Animals versus Man*, 156–8.

51 Goodman and McGregor, transl., *The Case of the Animals versus Man*, 157, in note 163.

52 Keegan, "'Elsewhere Lies Its Meaning'," 21–9.

53 See above 54 with the n. 24.

54 See Kristó-Nagy, "Conflict and Cooperation."

55 See Kristó-Nagy, "Marriage after Rape."

56 Keegan, "'Elsewhere Lies Its Meaning'," 23–6.

57 For editions, translations and studies of these two anti-Islamic texts attributed to Ibn al-Muqaffaʿ, see al-Qāsim b. Ibrāhīm, *al-Radd ʿalā al-zindīq al-laʿīn Ibn al-Muqaffaʿ*, in *La lotta tra l'Islam e il Manicheismo: Un libro di Ibn al-Muqaffa' contro il Corano confutato da al-Qāsim b. Ibrāhīm*, ed. and transl. by Michelangelo Guidi (Roma: R. Accademia Nazionale dei Lincei, 1927); Josef van Ess, "Some Fragments of the *Muʿāraḍat al-Qurʾān* Attributed to Ibn al-Muqaffaʿ," in *Studia Arabica et Islamica: Festschrift for Iḥsān ʿAbbās*, ed. by Wadād al-Qāḍī (Beirut: American University of Beirut, 1981), 151–63; idem, *Theologie und Gesellschaft im 2. und 3. Jahrhundert Hidschra: Eine Geschichte des religiösen Denkens im frühen Islam*, 6 vols. (Berlin and New York: Walter de Gruyter, 1991–97), vol. 5, 104–8; Dominique Urvoy, "Autour d'Ibn al-Muqaffaʿ," in idem, *Les penseurs libres dans l'Islam classique: L'interrogation sur la religion chez les penseurs arabes indépendants* (Paris: Albin Michel, 1996), 29–66; idem, "La démystification de la religion dans les textes attribués à Ibn al-Muqaffaʿ," in *Atheismus im Mittelalter und in der Renaissance*, ed. by Friedrich Niewöhner and Olaf Pluta (Wolfenbüttel: Herzog August Bibliothek, 1999), 85–94. See also Kristó-Nagy, *La pensée d'Ibn al-Muqaffa'*, 287–340 (for the analysis) and 438–61 (for the texts and their French translation), as well as István T. Kristó-Nagy, "A Violent, Irrational and Unjust God: Antique and Medieval Criticism of Jehovah and Allāh," in *La morale au crible des religions*, ed. by Marie-Thérèse Urvoy (Versailles: Éditions de Paris, 2013), 143–64.

58 Paul L. Heck shows the influence of scepticism, stemming partly from Greek thought, on the littérateurs, theologians and philosophers in the Islamic world, and the reactions it generated in Islamic thought. See Paul L. Heck, *Skepticism in Classical Islam: Moments of Confusion* (Abingdon, Oxon: Routledge, 2014).

59 ʿAzzām, 27–43; Cheikho, 30–44; Jallad, 66–77. See also Kristó-Nagy, *La pensée d'Ibn al-Muqaffa'*, 113–25.

60 See ʿAbd al-Jabbār b. Aḥmad al-Asadābādī, *Tathbīt dalāʾil al-nubuwwa* (Beirut: Dār al-ʿArabiyya, 1966), 72, ll. 1–6, and al-Bīrūnī, *Fī taḥqīq mā li-l-Hind min maqūla maqbūla fī l-ʿaql aw mardhūla* (Hyderabad Deccan: Maṭbaʿat majlis dāʾirat al-maʿārif al-ʿUthmāniyya, 1377/1958), 123, ll. 10–5. See also Kristó-Nagy, *La pensée d'Ibn al-Muqaffa'*, 120–4.

61 On Ibn al-Muqaffaʿ's personality and religion, see Kristó-Nagy, *La pensée d'Ibn al-Muqaffa'*, 65–79, as well as the analysis of his anti-Islamic writings 287–340, and the texts themselves and their translation 438–61; or, for a summary, the section "Imperial Religion, Heretical Resistance" in Kristó-Nagy, "Marriage after Rape," 178–80. See also Kristó-Nagy, "Denouncing the Damned Zindīq!"; and Kristó-Nagy, "A Violent, Irrational and Unjust God."

62 See Kristó-Nagy, "Conflict and Cooperation."

63 As in the Greek treatises titled *Peri basileias* (*On Kingship*), see Haake, "Writing down."

64 In the introduction under the name of Bahnūd b. Saḥwān and/or ʿAlī b. al-Shāh al-Fārisī. On this introduction, see A. F. L. [Alfred Felix Landon] Beeston, "The 'ʿAlī ibn Shāh' Preface to Kalīlah wa Dimnah," *Oriens* 7.1 (1954): 81–4, who suggests, ibid., 83, that it "was composed towards the end of the seventh century a.h." (that is the thirteenth century CE). De Blois, *Burzōy's Voyage to India*, 24–5, agrees with Beeston, while Kristó-Nagy, *La pensée d'Ibn al-Muqaffa'*, 127–30, underlines the affinity between parts of this preface and Ibn al-Muqaffaʿ's thought.
Most studies discussing this introduction, such as Abdallah Cheikh-Moussa, "Du discours autorisé ou comment s'adresser au tyran," *Arabica* 46.2 (1999), 139–75; Makram Abbès, "Le sage et le politique dans *Kalila et Dimna*," in Denis Lopez, ed., *Le pouvoir et ses écritures*, Bordeaux: Presses Universitaires de Bordeaux, 2012, 27–37; and Yūsif Aḥmad Ismāʿīl, "Tarhīn al-zaman fī *Kalīla wa-Dimna*," *al-Majalla al-ʿArabiyya li-l-maʿlūm al-insāniyya*, 31-121 (2013), 45–75, take for granted that it was already part of the text translated by Ibn al-Muqaffaʿ and present him as its author without considering the arguments for the posteriority of this introduction to Ibn al-Muqaffaʿ's version presented by Beeston and de Blois. This is not the case in Abdelfattah Kilito,

"How Should We Read *Kalila and Dimna*" = Chapter 2, in Abdelfattah Kilito, *Arabs and the Art of Storytelling: A Strange Familiarity*, translated by Mbarek Sryfi and Eric Sellin (Syracuse, NY: Syracuse University Press, 2014), 18–29, originally published in French as *Les Arabes et l'art du récit: Une étrange familiarité* (Paris: Actes Sud, Sindbad, 2009). I think that the question of Ibn al-Muqaffaʿ's role in producing this introduction remains open.

This introduction is not included in ʿAzzām. I will quote it below, p. 61, in the version published in *Āthār Ibn al-Muqaffaʿ* (Beirut: Dār al-kutub al-ʿilmiyya, 1989), which provides readings that seem more accurate than the version included in Cheikho. This edition of *Kalīla wa-Dimna* by Dār al-kutub al-ʿilmiyya is reprinted from the edition of *Kalīla wa-Dimna* in *Āthār Ibn al-Muqaffaʿ* edited by ʿUmar Abū l-Naṣr (Beirut: Dār maktabat al-ḥayāt, 1966) which itself reproduces the edition of *Kalīla wa-Dimna* by Aḥmad Ḥasan Ṭabbāra and Muṣṭafā Luṭfī al-Manfalūṭī (Cairo: al-Maktaba al-ahliyya, 1926).

65 See Jennifer London, "How to Do Things with Fables: Ibn al-Muqaffaʿ's Frank Speech in Stories from *Kalīla wa Dimna*," *History of Political Thought* 29.2 (2008): 189–212, and Kristó-Nagy, "Wild Lions and Wise Jackals."

66 On Aesopian language by Ibn al-Muqaffaʿ, see Kristó-Nagy, "The Crow Who Aped the Partridge."

67 See ʿAzzām, 41–2, Cheikho, 43–4 and Jallad, 74–5. See also de Blois, *Burzōy's Voyage to India*, 34–7.

68 For a Hindu version originally in Sanskrit, see *The Mahabharata of Krishna-Dwaipayana Vyasa: Translated into English Prose*, transl. by Kisari Mohan Ganguli (Calcutta: Bharata Press, 1883–96), Book 11 = *Stree Parva*, chapter 5–6, pp. 10–2. For a Jain version, see a translated quote from the *Samarādityakathā*, 2.55–80, written in Prākrit by Haribhadra, in *Sources of Indian Tradition*, ed. by Wm. Theodore de Bary et al., New York: Columbia University Press, 1958 reprinted Delhi: Motilal Banarsidass, 1963 and 1972, 56–8. See also Ernst Kuhn, "Der Mann im Brunnen: Geschichte eines indischen Gleichnisses," in *Festgruss an Otto von Böhtlingk*, ed. by Rudolf von Roth (Stuttgart: W. Kohlhammer, 1888), 68–76, and de Blois, *Burzōy's Voyage*, 34–7 and 73–80.

69 Kevin van Bladel, "Eighth-Century Indian Astronomy in the Two Cities of Peace," in *Islamic Cultures, Islamic Contexts: Essays in Honor of Professor Patricia Crone*, ed. by Behnam Sadeghi et al. (Leiden and Boston: Brill, 2015), 259. On medicine in the Sāsānian empire, see Peter E. Pormann and Emilie Savage-Smith, *Medieval Islamic Medicine* (Edinburgh: Edinburgh University Press, 2007), 15–23.

70 Jallad, 117. In both ʿAzzām, 98, and Cheikho, 100–1 we read "the resolute/judicious king" (*malik ḥāzim*) instead of a "prudent person."

71 See Aristotle, *Nicomachean Ethics*, with an English translation by H. Rackham, 1926, revised ed. (Cambridge, MA: Harvard University Press, 1934), VII/xii/*a*/I, 432–3 (1152b26–32). See also Aristotle, *Eudemian Ethics* (1235b35), in *The Complete Works of Aristotle: The Revised Oxford Translation*, ed. by Jonathan Barnes (Princeton, NJ: Princeton University Press, 1984), vol. 2, *Eudemian Ethics*, VII/2, 1957, or, together with the Greek text, Aristotle, *Athenian Constitution, Eudemian Ethics, Virtues and Vices*, with an English translation by H. Rackham, 1935, revised and reprinted Cambridge, MA: Harvard University Press, 1952, VII/II/4, 366–7.

72 See Edgerton, *The Pancatantra Reconstructed* (vol. 2, 328). Regarding the date of the composition of the Pañcatantra, to my knowledge there is no further clarity since the following time frame suggested by Franklin Edgerton in 1924, that: "I think it is at present impossible to say more about the date than that it was earlier than the sixth century A. D., in which the Pahlavi translation was made, and later than the beginning of the Christian era," see Edgerton, *The Pancatantra Reconstructed*, vol. 2, 182.

73 For the Syriac text, see Schulthess, *Kalīla und Dimna*, vol. 1, 50, for the German translation, see vol. 2, 51.

74 See n. 28 above.

75 See Gregory of Nyssa, *The Lord's Prayer, The Beatitudes*, transl. by Hilda C. Graef (New York: Newman Press, 1954), 172.

76 See Celsus (d. c. 50), *On Medicine*, with an English translation by W.G. Spencer (Cambridge, MA: Harvard University Press, 1935), vol. 2: Books 5–6, Book v, 34 D, 106–7.

77 See Epictetus, *Discourses, Books 1–2*, transl. by W.A. Oldfather (Cambridge, MA: Harvard University Press, 1925), II.5.22–3, 238–9.

78 Clement of Alexandria, *The Exhortation to the Greeks, The Rich Man's Salvation, To the Newly Baptized*, transl. by G.W. Butterworth (Cambridge, MA: Harvard University Press, 1919), chapter I, 20–1.

79 For the most authoritative scholarly edition of the text, see Muḥammad Kurd ʿAlī, ed., *Rasāʾil al-Bulaghāʾ*, 3rd ed., Cairo: Maṭbaʿat lajnat al-taʾlīf wa-l-tarjama wa-l-nashr, 1365/1946, reprinted as the 4th ed. (1954), 39–106. For a French translation, see Jean Tardy, “Traduction d'al-Adab al-Kabīr d'Ibn al-Muqaffaʿ,” *Annals islamologique* 27 (1993): 181–223. Regarding the title of this text, see István T. Kristó Nagy, “On the Authenticity of *Al-Adab al-ṣaġīr* Attributed to Ibn al-Muqaffaʿ and Problems concerning Some of His Titles,” *Acta Orientalia Scientiarum Hungariae* 62.2 (2009): 213–6.

80 For the scholarly literature on this text, see the relevant chapter of Kristó-Nagy, *La pensée d'Ibn al-Muqaffaʿ*, 213–66.

81 Kurd ʿAlī, *Rasāʾil al-Bulaghāʾ*, 40–4. For an English translation of this section, see Geert Jan van Gelder, transl., *Classical Arabic Literature: A Library of Arabic Literature Anthology* (New York and London: New York University Press, 2012), 168–70 (this translation, 170–5, also includes the *adab* for the ruler). See also Kristó-Nagy, *La pensée d'Ibn al-Muqaffaʿ*, 189–98.

82 Kurd ʿAlī, *Rasāʾil al-Bulaghāʾ*, 40, l. 4–41, l. 14.

83 Ibid., 42, l. 1–43, l. 11.

84 Andras Hamori, “Prudence, Virtue, and Self-Respect in Ibn al-Muqaffaʿ,” in *Reflections on Reflections: Near Eastern Writers Reading Literature: Dedicated to Renate Jacobi*, ed. by Angelika Neuwirth and Andreas Christian Islebe (Wiesbaden: Reichert Verlag, 2006), 165. See also Hans Daiber, “Das *Kitāb al-Ādāb al-kabīr* des Ibn al-Muqaffaʿ als Ausdruck griechischer Ethik, islamischer Ideologie und iranisch-sassanidischer Hofetikette,” *Oriens* 43 (2015): 273–92, reprinted in idem, *From the Greeks to the Arabs and Beyond*, 224–42, and Judith Josephson, “The Multicultural Background of the *Kitāb al-Ādāb al-kabīr* by ʿAbdallāh Ibn al-Muqaffaʿ,” in *Current Issues in the Analysis of Semitic Grammar and Lexicon I: Oslo–Göteborg Cooperation 3rd–5th June 2004*, ed. by Lutz Edzard and Jan Retsö (Wiesbaden: Harrassowitz, 2005), 166–92.

85 Kurd ʿAlī, *Rasāʾil al-Bulaghāʾ*, 42, l. 6.

86 See n. 64 above.

87 See *Āthār Ibn al-Muqaffaʿ*, 13 as well as Cheikho, 11; de Sacy, 15–6; and Jallad, 48.

88 Kurd ʿAlī, *Rasāʾil al-Bulaghāʾ*, 105, l. 14–106, l. 10.

89 Similarly to the conclusion of Aristotle's *Eudemian Ethics* (1248b9–1249b25), see Barnes, ed., *The Complete Works of Aristotle*, vol. 2, *Eudemian Ethics*, VIII/15, 1980–1, or, together with the Greek text, Aristotle, *Athenian Constitution*, VIII/II/1–7, 468–77.

90 See J.D. Latham, “Ibn al-Muqaffaʿ and Early ‘Abbasid Prose,” in *ʿAbbasid Belles-Lettres* , ed. by Julia Ashtiany (Cambridge and New York: Cambridge University Press, 1990), 62–4 and, regarding the style of *Risāla fī l-ṣaḥāba* using both Greek rhetoric and “rhythmical patterns and measured openings and terminations deriving their measures from the metres of Arabic poetry or savouring of the prosodic,” 72.

91 See Kurd ʿAlī, *Rasāʾil al-Bulaghāʾ*, 1–37. On the authenticity of this work, see Kristó Nagy, “On the Authenticity of *Al-Adab al-ṣaġīr*,” 197–216.

92 Kurd ʿAlī, *Rasāʾil al-Bulaghāʾ*, 4, l. 3. See Miklós Maróth's comments on this sentence in his introduction to *The Correspondence*, 89–90. It ends with the following observations: “Ibn al-Muqaffaʿ himself is author of a handbook on logic, traditionally treating the Aristotelian logic only up to *Prior Analytics* A7. In this work he speaks of categorical syllogisms only, the other ways of argumentation, including chains of hypothetical syllogisms, being unknown to him theoretically. Consequently, he imitated practical examples, when composing chains of concepts in consequential relation.”

93 Q. 54: 49. "Surely We have created everything in measure" in Arberry's translation. Sarwar translates *qadar* as purpose. See http://corpus.quran.com/translation.jsp?chapter=54&verse=49 (accessed September 21, 2022). For discussions and translations of a number of exegeses of this verse, see Feras Hamza and Sajjad Rizvi, with Farhana Mayer, eds., *An Anthology of Qur'anic Commentaries*, Vol. 1, *On the Nature of the Divine* (Oxford and New York: Oxford University Press and London: In association with The Institute of Ismaili Studies, 2008), 455–90.

94 I.e. the aim of the people is the rightness of the afterlife and the need of the people is the rightness of this life; the rightness of this life is needed for the rightness of the afterlife. The use of this reverse structure is also present in other works by Ibn al-Muqaffaʿ, see Kristó-Nagy, *La pensée d'Ibn al-Muqaffa'*, 396 with the note 1372, and 438 with the note 1616.

95 Kurd ʿAlī, *Rasāʾil al-Bulaghāʾ*, 4, ll. 4–6.

96 Ibid., 4, l. 6–5, l. 9.

97 This Islamization of Greek philosophical matter was preceded by its Christianization, see Rudolph, "The Late Ancient Background," 50–1 and its Zoroastrianization, see n. 8 above.

98 Michael G. Carter, "Language Control as People Control in Medieval Islam: The Aims of the Grammarians in Their Cultural Context," *Al-Abḥāth* 31 (1983): 76–84.

99 See above, 58 with the n. 57.

100 See Kristó-Nagy, *La pensée d'Ibn al-Muqaffa'*; idem, "Marriage after Rape"; and idem, "On the Authenticity of *Al-Adab al-ṣaġīr*." See also Dominique Urvoy, "Autour d'Ibn al-Muqaffaʿ."

101 Kurd ʿAlī, *Rasāʾil al-Bulaghāʾ*, 27, ll. 14–6.

102 Shaul Shaked, ed. and transl., *The Wisdom of the Sasanian Sages (Dēnkard VI) by Aturpāt-i Ēmētān* (Boulder, CO: Westview Press, 1979), 5, § 5.

103 See the preface and the introduction of Shaul Shaked, ed. and transl., *The Wisdom of the Sasanian Sages*, ix–x and xv–xviii.

104 See n. 34 above.

105 See Kurd ʿAlī, *Rasāʾil al-Bulaghāʾ*, 14, ll. 12–6.

106 Shaul Shaked, ed. and transl., *The Wisdom of the Sasanian Sages*, 5, § 224.

107 Kurd ʿAlī, *Rasāʾil al-Bulaghāʾ*, 22, ll. 11–2.

108 See ʿAzzām, 7–9; and Cheikho, 47–9. Both versions include passages that are missing from the other and present parallelisms with the above presented quotes from the *Kitāb al-Adab al-ṣaghīr*. On the divergence of the textual variants of Ibn al-Muqaffaʿ's introduction to *Kalīla wa-Dimna*, see Beatrice Gruendler, "Les versions arabes," 405–11. For future research on the chapter, it is noteworthy that it is one of those six chapters or passages of the text on which the project *Kalīla and Dimna – AnonymClassic* is focusing, see Gruendler et al., "An Interim Report," 247.

109 See, for instance in, Shaul Shaked, ed. and transl., *The Wisdom of the Sasanian Sages*, 17, § 40.

110 See al-Ghazālī, *Letter to a Disciple: Ayyuhā 'l-walad*, ed. and transl. by Tobias Mayer (Cambridge: Islamic Texts Society, 2005), 6–9. Sustaining the authorship of Abū Ḥāmid Muḥammad b. Muḥammad al-Ghazālī, and placing its composition into the last period of al-Ghazālī's life, Mayer refers in his introduction, xxii–xxiii, note B, to W. M. [William Montgomery] Watt, "The Authenticity of the Works Attributed to al-Ghazālī," *Journal of Royal Asiatic Society* 84.1/2 (1952): 24–5 as well as 43, but the first is a typo, as the relevant pages are rather 30–1 and 42–3 and 44.
The notion of the legacy of useful knowledge as a lasting action is in the following hadith:
إِذَا مَاتَ الإِنْسَانُ انْقَطَعَ عَنْهُ عَمَلُهُ إِلاَّ مِنْ ثَلاَثَةٍ إِلاَّ مِنْ صَدَقَةٍ جَارِيَةٍ أَوْ عِلْمٍ يُنْتَفَعُ بِهِ أَوْ وَلَدٍ صَالِحٍ يَدْعُو لَهُ
"When a man dies, all his good deeds come to an end, except for three: Ongoing charity, beneficial knowledge, or righteous son who will pray for him."
For variants and translations, see, for instance, in Muslim, *Ṣaḥīḥ = English Translation of Sahîh Muslim*, transl. by Nasiruddin Khattab, 7 vols. (Riyadh: Darussalam, 2007), vol. 4, 371, hadith [4223] 14 - (1631); al-Tirmidhī, *Jāmiʿ = English translation of Jāmiʿ At-Tirmidhī*, transl. by Abu Khaliyl, 6 vols (Riyadh, Darussalam, 2007), vol. 3, 167–8, hadith 1376; Abū Dāwūd, *Sunan = English Translation of Sunan Abu Dawud*, transl. by Yaser Qadhi (vols. 1–2) and Nasiruddin Khattab (vols. 3–5), 5 vols. (Riyadh: Darussalam, 2008), vol. 3, 424–5, hadith 2880; al-Bukhārī,

al-Adab al-mufrad = Manners in Islam: (Al Adab Al Mufrad): Arabic - English Text, transl. and commentated by Maulana Khalid Khan Garhi, transl. into English by Rafiq Abdur Rahman (Beirut: Dār al-kutub al-ʿilmiyya), 79, hadith 38.

111 This is in spite of the fact that al-Ghazālī clearly played a key role in the Islamization of Greek philosophy in that he sought to purify it of what he considered the heedless imitation of the Greeks and of the theses that he saw as contradictory to Islam. See Alexander Treiger, *Inspired Knowledge in Islamic Thought: Al-Ghazālī's Theory on Mystical Cognition and Its Avicennian Foundation* (London and New York: Routledge, 2012); and Jules Janssens, "Al-Ghazzālī's *Tahāfut*: Is It Really a Rejection of Ibn Sīnā's Philosophy?," *Journal of Islamic Studies* 12.1 (2001): 1–17.

112 ومن العلم أن تعلَم أنك لا تعلم بما لا تعلم

The end of this sentence is different in Kurd ʿAlī, *Rasāʾil al-Bulaghāʾ*, 25, l. 12. There is an unnecessary alteration as compared to the sources he used (see his note 3 on the same page), and the provided vocalization is also unjustified:

ومن العلم أن تعلَم أنك لا تعلم ما لا تُعَلَّمُ

That both the vocalization of the last term and the omission of the preposition ب from بلا is to be rectified is corroborated by the version in the *Dēnkard* (see below, in the main text).

113 Plato, *Charmides, Alcibiades I and II, Hiparchus, The Lovers, Theages, Minos, Epinomis,* with an English translation by W.R.M. Lamb, London: Heinemann and New York: Putnam, 1927, reprinted (Cambridge, MA: Harvard University Press and London: Heinemann, 1955), 76–7 (172c); building on 56–7 (167a): "And so this is being temperate, or temperance, and knowing oneself – that one should know what one knows and what one does not know."; 72–3 (171d): "the temperate man knew what he knew and what he did not know, and that he knows the one and does not know the other"; 74–5 (172a): "Did we not so speak of temperance, I said, Critias, when we remarked how great a boon it was to know what one knows and what one does not know?"; and 172b: "there is this good point in the knowledge of knowledge and of lack of knowledge, which we now find to be what temperance is."

For studies on the notion of *docta ignorantia* in Islamic philosophy, see Cristina D'Ancona, "Il tema della *docta ignorantia* nel neoplatonismo arabo: Un contributo all'analisi delle fonti di *Teologia di Aristotele, mîmar* II," in *Concordia discors: Studi su Niccolò Cusano e sull'umanesimo europeo offerti a Giovanni Santinello*, ed. by Gregorio Piaia (Padova: Antenore, 1993), 3–22, and Rafael Ramón Guerrero, "Docta ignorancia en el neopolatonismo árabe?," in *El problema del conocimiento en Nicolás de Cusa: Genealogía y proyección*, ed. by Jorge M. Machetta and Claudia D'Amico (Buenos Aires: Biblos, 2005), 67–84.

114 Shaul Shaked, ed. and transl., *The Wisdom of the Sasanian Sages*, 5, § 2.

115 Peimin Ni, transl., *Understanding the* Analects *of Confucius: A New Translation of* Lunyu *with Annotations* (Albany, NY: State University of New York Press, 2017), 171 (2.17). The idea is further explained in the *Xun Ji*: "Thus exemplary persons say they know when they know, and say they do not know when they don't know." See ibid., 172.

116 The text is published in Kurd ʿAlī, *Rasāʾil al-Bulaghāʾ*, 117–34. Presently, the most authoritative scholarly edition of the text is Charles Pellat, ed. and transl., *Ibn al-Muqaffaʿ: Mort vers 140/757: «Conseilleur» du calife* (Paris: G.-P. Maisonneuve et Larose, 1976), hereinafter Pellat, *«Conseilleur»*.

117 See Kurd ʿAlī, *Rasāʾil al-Bulaghāʾ*, 107–11, and for an edition including further fragments and a French translation, see Kristó-Nagy, *La pensée d'Ibn al-Muqaffaʿ*, 372–404. The latter also contains an analysis of this text (267–77).

118 For an overall study of the epistle, see Kristó-Nagy, *La pensée d'Ibn al-Muqaffaʿ*, 213–66.

119 The text is studied in Kristó-Nagy, *La pensée d'Ibn al-Muqaffaʿ*, 267–77, and Kristó-Nagy, "Marriage after Rape," but awaits further attention.

120 For an example of this combination in *al-Yatīma*, see Kristó-Nagy, *La pensée d'Ibn al-Muqaffaʿ*, 376–7. See also ibid., 270 with n. 864.

121 See Kristó-Nagy, *La pensée d'Ibn al-Muqaffa'*, 173 and 225–7; Jennifer A. London, "The Abbasid 'Circle of Justice': Re-reading Ibn al-Muqaffaʿ's *Letter on Companionship*," in *Comparative Political Theory in Time and Place*, ed. by Daniel J. Kapust and Helen M. Kinsella (New York: Palgrave Macmillan, 2017), 25–50. On the *circle of justice* in general, see Jennifer A. London, "The 'Circle of Justice'," *History of Political Thought* 32.3 (2011): 425–47; and Linda T. Darling, *A History of Social Justice and Political Power in the Middle East: The Circle of Justice from Mesopotamia to Globalization* (Abingdon and New York: Routledge, 2013).

122 See Pellat, *«Conseilleur»*, 64–5 (§ 57–8). See also István T. Kristó-Nagy, "Who Shall Educate Whom? The Official and the Sincere Views of Ibn al-Muqaffaʿ about Intellectual Hierarchy," in *Synoptikos: Mélanges offerts à Dominique Urvoy*, ed. by Nicole Koulayan and Mansour Sayah (Toulouse: Presses Universitaires du Mirail, 2011), 279–93. Presenting an interesting contrast, while Ibn al-Muqaffaʿ had to recognise that it was better to cajole the powerful as intellectually superior (see also Kristó-Nagy, "Wild Lions and Wise Jackals"), the elderly al-Ghazālī clearly could not bother to keep any servile attitude. In a letter dated a year before his death, he openly presents the (Sufi) spiritual elite as the elite of the elite (*khāṣṣ-khavāṣṣ*) at the highest level in a tripartite hierarchy of humankind and assumes a position of superiority over the vizier, see Jonathan AC Brown, "The Last Days of al-Ghazzālī and the Tripartite Division of the Sufi World: Abū Ḥāmid al-Ghazzālī's Letter to the Seljuq Vizier and Commentary," *The Muslim World* 96 (2006): 89–113. Regarding the *khāṣṣa* and *ʿāmma* in Islamic political thought, see Louise Marlow, *Hierarchy and Egalitarianism in Islamic Thought* (Cambridge and New York: Cambridge University Press, 1997), 37–40 and 54–5 (followed by a section on the influence of "The Platonic Tripartite Social Model," 55–7) and (in a discussion on the *Risāla fī l-ṣaḥāba*) 101. See also Crone, *God's Rule*, 115, 122, 215 and 335.

123 See Kristó-Nagy, *La pensée d'Ibn al-Muqaffa'*, 376–83.

124 In fact, it is rather a-Qurʾanic, see the Qurʾan 2: 104 and 4: 46. There is, however, a well-known hadith stating that:

كُلُّكُمْ رَاعٍ، وَكُلُّكُمْ مَسْئُولٌ عَنْ رَعِيَّتِهِ، الإِمَامُ رَاعٍ وَمَسْئُولٌ عَنْ رَعِيَّتِهِ، [. . .]

"Each of you is a shepherd, and each of you is responsible for your flock. The *Imām* [in other versions the *Amīr*] is the shepherd of his flock and is responsible for his flock, [. . .]."

For variants and translations, see, al-Bukhārī, *Ṣaḥīḥ* = *The Translation of the Meanings of Sahîh Al-Bukhâri: Arabic-English*, transl. by Muhammad Muhsin Khan, 9 vols. (Riyadh: Darussalam, 1997), vol. 2, 28, hadith 893, vol. 3, 340, hadith 2409, vol. 3, 419, hadith 2554 and 420, hadith 2558, vol. 4, 23, hadith 2751, vol. 7, 81, hadith 5188, vol. 7, 93–4, vol. 9, 160, hadith 7138; al-Bukhārī, *al-Adab al-mufrad*, 185, hadith 206, 190, hadith 212; Muslim, *Ṣaḥīḥ*, vol. 5, 155, hadith [4724] 20 – (1829), al-Tirmidhī, *Jāmiʿ*, vol. 3, 439, hadith 1705. Ibn ʿUmar is also reported as comparing the leader of the community to a shepherd, see Muslim, *Ṣaḥīḥ*, vol. 5, 149–50, hadith [4714] 12.

125 See for instance in *Inana and Enki*, Segment F, l. 19 available at the website of The Electronic Text Corpus of Sumerian Literature (ETCSL), Faculty of Oriental Studies, University of Oxford (2006) http://etcsl.orinst.ox.ac.uk/cgi-bin/etcsl.cgi?text=t.1.3.1&display=Crit&charenc=gcirc&lineid=t131.p21#t131.p21, Segment I, l. 9, available at http://etcsl.orinst.ox.ac.uk/cgi-bin/etcsl.cgi?text=t.1.3.1&display=Crit&charenc=gcirc&lineid=t131.p54#t131.p54; *Lugalbanda in the Mountain Cave*, Segment A, l. 240 available at http://etcsl.orinst.ox.ac.uk/cgi-bin/etcsl.cgi?text=t.1.8.2.1&display=Crit&charenc=gcirc&lineid=t1821.p22#t1821.p22. For a number of further examples, including kings described as shepherds, see http://etcsl.orinst.ox.ac.uk/cgi-bin/etcsl.cgi?simplesearchword=shepherd&simplesearch=translation&searchword=&charenc=gcirc&lists. All three webpages in this note were accessed on September 21, 2022.

126 See in the Old Testament: *Genesis* 48: 15–6, *Numbers* 27: 17, *2 Samuel* 5: 2, 7: 7, *1 Kings* 22: 17, *1 Chronicles* 11: 2, 17: 6, 18: 16, *Psalms* 23: 1, 28: 9, 49: 14, 78: 70–2, 80: 1, *Isaiah* 40: 10–1, 44: 28, 56: 11, 63: 11, *Jeremiah* 2: 8, 3: 15, 6: 3, 10: 21, 17: 16, 22: 22, 23: 1–4, 25: 34–6, 31: 10, 43: 12, 49: 19, 50: 6, 50: 44, 51: 23, *Ezekiel* 34: 1–31, *Amos* 3: 12, *Micah* 5: 4–6, 7: 14, *Nahum*

3: 18, *Zechariah* 10: 2–3, 11: 3–11, 15–7, and in the New Testament: *Matthew* 2: 6, 9: 36, 25: 32, 26: 31, *Mark* 6: 34, 14: 27, *John* 10: 1–16, *Ephesians* 4: 11, *Hebrews* 13: 20–1, *1 Peter* 2: 25, 5: 1–4, *Revelation* 7: 17.

127 According to Plato, *The Laws*, ed. by Malcolm Schofield, transl. by Tom Griffith (Cambridge and New York: Cambridge University Press, 2016), 181, n. 25 (to 2.735a–c): "The image of the people as herd or flock and the ruler as herdsman or shepherd was a popular one in Greek literature and philosophy from Homer on (*Iliad* 2.243, etc.). The star passages in texts of political theory are Xenophon *Cyropaedia* 1.1.2 and Plato *Statesman* 265b–268d, 274c–277a (where the idea undergoes critical scrutiny)." See also idem, 395 (10.905e–906a).

128 See Pellat, *«Conseilleur»*, 16–7 (§ 1). See also, *ibid.*, 20–1 (§ 8) and 32–3 (§ 22).

129 See also above, 64, the quotation from the *Kitāb al-Adab al-ṣaghīr*: "by knowledge (*ʿilm*) the judgments are judiciously made (*tustaḥkamu al-aḥkām*)."

130 See Kristó-Nagy, *La pensée d'Ibn al-Muqaffaʿ*, 378–9, 384–5, 386–7. See also Pellat, *«Conseilleur»*, 32–3 (§ 22).

131 See Pellat, *«Conseilleur»*, 24–5 (§ 11).

132 See Pellat, *«Conseilleur»*, 44–7 (§ 38–40). Interestingly, he uses a highly similar example (and a contrary conclusion) in 46–7 (§40) to the "lie to a murderer" example discussed by Immanuel Kant in his essay *On a Supposed Right to Lie from Philanthropy* published originally in 1797, responding to Benjamin Constant's criticism, see Immanuel Kant, *Practical Philosophy*, ed. and transl. by Mary J. Gregor (Cambridge: Cambridge University Press, 1996), 605–15.

133 See Pellat, *«Conseilleur»*, 25–31 (§ 13–21). See also Kristó-Nagy, *La pensée d'Ibn al-Muqaffaʿ*, 229–42.

134 See the *Risāla fī l-ṣaḥāba* (see Pellat, *«Conseilleur»*, 28–31 (§ 18–21)), *al-Yatīma* (see Kristó-Nagy, *La pensée d'Ibn al-Muqaffaʿ*, 390–1), and the *Kitāb al-Adab al-ṣaghīr* (see Kurd ʿAlī, *Rasāʾil al-Bulaghāʾ*, 21). The role of reason and religion in Ibn al-Muqaffaʿ's writings are discussed in István T. Kristó-Nagy, "Reason, Religion and Power in Ibn al-Muqaffaʿ," *Acta Orientalia Academiae Scientiarum Hungaricae* 62.3 (2009): 291–4.

135 See Pellat, *«Conseilleur»*, 24–5 (§ 12) and 32–3 (§ 22).

136 Kurd ʿAlī, *Rasāʾil al-Bulaghāʾ*, 49, ll. 6–9 (12). See also Kristó-Nagy, "Reason, Religion and Power": 294–5.

137 See Kurd ʿAlī, *Rasāʾil al-Bulaghāʾ*, 71, ll. 3–5.

138 See Kristó-Nagy, "Wild Lions and Wise Jackals."

Bibliography

Abbreviations for Ibn Muqaffaʿs Works

ʿAzzām: See *Kalīla wa-Dimna* > ʿAzzām.

Cheikho: See *Kalīla wa-Dimna* > Cheikho.

de Sacy: See *Kalīla wa-Dimna* > de Sacy.

Jallad: See *Kalīla wa-Dimna* > Jallad.

Pellat, *«Conseilleur»*: See *Risāla fī l-ṣaḥāba* > Pellat.

Ibn Muqaffaʿ's Oeuvre

Kitāb al-Ādāb al-kabīr

Ibn al-Muqaffaʿ. "*Al-Durra al-yatīma aw al-Adab al-kabīr.*" In *Rasāʾil al-Bulaghāʾ*. Ed. by Muḥammad Kurd ʿAlī. 3rd ed. Cairo: Maṭbaʿat lajnat al-taʾlīf wa-l-tarjama wa-l-nashr, 1365/1946. Reprinted (= 4th ed.), 1954, 39–106.

Gelder, Geert Jan van, transl. "Mirror for Princes (and Others): Passages from Ibn al-Muqaffaʿ's *Right Conduct.*" In *Classical Arabic Literature: A Library of Arabic Literature Anthology*. Selected and transl. by Geert Jan van Gelder. New York and London: New York University Press, 2012, 168–75.

Tardy, Jean, transl. "Traduction d'al-Adab al-Kabīr d'Ibn al-Muqaffaᶜ." *Annales islamologiques* 27 (1993): 181–223.

Kitāb al-Adab al-ṣaghīr

Ibn al-Muqaffaʿ. *Al-Adab al-ṣaghīr*. In *Rasāʾil al-Bulaghāʾ*. Ed. by Muḥammad Kurd ʿAlī. 3rd ed. Cairo: Maṭbaʿat lajnat al-taʾlīf wa-l-tarjama wa-l-nashr, 1365/1946. Reprinted (= 4th ed.), 1954, 1–37.

Kalīla wa-Dimna

ʿAzzām, ʿAbd al-Wahhāb, ed. *Kalīla wa-Dimna*. 2nd revised ed. Algiers: al-Sharika al-waṭaniyya li-l-nashr wa-l-tawzīʿ and Beirut: Dār al-shurūq, 1973.

Cheikho, Louis, ed. *La version arabe de Kalîlah et Dimnah d'après le plus ancien manuscrit arabe daté*. Beirut: Imprimerie catholique, 1905.

Fishbein, Michael, ed. *Kalīlah and Dimnah: Fables of Virtue and Vice*. Transl. by Michael Fishbein and James E. Montgomery. Library of Arabic Literature. New York and London: New York University Press, 2021.

Ibn al-Muqaffaʿ, *Le livre de Kalila et Dimna*. Transl. by André Miquel. 2nd ed. Paris: Klincksieck, Paris, 1980.

Jallad, Saleh Saʿadeh, transl. *The Fables of Kalilah and Dimnah: Adapted and Translated from the Sanskrit through the Pahlavi into Arabic by ʿAbdullāh ibn al-Muqaffaʿ AD 750*. London: Melisende, 2002. Reprinted, 2004.

Silvestre de Sacy, M. ed. *Calila et Dimna, ou Fables de Bidpai, en arabe*. Paris: Imprimerie Royal, 1816.

Ṭabbāra, Aḥmad Ḥasan and Muṣṭafā Luṭfī al-Manfalūṭī, eds. *Kalīla wa-Dimna*. Cairo: al-Maktaba al-ahliyya, 1926. Reprinted in ʿUmar Abū l-Naṣr, ed. *Āthār Ibn al-Muqaffaʿ*. Beirut: Dār maktabat al-ḥayāt, 1966, 3–244. Reprinted Beirut: Dār al-kutub al-ʿilmiyya, 1989.

Wyndham Knatchbull, A. M. *Kalila and Dimna: Or, The Fables of Bidpai: Translated from the Arabic Kalīla wa-Dimna*. Oxford: W. Baxter, 1819.

The Letter of Tansar

Ibn al-Muqaffaʿ. *The Letter of Tansar*. Transl. by Mary Boyce. Rome: Istituto italiano per il Medio ed Estremo Oriente, 1968.

Al-Manṭiq

Ibn al-Muqaffaʿ. *Al-Manṭiq*. In *al-Manṭiq (Logic) by Ibn al-Muqaffaʿ, Ḥudūd al-Manṭiq (Definitions of Logic) by Ibn Bihrīz*. Ed. by Muḥammad Taqī Dānishpazhūh. Tehran: Anjuman-i shāhanshāhī-i falsafah-i Īrān, 1978. Reprinted Tehran: Muʾassasah-i pazhūhishī-i ḥikmat va falsafah-i Īrān, 1381 AHS/2002–03.

Risāla fī l-ṣaḥāba

Ibn al-Muqaffaʿ. *Risāla fī l-ṣaḥāba*. In *Rasāʾil al-Bulaghāʾ*. Ed. by Muḥammad Kurd ʿAlī. 3rd ed. Cairo: Maṭbaʿat lajnat al-taʾlīf wa-l-tarjama wa-l-nashr, 1365/1946. Reprinted (= 4th ed.) 1954, 117 34.

Ibn al-Muqaffaʿ. *Risāla fī l-ṣaḥāba*. In *Ibn al-Muqaffaʿ: Mort vers 140/757: «Conseilleur» du calife*. Ed. and transl. by Charles Pellat. Paris: G.-P. Maisonneuve et Larose, 1976.

Al-Yatīma

Ibn al-Muqaffaʿ. *Al-Yatīma*. Ed. and transl. by István T. Kristó-Nagy. In Kristó-Nagy. *La pensée d'Ibn al-Muqaffa': Un «agent double» dans le monde persan et arabe*. Versailles: Éditions de Paris, 2013, 372–404.

Ibn al-Muqaffaʿ. *Yatīma thāniya*. In *Rasāʾil al-Bulaghāʾ*. Ed. by Muḥammad Kurd ʿAlī. 3rd ed. Cairo: Maṭbaʿat lajnat al-taʾlīf wa-l-tarjama wa-l-nashr, 1365/1946. Reprinted (= 4th ed.) 1954, 107–11.

Other Sources and Studies

ʿAbd al-Jabbār b. Aḥmad al-Asadābādī. *Tathbīt dalāʾil al-nubuwwa*. Beirut: Dār al-ʿArabiyya, 1966.

Abbès, Makram. "Le sage et le politique dans *Kalila et Dimna*." In *Le pouvoir et ses écritures*. Ed. by Denis Lopez. Bordeaux: Presses Universitaires de Bordeaux, 2012, 27–37.

Abū Dāwūd. *Sunan = English Translation of Sunan Abu Dawud*. Transl. by Yaser Qadhi (vols. 1–2) and Nasiruddin Khattab (vols. 3–5). 5 vols. Riyadh: Darussalam, 2008.

Aristotle. *Eudemian Ethics*. In *Athenian Constitution, Eudemian Ethics, Virtues and Vices*. With an English translation by H. Rackham. Cambridge, MA: Harvard University Press, 1935. Revised and reprinted, 1952, 189–482.

Aristotle. *Eudemian Ethics*. In *The Complete Works of Aristotle: The Revised Oxford Translation*. Ed. by Jonathan Barnes. Princeton, NJ: Princeton University Press, 1984, vol. 2, 1922–81.

Aristotle. *Nicomachean Ethics*. With an English translation by H. Rackham. Cambridge, MA: Harvard University Press, 1926. Revised ed., 1934.

Baffioni, Carmela. "Ikhwân al-Safâ'." In *The Stanford Encyclopedia of Philosophy*. Ed. by Edward N. Zalta. Available online at http://plato.stanford.edu/entries/ikhwan-al-safa/. Accessed September 21, 2022.

Beeston, A. F. L. [Alfred Felix Landon]. "The 'ʿAlī ibn Shāh' Preface to Kalīlah wa Dimnah." *Oriens* 7.1 (1954): 81–4.

Al-Bīrūnī. *Fī taḥqīq mā li-l-Hind min maqūla maqbūla fī l-ʿaql aw mardhūla*. Hyderabad Deccan: Maṭbaʿat majlis dāʾirat al-maʿārif al-ʿUthmāniyya, 1377/1958.

Bladel, Kevin van. "Eighth-Century Indian Astronomy in the Two Cities of Peace." *Islamic Cultures, Islamic Contexts: Essays in Honor of Professor Patricia Crone*. Ed. by Behnam Sadeghi, Asad Q. Ahmed, Adam Silverstein and Robert G. Hoyland. Leiden and Boston: Brill, 2015, 257–94.

Blois, François de. *Burzōy's Voyage to India and the Origin of the Book of Kalīlah wa Dimnah*. London: Royal Asiatic Society, 1990.

Bosworth, Clifford E. "Naṣīḥat al-Mulūk." In *The Encyclopaedia of Islam, New Edition*. Ed. by H. A. R. Gibb et als. 13 vols. Leiden: Brill, 1960–2009. https://referenceworks.brillonline.com/entries/encyclopaedia-of-islam-2/*-COM_0850. Accessed September 21, 2022.

Brown, Jonathan AC. "The Last Days of al-Ghazzālī and the Tripartite Division of the Sufi World: Abū Ḥāmid al-Ghazzālī's Letter to the Seljuq Vizier and Commentary." *The Muslim World* 96 (2006): 89–113.

Al-Bukhārī. *Al-Adab al-mufrad = Manners in Islam: (Al Adab Al Mufrad): Arabic - English Text*. Transl. and commentated by Maulana Khalid Khan Garhi. Transl. into English by Rafiq Abdur Rahman. 3rd ed. Beirut: Dār al-kutub al-ʿilmiyya, 2015. (1st edition: Karachi: Darul-Ishaat, 2004).

Al-Bukhārī. *Ṣaḥīḥ = The Translation of the Meanings of Sahîh Al-Bukhâri: Arabic-English*. Transl. by Muhammad Muhsin Khan. 9 vols. Riyadh: Darussalam, 1997.

Bürgel, Johann Christoph. "Language on Trial, Religion at Stake? Trial Scenes in Some Classical Arabic Texts and the Hermeneutic Problems Involved." In *Myths,*

Historical Archetypes and Symbolic Figures in Arabic Literature: Towards a New Hermeneutic Approach: Proceedings of the International Symposium in Beirut, June 25th–June 30th, 1996. Ed. by Angelika Neuwirth, Birgit Embaló, Sebastian Günther and Maher Jarrar. Stuttgart: Franz Steiner Verlag, 1999, 189–204.

Carter, Michael G. "Language Control as People Control in Medieval Islam: The Aims of the Grammarians in Their Cultural Context." *Al-Abḥāth* 31 (1983): 76–84.

Celsus. *On Medicine*. With an English translation by W. G. [Walter George] Spencer. Cambridge, MA: Harvard University Press, 1935.

Cheikh-Moussa, Abdallah. "Du discours autorisé ou comment s'adresser au tyran." *Arabica* 46.2 (1999): 139–75.

Clement of Alexandria. *The Exhortation to the Greeks, The Rich Man's Salvation, To the Newly Baptized*. Transl. by G.W. Butterworth. Cambridge, MA: Harvard University Press, 1919.

Confucius. *Analects*. In *Understanding the* Analects *of Confucius: A New Translation of* Lunyu *with Annotations*. Transl. by Peimin Ni. Albany, NY: State University of New York Press, 2017.

Crone, Patricia. *God's Rule: Government and Islam*. New York: Columbia University Press, 2004. Published in the UK under the title *Medieval Islamic Political Though*. Edinburgh: Edinburgh University Press, 2004.

D'Ancona, Cristina. "Il tema della *docta ignorantia* nel neoplatonismo arabo: Un contributo all'analisi delle fonti di *Teologia di Aristotele, mîmar* II." In *Concordia discors: Studi su Niccolò Cusano e sull'umanesimo europeo offerti a Giovanni Santinello*. Ed. by Gregorio Piaia. Padova: Antenore, 1993, 3–22.

D'Ancona, Cristina. "Greek Sources in Arabic and Islamic Philosophy." In *The Stanford Encyclopedia of Philosophy*. Ed. by Edward N. Zalta. Available online at https://plato.stanford.edu/entries/arabic-islamic-greek/. Accessed September 21, 2022.

Daiber, Hans. "Das *Kitāb al-Ādāb al-kabīr* des Ibn al-Muqaffaʿ als Ausdruck griechischer Ethik, islamischer Ideologie und iranisch-sassanidischer Hofetikette." *Oriens* 43 (2015): 273–92. Reprinted in: Idem. *From the Greeks to the Arabs and Beyond*, Volume 2, *Islamic Philosophy*. Leiden and Boston: Brill, 2021, 224–42.

Daiber, Hans. "The Syriac Tradition in the Early Islamic Era." In *Philosophy in the Islamic World*, Volume 1, *8th–9th Centuries*. Ed by. Ulrich Rudolph, Rotraud Hansberger and Peter Adamson. Transl. by Rotraud Hansberger. Leiden and Boston: Brill, 2017, 74–94.

Daiber, Hans. "*De praedicamento relationis in philosophia arabica et islamica*: The Category of Relation in Arabic-Islamic Philosophy (Extended Version)." *Enrahonar* 61 Supplement Issue (2018): 431–90. Available online at https://ddd.uab.cat/pub/enrahonar/enrahonar_a2018nsupissue/enrahonar_a2018nSupplp431.pdf. Accessed September 21, 2022. Reprinted in: Idem. *From the Greeks to the Arabs and Beyond*, Volume 2, *Islamic Philosophy*. Leiden and Boston: Brill, 2021, 153–223.

Darling, Linda T. *A History of Social Justice and Political Power in the Middle East: The Circle of Justice from Mesopotamia to Globalization*. Abingdon and New York: Routledge, 2013.

Edgerton, Franklin, ed. and transl. *The Pancatantra Reconstructed: An Attempt to Establish the Lost Original Sanskrit Text of the Most Famous of Indian Story-Collections on the Basis of the Principal Extant Versions*, Vol. 1, *Text and Critical Apparatus*, Vol. 2, *Introduction and Translation*. New Haven: American Oriental Society and London: Oxford University Press, 1924. Reprinted New York: Kraus Reprint Corporation, 1967.

Endress, Gerhard and Remke Kruk, eds. *The Ancient Tradition in Christian and Islamic Hellenism: Studies on the Transmission of Greek Philosophy and Sciences Dedicated to H.J. Drossaart Lulofs on His Ninetieth Birthday*. Leiden: Research School CNWS, 1997.

Epictetus. *Discourses, Books 1–2*. Transl. by W.A. Oldfather. Cambridge, MA: Harvard University Press, 1925.

Ess, Josef van. "Some Fragments of the *Muʿāraḍat al-Qurʾān* Attributed to Ibn al-Muqaffaʿ." In *Studia Arabica et Islamica: Festschrift for Iḥsān ʿAbbās*. Ed. by Wadād al-Qāḍī. Beirut: American University of Beirut, 1981, 151–63.

Ess, Josef van. *Theologie und Gesellschaft im 2. und 3. Jahrhundert Hidschra: Eine Geschichte des religiösen Denkens im frühen Islam*. 6 vols. Berlin and New York: Walter de Gruyter, 1991–97.

Forster, Regula and Neguin Yavari, eds. *Global Medieval: Mirrors for Princes Reconsidered*. Boston: Ilex Foundation, 2015.

Ganguli, Kisari Mohan, transl. *The Mahabharata of Krishna-Dwaipayana Vyasa: Translated into English Prose*. Calcutta: Bharata Press, 1883–96.

Al-Ghazālī. *Letter to a Disciple: Ayyuhā 'l-walad*. Ed. and transl. by Tobias Mayer. Cambridge: Islamic Texts Society, 2005.

Gimaret, Daniel, ed. *Kitāb Bilawhar wa-Būdhāsf*. Beirut: Dār al-mashriq, 1972.

Gimaret, Daniel, transl. *Le livre de Bilawhar et Būḏāsf selon la version arabe ismaélienne*. Geneva and Paris: Droz, 1971.

Gregory of Nyssa. *The Lord's Prayer, The Beatitudes*. Transl. by Hilda C. Graef. New York: Newman Press, 1954.

Grignaschi, Mario. "Les *Rasāʾil 'Arisṭāṭālīsa 'ilā-l-Iskandar* de Sālim Abū-l-ʿAlāʾ et l'activité culturelle à l'époque omayyade." *Bulletin d'Études Orientales* 19 (1965–66): 7–83.

Gruendler, Beatrice, "Les versions arabes de *Kalīla wa-Dimna*: Une transmission et une circulation mouvantes." In *Enoncés sapientiels en Méditerranée: Aliento*, vol. 3 = *Enoncés sapientiels et littérature exemplaire: Une intertextualité complexe*. Ed. by Marie-Sol Ortola. Nancy: Presses Universitaires de Nancy, 2013, 387–418.

Gruendler, Beatrice. "*Kalīla wa-Dimna*: A Unique Work of World Literature." In *Arab and German Tales: Transcending Cultures*. Ed. by Verena M. Lepper in collaboration with Sara Aisha Sabea. Berlin: Kadmos, 2018, 67–8.

Gruendler, Beatrice, Jan J. van Ginkel, Rima Redwan, Khouloud Khalfallah, Isabel Toral, Johannes Stephan, Matthew L. Keegan, Theodore S. Beers, Mahmoud Kozae and Marwa M. Ahmed. "An Interim Report on the Editorial and Analytical Work of the AnonymClassic Project." *Medieval Worlds* 11 (2020): 241–79. Available online at https://medievalworlds.net/0xc1aa5576_0x003ba1d6.pdf. Accessed September 21, 2022.

Gruendler, Beatrice et al. *Kalīla and Dimna – AnonymClassic*. Available online at https://www.geschkult.fu-berlin.de/en/e/kalila-wa-dimna/index.html. Accessed September 21, 2022.

Guerrero, Rafael Ramón. "Docta ignorancia en el neopolatonismo árabe?" In *El problema del conocimiento en Nicolás de Cusa: Genealogía y proyección*. Ed. by Jorge M. Machetta and Claudia D'Amico. Buenos Aires: Biblos, 2005, 67–84.

Gutas, Dimitri. "Classical Arabic Wisdom Literature: Nature and Scope." *Journal of the American Oriental Society* 101 (1981): 49–86.

Gutas, Dimitri. *Greek Thought, Arabic Culture: The Graeco-Arabic Translation Movement in Baghdad and Early ʿAbbasid Society (2nd–4th/8th–10th Centuries)*. London and New York: Routledge, 1998.

Gutas, Dimitri. "On Graeco-Arabic Epistolary 'Novels'." *Middle Eastern Literatures* 12.1 (2009): 59–70.

Gutas, Dimitri. "The Rebirth of Philosophy and the Translations into Arabic." In *Philosophy in the Islamic World*, Volume 1, *8th–9th Centuries*. Ed. by Ulrich Rudolph, Rotraud Hansberger and Peter Adamson. Transl. by Rotraud Hansberger. Leiden and Boston: Brill, 2017, 95–142.

Haake, Matthias. "Writing down the King: The Communicative Function of Treatises *On Kingship* in the Hellenistic Period." In *The Splendors and Miseries of Ruling Alone: Encounters with Monarchy from Archaic Greece to the Hellenistic Mediterranean*. Ed. by Nino Luraghi. Stuttgart: Franz Steiner Verlag, 2013, 165–206.

Haake, Matthias. "Writing to a Ruler, Speaking to a Ruler, Negotiating the Figure of the Ruler: Thoughts on 'Monocratological' Texts and Their Contexts in Greco-Roman Antiquity." In *Global Medieval: Mirrors for Princes Reconsidered*. Ed. by Regula Forster and Neguin Yavari. Boston: Ilex Foundation, 2015, 58–82.

Haake, Matthias. "Across All Boundaries of Genre? On the Uses and Disadvantages of the Term *Mirror for Princes* in Graeco-Roman Antiquity – Critical Remarks and Unorthodox Reflections." In *Concepts of Ideal Rulership from Antiquity to the Renaissance*. Ed. by Geert Roskam and Stefan Schorn. Turnhout, Brepols, 2018, 293–327.

Hamori, Andras. "Prudence, Virtue, and Self-Respect in Ibn al-Muqaffaʿ." In *Reflections on Reflections: Near Eastern Writers Reading Literature: Dedicated to Renate Jacobi*. Ed. by Angelika Neuwirth and Andreas Christian Islebe. Wiesbaden: Reichert Verlag, 2006, 161–77.

Hamza, Feras, Sajjad Rizvi, with Farhana Mayer, eds. *An Anthology of Qur'anic Commentaries*, vol. 1 = *On the Nature of the Divine*. Oxford and New York: Oxford University Press and London: in association with The Institute of Ismaili Studies, 2008.

Haribhadra. *Samarādityakathā*, 2.55–80. In *Sources of Indian Tradition*. Ed. by Wm. Theodore de Bary, Stephen Hay, Royal Weiler, Andrew Yarrow. New York: Columbia University Press, 1958. Reprinted Delhi: Motilal Banarsidass, 1963 and 1972, 56–8.

Heck, Paul L. *Skepticism in Classical Islam: Moments of Confusion*. Abingdon, Oxon: Routledge, 2014.

Hermans, Erik. "A Persian Origin of the Arabic Aristotle? The Debate on the Circumstantial Evidence of the Manteq Revisited." *Journal of Persianate Studies* 11 (2018): 72–88.

Hodgson, Marshall G. S. *The Venture of Islam*. Chicago and London: The University of Chicago Press, 1973.

Ikhwān al-Ṣafāʾ. *The Case of the Animals versus Man before the King of the Jinn: A Translation from the Epistles of the Brethren of Purity*. Transl. by Lenn E. Goodman and Richard McGregor. Oxford: Oxford University Press in association with The Institute of Ismaili Studies, 2012.

Inana and Enki. Available at the website of The Electronic Text Corpus of Sumerian Literature (ETCSL), Faculty of Oriental Studies, University of Oxford, 2006. https://etcsl.orinst.ox.ac.uk/cgi-bin/etcsl.cgi?text=t.1.3.1&display=Crit&charenc=gcirc&lineid=t131#t131. Accessed September 21, 2022.

Ismāʿīl, Yūsif Aḥmad. "Tarhīn al-zaman fī *Kalīla wa-Dimna*." *Al-Majalla al-ʿArabiyya li-l-maʿlūm al-insāniyya* 31-121 (2013): 45–75.

(Pseudo-?)al-Jāḥiẓ. "Akhlāq al-kuttāb." In *Three Essays of Abu ʿOthman ʿAmr Ibn Baḥr al-Jaḥiẓ (D. 869)*. Ed. by Joshua Finkel. Cairo: The Salafyah Press, 1344/1926. Reprinted 1382/1962–63, 39–51.

(Pseudo-?)al-Jāḥiẓ. "An Attack on Secretaries." In *The Life and Works of Jāḥiẓ: Translation of Selected Texts*. Transl. by Charles Pellat and transl. from the French by D.M. Hawke. Berkeley and Los Angeles: University of California Press, 1969.

Al-Jahshiyārī. *Kitāb al-Wuzarāʾ wa-l-kuttāb*. Ed. by M. Muṣṭafā al-Saqqā, Ibrāhīm al-Abyārī and ʿAbd al-Ḥafīẓ Shalabī. Cairo: Maṭbaʿat Muṣṭafā al-Bābī al-Ḥalabī wa-awlādihi, 1357/1938.

Al-Jahshiyārī. (al-Ǧahšiyārī). *Das Kitāb al-Wuzarāʾ wa-l-kuttāb des Abū ʿAbdallāh Muḥāmmad Ibn ʿAbdūs al-Ǧahšiyārī*. Ed. by Hans von Mžik. Leipzig, Otto Harrassowitz, 1926.

Janssens, Jules. "Al-Ghazzālī's *Tahāfut*: Is It Really a Rejection of Ibn Sīnā's Philosophy?" *Journal of Islamic Studies* 12.1 (2001): 1–17.

Josephson, Judith. "The Multicultural Background of the *Kitāb al-Ādāb al-kabīr* by ʿAbdallāh Ibn al-Muqaffaʿ." In *Current Issues in the Analysis of Semitic Grammar and Lexicon I: Oslo–Göteborg Cooperation 3rd–5th June 2004*. Ed. by Lutz Edzard and Jan Retsö. Wiesbaden: Harrassowitz, 2005, 166–92.

Kant, Immanuel. "On a Supposed Right to Lie from Philanthropy." In idem. *Practical Philosophy*. Ed. and transl. by Mary J. Gregor. Cambridge: Cambridge University Press, 1996, 605–15.

Keegan, Matthew L. "Before and after Kalīla wa-Dimna: An Introduction to the Special Issue on Animals, Adab, and Fictivity." *Journal of Abbasid Studies* 8 (2021): 1–11.

Keegan, Matthew L. "'Elsewhere Lies Its Meaning': The Vagaries of *Kalīla and Dimna*'s Reception." *Poetica* 52 (2021): 13–40.

Khaleghi-Motlagh, Djalal. "Borzūya." In *Encyclopædia Iranica Online*. Available at http://dx.doi.org/10.1163/2330-4804_EIRO_COM_7095. Accessed September 22, 2022.

Kilito, Abdelfattah. "How Should We Read *Kalila and Dimna*." = Chapter 2, in idem. *Arabs and the Art of Storytelling: A Strange Familiarity*. Transl. by Mbarek Sryfi and Eric Sellin. Syracuse, NY: Syracuse University Press, 2014, 18–29. Originally published in French as *Les Arabes et l'art du récit: Une étrange familiarité*. Paris: Actes Sud, Sindbad, 2009.

Kristó-Nagy, István T. "On the Authenticity of *Al-Adab al-ṣaġīr* Attributed to Ibn al-Muqaffaʿ and Problems concerning Some of His Titles." *Acta Orientalia Scientiarum Hungariae* 62.2 (2009): 199–218.

Kristó-Nagy, István T. "Reason, Religion and Power in Ibn al-Muqaffaʿ." *Acta Orientalia Academiae Scientiarum Hungaricae* 62.3 (2009): 285–301.

Kristó-Nagy, István T. "Who Shall Educate Whom? The Official and the Sincere Views of Ibn al-Muqaffaʿ about Intellectual Hierarchy." In *Synoptikos: Mélanges offerts à Dominique Urvoy*. Ed. by Nicole Koulayan and Sayah Mansour. Toulouse: Presses Universitaires du Mirail, 2011, 279–93.

Kristó-Nagy, István T. *La pensée d'Ibn al-Muqaffaʿ: Un «agent double» dans le monde persan et arabe*. Versailles: Éditions de Paris, 2013.

Kristó-Nagy, István T. "A Violent, Irrational and Unjust God: Antique and Medieval Criticism of Jehovah and Allāh." In *La morale au crible des religions*. Ed. by Marie-Thérèse Urvoy. Versailles: Éditions de Paris, 2013, 143–64.

Kristó-Nagy, István T. "Conflict and Cooperation between Arab Rulers and Persian Administrators in the Formative Period of Islamdom, c. 600–c. 950 ce." In *Empires and Bureaucracy in World History: From Late Antiquity to the*

Twentieth Century. Ed. by Peter Crooks and Timothy Parsons. Cambridge: Cambridge University Press, 2016, 54–80.

Kristó-Nagy, István T. "Marriage after Rape: The Ambiguous Relationship between Arab Lords and Iranian Intellectuals as Reflected in Ibn al-Muqaffaʿ's Oeuvre." In *Tradition and Reception in Arabic Literature: Essays Dedicated to Andras Hamori*. Ed. by Margaret Larkin and Jocelyn Sharlet. Wiesbaden: Harrassowitz Verlag, 2019, 161–88.

Kristó-Nagy, István T. "Wild Lions and Wise Jackals: Killer Kings and Clever Counsellors in *Kalīla wa-Dimna*." In *Prophets, Viziers, and Philosophers: Wisdom and Authority in Early Arabic Literature*. Ed. by Emily J. Cottrell. Groningen: Barkhuis & Groningen University Library, 2020, 147–209.

Kristó-Nagy, István T. "The Crow Who Aped the Partridge: Ibn al-Muqaffaʿ's Aesopian Language in a Fable of *Kalīla wa-Dimna*." *L'Adab toujours recommencé: Origines, transmission et métamorphoses*. Ed. by Catherine Mayeur-Jaouen, Francesca Bellino and Luca Patrizi. Leiden and Boston: Brill, forthcoming.

Kuhn, Ernst. "Der Mann im Brunnen: Geschichte eines indischen Gleichnisses." In *Festgruss an Otto von Böhtlingk*. Ed. by Rudolf von Roth. Stuttgart: W. Kohlhammer, 1888, 68–76.

Lambton, Ann K. S. "Islamic Mirrors for Princes." In *Atti del convegno internazionale sul tema: La Persia nel medioevo (Roma, 31 marzo–5 aprile 1970)*. Rome: Accademia Nazionale dei Lincei, 1971, 419–42. Reprinted in eadem. *Theory and Practice in Medieval Persian Government*. London: Variorum Reprints, 1980.

Latham, J.D. "Ibn al-Muqaffaʿ and Early ʿAbbasid Prose." In *ʿAbbasid Belles-Lettres*. Ed. by Julia Ashtiany. Cambridge and New York: Cambridge University Press, 1990, 48–77.

London, Jennifer. "How to Do Things with Fables: Ibn al-Muqaffaʿ's Frank Speech in Stories from *Kalīla wa Dimna*." *History of Political Thought* 29.2 (2008): 189–212.

London, Jennifer. "The 'Circle of Justice'." *History of Political Thought* 32.3 (2011): 425–47.

London, Jennifer. "The Abbasid 'Circle of Justice': Re-reading Ibn al-Muqaffaʿ's *Letter on Companionship*." In *Comparative Political Theory in Time and Place*. Ed. by Daniel J. Kapust and Helen M. Kinsella. New York: Palgrave Macmillan, 2017, 25–50.

Lugalbanda in the Mountain Cave. Available at the website of *The Electronic Text Corpus of Sumerian Literature (ETCSL)*, Faculty of Oriental Studies, University of Oxford, 2006. https://etcsl.orinst.ox.ac.uk/cgi-bin/etcsl.cgi?text=t.1.8.2.1&display=Crit&charenc=gcirc&lineid=t1821.#t1821. Accessed September 21, 2022.

Marlow, Louise. "Surveying Recent Literature on the Arabic and Persian Mirrors for Princes Genre." *History Compass* 7 (2009): 528–38.

Marlow, Louise. "Advice and Advice Literature." In *The Encyclopaedia of Islam Three*. Ed. by Kate Fleet et al. Leiden and Boston: Brill. Available online at https://referenceworks.brillonline.com/entries/encyclopaedia-of-islam-3/advice-and-advice-literature-COM_0026. Accessed September 21, 2022.

Marlow, Louise. *Hierarchy and Egalitarianism in Islamic Thought*. Cambridge and New York: Cambridge University Press, 1997.

Maróth, Miklós, ed. *The Correspondence between Aristotle and Alexander the Great: An Anonymous Greek Novel in Letters in Arabic Translation*. Piliscsaba: The Avicenna Institute of Middle Eastern Studies, 2006.

Muslim. *Ṣaḥīḥ = English Translation of Sahîh Muslim*. Transl. by Nasiruddin Khattab. 7 vols. Riyadh: Darussalam, 2007.

Peters, F.E. *Aristoteles Arabus: The Oriental Translations and Commentaries on the Aristotelian Corpus*. Leiden: Brill, 1968.

Plato. *Charmides, Alcibiades I and II, Hiparchus, The Lovers, Theages, Minos, Epinomis.* With an English translation by W.R.M. Lamb. London: Heinemann and New York: Putnam, 1927. Reprinted Cambridge, MA: Harvard University Press and London: Heinemann, 1955.

Plato. *The Laws*. Ed. by Malcolm Schofield. Transl. by Tom Griffith. Cambridge and New York: Cambridge University Press, 2016.

Pormann, Peter E. and Emilie Savage-Smith. *Medieval Islamic Medicine*. Edinburgh: Edinburgh University Press, 2007.

Al-Qāḍī, Wadād. "ʿAbd al-Ḥamīd al-Kātib." In *The Encyclopaedia of Islam Three*. Ed. by Kate Fleet et al. Leiden and Boston: Brill. Available online at https://referenceworks.brillonline.com/entries/encyclopaedia-of-islam-3/*-COM_22586. Accessed September 22, 2022.

Al-Qāsim b. Ibrāhīm. *Al-Radd ʿalā al-zindīq al-laʿīn Ibn al-Muqaffaʿ*. In *La lotta tra l'Islam e il Manicheismo: Un libro di Ibn al-Muqaffaʿ contro il Corano confutato da al-Qāsim b. Ibrāhīm*. Ed. and transl. by Michelangelo Guidi. Roma: R. Accademia Nazionale dei Lincei, 1927.

Al-Qurʾan and its English translations accessed at https://corpus.quran.com/translation.jsp. Accessed September 21, 2022.

Rudolph, Ulrich. "The Late Ancient Background." In *Philosophy in the Islamic World*, Volume 1, *8th–9th Centuries*. Ed. by Ulrich Rudolph, Rotraud Hansberger and Peter Adamson. Transl. by Rotraud Hansberger. Leiden and Boston: Brill, 2017, 29–73.

Rudolph, Ulrich, Rotraud Hansberger and Peter Adamson, eds. *Philosophy in the Islamic World*, Volume 1, *8th–9th Centuries*. Transl. by Rotraud Hansberger. Leiden and Boston: Brill, 2017.

Schulthess, Friedrich, ed. and transl. *Kalīla und Dimna: Syrisch und deutsch.* 2 vols. Berlin: Georg Reimer, 1911.

Shaked, Shaul, ed. and transl. *The Wisdom of the Sasanian Sages (Dēnkard VI) by Aturpāt-i Ēmētān*. Boulder, Colorado: Westview Press, 1979.

Street, Tony. "Arabic and Islamic Philosophy of Language and Logic." In *The Stanford Encyclopedia of Philosophy*. Ed. by Edward N. Zalta. Available at https://plato.stanford.edu/entries/arabic-islamic-language/. Accessed September 21, 2022.

Al-Tirmidhī. *Jāmi' = English Translation of Jāmi' At-Tirmidhī*. Transl. by Abu Khaliyl, 6 vols. Riyadh: Darussalam, 2007.

Tor, Deborah G. "The Islamisation of Iranian Kingly Ideals in the Persianate Fürstenspiegel." *Iran* 49 (2011): 115–22.

Treiger, Alexander. *Inspired Knowledge in Islamic Thought: Al-Ghazālī's Theory on Mystical Cognition and Its Avicennian Foundation*. London and New York: Routledge, 2012.

Ullman, Manfred. "Ḫālid ibn Yazīd und die Alchemie: Eine Legende." *Der Islam* 55 (1978): 181–218.

Urvoy, Dominique. "Autour d'Ibn al-Muqaffa'." In idem. *Les penseurs libres dans l'Islam classique: L'interrogation sur la religion chez les penseurs arabes indépendants*. Paris: Albin Michel, 1996, 29–66.

Urvoy, Dominique. "La démystification de la religion dans les textes attribués à Ibn al-Muqaffa'." In *Atheismus im Mittelalter und in der Renaissance*. Ed. by Friedrich Niewöhner and Olaf Pluta. Wolfenbüttel: Herzog August Bibliothek, 1999, 85–94.

Watt, W.M. "The Authenticity of the Works Attributed to al-Ghazālī." *Journal of Royal Asiatic Society* 84.1/2 (1952): 24–45.

Wildberg, Christian. "Neoplatonism." In *The Stanford Encyclopedia of Philosophy*. Ed. by Edward N. Zalta. Available at https://plato.stanford.edu/entries/neoplatonism/. Accessed September 21, 2022.

Yavari, Neguin. *Advice for the Sultan: Prophetic Voices and Secular Politics in Medieval Islam*. London: Hurst & Company, 2014.

3

The Sorcerer Scholar: Sirāj al-Dīn al-Sakkākī between Grammar and Grimoire

Emily Selove and Mohammed Sanad

Introduction

Sirāj al-Dīn al-Sakkākī was born in Khwarazm in 555/1160. His *Miftāḥ al-ʿulūm* (The Key to the Sciences) is an influential text on the study of the Arabic language. Besides being an expert of language, Sakkākī was also known as a magician; his biographers tell us that his powers gained him a position in the court of Chagatai Khan (r. 1227–42 CE), son of Chinggis Khan, where he is said to have captured birds out of the sky using magical inscriptions. Moreover, a contemporary account credits him with influencing a power struggle between the Abbasid caliph and the Khwarazmian Shah with a buried enchanted statue. One 19th-century biography (Khwānsārī's *Rawḍāt al-jannāt*) describes a work of Sakkākī on the subject of magic and talismans as being "of significant power and critical importance" (*kitāb jalīl al-qadr wa-ʿaẓīm al-khaṭar*).[1] Unlike his famous book of language, this book of magic has not yet been edited, translated, or studied by modern scholars, and this is the goal of the current Leverhulme-funded project, "A Sorcerer's Handbook."

Our translation of the title of this book, *Kitāb al-Shāmil wa-baḥr al-kāmil,* as *The Book of the Complete* is informed by a reading of its introduction, which refers to the "perfect" scholars of the ancient world on which it bases its information, hence, "The book of the Perfect/Complete person." It is probable that the title is a play on that of the 11th-century book of magic, *al-Shāmil fī l-baḥr al-kāmil* (Complete Book of the Perfect Sea) by Ṭabasī.[2] In the case of Sakkākī's grimoire, the focus moves from the book itself to the complete men, or the "perfect friends of God" (*awliyāʾihi al-kāmilīn*) to whom he refers immediately before presenting the title of his work.[3] These perfect embodiments of the microcosm serve as conduits between heaven and earth,[4] and are uniquely qualified to practice these dangerous forms of elite knowledge. We can read Sakkākī himself as the *Shāmil* (complete) man to whom the title refers. As this essay will demonstrate, he leaves nothing out of his microcosmic grimoire, which encompasses the darkest as well as the loftiest regions of the cosmos. He includes a mixed and varied collection of texts dealing with occult matters, including instructions for creating talismans in tune with their various astrological sympathies, for controlling *jinn* and devils, for causing sickness, for curing such magically-caused afflictions, and for calling upon the power of each of the planets (among other topics).

According to his biographies, and as his name, al-Sakkākī (the die caster) suggests, he began life as a metal worker, beginning his career in scholarship at the relatively late age of 30.[5] And as a former metal worker, the art of melting and pouring metal continued to loom large in Sakkākī's mind; he mentions it in the first words of the introduction to his famous book of language, the *Miftāḥ al-ʿulūm* ("speech poured out only in the mould of truth [. . .]" We quote the introduction more fully below). The verb *yufrigh*, to pour molten metal into a mould, is also used repeatedly in Sakkākī's *Shāmil*, which provides numerous detailed practical descriptions of the creation of talismans and statues, many of which involve melting and pouring gold and other metals.[6]

Though he went on to become an authority of the Arabic language, Sakkākī's Arabic language skills were far from "complete" by the time he wrote his grimoire. According to the colophon of our oldest manuscript witness,[7] the *Shāmil* was penned in 602 AH (1205 CE), when the author would have been about 45 years old. That he was a native Persian speaker and a latecomer to scholarship is everywhere apparent in his grimoire, and it may be that fifteen years was insufficient time for him to master the scholarly registers of Arabic,[8] for *The Book of the Complete* is written in a mixed formal and colloquial register that could be described as a type of Middle Arabic. It often ignores gender agreement and other basic standards of formal Arabic grammar, lapsing sometimes into Persian, perhaps especially when addressing the *jinn* (whom, we assume, were local to his area and therefore spoke the local language). Thus, the Arabic of his grimoire is very unlike that of his *Miftāḥ al-ʿulūm*, which is a *tour de force* of formal Arabic prosody, and which, we must assume, was written much later in his life. The linguistic register of his grimoire is possibly also a sign that it was in part collected as notes by his students or by his son (himself an author of occult writings). This is suggested by the frequent attributions at the beginning of sections chapters (e.g., *qāla mawlānā jāmiʿ al-kitāb shaykh Sirāj al-Dīn al-Sakkākī* [. . .] ["Our master, the compiler of the book, Shaykh Sirāj al-Dīn al-Sakkākī said [. . .]"]).[9] Other sections, and the colophon itself, suggests that Sakkākī wrote some of his grimoire in his own hand.[10]

Sakkākī's Reputation

Few modern scholars have mentioned Sakkākī's book of magic,[11] focusing instead on his work on grammar and language, the *Miftāḥ*. His *Encyclopaedia of Islam* entry states that "In spite of a number of lost or doubtful works that have been ascribed to him, al-Sakkākī is really a man of one book, the *Miftāḥ al-ʿulūm*."[12] An abridgement of this *Miftāḥ* is still widely used to study the Arabic language today, and Sakkākī's name is now famous for that reason alone. Like his work on language, he is therefore assumed to have been a hyper-logical and probably somewhat boring man.[13]

For Sakkākī and his contemporaries, however, his reputation as a sorcerer was a crucial asset, and one that often outweighed his reputation as a scholar of language. So notorious was his reputation for magic that some biographers writing before 1900 CE mention his grammatical writings only in passing while focusing instead on his role as a court magician and astrologer. A contemporary account of Sakkākī's life in Nasawī's *Sīrat al-Sulṭān Jalāl al-Dīn Mankubirtī* tells how he aided the Khwarazmian Shah ʿAlāʾ al-Dīn Muḥammad (r. 596–617/1200–1220) in his attempt to overtake the Abbasids by causing an enchanted statue to be buried in Baghdad. (He promised it would help the Shah, but its curse rebounded on Khwarazm and strengthened the armies of Baghdad instead.)[14] And Sakkākī's *Shāmil* is indeed filled with recipes for enchanted statues, some of which repel or attract military forces. Nasawī's biography also credits Sakkākī with the ability to "stop water flowing with his curses," and in fact his *Shāmil* provides instructions on the art of "halting the flow of all running water in whichever land you wish," by means of burying a brass model ship loaded with a dead fox and mustard seeds, and by reciting the names of angels at the correct astrological moment.[15] His biography and his grimoire therefore reinforce one another in the portrait they paint of Sakkākī as a sorcerer.

A much later (sixteenth-century) Persian history, Khwāndamīr's *Ḥabīb al-siyar*, introduces him as the author of the *Miftāḥ*, but then devotes the rest of its account to his role as a court magician, including a story in which he brings cranes down from the sky by drawing a magic circle on the ground. The use of magic circles (*mandal*s) and instructions for attracting or repelling birds and other animals can also be found in his *Shāmil*.[16] Khwāndamīr adds that when the vizier of Baghdad offended Sakkākī, he caused all the fires in the city to die out, and would not let them be relit until the vizier kissed a dog's arse, and issued a proclamation acknowledging Sakkākī's magical prowess. This shocking biography concludes with a fatal battle between Sakkākī and his rival at the court of Chagatai Khan. Sakkākī caused this rival to be banished from the court, convincing the ruler that his astrological chart showed him to be on the verge of a period of bad luck. Later Sakkākī attacked him with a fiery apparition by using the power of Mars. This rival finally convinced the Khan that Sakkākī's magical powers made him dangerous, so Sakkākī was put in jail, where he died.[17]

Powerful Illusions

Though the biographies depict the very real and dangerous forces that he wielded, it is also clear that illusion, performance, and manipulation of the truth were important tools for Sakkākī as a court magician. Magic and trickery often go hand in hand;[18] indeed the term *nīranj* "from a Persian word for creating illusions," is also used in the *Shāmil* and similar texts to refer to a talisman-like spell characterized as the action of spirit on spirit.[19] And just as a magician might influence the spirit of an animal in order to capture it by magical means, a trickster might influence the spirit of a gullible person by means of trickery. Sakkākī's grimoire includes a *nīranj* for creating illusion, which, like the fiery visions sent against his rival at court, are born of a blend of genuine power and terrifying deception:

> As for the *nīranj* of deceiving appearances, for this, one takes ten human hairs and the clippings of his fingernails of two barleycorns'-weight, and writes these letters on a sheet of scroll, and wraps it in the hair, and suffumigates it with the fingernail clippings, and afterwards you burn the incense of the lunar mansion, while you read the names of the six angels, and say, "Penetrate, spirits of fear, illusion, and terror, this work and this *nīranj*, until its victim cannot rest nor be quiet nor smile at anything he sees!" Then bury the work in front of his eyes, and this is what is in the scroll: [symbols on a spiral square]. By these means you will reach you goal, and [by] your retention of the letters and figures, so be advised.[20]

The power behind Sakkākī's illusions lies in language, and in the mastery and manipulation of symbols and signs ("letters and figures"). By this art, he sought to survive in the turmoil of his era. Anxiety about the power of language in times of turmoil stretched far beyond the confines of the royal courts and is widespread in Arabic literature. The most famous literary manifestation of this anxiety is the genre of the *maqāmāt,* whose trickster protagonists sometimes appear as charlatan magicians, influencing the spirits of their listeners with tricky language alone. In the *Maqāmāt* of al-Hamadhānī (d. 398/1008) the narrator, ʿĪsā b. Hishām, famously fails to recognise the trickster Abū l-Fatḥ al-Iskandarī as he delivers speeches, preaches, and begs under many disguises. One of these stories is directly related to Sakkākī's text: the *maqāma* of the amulet (*al-ḥirziyya*). In this story, the trickster extorts money from terrified passengers on a ship in a stormy sea by selling them amulets (consisting of slips of paper, presumably inscribed with magic words or symbols), which he promises will keep them safe from drowning. If the ship had sunk, he reasons at the end of the tale, nobody would have been around to blame him in any case. In Sakkākī's *Book of the Complete*, we have an example of the sort of spell the trickster may have pretended to offer to his fellow passengers: "The moon is also for protection of a ship at sea from sinking. Go to a secluded location and draw a picture of the ship on some paper, and suffumigate it with frankincense, sandarac, and thalia, with these words surrounding it [. . .]."[21] We can safely assume that Abū l-Fatḥ spared himself the expense of the incense when creating his scraps of "talismanic" paper. He could rely on his eloquence alone to hoodwink his audience, if not to save a sinking ship.

The Magical *Miftāḥ*

In the light of his biography as a court magician, with all its tales of power, illusion, and eloquence, Sakkākī's seemingly dry and upstanding work on language, the *Miftāḥ al-ʿulūm*, takes on an occult appearance. His references to the *siḥr* (sorcery) of rhetoric no longer sounds like a metaphor. He refers to his master in the art of "greater derivation" (on which see more below) as a kind of wizard (*nawʿ min saḥara*) of language.[22] The study of this art, and other elements of *ṣarf* (morphology), he writes, allows you to perceive the intelligent design of the "coiner" of language (*al-wāḍiʿ*), whether that coiner was God or an ancient wise man.[23]

As Sakkākī explains in his *Miftāḥ*, the letters themselves and the forms of words have *khawāṣṣ* (special properties), the same word used to refer to the hidden properties of gemstones, plants, and other magical tools found in occult texts. His *Miftāḥ*'s introduction includes a categorisation of letters according to these special properties,[24] a theme he resumes much later, when introducing his chapter on metaphor. Letters have *khawāṣṣ*, he writes there, but they are not intrinsically connected to the meanings of the words themselves. Rather they could be called symbols (*ramz*), linked by their properties of hardness or softness, and by the places they are formed in the mouth, to the things they describe.[25] These special properties of letter are similar to the *khawaṣṣ* of the gemstones which he describes in his *Shāmil*, linked by their texture, their color, and the places from which they are extracted, to the magical effects that they can be manipulated to produce. Like letters and words, gemstones are strung together for powerful results, and mined from the depths of the unseen treasures of creation.[26]

The *Miftāḥ* itself, writes Sakkākī, is meant to provide the *kāmil* (perfect) person (and here we hear an echo of the *Kitāb al-Shāmil wa-baḥr al-kāmil*) to the key (*miftāḥ*) to the sciences (*al-ʿulūm*), or to "all scientific issues" as he puts it (*jamīʿ al-maṭālib al-ʿilmiyya*).[27] Given his reputation, "all scientific issues" certainly include the occult sciences, with its manipulations of gemstones, incense, planets, spirits, and human hearts. Language is the key to these powers.

Those Who Know and Those Who Don't

Sakkākī claims that the labor of the *Miftāḥ* was undertaken as a penance to lessen his torments in the grave, for it may help people to avoid errors in language, a dangerous tool.[28] Although after Sakkākī's death, al-Khaṭīb al-Qazwīnī (d. 739/1338) abridged and adopted his work into the usefully didactic *Talkhīṣ* of the *Miftāḥ*, and thus fulfilled this stated goal. Sakkākī wrote the *Miftāḥ* itself as a master of an esoteric art, and in forbiddingly intricate language, often inaccessible to those not already initiated into the dark arts of Arabic grammar. The introduction to the *Miftāḥ* refers to the power of language to influence the listener, and names the Qur'an as containing the most powerful language of all. It then categorises people into two sorts – those with the capacity to follow the fiercely obscure and difficult text to follow, and those without, for whom it would be dangerous to try. These are implicitly linked to those who would try in vain to understand or imitate the language of the Qur'an, and, having failed, take up barbaric arms in their frustration. Sakkākī frames this argument within the standard opening format of virtually all Muslim Arabic books of the era, namely, in praise to God, the Prophet, and his family:

> The worthiest speech that tongues fervently repeat and whose pages are not folded by the passage of time is speech poured out only in the mould of truth and woven only on the pattern of veracity. It is fitting that you should accept it willingly when its flow bends the ear, and when it unveils its face, leaving no doubt hanging on the train of its gown. First, it is praise of God Almighty and the adoration due to Him forever from time immemorial, which praises are strung ever anew as on a string of pearls. Second, it is prayers of peace upon His beloved, Muḥammad the warner and bringer of glad tidings, in the illuminating Arabic book that bears witness to the truth of his call with the perfection of its eloquence, and which incapacitates the pontificating masses from desiring to match it by silencing the prattle of every pompous voice, and darkening the path so that the face of the way of imitation is obscured, until they give up trying to match it with letters, and try to fight it with swords, and give up speaking with lips, to try to beat it with spear tips, with their injustice, their hatred, their stubbornness, and their wrangling. And third, it is for the family of the prophet and his illustrious, guiding companions, the leaders of Islam.[29]

He returns to this theme of contrasting eloquence with ignorance at the end of his explanation of the derivation of words from root letters. He curtails the discussion, he says, for those who are clever will find it sufficient, while those who are not are the "slow ones who, by God, would never derive any benefit even if you read the entire

Torah and the Bible to them!"[30] (It is apparent in his grimoire that he considers both texts to hold enormous power, second only, perhaps, to the Qurʾan itself).

His approach can be contrasted with that of Abū Hilāl al-ʿAskarī's (d. 395/1005) *al-Ṣināʿatayn* (The "Two Arts" [i.e., of poetry and prose]), whose introduction blesses and welcomes the reader, making its didactic aim clear.[31] Meanwhile Sakkākī's *Miftāḥ* intimidates the reader, going on to warn that most people will be unable to understand him, and for such people, the small knowledge that they will gain might be a danger to them.[32] He returns to these dangers again in his conclusion, as we explain farther below.

As Hisashi Obuchi's contribution to this present volume shows, al-Kashshī, a contemporary of Sakkākī, praised writing for its ability to spread true knowledge, but equally blamed it for spreading false and misleading information. We may ask ourselves why Sakkākī allowed his *Miftāḥ*, let alone his grimoire, to be recorded on paper, if he considered his knowledge so dangerous. For though the information he provides contains profound truth, it may easily fall into the wrong hands. It seems that he did, however, believe a select few not only could but should benefit from even his most esoteric teachings, and indeed states in his grimoire that its rituals (even, it is implied, those aimed at contacting Satan) are "permitted to the wise [. . .]. Therefore, if someone were to forbid you to learn this, do not listen to them."[33] Again in the chapter on rituals of India, he says "we have mentioned one [ritual] that is hidden from creation, but not hidden from the deserving, and whoever forbids it to one of merit is unjust."[34] Even in a cautionary tale directly pertaining to the dangers of written material, in which a student of magic misleads himself by reading grimoires without proper instruction, he includes an admonition that one should not deny occult knowledge to a student who has proven himself worthy.[35] Perhaps the obscurity of the language of the *Miftāḥ* was itself a guard against the uninitiated. As for the *Shāmil*, it seems a written trace of an oral tradition, and is missing sections that we must assume were to be completed in private dialogue with a master – for example, a ritual to summon seven *jinn* requires the inscription of seven verses of the Qurʾan on seven pieces of paper, but only six verses are provided.[36] The ritual to invoke Venus requires that five gowns of five different colours be worn, but only four colours are divulged.[37]

It is easy to understand why such occult rituals could be dangerous, but why guard mastery of language so closely? In effect, the powers and dangers of both are one and the same. In his *Miftāḥ,* Sakkākī promises that the art of metaphor and simile (*majāz*) "if mastered, will allow you to grasp the reins of rhetorical sorcery."[38] This is because they pertain to the connections (*mulāzamāt*) between *maʿānī* ("meanings"). As Key explains in his *Language between God and the Poets,* although we may have "false cognitions" of *maʿnā*,[39] accurate accounts provide a way to understand God and his creation.[40] Ibn Manẓūr defines *siḥr* (sorcery) as "transforming something from its *ḥaqīqa* (true meaning) to something else."[41] This is similar to the definition of *majāz* (metaphor), which implies a mental insight into the *ḥaqīqa* (the meaning set for a word by the "coiner") followed by an effort to apply that word to something else. As in magic, where deceptive powers may alter the true appearance of a thing to terrifying effect, while true understanding of magic reveals and magnifies the hidden connections in God's creation, metaphor and the poetic power of language can either mislead or illuminate with the connections they create.[42]

The Sun Is a Pot of Gold

Sakkākī begins his discussion of metaphor with the simplest of examples – obvious comparisons based on the senses. For example, roses are red, like cheeks.[43] A cheek is like a rose. From there, his comparisons grow increasingly mental, manneristic, and complex – these are the more advanced levels of the metaphor. One of the most extended compares the sun at length to pot of melting gold:

> When you compared [the sun] to a crucible of molten gold [. . .] in its total form, including its roundness, the purity of its colour, its unity of movement, and the appearance of an alteration between expansion and contraction, because when gold is heated and melts in a crucible, and begins moving all around without boiling, it takes on the round shape of the crucible, and that movement is wondrous, as if it is trying to spread and overflow the sides of the crucible with its fine liquid nature, but then it realises that it must return to its confines, because of the perfect coherence of its constituents and the strength of its internal bonds, and the crucible, moving in answer to its movement, creates together with the melted gold the form that I mentioned. For the sun, if a person examines it carefully in order to understand its essence, is found to be constituted of two forms [. . .].[44]

Thus the sun is like the crucible on one hand, and the melted gold on the other – or to put it in more modern terms, a constant balance between explosive fusion and gravity.

This description of the movement of molten gold within a crucible, dramatically expanded from the versions found in works by his predecessors al-Jurjānī (fl. 441/1050) and Fakhr al-Dīn al-Rāzī (d. 606/1210), is clearly written by a man with personal experience of molten metal.[45] He shows an enthusiasm for this metaphor absent in Jurjānī's and Rāzī's analyses. For example, Sakkākī describes the movement of the molten gold in the crucible as "wondrous" (*ʿajība*), and goes on to speak of it in grammatical terms that depict the gold as a conscious being, using verbs that suggest awareness, such as "trying to" (*yahummu*) and "then it realizes that" (*thumma yabdū lahu*). In contrast, Jurjānī's and Rāzī's analyses of this same metaphor are systematic and impersonal, using the metaphor to illustrate their point without evincing any special predilection for or interaction with the image. In general, we could describe Sakkākī's version of this synonym as more literary than that of his predecessors – an honour he pays to this image presumably because of his own experience with metalwork. As he himself points out in his book of language, a person's personal and professional experiences provide the basis from which they choose metaphorical images that speak most powerfully to them.[46]

Moreover, we find in his grimoire that he specifically associates the sun with the minting of money and coins (*al-ḍarb wa-l-sikka*), the same root (s-k-k) from which his own name, al-Sakkākī, is derived.[47] That is to say, these crafts are governed by that heavenly body, whose aid can be sought in their practice. He ends his prescribed address to the sun with this prayer, appropriate for a craftsman who had sought (as his biography relates) royal patronage for his crafts:[48]

> You are [. . .] the Sun [. . .] endowed with awesome strength [. . .]. Fulfil my needs for might, elevation, security, comfort, acceptance, beautiful gifts, and generous grants, especially from kings and sultans, looking upon me with a favouring eye, and with tenderness and spontaneous love, and with requests for works of craftmanship, so that you make them and all great and noble men and kings and sultans avid for all of my weavings, and carefully preserving all of my crafts, thus making my deeds beautiful, comely, and prized in the eyes of all creation [. . .].

If we are correct that his grimoire was written long before his book of language, he was perhaps praying to the sun to show his metalwork in the best light long before he took up the sun-as-molten-metal metaphor and reworked it in his famous book of language. In his *Miftāḥ,* Sakkākī follows this extended metaphor with several more heavenly body-based examples of complex correspondence, where the likeness is not one to one, but implies a broad range of sensual and intellectual resemblances (e.g., a battle is like a night of falling stars, or Mars and Jupiter are like a person going home from a party holding a candle).[49] These heavenly-body based images go on for several pages and dominate his discussion of complex metaphor, again reminding us of his grimoire, full of heavenly bodies and their many corresponding forces on earth.

His description of the molten gold in the crucible as "wondrous" (*ʿajīb*) further links us to his grimoire, where he describes the actions of his talismans with the same adjective. There he seems to employ the adjective as a category – a wonder of God's creation, a clue or a sign that reveals, in its miraculous workings, a hidden connection between disparate entities.

The experience of wonder (*ʿajab*) provides a strong link between rhetoric and magic more generally. Lara Harb has shown that the ability to create the feeling of wonder by use of complex metaphors and similes is fundamental to the power of language. The wonder that strange metaphors excites drives the listener to exert himself in making the necessary connections, and thereby to learn more about God's creation.[50] But even this function is not without danger; Harb writes of Sakkākī's predecessor in the arts of language, al-Jurjānī: "He goes on to compare the seductiveness of poetry to that of idols for their worshipers, and compares the magical ability of the poet to alter substances and change qualities to that of alchemy and elixir."[51]

As we saw implied in his introduction to the *Miftāḥ*, translated above, such rhetorical sorcery is reserved for the advanced practitioner. We are reminded of an anecdote in his *Shāmil* (to which we previously referred) about a man who tried to contact spirits without a teacher at the age of fifteen and gave up when his efforts met with little success. Later, when in his fifties, he met a shaykh who could show him the right way. This shaykh threw his students' old books into the sea and made him promise never again to meddle ignorantly with these practices, for by doing so, he was merely serving Satan and his demonic forces. Such arts, he explains, cannot be obtained properly except after a rigorous period of prayer, abstention, and study of the Holy Text.[52]

Similarly, one must not rush too precipitously into the advanced practice of language and metaphor. The macrocosmic associations that Sakkākī's complex, planetary metaphors evoke are built upon the microcosmic workings of the words and letters themselves, the special properties of every letter, the echo of significances of words of related roots (*al-ishtiqāq al-akbar*), and the subtle alchemy of morphology and syntax, all of which the *Miftāḥ* has just spent four hundred pages exhaustively and often tediously laying bare.

Poetry on Purpose

It is in first mentioning the *ishtiqāq al-akbar* (greater derivation) that he brings up his (otherwise unknown) teacher in the arts of language. The science of relating words that share root letters (say, for example, the words "king" and "speech" (*malik* and *kalām*) has occult resonances,[53] and Sakkākī fawns over his master in the linguistic art of greater derivation, the "shaykh al-Ḥātimī (may God have mercy on him)" calling him "a kind of sorcerer in this art the likes of which has never been seen before."[54] He then lapses into fervent and poetic praise of the man, who clearly held the same status in his eyes as his masters in magic and their ancient forebears, whom he similarly praises in his grimoire.[55] He praises Ḥātimī again and with equal ebullience in his discussion on poetry,[56] where he states that his teacher defined poetry as speech which is intentionally metrical – speech which is metered *on purpose* – a crucial theme to which we will return again shortly. But we will first briefly clarify the links between magic and poetry (or *siḥr ḥalāl* [halal sorcery], as it is often known).

Apparent metaphors used in poetry, e.g., the comparison of a beautiful beloved to a gazelle, reappear in books of magic, where gazelle skins are used as the material support for love spells. Many commonly-used metaphors of poetry are similarly found in magic. Musk and camphor, for example, two types of incense linked to Venus, at least in one version of such lists that Sakkākī provides,[57] are frequent adornments of love poetry, as are myrtle- used in love *nīranj* of the tenth lunar mansion, and sweet basil, an image of which is used in a love *nīranj* of the 13th lunar mansion. These ingredients of love magic represent the beloved's enchanting appearance and manners in love poetry ("Down above her lip like sweet basil [. . .]. Her breath is ambergris and musk/ Her teeth are pearls and camphor [. . .]").[58] Jupiter, the Pleiades, and obviously the moon, are likewise used as metaphors for human beauty, but not Mars, despite its bright and attractive red colour. Its martial qualities would render the comparison ridiculous, in love poetry and gentle love magic alike.

Meanwhile we find in satire that an ugly man scowls like he just bit an onion or ate a radish! He has a face like he squirted mustard up his nose.[59] Mustard and radishes are used for spells of hatred, spells of violent love conducted with the aid of Mars.[60]

There is nothing particularly startling in all this: indeed, some of these associations seem too obvious to point out – they are linked so clearly to the spices' pleasant or unpleasant taste or odour. But that simply proves the primacy of affect, the deep, intuitive, emotional connections we experience that are prior to and at the root and heart of language, the music and metaphor that gave birth even to scientific discourse. Which is to say, the obviousness of these links exactly reveals the hidden connections between ourselves and the rest of creation, those hidden links and currents needed to produce effective poetry and magic.

The *shāʿir* (poet) is "the knower," the "feeler," who has a special talent for sniffing out these connections, these metaphors that Sakkākī says are the key to rhetorical sorcery.[61] But the basic definition of poetry is less mysterious – it is speech with meter and rhyme.

Poetry must have rhyme and meter on purpose, he writes.[62] If you are buying aubergines in the market, and accidentally enquire after their price in metrical speech, this is not poetry (I loosely translate this transaction as "How much for your aubergines. One coin, but will you try our beans?").[63] Only if you do this *intentionally* is it poetry, Sakkākī emphasises.

A Powerful Muse

But what if poetry is inspired by the *jinn*? How much control do poets have over their *jinn*? If the *jinn* inspires you to recite a poem, do you recite it intentionally? A.S. Tritton writes in "Spirits and Demons in Arabia," "During a discussion between two poets one said: 'I say a poem every hour, but you compose one a month; How is this?' The other said: 'I do not accept from my *shaiṭān* what you accept from yours.'"[64]

Likewise, the soothsayers may deliver oracles when they are inspired by a *jinn*, but are they *majnūn* (insane)? Of course, the prophet himself was accused of being *majnūn*. Michael Dols writes that when he received his revelations, his critics first accused him of being possessed, but then, when told that "here is no choking, spasmodic movements and whispering [*waswasa*]," they suggested instead that he was a poet. This accusation was in turn rejected due to the lack of metre in his speech, nor did his actions quite match those of a sorcerer, as he did not spit on knots, nor those of a soothsayer, because he did not produce unintelligible murmuring rhymed speech.[65]

As for Sakkākī, he is at pains to prove that the prophet was not himself the author of the Qur'an, and he ends his *Miftāḥ* with a passionate defence of this argument.[66] Anyone, he writes, who would claim otherwise knows nothing of language (or of "secrets" [*asrār*], he vaguely adds), "and their leaders are animals who only lick the trash of philosophy[. . .] and spout nonsense with their tongues stuck out like panting dogs [. . .]").

In both the introduction and conclusion of his *Miftāḥ*, Sakkākī argues that it is of prime importance to gain, by painstaking effort, mastery over the Arabic language in order, first and foremost, to understand the Qur'an as well as possible, and to avoid hateful errors such as these. By studying the arts of grammar, one can refute those who criticize the Qur'an as self-contradictory, repetitive, and, in short, written by a human. In his introduction, Sakkākī warned us that a partial study of grammar leads to overconfidence and can be dangerous in the wrong hands, and in his conclusion, he provides examples of those who think they understand language, but whose incomplete knowledge leads them further into error. In refuting these arguments, he demonstrates another point from his introduction, that an in-depth study of language reveals the profound logic at the root of its smallest details, and the wisdom of the one who first designed it.[67] An incomplete knowledge of grammar, it is implied, could lead one to misinterpret God's word, and thus lead to grave error or even damnation.

Meanwhile, in his *Shāmil*, verses of the Qur'an are woven together into powerful invocations by which to subdue devils and *jinn*; he spells out the obvious dangers of this practice as well: that these *jinn* will destroy you if you show fear, or fail to produce the ritual correctly. In both cases, knowledge of language is the key to true knowledge of the Holy Text, and thus the surest route to confidence, power, and safety.

In refuting the claim that the prophet was the author of the Qur'an (as opposed to God Himself), Sakkākī first admits that the prophet was the most eloquent of Arabs. Even so, he writes, he could never have fooled the other Arabs, those masters of language, into thinking that God was the author of a text that he wrote himself.

After all, the early satirists Jarīr and Farazdaq were so advanced in their mastery of language, and so consequently tuned into the "unknown", that they could anticipate one another's verses, predicting word for word a poem the other would recite (indeed it was said that they shared an inspiring *jinn*). Moreover, they could pick, at first hearing, one plagiarised line out of a lengthy poem, identifying its original author merely by the style. How then could the prophet have tricked his fellow eloquent Arabs into believing that God and not he was the author of the holy text? Their mastery of language preserved them from this dangerous error.

One particularly amusing anecdote from this section, provided as another example the Arabs' sensitivity for the subtleties of language, depicts an Arab woman named Sukayna criticising the poetry of both Jarīr and Farazdaq in turn. Turning her attention to a line of love poetry, which praises the poet's relationship with his beloved by rejoicing that they "both like the same things," Sukayna asks if the poet is implying that he likes being penetrated, or relishes playing the passive role in sex (as his female beloved presumably does).[68] Thus does Sukayna show how an ill-chosen turn of phrase can render a poet not an object of envy but a laughing stock. We find obvious parallels with the care that must be taken in uttering magical incantations: one may seek control over the *jinn*, but find oneself through carelessness – a misspoken word or phrase – dominated by them instead, or as you might say, "screwed" – the passive rather than the active partner in the relationship.

Sakkākī the Man

Sakkākī emphasises control in his *Miftāḥ*. In his promise to unveil the secrets of metaphor, he writes, "We shall drive them to you in an orderly file, the leader of their pack of benefits in chains, arranging them in an order that tightens the bridle back on the faces of their precious pearls."[69] All in all, he seems like a man who strives to keep a firm grasp on his *jinn*. In his *Shāmil*, the *jinn* are only to be addressed in a state of absolute ritual purity and under carefully determined astrological circumstances. They are to be faced without fear and ordered firmly in the name of whichever Holy Text they would best respond to (the Qur'an for Muslim *jinn*, but the texts of the Christians, Jews, or Zoroastrians if attempting to control Christian, Jewish, or Zoroastrian *jinn*. When attempting to expel *jinn* of undetermined faith from an epileptic, he recommends "any incantation that is formidable and awe-inspiring").[70] Even in, for example, invoking the power of Venus, Sakkākī's ritual is relatively restrained compared to a similar ceremony in Rāzī's *al-Sirr al-maktūm*.[71] Sakkākī largely avoids methods which might put mental control at risk, namely, the use of sex and wine as ritual tools (indeed he implies in his *Miftāḥ* that he has never tasted wine, when he writes that it is as sweet as a lover's kiss "or so people claim.")[72]

Again, this seems to be a symptom of his desire for self-control, more than an unwillingness to overstep the bounds of decorum. In fact, his willingness to go beyond the limits of proper conduct in his magical practice earned him the opprobrium of some commentators. Zadeh writes "Al-Sakkākī was also held out, even in occult literature, as an object lesson for transgressing the bounds of probity."[73] But like other famous transgressors in the history of Arabic literature (Abū Nuwās springs naturally to mind), he was nevertheless a pious Muslim of passionate faith; he was a man of microcosmic contradictions.

Nor was he devoid of a sense of humour – a trait especially apparent in his chapter on *faṣl wa-waṣl* (detachment and conjunction), in which he explains the importance of joining words and phrases with appropriate links:[74]

> If someone said, "Zayd has gone away, there are 30 degrees in the constellation Aries, the Caliph's sleeve is extremely long, I really need to vomit, the people of Byzantium are Christian, there is a bulginess about the eye of the fly, Galen was a skilled physician, it is *sunna* to read the Qur'an in *tarāwīḥ*, and monkeys look like people," and he used "and" to connect [these sentences together], he would be kicked out of the category of the smart people club, recorded among the ranks of the perfectly silly, or counted as a laughingstock. If taken to the extreme, such an ordering might be considered the work of a joker, a vessel of rare nonsense, as opposed to if he had thrown the sentences out like so many nuts and stones without seeking to link them together.

Although we have painted Sakkākī as a man with an interest in the darkest of the dark arts, and with a somewhat terrifying desire for control, it is clear in this passage that he also had a playful side. But his interests in the images and tools of occult ritual loom even beneath this light-hearted discussion, which he first introduces with a similarly silly list of unrelated items: "There should be a shared feature between the items joined together, such as the sun and the moon, heaven and earth, *jinn* and man [. . .] as opposed to, for example, the sun and the gallbladder of a hare, *Sūrat al-ikhlāṣ* and the left leg of a frog, Zoroastrianism and a thousand eggplants [. . .]."[75] We cannot help but remark how even his humour revolves around animal and plant parts, holy texts and traditions, and heavenly bodies, all in a way that inevitably reminds us of his grimoire.

Conclusion

The closing pages of the *Miftāḥ* are redolent with magic.[76] Sakkākī's final three refutations of criticisms of the Qur'an revolve around the images of Solomon's tempest, Moses's staff, and the heavenly tablets on which the highest version of the Qur'an is preserved. As for the wind which King Solomon commanded, Sakkākī claims that critics characterize its description as both "gentle" and "storm-like"[77] as contradictory; Sakkākī explains that it was a strong but not a destructive wind. They further complain, he claims, that Moses's staff was described as three different types of snake of three different sizes.[78] (It was a large snake but not a heavy one, he explains). And he refutes the criticism that the Qur'an should not have been called both *tanzīl* and *inzāl*,[79] two words meaning subtly different versions of "sent down," by explaining that each refers to different stages in its progress from Heaven to Earth.

Although he gives the appearance in this section of refuting the criticisms of a non-Muslim, non-native Arabic speaker, as he concludes his argument, the criticisms he pretends to refute grow increasingly arcane – advanced knowledge of Arabic grammar is required even to understand them. It is implausible that anyone "ignorant without limit" of the Arabic language (as he then calls them) would ever have raised these objections in the first place – they are at once too subtle and too absurd. It seems more likely that Sakkākī chose these three images as locations of enormous power – Solomon's wind, Moses's staff, and the language of the Qur'an as bridge between Heaven and Earth. These images all feature in his grimoire, and they are here at the end of his book of language as examples of the power of language itself.

He follows these arguments with a brief refutation of a purported criticism of a verse in which the angels bow down to Adam; again, it seems less likely that he is answering a real criticism here (regarding a technicality of when precisely humans were created)[80] and more likely that he is seeking to conclude his book with another image of great importance to him – the image of man's power over angels. This closing image of his grammar leads naturally into the opening image of his angel-filled grimoire: "Praise God who made the angels messengers with two, three, or four wings, adding to His creation as He wills, for God has power over all things."[81]

But the final argument of the entire *Miftāḥ*, with which he abruptly concludes his 726-page tome, is that the Qur'an is not poetry, because, although certain fragments of verse fit into metrical patterns, they do not do so because they *intend* to be poetry.[82] They are not poetry on purpose.

This is the goal of both books: to harness and dominate the dangerous forces of language and magic – to create rhetorical sorcery by the force and training of the purpose and the will. Despite the fact that Sakkākī is not now remembered as a Sufi, his text, like many works of occult significance of the era, cites Sufis as authorities on these matters. If we were to link his practises to a Sufi path broadly defined, we would have to call him a sober rather than an intoxicated practitioner, despite the fact that he deals with the darkest of the dark arts.

A substantial proportion of his *Shāmil* is aimed at communication with the devil and his offspring, and often for purposes of harming or sexually ensnaring a victim.

His grimoire was as dark as the time and place he lived in; his desire for control made poignant by the chaotic environment in which he attempted to survive.

In explaining the apparent pessimism of Farīd al-Dīn ʿAṭṭār's *Book of Suffering*, Navid Kermani describes the environment of 13th-century Iran and Central Asia – the world Sakkākī also inhabited – as "an agitated, bloody time in which robbery, whoring and drunkenness spread as widely as mysticism, asceticism and inwardness."[83] Warring local rulers burned, pillaged, and abused the populations that they sought to rule, while simultaneously providing protection and patronage to the poets and scholars who adorned their courts.[84] As Miller writes, Khwarazmian Shah ʿAlāʾ al-Dīn's resort to magic and divination, including his employ of Sakkākī's malfunctioning statue, was another result of the "confusion, desperation, and sheer terror" inspired by the conflicts in the region.[85] She refers especially to the Mongol conquests, but Noble reminds us that the Shah simultaneously had reason to fear Nizārī Ismāʿīlī assassination.[86] Amongst these warring factions, Islamic, Christian, Jewish, and other religious traditions coexisted, survived side by side, and seeped into one another by "osmotic processes."[87]

Let us remember Sakkākī's own linguistic distance from the Arab masters of language whom he idolises – he was himself likely a native speaker of Persian, Khwarazmian, and/or Khwarazm Turkic.[88] The mixed linguistic background he inhabited is everywhere apparent in his garbled grimoire. In his thorough study of the *Miftāḥ*, *al-Balāgha ʿind al-Sakkākī*, Aḥmad Maṭlūb identifies a poetic exemplar that Sakkākī himself penned, and criticising it as derivative and ugly, concludes that this famed scholar of language lacked poetic genius. To Maṭlūb, the competent but uninspired verses are proof of his thesis, that driven by his Muʿtazili leanings, Sakkākī approached language from a dryly logical and systematic, rather than a literary standpoint.[89] This is in keeping with our argument that Sakkākī was a man who sought to dominate rather than submit to inspiration, although I would point out that the moments I have focused on in this essay – those rare moments of high emotion in the *Miftāḥ*, work their magic on the mind with a fierce and delicate exactitude. Without doubt, Sakkākī wielded a powerful pen. As for the verses Maṭlūb criticises, these rail against a hard and treacherous fate, ending every line with the poetic apostrophe, "O thou Time!" (*ayyuhā al-zaman*),[90] employing the *radīf* rhyme scheme more common to Persian than Arabic.[91] We can read this refrain in light of his work on magic, where such apostrophes addressed to planetary spirits, *jinn*, and angels are pervasive.[92] The theme of the poem itself further highlights the hardships that the author faced during his lifetime.

Read against this historical background, we can perceive a man struggling to stay in control of his situation (and ultimately failing – as he died in prison, having lost in a magical battle of wits). As a translator and interpreter of his work, one may follow him in perceiving the links between poetry and magic, but find we must take a passive role to his dominating prose style, and embrace the illegibility and ambiguity of his writing with something like an ecstatically resigned shrug.

Notes

1 Muḥammad Bāqir al-Mūsawī Khwānsārī, *Rawḍāt al-jannāt fī aḥwāl al-ʿulamāʾ wa-l-sādāt* (Tehran: Maktabat Ismāʿīliyān, 1970), vol. 8, 222. This biography is further mentioned below.

2 See Travis Zadeh, "Commanding Demons and Jinn: The Sorcerer in Early Islamic Thought," in *No Tapping around Philology: A Festschrift in Honor of Wheeler McIntosh Thackston Jr.'s 70th Birthday*, ed. by Alireza Korangy and Daniel J. Sheffield (Wiesbaden: Harrassowitz, 2014), 144–51 for a highly informative summary of al-Ṭabasī's work. This essay also includes an introduction to Sakkākī as mentioned below. The Leverhulme-funded "Sorcerer's Handbook project" (P.I. Emily Selove), aims to produce an edition and translation of the *Shāmil*, as well as a volume of essays by multiple authors. In this volume, Travis Zadeh will shed light on the various Persian works of magic attributed to Sakkākī and his son (see "Cutting Ariadne's Thread, or How to Think Otherwise in the Maze," in *Islamicate Occult Sciences in Theory and Practice*, ed. by Liana Saif et al. [Leiden: Brill, 2020], 635–6), which appear at first glance to be similar in some ways to the *Shāmil*, but nevertheless, different in content.

3 MS. Dār al-Kutub al-Miṣriyya, Cairo 1735, 1b–2a. This manuscript will hereafter be referred to as C. We obtained this manuscript as a photocopy from the Juma al-Majid Cultural Centre in Dubai, but we refer to it as C, standing for "Cairo," because of the label reading Dār al-Kutub al-Miṣriyya on the final folio. By comparing the image on folio 62a to Christie's Auction house's online records, we can see that the original manuscript was purchased in 2001 by an anonymous buyer, who did not respond to our attempts to contact them through the auction house. It is unclear how the manuscript made its way from Cairo to Christie's.

4 See Chapter Seven, "Sabian Perfected Man and the Avicennan Theory of Prophethood" in Michael-Sebastian Noble, *Philosophising the Occult: Avicennan Psychology and 'The Hidden Secret' of Fakhr al-Dīn al-Rāzī* (Berlin: De Gruyter, 2021) for the philosophical background of Fakhr al-Dīn al-Rāzī's reliance on this concept in his *al-Sirr al-maktūm*, which work profoundly influenced Sakkākī's own grimoire.

5 Khwansarī, *Rawḍāt al-jannāt*, vol. 8, 221. Heinrichs suggests that the details of this tale, in which Sakkākī changes professions in hopes of gaining greater favour from his royal patrons, may be "a transposition of a similar *curriculum vitae* told about the Shāfiʿī scholar al-Ḳaffāl ("the Locksmith") al-Marwazī" (Wolfhart Heinrichs, "al-Sakkākī," in *The Encyclopaedia of Islam, New Edition*, ed. by H. A. R. Gibb et al., 13 vols. [Leiden: Brill, 1960–2009], vol. 2, 893–4), but the transposition may have occurred because the arc of these two scholars' lives resembled one another in this regard.

6 In her presentation "The Name of the Key, al-Sakkākī's Literary Craftsmanship and Pragmatic Poetics in *Miftāḥ al-ʿUlūm*," (a published version of which is to be hoped for in the collection of essays that will accompany The Sorcerer's Handbook project's edition and translation of the *Shāmil*), Chiara Fontana painted an evocative portrait of the *Miftāḥ* as a text that paradoxically employs an approach based on goal-oriented craftsmanship and the manipulation of tools in pursuit of specific aims (and thus appears to espouse a dry, earthy, and quotidian approach to language), but which masks profound and deliberately hidden depths. This is the perfect accompaniment or counterpoint to Sakkākī's work on magic, as she illustrated.

7 C 216a.

8 As indeed Khwānsārī suggests, in portraying his slow struggle to acquire his new language. When he saw a trickle of water wearing away a stone, Khwānsārī writes, he resolved to show the

same persistence, and thus gradually overcame the hurdles of the Arabic language to become the linguistic master that we know today.

9 MS British Library, Delhi Arabic 1915b, 216b, in introducing a chapter on how to cause sexual impotence. This manuscript will hereafter be referred to as D. Currently housed in the British Library, it appears to have been looted from the Mughal Palace in the 19th century, following an uprising against the British East India company (as I discovered in Bink Hallum's workshop "An Introduction to Arabic Scientific MSS" on June 10, 2019 in London). It appears that it was copied directly from MS School of Oriental and African Studies, London MS 46347 (hereafter referred to as SOAS), which may in turn have been copied directly from C.

10 Sakkākī seems to have written entire sections of the later chapters of curses in his own voice, for example. Meanwhile, the widely circulated work on lunar mansions may have been included in the *Shāmil* after his death, as suggested by the *isnād* beginning *Qāla muṣannif al-kitāb al-shaykh al-kabīr Sirāj al-Dīn al-Sakkākī ʿalayhi al-raḥma*, "The compiler of the book the great shaykh Sirāj al-Dīn al-Sakkākī, rest his soul [. . .]." The colophon of C refers to him as the "*faqīr*" ("the poor wretch"), a label most likely to be self-applied (suggesting that C was copied from a branch of manuscripts that could be traced to a version that Sakkākī wrote himself: "The poor wretch Sirāj al-Dīn Abū Yaʿqūb wrote in the year 602 [. . .]." C 216a. SOAS omits the word *al-faqīr*).

11 Notable exceptions, such as Travis Zadeh and Michael Noble, are cited throughout. See Noble, *Philosophising the Occult*, 31–3 for a biography of Sakkākī as a magician. Zadeh provides another excellent introduction to the subject in "Commanding Demons and Jinn," 133–4. Zadeh also notes in his *Wonders and Rarities: How a Book of Natural Curiosities Shaped the World* (Cambridge: Harvard University Press, 2023), 85 that the Mamluk physician of Cairo, Ibn al-Akfānī (d. 749/1348), hails Sakkākī's handbook of spells as "a work of significant standing whose benefit is manifestly of great utility, but whose methods are of extreme difficulty." Al-Akfānī offers no further comment on the work. See Ibn al-Akfānī, *Kitāb al-Irshād al-qāṣid ilā asnā al-maqāṣid*, in *De egyptische arts Ibn al-Akfānī*, ed. by Jan J. Witkam (Leiden: Ter Lugt Pers, 1989), 414 (and 51 of the Arabic text).

12 Heinrichs, "al-Sakkākī."

13 See footnote 89, which explains the origins and refutation of this characterisation.

14 Muḥammad b. Aḥmad Nasawī, *Sīrat al-Sulṭān Jalāl al-Dīn Mankubirtī*, ed. by Ḥāfiẓ Aḥmad Ḥamdī ([Cairo]: Dār al-fikr al-ʿArabī, 1953), 253–4. The biographer provides this as a cautionary tale against hubris, and against vain clinging to the pleasures and powers of earthly life, ending his account with this comment: "I don't know which is more astounding: the credulousness of that learned man, or the deception of these people by what he spat curses into? Is any nation safe from the passage of time, or can this earthly life remain as it is without changing? How many communities have had 'all their bonds severed?' (Q 2: 166), for 'God effaces or makes firm what He wills, and the Mother of the Book is His' (Q 13: 39)." Also see Isabel Miller, "Occult Science and the Fall of the Khwārazm-Shāh Jalāl al-Dīn," *Iran* 39 (2001): 249–56 and Emily Selove, *Popeye and Curly: 120 Days in Medieval Baghdad* (Fargo: Theran Press, 2021), episode 79.

15 C 20a–b, D 82b.

16 These magic circles are also described and illustrated in a Persian work attributed to Sakkākī, the *Taskhīrāt* in Oxford University's Bodleian Library MS Walter 91. See Zadeh, "Cutting Ariadne's Thread," 635.

17 Ghiyāth al-Dīn Khwāndamīr, *Ḥabīb al-siyar*, in *A Century of Princes: Sources on Timurid History and Art*, selected and transl. by W. M. Thackston (Cambridge, Ma.: Aga Khan Program for Islamic Architecture, 1989), 46. This is all repeated in Abū l-Ḥasanāt ʿAbd al-Ḥayy al-Laknawī, *al-Fawāʾid al-bahiyya fī tarājim al-Ḥanafiyya* (Cairo: Maṭbaʿat al-saʿāda, 1906), 232.

18 Ibn al-Nadīm's *Fihrist* mentions talismans in the same breath as trickery (*ḥiyal*) (Abū l-Faraj Muḥammad b. Isḥāq b. al-Nadīm, *Kitāb al-Fihrist*, ed. by Ayman Fuʾād Sayyid [London: al-Furqān, 2009], 333) and as Savage-Smith writes, "Magic also included the art of trickery or forgery." Emilie Savage-Smith, "Introduction," in *Magic and Divination in Early Islam*, ed. by

Emilie Savage-Smith (Burlington: Ashgate Publishing, 2004), xxviii–ix (*ḥīla* can also refer to a stratagem, a means, or an expedient, and is therefore not always a negative term. Our thanks to Geert Jan van Gelder for pointing this out).

19 See Charles Burnett, "*Nīranj*: A Category of Magic (Almost) Forgotten in the Latin West," in *Natura, scienze e societa medievali. Studi in onore di Agostino Paravicini Bagliani,* ed. by Claudio Leonardi and Francesco Santi (Florence: Edizione del Galluzzo, 2008), 37–66. The *nīrānj*, unlike the talisman, can only be created at night, and often pertains to emotions like love or anger.

20 C 34b–35a, D 112a.

21 SOAS 212b; MS John Ryland's Library, Manchester MS 372 [404], 160b.

22 Al-Sakkākī, *Miftāḥ*, 49.

23 Ibid., 42.

24 Ibid., 43–7.

25 Ibid., 466–7. The organizational logic of the "coiner," whether God or wise man, reappears here as well.

26 Luca Patrizi makes the link between gemstones and words explicit in his "A Gemstone Among the Stones: The Symbolisms of Precious Stones in Islam and Its Relation with Language," *Historia religionum* 10 (2018): 107–26.

27 Al-Sakkākī, *Miftāḥ*, 39.

28 Ibid., 38.

29 Ibid., 35–6.

30 Ibid., 74.

31 See Mohammed Sayyaf Sanad, "A Multidisciplinary Investigation of Abū Hilāl al-ʿAskarī's Literary Heritage (d. 395–400 AH – 1005 AC), Insights from Lexicography, Linguistics, and Literary Criticism," Ph.D. dissertation, University of Exeter, 2022. It seems that Sakkākī's introduction is influenced directly by Abū Hilāl's, as both begin with the word "*aḥaqq*" (the most deserving/best).

32 It is especially a danger in that the overconfidence derived from a little bit of grammatical knowledge may lead them to falsely interpret the word of God, as he warns on pp. 38–39. This is further addressed at the end of this essay.

33 C 106b. This introduces a chapter containing rituals which he divides into two categories, the *ḥalāl* and the *ḥarām*, and which are designed not only to contact pious jinn, but also Satan himself as well as his children.

34 C 142a.

35 C 137b ff. – see footnote 52 where the anecdote is quoted in full.

36 C 126a–b, though it should be noted that the first "verse" is in fact half each of verses 23: 80 and 2: 117 joined together, which is possibly a source of confusion in numbering the list. In most such cases, full lists are in fact provided.

37 C 18a.

38 Al-Sakkākī, *Miftāḥ*, 439.

39 Alexander Key, *Language between God and the Poets: Maʿnā in the Eleventh Century* (Berkeley: University of California Press, 2018), 147.

40 "[. . .] and this is "theology," or *ʿilm al-kalām* ("the science/discipline/knowledge of speech")" (Key, *Language between God and the Poets*, 11). Key translates the word *maʿnā* (more commonly translated as "meaning") as "mental contents"; he also describes *maʿnā* as "a set of ontological and cognitive pigeonholes" (*Language between God and the Poets*, 130). These "pigeonholes" and their study are inextricably linked to a reverence for the language of the Qurʾān and of poetry.

41 In his *Lisān al-ʿArab*, he writes that according to al-Azharī (d. 370/980), "*Aṣl al-siḥr ṣarf al-shayʾ ʿan ḥaqīqatihi ilā ghayrihi*" (Muḥammad b. Mukarram b. Manẓūr, *Lisān al-ʿArab* [Beirut: Dār iḥyāʾ al-turāth al-ʿArabī and Muʾassasat al-turāth al-ʿArabī, 1996], vol. 4, 350). This was brought to my attention by Matthew Melvin-Khoushki in his "Talismans as Technology: The Construction and

Operation of Magical Machines in Early Modern Persian Grimoires and Chronicles," a presentation at the Middle East Studies Association conference, New Orleans, 2019.

42 As Liana Saif explains, Pharaoh's sorcerers were thought to have used a power called *sīmiyāʾ*, which "according to Ibn ʿArabī [. . .] is the knowledge of letters and names that have power over the senses of the observer, causing illusions without any essential transformations." This is to be contrasted with the power of the "true lettrist [. . .] to [generate] essences" or "[produce] beings." Liana Saif, "From *Ġāyat al-ḥakīm* to *Šams al-maʿārif*: Ways of Knowing and Paths of Power in Medieval Islam," *Arabica* 64.3/4 (2017): 335.

43 Al-Sakkākī, *Miftāḥ*, 437. Lara Harb explains the function of the increasing levels of complexity in similes and metaphor in her *Arabic Poetics: Aesthetic Experience in Classical Arabic Literature* (Cambridge: Cambridge University Press, 2020), 157–9, relating it to al-Jurjānī's previous discussions, and describing the increasing levels of strangeness and effort required in comprehending each new level of comparison. Also see William Smyth, "Some Quick Rules *Ut Pictura Poesis*: The Rules for Simile in *Miftāḥ al-ʿUlūm*," *Oriens* 33 (1992): 215–29.

44 Al-Sakkākī, *Miftāḥ*, 443.

45 ʿAbd al-Qāhir al-Jurjānī, *Asrār al-balāgha*, ed. by Maḥmūd Shākir (Jeddah: Dār al-madanī, 1991), 180–1; Muḥammad Fakhr al-Dīn al-Rāzī, *Nihāyat al-ījāz fī dirāyat al-iʿjāz*, ed. by Naṣr Allāh Ḥājī (Beirut: Dār ṣādir, 2004), 128–9.

46 Al-Sakkākī, *Miftāḥ*, 357 ff., on which see Chiara Fontana, "The Name of the Key, al-Sakkākī's Literary Craftsmanship and Pragmatic Poetics in *Miftāḥ al-ʿulūm*," a presentation at the Sorcerer's Handbook Workshop, Exeter, 2021.

47 C 208a.

48 Recounted in al-Khwānsārī's biography "on the authority of the *Zīnat al-madjālis* of Madjd al-Dīn Muḥammad al-Ḥusaynī al-Madjdī (a contemporary of Bahāʾ al-Dīn al-ʿĀmilī, who died in 1030/1621)" (Heinrichs, "al-Sakkākī").

49 Al-Sakkākī, *Miftāḥ*, 443–5.

50 Zadeh's *Wonders and Rarities* explores many associations with the term "wonder" (*ʿajab*), also linking it to the feeling of curiosity that inspires us to learn more about God.

51 "[E]xcept that it is psychological in nature, employing the imagination and intellect instead of earthly and heavenly bodies" (Harb, *Arabic Poetics*, 74).

52 The Shaykh Abū ʿAbd Allah b. Muḥammad al-Andalusī, "I undertook to study the science of the *rūḥāniyya* from the age of fifteen until I turned sixteen, and I was struggling with the seals of the kings of the *jinn* and their illusions [. . .] and memorising the names of their helpers. And I did not manage thereby to discover a spirit or a means to subjugate it or [to cause it to] perform a task, and I remained like a blind man without a stick, straying, and reached neither the beginning nor the end.

When I turned fifty-nine, I met a man from the land of al-Andalus named Aḥmad, and I talked to him about the science of the *rūḥāniyya* that I had tried in the past, and I told him that I had gained nothing by it but epilepsy, or causing a seal or an object to move very slightly, and I was not content with that, having never discovered or seized on a spirit.

"Poor thing," said Aḥmad to me, "By God, you have forfeited both this world and the next, and troubled yourself ignorantly and to no avail!"

"My shaykh," I replied, "Guide me to what will benefit me, and I will speak well of you for as long as I live, and whatever I gain will be unto the God the Exalted."

"On one condition," he said.

"And what is that?" I asked.

"My son," he replied, "Bring me all of the books of wisdom that you mentioned that you read in the past."

I brought them and placed them before him, and he brought out a Qurʾan and made me swear upon it that I would never again do anything like what I did before with regards to the science of the *rūḥāniyya*, and he threw all the books in the sea and destroyed them." C 137b ff.

53 The *Ghāyat al-ḥakīm* notes that ṭ-l-s-m backwards gives us m-s-l-ṭ, and *musallaṭ* means "that to which power over something is conferred," a meaning clearly related to *ṭillasm* (talisman) which is granted power by the "celestial secrets" in its body (See Saif, "From *Ġāyat al-ḥakīm* to *Šams al-maʿārif*," 300, where she is discussing and translating Maslama b. Qāsim al-Qurṭubī, *Picatrix: Das Ziel des Weisen,* ed. by Hellmut Ritter [Leipzig: B.G. Teubner, 1933], 7–8. My thanks to Hisashi Obuchi for drawing my attention to this passage. Since *mīm* is not a root letter of *musallaṭ*, this does not technically qualify as *al-isthiqāq al-akbar*, but is nonetheless evocative.

54 Al-Sakkākī, *Miftāḥ*, 49. Aḥmad Maṭlūb speculates on the identity of al-Hātimi in his *al-Balāgha ʿind al-Sakkākī* (Cairo, 1964), 53. The notion of the greater derivation was first introduced in Ibn Jinnī's (d. 392/1002) *al-Khaṣāʾiṣ fī ʿilm uṣūl al-ʿArabiyya,* ed. by Muḥammad ʿAlī al-Najjār (Beirut: Dār al-hudā, 1974).

55 In occult matters, he relies especially on a certain Awḥad al-Dīn, whom he mentions numerous times in the *Shāmil*, but also in Persian occult works attributed to him, as found, for example, in BL Or. 11041, 86a–b / Bodleian, Walker 91, 183a, which, unlike the *Shāmil*, provides his master's full name. In a private communication to me, Travis Zadeh alerted me to this passage and translated it as "Our teacher, our master, our lord, the just prince, the great noble servant, unique of the age, singular in the time, master of meanings, sun of meanings, Awḥad al-Dīn Maḥmūd ibn ʿUmar ibn Muḥammad ibn Ilyās ibn ʿAbd Allāh [ibn] Hilāl al-Andalusī."

56 Al-Sakkākī, *Miftāḥ*, 619.

57 "As for Venus, its incense are dried storax, labdanum, camphor, and musk" (citing Jābir b. Ḥayyān in this section) (C 91a).

58 Al-Azdī, *The Portrait of Abū l-Qāsim al-Baghdādī al-Tamīmī*, ed. Emily Selove and Geert Jan Van Gelder (Oxford: Gibb Memorial Trust, 2021), §185.

59 Ibid., §229.

60 D 100a, C 194b.

61 In his *Beholding Beauty: Saʿdi and the Persian Lyric Tradition* (Leiden: Brill, 2020) Domenico Ingenito, focusing on the Persian poet Saʿdi of Shiraz (d. 1292), shows how the poet may perceive through the image of the beloved, the *ghayb*, or unseen and divine world, and thus may intuit an indication of God in his love poetry. He describes this poetic capacity in terms of the philosophy of al-Ghazālī and Ibn Sīna (see especially 333–48). Also see Emily Selove, "Magic as Poetry, Poetry as Magic: A Fragment of Arabic Spells," *Magic, Ritual, and Witchcraft* 15.1 (2020): 33–57.

62 Al-Sakkākī, *Miftāḥ,* 619.

63 *Bi-kam tabīʿu alfa bādhinjāna? Abīʿuhā bi-ʿasharatin ʿadliyāt.* Ibid., 619. See Selove, *Popeye and Curly*, episode 97.

64 A. S. Tritton, "Spirits and Demons in Arabia," *Journal of the Royal Asiatic Society* 66.4 (1934): 723 (He cites al-Jāḥiẓ's *Kitāb al-bayān*, 1. 116 referring to the Cairo 1905–07 edition). Similarly, Bürgel's "The Poet and his Demon" quotes Imruʾ al-Qays's boasting, "The demons let me choose their poems/ and I select from them whatever I like." Johann Christoph Bürgel, "The Poet and His Demon," in *Conscious Voices: Concepts of Writing in the Middle East*, ed. by Stephan Guth, Priska Furrer and Johann Christoph Bürgel (Beirut and Stuttgart: Franz Steiner, 1999), 13.

65 Michael W. Dols, *Majnūn*: *The Madman in Medieval Islamic Society*, ed. by Diana E. Immisch (Oxford: Clarendon Press, 1992), 221, citing the *Encylopaedia of Islam 1* article on al-Walīd b. al-Mughīra, the prophet's defender in the anecdote. Also see p. 216, as well as Bürgel's "The Poet and His Demon."

66 Al-Sakkākī, *Miftāḥ,* 700–3.

67 Ibid., 42.

68 Ibid., 707.

69 Ibid., 471.

70 C 114b: *Ayya ʿaẓīma in kāna bi-hayba ʿaẓīma.*

71 Both versions of the ritual were discussed by Liana Saif in her "Under the Light of Venus: Transgressive Performativity in Medieval Arabic Occultism," a presentation at the Gender and Transgression in the Middle Ages Conference, St. Andrews, 2016.

72 Al-Sakkākī, *Miftāḥ*, 441.

73 Zadeh, "Cutting Ariadne's Thread," 634 footnote 78, where he cites the opening of the astrological treatise, *Hay'āt al-aflāk*, British Library, MS Or. 5416, 4b. As mentioned above, the contemporary account of Sakkākī's failed magical statue is also described in disapproving terms, as an act of dangerously impious hubris (Nasawī, *Sīrat al-Sulṭān*, 254).

74 Al-Sakkākī, *Miftāḥ*, 381.

75 Ibid., 359–60.

76 Ibid., 721.

77 Gentle (*rukhā'an*) in Q 38: 36, and storm-like (*'āṣifa*) in Q 21: 81.

78 *Thu'bānun* in 7: 107 and 26: 32, *al-jānn* in 27: 10 and 28: 31, and *ḥayya* in 20: 20.

79 Verb forms two and four of the root n-z-l are used to refer to the Qur'an in multiple verses (though the verbal noun *inzāl* is never used in the Qur'an).

80 This pertains to Q 7: 11, translated by Yusuf Ali as, "And We created you, then fashioned you, then told the angels: Fall ye prostrate before Adam!"

81 C 1b, a paraphrase of Q 35: 1.

82 Al-Sakkākī, *Miftāḥ*, 722–6.

83 Navid Kermani, *The Terror of God: Attar, Job and the Metaphysical Kirmani* (Cambridge: Polity, 2011), 65–6. Noble also discusses the impact of the terror of the Mongol invasions and uncertainty of the time in promoting the "aggressive use of the talismanic science" (*Philosophising the Occult,* 265). Melvin-Koushki's "Mobilizing Magic" comments on the uncertain environment of post-Mongol conquest and the manner in which it empowered magicians. Zadeh discusses this extensively in his *Wonders and Rarities.*

84 Maṭlūb, *al-Balāgha,* 30–40.

85 Miller, "Occult Science," 249.

86 Ibid., 266.

87 Kermani, *The Terror of God,* 192.

88 As Heinrichs suggests in his "al-Sakkākī."

89 This has become the standard interpretation of the *Miftāḥ*, so frequently characterised as a dry and boring reduction of language to a set of logical rules (inspired by the Mu'tazilī love of rationalism, and read in contrast to al-Jurjānī's depiction of language as a vehicle of wonder) that this has become almost a trope in speaking about Sakkākī's work. In her "The Name of the Key" Fontana provides a full analysis of this scholarly trope, as well as a defence of this book, which in fact holds enormous mystery and magic.

90 Al-Sakkākī, *Miftāḥ,* 694 and Maṭlūb, *al-Balāgha,* 59.

91 When it is found in Arabic, it is typically used by Persians writing in Arabic, as explained in Van Gelder's *Sound and Sense*, 180 ff.

92 Selove, "Magic as Poetry, Poetry as Magic."

Bibliography

For the abbreviations C, D, and SOAS, see al-Sakkākī, *Kitāb al-Shāmil*.

Al-Sakkākī's Works

Al-Sakkākī, Sirāj al-Dīn. *Miftāḥ al-ʿulūm*. Ed. by ʿAbd al-Ḥamīd al-Hindāwī. Beirut: Dār al-kutub al-ʿilmiyya, 1971.

Al-Sakkākī, Sirāj al-Dīn. *Kitāb al-Shāmil wa-baḥr al-kāmil*. MS British Library, Delhi Arabic 1915b, London (referred to as D); MS Dār al-Kutub al-Miṣriyya, Cairo, now available as a photocopy in Juma al-Majid Cultural Centre, Dubai, ms. 1735 (referred to as C); MS School of Oriental and African Studies, London MS 46347 (referred to as SOAS); MS John Ryland's Library, Manchester MS 372 [404].

Al-Sakkākī, Sirāj al-Dīn. *Sirr al-asrār fī ʿilm al-ṭilasmāt*. MS British Library Or. 11041, 86a–b; MS Bodleian Walker 91, 183a.

Other Sources and Studies

Al-Azdī. *The Portrait of Abū l-Qāsim al-Baghdādī al-Tamīmī*. Ed. by Emily Selove and Geert Jan van Gelder. Oxford: Gibb Memorial Trust, 2021.

Bürgel, Johann Christoph. "The Poet and His Demon." In *Conscious Voices: Concepts of Writing in the Middle East*. Ed. by Stephan Guth, Priska Furrer and Johann Christoph Bürgel. Beirut and Stuttgart: Franz Steiner, 1999, 13–28.

Burnett, Charles. "*Nīranj*: A Category of Magic (Almost) Forgotten in the Latin West." In *Natura, scienze e societa medievali. Studi in onore di Agostino Paravicini Bagliani*. Ed. by Claudio Leonardi and Francesco Santi. Florence: Edizione del Galluzzo, 2008, 37–66.

Dols, Michael W. *Majnūn: The Madman in Medieval Islamic Society*. Ed. by Diana E. Immisch. Oxford: Clarendon Press, 1992.

Fontana, Chiara. "The Name of the Key, al-Sakkākī's Literary Craftsmanship and Pragmatic Poetics in Miftāḥ al-ʿulūm." A presentation at the Sorcerer's Handbook Workshop, Exeter, 2021.

Al-Hamadhānī, Badīʿ al-Zamān. *Maqāmāt*. Beirut: Dār al-mashriq, 1968.

Harb, Lara. *Arabic Poetics: Aesthetic Experience in Classical Arabic Literature*. Cambridge: Cambridge University Press, 2020.

Heinrichs, Wolfhart. "al-Sakkākī." In *The Encyclopaedia of Islam, New Edition*. Ed. by H. A. R. Gibb et al., 13 vols. Leiden: Brill, 1960–2009, vol. 2, 893–4.

Ibn al-Akfānī. *Kitāb al-Irshād al-qāṣid ilā asnā al-maqāṣid*. In *De egyptische arts Ibn al-Akfānī*. Ed. by Jan J. Witkam. Leiden: Ter Lugt Pers, 1989.

Ibn Jinnī. *Al-Khaṣā'iṣ fī 'ilm uṣūl al-'Arabiyya*. Ed. by Muḥammad 'Alī al-Najjār. Beirut: Dār al-hudā, 1974.

Ibn Manẓūr, Muḥammad b. Mukarram. *Lisān al-'Arab*. 18 vols. Beirut: Dār iḥyā' al-turāth al-'Arabī and Mu'assasat al-turāth al-'Arabī, 1996.

Ibn al-Nadīm, Abū l-Faraj Muḥammad b. Isḥāq. *Kitāb al-Fihrist*. Ed. by Ayman Fu'ād Sayyid. London: al-Furqān, 2009.

Ingenito, Domenico. *Beholding Beauty: Sa'di and the Persian Lyric Tradition*. Leiden: Brill, 2020.

Al-Jurjānī, 'Abd al-Qāhir. *Asrār al-balāgha*. Ed. by Maḥmūd Shākir. Jeddah: Dār al-madanī, 1991.

Key, Alexander. *Language between God and the Poets: Ma'nā in the Eleventh Century*. Berkeley: University of California Press, 2018.

Khwāndamīr, Ghiyāth al-Dīn. *Ḥabīb al-siyar*. In *A Century of Princes: Sources on Timurid History and Art*. Selected and transl. by W. M. Thackston. Cambridge, MA.: Aga Khan Program for Islamic Architecture, 1989.

Khwānsārī, Muḥammad Bāqir al-Mūsawī. *Rawḍāt al-jannāt fi aḥwāl al-'ulamā' wa-l-sādāt*. 9 vols. Tehran: Maktabat Ismā'īliyān, 1970.

Kermani, Navid. *The Terror of God: Attar, Job and the Metaphysical Revolt*. Cambridge: Polity, 2011.

Maṭlūb, Aḥmad. *Al-Balāgha 'ind al-Sakkākī*. Cairo, 1964.

Melvin-Koushki, Matthew. "Mobilizing Magic: Occultism in Central Asia and the Continuity of High Persianate Culture under Russian Rule." *Studia Islamica* 111.2 (2016): 231–84.

Melvin-Koushki, Matthew. "Talismans as Technology: The Construction and Operation of Magical Machines in Early Modern Persian Grimoires and Chronicles." A presentation at the Middle East Studies Association conference, New Orleans, 2019.

Miller, Isabel. "Occult Science and the Fall of the Khwārazm-Shāh Jalāl al-Dīn." *Iran* 39 (2001): 249–56.

Al-Laknawī, Abū l-Ḥasanāt 'Abd al-Ḥayy. *Al-Fawā'id al-bahiyya fī tarājim al-Ḥanafiyya*. Cairo: Maṭba'at al-sa'āda, 1906.

Nasawī, Muḥammad b. Aḥmad. *Sīrat al-Sulṭān Jalāl al-Dīn Mankubirtī*. Ed. by Ḥāfiẓ Aḥmad Ḥamdī. [Cairo]: Dār al-fikr al-'Arabī, 1953.

Noble, Michael-Sebastian. *Philosophising the Occult: Avicennan Psychology and 'The Hidden Secret' of Fakhr al-Dīn al-Rāzī*. Berlin: De Gruyter, 2021.

Patrizi, Luca. "A Gemstone Among the Stones: The Symbolisms of Precious Stones in Islam and Its Relation with Language." *Historia religionum* 10 (2018): 107–26.

Al-Qurṭubī, Maslama b. Qāsim. *Picatrix: Das Ziel des Weisen*. Ed. by Hellmut Ritter. Leipzig: B.G. Teubner, 1933.

Al-Rāzī, Muḥammad Fakhr al-Dīn. *Nihāyat al-ījāz fī dirāyat al-iʿjāz*. Ed. by Naṣr Allāh Ḥājī. Beirut: Dār Ṣādir, 2004.

Saif, Liana. "From *Ġāyat al-ḥakīm* to *Šams al-maʿārif*: Ways of Knowing and Paths of Power in Medieval Islam." *Arabica* 64.3/4 (2017): 297–345.

Saif, Liana. "Under the Light of Venus: Transgressive Performativity in Medieval Arabic Occultism." A presentation at the Gender and Transgression in the Middle Ages Conference, St. Andrews, 2016.

Sanad, Mohammed Sayyaf. "A Multidisciplinary Investigation of Abū Hilāl Al-ʿAskarī's Literary Heritage (d. 395–400 AH–1005 AC), Insights from Lexicography, Linguistics, and Literary Criticism." Ph.D. dissertation, University of Exeter, 2022.

Savage-Smith, Emilie. "Introduction." In *Magic and Divination in Early Islam*. Ed. by Emilie Savage-Smith. Burlington: Ashgate Publishing, 2004.

Selove, Emily. "Magic as Poetry, Poetry as Magic: A Fragment of Arabic Spells." *Magic, Ritual, and Witchcraft* 15.1 (2020): 33–57.

Selove, Emily. *Popeye and Curly: 120 Days in Medieval Baghdad*. Fargo: Theran Press, 2021.

Smyth, William. "Some Quick Rules *Ut Pictura Poesis*: The Rules for Simile in *Miftāḥ al-ʿUlūm*." *Oriens* 33 (1992): 215–29.

Al-Ṭabasī, Abū l-Faḍl Muḥammad. *Al-Kitāb al-Shāmil fī l-baḥr al-kāmil*. MS Staatsbibliothek, Berlin Or. Fol. 52; MS Princeton University Library, Islamic Manuscripts, New Series no. 160; MS Salar Jung Museum, Hyderabad 2208.

Tritton, A.S. "Spirits and Demons in Arabia." *Journal of the Royal Asiatic Society* 66.4 (1934): 715–27.

Van Gelder, Geert Jan. *Sound and Sense in Classical Arabic Poetry*. Wiesbaden: Harrassowitz, 2012.

Zadeh, Travis. "Commanding Demons and Jinn: The Sorcerer in Early Islamic Thought." In *No Tapping around Philology: A Festschrift in Honor of Wheeler McIntosh Thackston Jr.'s 70th Birthday*. Ed. by Alireza Korangy and Daniel J. Sheffield. Wiesbaden: Harrassowitz, 2014, 131–60.

Zadeh, Travis. "Cutting Ariadne's Thread, or How to Think Otherwise in the Maze." In *Islamicate Occult Sciences in Theory and Practice*. Ed. by Liana Saif et al. Leiden: Brill, 2020, 607–50.

Zadeh, Travis. *Wonders and Rarities: How a Book of Natural Curiosities Shaped the World*. Cambridge: Harvard University Press, 2023.

4

Knowledge for All: Zayn al-Dīn al-Kaššī (d. before 1228) on Philosophical Writing

Hisashi Obuchi

Introduction

"What is philosophy?" is a question that has been posed by many and answered in various ways. The very fact that such a question can be raised indicates that "philosophy" is not merely a term to denote the particular system of a philosopher's thought or a generic name for its disciplines.[1] Philosophers *(falāsifa, ḥukamāʾ)* in the premodern Islamic world, similar to those in late antiquity, considered philosophy *(falsafa, ḥikma)* a path to human perfection and everlasting happiness.[2] For example, in the arguably most important philosophical summa ever written in Arabic, *al-Šifāʾ (The Healing)*, Ibn Sīnā (Avicenna, d. 428/1037) states, "The purpose of philosophy *(falsafa)* is to grasp the realities *(ḥaqāʾiq)* of all things to the extent that humans can grasp them," and "the end of theoretical philosophy is to perfect the soul simply by knowing, whereas that of practical philosophy is to perfect the soul, not simply by knowing, but by knowing, so that one will act, the things upon which one should act."[3] With this goal in mind, the philosopher knew what to write in the *Šifāʾ*: the gist of the philosophical principles with occasional discussions of side issues and his solutions to philosophically difficult problems.[4]

To what extent, however, does the written word contribute to such an ambitious enterprise of philosophy? Writing has not always been reputed as a good way to communicate knowledge. In *Phaedrus*, Socrates concludes that "no discourse worth serious attention has ever been written in verse or prose" and that "only what is said for the sake of understanding and learning, what is truly written in the soul concerning what is just, noble, and good can be clear, perfect, and worth serious attention" (277e–8a).[5] Although one may think thus negatively of writing,[6] Arabic philosophers do not give justification for writing their knowledge and so appear to take it for granted that philosophy is to be written and read. Of course, they had reasons to compose books in particular. In the case of the *Šifāʾ*, Ibn Sīnā's close disciple was keen for him to write a new philosophical summa.[7] This, however, does not explain why philosophy needs to be recorded – Did Arabic philosophers write philosophy only "lest it be forgotten"?[8]

The protagonist of this chapter, Zayn al-Dīn ʿAbd al-Raḥmān b. Muḥammad al-Kaššī (d. before 625/1228), is an exceptional Muslim philosopher who addressed the question of why, after all, philosophers must write. He is above all known as a senior disciple of the celebrated Sunni theologian-philosopher Faḫr al-Dīn al-Rāzī (d. 606/1210). As recent studies have shown, al-Kaššī was an acknowledged expert in Arabic logic, so later logicians frequently referred to him as such rather than as a follower of the master.[9] However, research into his logic, not to mention his thought in general, is still at its earliest stage.

Al-Kaššī deals with the issue as an introduction to his philosophical summa, *Ḥadāʾiq al-ḥaqāʾiq* (*The Gardens of Realities*).[10] The introduction consists of two *muqaddima*s ("prolegomena"). In the second *muqaddima*, the author defines key epistemological terms, classifies philosophy into the conventional divisions of theoretical and practical philosophies, and outlines the contents and structure of the work. The first *muqaddima* has a more general perspective: it explains why philosophers have to write and sketches how al-Kaššī as one of them has complied with the requirements in the present work. As Muḥammad ʿImādī Ḥāʾirī suggests in his overview of the *Ḥadāʾiq*,[11] the twofold introduction is itself worthy of a study considering that it was also circulated as an isolated treatise.[12] However, previous work has not attempted to examine it as such. What I propose to do here, therefore, is to analyse the introduction of the *Ḥadāʾiq* with a principal focus on the first *muqaddima* and to explore the value of writing in philosophy, as understood by al-Kaššī.[13]

In what follows, I will proceed along the first *muqaddima* and begin by reviewing al-Kaššī's notions of *ʿilm* (knowledge and science) and *ḥikma* (wisdom and philosophy). It will be shown that in line with his predecessors, he conceives the aim of philosophy *(ḥikma)* to be human perfection and eternal felicity. Importantly, he further argues that despite the universal obligation to philosophize to achieve perfection, the great majority of people, "*muqallid*s," will not philosophize. *Taqlīd* – unreflective acquiescence to others – may be seen as a somewhat old-fashioned concept that is frequently encountered in the intellectual history of Islam. As discussed later, however, al-Kaššī employs the concept of *taqlīd* to redefine the role of the intellectual elites, or "*muḥaqqiq*s," who have insights into the truth. As he acknowledges in the preface, the *Ḥadāʾiq* was dedicated to his patrons, namely, the Ḫwārazmšāh ʿAlāʾ al-Dīn Muḥammad (r. 596–617/1200–20), the prince Ǧalāl al-Dīn Manguburnī (d. 628/1231), and the empress-dowager Terken Khatun (d. 630/1232–33).[14] However, al-Kaššī's essential aim in the *Ḥadāʾiq* was not to serve the sovereign. Writing, for him, was the necessary means to save all human beings, both *muḥaqqiq*s and *muqallid*s.

Knowledge (*ʿilm*) and Philosophy (*ḥikma*)

At the opening of the first *muqaddima*, al-Kaššī establishes the immense value of *ʿilm* – knowledge and the act of knowing. He gathers from revealed texts that *any* knowledge is noble, precious, and powerful insofar as it is *ʿilm*.[15] The privileged position of *ʿilm* is also highlighted by his definition of *maʿrifa* or recognition. God is *ʿālim* (knowing), and the *ʿilm* in this case refers to His creative action, but one may not attribute *maʿrifa* to Him, since *maʿrifa* always refers to the knowledge of what already exists.[16]

Al-Kaššī's central thesis in the first *muqaddima* is that *ʿilm* as such must be pursued by *all* humans. For *ʿilm* will bring pleasure and happiness to its holder, or rather, it is itself pleasure and happiness. In opposition to the *mutakallimūn* (classical Muslim theologians), who held that a human was an aggregate of atoms and accidents, al-Kaššī acknowledges the immaterial human soul like the *falāsifa* and many post-Avicennan theologians, including al-Rāzī. What distinguishes al-Kaššī from them is that he was a Platonist like major figures of the pre-Avicennan *falāsifa* – he employs the Platonic notion of the tripartite soul, in which humans have animal, beastly, and rational souls, which are also called appetitive, irascible, and angelic faculties, respectively.[17] The appetitive faculty urges humans to satisfy desires such as eating and coition, and the irascible faculty drives them to power and authority.[18] The point is that those pleasures achieved by the appetitive and irascible faculties will be lost when those two corporeal faculties cease to function, that is, when the person's body dies.[19] In contrast, the rational soul or angelic faculty seeks intellectual pleasures, particularly to recognize God's existence and uniqueness through His attributes and to know angels, prophets, and saints. As a noetic substance, the rational soul will not disappear: *Do not call "dead" the killed in God's path; verily they are alive, and you are not aware* (2: 154).[20] Therefore, the "real universal knowledge" and "holy divine recognitions" of God and the immaterial entities will last forever as spiritual pleasure and happiness – both in this transient world and in the hereafter.[21]

However, when *He taught (ʿallama) Adam all the names and then showed them to angels* (2: 31), He merely concealed his appetites and anger by *ʿilm*.[22] Even if they possess *ʿilm*, humans are not angels, who as purely spiritual entities, are filled with sheer happiness by God. Nevertheless, humans can become like angels. In the stage of perfection *(kamāl)*, the rational soul becomes an intellect in actuality *(ʿaql bi-l-fiʿl)* and, as such, "encounters God the Exalted."[23] Of course, perfection is no easy task. To attain it, one needs to subjugate the animal and beastly souls by physical discipline and by the observation of the regulations of the law.[24] Furthermore, the Qur'an says, *By time, verily humans are in loss except those who believe, perform good deeds, urge one another to take up the truth, and urge one another to take up the patience* (103: 1–3). Al-Kaššī quotes this divine word as evidence that "perfection" means not only being perfect but also perfecting others (*mukammil*). "*Believe*" indicates perfection in the contemplative faculty, while "*perform good deeds*" indicates perfection in the practical faculty; "*urge one another to take up the truth*" indicates perfecting (*takmīl*) in the contemplative faculty, while "*urge one another to take up the patience*" indicates perfecting in the practical faculty.[25]

In al-Kaššī's view, *ḥikma* is the very exercise to attain perfection. In the second *muqaddima*, he writes that *ḥikma* is "to seek perfection (*istikmāl*) both in the contemplative faculty by recognizing realities and in the practical faculty by doing good things."[26] Alternatively, *ḥikma* is said to be "to seek perfection by conceiving things, by assenting to theoretical and practical realities, and by gleaning moral virtues as much as humanly possible."[27] Because perfect felicity will be realized by *ḥikma*, the highest rank of *ʿilm* is held by *ḥikma*.[28] According to the Qur'an (2: 269, 58: 11), one who possesses *ḥikma* has already achieved the good and will enter paradise.[29] Al-Kaššī, in effect, justifies *ḥikma* in the sense of philosophy. For, according to his division of sciences, both physics (*al-ʿilm al-ṭabīʿī*) and metaphysics or theology (*al-ʿilm al-ilāhī*), along with mathematics (*al-ʿilm al-riyāḍī*), are parts of theoretical philosophy (*al-ḥikma al-naẓariyya*), whereas practical philosophy (*al-ḥikma al-ʿamaliyya*) consists of ethics (*ʿilm al-aḫlāq, al-ḥikma al-ḫulqiyya*), household management (*ʿilm tadbīr al-manzil, al-ḥikma al-manziliyya*), and politics (*al-ʿilm al-siyāsī, al-ḥikma al-madaniyya*).[30]

ʿIlm as eternal happiness can be conceived in terms of the reward in the hereafter. In the exordium of the *Ḥadāʾiq*, al-Kaššī explicitly writes, "[God] has obligated (*kallafa*) [the creation] to recognize His divinity and commanded (*amara*) them to know His oneness."[31] As mentioned, everyone is created with the rational soul or intellect by which, al-Kaššī writes, "one, if unhurt and healthy, perceives universal matters hidden from the senses and performs mental actions that are to be considered right by most people."[32] Having the intellect, no individual is exempted from the obligation to recognize God and thank Him for His beneficence.[33] As to perfection, al-Kaššī says, "All the souls must (*yağibu*) be passionately fond of it, all the ambitions [must] be directed towards it, and all the people [must] make firm and purify knowledge."[34] This is because, as al-Kaššī understands the Qur'an (103: 1–3), one who does not achieve perfection lives miserably both in this world and in the world to come; humans will be disengaged from such a loss (*ḫusrān*) if they achieve human perfection.[35] Therefore, knowledge (*ʿilm*), especially philosophy (*ḥikma*) that may lead to perfection, is to be pursued in terms of divine obligation. From this perspective, happiness is the reward for those who comply with the obligation to know God. Thus, philosophy is by no means a leisure-time activity but, rather, an obligation imposed upon all human beings to know God and achieve felicities.

The Duty to Write

Having asserted that philosophy *(ḥikma)* is indispensable and obligatory for humans to live happily, al-Kaššī faces a severe problem: not everyone is given the gift of philosophizing. He describes this sad reality by a radical classification of people (*al-nās*) into two types in terms of learning.[36] Accordingly, some people are *muḥaqqiq*s, or those who (try to) verify the truth. "Their souls," writes al-Kaššī, "never rest but on the delight of certitude (*yaqīn*) so they will never accept but what is elucidated by clear demonstration (*burhān*)."[37] Verification (*taḥqīq*) was popularly conceived to be the method to obtain real knowledge through logical understanding and demonstration, and al-Rāzī used this term to denote his method of thorough research.[38] To understand what exactly verification – the act that *muḥaqqiq*s naturally perform in search for truth – is would require a detailed examination of al-Kaššī's argumentations in the *Ḥadāʾiq*, which goes beyond the scope of the present chapter. As far as the introduction we are investigating concerns, he seems to use the term rather generally in the literal sense of "to seek the truth."

As opposed to those who are intellectually gifted, there are people who adopt others' opinions unreflectively – *muqallid*s:

> The rest are *muqallid*s, who entrust their affairs to others. They are led by anyone who leads them, even without trying to make sure of [the leader's] error or integrity. They start to move when set in motion, and they remain still as long as they are left. They think their predecessors great and insist on their qualities without reflection (*naẓar*). They acquiesce to their lighthouse and follow their traces. The Qurʾan reports the words of such people: *"Indeed, we have found our forefathers in a community, and we are following their traces"* (43: 23), *even though their forefathers knew nothing, not being guided* (5: 104).[39]

Despite the unfortunate consequence of their ignorance, *muqallid*s do not even wish to fulfil the divine command. Al-Kaššī writes, "Those satisfied with being among the multitude of *muqallid*s, particularly about knowledge on the divine, are not counted among the world's inhabitants. They are content with being at a rank short of the lowest rank of human beings." They are thus like irrational animals. Al-Kaššī quotes the Qurʾan 25: 43–5: *Did you see the man who assumed his desire to be his god? And will you be his representative? Or do you deem most of them would listen or apprehend (yaʿqilūna)? Verily they are nothing but like cattle. In fact, they are errored.*[40]

Critiques of *taqlīd* are found throughout the history of Arabic philosophy.[41] The most famous example is *Tahāfut al-falāsifa* (*The Incoherence of the Falāsifa*) by the great Sunni thinker Abū Ḥāmid al-Ġazālī (d. 505/1111). There, he accuses the *falāsifa* of *taqlīd* to authoritative philosophers, such as Plato and Aristotle, and the unbelief (*kufr*) it causes.[42] Al-Rāzī similarly criticizes the *taqlīd* of his contemporary philosophers in his early important philosophical summa, *al-Mabāḥiṯ al-mašriqiyya* (*Eastern Investigations*). According to him, while some rigid scholars thoroughly reject leading authorities, *muqallid*s (probably traditional Avicennan philosophers in his milieu) consider themselves commanded to follow their predecessors, who in turn did not emulate authorities but held fast to evidence and demonstrations and hence often had opposing views with their forerunners. In this sense, the *muqallids* are in contradiction (*tanāquḍ*) with their ideal.[43]

A superficial interpretation might suggest that al-Kaššī criticizes the *taqlīd* of scholars in the same manner as al-Ġazālī and al-Rāzī did. However, a close reading of the text makes it evident that al-Kaššī raises the problem of *taqlīd* from a different perspective. The most crucial point is that he deals with the *taqlīd* of people in general (*al-nās*), not scholars or self-proclaimed philosophers. With this in mind, we should be cautious about al-Kaššī's intention to put together the two Qurʾanic verses in the above citation. According to verse 43: 23, *muqallid*s in the past tracked their forefathers' way consciously and proudly. This verse was originally followed by an account of unbelievers who rejected prophets (43: 24), but al-Kaššī instead connects verse 5: 104, which similarly describes the entrenched belief of such deniers of prophets in the past. Nevertheless, this verse tells us a crucial fact: the models of those credulous *muqallid*s were no less ignorant than the latter. Al-Kaššī thus draws attention to the fact that those who lead *muqallid*s are often likewise unlearned.

As we saw above, people must recognize God and know His uniqueness, and philosophy is a path to this understanding, but *muqallid*s will not, or rather they cannot, philosophize. To make matters worse, they conform to the teachings of unreliable individuals and end up being ignorant of God. When the Prophet Muḥammad was alive, this would not be a problem because he was the person entrusted by God to impart his knowledge (*ʿilm*) to people (4: 113).[44]

The answer al-Kaššī arrives at is that the responsibility for the disaster caused by the *taqlīd* of *muqallid*s rests rather upon those advanced *muḥaqqiq*s who have achieved human perfection, i.e., have already acquired demonstrative knowledge of God. Al-Kaššī writes,

> Indeed, it is obligatory upon a perfect intellectual (*al-ʿāqil al-kāmil*) to be guided to the straight way by proofs, namely, demonstrations and other kinds of evidence. For they are the mark of the veracity of speakers as God, the Exalted, says: *Say, "Present your demonstration (burhān) if you are veracious!"* (2: 111).

> Then, besides that, he [must] take upon himself the therapy of the patients of *taqlīd* (*mudāwāt marḍā al-taqlīd*) and make an effort to guide them to the correct view (*al-ra'y al-sadīd*).[45]

Here, al-Kaššī describes two phases that intellectual elites must complete. First, they need to adopt sound reasoning. This primary phase should be passed not only for themselves to attain sound knowledge and everlasting felicities; proofs (*ḥuǧǧa*), especially demonstrations (*burhān*), are also required to indicate their reliability to their fellow *muḥaqqiq*s (since *muqallid*s never deliberate whether the leaders are reliable).

In the second phase, the intellectuals are to take care of *muqallid*s. Looking at the expression "the therapy of the patients of *taqlīd*," one might think that al-Kaššī aims to eradicate the disease of *taqlīd*. Does al-Kaššī claim that all *muqallid*s should develop into *muḥaqqiq*s by, say, education and training that the latter may provide? This scenario is quite unlikely. After all, al-Kaššī urges perfect intellectuals only to lead *muqallid*s to "the correct view." A *muqallid* would not become a *muḥaqqiq* by having a correct view. To be a *muḥaqqiq* means, literally speaking, to be a person who seeks to verify the truth and, as quoted earlier, to be satisfied only with certitude (*yaqīn*) and demonstration (*burhān*). The unlikeliness of the complete cure of *taqlīd* may be well understood by considering the notion of *taqlīd* in legal theory. Wael B. Hallaq states that not all the *muqallid*s of a community may become *muǧtahid*s who can give legal opinions: "For this would require that they devote all their energies and time to attaining a sophisticated knowledge of the law which would in turn mean that no one would be able to acquire any other skill. As a consequence, society, whose functioning depends on all sorts of professions, would become impossible."[46] Instead, *muqallid*s are supposed to follow *muǧtahid*s.[47] Therefore, what al-Kaššī calls "therapy" should be, as it were, a symptomatic therapy that aims to save *muqallid*s from ignorance and misery.

Here we see the reason why philosophy is to be written. Having identified the problem caused by the *taqlīd* of *muqallid*s, al-Kaššī concludes that inscribing knowledge is what those advanced *muḥaqqiq*s must do:

> So, [the perfect intellectual must] author a book about each of a variety of fields of knowledge, burdening himself to establish demonstration in each topic as much as the book can contain. He [must] make the steps of his mind firm in its place to fulfil his promise and responsibility – demonstrate claims, decipher the meaning, reform the unsound, promote the correct in the face of indifference, and indicate a variety of verifications (*yušīra ilā anwā'i al-taḥqīqi*).[48]

It is noteworthy that al-Kaššī does not state that the intellectual elites must uncover the truth by the written word. They are obliged to at least "indicate" their investigations. Al-Kaššī goes on to say,

> On various kinds of knowledge and virtue, scholars (*'ulamā'*) and philosophers (*ḥukamā'*) in the past composed many books, in which they redacted evidence and detailed investigations and questions. From generation to generation, every latecomer has asked for the predecessor's help, and every follower the leader's. They have thus refined religious doctrines and redacted the quests for certitude (*al-maṭālib al-yaqīniyya*).[49]

Again, al-Kaššī does not say that scholars and philosophers wrote the truth, but they provided evidence, investigations, and questions. He does not clarify whether they *may not* spell out the truth or *cannot* do so because of its ineffable nature. In any case, the necessity of writing for truth-seeking (*taḥqīq*) is recognized in the fact that the quest for truth is an enormous task undertaken together with past and future generations, and the written word can mediate their achievements, whereas the spoken word disappears immediately after being uttered and is almost always not transmitted even beyond a generation.

Here, we can identify an important difference between al-Rāzī and al-Kaššī. For al-Rāzī, the writing strategy was to be designed only for a more effective presentation of research, and much of his effort was devoted to truth-seeking (*taḥqīq*). As a result, he became frustrated by human cognitive ability and displayed epistemological "pessimism" or "skepticism" toward the end of his life.[50] If one calls him an idealist in the sense that he tried to live up to the ideal of philosophy (and failed), then al-Kaššī was a realist who learned that such *muḥaqqiq*s as his master would be satisfied only with certitude, but this natural insistence did not guarantee complete knowledge to them. Al-Kaššī instead considered that human beings were always in the process of truth-seeking. Therefore, it is important for all scholars to write and preserve their thoughts, and this is what has been practiced in human history by a number of writers. Even though one writer cannot obtain the absolute truth, the writer should not be disappointed. Truth-seeking is not work done by an individual; it is instead an ongoing work undertaken by many *muḥaqqiq*s through the aid of what previous *muḥaqqiq*s have written. The writer's eternal, blissful life is, al-Kaššī says, in the gratitude the readers express: *Indeed they are alive with their Lord, well provided for and happy* (3: 169–70).[51]

Al-Kaššī thus maintains the obligation to record one's search for truth in the written word. An undeniable advantage of the written word is, as he notes, its permanence so that the readers in the future will make use of it for their own research. His idea about philosophical writing, however, has not yet been fully explained. For if writing is to serve only *muḥaqqiq*s who will conduct their own verification, the intellectuals cannot fulfill the duty to help *muqallid*s to have a "correct view." Additionally, the persistence of the written word does not rule out the spoken word as a means to communicate knowledge. Al-Kaššī could have argued, say, that perfect intellectuals must write for *muḥaqqiq*s on the one hand and orally instruct naive *muqallid*s on the other hand. Therefore, the primary reason for philosophers to write should be something other than the persistence of the written word.

Who Are *Muqallids*?: The Ġazālian Background of al-Kaššī's Notion of *Taqlīd*

In his preliminary overview of the *Ḥadāʾiq*, Muḥammad ʿImādī Ḥāʾirī notes al-Kaššī's favorable attitude toward mysticism (*ʿirfān*) and Sufism (*taṣawwuf*).[52] Al-Kaššī's attachment to Sufism is most noticeable in the middle of the first *muqaddima*, where he introduces a hierarchy of "those who know" (*ʿulamāʾ*) according to the amount, intensity, and causality of their knowledge. As the first, he ranks "the possessors of tasting" (*ṣāḥib al-ḏawq*), saying that "their cognition (*ʿirfān*) of demonstration (*burhān*) reaches the level of finding (*wiǧdān*) and viewing (*ʿiyān*)." Those real gnostics are followed by "the possessors of only reasoning (*qiyās*) and cognition of demonstration" and then "the possessors of only assent and belief (*īmān*)."[53] Al-Kaššī goes on to say that although some nonprophetic people "have a portion of insight (*baṣīra*)" into the transcendent, the rest can do nothing but receive "purely by way of *taqlīd*" what prophets tell them.[54] I do not absolutely deny ʿImādī Ḥāʾirī's assessment that the *Ḥadāʾiq* is under the positive influence of Sufism. This simplification, however, prevents a proper understanding of al-Kaššī's critical idea we observed in the previous section and now encounter again, namely, that of *taqlīd*. ʿImādī Ḥāʾirī overlooks the fact that al-Kaššī adopts the above hierarchical classification of humans from Abū Ḥāmid al-Ġazālī's *Miškāt al-anwār* (*The Niche of Lights*).[55]

Al-Kaššī's notion of *taqlīd* will be clarified in light of al-Ġazālī. Unlike earlier Ašʿarite *mutakallimūn*, who maintained that *taqlīd* would not yield knowledge (*ʿilm* and *maʿrifa*) in the proper sense of the term,[56] al-Ġazālī considered that *muqallid*s would also have knowledge since *muqallid*s are "all those who lack penetrating intellectual insight."[57] In other words, knowledge and *taqlīd* do not stand in direct contradiction with each other. This view of *taqlīd* is observed in al-Kaššī's *muqallid*/*muḥaqqiq* distinction; *taqlīd* does not present a contrast to knowledge (*ʿilm*, under which *maʿrifa* is subsumed) but to verification (*taḥqīq*).

The Ġazālian understanding of *taqlīd* is also plainly reflected in al-Kaššī's notion of "knowledge based on *taqlīd* and report" (*al-ʿilm al-taqlīdī al-ḫabarī*). Employing the widely received distinction of knowledge between conception (*taṣawwur*) and assent (*taṣdīq*),[58] he classifies the latter further into six types. Accordingly, some assent, such as that to the law of contradiction, is intuitive.[59] In most cases, however, one appeals for the aid of something to acquire assent, viz., knowledge proper. Al-Kaššī divides *a posteriori* knowledge into five types according to its source. Two of them, necessary (*ḍarūrī*) and direct (*wiǧdānī*), are acquired through external and internal senses, respectively.[60] If one draws a conclusion by reflection (*naẓar*) and inference (*istidlāl*) with compelling proofs and demonstrations, it is reflective (*naẓarī*) and demonstrative (*burhānī*) knowledge.[61] The remaining two types of knowledge, widely transmitted (*tawāturī*) and *taqlīd*-based (*taqlīdī*), are both based on information from others but are different in their objects: the former concerns the sensible, and the latter the nonsensible.[62] The sort of knowledge to which attention must be directed now is, of course, *taqlīd*-based knowledge. Al-Kaššī evidently regards it as knowledge proper (*ʿilm*), even though it may differ from the other sorts of knowledge in intensity (*ḍuʿf* and *šidda*). In fact, *muqallid*s among Muslims, as well as *muqallid*s of other religious convictions, hold nothing but such *taqlīd*-based knowledge concerning theological matters.[63] Thus, *muqallid*s do not offer a contrast not with "those who know" (*ʿulamāʾ*) and, more particularly, individuals commonly called "scholars" (*ʿulamāʾ*) but with *muḥaqqiq*s who aspire after demonstration and certitude.

With the nature of *taqlīd* thus understood, the concept that is opposed to it, namely, "insight" (*baṣīra*), should not exclusively be associated with the mystical cognitive ability of gnostics. Al-Kaššī follows al-Ġazālī in this regard;[64] he writes in the opening paragraph of the *Ḥadāʾiq* that humans can become intellectual leaders not only by the mystical path called "struggle" (*muǧāhada*) that leads to the "witnessing" (*mušāhada*) but also by the rationalist approach beginning from "reflection" (*naẓar*) to achieve understanding (*darak*).[65]

Al-Kaššī's point of departure from al-Ġazālī is that the former, giving up the "mystical" methods, chose thinking (*fikr*) as his path to realities and authored the philosophical summa. Leaving the *Miškāt* aside, al-Kaššī writes,

> O God! [. . .] By Your favor and mercy, let us access the recognition of Your great honor and let us taste the sweetness of the view (*naẓar*) of Your noble face [. . .] just as You let Your close servants access and let Your venerated slaves taste it [. . .]! These are high stages and lofty levels that would be offered only to those who keep swimming by their thinking (*fikr*) in the vast ocean and the magnificence and manuring by their spirit the fields of the perfect essence, sublime attributes, and beautiful names.[66]

He continues to say, "One of the paths of those who explore for God the Exalted, aspire to Him, and seek for the closeness by Him is to explore how His creations come into being by the steps of thinking (*afkār*) and by the strides of reflections (*anẓār*)."[67] Indeed, God commands us to "reflect upon" (*naẓara*) and "think over" (*tafakkara*) created beings (3: 191, 10: 101, 29: 20, 30: 8, 30: 50, 50: 6, 88: 17–20).[68] The Prophet reportedly said, when verse 3: 191 was revealed, "Woe unto a man who chews it in the mouth without thinking!"[69] As mentioned, the *Ḥadāʾiq* is composed of logic, physics, and metaphysics, and the latter two are disciplines used to carry out that obligation. In physics, one reflects upon natural, created objects and phenomena, each of which is a sign (*āya*) of God's oneness.[70] After physics, one may proceed to the final step of the rational quest, metaphysics or theology (*al-ʿilm al-ilāhī*), by which the soul ascends to its highest level.[71] Al-Kaššī relates this sequence of physics and then metaphysics to the Qurʾan: *We will let them see Our signs* (*āyāt*) *in the horizon and in themselves so that it becomes clear to them that it is the truth* (41: 53).[72]

To conduct full investigations into natural objects and divine entities and to fulfil the obligation to recognize God's existence and unity in a demonstrative manner, humans are granted a tool, which the Qurʾan mentions as "scales" (*mīzān*) together with itself: *We have sent Our messengers with clear signs and, with them, given down the Book and the scales so that people could stand with justice* (57: 25).[73] Namely, the tool is logic (*manṭiq*). As traditionally conceived, al-Kaššī considers it "the tool for humans to acquire reflective knowledge, which secures them from error and mistakes resulting from delusion."[74] Al-Kaššī also draws on *al-Išārāt wa-l-tanbīhāt* (*Pointers and Reminders*) by Ibn Sīnā and writes that logic is "a canonical tool for human beings which, if they observe, will save them from errors in their thinking."[75] Thinking is "the ordering of known matters into such a specific manner that the unknown becomes known,"[76] and logic concerns that specific manner. As the tool, logic should be learned prior to physics and metaphysics, and al-Kaššī begins the *Ḥadāʾiq* with it.

Al-Kaššī's manner of truth-seeking (*taḥqīq*) is therefore simple: think and demonstrate as much as possible, and if impossible, defer the conclusion. He completes the first *muqaddima* as follows:

> We must inquire into the realities of things through *sound*, correct *research (baḥṯ) and proper*, complete *reflection (naẓar)*. If, *in any discussion, we find [one view] more compelling, and if the glory of truth* appears *from the horizon of demonstration (burhān), we shall* prefer *it and adopt it. However, if both sides of the scales are equal* or if the truth cannot be distinguished from false, then we send it to the site of possibility unless something demonstrative holds [it] back from there.[77]

Strikingly, this passage is almost literally taken from the preamble to al-Rāzī's seminal philosophical summa *al-Mulaḫḫaṣ* (*The Précis*), and the rest is from the last chapter of Ibn Sīnā's *Išārāt*.[78] Both Ibn Sīnā and al-Rāzī, as we clearly see here, admitted that rational investigations would not always reveal the truth. Al-Kaššī writes in the same vein,

> Our discussion [in the *Ḥadāʾiq*] has sometimes made sure of the truth but sometimes merely made use of proof. This reminds us that especially in regard

> to mysterious and profound enigmata and inscrutable and difficult questions, it is one of the most challenging things to do full justice to research (*baḥṯ*) and to present to thinking (*fikr*) what it deserves through affirmation, verification (*taḥqīq*), redaction, and analysis. It is so even for those who verify reports (*muḥaqqiqat al-aḫbār*) and plunge into the ocean of secrets, supported by a strong intuition, straight nature, brilliant talent, and critical insight. Then what about one like me?[79]

Al-Kaššī goes on to write that one may not reject everything that cannot be demonstrated. The effect of medication, for instance, is not demonstrated, but it is nonsense to deny it at all since the effect is empirically obvious.[80] Like his great predecessors, he thus realistically accepts the limitation of his, or the human's, intellectual capability.

Al-Kaššī is indeed favorable to Sufism and esteems the noblest cognitive ability of true gnostics. He summarizes the *Miškāt* and says that some people are indeed gifted with the superlative ability to gain demonstrative knowledge through direct experience (*ḏawq, wiǧdān, ʿiyān*) and can unveil and enjoy the ineffable truth in a particular state that Sufis call "annihilation" (*fanāʾ*).[81] Historically, some boldly pronounced in such a state, "I am the truth!" (*anā al-ḥaqq*) and "Glory to me, how great my sublimity is!" (*subḥānī mā aʿẓama šaʾnī*). However, al-Kaššī, as well as al-Ġazālī, is well aware that for the absolute majority of people, annihilation is irrelevant and may even be harmful. Al-Ġazālī warns that "the speech of lovers in the state of intoxication should be kept secret and should not be imitated," and al-Kaššī adds, "except in order to arouse longing and love" for the truth.[82] As ʿImādī Ḥāʾirī points out, al-Kaššī was in favor of Sufism. However, he did not think himself as one of those "possessors of tasting." This is not to say that he could not even attempt to reach the truth. Like Ibn Sīnā and al-Rāzī, he was able to attain demonstrative knowledge, though to a certain extent, through reasoning (*qiyās*), which is properly the insight (*baṣīra*) that differentiates them from all *muqallid*s.

For the purpose of the present study, one point must be stressed. For al-Kaššī, all who lack insight (*baṣīra*), or all who do not commit to verification (*taḥqīq*), are *muqallid*s, but they attain knowledge (*ʿilm*) through *taqlīd*, and in this sense, they are rightly called "those who know" (*ʿulamāʾ*).[83] It follows that the "scholars" (*ʿulamāʾ*) are not necessarily *muḥaqqiq*s but possibly *muqallid*s. Now we are very close to the reason al-Kaššī urges intellectuals to write: through the written word, they can address *muqallid*s. In the next section, I shall examine the audience of the *Ḥadāʾiq* and show that al-Kaššī wrote it not only for *muḥaqqiq*s but also *muqallid*s.

Al-Kaššī's Art of Writing

According to the introduction, al-Kaššī composed the *Ḥadā'iq* with two specific groups of readers in mind. The first and primary audience is his "brethren" (*iḫwān*):

> We have written in the *Ḥadā'iq* so many gems of the principles of philosophy and fine points of its branches as is proper, sufficient, and adequate for our brethren (*iḫwān*) who aspire to and seek for philosophy in the time when its heritage is endangered, with most of the people turning their ambitions away from affection for it. In that [sc., writing the *Ḥadā'iq*], we have observed the middle between insufficiency and prolixity, being wary of tiresome fussiness and avoiding detrimental succinctness – in addition to what we wrote in our book titled *al-Risāla al-Iḫtiyāriyya* about the basics of philosophy – in such a scope and scale that will not be considered insufficient or immoderate.[84]

Al-Kaššī does not explicitly state who the "brethren" are. His reference to his previous work, *al-Risāla al-Iḫtiyāriyya* (probably dedicated to a certain Iḫtiyār al-Dīn or Iḫtiyār al-Mulk), implies that the *Ḥadā'iq* is primarily intended for his disciples and fellows who have learned the *Risāla*. His "brethren" may well include students of philosophy in general whom he did not know in person. In any case, the critical point is that his "brethren" are *muḥaqqiq*s and therefore have a passionate interest in philosophy (*ḥikma*) and human perfection but are still beginners or intermediate learners of the subject.

The second target audience is those who do not have a particular interest in philosophy or may even hate it. As al-Kaššī implies in the above citation, most people belong to this group. Even if they do not think well of philosophy, they may look at his written work. Therefore, with such potential readers in mind, he has

> added such units of philosophy that [people] should have a good opinion of philosophy that it is more proper as discourse and clearer as evidence.[85]

Al-Kaššī thus paid much attention to the composition of the *Ḥadā'iq* in such an appropriate way that beginners, intermediate learners, and even strangers can follow his arguments. In addition, as we saw in the previous section, he presents the processes and results of his research in such a demonstrative way that *muḥaqqiq*s will be satisfied.

As a result, he claims that the *Ḥadā'iq* benefits readers at two different stages of philosophical learning. "The compilation," he writes, "has become such that it has satisfaction, sufficiency, reminder, and guidance for those who content themselves with the truth (*ḥaqq*), as well as [those who] benefit from the clarity of proof (*ḥuǧǧa*),"[86] and he thinks this feature makes the summa "the best of the published books composed in the same fashion."[87]

To understand why it is remarkable that the needs of the readers of two different stages of learning are addressed in one treatise, we need to recall the prime goal of philosophical writing. As we already saw, al-Kaššī claims in the first prolegomena that every truly knowledgeable writer must present arguments with proofs, especially demonstrative reasonings, for both the writer himself and his fellow-*muḥaqqiq*s and then treat *muqallid*s so that they hold the correct view and will be saved from ignorance. Therefore, the two groups of beneficiaries of the *Ḥadāʾiq*, namely, "those who content themselves with truth" and "those who benefit from the clarity of proof," must include both *muqallid*s and *muḥaqqiq*s. The readers "who content themselves with truth" are certainly *muḥaqqiq*s. Then, are the rest of the beneficiaries or the novices who "benefit from the clarity of proof" *muqallid*s or *muḥaqqiq*s? I argue that they include both. On the one hand, it is conceivable that a *muqallid* who is indifferent to philosophy would look at the *Ḥadāʾiq*, and this case is quite desirable in terms of the obligation of the intellectuals to guide *muqallid*s. If a *muqallid* reads the *Ḥadāʾiq*, he will be guided by the author's clear explanations and finally reach, perhaps without being aware, the correct view. Again, to be a *muqallid* is not to be irrational. All individuals are granted an intellect by which they may gain knowledge of entities outside the sensible world, not in a demonstrative way, but through *taqlīd*, and most Muslims, even scholars (*ʿulamāʾ*), have only this kind of knowledge, as we saw in the previous section. On the other hand, novices in philosophy may be *muḥaqqiq*s. As in the case of *muqallid*s, to be a *muḥaqqiq* is not to be knowledgeable; *muḥaqqiq*s likewise need to begin learning at some point. It is now clear that the *Ḥadāʾiq* is beneficial to both *muḥaqqiq*s and *muqallid*s, and al-Kaššī thus fulfills the obligation by a single work. In this sense, he proudly says that the *Ḥadāʾiq* is the best philosophical summa.

We now understand why perfect intellectuals must inscribe knowledge rather than orally teach. Reading premodern philosophers, Leo Strauss claims that they "believed that the gulf separating 'the wise' and 'the vulgar' was a basic fact of human nature which could not be influenced by any progress of popular education: philosophy, or science, was essentially a privilege of 'the few.'"[88] The distinction between "the wise" and "the vulgar" is reminiscent of al-Kaššī's distinction between *muḥaqqiq*s and *muqallid*s. Additionally, Strauss' idea that philosophers' books are truly addressed to "neither the unphilosophic majority nor the perfect philosopher as such, but the young men who might become philosophers,"[89] is relatable to al-Kaššī's target and subsidiary audiences, namely, the "brethren" and the "strangers." By referring to Strauss, however, I do not by any means argue without historical data that al-Kaššī was subjected to "persecution" in society, nor do I insist without looking into the main body of the summa that he has written "a philosophic teaching concerning the most important subject" behind "a popular teaching of an edifying character," or "between the lines."[90] Rather, I want to draw attention to the fundamental fact from which Strauss developed his idea that "Writings are naturally accessible to all who can read."[91]

In *Phaedrus*, Plato has Socrates say, "When it has once been written down, every discourse roams about everywhere, reaching indiscriminately those with understanding no less than those who have no business with it" (275e). For Strauss, because of that, philosophers developed their art of writing to avoid causing unwanted reactions from the unphilosophic majority. Ibn Sīnā employed the method of "indication" (*išāra*) to obscure the philosophical truth, inspired by the epistle historically attributed to Abū Naṣr al-Fārābī (d. 339/950–51) on the reconciliation of Plato and Aristotle.[92] Ibn Sīnā thus aimed not only to train the deserving students of philosophy but also to save the commons from being dazzled by the truth and thus mistaking their religious obligation.[93] Ibn Sīnā's art of writing was, according to Dimitri Gutas, to make strangers "turn away from philosophy altogether."[94]

For al-Kaššī, however, a "perfect intellectual" must guide not only his *muḥaqqiq* brethren *inside* his circle but also the *muqallid* strangers *outside* it, and the written word, rather than the spoken, enables philosophers to reach people *outside* their circle. In this regard, referring to the above-quoted lines of *Phaedrus*, Pierre Hadot rightly suggests the motivation for Plato to write his dialogues despite the shortcomings he saw in the written word: "it was perhaps because he wanted above all to address not only the members of his school, but also absent people and strangers."[95] Words disappear once they are pronounced, so the master can communicate knowledge to the deserving readers *inside* the circle. Ibn Abī Uṣaybiʿa (d. 668/1270) reports on al-Rāzī's scholarly circle:

> When [al-Rāzī] sat to lecture, a group of his senior students (*talāmīḏihi al-kibār*) would take their places near him, such as Zayn al-Dīn al-Kaššī, Quṭb al-Dīn al-Miṣrī, and Šihāb al-Dīn al-Nīsābūrī. These would be followed by the rest of the students and the rest of the people according to their grades. When someone brought up a subject for disputation, the senior students would debate it. If the disputation became complicated, or an abstruse notion arose, the Professor would join in the disputation and provide a solution in a manner brilliant beyond description.[96]

In most cases, oral teachings are thus not transmitted beyond to people who are not present at the session. If, however, words are written down, they can be received by strangers outside the circle. As Strauss noted, this is admittedly a serious weakness of the written word. But this can turn into an advantage. Al-Kaššī's art of writing was not to reject the unphilosophical majority but to address and enlighten them.

Conclusion

Zayn al-Dīn al-Kaššī has thus far been known as a senior disciple of the great Faḫr al-Dīn al-Rāzī and, at best, as a unique Arabic logician who succeeded the master. This characterization is challenged by the new perspective al-Kaššī takes on philosophical writing. For him, texts are not merely memoranda for the future but are the channel to strangers. Of course, the idea that the written word is received by a wider audience than the spoken did not appear to al-Kaššī without precedent in the history of Arabic literature. "The book (*kitāb*) is read anywhere and studied anytime; the speech (*lisān*) does not pass the listener nor go beyond him to others," says Abū ʿUṯmān al-Ǧāḥiẓ (d. 255/868–69),[97] who wrote for a reading public and made accessible a variety of knowledge to a broader range of people.[98] In the field of Arabic philosophy (*falsafa, ḥikma*), al-Kaššī seems to be the first to aim to convey knowledge to a reading public beyond the "brethren."

Notes

* This work was supported in part by JSPS KAKENHI Grant number 18J10539 (April 2018–March 2020). I am very grateful to many colleagues for their helpful and insightful comments on the earlier drafts of this chapter.

1 Pierre Hadot, *What Is Ancient Philosophy?*, transl. by Michael Chase (Cambridge, MA: The Belknap Press of Harvard University Press, 2002), 1–2.

2 Sajjad Rizvi, "Mysticism and Philosophy: Ibn ʿArabī and Mullā Ṣadrā," in *The Cambridge Companion to Arabic Philosophy*, ed. by Peter Adamson and Richard C. Taylor (Cambridge: Cambridge University Press, 2005), 225; Nadja Germann, "Logic as the Path to Happiness: Al-Fārābī and the Divisions of the Sciences," *Quaestio* 15 (2015): 17.

3 Ibn Sīnā, *al-Šifāʾ: Al-Manṭiq: I - al-Madḫal*, ed. by Ibrāhīm Madkūr et al. (Cairo: al-Maṭbaʿa al-amīriyya, 1371/1951), 12. Cf. ibid., 14.

4 Ibn Sīnā, *al-Šifāʾ: al-Madḫal*, 9. Cf. Dimitri Gutas, *Avicenna and the Aristotelian Tradition: Introduction to Reading Avicenna's Philosophical Works*, 2nd ed. (Leiden: Brill, 2014), 42–3.

5 Transl. by Alexander Nehamas and Paul Woodruff in Plato, *Complete Works*, ed. by John M. Cooper and D. S. Hutchinson (Indianapolis: Hackett Publishing Company, 1997).

6 *Phaedrus* and Plato's criticism of writing in it were transmitted into Arabic. See Alfarabi, *Philosophy of Plato and Aristotle*, transl. by Muhsin Mahdi, rev. ed. (Ithaca, NY: Cornell University Press, 2001), 62. See also Michael Cook, "The Opponents of the Writing of Tradition in Early Islam," *Arabica* 44.4 (1997): 437–530.

7 Ibn Sīnā, *al-Šifāʾ: al-Madḫal*, 1–4. Cf. Gutas, *Avicenna*, 29–34.

8 Gutas, *Avicenna*, 261.

9 For example, see Afḍal al-Dīn al-Ḫūnaǧī, *Kašf al-asrār ʿan ġawāmiḍ al-afkār*, ed. by Khaled El-Rouayheb (Tehran: Iranian Institute of Philosophy, 1389 AHS/2010), index, s.v. "al-Kaššī, Zayn al-Dīn" and the editor's introduction, xviii; Muḥammad ʿImādī Ḥāʾirī, *Az nusḫa'hā-yi Istānbūl: Dastnivīs'hā-yī dar falsafa, kalām, ʿirfān* (Tehran: Mīrāṯ-i maktūb, 1391 AHS/2012), 25. For al-Kaššī's original points in logic, see the editor's introduction to al-Ḫūnaǧī, *Kašf*, xix–xx; Asadullāh Fallāḥī, "Taṣḥīḥ va taḥqīq-i risāla-ʾi *al-Lāmiʿ fī l-šakl al-rābiʿ* nivišta-ʾi Maǧd al-Dīn-i Ǧīlī," *Falsafa va kalām-i Islāmī* 48.2 (1394 AHS/2015–16): 207, 217; Khaled El-Rouayheb, *The*

Development of Arabic Logic (1200–1800) (Basel: Schwabe, 2019), 41–2. There are two recent MA dissertations on al-Kaššī's logic: Ali Rıza Şahin, "Zeynuddin el-Keşşî'nin *Hadâiku'l-Hakâik* adlı eserinin mantık bölümünün tasavvurat kısımının tahkîki, tercümesi ve değerlendirmesi," MA dissertation, Ankara University, 2017; Yazdān Fażlī, "Taṣḥīḥ va taḥqīq-i *Ḥadā'iq al-ḥaqā'iq*-i Zayn al-Dīn-i Kaššī," MA dissertation, Tehran University, 1396 AHS/2018. The latter was unavailable to me for the present study.

10 Ms. Istanbul: Fazıl Ahmed Paşa 864, 218 foll. (henceforth, Ms. F). Cf. Carl Brockelmann, *Geschichte der arabischen Litteratur*, 2 vols. and 3 sup. vols. (Leiden: E.J. Brill, 1937–49), sup. vol. 2, 1013. For the structure and peculiarities of the *Ḥadā'iq*, see Hisashi Obuchi, "In the Wake of Faḫr al-Dīn al-Rāzī: A Critical Edition of Zayn al-Dīn al-Kaššī's Introduction to *Ḥadā'iq al-ḥaqā'iq*," *Annals of Japan Association for Middle East Studies* 35.1 (2019): 187–90.

11 ʿImādī Ḥā'irī, *Az nusḫa'hā-yi Istānbūl*, 47, n. 37.

12 Ms. Istanbul: Hamidiye 1447, foll. 352r–6r (henceforth, Ms. H).

13 In the present chapter, unless otherwise noted, I use "Intro." to refer to my edition of the introduction in Obuchi, "In the Wake of Faḫr al-Dīn al-Rāzī," 191–201. According to this edition, I indicate page and line numbers, as well as the transliteration of the Arabic.

14 Intro., 191, l. 20–192, l. 29, esp. 192, ll. 27–8 (*wa-l-āna qad ḥāna ḥīnu stiftāḥi l-kitābi wa-tabwībi l-abwābi ḫidmatan li-ḫazā'ini kutubihim al-ʿāliyati*).

15 Intro., 193, l. 10 (*fa-ʿulima bi-hāḏihi l-dalā'ili l-qāhirati l-bāhirati anna l-ʿulūma kullahā šarīfatun ʿaliyyatu l-qudrati ʿaẓīmatu l-ḫaṭari*). On the concept of *ʿilm* in the Qur'an, see Franz Rosenthal, *Knowledge Triumphant: The Concept of Knowledge in Medieval Islam* (Leiden and Boston: Brill, 2007), 19–32.

16 Intro., 198, ll. 14–6 (*wa-ammā l-maʿrifatu fa-hiya ʿibāratun ʿan ʿilmin ḥādiṯin infiʿāliyyin lā fiʿliyyin ʿalā maʿnā anna ḏālika l-ʿilma lā yakūnu sababan li-wuǧūdi l-maʿlūmi bihi, bal yakūnu wuǧūdu l-maʿlūmi sababan li-wuǧūdi l-ʿilmi immā bi-wāsiṭati l-mušāhadati aw al-mubāšarati wa-l-mulāqāti, wa-li-hāḏā l-maʿnā lā yūṣafu llāhu taʿālā bi-kawnihi ʿārifan li-anna ʿilmahu subḥānahu wa-taʿālā ʿilmun qadīmun fiʿliyyun lā infiʿāliyyun*). Cf. Rosenthal, *Knowledge Triumphant*, 113ff. For al-Kaššī, *ʿilm* is itself self-evident because it, as the act of knowing, precedes any attempt to know it (Intro., 197, l. 30: *wa-ammā l-ʿilmu fa-huwa mina l-maʿlūmāti l-badīhiyyati l-ġaniyyati ʿani l-iktisābi*). Cf. al-Rāzī's position in Josef van Ess, *Die Erkenntnislehre des ʿAḍudaddīn al-Īcī: Übersetzung und Kommentar des ersten Buches seiner Mawāqif* (Wiesbaden: Franz Steiner, 1966), 60–6, esp. 64–5.

17 Intro., 193, ll. 24–5 (*wa-l-nufūsu ayḍan ṯalāṯatun: bahmiyyatun wa-tusammā quwwatan šahwāniyyatan, wa-sabʿiyyatun wa-tusammā quwwatan ġaḍabiyyatan* [. . .] *wa-nāṭiqatun wa-tusammā quwwatan malakiyyatan*).

18 Intro., 193, ll. 21–2 (*wa-ammā l-dalīlu l-ʿaqliyyu ʿalā ḏālika fa-huwa anna l-laḏḏāti ṯalāṯatun: ḥissiyyatun ka-l-maṭuʿūmi l-šahiyyi wa-l-mašrūbi l-haniyyi wa-l-mankūḥi l-bahiyyi ilā ġayri ḏālika, wa-ḫayāliyyatun ka-anwāʿi l-taǧammulāti wa-l-imārāti wa-l-sulṭanati*).

19 Intro., 193, ll. 22–3 (*fa-kullu hāḏihi laḏḏātun ǧusmāniyyatun fāniyatun*).

20 Intro., 193, ll. 25–7 (*wa-nāṭiqatun wa-tusammā quwwatan malakiyyatan wa-hiya ǧawharun rūḥāniyyun bihi yumtāzu l-insānu ʿan ġayrihi mina l-ḥayawānāti wa-huwa l-bāqī baʿda mawti l-badani ʿalā mā qāla llāhu taʿālā, "Wa-lā taqūlū li-man yuqtalu fī sabīli llāhi amwātun bal aḥyā'un walākin lā tašʿurūna"*).

21 Intro., 193, ll. 23–4 (*wa-ʿaqliyyatun ka-l-ʿulūmi l-kulliyyati l-ḥaqīqiyyati wa-l-maʿārifi l-ilāhiyyati l-qudsiyyati wa-hāḏihi laḏḏātun rūḥāniyyatun bāqiyatun wa-saʿādātun rabbāniyyatun ṣāfiyatun*).

22 Intro., 193, ll. 8–9 (*satara ʿayba l-šahwati wa-l-ġaḍabi fī Ādama ʿalayhi l-salāmu bi-l-ʿilmi kamā qāla taʿālā, "Wa-ʿallama Ādama l-asmā'a kullahā ṯumma ʿaraḍahum ʿalā l-malā'ikati*).

23 Intro., 193, ll. 31–2 (*fa-hāḏā huwa l-kamālu llaḏī bihi yaṣīru l-ǧawharu l-ʿaqliyyu ʿaqlan bi-l-fiʿli wa-bihi yalqā llāha taʿālā wa-bihi yaltaḏḏu wa-yabtahiǧu*).

24 Intro., 193, l. 32 (*baʿda qahri l-nafsi l-bahmiyyati wa-l-sabʿiyyati bi-l-riyāḍāti l-badaniyyati wa-l-muḥāfaẓati ʿalā l-ḥudūdi l-šarʿiyyati*). Read *al-šarʿiyyati* with Şahin instead of *al-šahiyyati*.

25 Intro., 193, ll. 16–9 (*"Wa-l-ʿaṣri inna l-insāna la-fī ḫusrin illā llaḏīna āmanū wa-ʿamilū l-ṣāliḥāti," fa-inna qawlahu "āmanū" išāratun ilā l-kamāli fī l-quwwati l-naẓariyyati wa-"ʿamilū l-ṣāliḥāti" išāratun ilā l-kamāli fī l-quwwati l-ʿamaliyyati wa-"tawāṣaw bi-l-ḥaqqi" išāratun ilā l-takmīli fī l-quwwati l-naẓariyyati wa-"tawāṣaw bi-l-ṣabri" išāratun ilā l-takmīli fī l-quwwati l-ʿamaliyyati*).

26 Intro., 199, l. 18 (*ʿibāratun ʿan istikmāli l-nafsi l-insāniyyati fī quwwatihā l-naẓariyyati bi-maʿrifati l-ḥaqāʾiqi wa-fī quwwatihā l-ʿamaliyyati bi-fiʿli l-ḫayrāti*).

27 Intro., 199, ll. 21–2 (*wa-qad qīla fī ḥaddi l-ḥikmati ayḍan istikmālu l-nafsi l-insāniyyati bi-taṣawwuri l-umūri wa-l-taṣdīqi bi-l-ḥaqāʾiqi l-naẓariyyati wa-l-ʿamaliyyati wa-taḥṣīli l-faḍāʾili l-ḫulqiyyati bi-qadri l-ṭāqati l-bašariyyati*).

28 Intro., 193, ll. 10–2 (*illā anna aʿlā l-ʿulūmi qadaran wa-aʿẓamahā ḫaṭaran ʿilmu l-ḥikmati llatī hiya l-maʿārifu l-ilāhiyyatu wa-l-anwāru l-qudsiyyatu, iḏ maʿa šarafi maʿlūmātihā wa-šiddati l-ḥāǧati ilayhā hiya muḫtaṣṣatun bi-quwwati l-dalāʾili ʿalayhā wa-kawni kamāli l-saʿādati ladayhā*).

29 Intro., 193, ll. 13–4 (*wa-li-hāḏā l-maʿnā sammā llāhu taʿālā l-ḥikmata ḫayran kaṯīran kamā qāla taʿālā, "Wa-man yuʾta l-ḥikmata fa-qad ūtiya ḫayran kaṯīran," wa-li-annahā tuʾaddī ṣāḥibahā ilā l-ǧannati l-maʾwā wa-turaqqīhi l-daraǧata l-ʿulyā ʿalā mā qāla llāhu taʿālā, "Yarfaʿi llāhu llaḏīna āmanū minkum wa-llaḏīna utū l-ʿilma daraǧātin"*). For the concept of *ḥikma* in the Qurʾān, see Rosenthal, *Knowledge Triumphant*, 35–40.

30 Intro., 199, l. 23–200, l. 27. Note that al-Kaššī distinguishes *ḥikma* from *falsafa*, defining the latter as "to know the realities of things and practice what most properly follows from them" (Intro., 199, l. 17: *wa-maʿnā l-falsafati l-ʿilmu bi-ḥaqāʾiqi l-ašyāʾi wa-l-ʿamalu bi-mā huwa l-aṣaḥḥu minhā*). Although *falsafa* is thus a sort of *ʿilm*, it is not precisely the science to be studied in the *Ḥadāʾiq* since al-Kaššī's goal is to achieve human perfection. The reason he gives a lesser rank of knowledge to the *falsafa* is probably because of the historical context in which the name "*falāsifa*" had a negative connotation.

31 Intro., 191, ll. 2–3 (*kallafahum bi-maʿrifati ulūhiyyatihi wa-amarahum bi-l-ʿilmi bi-waḥdāniyyatihi*).

32 Intro., 197, ll. 19–20 (*bihi yudriku l-insānu l-umūra l-kulliyyata wa-l-ġāʾibata ʿani l-ḥawāssi wa-yafʿalu l-afʿāla l-fikriyyata l-mustaṣawbata min aʿammi l-nāsi iḏā kāna ṣaḥīḥan salīman*).

33 Intro., 197, ll. 20–1 (*yaqṭaʿu bihi aʿḏārahum wa-yalzamu ʿalayhim ḥuqūqahu min maʿrifatihi wa-šukri niʿmatihi*). Read *yalzamu* with Şahin instead of *talzamu*.

34 Intro., 194, ll. 1–2 (*yaǧibu an takūna l-nufūsu bihi mašġūfatan wa-l-himamu ilayhi maṣrūfatan wa-l-anāmu ʿalā iḥkāmi l-ʿulūmi wa-inqāʾihā mawqūfatan*).

35 Intro., 193, l. 15 (*fa-man ḥaṣṣalahu fa-qad iġtanama l-saʿādata l-qiswā wa-man ḍayyaʿahu fa-qad ḫasara l-āḫirata wa-l-dunyā*); ll. 19–20 (*fa-hāḏihi l-sūratu dāllatun ʿalā anna l-insāna innamā yataḫallaṣu ʿani l-ḫusrāni iḏā kāna kāmilan mukmilan fī l-quwwati l-naẓariyyati wa-l-ʿamaliyyati*).

36 Intro., 194, l. 2 (*li-anna l-nāsa fī mudārasati l-ʿulūmi wa-mumārasatihā ʿalā ṣanfayni*). Note that the criterion for this bifurcation is not the "ability" to learn.

37 Intro., 194, ll. 2–3 (*muḥaqqiqūna lā taskunu nufūsuhum illā ilā balaǧi l-yaqīni fa-lā yaqbalūna ġayra mā yaḍiḥu bi-l-burhāni l-mubīni*).

38 Gutas, *Avicenna*, 213–9; Ayman Shihadeh, "Al-Rāzī's (d. 1210) Commentary on Avicenna's *Pointers*: The Confluence of Exegesis and Aporetics," in *The Oxford Handbook of Islamic Philosophy*, ed. by Khaled El-Rouayheb and Sabine Schmidtke (New York: Oxford University Press, 2017), 301; Robert Wisnovsky, "Avicennism and Exegetical Practice in the Early Commentaries on the *Ishārāt*," *Oriens* 41 (2013): 349–78; Kamran I. Karimullah, "The Emergence of Verification (*taḥqīq*) in Islamic Medicine: The Exegetical Legacy of Faḫr al-Dīn al-Rāzī's (d. 1210) Commentary on Avicenna's (d. 1037) *Canon of Medicine*," *Oriens* 47 (2019): 9–74.

39 Intro., 194, ll. 3–6 (*wa-āḫarūna muqallidūna ġayrihim muwaffiḍūna ilayhim amarahum munqādūna li-kulli man qādahum ġayri mustaṯbitīna ġayyihim wa-rušādihim yataḥarrakūna in ḥurrikū wa-yaskunūna mihmā turakū yaʿẓamūna aslāfahum wa-yaltazimūna min ġayri*

naẓarin awṣāfahum yataqalladūna manārahum wa-yattabiʿūna āṯārahum, kamā ḥakā l-Qurʾānu ʿan amṯālihim qawlahum, "Innā waǧadnā ābāʾanā ʿalā ummatin wa-annā ʿalā āṯārihim muqtadūna," "awa law kāna ābāʾuhum lā yaʿlamūna šayʾan wa-lā yahtadūna").

40 Intro., 194, ll. 7–9 (*wa-man raḍiya li-nafsihi an yakūna min ǧumlati l-muqallidīna wa-ḫuṣūṣan fī l-ʿulūmi l-ilāhiyyati fa-qad aḫraǧahā min aʿdādi l-ʿālamīna wa-qtanaʿa lahā bi-martabatin qāṣiratin ʿan adwani marātibi l-ādamiyyīna kamā qāla llāhu tabāraka wa-taʿālā, "A-raʾayta man ittaḫaḏa ilāhahu hawāhu, a-fa-anta takūnu ʿalayhi wakīlan am taḥsabu anna akṯarahum yasmaʿūna aw yaʿqilūna in hum illā ka-l-anʿāmi bal hum aḍallu sabīlan"*).

41 Peter Adamson, *Philosophy in the Islamic World: A History of Philosophy without Any Gaps* (New York: Oxford University Press, 2016), xi.

42 Abū Ḥāmid al-Ġazālī, *Tahāfut al-falāsifa: The Incoherence of the Philosophers*, ed. and transl. by Michael E. Marmura (Provo, Utah: Brigham Young University Press, 2000), 1–3. Cf. Richard M. Frank, "Al-Ghazālī on *Taqlīd*: Scholars, Theologians, and Philosophers," *Zeitschrift für Geschichte der arabisch-islamischen Wissenschaften* 7 (1991–92): 244–7; Frank Griffel, "*Taqlīd* of the Philosophers: al-Ghazālī's Initial Accusation in His *Tahāfut*," in *Ideas, Images, and Methods of Portrayal: Insights into Classical Arabic Literature and Islam*, ed. by Sebastian Günther (Leiden: Brill, 2005), 282–96.

43 Faḫr al-Dīn al-Rāzī, *al-Mabāḥiṯ al-mašriqiyya fī ʿilm al-ilāhiyyāt wa-l-ṭabīʿiyyāt*, ed. by Muḥammad al-Muʿtaṣim bi-Allāh al-Baġdādī, 2 vols. (Qum: Manšūrāt-i Ḏawī al-Qurbā, 1429/[2008–09]), vol. 1, 88–9; Tariq Jaffer, *Rāzī: Master of Qurʾānic Interpretation and Theological Reasoning* (New York: Oxford University Press, 2015), 23–4; Shihadeh, "Al-Rāzī's Commentary," 299.

44 Intro., 193, ll. 7–8 (*wa-manna ʿalayhi bi-iʿṭāʾi l-ʿilmi ʿalā mā qāla taʿālā, "Wa-ʿallamaka mā lam takun taʿlamu wa-kāna faḍlu llāhi ʿalayka ʿaẓīman"*).

45 Intro., 194, ll. 10–2 (*bal al-wāǧibu ʿalā l-ʿāqili l-kāmili an yahtadiya ilā sawāʾi l-sabīli bi-l-ḥuǧaǧi wa-l-barāhīni wa-ġayrihā min anwāʿi l-dalāʾili li-annahu ʿalāmatu ṣidqi l-qāʾilīna kamā qāla llāhu taʿālā, "Qul hātū burhānakum in kuntum ṣādiqīna," ṯumma yatakallafa baʿda ḏālika li-mudāwāti marḍā l-taqlīdi wa-yasʿā li-iršādihim ilā l-raʾyi l-sadīdi*). Read *wa-l-barāhīni wa-ġayrihā* with Ms. H rather than *wa-l-burhāni wa-ġayrihimā* of Ms. F.

46 Wael B. Hallaq, *A History of Islamic Legal Theories: An Introduction to Sunnī* Uṣūl al-Fiqh (Cambridge: Cambridge University Press, 1997), 122.

47 Norman Calder, "Taḳlīd," in *The Encyclopaedia of Islam, New Edition*, ed. by H. A. R. Gibb et al., 13 vols. (Leiden: E.J. Brill, 1960–2009), vol. 10, 137–8. See also Toshihiko Izutsu, *The Concept of Belief in Islamic Theology: A Semantic Analysis of Îmân and Islâm* (Tokyo: The Keio Institute of Cultural and Linguistic Studies, 1965), 119–30.

48 Intro., 194, ll. 12–5 (*fa-yuṣannifa fī anwāʿi l-ʿulūmi kitāban kitāban wa-l-yatakaffala bi-iqāmati l-burhāni bi-qadri l-imkāni ʿalā mā fīhi bāban bāban wa-yuṯbita qadama ḫāṭirihi fī makānihi ḥattā yafiya bi-waʿdihi wa-ḍamānihi, yubruhana ʿalā l-daʿwā wa-yakšifa ʿani l-maʿnā wa-yuṣliḥa l-fāsidata wa-yurawwiǧa l-ṣaḥīḥa l-kāsida wa-yušīra ilā anwāʿi l-taḥqīqi*). Read *al-kāsida* with Ms. H for *wa-l-kāsida* of Ms. F.

49 Intro., 194, ll. 17–9 (*kamā ṣannafa l-ʿulamāʾu wa-l-ḥukamāʾu l-awāʾilu kutuban kaṯīratan fī anwāʿi l-ʿulūmi wa-l-faḍāʾili maʿa taḥrīri l-dalāʾili wa-tafṣīli l-mabāḥiṯi wa-l-masāʾili wa-stiʿāna kullu mutaʾaḫḫirin bi-mutaqaddimihi wa-kullu maʾmūmin bi-imāmihi ḫalafan ʿan salafan, fa-haḏḏabū l-maḏāhiba l-dīniyyata wa-ḥarrarū l-maṭāliba l-yaqīniyyata*).

50 Ayman Shihadeh, *The Teleological Ethics of Fakhr al-Dīn al-Rāzī* (Leiden: Brill, 2006), 182–203; idem, "al-Rāzī's Commentary," 301–2.

51 Intro., 194, ll. 19–21 (*ḥattā rtafaʿa bihā aqdāruhum wa-taḫallada bihā āṯāruhum wa-taṭāyara ilā āfāqi l-dunyā wa-l-ʿuqbā anwāruhum, fa-ṣārat al-afʾidatu ʿalā waddihim mutawāfiqatan wa-l-alsinatu ʿalā šukrihim mutaṭābiqatan, wa-hum al-āna aḥyāʾun nāṭiqūna wa-fī ḥiyāḍi l-qudsi sābiḥūna wa-fī riyāḍi l-unsi sāʾiḥūna kamā qāla taʿālā, "Bal aḥyāʾun ʿinda rabbihim yarzaqūna fariḥīna"*).

52 ʿImādī Ḥāʾirī, *As nusḫa'hā-yi Istānbūl*, 42.

53 Intro., 194, ll. 23–7 (*ṯumma ʿlam bi-anna marātiba l-ʿulamāʾi fī anwāʿi l-ʿulūmi mutafāwitatun bi-l-qillati wa-l-kaṯrati wa-l-ḍuʿfi wa-l-šiddati li-kawni baʿḍihim muḍiyyan wa-kawni l-āḫara mustaḍiyyan* [. . .] *wa-kawni baʿḍihim ṣāḥiba l-ḏawqi wa-huwa bulūġu l-ʿirfāni bi-l-burhāni ilā ḥaddi l-wiğdāni wa-l-ʿiyāni wa-kawni l-ṯānī ṣāḥiba muğarradi l-qiyāsi wa-l-ʿirfāni bi-l-burhāni wa-kawni l-ṯāliṯi ṣāḥiba muğarradi l-taṣdīqi wa-l-īmāni wa-huwa aḍʿafu marātibi l-ʿilmi wa-l-ʿirfāni*).

54 Intro., 195, ll. 7–8 (*wa-l-mutalaqqinūna mina l-anbiyāʾi ʿalā ṣanfayni: baʿḍuhum ʿalā maḥḍi l-taqlīdi fī-mā yasmaʿuhu wa-baʿḍuhum ʿalā ḥaẓẓin mina l-baṣīrati fī ḏālika*). Cf. al-Ġazālī, *Miškāt*, 30.

55 Compare Intro., 194, l. 23–195, l. 27, with Abū Ḥāmid al-Ġazālī, *Miškāt al-anwār: The Niche of Lights*, ed. and transl. by David Buchman (Provo, Utah: Brigham Young University Press, 1998), 18, 20, 29–30, 38.

56 Richard M. Frank, "Knowledge and *Taqlîd*: The Foundations of Religious Belief in Classical Ashʿarism," *Journal of the American Oriental Society* 109.1 (1989): 37–62. For Abū Manṣūr al-Māturīdī (d. 333/944), too, people follow false doctrines because of their *taqlīd*. See Ulrich Rudolph, "Ratio und Überlieferung in der Erkenntnislehre al-Ašʿarī's und al-Māturīdī's," *Zeitschrift der Deutschen Morgenländischen Gesellschaft* 142.1 (1992): 79.

57 Frank, "Al-Ghazālī on *Taqlīd*," 250.

58 Intro., 198, l. 19 (*fa-naqūlu l-ʿilmu yanqasimu ilā taṣawwurin wa-taṣdīqin*). Following Ibn Sīnā (*al-Šifāʾ: al-Madḫal*, 17), al-Kaššī holds that conception can be acquired (*kasbī*) (Intro., 198, ll. 19–22) and that assent is a positive or negative judgment (*ḥukm*) on the conceived (Intro., 198, l. 23). Here, al-Kaššī disagrees with his master, who maintained that conception was all intuitive and that assent is the sum of a ceonception and a judgment on it. See van Ess, *Die Erkenntnislehre*, 95ff. and 142ff.

59 Intro., 198, ll. 30–1 (*fa-in kāna yakfī fī wuqūʿihi muğarradu taṣawwuri ṭarafayhi wa-humā l-mawḍūʿu wa-l-maḥmūlu, fa-huwa l-ʿilmu l-badīhiyyu wa-l-taṣdīqu l-awwaliyyu l-ġaniyyu ʿani l-iktisābi*).

60 Intro., 198, l. 33–199, l. 1 (*wa-in kāna lā yakfī fī wuqūʿihi muğarradu taṣawwuri ṭarafayhi, bal lā budda fī wuqūʿihi min amrin āḫara, fa-ḏālika l-amru l-āḫaru in kāna aḥada l-ḥawāssi l-ẓāhirati, fa-huwa l-ʿilmu l-ḍarūriyyu* [. . .]; *wa-in* [199] *kāna ḏālika l-amru aḥada l-mašāʿiri l-bāṭinati, fa-huwa l-ʿilmu l-wiğdāniyyu ka-ʿilmu kulli aḥadin bi-ğūʿihi wa-ʿaṭašihi wa-alamihi wa-laḏḏatihi*).

61 Intro., 199, ll. 3–5 (*wa-inna ḏālika l-amra innamā huwa l-naẓaru wa-l-istidlālu bi-l-ḥuğaği wa-l-barāhīni l-qāṭiʿati, fa-huwa l-ʿilmu l-naẓariyyu wa-l-burhāniyyu wa-l-taṣdīqu l-kasbiyyu wa-l-istidlāliyyu*).

62 Intro., 199, ll. 1–3 (*wa-in kāna ḏālika l-amru iʿlāman wa-iḫbāran ʿan amrin maḥsūsin, fa-huwa l-ʿilmu l-tawāturiyyu* [. . .]; *wa-in kāna ʿan amrin ġayri maḥsūsin, fa-huwa l-ʿilmu l-taqlīdiyyu wa-l-ḫabariyyu*).

63 Intro., 199, l. 3 (*ka-ʿtiqādi l-muqallidati mina l-muslimīna wa-ġayrihim*).

64 For al-Ġazālī's view, see al-Ġazālī, *Miškāt*, 23; Frank, "Al-Ghazālī on *Taqlīd*," 217.

65 Intro., 191, ll. 5–7 (*fa-waffaqahum li-l-naẓari wa-l-muğāhadati wa-šarrafahum bi-l-daraki wa-l-mušāhadati ḥattā suʿidū bi-hāḏā l-iḥsāni wa-l-inʿāmi bi-an ṣaʿidū min ḥaḍīḍi manāzili l-bahāʾimi wa-l-anʿāmi ilā awği darağati ʿulamāʾi l-anāmi wa-maṣābīḥi l-ẓalāmi*). On "struggle" and "witnessing," see William C. Chittick, *The Sufi Path of Knowledge: Ibn al-ʿArabi's Metaphysics of Immagination* (Albany, NY: State University of New York Press, 1989), 111, 168.

66 Intro., 195, l. 28–196, l. 1 (*allāhumma* [. . .] *ahhilnā li-maʿrifati ğinānika l-ʿaẓīmi wa-aḏiqnā ḥalāwata l-naẓari ilā waǧhika l-karīmi bi-faḍlika wa-raḥmatika* [. . .] *kamā ahhalta ʿibādaka l-muqarrabīna wa-aḏaqta ʿibādaka l-mukramīna* [. . .] *wa-hāḏihi maqāmātun saniyyatun wa-darağātun ʿaliyyatun lā tasnaḥu illā li-man lam yazal yasbaḥu bi-fikrihi fī biḥāri* [196] *l-ʿaẓamati wa-l-kibriyāʾi wa-yasbaḥu bi-rūḥihi fī mayādīni kamāli l-ḏāti wa-ğalāli l-ṣifāti wa-ğamāli l-asmāʾi*).

67 Intro., 196, ll. 4–5 (*ṯumma ʿlam bi-anna min ṭuruqi l-sāʾirīna ilā llāhi taʿālā wa-l-muštāqīna ilayhi wa-l-ṭālibīna li-l-zulafā ladayhi innamā huwa l-sayra fī l-kayfiyyati takawwuni maḫlūqātihi wa-mubdaʿātihi bi-aqdāmi l-afkāri wa-ḫuṭawāti l-anẓāri*).

68 Intro., 196, ll. 6–11.

69 Intro., 196, l. 12 (*ruwiya annahu lammā nazalat hāḏihi l-āyatu qāla ʿalayhi l-salāmu, "Waylun li-man lākahā bayna laḥyayhi wa-lam yatafakkar"*). Al-Kaššī's contemporary scholar in Syria, Sayf al-Dīn al-Āmidī (d. 631/1233), uses the same tradition to demonstrate the obligatoriness of reflection (*naẓar*) to recognize God. However, he relates it to verse 3: 190, not 3: 191. See van Ess, *Die Erkenntnislehre*, 302. For al-Āmidī's antagonism toward al-Rāzī and his disciples, see Gerhard Endress, "Reading Avicenna in the Madrasa: Intellectual Genealogies and Chains of Transmission of Philosophy and the Sciences in the Islamic East," in *Arabic Theology, Arabic Philosophy: From the Many to the One: Essays in Celebration of Richard M. Frank*, ed. by James E. Montgomery (Louvain: Peeters, 2007), 408–10.

70 Intro., 196, ll. 21–7 (*ṯumma bi-l-ʿilmi l-ṭabīʿiyyi llaḏī huwa l-baḥṯu ʿani l-āyāti l-ilāhiyyati kamā qāla taʿālā* [. . .] *wa-amṯālu ḏālika mina l-dalāʾili l-dāllati ʿalā kawni kulli wāḥidin mina l-maḫlūqāti wa-l-mabdaʿāti wa-l-maṣnūʿāti āyatan dāllatan ʿalā waḥdāniyyati llāhi taʿālā*).

71 Intro., 196, ll. 30–1 (*ṯumma bi-l-ʿilmi l-ilāhiyyi llaḏī huwa l-darağātu l-ʿaliyyatu wa-l-kamālātu l-bahiyyatu wa-l-laḏḏātu l-haniyyatu li-l-nufūsi l-ṭāhirati l-naqiyyati l-malakiyyati*).

72 Intro., 201, ll. 15–8 (*ṯumma qaffaynā hāḏihi l-ğumlata bi-l-kitābi l-ṭabīʿiyyi li-kawnihi baḥṯan ʿani l-maṣnūʿāti wa-l-maḫlūqāti llatī hiya l-āyātu wa-l-dalālātu ʿalā ṣāniʿihā l-qadīmi wa-mudabbirihā l-ḥakīmi, wa-min ḥaqqi l-āyāti wa-l-dalālāti an yaqdama ḏikruhā ʿalā ḏikri l-maṭālibi wa-l-maqāṣidi; ṯumma rattabnā ʿalayhi l-ʿilma l-ilāhiyya tartība l-maṭālibi ʿalā l-dalāʾili wa-tawfīra l-maqāṣidi ʿalā l-wasāʾili ka-mā qāla taʿālā, "Sa-nurīhim āyātinā fī l-āfāqi wa-fī anfsihim ḥattā yatabayyana lahum annahu l-ḥaqqu"*).

73 Intro., 196, ll. 13–6 (*wa-ḏālika l-tartību l-maḫṣūṣu lā budda lahu mina l-mīzāni li-yaẓhara bihi l-ḥaqqu mina l-buṭlāni wa-l-ribḥu mina l-ḫusrāni ʿinda l-imtiḥāni wa-huwa l-manṭiqu llaḏī huwa ʿilmu l-ḥuğğati wa-l-burhāni wa-l-dalīli wa-l-bayāni, wa-li-ġāyati šarafihi qarana ḏikru taʿlīmihi bi-taʿlīmi l-Qurʾāni wa-ḫalqi l-insāni kamā qāla taʿālā, "Al-raḥmānu ʿallama l-Qurʾāna, ḫalaqa l-insāna, ʿallamahu l-bayāna"*). For different views on logic, see Rosenthal, *Knowledge Triumphant*, 203–8.

74 Intro., 196, ll. 20–1 (*fa-li-hāḏā l-maʿnā ftataḥnā hāḏā l-mağmūʿa bi-ʿilmi l-manṭiqi llaḏī huwa l-ālatu li-l-insāni fī ktisābi l-ʿulūmi l-naẓariyyati wa-l-ʿāṣimati lahu ʿani l-ḫaṭaʾi wa-l-zalali l-wahmiyyati*).

75 Intro., 200, l. 31 (*wa-huwa ālatun qānūniyyatun li-l-insāni taʿṣimuhu murāʿātuhā ʿan an yaḍilla fī fikrihi*). Cf. Abū ʿAlī Ibn Sīnā, *al-Išārāt wa-l-tanbīhāt*, ed. by Muğtabā al-Zāriʿī (Qum: Muʾassasa-yi būstān-i kitāb, 3rd ed., 1392 AHS/[2013–14]), 39.

76 Intro., 196, ll. 12–3 (*wa-l-fikru tartību umūrin maʿlūmatin ʿalā wağhin maḫṣūṣin li-yaṣīra l-mağhūlu bihi maʿlūman*).

77 Intro., 197, ll. 12–4 (*bal al-wāğibu ʿalaynā an nabḥaṯa ʿan ḥaqāʾiqi l-ašyāʾi bi-l-baḥṯi l-ṣaḥīḥi l-salīmi wa-l-naẓari l-tāmmi l-mustaqīmi, fa-in lāḥa lanā fī maṭlūbin aṯaru l-ruğḥāni wa-ẓahara ṣubḥu l-ḥaqqi ʿan ufqi l-burhāni, malnā ilayhi wa-ʿawwalnā ʿalayhi, wa-in takaffaʾat al-kaffatāni wa-lam yatabayyan al-ḥaqqu fīhi mina l-buṭlāni, sarraḥnāhu ilā buqʿati l-imkāni mā lam yarudda ʿanhā qāʾimu l-burhāni*). Read *takaffaʾat* with Şahin instead of *takaffaʾa bihi*. The emphasized is the rendering from al-Rāzī's *Mulaḫḫaṣ* by Shihadeh, "Al-Rāzī's Commentary," 300–1.

78 Cf. Faḫr al-Dīn al-Rāzī, *Manṭiq al-Mulaḫḫaṣ*, ed. by Aḥad Farāmarz Qarāmalikī and Ādīna Aṣġarīnižād (Tehran: Intišārāt-i Dānišgāh-i Imām Ṣādiq, 1383 AHS/[2002–03]), 3–4; Ibn Sīnā, *al-Išārāt*, 391 (*fa-l-ṣawābu laka an tusarriḥa amṯāla ḏālika ilā buqʿati l-imkāni mā lam yaḏudka ʿanhā qāʾimu l-burhāni*).

79 Intro., 197, ll. 6–9 (*wa-innamā raddadnā l-kalāma bayna l-iqnāʿi bi-l-ḥaqqi wa-l-intifāʿi bi-l-ḥuğğati tanbīhan ʿalā anna īfāʾa l-baḥṯi ḥaqqahu wa-iʿṭāʾi l-fikri mustaḥaqqahu fī l-taqrīri wa-l-taḥqīqi wa-l-taḥrīri wa-l-tadqīqi min aṣʿabi l-umūri ḫuṣūṣan fī l-maʿāriḍāti l-ḫafiyyati l-ʿamīqati*

wa-l-mabāḥiṯāti l-ġāmiḍati l-daqīqati ʿalā man ayyada bi-ḥadsin qawiyyin wa-ṭabʿin sawiyyin wa-qarīḥatin waqqādatin wa-baṣīratin naqqādatin min muḥaqqiqati l-aḫbāri wa-ġāṣṣati biḥāri l-asrāri, fa-kayfa ʿalā miṯlī).

80 Intro., 197, ll. 9–12 (*lākinna laysa kullu mā lā burhāna ʿalayhi aw laysa yumkinu an yubarhana ʿalayhi nafyan wa-iṯbātan yağibu inkāruhu fa-inna ṭabāʾiʿa l-adwiyati wa-l-aġḏiyati wa-l-ašribati wa-afʿālihā wa-ṭuʿūmihā wa-rawāʾiḥihā laysa šayʾun minhā mimmā yumkinu an yubarhana ʿalayhi bi-ḥuǧǧatin qāṭiʿatin wa-dalālatin sāṭiʿatin maʿa annahu lā yağūzu inkāruhā li-ẓuhūrihā bi-l-ḥissi wa-l-mušāhadati*).

81 Intro., 195, ll. 12–7 (*li-anna ṣāḥiba l-ḏawqi yušāriku l-nabiyya ʿalayhi l-salāmu fī mukāšafāti baʿḍi l-muġayyibāti wa-mušāhadatihā fī baʿḍi l-aḥwāli* [. . .] *wa-yusammā ḏālika fanāʾan fī llāhi taʿālā fī ʿurfi l-ʿārifīna*). Cf. al-Ġazālī, *Miškāt*, 30.

82 Intro., 195, ll. 18–20 (*qāla baʿḍuhum fī l-tawḥīdi, "lā huwa illā huwa," wa-qāla āḫaru, "anā l-ḥaqqu," wa-qāla āḫaru, "subḥānī, mā aʿẓama šaʾnī," li-ġāyati ḥusnihim wa-tazayyunihim wa-bahāʾihim wa-tağammulihim bi-ğamāli ruʾyatihi wa-wiğdānihi wa-nihāyati taḥayyurihim fī anwāri mušāhadatihi wa-ʿiyānihi, lākinna kalāma l-ʿuššāqi fī ḥāli l-sukri yuṭwā wa-lā yuḥkā illā li-l-tašwīqi wa-l-taʿšīqi*). Cf. al-Ġazālī, *Miškāt*, 18. The first ecstatic uterrance al-Kaššī here quotes, "There is no it but It" (*lā huwa illā huwa*), is also very likely taken from al-Ġazālī, *Miškāt*, 20.

83 Although a detailed comparative analysis would be beyond the scope of the present study, it is also interesting to refer to al-Fārābī here. He writes, "The things in common which all the people of the excellent city ought to know" are to be recognized either through demonstrations (*barāhīn*) and insights (*baṣāʾir*) or through "symbols which reproduce them by imitation" (*bi-l-miṯālāti llatī tuḥākīhā*). The former way is of philosophers (*ḥukamāʾ*). The rest of humans usually have no choice but to recourse to symbols. Both of these ways equally yield knowledge (*maʿrifa*), but the knowledge attained through demonstrations and insights is superior because the knowledge gained through symbols is more or less refutable. Therefore, some of the unphilosophic people may finally reject all the symbols and, if they are capable, recognize the truth. Nevertheless, they will not be philosophers but *muqallid*s who should acquiese to the true-philosophers (*muqallidīn li-l-ḥukamāʾ*). See Abū Naṣr al-Fārābī, *Mabādiʾ ārāʾ ahl al-madīna al-fāḍila*, published as *Al-Farabi on the Perfect State*, ed. and transl. by Richard Walzer (Oxford: Clarendon Press, 1985), 276–83. I owe this reference to Prof. Nadja Germann.

84 Intro., 196, l. 34–197, l. 3 (*annā ḏakarnā fīhi min nafāʾisi uṣūli l-ḥikmati wa-laṭāʾifi furūʿihā qadran* [197] *ṣāliḥan kāfiyan wāfiyan li-iḫwāninā l-rāġibīna fīhā wa-l-ṭālibīna lahā ʿalā ḥīni ṭumūsi min āṯārihā wa-nṣirāfi himami akṯari l-nufūsi ʿan īṯārihā, wa-rāʿaynā fī ḏālika l-tawassuṭa bayna l-taqṣīri wa-l-taṭwīli taḥarruzan ʿan iṭnābin yumillu wa-tağannuban ʿan īğāzin yuḫillu, baʿda mā ḏakarnā fī kitābinā l-musammā bi-l-Risālati l-Iḫtiyāriyyati fī mabdaʾi l-amri minhā, ṭarafan wa-qadran lā yuʿaddu taqṣīran wa-lā sarafan*). Read *īğāzin* instead of *īğādin*. Compare al-Kaššī's wording here with that of al-Rāzī, *Mabāḥiṯ*, vol. 1, 88 (translated in Shihadeh, "al-Rāzī's Commentary," 300; Jaffer, *Rāzī*, 26).

85 Intro., 197, l. 4 (*wa-ḍammamnā ilayhi min funūni l-ḥikmati mā ḥasunat bihi l-ẓunūnu fī annahā aṣaḥḥu maqālatan wa-awḍaḥu dalālatan*).

86 Intro., 197, ll. 4–5 (*ḥattā balaġa l-mağmūʿu mablaġan fīhi muqniʿun wa-kifāyatun wa-tanbīhun wa-hidāyatun li-man bi-l-ḥaqqi yaqtaniʿu aw bi-ẓuhūri l-ḥuǧǧati yantafiʿu*).

87 Intro., 197, ll. 5–6 (*wa-ẓannī anna hāḏā l-kitāba ḫayru mā ṣunnifa fī nawʿihi mina l-kutubi l-mabsūṭati*).

88 Leo Strauss, *Persecution and the Art of Writing* (Chicago: The University of Chicago Press, 1988), 34.

89 Strauss, *Persecution*, 36.

90 For a fierce criticism of such Straussian (over)interpretation of Arabic writers, see Dimitri Gutas, "The Study of Arabic Philosophy in the Twentieth Century: An Essay on the Historiography of Arabic Philosophy," *British Journal of Middle Eastern Studies* 29.1 (2002): 19–25.

91 Strauss, *Persecution*, 35.

92 The passage is translated in Gutas, *Avicenna*, 359–60; Alfarabi, *The Political Wirtings: Selected Aphorisms and Other Texts*, transl. by Charles E. Butterworth (Ithaca and London: Cornell University Press, 2001), 131–3.

93 Gutas, *Avicenna*, 346–50.

94 Ibid., 261.

95 Hadot, *What Is Ancient Philosophy?* 72.

96 As translated by George Makdisi, *The Rise of Colleges: Institutions of Learning in Islam and the West* (Edinburgh: Edinburgh University Press, 1981), 93 (the transliteration is modified). For Quṭb al-Dīn al-Miṣrī (d. 618/1221), see Endress, "Reading Avincenna," 405–6, 411–2; Karimullah, "The Emergence of Verification," 6. Šihāb al-Dīn al-Nīsābūrī is otherwise unknown.

97 Abū ʿUṯmān al-Ǧāḥiẓ, *al-Bayān wa-l-tabyīn*, ed. by ʿAbd al-Salām Muḥammad Hārūn, 4 vols., 7th ed. (Cairo: Maktabat al-Ḫānǧī, 1418/1998), vol. 1, 80. Cf. James E. Montgomery, *Al-Jāḥiẓ: In Praise of Books* (Edinburgh: Edinburgh University Press, 2013), 460. I owe this reference to Prof. Germann.

98 Gregor Schoeler, "Writing for a Reading Public: The Case of al-Jāḥiẓ," in *Al-Jāḥiẓ: A Muslim Humanist for Our Time*, ed. by Arnim Heinemann et al. (Beirut: Orient-Institut Beirut, 2009), 51–63.

Bibliography

Sources

Intro. Zayn al-Dīn al-Kaššī's introduction to *Ḥadāʾiq al-ḥaqāʾiq* as edited in Obuchi, "In the Wake of Faḫr al-Dīn al-Rāzī," 191–201.

Ms. F Zayn al-Dīn al-Kaššī, *Ḥadāʾiq al-ḥaqāʾiq*, Ms. Istanbul: Köprülü Yazma Eserler Kütüphanesi, Fazıl Ahmed Paşa 864, 218 foll.

Ms. H Zayn al-Dīn al-Kaššī's Introduction to *Ḥadāʾiq al-ḥaqāʾiq*, Ms. Istanbul: Süleymaniye Yazma Eserler Kütüphanesi, Hamidiye 1447, foll. 352r–6r.

Al-Fārābī, Abū Naṣr [Alfarabi]. *Mabādiʾ ārāʾ ahl al-madīna al-fāḍila*. Published as *Al-Farabi on the Perfect State*. Ed. and transl. by Richard Walzer. Oxford: Clarendon Press, 1985.

Al-Fārābī, Abū Naṣr [Alfarabi]. *Philosophy of Plato and Aristotle*. Transl. by Muhsin Mahdi. Rev. ed. Ithaca, NY: Cornell University Press, 2001.

Al-Fārābī, Abū Naṣr [Alfarabi]. *The Political Writings: Selected Aphorisms and Other Texts*. Transl. by Charles E. Butterworth. Ithaca and London: Cornell University Press, 2001.

Al-Ǧāḥiẓ, Abū ʿUṯmān. *Al-Bayān wa-l-tabyīn*. Ed. by ʿAbd al-Salām Muḥammad Hārūn. 4 vols. 7th ed. Cairo: Maktabat al-Ḫānǧī, 1418/1998.

Al-Ġazālī, Abū Ḥāmid. *Miškāt al-anwār: The Niche of Lights*. Ed. and transl. by David Buchman. Provo, Utah: Brigham Young University Press, 1998.

Al-Ġazālī, Abū Ḥāmid. *Tahāfut al-falāsifa: The Incoherence of the Philosophers*. Ed. and transl. by Michael E. Marmura. Provo, Utah: Brigham Young University Press, 2000.

Al-Ḫūnaǧī, Afḍal al-Dīn. *Kašf al-asrār ʿan ġawāmiḍ al-afkār*. Ed. by Khaled El-Rouayheb. Tehran: Iranian Institute of Philosophy, 1389 AHS/2010.

Ibn Sīnā, Abū ʿAlī. *Al-Išārāt wa-l-tanbīhāt*. Ed. by Muǧtabā al-Zāriʿī, 3rd ed. Qum: Muʾassasa-yi būstān-i kitāb, 1392 AHS/[2013–14].

Ibn Sīnā, Abū ʿAlī. *Al-Šifāʾ: al-Manṭiq: I - al-Madḫal*. Ed. by Ibrāhīm Madkūr et al. Cairo: al-Maṭbaʿat al-amīriyya, 1371/1951.

Plato. *Complete Works*. Ed. by John M. Cooper and D. S. Hutchinson. Indianapolis: Hackett Publishing Company, 1997.

Al-Rāzī, Faḫr al-Dīn. *Al-Mabāḥiṯ al-mašriqiyya fī ʿilm al-ilāhiyyāt wa-l-ṭabīʿiyyāt*. Ed. by Muḥammad al-Muʿtaṣim bi-Allāh al-Baġdādī. 2 vols. Qum: Manšūrāt-i Ḏawī al-Qurbā, 1429/[2008–09].

Al-Rāzī, Faḫr al-Dīn. *Manṭiq al-Mulaḫḫaṣ*. Ed. by Aḥad Farāmarz Qarāmalikī and Ādīna Aṣġarīnižād. Tehran: Intišārāt-i Dānišgāh-i Imām Ṣādiq, 1383 AHS/[2002–03].

Studies

Adamson, Peter. *Philosophy in the Islamic World: A History of Philosophy without Any Gaps*. New York: Oxford University Press, 2016.

Brockelmann, Carl. *Geschichte der arabischen Litteratur*. 2 vols. and 3 sup. vols. Leiden: E.J. Brill, 1937–49.

Calder, Norman. "Taḳlīd." In *The Encyclopaedia of Islam, New Edition*. Ed. by H. A. R. Gibb et al. 13 vols. (Leiden: Brill, 1960–2009), vol. 10, 137–8.

Chittick, William C. *The Sufi Path of Knowledge: Ibn al-ʿArabi's Metaphysics of Imagination*. Albany, NY: State University of New York Press, 1989.

Cook, Michael. "The Opponents of the Writing of Tradition in Early Islam." *Arabica* 44.4 (1997): 437–530.

El-Rouayheb, Khaled. *The Development of Arabic Logic (1200–1800)*. Basel: Schwabe, 2019.

Endress, Gerhard. "Reading Avicenna in the Madrasa: Intellectual Genealogies and Chains of Transmission of Philosophy and the Sciences in the Islamic East." In *Arabic Theology, Arabic Philosophy: From the Many to the One: Essays in Celebration of Richard M. Frank*. Ed. by James E. Montgomery. Louvain: Peeters, 2007, 371–424.

van Ess, Joseph. *Die Erkenntnislehre des ʿAḍudaddīn al-Īcī: Übersetzung und Kommentar des ersten Buches seiner Mawāqif*. Wiesbaden: Franz Steiner, 1966.

Fallāḥī, Asadullāh. "Taṣḥīḥ va taḥqīq-i risāla-ʾi *al-Lāmiʿ fī l-šakl al-rābiʿ* nivišta-ʾi Maǧd al-Dīn-i Ǧīlī." *Falsafa va kalām-i Islāmī* 48.2 (1394 AHS/2015–16): 201–44.

Fażlī, Yazdān. "Taṣḥīḥ va taḥqīq-i *Ḥadāʾiq al-ḥaqāʾiq*-i Zayn al-Dīn-i Kaššī." MA dissertation, Tehran University, 1396 AHS/2018.

Frank, Richard M. "Knowledge and *Taqlîd*: The Foundations of Religious Belief in Classical Ashʿarism." *Journal of the American Oriental Society* 109.1 (1989): 37–62.

Frank, Richard M. "Al-Ghazālī on *Taqlīd*: Scholars, Theologians, and Philosophers." *Zeitschrift für Geschichte der arabisch-islamischen Wissenschaften* 7 (1991–92): 207–52.

Germann, Nadja. "Logic as the Path to Happiness: Al-Fārābī and the Divisions of the Sciences." *Quaestio* 15 (2015): 15–30.

Griffel, Frank. "*Taqlīd* of the Philosophers: Al-Ghazālī's Initial Accusation in His *Tahāfut*." In *Ideas, Images, and Methods of Portrayal: Insights into Classical Arabic Literature and Islam*. Ed. by Sebastian Günther. Leiden: Brill, 2005, 273–96.

Griffel, Frank. "On Fakhr al-Dīn al-Rāzī's Life and the Patronage He Received." *Journal of Islamic Studies* 18.3 (2007): 313–44.

Gutas, Dimitri. "The Study of Arabic Philosophy in the Twentieth Century: An Essay on the Historiography of Arabic Philosophy." *British Journal of Middle Eastern Studies* 29.1 (2002): 5–25.

Gutas, Dimitri. *Avicenna and the Aristotelian Tradition: Introduction to Reading Avicenna's Philosophical Works*. 2nd ed. Leiden: Brill, 2014.

Hadot, Pierre. *What Is Ancient Philosophy?* Transl. by Michael Chase. Cambridge, MA: The Belknap Press of Harvard University Press, 2002.

Hallaq, Wael B. *A History of Islamic Legal Theories: An Introduction to Sunnī* Uṣūl al-Fiqh. Cambridge: Cambridge University Press, 1997.

ʿImādī Ḥāʾirī, Muḥammad. *Az nusḫa'hā-yi Istānbūl: Dastnivīs'hā-yī dar falsafa, kalām, ʿirfān*. Tehran: Mīrāṯ-i maktūb, 1391 AHS/2012.

Izutsu, Toshihiko. *The Concept of Belief in Islamic Theology: A Semantic Analysis of Îmân and Islâm*. Tokyo: The Keio Institute of Cultural and Linguistic Studies, 1965.

Jaffer, Tariq. *Rāzī: Master of Qurʾānic Interpretation and Theological Reasoning*. New York: Oxford University Press, 2015.

Karimullah, Kamran I. "The Emergence of Verification *(taḥqīq)* in Islamic Medicine: The Exegetical Legacy of Faḫr al-Dīn al-Rāzī's (d. 1210) Commentary on Avicenna's (d. 1037) *Canon of Medicine*." *Oriens* 47 (2019): 1–113.

Makdisi, George. *The Rise of Colleges: Institutions of Learning in Islam and the West*. Edinburgh: Edinburgh University Press, 1981.

Montgomery, James E. *Al-Jāḥiẓ: In Praise of Books*. Edinburgh: Edinburgh University Press, 2013.

Obuchi, Hisashi. "In the Wake of Faḫr al-Dīn al-Rāzī: A Critical Edition of Zayn al-Dīn al-Kaššī's Introduction to *Ḥadāʾiq al-ḥaqāʾiq*." *Annals of Japan Association for the Middle East Studies* 35.1 (2019): 185–207.

Rizvi, Sajjad. "Mysticism and Philosophy: Ibn ʿArabī and Mullā Ṣadrā." In *The Cambridge Companion to Arabic Philosophy*. Ed. by Peter Adamson and Richard C. Taylor. Cambridge: Cambridge University Press, 2005, 224–46.

Rosenthal, Franz. *Knowledge Triumphant: The Concept of Knowledge in Medieval Islam*. Leiden and Boston: Brill, 2007.

Rudolph, Ulrich. "Ratio und Überlieferung in der Erkenntnislehre al-Ašʿarī's und al-Māturīdī's." *Zeitschrift der Deutschen Morgenländischen Gesellschaft* 142.1 (1992): 72–89.

Şahin, Ali Rıza. "Zeynuddin el-Keşşî'nin *Hadâiku'l-Hakâik* adlı eserinin mantık bölümünün tasavvurat kısımının tahkîki, tercümesi ve değerlendirmesi." MA dissertation, Ankara University, 2017.

Shihadeh, Ayman. *The Teleological Ethics of Fakhr al-Dīn al-Rāzī*. Leiden: Brill, 2006.

Shihadeh, Ayman. "Al-Rāzī's (d. 1210) Commentary on Avicenna's *Pointers*: The Confluence of Exegesis and Aporetics." In *The Oxford Handbook of Islamic Philosophy*. Ed. by Khaled El-Rouayheb and Sabine Schmidtke. New York: Oxford University Press, 2017, 298–325.

Schoeler, Gregor. "Writing for a Reading Public: The Case of al-Jāḥiẓ." In *Al-Jāḥiẓ: A Muslim Humanist for Our Time*. Ed. by Arnim Heinemann et al. Beirut: Orient-Institut Beirut, 2009, 51–63.

Strauss, Leo. *Persecution and the Art of Writing*. Chicago: The University of Chicago Press, 1988.

Wisnovsky, Robert. "Avicennism and Exegetical Practice in the Early Commentaries on the *Ishārāt*." *Oriens* 41 (2013): 349–78.

5

Cancelling the Apocalypse: Refracted Anticipation for the Awaited Mahdī in Sayyid Muḥammad al-Mushaʿshaʿ's Discourse

Tetsuro Sumida

Introduction

The murder of the last ʿAbbasid Caliph by the invading Mongols was followed by "the deeply messianic" centuries in the Persianate world.[1] The *longue durée* of the spiritual *interregnum* that followed this portentous murder increasingly reinforced apocalyptic fears for the looming end of the first Islamic millennium (1591 AD). There emerged millenarian movements that commonly expected the advent of a wholly new dispensation, which is foretold to be inaugurated through the universal rule of the awaited messiah. The messianism of the age was intertwined with other currents such as Sufism and ʿAlīdism, and several messianic claimants to religio-political supremacy appeared intermittently.[2] The Safavid Sufi network, nourished from this millenarian soil, transformed from a moderate Sufi order into a militant messianic movement in the mid-fifteenth century, culminating in the young Shaykh Ismāʿīl's establishment of the Safavid state with the help of armed followers in 907/1501. Although the foundation of the Safavid state is commonly regarded as the most successful product of this *Zeitgeist*, recent studies have revealed that neighbouring states, such as the Ottomans and Mughals, were similarly drawn into the millenarian tendency.[3]

The Mahdist movement of Sayyid Muḥammad al-Mushaʿshaʿ (d. 870/1466), one of the self-proclaimed Mahdīs in the middle fifteenth century, successfully established the Mushaʿshaʿid dynasty in Khūzistān province by gathering supporters from nomadic Arabs in ʿIrāq-i ʿArab. This success obliged him to restrain the irrepressible force of the very messianism that had conferred upon him authority over the region while striving to maintain his own charismatic authority. In his case, the routinization of eschatological expectation meant denial of the actual manifestation of the Hidden

Imam of Twelver Shiʿa as the awaited Mahdī, whose messianic prestige bestowed on Sayyid Muḥammad a collateral authority.

This chapter seeks to explore Sayyid Muḥammad's *Kalām al-mahdī* (*Mahdī's Discourse*) that conveys his claim to religio-political authority in light of the awaited apocalypse. It also highlights his attempt to attenuate the eschatological atmosphere whose centripetal force he had drawn on. Several theses presented in *Kalām al-mahdī* have attracted scholarly interest since Aḥmad Kasrawī discovered the work and published an influential monograph illustrating some of Sayyid Muḥammad's beliefs in detail. According to Kasrawī, who offered insightful suggestions on this "unprecedented" Mahdist, Sayyid Muḥammad essentially positioned himself as a deputy of the Hidden Imam while typologically belonging to Twelver Shiʿa in so far as he believed in the twelve Imams ending with Muḥammad al-Mahdī.[4] Kasrawī and other scholars also established that Sayyid Muḥammad put forth unusual ideas, such as "the deification of ʿAlī b. Abī Ṭālib" and "the immortality of all of the twelve Imams," not shared by mainstream Twelver Shiʿa.[5] However, these studies generally limit themselves to enumerating Sayyid Muḥammad's theses and do not systematically explain the whole design of his Mahdī theory, even though some of his theses in *Kalām al-mahdī* interconnectedly complement his self-proclamation. Although it may be laborious to identify these theoretical interactions due to their dispersed arrangement throughout the text, the Mahdism developed in *Kalām al-mahdī* is characterized by the speculative manner of its construction. Accordingly, I stress the theoretical connection between the theses in *Kalām al-mahdī*, which has been treated separately in previous studies, and demonstrate that their interconnection supports the whole idea of Sayyid Muhammad's Mahdism.

This chapter first provides a brief overview of Sayyid Muḥammad's career and work before outlining its approach to *Kalām al-mahdī*. In the following analysis, I will first argue that the thesis of the twelve Imams' immortality is a prerequisite for denying the manifestation of the awaited Mahdī. I then analyse Sayyid Muḥammad's alleged status as "the veil of the Hidden Imam" by focusing on his interpretation of episodes in the Qurʾan and hadith. Finally, I demonstrate that *Kalām al-mahdī* has two conceptualizations of the *mahdī* of different quality. Advocating the thesis of "God's ordeal," Sayyid Muḥammad sought to routinize his messianic charisma by identifying himself with the more realistic of these two concepts. I believe that shedding new light on the Mahdism of Sayyid Muḥammad deepens our understanding of the reconstruction phase of religio-political authority in the post-Baghdad era, during which messianism played an important role.

Sayyid Muḥammad and *Kalām al-mahdī*

Sayyid Muḥammad, born in Wāsiṭ around the turn of the fifteenth century, was reportedly an expert in rational and traditional science (*jāmiʿ-i maʿqūl wa manqūl*).[6] In his youth, he migrated to al-Ḥilla where he was trained in Sufism under the supervision of Ibn Fahd al-Ḥillī (d. 841/1438), the well-known-Shiʿi Sufi and jurist.[7] His master eventually excommunicated Sayyid Muḥammad because he began to claim to be the awaited Mahdī (*mahdī-yi maʿhūd*) in Wāsiṭ.[8] When Ibn Fahd pronounced a *fatwā* calling for his murder, Sayyid Muḥammad fled to Jazāʾir (formerly Baṭāʾiḥ) province in southern ʿIrāq, where he gained followers among the nomadic Arabs, attracting them to his messianic claim.[9] Over the Iranian plateau and neighboring areas, the Timurids and Qaraqoyunlu had been struggling with each other for political supremacy, and Khūzistān province, where the Mushaʿshaʿids would establish its base, was particularly contested. After several expeditions and battles with the inhabitants of Wāsiṭ, Jazāʾir, and Huwayza, Sayyid Muḥammad took advantage of the prevailing political unrest and conquered Huwayza in 845/1441–42. Sayyid Muḥammad repelled an intervention by Aspand Mīrzā (d. 848/1445), Qaraqoyunlu governor of Baghdad, and finally established his authority in Khūzistān that same year. The Mushaʿshaʿ movement lost its initial expansionary momentum after the leader's son Mawlā ʿAlī (d. 861/1456–57),[10] who had assumed his father's leadership of the movement, was killed by the Qaraqoyunlu army in the course of an expedition to Kūh-Gīrūya province in 861/1456–57. His aged father reassumed leadership and reportedly concentrated on internal affairs and writing until his death in 870/1466.[11] Sayyid Muḥammad's descendants governed Khūzistān as a buffer state between the successive Persian governments and the Ottomans until Reza Shah officially deposed them and established direct control via a military governor in the early twentieth century.[12]

Sayyid Muḥammad's Arabic work *Kalām al-mahdī* is a compilation of his teachings, most of which are *tafsīr* and epistles sent to hostile *ʿulamāʾ* and local authorities.[13] Four manuscripts have been preserved in Iran, only one of which has survived without lacunae, consisting of seventy-five sections headed by the *basmala*.[14] The precise circumstances of the work's compilation are uncertain. Nonetheless, it seems to have been assembled at some point after Sayyid Muḥammad's conquest of Huwayza in 845/1441–42 because *Kalām al-mahdī* contains five sections that, though not in chronological order, date to between 855/1451–52 and 865/1460–61.[15] This estimated compilation date is supported by contents that tend to routinize Mahdistic anticipation, although it is difficult to ascertain the precise dates when individual sections of *Kalām al-mahdī* were written in the course of Sayyid Muḥammad's activities.

In this chapter, we discuss aspects of Sayyid Muḥammad's Mahdī theory from the entire text of *Kalām al-mahdī*. However, this approach risks confusing the contents of sections with different writing dates. This study will focus on three particular themes to compensate for the approach's limitation, given the uncertainty of the dates of composition of individual sections of *Kalām al-mahdī*: "the immortality of the twelve Imams," "the necessity of the deputy for the Hidden Imam," and "God's ordeal." Those theses support interconnectedly the system of Sayyid Muḥammad's self-proclamation. The advantage of focusing on these themes is that they are commonly included, albeit in a brief form, in two single sections with specific dates. The fact that they are all contained in the two sections in question implies that these three theses were components of the author's argument at one point in time.

The first section (KMa, 1b–6a/KMb, 1b–12b, dated to Muḥarram 855/February 3–March 4, 1451) is a summary of Sayyid Muhammad's arguments in *Kalām al-mahdī* and supplemented by annotations whose wordings and details conform with the other sections of *Kalām al-mahdī*. This fact means that these annotations are not subsequent interpretations but rather the author's original tenet. Consequently, a careful reading of this section and the annotation to it enables a complete reconstruction of the Mahdism displayed in *Kalām al-mahdī* by cross-referring to texts contained in other sections. Second, the sixty-third section (KMa, 148b–50b/KMb, 331a–6a, dated to 861/1456–57) contains features that are helpful in contextualizing the Mahdism presented in *Kalām al-mahdī*. The section composed of a copy of a letter sent to a religious scholar (*ʿālim*), Shams al-Dīn Ibn Shammāʿ,[16] which is uniquely significant because the same letter is contained in *Kunūz al-dhahab fī taʾrīkh Ḥalab*, a contemporary source on Syrian history. The description in *Kunūz al-dhahab* provides a clue to apprehend the circumstances under which Sayyid Muḥammad wrote the epistle. According to *Kunūz al-dhahab*, the letter at issue was addressed to the hostile *ʿulamāʾ* of Aleppo to vindicate the author for his past deeds.[17] Considering those two sections, the author simultaneously had the three ideas dealt with in this chapter at least the years between 1445–57, which is after the conquest of Huwayza in 1441–42. Moreover, the sixty-third section leads to the estimation that the Mahdism presented in *Kalām al-mahdī* was somewhat defensive and was modified in a way consistent with the author's political situation, already long-established before the sections were written.

A Paradox in the Manifestation of the Hidden Imām as the Awaited Mahdī

It is appropriate first to ascertain the textual evidence confirming that Sayyid Muḥammad identifies the awaited Mahdī with the Hidden Imam of the Twelver Shiʿa. In several places in *Kalām al-mahdī*, Sayyid Muḥammad presents his belief that Muḥammad b. al-Ḥasan al-ʿAskarī is the Mahdī whose manifestation is foretold in various hadith:

> It is evident that the Mahdī is the twelfth Imam, who was born in 255[/869]. He is Muḥammad b. al-Ḥasan al-ʿAskarī and the twelfth of the Imams, whose mother was Narjis bt. Qayṣar, the king of Rūm. [. . .] She gave birth to al-Mahdī Muḥammad b. al-Ḥasan al-ʿAskarī. He is the designated (*al-maqṣūd*) [to the Mahdī] and the successor of [his] fathers (*al-ābāʾ wa-l-ajdād*) [i.e., the eleven Imams of the Twelver Shiʿa].[18]

Sayyid Muḥammad shares with the Twelver Shiʿa the belief that Muḥammad b. al-Ḥasan al-ʿAskarī would be the awaited Mahdī whose second advent fills the earth with justice, and in that sense, he seems to be Twelver Shiʿi. Nevertheless, he declares his disagreement with Twelver Shiʿi doctrine by arguing that the Hidden Imam would not manifest as the Mahdī. In *Kalām al-mahdī*, the impossibility of the manifestation of the Hidden Imam is demonstrated by applying a paradox over *selection* to the relationship between God and the Hidden Imam. He attempts to establish this claim through quite a speculative demonstration, in which the thesis of "the immortality of the twelve Imams," another conspicuous tenet presented in *Kalām al-mahdī*, is invoked and used to assert the impossibility of the manifestation of the awaited Mahdī. The following passage and accompanying annotation (*ḥāshiya*) illustrate the theoretical connection between the premise and the proposition:

> The one whose manifestation is awaited [i.e., the Hidden Imam] would not manifest but in this way: *the annotation to his word "in this way"*; what we intend by "way" is that the deaths of the fathers [i.e., the eleven Imams] are not metaphorical (*majāz*) but true (*ḥaqīqa*) just like the death of the common people (*ʿawāmm*), the ignoramus (*juhhāl*), beasts, and animals.[19]

In the annotation mentioned above, the author sets forth that the Hidden Imam could manifest himself only when the other eleven Imams are *not just metaphorically* but *really* dead. Sayyid Muḥammad, however, argues in reverse that the proposition of the manifestation of the Hidden Imam is false by proving that the premise of the deaths of the eleven Imams is false. Two points demand clarification here: first, the reasoning behind Sayyid Muḥammad's idea of the immortality of the eleven Imams, and, second, the incompatibility of the thesis with the manifestation of the Hidden Imam.

Immortality of the Eleven Imāms

The thesis of the immortality of the eleven Imams in *Kalām al-mahdī* involves the common belief that the spirit (*rūḥ*) survives after the collapse of the body. Sayyid Muḥammad argues that the spirit is immortal only in the case of pious believers (*ṣāliḥūn*); conversely, the persistence of the spirit is not applicable to unbelievers and animals. He, therefore, insists that pious believers, including the Imams, merely share with unbelievers and animals the phenomenon of the spirit's separation from the body:

> This death means the separation of the spirit (*rūḥ*) from this sensible body. The body would become dust or go where it should be, namely, caves of beasts, gizzards of birds, or human stomachs. The spirit is handed over the hand of ʿIzrāʾīl. [. . .] If we equated their [i.e., all of the eleven Imams'] deaths and murders with the death of animals or the execution of [God's] order [i.e., death] in general circumstances, we would not be distinguishing them from those who are in lower grades. Rather [we would be claiming that] they [i.e., the eleven Imams] and the animals are the same in that [all of them] would be transferred from this world.[20]

In Sayyid Muḥammad's view, the verses of the Qurʾan that testify to the immortality of believers should be interpreted quite literally, and the phenomenon of their spirits' separation from the bodies signifies only a metaphorical death. He writes: "God said: '*Truly thou wilt die, and truly they will die*' [Q. 39: 30]. He intended by this [verse] the metaphor (*al-majāz*) for [the Prophet] Muḥammad and the truth (*al-ḥaqīqa*) for the others." The author thus considers that the believer's immortality, as expounded in Qurʾan and the hadith,[21] refers to the immortality of the spirit and declares that the eleven Imams are not dead, having been merely concealed by God in the same manner as the Hidden Imam:

> He [i.e., the Hidden Imam] has been concealed [by God] in the invisible world (*al-ghayb*) in the same way that his fathers were concealed at the deaths and murders – their deaths and murders were hidden from the eyes of the ignoramus who did not know the clue. "*But God will complete His Light*" [Q. 61: 8]. And all of them [i.e., all of the Imams] are not dead but alive. Truly, the effacement (*fanā*) and annulment (*taʿṭīl*) were not incumbent upon them.[22]

Sayyid Muḥammad thus establishes his thesis of the immortality of the eleven Imams, which serves as the premise to deny the manifestation of the Hidden Imam. The author's view that all pious believers never die does not entail that the status of immortality is exclusive to the Imams. In this sense, this argument might seem pointless. As will be shown, however, this reasoning is significant for Sayyid Muḥammad's Mahdism because it concludes that all twelve Imams, including the Hidden Imam, are equivalent in the sense that all are immortal.

Impossibility of the Hidden Imām's Manifestation

To deny the actual manifestation of the awaited Mahdī, Sayyid Muḥammad interestingly employs a particular paradox concerning *selection* that was common among contemporary logicians. The outline of this is as follows: God is not able to *select* the Hidden Imam to manifest as the awaited Mahdī because the Hidden Imam and the other eleven Imams are equal in the eyes of God in the sense that none of them is dead, for the act of *selection* in principle cannot be applied to objects that cannot be distinguished from each other by the selector. The following quotation clearly expresses Sayyid Muḥammad's argument that the immortality of all the Imams is incompatible with the actual manifestation of the Hidden Imam:

> Because [. . .] all of them [i.e., the eleven Imams] are alive and have never been altered, annulled, and exchanged, then the last one of them [i.e., the Hidden Imam] is not preponderant (*lā yatarajjaḥu*) [over the other Imams] at the manifestation. For, that [i.e., his preponderance] would result in preponderance without preponderant (*tarjīḥ min ghayr murajjaḥ*), and therefore, is impossible. He would never manifest himself without his fathers, so it is incumbent on God to manifest a weak deputy for [each of] them.[23]

Noteworthy in this quote is the phrase "preponderance without preponderant" because it seems key in establishing the incompatibility between the immortality of all the Imams and the sole manifestation of the Hidden Imam.[24] *Kalām al-mahdī* does not elaborate on the meaning of this phrase; therefore, it is necessary to seek clues to its significance elsewhere in pertinent discussions from Islamic philosophical thought.

In short, the expression *tarjīḥ min ghayr murajjaḥ* quoted above seems to refer to a paradox concerning *selection*, that is, the problem of "choice without preference." This paradox is commonly known today as "Buridan's Ass," which states that if someone is obliged to select something among things absolutely equal to one another, he has no motive or necessity to choose one over the others and thus cannot select one. The paradox, initially raised by ancient Greek philosophers, was widely discussed in philosophical and theological arguments in the medieval Islamic milieu.[25] Muʿtazilī theologians such as Abū l-Ḥusayn al-Baṣrī (d. 436/1044) argued that to take any action and not to do so are unselectable for a capable agent in principle, and for an action to take place, he or she needs a motive (*dāʿī*) that causes the preponderance (*tarajjuḥ*) for it.[26] Philosophers such as Ibn Sīnā (370–428/980–1037) and Ashʿarī theologians such as Juwaynī (419–78/1028–85) attempted to prove the existence of God as "'preponderator' (*murajjiḥ*), who [. . .] determines the existence of everything that exists in the world."[27] These serial arguments entail the impossibility of selection without preference, and al-Ghazālī

(451–504/1058–1111) quotes, though unfavourably, such view as a statement by philosophers: "If in front of a thirsty person there are two glasses of water that are similar in every respect in relation to his purpose, it would be impossible for him to take either."[28] Whereas al-Ghazālī refutes this discourse as a fallacy,[29] his account shows that the thesis of the invalidity of choice without preference was prevalent in his time. Sayyid Muḥammad, in turn, favourably employs the paradox to negate the manifestation of the Hidden Imam by combining it with his thesis of the immortality of the Imams.

Sayyid Muḥammad's reasoning for denying the manifestation of the Hidden Imam as the awaited Mahdī may be summarized as follows: because the other eleven Imams are equivalent to the Hidden Imam in the sense that none of them is dead, God is torn between them in His selection of the Mahdī; hence, the Hidden Imam never manifests himself as the Mahdī. Ignoring the propriety of applying such reasoning to God, Sayyid Muḥammad quite speculatively demonstrated the impossibility of the Hidden Imam's manifestation as the awaited Mahdī.

Modelling the Deputyship: The Theory of the Veil

This section explores the concept of the deputyship in *Kalām al-mahdī*, focusing on the unique idea of "veil" (*ḥijāb*), a title the author claims, styling himself as the deputy of the Hidden Imam, whose manifestation is speculatively canceled in his theory. The model of the veil, which connotes a kind of duality recalling the relationship between mandator (*muwakkil*) and deputy (*wakīl*), is conceived based on Sayyid Muḥammad's interpretation of specific Qur'anic episodes and hadith. This concept is vital for his Mahdism as it emphasizes the necessity of his deputyship of the Hidden Imam. In the following, we examine the theory of the veil in *Kalām al-mahdī* and its significance for Sayyid Muḥammad's attempt to justify his own claim to the deputyship.

The word "*ḥijāb*" employed in *Kalām al-mahdī* is a technical term referring to the body, the visible form in which an essence (*dhāt*) is veiled (*muḥtajib*). The conception of the veil in Sayyid Muḥammad's thought symbolizes an analytical framework that offers the understanding of humanity as the combination of the spirit with the body. *Kalām al-mahdī* further relates that the spirit is similar to the angels:

> Then we say: "What is the quality of a spirit which God has put in that body?" [The answer is that] it is one of the angels of God. He has veiled it (*ḥajabahu*) in the observable body in the same way that [on several occasions] Gabriel veiled himself in the perceptible bodies reported in the sound traditions. Human death is similar to the separation of Gabriel from those bodies.[30]

The instance given in *Kalām al-mahdī* to indicate this arrangement of the essence and the corporeal body are episodes involving Gabriel, who reportedly appeared in various human forms during his duties, and the invocation of Moses at which he was addressed from the burning bush. Sayyid Muḥammad adduces these examples to present the view that an unchangeable essence can take several different forms. His infamous thesis of "the deification of ʿAlī" is also explained in relation to this *ḥijāb* theory, in the sense that God was using ʿAlī as His veil:

> ʿAlī, the father of Ḥasan and Ḥusayn and the husband of Fāṭima, is God the Lord of the worlds (*Allāh rabb al-ʿālamīn*) because God has power over everything. That [ʿAlī's] body belonged to the house of ʿAbd al-Muṭṭalib is similar to [the fact] that Gabriel was veiled (*iḥtajaba*) in <the form of a miserable elder and an orphan before the dawn>[31] and in the form of a captive captured by Muslims.[32] Gabriel descended to Mary in the form of a man called Taqī who was not pious (*taqī*) but vicious (*fāsiq*), and descended [to the Prophet Muḥammad] in the form of Diḥya al-Kalbī more than once.[33] [. . .] That veil was not Gabriel. Rather, he was veiled in it (*al-muḥtajib fīhi*). Similarly, the human is not the body. Rather, he is the spirit veiled in it (*al-rūḥ al-maḥjūba fīhi*). Similarly, [God] the Most Gracious is not a corporeal thing (*jasad*). Rather, he is veiled with it (*al-muḥtajib bihi*) in the same way that the speaking fire of Moses (*nār Mūsā al-marʿiyya*) is the veil of the essence of [God] the Creator. He was, in reality, not that fire nor that bush.[34]
>
> It is obvious by clear evidence that ʿAlī, the legatee (*waṣī*) of Muḥammad, was God who veiled Himself in that perceptible body (*Allāh al-muḥtajib bi-dhālika l-badan al-maʿrūf*). This is the same as how Gabriel was veiled in the miserable one, and someone similar to that. The Qurʾan confirms this, and the commentators agree about this. And whoever does not believe that ʿAlī was God, that Muḥammad was His messenger, that Fāṭima was His maid-servant, that the eleven Imams were His angels, that the prophets were His messengers, that the descended Book was His Word, and that existence is His Creation, is not a believer.[35]

Based on his explanation and the supporting examples, the notion of the veil is conceived in terms of the deputyship whereby the unperceivable essence interacts with the material world. In this context, it may be deduced that the infamous thesis of "the divinity of ʿAlī" in *Kalām al-mahdī* was to provide a model for Sayyid Muḥammad's self-identification as a veil of the Hidden Imam. The passage below underlines the author's claim to be the veil of the Hidden Imam and the necessity of his taking the role in accordance with God's wisdom (*al-ḥikma*):

> All of the monotheists and those who believe in the infallibility of the prophethood and the legateehood and the infallibility of all of the twelve successors of Muḥammad [. . .] know that this Sayyid (*hādhā l-sayyid*),[36] who has manifested himself as you know, stands in the place (*maqām*) of the Hidden Imam by the entrustment of deputyship (*bi-l-istināba*) just as a body takes the place of a spirit (*rūḥ*) with the deputyship (*niyāba*). [. . .] This Sayyid is a veil and a tool for this invisible secret [i.e., the Hidden Imam] and [his] deputy (*manāb*) during the Occultation. Without his deputyship under such absence, the wisdom would be incomplete, and the evil (*qubḥ*)[37] would not vanish from God.[38]

Unfortunately, the text cited above contains no explicit explanation of the reason why the Hidden Imam should need his veil. Nonetheless, a clue to this question lies in the texts that describe the necessity of the human body's deputyship to its spirit. Sayyid Muḥammad defines a human being as a spirit in essence by relating that "the essence (*ḥaqīqa*) [of the human] is the spirit (*rūḥ*) and the metaphor (*majāz*) is the body."[39] Despite this, however, Sayyid Muḥammad also emphasizes the indispensability of the body and its importance in human activities. In his view, all human actions originate from the spirit, the true agent of any act, and are performed through the mediation of the body. In other words, human activities cannot be actualized in the physical world without the body as an intermediary. The author implies that the deputyship of the body can be deduced from provisions instituted by the divine law (*sharīʿa*):

> As to a murderer, when he intentionally commits murder, retributive punishment (*qiṣāṣ*) is inflicted on his body, not on his spirit, although the spirit is the agent (*fāʿil*) of the murder. [. . .] Truly all [the actions] generate from the spirit with the intermediation of the body. Therefore, [the body] is punished in place of punishment for the spirit (*bi-muʿāqibatihā*) and is rewarded in place of reward for the spirit (*bi-mathūbatihā*) because of [their] partnership (*li-l-ishtirāk*). Hence, the spirit is the body, and vice versa (*fa-hiya huwa wa-huwa hiya*).[40]

The citation above explains the interrelation between the body and the spirit, focusing on the corporal sanctions prescribed by the divine law, which oblige the body to receive the punishments or rewards that have been incurred by the spirit, as the source of all human actions. The author's observation on the body establishes its deputyship with reference to its acceptance of charges proper to the spirit as well as its indispensability in facilitating any action. In parallel with this partnership between spirit and body, Sayyid Muḥammad constrains the Hidden Imam to require a deputy as his body or veil, identifying the former with the latter for practical purposes: "the hand of the deputy is the hand of the mandator" (*yadu al-wakīli hiya yadu al-muwakkili*).[41] He thus formulates a correspondence between the metaphysical Mahdī and a corporeal deputy within his Mahdistic theory.

Having reconstructed Sayyid Muḥammad's theorization regarding *how* the Hidden Imam requires his deputy, it remains necessary to explain *why* this deputy must be the author. In the following, we shall explore Sayyid Muḥammad's justification for his claim to be the deputy of the Hidden Imam, consulting texts from *Kalām al-mahdī*.

Justification of the Deputyship: God's Ordeal and a "Weak" Mahdī

Remarkably, the Mahdism presented in *Kalām al-mahdī* alleges a complementary relationship between Sayyid Muḥammad and the Hidden Imam. This complementarity is established through the thesis of "God's ordeal," which enables the author to justify his own deputyship. A careful reading of the relevant passages illustrates two types of concepts of *mahdī*: a messianic *mahdī* attributed to the Hidden Imam and a non-messianic, "weak" *mahdī* attributed to Sayyid Muḥammad himself. In addition to the title of the veil of the Hidden Imam, Sayyid Muḥammad overtly calls himself "Mahdī" in several passages of *Kalām al-mahdī*.[42] Given that he develops his self-definition as alleged deputy for the Hidden Imam, however, the term "*mahdī*" that Sayyid Muḥammad employs to address himself in the texts should be understood as reflecting precisely the status of a mere deputy of the true Mahdī. Accordingly, it is likely that the title *mahdī* claimed by Sayyid Muḥammad does not exceed its original meaning that has no messianic connotation.[43] This duality secures the deputyship of Sayyid Muḥammad as it is incumbent upon God to manifest him as a non-messianic *mahdī*, complementing the Hidden Imam's inadequacy for the accomplishment of God's ordeal.

God's Ordeal

Although the manifestation of the Hidden Imam is theoretically negated in the text by application of the selection paradox, *Kalām al-mahdī* contains some passages depicting the Hidden Imam's messianic power, to be wielded at his hypothetical manifestation: "When he manifests himself, he will never follow any school (*madhāhib*). Rather, all schools will return to him. He will correct the divine law after its split and its differences"[44]; "If Mahdī took possession of the earth, he would behave in the same way that his ancestor [i.e., the Prophet Muḥammad] did, and then he would abolish the falsehood (*al-bāṭil*) and establish the truth (*al-ḥaqq*)."[45] These symbolic, fragmentary depictions about the imaginary manifestation of the Hidden Imam attribute the messianic potency to him, corresponding with the commonly accepted Shiʿi belief that he is destined to correct injustice throughout the world. Furthermore, Sayyid

Muḥammad holds that the Hidden Imam has the capacity to intervene in the visible world even during his Occultation:

> [. . .] the school [i.e., the Twelver Shiʿa][46] agrees that he [i.e., the Hidden Imam] enters the honourable domes [i.e., mausoleums of the Imams] and visits the well-known graves [of theirs] during the Occultation. It is impossible for any possessor of power to seize him or to beat [him] with his hand on those occasions. Nay, if he hopes to beat such a person, then it is possible. Such a status has never been accorded to any of the other prophets or Imams.[47]

Sayyid Muḥammad explains elsewhere that the Hidden Imam's ability to intervene in the affairs of the visible world during his Occultation is similar to that of ʿIzrāʾīl, the angel who "grasps the spirits from the bodies, and no one has capacity to hinder him."[48] This consideration leads to his conclusion that there is no need for the Hidden Imam, who possesses overwhelming power, to struggle with enemies or to require any supporters at his return.[49] Once the Hidden Imam appears as the awaited Mahdī, his messianic power will certainly force all people to surrender. *Kalām al-mahdī* presents the irresistible power of the Hidden Imam upon his Return as a reason why the Hidden Imam has not appeared. The author refutes the belief of the Twelver Shiʿa and explains the Hidden Imam's inadequacy to manifest himself:

> Indeed, the Twelver Shiʿa say: "Because of his occultation, he will manifest himself. Along with him, Khaḍir will manifest himself from his travel, as well as Jesus from the sky." The point with which we refute them is as follows: if he would manifest himself in such a manner after Occultation, and with him Khaḍir and Jesus [would appear] from the sky, there would never be anyone who could confront him.[50]

In the above, Sayyid Muḥammad questions the validity of the manifestation of a messianic saviour invested with such unequalled strength that no opponent could resist it. On this basis, he develops another paradoxical argument: the Hidden Imam is the awaited Mahdī; therefore, his manifestation is precluded by his own overwhelming authority that would nullify all struggles against him. According to Sayyid Muḥammad, this is because God originally intended an ordeal (*ikhtibār* or *imtiḥān*) in which the obligation (*taklīf*) is used as a test of each Muslim that determines whether he or she deserves the salvation:

> On that occasion [i.e., the manifestation of the Mahdī], whomsoever he [i.e., the Hidden Imam] summons to him must accede to him. When the powerful and the miserable from the *umma* come before him, this results in the compulsion

> (*jabr*). In such a case, however, the ordeal would not be accomplished because the ordeal is not carried out through flight or impulsion, and the obliged one (*mukallaf*) would not be rewarded without voluntary action (*bi-l-fiʿl al-ikhtiyārī*). Nay, what is incumbent [upon God] is the ordeal in the same situation as when the Prophet Muḥammad manifested himself.[51]

This passage shows that Sayyid Muḥammad frames the notion of the ordeal by analogy with the adversities experienced by the Prophet Muḥammad when he propagated Islām: if the Hidden Imam were to manifest himself as the Mahdī, individuals would have no choice in the ordeal as none would be able to resist Mahdī's transcendent strength. Thus, for the ordeal to be realized, God requires a "weak" appointee akin to the Prophet Muḥammad, who was obliged to suffer numerous hardships during his promulgation of Islam:

> When [the Prophet Muḥammad] was over forty years old, he fled to the cave (*haraba ilā al-ghāri*) and emigrated [from Mecca to Medina]. At the time he escaped, everyone doubted him and said: "He was a liar." If his power (*amruhu*) were as [overwhelming] as the blowing of the trumpet [at the Day of Judgment], no servants (*ʿibād*) would have doubted him. The Evolver's [i.e., God's] intention of weakening him was to evaluate everyone through him because only a few people could fulfil their devotions owing to his weakness. This was the ordeal planned [by God]; it is incumbent upon God the Sublime to let him [i.e., the deputy of the Hidden Imam] walk on the earth with weakness so that the obligation and the ordeal should be arranged to every person (*yaqūma al-taklīfu wa-l-ikhtibāru ʿalā ḥidatin*). And then, all people will carry the burden of obedience and disobedience. Among the community (*umma*), there are the obedient and the disobedient, as well as the fortunate and the unfortunate. If a prophet who has compulsion and power came to a community and the obliged one thought that there is no obstacle [against what the Prophet does], they would submit to him because of his strength and power. Consequently, it would be impossible to distinguish the pious from the vicious among the *umma*. Such a situation is not the ordeal of God the Wise and Absolute, who never commits an evil act (*qabīḥ*) and never fails to accomplish the incumbent. It is reasonably evil to send prophets with overwhelming power. Yet God will never commit any evil acts.[52]

In this way, Sayyid Muḥammad denies the actual manifestation of the Mahdī, based on the paradoxical reasoning that the Hidden Imam would never manifest himself because of his own transcendent power. Thus, it is suggested that a weaker substitute, recalling the Prophet Muḥammad, will be appointed to judge the belief of all Muslims individually.

Sayyid Muḥammad's theological scheme based on his unique reasoning does not simply postpone the manifestation of the awaited Mahdī indefinitely but also entirely cancels it. This denial enables Sayyid Muḥammad to declare himself the deputy of the Hidden Imam as a weak or realistic *mahdī*.

Mahdī of the Community

The accomplishment of God's ordeal demands a disempowered deputy who requires the support of followers to install justice on earth. Undoubtedly, Sayyid Muḥammad believed himself to possess the necessary qualities to fulfil this condition. Indeed, *Kalām al-mahdī* contains several passages in which Sayyid Muḥammad overtly affirms the humiliations and defeats he had experienced in the course of his mission. For example, he forthrightly expresses his powerlessness: "Who else have you seen besides this Sayyid, on whom God has imposed the ordeal more greatly? For fifteen years now people have cursed him, have tried to capture him, and have decreed death for him and his children."[53] According to the theory of God's ordeal, these hardships confirm Sayyid Muḥammad's suitability for the deputyship. Considering the necessity for the weak deputy, it is concluded that the term of the *mahdī* that Sayyid Muḥammad attributes to himself in the several passages of *Kalām al-Mahdī* means not the Mahdī expected to have the messianic power but the weak *mahdī* whose weakness fulfils the conditions for completing God's ordeal as a deputy for the Hidden Imam. Through the connotations of this quasi-messianic title, the self-proclaimed Mahdī successfully tamed the eschatological echo induced by the longing for a messianic savior within the context of his own non-messianic, practical governance over his already established domain. He thus suggests the advent of a weak *mahdī* of limited potency, analogous to the Prophet Muḥammad who symbolizes in *Kalām al-mahdī* the weakness of an ordinary figure:

> Some mountain Kurds (*akrād al-jibāl*) and other ignoramuses say: "When <the Mahdī>[54] manifests himself, he will possess the land in seven days or earlier." However, that is a hypocritical saying and a lie against God and the Apostle. Rather, he follows the model of the Prophet and the other prophets. Indeed, Muḥammad[55] lived in Mecca for fifty-three years, during which most of the Qur'an descended. Then he escaped into the cave and emigrated from there to Medina. [. . .] He lived [in Medina] for ten years after that, and he had acquired little land. How would the situation of his descendant who is inferior to him in rank, virtue, and fame be to possess the earth without aiders despite plenty of enemies? He who is suspicious of what he [i.e., Sayyid Muḥammad] says must remember the episode of the Apostle Muḥammad and what God narrated about him in His glorious Book.[56]

The *de facto* messiah who is not as transcendent as conventionally expected – this was the *mahdī* that Sayyid Muḥammad proclaimed and with which he adorned his religio-political authority. The *mahdī* who actually manifested presented – paradoxically because of his weakness – his followers with the opportunity to attain the salvation. Some passages in *Kalām al-mahdī* term such a *mahdī* "the Mahdī of the community" (*mahdī al-umma*):[57]

> If his [i.e., the Hidden Imam's] status during the Occultation is such [i.e., similar to that of ʿIzrāʿīl] and the capacity [to intervene in the affair of this world without any obstacle] is with him, how will he fight or require aiders? Nay, this weak one (*hādhā al-ḍaʿīf*) [i.e., Sayyid Muḥammad] manifests himself so that his weakness requires <aiders>[58] who aid him, and God imposes the ordeal on the hearts of people through him. God the Sublime said: '*If ye will aid God, He will aid you*' [Q. 47: 7]. And aid for God is aid for the weak among the prophets and saints and for the pious among worshippers of God. The manifestation of "the Mahdī of the Community" follows the quality of the manifestation of [the Prophet] Muḥammad, who lived in Mecca for the fifty-two years, and then escaped to the cave as proof for the people of this world. [. . .] For he who is hidden, concealed from eyesight and clothed with the perfection and various lights, and for he who wears the cloths of the great angels [i.e., the Hidden Imam] as previously mentioned, it is not permissible to manifest himself. Rather, a weak person manifests himself in the same way as the manifestation of [the Prophet] Muḥammad. Thus, the Hidden Imam is the secret, and this weak one [i.e., Sayyid Muḥammad] is his veil and *locum tenens* (*maqāmuhu*).[59]

Sayyid Muḥammad's religio-political prestige, built on various lines of reasoning, became legitimate with the notion of "the Mahdī of the community," which was paradoxically legitimated by his qualities as an ordinary man unable to realize his own theocratic state without the help of followers who shared his messianic cause. This meant the routinization of the eschatological expectations on which he had relied and the selective extraction of the religio-political authority inherently carried by the Hidden Imam, the host of the apocalypse. We can conclude that the theory of the Mahdī constructed in *Kalām al-mahdī* reflected the eschaton as modified to fit this sober world, rather than the ideal – and fruitless – apocalypse that never comes to pass, no matter how long awaited.

Conclusions

From the accounts in *Kalām al-mahdī*, this chapter has offered a reconstruction of the Mahdism held by Sayyid Muḥammad. What is depicted here is the theorization of the notion of the realistic Mahdī, which enables the author to justify his own sovereignty on behalf of the messianic Mahdī. His routinized Mahdī theory contained in *Kalām al-mahdī* reflected the author's urgency to manipulate his own messianic authority in harmony with his rulership. Accordingly, it is difficult to figure out from the analysis of *Kalām al-mahdī* to what extent the theses presented there were consistent with earlier tenets he held before establishing the local dynasty. Still, we can find an echo of his early discourse among the claims discussed in this chapter: that is, the notion of the ordeal of God. This reasoning is undoubtedly self-serving sophistry that cancels the awaited Mahdī's actual manifestation and justifies the author's deputyship. However, this thesis, by promising salvation only to those who accept Sayyid Muḥammad, could effectively incite his supporters to political and military struggles against the status quo.

In conclusion, I would like to point out an omission in *Kalām al-mahdī* concerning the Mahdī's self-styling. Although Sayyid Muḥammad repeatedly claims to be the veil of the Hidden Imam, his discussion never goes beyond the simple self-definition to be it. Strangely enough, when Sayyid Muḥammad argues that he is the veil of the Hidden Imam, he never explicitly states that the Hidden Imam has been veiled in himself. As this chapter has attempted, a close examination of *Kalām al-mahdī*'s texts shows that his self-definition revolves around the reasoning of the relationship between the spirit and the body. However, both Sayyid Muḥammad's self-definition and ʿAlī and Gabriel's veilings, which he elucidates explicitly based on the relation between the veil and the veiled, are not discussed in the same section. Therefore, without cross-checking with the other sections, it is not clear why Sayyid Muḥammad can be the veil of the Hidden Imam. While the concept of "Ordeal" offers to readers the reason that Sayyid Muḥammad is the deputy of the Hidden Imam, the author seems to avoid the structural explanation of the Hidden Imam's covering in himself. This omission of definite explanation seems to be an expression of hesitation caused by the subtle faith of the pseudo-Mahdī, who was aware that he was not the messiah. It is presumable that Sayyid Muḥammad, in his youth, was convinced of his genuine messianic role, devoting himself to filling the earth with justice. As history has proven, however, he was indeed not such a protagonist. Therefore, he lost confidence in his messiahship in his later years. This diffidence might be reflected in the inarticulate language of *Kalām al-mahdī*. Indeed, this is a tentative idea deduced from the blank of the explanation that readers might expect to be contained in the texts. Nevertheless, the millennial sovereigns, including Sayyid Muḥammad, were also Muslims who hoped for salvation for themselves. And their introspections should be counted as a factor regulating their arrogant self-assertions.

Notes

* This work was supported by Grant-in-Aid for JSPS Fellows 21J14204.

1 For an overview of religio-political developments in the post-Mongol era, see Orkhan Mir-Kasimov, "Conflicting Synergy of Patterns of Religious Authorities in Islam," in *Unity in Diversity: Mysticism, Messianism and the Construction of Religious Authority in Islam*, ed. by Orkhan Mir-Kasimov (Leiden: Brill, 2014), 1–20; and Matthew Melvin-Koushki, "Early Modern Islamicate Empire: New Forms of Religiopolitical Legitimacy," in *The Wiley Blackwell History of Islam*. ed. by Armando Salvatore et al. (Hoboken: Wiley Blackwell, 2018), 353–75.

2 On messianic movements in general in the Persianate world of the fourteenth and fifteenth centuries, see Said A. Arjomand, *The Shadow of God and the Hidden Imām: Religion, Political Order, and Societal Change in Shi'ite Iran from the Beginning to 1890* (Chicago: University of Chicago Press, 1984), 66–84; Biancamaria Scarcia Amoretti, "Religion in the Timurid and Safavid Periods," in *The Cambridge History of Iran*, vol. 6, ed. by Peter Jackson et al. (Cambridge: Cambridge University Press, 1986), vol. 6, 610–55; Shahzad Bashir, *Messianic Hopes and Mystical Visions: The Nūrbakhshīya between Medieval and Modern Islam* (Columbia: University of South Carolina Press, 2003), 3–28; and Rasūl Jaʿfariyān, *Mahdiyān-i durūghīn: Bih ḍamīma-i sih risāla: Sharḥ-i ḥadīth-i dawlatunā fī ākhir al-zamān, Risāla-yi mubashshira-yi shāhiyya, Risālat al-hudā, Sayyid Muḥammad Nūrbakhsh* (Tehran: Intishārāt-i ʿilm, 1391 AHS/2012–13), 91–122.

3 Cornell H. Fleischer, "Mahdi and Millennium: Messianic Dimensions in the Development of Ottoman Imperial Ideology," in *Great Ottoman-Turkish Civilization*, ed. by Kemal Çiçek et al., 4 vols. (Ankara: Yeni Türkiye, 2000), vol. 3, 42–55; Azfar A. Moin, *The Millennial Sovereign: Sacred Kingship and Sainthood in Islam* (New York: Columbia University Press, 2012); and Jaʿfariyan, *Mahdiyān-i durūghīn*, 125–84; Sanjay Subrahmanyam, "Turning the Stones Over: Sixteen-Century Millenarianism from Tagus to the Ganges," *Indian Economic and Social History Review* 40 (2003): 159.

4 Aḥmad Kasrawī, *Tārīkh-i pānṣad sāla-yi Khūzistān* (Tehran, 1313 AHS/1934), 21.

5 For an overview of Sayyid Muḥammad's religious thought, see Kasrawī, *Tārīkh-i pānṣad sāla*, 21–40; Michel M. Mazzaoui, "Mushaʿshaʿiyān: A Fifteenth Century Shīʿi Movement in Khūzistān and Southern Iraq," *Folio Orientalia* 22 (1981–84): 139–62; Shahzad Bashir, "The Imam's Return: Messianic Leadership in Late Medieval Shiʿism," in *The Most Learned of the Shiʿa*, ed. by Linda Walbridge (New York: Oxford University Press, 2001), 21–33; and Muḥammad ʿAlī Ranjbar, *Mushaʿshaʿiyān: Māhiyyat-i fikrī-ijtimāʿī wa farāyand-i taḥawwulāt-i tārīkhī* (Tehran: Muʾassasa-yi intishārāt-i āgāh, 1382 AHS/2003–04), 212–43.

6 Qāḍī Nūr Allāh Shūshtarī, *Majālis al-muʾminīn*, ed. by Ibrāhīm ʿArabpūr (Mashhad: Bunyād-i Pazhūhish'hā-yi Islāmī, 1393 AHS/2014–15), vol. 5, 367.

7 The other contemporary self-proclaimed Mahdī, Muḥammad Nūrbakhsh (d. 869/1464), is also reported to have studied under Ibn Fahd. For further information on Ibn Fahd al-Ḥillī, see Muṣṭafā al-Shaybī, *al-Fikr al-shīʿī wa-l-nazaʿāt al-ṣūfiyya ḥattā maṭlaʿ al-qarn al-thānī ʿashar al-hijrī* (Baghdad: Maktabat al-nahḍa, 1386/1966), 288–301.

8 *Tārīkh-i kabīr*, another contemporary source, also reports that Sayyid Muḥammad called himself "the precursor (*pīsh-raw*) of the Imām Mahdī" (Caʿferî b. Muhammed el-Hüseynî, *Târîh-i Kebîr (Tevârîh-i Enbiyâ ve Mülûk)*, ed. by İsmail Aka [Ankara: Türk Tarih Kurumu Basımevi, 2011], 125/330a). Regarding the date when Sayyid Muḥammad began to proclaim himself as Mahdī, *Majālis* mentions two different years, 820/1417–18 and 828/1424–25 (Shūshtarī, *Majālis*, vol. 5, 367).

9 For further information on the political development of the Mushaʿshaʿid movement, see Kasrawī, *Tārīkh-i pānṣad sāla*, 9–21; Mazzaoui, "Mushaʿshaʿiyān," 143–52; and Ranjbar, *Mushaʿshaʿiyān*, 141–76.

10 Mawlā ʿAlī is reported to have been even more radical in faith than his father. According to Shūshtarī, he not only claimed that the spirit (*rūḥ*) of ʿAlī b. Abī Ṭālib had incarnated into him

but also declared his own divinity (Shūshtarī, *Majālis*, vol. 5, 377; Amoretti, "Religion in the Timurid and Safavid Periods," 628).

11 According to *Majālis*, letters were exchanged between the rulers of ʿIrāq and Sayyid Muḥammad regarding Mawlā ʿAlī's attack on Najaf. The same work reports that the compilation of these letters was preserved by Sayyid Muḥammad's followers under the name of "*Kalām-i mahdī*." See Shūshtarī, *Majālis*, vol. 5, 376–7.

12 On the Mushaʿshaʿid dynasty after Sayyid Muḥammad, see Wladimir Minorsky, "Mushaʿshaʿ," in *E. J. Brill's First Encyclopaedia of Islam 1913–1936*, ed. by Martijn Th. Houtsma at al. (Leiden and New York: Brill, 1987), vol. 9, 160–3; and Ranjbar, "*Mushaʿshaʿiyān*," 177–200, 291–353.

13 Although the work contains no preface or author name, some of *Kalām al-mahdī*'s contents accord with information reported by contemporary sources as pertaining to Sayyid Muḥammad, enabling us to identify him as its author. For example, Shūshtarī states that Sayyid Muḥammad was accused of Mawlā ʿAlī's misdeeds by the authorities in ʿIrāq and sought to excuse himself by writing letters asserting his inability to control his son's deeds (Shūshtarī, *Majālis*, vol. 5, 376–7). In this connection, *Kalām al-mahdī* contains a correspondence that alludes to this episode, implying that he was powerless to do anything other than approve of Mawlā ʿAlī's devastation of Najaf (KMa, 147a–8b/KMb, 328a–31a [see the next footnote for the abbreviations]. Cf. Bashir, "Imam's Return," 24).

14 In this chapter, I utilize the complete manuscript preserved in the Marʿashī Library (MS 1211 [abbr. KMa]), copied in Muḥarram 1, 1011 AH/June 21, 1601 AD, and the manuscript preserved in the Majlis Library (MS 10222 [abbr. KMb]), which lacks the portion from fol. 175b to the end of the Marʿashī manuscript. For the detailed information of the Marʿashī manuscript, see Maḥmūd Marʿashī et al., *Fihrist-i nuskhahā-yi khaṭṭī-yi Kitāb-khāna-yi ʿumūmī-yi Ḥaḍrat-i Āyat Allāh al-ʿUẓmā Najafī Marʿashī* (Qom: Kitāb-khāna-yi ʿumūmī-yi Ḥaḍrat-i Āyat Allāh al-ʿUẓmā Najafī Marʿashī, 1354–76 AHS/1975–98), vol. 4, 9–10. For the Majlis manuscript, see Muḥammad Ṭabāṭabāʾī Bihbihānī, *Fihrist-i nuskhahā-yi khaṭṭī-yi Kitāb-khāna-yi Majlis-i Shūrā-yi Islāmī* (Tehran: Kitāb-khāna, mūza wa markaz-i asnād-i Majlis-i Shūrā-yi Islāmī, 1381 AHS/2002–03), vol. 32, 262.

15 Specifically, KMa, 3a/KMb, 5b indicates 855/1451–52 and KMa, 47b/KMb, 111b indicates 865/1460–61.

16 Ibn Shammāʿ (791–863/1388–1458) was a Sufi who lived in Aleppo. According to *Kunūz al-dhahab*, in 861/1456–57 Ibn Shammāʿ held a consultation (*majlis*) at a courthouse (*dār al-ʿadl*) with *qāḍī*s there about how to deal with Sulṭān Junayd Ṣafawī, who had gathered followers in Syria after being expelled from Ardabīl. In this connection, *Kunūz al-dhahab* also offers an interesting suggestion that associates Junayd with Mushaʿshaʿid movement. Still, the details are not known (Sibṭ b. al-ʿAjamī al-Ḥalabī, *Kunūz al-dhahab fī taʾrīkh Ḥalab*, ed. by Shawqī Shaʿath [Aleppo: Dār al-qalam al-ʿArabī, 1417/1996], vol. 2, 284–6). For more information on Ibn Shammāʿ, see al-Sakhāwī, *al-Ḍawʾ al-lāmiʿ li-ahl al-qarn al-tāsiʿ* (Cairo: Maktabat al-qudsī, 1353–55/1934–37), vol. 9, 142–3; Aḥmad Khāmayār, "Maktūb-i Sulṭān Junayd Ṣafawī bih Shammāʿ Ḥalabī," *Payām-i Bahāristān* 5 (1392 AHS/2003–04): 130–9, esp. 132–5; Rasūl Jaʿfariyān, *Tārīkh-i qizilbāshān-i Ṣafawī: Dar chand matn-i tārīkhī-madhhabī-yi ʿArabī-yi dawra-yi ʿUthmānī* (Qom: Nashr-i muʾarrikh, 1397 AHS/2018–19), 108–11.

17 Sibṭ b. al-ʿAjamī al-Ḥalabī, *Kunūz al-dhahab*, vol. 2, 286–9. Although the copy of this letter is contained in the manuscript of *Kalām al-mahdī* [KMa, 148b–50b/KMb, 331a–6a], Khāmayār and Jaʿfariyān erroneously attribute it to Shaykh Junayd Ṣafawī. See Khāmayār, "Maktūb-i Sulṭān Junayd Ṣafawī"; Jaʿfariyān, *Tārīkh-i qizilbāshān-i Ṣafawī*, 108–14.

18 KMa, 122a; KMb, 272b (*bi-dalīlin inna l-Mahdiyya thānī ʿashari l-aʾimmati wa-qad wulida sanata khamsin wa-khamsīna wa-miʾatayni min al-hijrati wa-huwa Muḥammadu bnu l-Ḥasani l-ʿAskariyyi thānī ʿashari l-aʾimmati l-ithnay ʿashara lladhī ummuhu Narjisu bintu Qayṣara maliki l-Rūmi.* [. . .] *Wa-jāʾat bi-l-Mahdiyyi Muḥammadi bni l-Ḥasani l-ʿAskariyyi wa-huwa l-maqṣūdu wa-l-khalīfatu ʿan al-abāʾi wa-l-ajdādi*).

19 KMa, 3b; KMb, 5b (*fa-lā yaẓharu l-ma'hūdu bi-ẓuhūrihi illā 'alā hādhā l-namṭi: ḥāshiyatu li-qawlihi 'alā hādhā l-namaṭi; wa-na'nī bi-l-namaṭi l-ḥukma bi-mawti l-abā'i wa-l-ajdādi ḥaqīqatan lā majāzan ka-mawti l-'awwāmi wa-l-juhhāli wa-l-bahā'imi wa-l-ḥayawāni*).

20 KMa, 3b; KMb, 5b–6a (*fa-inna mawta hādhihi 'ibāratun 'an salbi l-arwāḥi min hādhihi l-abdāni l-mushāri ilayhā l-maḥsūsi. Wa-taṣīru l-abdānu ilā l-atribati aw mā yaqūmu maqāmahā min wajirati l-sibā'i wa-qawāniṣi l-ṭayri wa-buṭūni l-nāsi. Wa-tasīru l-arwāḥu ilā yadi 'Izrā'īla.* [. . .] *Wa-idhā sāwaynā bi-mawtihim wa-qatlihim mawta l-ḥayawāni wa-ijrā'a l-ḥukmi fī jamī'i l-aḥwāli, wa-lam na'jal lahum khuṣūṣiyyatan 'an nāqiṣi l-darajāti. Bal hum wa-l-ḥayawānu bi-l-intiqāli min dāri l-dunyā sawā'un*).

21 In *Kalām al-mahdī*, Sayyid Muḥammad declares not only the immortality of the Prophet but also that of the pious believers (*ṣāliḥūn*) in general. For example, he argues, based on the hadith and the Qur'anic verse relating the living in the Hereafter, that prophets and saints never die, and that the spirits of the righteous believers retransform to angels. See KMa, 36b; KMb, 86b (*wa-idhā ṣārat l-rūḥu hiya l-insānu fa-ayyu mawtin yalḥaqu bi-l-anbiyā'i wa-l-awliyā'i wa-li-hādhā warada fī l-ḥadīthi inna l-mu'mina ḥayyun fī l-dārayni wa-fī l-Qur'āni wa-lā taḥsabunna lladhīna qutilū fī sabīli llāhi amwātan bal aḥyā'un 'indahum yurzaqūna. Ay ya'ūdūna ilā hay'ati l-malā'ikati kamā kānat arwāḥu l-ṣāliḥīna min qabli iḍāfatihā ilā l-abdāni fa-bi-salbihā ta'ūdu ilā l-hay'ati l-ūlā*).

22 KMa, 97b; KMb, 220b (*wa-huwa mastūrun fī l-ghaybi kamā sutirat al-abā'uhu* (sic.) *wa-l-ajdādu bi-l-qatli wa-l-mawti lladhayni khafiyā 'an a'yuni l-juhhāl min-man jahila l-athara. Wa-llāhu mutimmun nūrahu wa-l-jamī'u minhum aḥyā'un ghayru amwātin wa-innahum lam yalḥaqhum al-fanā'u wa-l-ta'ṭīlu*).

23 KMa, 97b–98a; KMb, 220b ([*bal hum ka-Jabra'īla l-nāzili ilā l-arḍi wa-a'zamu* [?] *wa-qad raja'a ilā ḥaqīqati l-ḥāli wa-lam yalḥaqhu mawtun wa-lā fanā'un ka-l-juhhāli wa-l-bahā'imi wa-l-ḥayawāni.*] *wa-idhā* [*kāna l-amru ka-dhālika*] *wa-anna l-jamī'a minhum aḥyā'un wa-lam yataghayyarū wa-lam yata'aṭṭalū wa-lam yatabaddalū, fa-lā yatarajjaḥu ākhiruhum bi-l-ẓuhūri fa-yalzamu l-tarjīḥu min ghayri murajjaḥin wa-huwa maḥālun. Wa-idhā lam yumkin ẓuhūruhu min dūnihim,* [*wajaba 'alā llāhi an yuẓhira lahum maqāman ḍa'īfan kamā ẓahara Muḥammadun alladhī haraba ilā l-ghāri li-ḍa'fihi wa-hādhā l-sayyidu lladhī ẓahara bi-ḥasabi al-niyābati 'an thāniya 'ashara l-a'immati. Bal 'an kulli wāḥidin minhum*]).

24 In KMa, 127a/KMb, 283a, instead of this phrase, a more definitive expression "preponderance without preponderation (*tarjīḥ bi-lā-rujḥān*)" is used in the same context.

25 The problem now known as "Buridan's Ass" is a paradox formulated in scholastic arguments. On its historical development, see Nicolas Rescher, "Choice without Preference: The Problem of 'Buridan's Ass,'" in idem, *Studies in the History of Logic* (Frankfurt: De Gruyter, 2006), 91–139, esp. 94–105.

26 Wilferd Madelung. "The Late Mu'tazila and Determinism: The Philosopher's Trap," in *Yād-nāma: In Memoria di Alessandro Bausani*. ed. by Bianncamaria Scarcia Amoretti et al., 2 vols. (Rome: Bardi Editore, 1991), vol. 1, 249–51. Frank Griffel, *Al-Ghazālī's Philosophical Theology* (New York and Oxford: Oxford University Press, 2009), 170. Fakhr al-Dīn al-Rāzī (d. 606/1210) also argued the psychological problem of selection caused by motive with reference to the notion of a "preponderator" (*murajjiḥ*). See Ayman Shihadeh, *The Teleological Ethics of Fakhr al-Dīn al-Rāzī* (Leiden and Boston: Brill, 2006), 20–9.

27 According to Frank Griffel, the argument concerning the existence by Arabic philosophers is outlined as follows: "because everything in the world can be perceived as non-existing, its nonexistence is by itself equally possible as its existence. Existing things necessarily need something that 'tips the scales' (*yurajjiḥ*) or preponderates between the two equally possible alternatives of being and nonbeing. God is this 'preponderator' (*murajjiḥ*), who in this sense determines the existence of everything that exists in the world." See Griffel, *Al-Ghazālī's Philosophical Theology*, 170.

28 Al-Ghazālī, *The Incoherence of the Philosophers*, transl. by Michael Marmura (Pravo, Utah: Brigham Young University Press, 1997), 22–3.

29 Ibid., 23–4.

30 KMa, 13b; KMb, 31b (*wa-naqūlu ṣifatu l-rūḥi llatī waḍiʿahā llāhu dhālika l-badani huwa malakun min malāʾikati llāhi ḥajabahu fī dhālika l-badani l-maʿlūmi kamā iḥtajaba Jabraʾīlu fī tilka l-abdāni l-maʿrūfati l-manqūlati l-muttafiqi ʿalā ṣiḥḥati naqlihā wa-mawtu Ādama ka-salbi Jabraʾīla min tilka l-abdāni sawāʾun*).

31 The passage in this bracket is absent from the manuscript of the Marʿashī Library. Henceforth, this type of bracket in translation and transcription will be used when the words missing in KMa are supplemented with those found in KMb.

32 Sayyid Muḥammad interprets the three people mentioned in the Qurʾānic verse 76: 8 as the different forms Gabriel took when he visited ʿAlī, as follows: "the time when [Gabriel] stood still near the house of ʿAlī and Fāṭima. At that time, they were praying and fasting because Ḥasan and Ḥusayn had suffered illness. As [found in] the Word of God the Supreme in the Qurʾanic chapter of "*Hal atā*" [i.e., *Sūrat al-insān*] "*And they feed, for the love of God, the indigent, the orphan, and the captive*" [Q. 76: 8], [Gabriel appeared on the first night in the form of a miserable elder and] on the second night in the form of a nonage orphan, and on the third night in the form of a captive captured by Muslims" [KMa, 96b; KMb, 217b].

33 Diḥya b. Khalīfa al-Kalbī was one of the companions of the Prophet. He was known for his beauty, and it is said that Gabriel assumed his features when he visited the Prophet. See Henri Lammens et al. "Diḥya," in *The Encyclopaedia of Islam, New Edition*, ed. by H. A. R. Gibb et al., 13 vols. (Leiden: Brill, 1960–2009), vol. 2, 274–5.

34 KMa, 9b–10a; KMb, 20b–2a (*ʿAliyyun abū l-Ḥasani wa-l-Ḥusayn zawju l-Fāṭimati l-ṭuhri ibnatu l-rasūli huwa llāhu rabbu l-ʿālamīna ḥaythu anna llāha ʿalā kulli shayʾin qadīrun. Wa-l-jasadu min bayti ʿAbdi l-Muṭṭalibi kamā iḥatajaba Jabraʾīlu fī ṣūrati <shaykhin miskīnin wa-fī ṣūrati yatīmin qabli l-bulūghi wa-fī ṣūrati> asīrin istaʾsarahu l-islāmu wa-qad nazala Jabraʾīlu ʿalā Maryama ibnati ʿImrāna ʿalayhā l-salāmu bi-ṣūrati rajlun yuqālu lahu Taqiyyun wa-huwa laysa bi-taqiyyin. Bal fāsiqun wa-nazala ʿiddata mirārin ʿalā ṣūrati Diḥya l-Kalbī.* [. . .] *Wa-laysa l-ḥijābu huwa Jabraʾīla wa-innamā huwa l-muḥtajibu fīhi wa-ka-dhālika laysa l-insānu hādhā l-badana wa-innamā huwa l-rūḥu l-muḥjūbatu fīhi fa-ka-dhālika l-Raḥumānu laysa huwa l-jasada wa-innamā huwa l-muḥtajibu bihi kamā anna nāra Mūsā ʿalayhi l-salāmu l-marʾiyata hiya ḥijābun li-dhāti l-bārī subḥānahu wa-laysa huwa fī l-ḥaqīqati tilka l-nāra wa-lā tilka l-shajarata*).

35 KMa, 122b; KMb, 273b–4a (*wa-qad tabayyana bi-l-dalīli l-wāḍiḥi anna ʿAliyyan waṣiyya Muḥammadin huwa llāhu l-muḥtajibu bi-dhālika l-badani l-maʿrūfi kamā iḥtajaba Jabraʾīlu bi-badani l-miskīni wa-amthālihi. Wa-qad shahida l-Qurʾānu bi-dhālika wa-ajmaʿa l-mufassirūna ʿalayhā. Wa-man lam yaʿtaqid anna ʿAliyyan huwa llāhu wa-anna Muḥammadan rasūluhu wa-Fāṭimata amatuhu wa-l-aḥada ʿashara imāman malāʾikatuhu wa-l-anbiyāʾa rusulhu wa-l-kutuba al-munzilata kalāmuhu wa-l-wujūda khalquhu fa-qad kafara*).

36 This expression, frequently employed in *Kalām al-mahdī*, is Sayyid Muhammad's way of referring to himself in the third person.

37 In *Kalām al-mahdī*, belief in "the justice of God" (*ʿadl*), which constitutes the principle of religion (*uṣūl al-dīn*) of the Twelver Shiʿa, is defined as "God's segregation from any evil acts or breach of any incumbencies" (*tanzīh al-bāriʾ ʿan fiʿl al-qabīḥ wa-l-ikhlāl bi-l-wājib*) (KMa, 7a; KMb, 15a).

38 KMa, 100b–1b; KMb, 225b–7b (*yaʿlamu sāʾiru l-muwaḥḥidīna wa-man iʿtaqada bi-ʿiṣmati l-nabiyyīna wa-l-waṣiyyīna wa-bi-ʿiṣmati khulafāʾi Muḥammadin al-ithnā ʿashara ajmaʿīna* [. . .] *anna hādha l-sayyida lladhī ẓahara kamā taʿlamūna huwa qāʾimun maqāma l-ghāʾibi bi-ḥasabi l-niyābati kamā qāma l-jasadu ʿan l-rūḥi bi-l-istinābati.* [. . .] *Ṣāra hādhā l-sayyidu ḥijāban wa-ālatan li-hādhā l-sirri l-ghāʾibi wa-l-manāba fī ḥālati l-ghaybati wa-lā tatimmu l-ḥikmatu wa-lā yazūlu l-qubḥu ʿan Allāhi illā bi-niyābatihi fī ḥāli l-ghiyābi*).

39 KMa, 67b; KMb, 155b (*fa-l-jamʿu bayna l-ḥadīthi wa-l-Qurʾān anna l-insāna yubḥathu ʿan ḥaqīqatihi wa-majāzihi. Fa-ammā l-ḥaqīqatu hiya l-rūḥu wa-l-majāzu huwa l-badanu li-ʿilāqatin bayna l-rūḥi wa-l-badani*).

40 KMa, 100b–1a; KMb, 226b (*fa-inna l-qātila idhā qatala ʿamdan innamā yuqtaṣṣu min al-badani bi-l-qawdi lā min l-rūḥi maʿa kawni l-rūḥi hiya l-fāʿilata li-l-qatli.* [*Idh bi-mufāriqatihā l-badana lā yaqaʿu min al-jasadi qatlun wa-lā maqātilata wa-lā baṭshun wa-lā mubāṭashatun wa-lā fiʿlun wa-lā mufāʿalatun wa-lā nakḥun wa-lā munākiḥatun wa-lā walada wa-lā muwāladatun wa-lā ʿiṣyānun wa-lā muʿāṣātun wa-lā ṭāʿatun wa-lā muṭāwaʿatun wa-lā ḥarakatun mutaḥarrikatun.*] *Bal innamā yaṣduru l-jamīʿu min al-rūḥi bi-wāsiṭati l-badani wa-li-hādhā ʿūqiba bi-maʿāqabatihā wa-athība bi-mathūbatihā li-l-ishtirāki fa-hiya huwa wa-huwa hiya*).

41 KMa, 98a; KMb, 221a.

42 An example of Sayyid Muḥammad's overt claims to be the Mahdī is as follows: "'*It was not fitting for the people of Madīna and the Bedouin Arabs of the neighbourhood, to refuse to follow God's messenger, nor to prefer their own lives to his*' [Q. 9: 120]. [. . .] In the same manner that God made it incumbent upon the people neighboring the apostle, it is incumbent upon the followers of the way of this Sayyid who is the Mahdī from the family of [the Prophet] Muḥammad (*al-mahdī min āl Muḥammad*) to rise with him in order to propagate his command and to spread his right (*ḥaqq*)" (KMa, 95b; KMb, 215b–6a).

43 For the historical development of the concept of "*mahdī*," see Wilferd Madelung, "Mahdī," in *The Encyclopaedia of Islam, New Edition*, vol. 5, 1230–8.

44 KMa, 30b; KMb, 74a–b ([*inna l-mahdiyya min waladi Muḥammadin ʿalayhi l-salātu wa-l-salāmu*] *idā ẓahara lā yaqtaḍī bi-aḥadi l-madhāhibi bal al-madhāhibu kulluhā taʿūdu ilayhi wa-yuṣaḥiḥu l-sharīʿatu min baʿdi iftirāqihā wa-l-ikhtilāfi fīhā*).

45 KMa, 51b; KMb, 120b (*al-mahdiyyu idhā tawallā l-arḍa yafʿalu ka-fiʿli jaddihi ʿalayhi l-salāmu fa-yudḥiḍu l-bāṭila wa-yanṣibu l-ḥaqqa* [*ḥaythu yuʿabbaru bi-l-maẓrūfi ʿan al-ẓurfi*]).

46 According to some passages in *Kalām al-mahdī*, the author attributes to the Twelver Shiʿa the belief that the Hidden Imam would interfere with affairs in this world in the unseen state (Cf. KMa, 145b; KMb, 324b–5a).

47 KMa, 153b; KMb, 342b ([*idh law ẓahara huwa bi-ʿaynihi la-saqaṭa l-taklīfu wa-l-ikhtibāru li-quwwati qahrihi*] *li-anna l-madhhaba ajmaʿa ʿalā annahu fī ḥālati l-ghaybati yazūru l-qibāba l-musharrafata wa-l-qubūra l-maʿhūdata wa-laysa li-aḥadin min dhawī l-quwwati fī tilka l-ḥālati an yaqbiḍahu aw yabṭisha bi-yadihi. Bal huwa law arāda an yabṭisha bi-aḥadin minhum la-amkanahu dhālika wa-lam yaḥṣul hādhihi l-manzilatu li-sāʾiri l-anbiyāʾi wa-l-aʾimmati*).

48 KMa, 145b; KMb, 324b–5a (*ṣārat nawʿiyyatihi ka-nawʿiyyati ʿIzrāʾīla lladhī yaʾkhudhu l-arwāḥa min al-abdāni wa-lā li-aḥadin quwwatu manʿihi bi-l-ijmāʿi wa-l-adillati*).

49 KMa, 145b–6a; KMb, 324b–5a. See n. 59.

50 KMa, 150a; KMb, 335a (*wa-qad qālat al-ithnā ʿashariyyatu innahu huwa li-ghaybatihi yaẓharu wa-yaẓharu maʿahu l Khaḍiru min al-siyāḥati wa-ʿĪsā min al-samāʾi. Wa-lladhī yaruddu minnā ʿalayhim huwa annahu law ẓahara bi-hādhihi l-mathābati baʿda hādhihi l-ghaybati wa-maʿahu l-Khiḍru wa-ʿĪsā min al-samawāti lam yajid fī l-arḍi lahu mukhālifan li-quwwati l-shawkati l-mubhirati.* [*Idh kayfa yakūnu l-ikhtibāru wa-ṣiḥḥatuhu bi-ẓuhūri nabiyyin fī l-ummati qawiyyin qāhirin yusallimu ilayhi ʿalā quwwatihi l-khāṣṣu wa-l-ʿāmmu. Fa-ayyuhum al-taqiyyu yakūnu min al-ʿāṣiyyi fa-lā yajūzu an yakhtabira llāhu l-ummata fī kulli zamānin illā bi-ḍaʿīfin yaḥtāju ilā nāṣirin kamā faʿala bi-Muḥammadin.*])

51 KMa, 47b; KMb, 112a–b (*wa-fī tilka l-ḥālati ayyu man daʿāhu ilayhi ajābahu fa-yalzamu l-jabru idh yaʾtīhi qawiyyu l-ummati wa-ḍaʿīfuhā wa-lā yaṣiḥḥu fī dhālika l-ikhtibāru li-anna l-ikhtibāra lā yablughu l-iljāʾa wa-l-qahra fa-lā yuthābu l-mukallafu illā bi-l-fiʿli l-ikhtiyāriyyi. Bal yajibu l-ikhtiyāru bi-an yakūna ḥālata l-ẓuhūri ka-Muḥammadin* [*lladhī haraba ilā l-ghāri min faqdi l-nāṣiri.*])

52 KMa, 18a; KMb, 43b–4a (*ʿāsha min al-ʿumri fī Makkata thalāthan wa-khamsīna sanatan wa-huwa yanzilu ʿalayhi l-waḥyu wa-l-Qurʾānu fī mā zāda ʿalā l-arbaʿīna min ʿumrihi ʿalayhi l-salāmu wa-haraba ilā l-ghāri wa-hājara wa-shakka bihi jamīʿu l-khalqi ḥīna harabihi qālū innahu mubṭilun. Idh law jāʾa amaruhu ka-nafkhi l-ṣūri lam yashukka bihi aḥadun min al-ʿibādi wa-gharaḍu l-bārī subḥānahu min iḍʿāfihi ikhtiyāru l-khalqi bihi li-anna bi-ḍaʿfihi lā yaṣfū*

ʿalā l-tamassuki illā l-qalīlu l-nādilu wa-hādhā huwa l-ikhtiyāru l-mashrūʿu wa-huwa wājibun ʿalā llāhi taʿālā wa-huwa an yusayyirahu fī l-arḍi bi-sayrati l-ḍaʿfi ḥattā yaqūma l-taklīfu wa-l-ikhtibāru ʿalā ḥidatin. Fa-yaḥmilu kullun ʿabwahu min al-ṭāʿati wa-l-maʿṣiyati fa-yakūnu fī l-ummati muṭīʿan wa-ʿāṣiyan wa-shaqiyyan wa-saʿīdan idh law jāʾa l-nabiyyu ilā l-ummati bi-yadi l-qahri wa-l-quwwati wa-ʿalima l-mukallafūna bi-ʿadami l-imtināʿi lahum min saṭwatihi wa-ʿuluwwi qahrihi la-sallamat ilayhi jamīʿu l-khalqi li-quwwatihi wa-qahrihi fa-lā yubānu ṣāliḥu l-ummati min ṭāliḥihā wa-laysa hādhā ikhtibāra l-ḥakīmi l-muṭlaqi lladhī lā yafʿalu l-qabīḥa wa-lā yukhillu bi-l-wājibi. Fa-yakūnu irsālu l-anbiyāʾi ʿalā l-wajhi l-qahriyyi qabīḥan ʿaqlan. Wa-lā yafʿalu llāhu l-qabīḥa).

53 KMa, 126a; KMb, 281a (*man yakūnu imtaḥana llāhu aʿẓamu min hādhā l-sayyidi lladhī tarawnahu fa-innahu tamma khamsata ʿashara sanatan yalʿanūnahu l-nāsu wa-wasubbūnahu wa-yaʾmurūna bi-qatlihi wa-qatli awlādihi*). This passage is taken from the English translation by Shahzad Bashir with some modifications (Shahzad Bashir, "Between Mysticism and Messianism: The Life and Thought of Muḥammad Nūrbakš (d. 1464)," Ph.D. dissertation, Yale University. 1997, 41).

54 The word "*al-mahdī*" in this sentence is missing in the Marʿashī manuscript.

55 The word "*Muhammad*" in this passage is incorrectly written as "*al-mahdī*" in the Marʿashī manuscript.

56 KMa, 98a; KMb, 221a–b (*wa-man qāla min akrādi l-jibāli wa-sāʾiri l-juhhāli inna* <*l-Mahdiyya*> *idhā ẓahara yamliku l-arḍa bi-sabʿati ayyāmin aw aqalla. Fa-dhāka nifāqun min al-qāʾili wa-kidhbun ʿalā llāhi wa-l-rasūli. Bal lahu l-uswatu bi-l-nabiyyi wa-bi-sāʾiri l-anbiyāʾi fa-inna* <*Muḥammadan ʿalayhi l-salāmu*> *ʿāsha fī Makkata thalāthan wa-khamsīna sanatan wa-qad nazala ʿalayhi aktharu l-Qurʾāni wa-haraba baʿda dhālika ilā l-ghāri wa-hājara minhu ilā l-Madīnati.* [. . .] *Wa-makatha baʿda dhālika ʿashara sinīna wa-lam yamlik min al-arḍi illā l-baʿḍa fa-kayfa yakūnu ḥālu man huwa min waladihi lladhī huwa aqallu darajatan wa-aqallu faḍlan wa-ishtihāran an yamlika l-arḍa bilā nāṣirin wa-muʿīnin maʿa kathrati l-aʿdāʾi fa-man shakka bi-mā aqūlu fa-l-yaqif ʿalā qiṣṣati l-rasūli Muḥammadin ṣallā llāhu ʿalayhi wa-ālihi wa-sallama wa-mā ḥakāhu llāhu ʿanhu fī kitābihi l-ʿazīzi*).

57 The idea of "the Mahdī of the community" also appears briefly in a similar context in the previously mentioned letter to the *ʿulamāʾ* in Aleppo: "It is not permissible that the Mahdī of the community manifests himself as stronger than [the Prophet] Muḥammad (*lā yajūzu an yaẓhara mahdiyyu l-ummati aqwā min Muḥammadin*). According to this view (*bi-hādhā l-naẓar*), it is incumbent on the wisdom not to permit the forementioned [i.e., the Hidden Imam] to manifest as in the doctrines of the Twelver Shiʿa. Nay, his veil and deputy will be manifest in the earth as a weak man (*ḍaʿīf*) who however exceeds him [i.e., the Prophet Muḥammad] (*bal yaẓharu ḥijābuhu wa-maqāmuhu fī l-arḍ bi-ḍaʿīfin yaʿlūhu*)." See KMa, 150b; KMb, 335a; Sibṭ b. al-ʿAjamī al-Ḥalabī, *Kunūz al-dhahab*, vol. 2, 289.

58 The word "*ilā nāṣir*" is missing in the Marʿashī manuscript.

59 KMa, 145b–6a; KMb, 324b–5a ([*wa-ṣārat nawʿiyyatuhu ka-nawʿiyyati ʿIzrāʾīla lladhī yaʾkhudhu l-arwāḥa min al-abdāni wa-lā li-aḥadin quwwatu manʿihi bi-l-ijmāʿi wa-l-adillati. Fa-qad tasāwayā fī maʿnā l-iqtidāri ʿalā mā zaʿamat al-shīʿatu.*] *wa-idhā kānat ṣifatuhu fī ḥālati ghaybatihi ka-dhālika wa-l-qudratu maʿahu kayfa yuqātilu aw yaḥtāju ilā l-anṣari. Bal innamā yaẓharu hādhā l-ḍaʿīfu ḥattā yakhtabira llāhu bihi qulūba l-khalqi wa-yaḥtāja li-ḍaʿfihi* <*ilā nāṣirin*> *yanṣuruhu wa-qad qāla llāhu subḥānahu in tanṣurū llāha yanṣurukum al-āyata wa-nuṣratu l-raḥmāni hiya nuṣratu ḍaʿīfi l-anbiyāʾi wa-l-awliyāʾi wa-l-ṣāliḥi min ʿibādi llāhi fa-lā yaẓharu mahdiyyu l-ummati illā ʿalā ṣifati ẓuhūri Muḥammadin ʿalayhi l-ṣalawātu wa-l-salāmu lladhī ʿāsha fī Makkata ithnayni wa-khamsīna sanatan wa-baʿdahā haraba ilā l-ghāri li-takūna ḥujjatuhu ʿalā ahli l-dunyā.* [. . .] *Fa-lā yajūzu an yaẓuhara hādhā l-ghāʾibu l-mastūru ʿan al-abṣāri l-mutajalbibu bi-l-kamāli wa-l-anwāri lladhī labisa qamīṣa l-malāʾikati l-ʿiẓāmi kamā taqaddama dhikruhu fī mā sabaqa. Bal innamā yaẓharu ḍaʿīfun kamā ẓahara Muḥammadun ʿalayhi l-salāmu fa-hādhāka l-mastūru huwa l-sirru wa-hādhā l-ḍaʿīfu huwa ḥijābuhu wa-maqāmuhu*).

Bibliography

Kalām al-mahdī

KMa: Sayyid Muḥammad al-Mushaʿshaʿ. *Kalām al-mahdī.* MS Marʿashī Library, Qom 1011.

KMb: Sayyid Muḥammad al-Mushaʿshaʿ. *Kalām al-mahdī.* MS Majlis Library, Tehran 10222.

Qurʾan

The Holy Qurʾān: Text, Translation and Commentary. Ed. and transl. by Abdullah Yusuf Alī. Damascus and Beirut: Dar Ibn Qudama, 1938.

Other Sources and Studies

Arjomand, Said Amir. *The Shadow of God and the Hidden Imām: Religion, Political Order, and Societal Change in Shiʿite Iran from the Beginning to 1890.* Chicago: University of Chicago Press, 1984.

Bashir, Shahzad. "Between Mysticism and Messianism: The Life and Thought of Muḥammad Nūrbaḵš (d. 1464)." Ph.D. dissertation, Yale University, 1997.

Bashir, Shahzad. "The Imam's Return: Messianic Leadership in Late Medieval Shiʿism." In *The Most Learned of the Shiʿa: The Institution of the Marjaʿ Taqlid.* Ed. by Linda S. Walbridge. New York: Oxford University Press, 2001, 21–33.

Bashir, Shahzad. *Messianic Hopes and Mystical Visions: The Nūrbakhshīya between Medieval and Modern Islam.* Columbia: University of South Carolina Press, 2003.

Caʿferî b. Muhammed el-Hüseynî. *Târîh-i Kebîr (Tevârîh-i Enbiyâ ve Mülûk).* Ed. by İsmail Aka. Ankara: Türk Tarih Kurumu Basımevi, 2011.

Fleischer, Cornell H. "Mahdi and Millennium: Messianic Dimensions in the Development of Ottoman Imperial Ideology." In *Great Ottoman-Turkish Civilization.* Ed. by Kemal Çiçek et al. 4 vols. Ankara: Yeni Türkiye, 2000, vol. 3, 42–55.

Al-Ghazālī. *The Incoherence of the Philosophers.* Transl. by Michael E. Marmura. Provo, Utah: Brigham Young University Press, 1997.

Griffel, Frank. *Al-Ghazālī's Philosophical Theology*. New York and Oxford: Oxford University Press, 2009.

Jaʿfariyān, Rasūl. *Mahdiyān-i durūghīn: Bih ḍamīma-i sih risāla: Sharḥ-i ḥadīth-i dawlatunā fī ākhir al-zamān, Risāla-yi mubashshira-yi shāhiyya, Risālat al-hudā, Sayyid Muḥammad Nūrbakhsh*. Tehran: Intishārāt-i ʿilm, 1391 AHS/2012–13.

Jaʿfariyān, Rasūl. *Tārīkh-i qizilbāshān-i Ṣafawī: Dar chand matn-i tārīkhī-madhhabī-yi ʿArabī-yi dawra-yi ʿUthmānī.* Qom: Nashr-i muʾarrikh, 1397 AHS/2018–19, 108–14.

Kasrawī, Aḥmad. *Tārīkh-i pānṣad sāla-yi Khūzistān*. Tehran, 1313 AHS/1934.

Khāmayār, Aḥmad. "Maktūb-i Sulṭān Junayd Ṣafawī bih Shammāʿ Ḥalabī." *Payām-i Bahāristān* 5 (1392 AHS/2003–04): 130–9.

Madelung, Wilferd. "Mahdī." In *The Encyclopaedia of Islam, New Edition*. Ed. by H. A. R. Gibb et al. 13 vols. Leiden: Brill, 1960–2009, vol. 5, 1230–8.

Madelung, Wilferd. "The Late Muʿtazila and Determinism: The Philosopher's Trap." In *Yād-nāma: In Memoria di Alessandro Bausani*. Ed. by Bianncamaria Scarcia Amoretti et al. 2 vols. Rome: Bardi Editore, 1991, vol. 1, 245–57.

Maḥmūd Marʿashī et al. *Fihrist-i nuskhahā-yi khaṭṭī-yi Kitāb-khāna-yi ʿumūmī-yi Ḥaḍrat-i Āyat Allāh al-ʿUẓmā Najafī Marʿashī*. 27 vols. Qom: Kitāb-khāna-yi ʿUmūmī-yi Ḥaḍrat-i Āyat Allāh al-ʿUẓmā Najafī Marʿashī, 1354–76 AHS/1975–98.

Mazzaoui, Michel M. "Mushaʿshaʿiyān: A Fifteenth Century Shīʿi Movement in Khūzistān and Southern Iraq." *Folio Orientalia* 22 (1981–84): 139–62.

Melvin-Koushki, Matthew. "Early Modern Islamicate Empire: New Forms of Religiopolitical Legitimacy." In *The Wiley Blackwell History of Islam*. Ed. by A. Salvatore et al. Hoboken: Wiley Blackwell, 2018, 353–75.

Minorsky, Vladimir. "Mushaʿshaʿ." In *E. J. Brill's First Encyclopaedia of Islam 1913–1936*. Ed. by Martijn T. Houtsma et al. 9 vols. Leiden and New York: Brill, 1987, vol. 9, 160–3.

Mir-Kasimov, Orkhan. "Conflicting Synergy of Patterns of Religious Authorities in Islam." In *Unity in Diversity: Mysticism, Messianism and the Construction of Religious Authority in Islam*. Ed. by Orkhan Mir-Kasimov. Leiden: Brill, 2014, 1–20.

Moin, A. Azfar. *The Millennial Sovereign: Sacred Kingship and Sainthood in Islam*. New York: Columbia University Press, 2012.

Qāḍī Nūr Allāh Shūshtarī. *Majālis al-muʾminīn*. Ed. by Ibrahīm ʿArabpūr. 5 vols. Mashhad: Bunyād-i Pazhūhish'hā-yi Islāmī, 1393 AHS/2014–15.

Ranjbar, Muḥammad ʿAlī. *Mushaʿshaʿiyān: Māhiyyat-i fikrī-ijtimāʿī wa farāyand-i taḥawwulāt-i tārīkhī*. Tehran: Muʾassasa-yi intishārāt-i āgāh, 1382 AHS/2004-5.

Rescher, Nicholas. "Choice without Preference: The Problem of 'Buridan's Ass.'" In idem, *Studies in the History of Logic*. Frankfurt: De Gruyter, 2006, 91–139.

Scarcia Amoretti, Biancamaria. "Religion in the Timurid and Safavid Periods." In *The Cambridge History of Iran*, Vol. 6. Ed. by Peter Jackson et al. Cambridge: Cambridge University Press, 1986, 610–55.

Al-Sakhāwī. *Al-Ḍawʾ al-lāmiʿ li-ahl al-qarn al-tāsiʿ*. 12 vols. Cairo: Maktabat al-qudsī, 1353–55/1934–37.

Al-Shaybī, Muṣṭafā. *Al-Fikr al-shīʿī wa-l-nazaʿāt al-ṣūfiyya ḥattā maṭlaʿ al-qarn al-thānī ʿashar al-hijrī*. Baghdad: Maktabat al-nahḍa, 1386/1966.

Shihadeh, Ayman. *The Teleological Ethics of Fakhr al-Dīn al-Rāzī*. Leiden and Boston: Brill, 2006.

Sibṭ b. al-ʿAjamī al-Ḥalabī. *Kunūz al-dhahab fī taʾrīkh Ḥalab*. Ed. by Shawqī Shaʿath. 2 vols. Aleppo: Dār al-qalam al-ʿArabī, 1417/1996.

Subrahmanyam, Sanjay. "Turning the Stones Over: Sixteen-Century Millenarianism from Tagus to the Ganges." *Indian Economic and Social History Review* 40 (2003): 129–61.

Ṭabāṭabāʾī Bihbihānī, Muḥammad. *Fihrist-i nuskhahā-yi khaṭṭī-yi Kitāb-khāna-yi Majlis-i Shūrā-yi Islāmī*, vol. 32. Tehran: Kitāb-khāna, mūza wa markaz-i asnād-i Majlis-i Shūrā-yi Islāmī, 1381 AHS/2002–03.

SCHOLARLY PRODUCTION

6

Didactic Discourse and Sarcastic Expressions in the Context of Abū Hilāl al-ʿAskarī's Literary Criticism

Mohammed Sanad

Abū Hilāl al-ʿAskarī and His Literary Critical Position

Abū Hilāl al-ʿAskarī (d. 400/1009) was a prominent rhetorician and critic of Arabic literature with a broad understanding of *adab* and other branches of knowledge in the fourth century AH, as is evident in his diverse books and in the list of his literary output, as stated by Kanazi.[1] In the literary field, Abū Hilāl's fame is based mainly on two of his books, *al-Ṣināʿatayn* and *Dīwān al-maʿānī,* in which his literary taste is shown clearly. *Dīwān al-maʿānī* includes quotations from poetry and prose which, as he argued in the introduction,[2] represent a high level of rhetoric and well-crafted speech. On the other hand, his book *al-Ṣināʿatayn,* which literally means 'the two arts' (prose and poetry), is directed at those who practice the art of writing by showing them how to avoid uncouth language and to produce valuable literature via a set of rules for sophisticated literary works that could be applied to prose and poetry alike. Hence, *Dīwān al-maʿānī* is essentially an anthology that consists of examples of sophisticated poetry and prose, while *al-Ṣināʿatyn* is work of rhetoric that discusses rhetorical devises with examples that can be employed in the production of literary works.[3]

However, ʿAbbās argued that *al-Ṣināʿatayn* did not contribute significantly to literary criticism because Abū Hilāl did not add his own ideas to the works of his predecessors,[4] and thus could not be regarded as a great mind, as also stated by Kanazi (as cited in Ashtiany).[5] However, what he produced was a rearrangement of the material in previous books of criticism from the third and fourth centuries, such as *Naqd al-shiʿr, ʿIyār al-shiʿr, al-Muwāzana* and *al-Wasāṭa.* By contrast, ʿAbd al-Qādir al-Baghdādī (d. 1093/1682–83), in his book *Khizānat al-adab,* stated that the two books by Abū Hilāl (*al-Furūq fī l-lugha* and *Dīwān al-ma ʿānī*) indicated his abundant knowledge, as quoted by Maḥmūd al-Ṭanāḥī (d. 1999): "And for him [i.e., Abū Hilāl] I have his books *al-Furūq fī l-lugha* in linguistics and *Dīwān al-ma ʿānī* which indicate his copious knowledge."[6]

ʿAbbās' and Kanazi's arguments could possibly be refuted by al-Baghdādī's statement, as well as by saying that Abū Hilāl added many of his personal insights and comments on quotations he drew from poetry and prose; although they are succinct, they can provide hints about his method for evaluating both sophisticated and poor literature through rigorous analyses. Moreover, rearranging the material of literary criticism is complex work that could only be performed by a knowledgeable critic such as Abū Hilāl, since a high degree of linguistic and literary proficiency is required to preserve its content. Similarly, in his book *al-ʿIqd al-farīd*, Ibn ʿAbd Rabbih (d. 328/940) affirmed that compiling examples of the speech act is more difficult than composing it (*ikhtiyār al-kalām aṣʿab min taʾlīfihi*).[7] A similar idea was expressed by Selove, who stated that *Ḥikāyāt Abī l-Qāsim* "deserves its own analysis" since it constitutes a microcosm in itself.[8] This is also applied to Abū Hilāl's works.

Another point is that Abū Hilāl's position regarding the issue of *al-lafẓ wa-l-maʿnā* (wording and meaning) is extremely clear in his book *Dīwān al-maʿānī,* particularly when he criticised the poetry of Abū Nuwās (d. c. 199/814), who used long expressions for his meanings with no justification.[9] In this regard, Orfali argued that "modern scholars have begun to recognize, however, the originality of a particular anthology consists precisely in the choice and arrangement of the produced text, which reveals in turn the individual interests of the compiler."[10] Finally, *al-Ṣinaʿatayn* is of particular importance because it consists of a summary of the most important works of criticism, and may be considered as a gateway to the field of literary criticism in the third and fourth centuries. That is to say, novice writers and poets could find valuable material in it that could improve their literary skills and taste significantly.

As far as his critical position is concerned, based on his books *Diwān al-maʿānī* and *al-Ṣināʿatayn*, Abū Hilāl expressed noticeable antagonism towards al-Mutanabbī (d. 354/965).[11] Abū Hilāl tended not to mention al-Mutanabbī's name when he discussed his poetry, and said only: *wa-qāla baʿḍuhum* (one of them said), or *wa-qāla baʿḍu al-mutaʾakhkhirīn* (one of the latest poets said),[12] despite knowing that al-Mutanabbī was the composer of this poetry, as he mentioned his name being linked to the same poetry in his book *Dīwān al-maʿānī.*[13] Similarly, Muḥārib[14] claimed that most of al-Mutanabbī's poetry mentioned in Abū Hilāl's books was criticised and described as discarded poetry without any justification being provided. It is not unusual to find a critic or poet who disapproves of al-Mutanabbī's poetry, as such criticism is part of the debate surrounding him at that time and in the following centuries. The reason for the antagonism shown towards al-Mutanabbī in the fourth century could be attributed to peer jealousy; however, liking or disliking certain poetry is a matter of taste, which should depend on the critic's literary knowledge and not on personality or first impressions.

Abū Hilāl's essential role in the fourth century AH is evident through his myriad books, whereby he contributed to different areas of Arabic sciences. In *al-Furūq fī l-lugha*, for example, he addressed linguistic issues and explained differences in words or expressions that appeared synonymous, although they had different meanings according to their context in a given discourse. In addition, Abū Hilāl commented on the poetry of Abū Miḥjan al-Thaqafī (d. after 15/637), thus attempting to collect the oeuvre of minor poets.[15] This indicates Abū Hilāl's awareness of the importance of preserving the Arabic literary heritage by paying attention to various poets from different levels, as each poet represents a certain level of language and artistic literary talent. Another book by Abū Hilāl was *al-Ḥathth ʿalā ṭalab al-ʿilm,* in which he discussed several important requirements for gaining knowledge. In addition, Abū Hilāl compiled a book of Arabic proverbs, *Jamharat al-amthāl,* which consists of 2,000 classical Arabic proverbs divided in twenty-nine chapters, the number of letters in the Arabic alphabet.[16] These books indicate the active role that Abū Hilāl played in the fourth century in the fields of rhetoric, proverbs, literary criticism, linguistics, and lexicography, although Kanazi stated that almost half of his books did not survive.[17] However, Abū Hilāl's surviving works constitute a strong motivation for a comprehensive study and extensive exploration in order to reveal some of the unknown aspects of his intellectual and literary works.

Pedagogical and Didactic Discourse in *al-Ḥathth ʿalā ṭalab al-ʿilm*, *al-Ṣināʿatayn* and *Faḍl al-ʿaṭāʾ ʿalā al-ʿusr*

This section discusses the didactic sense and discourse that predominate in Abū Hilāl's books, and which take different forms. This might be a reflection of Abū Hilāl's personality, which prompted him to act as a teacher or tutor to his readers by approaching different topics gradually and logically using a writing style that is frequently devoid of any complications. Abū Hilāl's book *al-Ḥathth ʿalā ṭalab al-ʿilm wa-l-ijtihād fī jamʿihi* is a clear example of this, as Abū Hilāl shares his invaluable experience regarding knowledge seeking and the most important aspects that students must consider in this regard with his readers. In the introduction to this book, the editor states that Abū Hilāl's style of writing is easy, clear, and not artificial.[18] These features of his writing style, however, might account for the accessibility of any book and may attract a wide range of readers; on the other hand, they do not necessarily indicate trivial, shallow or worthless content. In this work, the order of the paragraphs and topics is logical and smooth, and the themes of the paragraphs are usually stated clearly and are easy to understand. At the beginning of the book,

Abū Hilāl says prayers (*duʿāʾ*) for the readers in order to encourage them and attract their attention. Another feature that reflects Abū Hilāl's didactic approach is the employment of the vocative particle "*ayyuhā al-akh*" (O brother) to ensure that the reader is paying attention, and to emphasise that the discourse requires the reader's involvement and participation.[19] Moreover, the vocative particle could be employed to ensure the continuation of the dialogue in this context, which is an essential aspect of didactic discourse. The discourse in this book is supported by numerous quotations by various scholars, and Abū Hilāl related several narrations following the standards of authentication demanded by Hadith scholars.[20]

With regard to Abū Hilāl's book *al-Ṣināʿatayn*, the didactic sense can be seen in several forms. In terms of organisation and structure, the book is divided into ten main chapters, and each chapter is divided into several sections, as stated in the introduction.[21] The chapters and sections include a variety of discussions related to language, rhetoric and literary criticism. As explained previously, Abū Hilāl begins his work with prayers for the reader in an attempt to build a relationship with the reader based on intimacy, which makes the reader eager to read the book. In these prayers, Abū Hilāl says: "Know – may God let you know the good, point you out the way to it, predestine it for you and may you be one of his family!"[22]

Another didactic feature that characterises *al-Ṣināʿatayn* is that most of the discussions are accompanied by diverse and appropriate examples from various poetic and prosaic texts. It is possible that incorporating this structure when composing a book indicates that the scribe was aware of the different levels and backgrounds of the readers and aimed to ensure that the discussions were generally understood. With regard to *al-Ṣināʿatayn*, the book is largely devoted to teaching the two arts: prose and poetry, which are the two main modes of Arabic writing. Therefore, it is surprising that Abū Hilāl's personality as a teacher or tutor can be seen to predominate by presenting most of his discourses to the readers in such a way as to attract their attention. It is worth noting that the discourse in *al-Ṣināʿatayn* could be seen as an example of an eloquent and high-standard style of writing in terms of clarity and linguistic virtuosity. In confirmation of this, Abū Hilāl stated: "It is not the purpose in this book to follow the theologians' doctrine."[23] This might be a reference to Qudāma b. Jaʿfar (d. 337/948) and Abū l-Ḥasan Ibn Ṭabāṭabā (d. 322/934), as their books on literary criticism were composed according to the methodology of the theologians (*al-mutakallimīn*) in which logical discourses predominate; in particular, Qudāma attempted to enforce the rules of logic in poetry.

Some of the didactic features mentioned previously can be found in Abū Hilāl's book *Faḍl al-ʿaṭāʾ ʿalā al-ʿusr*, which also reflects the unique topics in his books, as mentioned above. Although the discourse in this book addresses an extremely specific topic, which is the superiority of generosity and donations despite being poor, it shares some common elements with *al-Ḥathth ʿalā ṭalab al-*

ʿilm wa-l-ijtihād fī jamʿihi in terms of the numerous high-quality literary quotations that support the subject of the book, which Abū Hilāl selected thoughtfully and carefully based on his in-depth experience in this field. These quotations could also be classified as belonging to the didactic genre, which reflects the essence of Abū Hilāl's teaching persona, particularly with reference to his comments or quotations in his composition that reflect his incorporation of the topic and his ability to draw parallels with other high-quality compositions; in some examples, he surpasses them.[24] Despite the specific nature of the topic of this book, its functional role could affect the essence and the productivity of individual lives because the absence of the quality of generosity and the prevalence of miserliness would prevent individuals from fulfilling their roles and would deprive them of positive participation and engagement in society, particularly in those activities that would serve the greater good of the society. This is probably what Abū Hilāl recommended that knowledge seekers, scholars and teachers should avoid, as their mission constantly requires generosity and donations, particularly when sharing knowledge.

This is in contrast to Ghayyāḍ's claims that Abū Hilāl's book *Faḍl al-ʿaṭāʾ ʿalā al-ʿusr* indicated Abū Hilāl's eagerness for money and his desire to attract princes' donations.[25] Yāqūt al-Ḥamawī (d. 626/1229), the famed littérateur, refuted this claim by saying that Abū l-Muẓaffar al-Abiwardī (d. 507/1113) described Abū Hilāl selling clothes in order to avoid begging or asking people for money.[26] Another point that could refute Ghayyāḍ's claim is that, in his book, Abū Hilāl[27] emphasises that scarcity and plenitude of donation are not considered when identifying generosity, stating: "Indeed giving a little is better than prevention" (*inna iʿṭāʾ al-qalīl khayr min al-manʿ*).[28] This notion prevails in his book and is supported by many examples; as he states, rich people who donate large amounts of their money do not gain the same reputation as do poor people who donated when they could.[29] Therefore, if Abū Hilāl's intention were to collect money from princes and rich people, he would not have traded in clothes, would have given preference to large donations over small ones, and would not have undervalued the gifts of rich people. The reason that Abū Hilāl stressed this concept could be attributed to the social condition of misunderstanding the quality of generosity at that time, to the extent that people would only donate large amounts of money; otherwise, they would give nothing, which would have a negative effect on the distribution of wealth in the society.

Overall, Abū Hilāl's didactic sense and the discourse in this book can be identified through the following two dimensions: first, the literary quotations and narrations that he included in his book, which combine both the didactic sense and the literary quality that represent the narrow meaning of the term *adab,* which is a style of writing that employs a high standard of language usage; and second, the ethical dimension that should constantly be observed by knowledge seekers and which represents the general meaning of *adab* that prompts individuals to improve their personal qualities.

As a result, the didactic sense and discourse that characterise Abū Hilāl's books could be presented as a reason for the popularity of his books and could be why his successors referred to his books in different literary and linguistic discussions even though other books by his contemporaries or predecessors had addressed similar topics of discourse. It is worth noting that the features discussed previously also apply to Abū Hilāl's other books, such as *al-Talkhīṣ fī maʿrifat asmāʾ al-ashyāʾ* and to his commentary on *Dīwān Abī Miḥjan,* in which his role as a critic is evident because he evaluated and refined some verses in order to improve their rhetorical effect.[30] Based on this commentary, it can also be seen that, as a critic and linguist, Abū Hilāl did not confine his work to the simple explanation of difficult vocabulary, but would add his perspective and literary opinion to the commentary by evaluating different uses of rhetorical devices.[31] Kittān conducted a semantic study of Abū Hilāl's commentary, and stated that the easy style and the clarity of this commentary encouraged him to embark on his own research.[32] In the introduction to the book *al-Talkhīṣ*, Abū Hilāl stated that he intended to structure the book in such a way that both beginners and advanced readers would be able to read it, which emphasises that his didactic sense would always lead him to consider the readers' level to ensure that readers would achieve a better understanding of the content of his books.[33] In addition to the didactic discourse, another phenomenon that can be observed is the employment of sarcastic expressions throughout the literary critical discourse. Therefore, the next section discusses the purpose and function of these expressions in the literary critical discourse, and whether this would contradict the didactic sense or not.

The Sarcastic Expressions That Abū Hilāl Used in His Critiques and How He Employed Them

In *al-Ṣināʿatayn*, Abū Hilāl presents excerpts of poetry and prose by different poets as examples of different rhetorical issues and discussions, followed by his literary judgement of these examples based on his opinion of the topic being discussed. Moreover, he injects his critical discourse with some sarcastic expressions that might amuse the reader to some extent, particularly when he provides examples of poorly composed poetry or verses in poems. Therefore, this section discusses the context of these expressions, their purpose and function, their critical role in the discussion, and whether these sarcastic expressions and phrases contradict the didactic purpose discussed in the previous section. This is accomplished by presenting these expressions, explaining their meanings, identifying the points that Abū Hilāl intends to clarify, and discussing their functions in different contexts.

Most of these sarcastic expressions can be found in the second section of the second chapter of *al-Ṣināʿatayn*, which is dedicated to discussing faulty and correct meanings in poetic verses in order to be guided by the accurate meanings and to avoid the incorrect ones.[34] As Abū Hilāl stated, 'A rhetorician is required to achieve accurate meaning as well as he/she is required to refine the wording.'[35] Abū Hilāl justified his presentation of verses including inaccurate meanings by drawing attention to the idea that 'He who is unaware of a mistake is likely to commit it' (*wa-man lā yaʿrifu al-khaṭaʾ kān jadīr^an^ bi-l-wuqūʿ fīhi*).[36]

It is worth noting that incorrect meanings can be found amongst both classic and modern poets and are caused by misconceptions of the topics approached by poets. In his book *Awhām shuʿarāʾ al-ʿArab fī l-maʿānī* (*The Delusions of Arab Poets in Meanings*), Taymūr discussed this issue extensively.[37] This implies that classical and contemporary poets were equal in the critical eyes of Abū Hilāl; therefore, he did not restrict his examples to poets from a specific era, and did not consider classical poets to be superior to contemporary poets, such as pre-Islamic (*jāhilī*) poets like Imruʾ al-Qays and al-Aʿshā were not excluded from this discourse. It can also be seen that Abū Hilāl uses various terms and descriptions to describe incorrect meanings, such as corrupted, imperfect, eccentric, disordered, contradicted, impossible, defective, deplored and malignant meanings, followed by examples that contained these attributes. However, it was not only verses with incorrect meanings that are presented in this section, as Abū Hilāl presents other verses in which meaning was expressed successfully in order to enable the reader to distinguish between incorrect and correct meanings.

The following lines contain verses that Abū Hilāl used as examples of incorrect meanings, accompanied by his comments, followed by an analysis of these comments.

1 - Some incorrect meanings are found in the words of al-Muraqqash al-Aṣghar:

His heart sobered up from her, but for a memory of her
Which caused the earth to spin dizzily below him, despite his standing still
صحا قلبُهُ عنها على أنّ ذُكْرةً / إذا خطَرَتْ دارَتْ بِهِ الأرضُ قائما

For how, if his heart has become sober thanks to forgetting his beloved, can the earth cause him dizziness at the thought of her?
وكيفَ صحا عنها مَنْ إذا ذُكِرَتْ له دارَتْ به الأرض[38]

2 - In the words of Junāda:
For the sake of her love I long to be met by
The message of her death delivered from her town
In order that our separation have no farewell
And the soul may harbour despair and then release her

مِنْ حُبِّها أتَمَنّى أنْ يُلاقِيَني / مِنْ نَحْوِ بَلْدَتِها ناعٍ فَيَنْعاها
لِكَيْ يَكونَ فِراقٌ لا لِقاءَ له / وتُضْمِرُ النَّفْسُ يَأساً ثُمَّ تَسْلاها

If the lover wishes death upon his beloved, what might the hateful one wish upon his enemy?
فإذا تَمَنّى المُحِبُّ لحبيبَتِهِ الموتَ، فما عسى أن يتَمَنّى المُبْغِضُ لِبَغيضَتِهِ[93]

3 - Some erroneous meanings are found in the words of al-Aʿshā:

What alarmed her most was nothing less than
The sight of my long greying hairs
وما رابَها مِنْ رِيبةٍ غَيْرَ أنّها / رَأتْ لِمَّتي شابَتْ وشابَتْ لِداتِيا

But what could be more alarming for a woman than her beloved's hair turning grey?!
وأيّ رِيبَةٍ عِنْدَ امرأةٍ أعظَمُ من الشَّيْب[40]

4 - Peculiar too are those words (those of al-Aʿshā):

Hurayra turned away from us and ceased to speak
And I, not knowing if that mother of Khulayd may find elsewhere that rope that binds.
Perhaps because she saw, in me, a man with night blindness
Harmed by the events of time and a deceitful, corrupted era?
صَدّتْ هُرَيْرَةُ عَنّا ما تُكَلِّمُنا / جَهْلاً بأُمِّ خُلَيْدٍ حَبْلَ مَن تَصِلُ
أَأَنْ رأت رَجُلاً أعْشى أضَرَّ به / رَيْبُ الزّمانِ ودَهْرٌ خاتِلٌ خَبِلُ

What is more loathsome for women than seeing her beloved begin to suffer night blindness?! Indeed the most perturbing thing to be found in his words is where he cries: who will this woman be bound to after me, while I am in this state of night blindness, poverty and old age? For you surely won't find more foolish words than these.
وأيُّ شَيْءٍ أَبْغَضُ عِنْدَ النّساءِ مِن العَشا يَتَبَيَّنُهُ الرجُل؟! وأعْجَبُ ما في هذا الكَلام أنّه قال: حَبلَ مَنْ تَصِلُ
هذه المَرأةُ بَعْدي وأنا بهذه الصّفَةِ مِن العَشا والفقرِ والشّيْبِ؟ فلا تَرى كَلاماً أحْمَقَ مِن هذا[41]

5 - Some misplaced meanings are found in the words of Imruʾ al-Qays:

I see that those women cannot stand it when their beloved's money starts to diminish
Or when they notice his grey hairs and hunching back
أراهُنّ لا يُحْبِبْنَ مَنْ قَلَّ مالُهُ / ولا مَنْ رَأيْنَ الشَّيْبَ فيه وقَوَّسا

The women hate their beloved before his back begins to hunch, when they are on the mere cusp of old-age, so why is it necessary to even mention the hunching? Either their hatred is reserved for the beloved with a hunch-back, or it is not worthy of mention nor remark.

وهُنَّ يُبْغِضْنَهُ قبلَ التَّقويسِ، فما مَعْنى ذِكرِ التَّقويسِ؟ فأمّا بُغْضُهُنَّ لِمَنْ قَوَّسَ فجَديرٌ وليسَ بِبَديعٍ[42]

6 - Impossible to explain that which ʿAbd al-Raḥmān al-Qass tries to say:

If death were to come and steal her soul
I would vanish first and bury myself

إنّي إذا المَوْتُ حَلَّ بنَفْسِها / يُزالُ بنَفْسي قَبْلَ ذاكَ فأَقْبَرُ

This is like saying: If Zayd enters the house, I will enter before him. This is the most impossible notion of being.

وهذا شَبيهٌ بقَوْلِ قائِلٍ لو قال: إذا دَخَلَ زَيْدٌ الدّارَ دَخَلْتُ قَبْلَه. وهذا عَيْنُ المُحالِ الذي لا يَجوزُ كَوْنُهُ[43]

7 - In the words of Abū l-ʿIyāl:

I remembered my brother and became
Plagued by fatigue and a headache in my head.

ذَكَرْتُ أخي فعاوَدَني / صُداعُ الرّأسِ والوَصَبُ

It is superfluous to mention the head in relation to a headache, for one cannot suffer a headache in the leg or any other part of the body. There is also another defect, which is that in remembering a beloved the pain that manifests would be in the heart, causing a burning sensation, rather than a headache.

فذِكْرُ الرأسِ مع الصُّداعِ فَضْلٌ، لأنَّ الصُّداعَ لا يكونُ في الرِّجْلِ ولا في غيرِها من الأعْضاءِ. وفيه وَجْهٌ آخرُ من العَيْبِ، وهو أنَّ الذّاكِرَ لِما قد فاتَ من مَحْبوبٍ يوصَفُ بأَلَمِ القَلْبِ واحْتِراقِهِ لا بالصُّداعِ[44]

8 - As ʿAlqama said:

The women carry perfumes, spraying their rose-scent
As though their aromas were sniffed through the nose

يَحْمِلْنَ أُتْرُجَّةً نَضْخُ العَبيرِ بها / كأنَّ تَطْيابَها في الأنْفِ مَشْمومُ

The notion of aroma here is extremely bland, it is also inevitable that they are smelt, for his words 'as though their aromas were sniffed' are an incorrect use of language, and 'through the nose' even more so, as one cannot sniff through the eye!

والتَّطْيابُ هاهنا في غايةِ السَّماجةِ، والطِّيبُ أيضاً مَشْمومٌ لا مَحالةَ، فقَوْلُهُ: كأنّه مَشْمومٌ هُجْنةٌ، وقَوْلُهُ: في الأنْفِ أَهْجَنُ؛ لأنَّ الشَّمَّ لا يكونُ بالعَيْنِ[54]

9- In the words of Jamīl:

If she were to return my sanity to me I would not love her
For I loved her as I wasn't in my right mind
فلَوْ تَرَكَتْ قَلْبي مَعي ما طَلَبْتُها / ولكِنْ طِلابيها لِما فاتَ مِن عَقْلي

He claims to love her in the absence of his sanity, but love can only exist in the presence of mental lucidity.
زَعَمَ أنّه يَهواها لِذَهابِ عَقْلِه، ولو كانَ عاقِلاً ما هَوِيَها[46]

10 - Abū Tammām said the following:

When the word 'dove' is altered slightly in pronunciation
It comes to mean 'death'
هُنَّ الحَمامُ فإنْ كَسَرْتَ عِيافةٍ / مِنْ حائهنّ فإنّهُنَّ حِمامُ

Who could be so ignorant as to not see that in changing the pronunciation of the word 'dove' (*al-ḥamām*) it becomes 'death' (*al-ḥimām*)?!
فمَنْ ذا الذي يَجْهَلُ أنّ الحَمامَ إذا كُسِرَتْ حاؤُها صارتْ حِماماً![47]

Several observations can be made regarding these literary critical and sarcastic comments by Abū Hilāl in *al-Ṣināʿatayn*. It seems that Abū Hilāl aimed to create new critical methods that would have an evaluative function in the process of critiquing different poetic verses. Abū Hilāl would detect certain phenomena in the poetic verses that included confusion in their semantic structure, which could be due to the poets' failure to deliver the meaning and would then attempt to draw attention to the points of inaccuracy via sarcastic comments. Some of these comments resemble proverbs or wise phrases in terms of structure and content, as can be seen in Examples 1, 2, and 3, which allows them to be applied in various similar contexts. In other words, these phrases are presented using a general formula or expression in order to extend their use to similar situations.

As mentioned previously, by studying the list of poets whose verses Abū Hilāl used as examples of incorrect meanings, it appears that Abū Hilāl did not consider the periods in which the poets wrote or their renown as masters of poetry, which is similar to criteria of Ibn Qutayba (d. 276/889) in the introduction to his book *al-Shiʿr wa-l-shuʿarāʾ*, in which he stated that he did not exalt a poet simply because he was a classical poet; nor did he underestimate others simply because they were modern, as he evaluated them equally.[48] Therefore, Abū Hilāl's criteria were the accuracy and the clarity of meaning; thus, he would not accept ambiguous, defective, or even illogical meanings or wordings, as in Examples 6 and 7, when he says that "The eye has no sense of smell" and "headache does not happen in leg." In these two examples, Abū Hilāl indicated his preference for realism by expressing his criticism in the form of axioms to justify his dislike of verses that he considered to exceed the bounds of probability.

As discussed previously, Abū Hilāl employs certain kinds of expressions in order to attract readers' or learners' attention by giving his blessing or by approaching different issues and discussions gradually and logically considering the various levels of the learners. However, in the sarcastic examples presented here, Abū Hilāl deviates from his didactic discourse to a sarcastic discourse as an indication of his absolute dislike of such artistic defects in poetic verses, as well as to advise *Adab* seekers that these defects or incorrect meanings were unacceptable in the literary craft because they undermined the value of the literary works. This sarcastic style could achieve further critical purposes, as it could serve as an alternative to the usual form of criticism that might not be as effective in this context as sarcasm would be. Therefore, Abū Hilāl employs this discourse as a device to avoid the monotonous tone of literary criticism. Abū Hilāl's precise observations in his sarcastic criticisms and conventional criticisms indicate his sensitivity to wording and meaning, as well as to the elaborate use of these two aspects.[49] This would reflect the cultural dimension of his personality, which involved observing the accurate and precise wording for each object and meaning and would explain his lexical interests that provided accurate knowledge of the names of things. Abū Hilāl revealed this interest in his book *al-Talkhīṣ fī maʿrifat asmāʾ al-ashyāʾ* (*The Abridgement Regarding Knowing the Names of Things*), in which he aimed to equip *adab* learners with the necessary knowledge of knowing the names of things that most *adab* learners lacked, as he stated in the introduction to this book.[50] Abū Hilāl emphasised that it was essential for *adab* learners to acquire cultural knowledge that would improve their writing and prevent them from producing defective compositions.

Previously, it was mentioned that Abū Hilāl employs various expressions and descriptions to describe meanings and defective compositions, such as corrupted, incorrect, and disordered meanings. In this discussion, two essential terms concerned when Abū Hilāl's discourse are discussed, namely meaning and accuracy, reflecting the accuracy of a particular word as representing a particular meaning. In his book on *al-maʿnā,* Key studied these two concepts in depth, particularly with regard to the eleventh century literature in the disciplines of logic, lexicography, theology and literary criticism.[51] Key translated the Arabic word '*maʿnā*' as 'mental content,' while he used the English word 'accuracy' as an equivalent to the Arabic word '*ḥaqīqa*.' Both terms play a key role in rhetoric and literary criticism, as they are genuine constructs that contribute to shaping the discourse and how readers perceive it. However, the concepts of truth and falsity (*al-ṣidq wa-l-kidhb*) have been approached intensively by rhetoricians in the context of allegory. Ḥāzim al-Qarṭājinnī (d. 684/1284) stated that these two concepts could be found in poetry; however, these concepts do not determine whether a given speech is poetic or not, as it is imagination (*al-takhyīl*) that constitutes poetry.[52] It is worth noting that Key's translation of *maʿnā* is similar to al-Qarṭājinnī's definition of the same word, when he stated that 'meanings verily arise in the mind regarding existing objects' (*al-maʿānī innamā tataḥaṣṣalu fī l-adhhān ʿan al-umūr al-mawjūda fī l-aʿyān*).[53] Al-Qarṭājinnī also used 'mental images' instead of 'mental content' as a description of what is meaning (*maʿnā*); therefore, for al-Qarṭājinnī, meanings are images that are processed in the mind regarding objects that are observed in the real world.

However, in his sarcastic comments, Abū Hilāl does not pass judgement on meanings in terms of truth and falsehood; instead, he examines certain deviations or confusion in the meanings that decreased the artistry of the given verses, thus decreasing their poetic value and ruining their artistic contribution.

To clarify this, in the first example, Abū Hilāl describes the meaning as being corrupted (*fāsid*) because the poet stated that he experienced two conditions and these conditions cannot be combined, which leads to a contradictory statement. The poet admitted that his heart had been released from being attached to his beloved woman; however, he would become dizzy whenever he remembered her. This causes Abū Hilāl to question the possibility of combining these two contradictory feelings, which he thinks corrupts the meaning. Therefore, it could be deduced that corrupted meanings are meanings that are rejected on the grounds of logic, which could be considered strong evidence to support a critic's literary verdict. In terms of wording and prosody, the verse seems perfect, artistic, and highly poetic, but the elements of sense and logic are absent. One might question the possibility of considering a particular speech to be poetry when the essential element of meaning (*al-maʿnā*) is absent. Answering this involves saying that poetry has two major aspects or constituent elements, one that considers aspects of the craft (*jānib al-ṣināʿa*), including prosody, wording, rhyme, and rhythm, while the other relates to aspects of meaning and involves observing the accuracy of wording in the representation of meanings and to prevent ambiguity and illogical discourses. In this regard, the example that Abū Hilāl presentes could be considered poetic, yet still a failure in terms of delivering logical meaning.

In Example 3, Abū Hilāl states that the meaning of the verse is incorrect (*wa-min khaṭaʾ al-maʿānī*). The poet used the words *rāba*, and *rība*, which are a verb and a noun verb, respectively. According to *Lisān al-ʿArab*, the root of the words is *rāʾ yāʾ bāʾ*, and the derivations are *rāba*, *yarību*, *rayb*, and *rība*. Thus, the words have several meanings but, in the context of the verse, the meaning could be *al-karāha* (hatred), *al-inziʿāj* (being annoyed or uncomfortable) or *al-istiyāʾ* (displeasure and hostility). The poet says that nothing annoyed the woman or caused her to feel hatred other than seeing his grey hair. As can be seen, in terms of grammar, the poet employed an expression called *al-nafy wa-l-istithnāʾ* (negation and exception), which consists of two fundamental particles of negation (*mā*) and restriction (*ghayr*);[54] conversely, this expression can be called *al-qaṣr* (restriction). The pragmatic function of this expression is *al-tawkīd* (affirmation). Abū Hilāl's objection is based on the consideration of what could be more annoying for a women than a man having grey hair.[55] The expected meaning, according to the grammatical structure that the poet employed in the first part of the verse, indicates that there is only one thing that annoyed this woman; according to Abū Hilāl, having grey hair would be excluded because being annoyed by age and grey hair is common for women. Abū Hilāl seems to have been disappointed when, in the second part of the verse, the poet says that having grey hair annoyed the woman. For this reason, Abū Hilāl finds the meaning of the verse to be incorrect because the poet employed a type of grammatical structure that was not completely successful in delivering the meaning, which could have been expressed using more appropriate syntax. Therefore, as discussed previously, the craft, or the artistic aspect, and the grammatical structure of the verse are absolutely correct; however, the grammatical structure failed to deliver the meaning accurately, which caused the meaning to be incorrect.

The last example that is discussed is Example 5; Abū Hilāl describes its meaning as being disordered or confusing (*muḍṭarib*). This example has the same theme as Example 3, which is the hated attribute of men having grey hair. The poet says that women do not love a man whose wealth has decreased nor one whose hair is grey and whose back is bowed (*qawwas*) due to age. Abū Hilāl criticises the poet for mentioning the feature of a bowed back after mentioning the grey hair, finds no reason to mention this feature, and argues that 'they had hated him before his back was bowed; therefore, what was the point of mentioning it' (*wa-hunna yubghiḍnahu qabla al-taqwīs, fa-mā maʿnā dhikr al-taqwīs*)? This is because grey hair usually precedes a bowed back; since women hate grey hair, it would be obvious that they hate bowed backs. For Abū Hilāl, this could be a possible reason for the confusion that occurred in the verse, as the inclusion of this word at the end of the verse implies that it conveys additional meaning, whereas it is actually redundant and meaningless in this context. Moreover, it causes confusion.

Based on the previous discussion, it is evident that there is a fundamental relationship between meaning and syntax (word order) when constructing clear and coherent discourse. In other words, the accuracy of the grammar that is used to express a certain meaning makes an essential contribution to the accuracy of the meaning. It is worth remarking that the fundamental correlation between syntax and meaning has been noted since the early stages of Arabic literary production when the word meaning '*al-maʿānī*' was used to mean grammar analysis (*al-iʿrāb*), as can be seen in two books in this genre, namely *Maʿānī al-Qurʾān* by al-Farrāʾ (d. 207/822) and another with the same title by al-Zajjāj (d. 311/923).

Conclusion

Abū Hilāl's books are characterised by a clear structure and a style that is devoid of complications and ambiguity, which enabled a wide range of readers to gain access to them. Moreover, his books are characterised by a didactic sense that is reflected in the structure and language thereof, as borne out by several examples including *al-Ṣināʿatayn, al-Ḥathth ʿalā ṭalab al-ʿilm* and *Faḍl al-ʿaṭāʾ ʿalā al-ʿusr.*

An observation that seems to contradict Abū Hilāl's didactic sense is the sarcastic criticism that he employs in his analyses, as can be seen in the examples presented above. It was noted that Abū Hilāl employs sarcasm when he considers the meaning of a given verse of poetry to be spoiled or corrupted, incorrect or disordered. A close reading of the verses that Abū Hilāl presents revealed that the meaning was considered to be spoiled or corrupted when it was illogical or could not be conceptualised mentally. On the other hand, the meaning was described as being incorrect when the poet employed a syntactical structure that did not reflect the meaning accurately, which led to a different meaning being expressed. Finally, disordered meaning was considered to occur when a poet added a lexical item that seemed to add new meaning to the verse, thus causing confusion due to the mismatch with other lexical items.

Abū Hilāl's sarcastic discourse is an indication of his absolute dislike of such artistic defects in poetic verses, as well as his aim to advise *adab* seekers that these defects or incorrect meanings were unacceptable in the literary craft because they undermined the value of the literary works. This sarcastic style could achieve further critical purposes, as it could serve as an alternative to the usual form or pattern of criticism that might not be as effective in this context as would sarcasm. Therefore, Abū Hilāl employs this discourse as a device to avoid the monotonous tone of literary criticism.

It should be acknowledged that, in his sarcastic comments, Abū Hilāl does not pass judgement on meaning in terms of truth and falsehood; instead, he examines certain deviations or confusion in the meanings that decrease the artistry of the given verses, thus lessening their poetic value and ruining their artistic contribution. Thus, it could be argued that Abū Hilāl's sarcasm does not contradict the didactic sense that prevails in his books.

Notes

1 George Kanazi, "The Works of Abū Hilāl al-ʿAskarī," *Arabica* 22.1 (1975): 61–70; idem, "Abū Hilāl al-ʿAskarī," in *Essays in Arabic Literary Biography*, ed. by Terri DeYoung and Mary St. Germain (Wiesbaden: Otto Harrassowitz Verlag, 2011), 29.

2 Abū Hilāl al-ʿAskarī, *Dīwān al-maʿānī* (Beirut: Dār al-aḍwāʾ, 1989), vol. 1, 18.

3 Abū Hilāl al-ʿAskarī, *al-Ṣināʿatayn*, ed. by ʿAlī al-Bijāwī and Muḥammad Ibrāhīm (Cairo: ʿĪsā al-Bābī al-Ḥalabī, 1971).

4 Iḥsān ʿAbbas, *Tārīkh al-naqd al-ʿArabī ʿinda al-ʿArab* (Beirut: Dār al-thaqāfa, 1981), 355–7.

5 Julia Ashtiany, "Book Review: *Studies in the* Kitāb aṣ-Ṣināʿatayn *of Abū Hilāl al-ʿAskarī*," *Journal of Arabic Literature* 25.2 (1994): 179–80.

6 "*Wa-lahu ʿindī Kitāb al-Furūq fī l-lugha wa-Kitāb Dīwān al-maʿānī, wa-humā dāllān ʿalā ghazārat ʿilmihi.*" Cited in Maḥmūd al-Ṭanāḥī, *Fī l-lugha wa-l-adab* (Beirut: Dār al-gharb al-Islāmī, n.d.), 794.

7 Aḥmad ibn ʿAbd Rabbih, *al-ʿIqd al-farīd*, ed. by Aḥmad Amīn, Aḥmad al-Zayn, and Ibrāhīm al-Abyārī (Cairo: Lajnat al-taʾlīf wa-l-tarjama wa-l-nashr, 1965), vol. 1, 2.

8 Emily Selove, *Ḥikāyāt Abī al-Qāsim* (Edinburgh: Edinburgh University Press, 2016), 12.

9 Al-Ṭanāḥī, *Fī l-lugha.*

10 Bilal Orfali, "A Sketch Map of Arabic Poetry Anthologies Up to the Fall of Baghdad," *Journal of Arabic Literature* 43.1 (2012): 29–59.

11 Al-Ṭanāḥī, *Fī l-lugha*, 158–9; ʿAbd Allāh Muḥārib, "al-Mutanabbī fī kitābay *al-Ṣināʿatayn* wa-*Dīwān al-maʿānī* li-Abī Hilāl al-ʿAskarī," *al-Majalla al-ʿArabiyya li-l-ʿulūm al-insāniyya* 28 (111) (2019): 103–67.

12 Abū Hilāl al-ʿAskarī, *al-Ṣināʿatayn*, 384.

13 Abū Hilāl al-ʿAskarī, *Dīwān al-maʿānī*, vol. 1, 316.

14 Muḥārib, "al-Mutanabbī fī kitābay *al-Ṣināʿatayn* wa-*Dīwān al-maʿānī*," 105.

15 He lived in the first decades of Islam. He was a wine drinker but later repented and became one of the first converts to Islam (Kanazi, "Abū Hilāl al-ʿAskarī," 31).

16 Kanazi, "Abū Hilāl al-ʿAskarī," 32.

17 Ibid., 33.

18 Abū Hilāl al-ʿAskarī, *al-Ḥathth ʿalā ṭalab al-ʿilm wa-l-ijtihād fī jamʿihi*, ed. by ʿAbd al-Majīd Diyāb (Cairo: Dār al-faḍīla, 1998), 20.

19 Ibid., 48.

20 Ibid., 48, 55.

21 Abū Hilāl al-ʿAskarī, *al-Ṣināʿatayn*, 11.

22 "*Iʿlam — ʿallamaka Allāh al-khayr, wa-dallaka ʿalayhi, wa-qayyaḍahu laka, wa-jaʿalaka min ahlihi —.*" Abū Hilāl al-ʿAskarī, *al-Ṣināʿatayn*, 7. This translation is taken from Vicente Cantarino, *Arabic Poetics in the Golden Age* (Leiden: E. J. Brill, 1975), 125.

23 "*Wa-laysa al-gharaḍ fī hādhā al-kitāb sulūk madhhab al-mutakallimīn.*" Abū Hilāl al-ʿAskarī, *al-Ṣināʿatayn*, 15.

24 See Abū Hilāl al-ʿAskarī, *Faḍl al-ʿaṭāʾ ʿalā al-ʿusr*, ed. by Maḥmūd Shākir (Cairo: al-Maṭbaʿa al-salafiyya, 1934–35), 49.

25 Muḥsin Ghayyāḍ, *Shiʿr Abī Hilāl al-ʿAskarī* (Beirut: Turāth ʿUwaydāt, 1975),15.

26 Yāqūt al-Ḥamawī, *Muʿjam al-udabāʾ* ([Cairo]: ʿĪsā al-Bābī al-Ḥalabī, 1936–38), vol. 8, 259.

27 Abū Hilāl al-ʿAskarī, *Faḍl al-ʿaṭāʾ ʿalā al-ʿusr*, 42, 49, 50.

28 Ibid., 27.

29 Ibid., 65.

30 Abū Hilāl al-ʿAskarī, *Dīwān al-maʿānī*, 5, 9.

31 Ibid., 20.

32 Muḥammad Kittān, "al-Dilāla fī *Sharḥ Diwān Abī Miḥjan al-Thaqafī*," *Jāmiʿat al-Azhar, Ḥawliyyat Kulliyyat al-Lugha al-ʿArabiyya* 21.7 (2017): 6739.

33 Abū Hilāl al-ʿAskarī, *al-Talkhīṣ fī maʿrifat asmāʾ al-ashyāʾ*, ed. by ʿAzza Ḥasan (Damascus: Dār Ṭalās, 1996), 29.
34 Abū Hilāl al-ʿAskarī, *al-Ṣināʿatayn*, 75.
35 Ibid., 75.
36 Ibid., 76
37 Aḥmad Taymūr, *Awhām shuʿarāʾ al-ʿArab fī l-maʿānī* ([Cairo]: Dār al-kitāb al-ʿArabī, 1959).
38 Abū Hilāl al-ʿAskarī, *al-Ṣināʿatayn*, 79. English translations from the original Arabic by Daisy Vaughan in this and in the following sections.
39 Abū Hilāl al-ʿAskarī, *al-Ṣināʿatayn*, 82.
40 Ibid., 89.
41 Ibid., 90.
42 Ibid., 90.
43 Ibid., 102.
44 Ibid., 113.
45 Ibid., 115.
46 Ibid., 118.
47 Ibid., 124.
48 ʿAbd Allāh ibn Qutayba, *al-Shiʿr wa-l-shuʿarāʾ*, ed. by Aḥmad Muḥammad Shākir (Cairo: Dār al-maʿārif, 1982), 62.
49 This also implies that sarcasm and humour can have a didactic value. This would support the discussion in the previous point regarding Abū Hilāl's didactic sense. Therefore, it can also be said that Ibn al-Jawzī's (d. 597/1201) humorous book *Akhbār al-ḥamqā wa-l-mughaffalīn* is partly meant to teach readers not to behave like stupid people. Ibn al-Jawzī employed humour to achieve this didactic aim.
50 Abū Hilāl al-ʿAskarī, *al-Talkhīṣ*, 29.
51 Alexander Key, *Language between God and the Poets: Maʿnā in the Eleventh Century* (Oakland, Ca.: University of California Press, 2018), 16.
52 Ḥāzim al-Qarṭājinnī, *Minhāj al-bulaghāʾ wa-sirāj al-udabāʾ*, ed. by Muḥammad al-Ḥabīb b. al-Khūja (Beirut: Dār al-gharb al-Islāmī, 1981), 63.
53 Al-Qarṭājinnī, *Minhāj al-bulaghāʾ*, 10.
54 Hussein Abdul-Raof, *Arabic Rhetoric: A Pragmatic Analysis* (Abingdon, Oxon: Routledge, 2006), 168.
55 Time and cultural differences should be considered in this context.

Bibliography

ʿAbbas, Iḥsān. *Tārīkh al-naqd al-ʿArabī ʿinda al-ʿArab*. Beirut: Dār al-thaqāfa, 1981.

Abū Hilāl al-ʿAskarī. *Dīwān al-maʿānī*. Beirut: Dār al-aḍwāʾ, 1989.

Abū Hilāl al-ʿAskarī. *Faḍl al-ʿaṭāʾ ʿalā al-ʿusr*. Ed. by Maḥmūd Shākir. Cairo: al-Maṭbaʿa al-salafiyya, 1934–35.

Abū Hilāl al-ʿAskarī. *Al-Ḥathth ʿalā ṭalab al-ʿilm wa-l-ijtihād fī jamʿihi*. Ed. by ʿAbd al-Majīd Diyāb. Cairo: Dār al-faḍīla, 1998.

Abū Hilāl al-ʿAskarī. *Al-Ṣināʿatayn*. Ed. by ʿAlī al-Bijāwī and Muḥammad Ibrāhīm. Cairo: ʿIsā al-Bābī al-Ḥalabī, 1971.

Abū Hilāl al-ʿAskarī. *Al-Talkhīṣ fī maʿrifat asmāʾ al-ashyāʾ*. Ed. by ʿAzza Ḥasan. Damascus: Dār Ṭalās, 1996.

Abdul-Raof, Hussein, *Arabic Rhetoric: A Pragmatic Analysis*. Abingdon, Oxon: Routledge, 2006.

Ashtiany, Julia. "Book Review: *Studies in the* Kitāb aṣ-Ṣināʿatayn *of Abū Hilāl al-ʿAskarī.*" *Journal of Arabic Literature* 25.2 (1994): 179–80.

Cantarino, Vicente. *Arabic Poetics in the Golden Age*. Leiden: E. J. Brill, 1975.

Ghayyāḍ, Muḥsin. *Shiʿr Abī Hilāl al-ʿAskarī*. Beirut: Turāth ʿUwaydāt, 1975.

Al-Ḥamawī, Yāqūt. *Muʿjam al-udabāʾ*. [Cairo]: ʿĪsā al-Bābī al-Ḥalabī, 1936–38.

Ibn ʿAbd Rabbih, Aḥmad. *Al-ʿIqd al-farīd*. Ed. by Aḥmad Amīn, Aḥmad al-Zayn, and Ibrāhīm al-Abyārī. Cairo: Lajnat al-taʾlīf wa-l-tarjama wa-l-nashr, 1965.

Ibn Qutayba, ʿAbd Allāh. *Al-Shiʿr wa-l-shuʿarāʾ*. Ed. by Aḥmad Muḥammad Shākir. Cairo: Dār al-maʿārif, 1982.

Kanazi, George. "The Works of Abū Hilāl al-ʿAskarī." *Arabica* 22.1 (1975): 61–70.

Kanazi, George. "Abū Hilāl al-ʿAskarī." In *Essays in Arabic Literary Biography I: 925–1350*. Ed. by Terri DeYoung and Mary St. Germain. Wiesbaden: Harrassowitz Verlag, 2011, 26–34.

Key, Alexander. *Language between God and the Poets: Maʿnā in the Eleventh Century*. Oakland, Ca.: University of California Press, 2018.

Kittān, Muḥammad. "Al-Dilāla fī *Sharḥ Diwān Abī Miḥjan al-Thaqafī*." *Jāmiʿat al-Azhar, Ḥawliyyat Kulliyyat al-Lugha al-ʿArabiyya* 21.7 (2017): 6738–866.

Muḥārib, ʿAbd Allāh. "Al-Mutanabbī fī kitābay *al-Ṣināʿatayn* wa-*Dīwān al-maʿānī* li-Abī Hilāl al-ʿAskarī." *Al-Majalla al-ʿArabiyya li-l-ʿulūm al-insāniyya* 28 (111) (2019): 103–67.

Orfali, Bilal. "A Sketch Map of Arabic Poetry Anthologies Up to the Fall of Baghdad." *Journal of Arabic Literature* 43.1 (2012): 29–59.

Al-Qarṭājinnī, Ḥāzim. *Minhāj al-bulaghāʾ wa-sirāj al-udabāʾ*. Ed. by Muḥammad al-Ḥabīb b. al-Khūja. Beirut: Dār al-gharb al-Islāmī, 1981.

Selove, Emily. *Ḥikāyāt Abī al-Qāsim*. Edinburgh: Edinburgh University Press, 2016.

Al-Ṭanāḥī, Maḥmūd. *Fī l-lugha wa-l-adab*. Beirut: Dār al-gharb al-Islāmī, n.d.

Taymūr, Aḥmad. *Awhām shuʿarāʾ al-ʿArab fī l-maʿānī*. [Cairo]: Dār al-kitāb al-ʿArabī, 1959.

7

Writing the Imams' Virtues under the Interconfessional Policy of al-Nāṣir li-Dīn Allāh: Ibn al-Biṭrīq al-Ḥillī and His *Faḍāʾil* Works

Ryo Mizukami

Introduction

At the turn of the 13th century, a novel religio-political situation developed in Iraq. To reinforce his authority, the ʿAbbasid caliph al-Nāṣir li-Dīn Allāh (r. 1180–1225) attempted to garner support from various religious groups, including Twelver Shiʿis. While he supported and enjoyed scholarly exchange with Sunni scholars, he also appointed Shiʿi *wazīr*s and restored the monument to the twelfth Shiʿi Imam in Samarra and the mausoleum of the seventh Imam, Mūsā al-Kāẓim, in Baghdad.[1]

This interconfessional policy had the potential to lead to a new phase in the relationship between Iraq's rulers and the Shiʿi population. To examine this turning point, this study focuses on the Iraqi Twelver Shiʿi scholar Yaḥyā b. al-Ḥasan ibn al-Biṭrīq al-Ḥillī (d. 600 or 601/1204 or 1205) and his *al-ʿUmda fī ʿuyūn ṣiḥāḥ al-akhbār fī manāqib imām al-abrār*. This is a *faḍāʾil* (virtues) work on ʿAlī and the "twelve leaders" who ended with the Mahdī (Savior), the members clearly reminiscent of the Twelve Shiʿi Imams.[2] By analyzing the characteristics of the *ʿUmda*, this study seeks to clarify why Ibn al-Biṭrīq wrote the work in the period of al-Nāṣir's interconfessional policy and how he employed his knowledge of the Imams as power to approach al-Nāṣir. Ibn al-Biṭrīq's compilation of *faḍāʾil* can be regarded as the response of one Iraqi Twelver Shiʿi scholar to the spread of reverence for the Imams promoted by the caliph. The completion of the *ʿUmda* did not represent the end of Ibn al-Biṭrīq's writing project. He subsequently wrote two other *faḍāʾil*s, *al-Mustadrak al-mukhtār fī manāqib waṣī al-mukhtār*[3] and *Khaṣāʾiṣ al-waḥy al-mubīn*,[4] in which he introduced new topics and methods. This study also considers how the characteristics of the *ʿUmda* were developed in these later *faḍāʾil*s.

Despite containing an important clue as to how al-Nāṣir influenced the religio-political situation in Iraq, researchers have paid little attention to the characteristics of the *ʿUmda*. Saleh, in his study on the medieval Sunni *tafsīr* (commentary of the Qurʾan) of al-Thaʿlabī (d. 427/1035), briefly describes Ibn al-Biṭrīq as a Shiʿi receiver of the *tafsīr*.[5] Pierce studied the *faḍāʾil* on the Twelve Imams written by Ibn Shahrāshūb (d. 588/1192), Ibn al-Biṭrīq's teacher, and regards Ibn al-Biṭrīq and subsequent Ḥillī authors of *faḍāʾil*s as under Ibn Shahrāshūb's influence.[6] Ansari and Schmidtke analyzed the Yemeni Zaydi reception of the *ʿUmda*.[7] However, these studies focus neither on the contents of the *ʿUmda* nor the background of its compilation. Probing these points, this study considers how Ibn al-Biṭrīq presents his knowledge of the Imams.

Ibn al-Biṭrīq was among the first generation of Ḥillī Shiʿi scholars writing religious works.[8] From his time to the 15th century, the city was a flourishing scholarly center for Twelver Shiʿism. After Ibn al-Biṭrīq, Twelver Shiʿi scholars from al-Ḥilla and their students, such as Raḍī al-Dīn ʿAlī Ibn Ṭāwūs (d. 664/1266), ʿAlī b. ʿĪsā al-Irbilī (d. 692 or 693/1293 or 1294), al-ʿAllāma al-Ḥillī (d. 726/1325), and a scholar called Jalāl al-Dīn (fl. late 15th century) repeatedly compiled *faḍāʾil*s on the Imams using similar methodology. Through composition of *faḍāʾil*, they attempted to approach not only the ʿAbbasids but also the later Mongol dynasties. The analysis of the *ʿUmda* thus helps elucidate the origins of *faḍāʾil* writing among the scholarly circle of Ḥilla, and the continuity of this activity by Iraqi Twelver Shiʿi scholars throughout the rules of several dynasties.

With the labels "confessional ambiguity," "Imamophilia," or "de-confessionalisation," recent scholars draw attention to the conspicuous Sunnis who, like Shiʿis, showed reverence for the House of the Prophet (*ahl al-bayt*) or the Shiʿi Imams.[9] These researchers often treat this religious situation as a remarkable feature from the Mongol period onward. However, as described by Hodgson as ʿAlid loyalism, al-Nāṣir's respect for the Shiʿi Imams was doubtlessly an early example of Imamophilia. This study seeks to explore the continuity of Imamophilia and the Shiʿi response to it from the late ʿAbbasid period into the Mongol period.

Ibn al-Biṭrīq and the *ʿUmda*

Ibn al-Biṭrīq was born in al-Ḥilla, in the first half of the 12th century. Details of his biographical information are reported in the biographical dictionary of Ibn al-Shaʿʿār (d. 654/1256) on the authority of Fikhār b. Maʿadd al-Mūsawī (d. 630/1233), a well-known Ḥillī scholar and student of Ibn al-Biṭrīq. According to Ibn al-Shaʿʿār, Ibn al-Biṭrīq traveled to many cities and collected a great number of hadiths. He first moved to Wāsiṭ and remained there for twenty years. After returning to Ḥilla, he moved to Mosul and then to Aleppo. Finally, he settled in Ḥilla and died there in 1204–05 at more than eighty years of age.[10] Although Ibn al-Biṭrīq had several teachers, the best-known and most influential was Ibn Shahrāshūb, known as the author of the *Manāqib āl Abī Ṭālib*, a *faḍā'il* on the Twelve Imams which relies on various Sunni and Shiʿi sources.[11]

During the lifetime of Ibn al-Biṭrīq, the *faḍā'il* literature on the Imams became a major literary genre among Shiʿi scholars. As Pierce discussed, Shiʿi scholars began to write biographies of the Imams in the 10th or 11th centuries.[12] Works of this kind were called *faḍā'il* because they had an important role, namely legitimizing and defending their subjects through the presentation of traditions on his/her virtues. Over the next century, a range of Twelver Shiʿi scholars, such as al-Faḍl b. al-Ḥasan al-Ṭabrisī (d. 548/1153–54), ʿImād al-Dīn Muḥammad al-Ṭabarī (d. mid-12th century),[13] Quṭb al-Dīn al-Rāwandī (d. 573/1177–78), Ibn al-Ḥamza al-Ṭūsī (d. late 12th century), Shādhān b. Jibra'īl al-Qummī (fl. late 12th century),[14] Muḥammad b. Jaʿfar al-Mashhadī, and Ibn Shahrāshūb compiled *faḍā'il*s on the Imam(s).[15] Ibn al-Biṭrīq's *faḍā'il* writing can be located within this Shiʿi literary trend.

Concerning Ibn al-Biṭrīq's three *faḍā'il*s now extant, the *ʿUmda*, the *Mustadrak*, and the *Khaṣā'iṣ*, the exact dates of their completion are unknown. Immediately after the preface to the *ʿUmda*, Ibn al-Biṭrīq presents all the *isnād*s (paths of transmission) for the works he quotes, describing when, where, and from whom he learned them. The latest date of hadith-learning mentioned among these *isnād*s is 585/1189.[16] One manuscript of the *ʿUmda* includes an *ijāza* (certificate of transmission) issued in 596/1200 by the author.[17] The work must therefore have been completed between 1189 and 1200. As Ibn al-Biṭrīq repeatedly quotes the *ʿUmda* in the *Mustadrak*, it seems that the former predates the latter.[18] In the preface to the *Khaṣā'iṣ*, he refers to both the *ʿUmda* and the *Mustadrak*.[19] It is thus evident that Ibn al-Biṭrīq first started writing the *ʿUmda*, followed by the *Mustadrak*, and finally the *Khaṣā'iṣ*.[20]

Ibn al-Biṭrīq's works soon became known among Sunni scholars. According to Ansari and Schmidtke's analysis, the *ʿUmda* was transmitted to Yemeni Zaydis in the 13th century via a Sunni scholar who had met Ibn al-Biṭrīq in Aleppo.[21] Reporting the words of Fikhār b. Maʿadd, Ibn al-Shaʿʿār wrote that Ibn al-Biṭrīq was devout and an author of good books, even though Ibn al-Shaʿʿār recognized him as Shiʿi.[22] Although no reports exist of Ibn al-Shaʿʿār's *madhhab*, his Sunni orientation can be inferred from him blessing Abū Bakr, ʿUmar, and ʿUthmān.[23]

Compilation of the *ʿUmda* under al-Nāṣir li-Dīn Allāh

In the long preface to the *ʿUmda*, Ibn al-Biṭrīq outlines the purpose and methodology of his compilation. At the beginning of the preface, he states that he compiled this work "because of the request from one great and pious *sayyid*."[24] He then uses the first half of the preface to explicitly explain his approach to compilation (see the next section). By contrast, the second half of the preface is filled with roundabout and ambiguous expressions, and Ibn al-Biṭrīq undoubtedly indicates that the work was written for the ʿAbbasid caliph al-Nāṣir li-Dīn Allāh.

Having explained his approach to compilation, Ibn al-Biṭrīq suddenly mentions that ʿAbbās b. ʿAbd al-Muṭṭalib and his descendants, namely the ʿAbbasid family, should be regarded as *ahl al-bayt*:

> We begin [the discussion in this book] with this first part on the virtues that deals with what has been said concerning the interpretation of His saying "Allāh's wish is but to remove uncleanness far from you, O People of the House (*ahl al-bayt*), and cleanse you with a thorough cleaning" (Q 33: 33). And then the second [part] will be on the interpretation of His saying "Say, 'I do not ask you for a reward for my mission – only love for our kinfolk'" (Q 42: 23). These two parts indicate that ʿAbbās b. ʿAbd al-Muṭṭalib should be included among the kinfolk [of the Prophet] (*ulī al-qurbā*), for whom Allāh the Exalted ordered a love.[25]

He then states that al-Thaʿlabī, the famous Sunni Qurʾanic exegete, considered ʿAbbās and his descendants to be members of the *ahl al-bayt*, and that the Twelver Shiʿi scholar al-Shaykh al-Ṭūsī (d. 460/1067) shared this opinion.[26] In other words, Ibn al-Biṭrīq emphasizes the agreement on the position of the ʿAbbasids between authoritative Sunni and Shiʿi scholars.

Thereafter, Ibn al-Biṭrīq intimates why he decided to compile the *ʿUmda*, with an indirect allusion to the then ʿAbbasid caliph:

> It is now established that they (*ahl al-bayt*) are the quintessence of goodness and that it is to them that the Prophet's authentic words in this hadith pertain (*ʿalayhim waqaʿa al-naṣṣ min al-nabī fī hādhā al-athar*). [The holder] of the holy and noble standing [adorned with] the purity, the lineage of the Prophet, the chasteness, the nature associated to the imams, and the role as helper of the religion of Allāh the Exalted – may Allāh the Exalted support the standing with divine help and retaining, providing it with dignity and nobility, and enabling it to contain its enemies (*al-mawāqif al-muqaddasa al-sharīfa al-ṭāhira al-nabawiyya al-zakiyya al-imāmiyya al-nāṣira li-dīn Allāh taʿālā -ʿaḍadahā Allāh taʿālā bi-l-naṣr wa-l-baqāʾ, wa-amaddahā bi-rifʿa wa-l-ʿalāʾ, wa-mallakahā nawāṣiya al-aʿdāʾ*) belongs to the people of this noble house to which the [above mentioned] words pertain and which is the object of the special mention in the divine revelation (*min ahl hādhā al-bayt al-karīm, alladhī waqaʿa al-naṣṣ ʿalayhi, wa-tawajjaha al-takhṣīṣ fī l-waḥy ilayhi*). Because of

> that standing's fortunate nature, Allāh the Exalted enabled the servant of its *dawla* [i.e. Ibn al-Biṭrīq] to gain His satisfaction by compiling the virtues of the noble house and the pure lineage to which it belongs and by displaying what the scholars had cast away behind their backs as if they did not know it [from the beginning] (*Bi-yumn naqībatihā al-maymūna, yasurru Allāh taʿālā li-ʿabd dawlatihā ḥiyāzat marāḍī Allāh taʿālā, fī taʾlīf manāqib baytihā al-karīm wa-nasabihā al-ṣamīm, wa-iẓhār mā mabadhahu al-ʿulamāʾ min dhālika warāʾ ẓuhūrihim ka-annahum lā yaʿlimūna*).[27]

From the fact that this text includes optative words whose pronoun *hā* refers to "the standing (*al-mawāqif*)," it is obvious that "the standing" means a specific and noble person. In addition, the expression modifying "the standing," "*al-nāṣira li-dīn Allāh*" strongly implies that this person is al-Nāṣir li-Dīn Allāh, the ʿAbbasid caliph when Ibn al-Biṭrīq completed the *ʿUmda*. Ibn al-Biṭrīq describes al-Nāṣir as the holder of the lineage of the Prophet (*nabawiyya*) and the nature of the imams (*imāmiyya*). These expressions assert al-Nāṣir's membership of the family of the Prophet and support his position as caliph. At the same time, the term "*imāmiyya*" implies that al-Nāṣir's nature is related to that of the Shiʿi Imams. By counting the caliph as among the *ahl al-bayt* and attributing the nature of the Shiʿi Imams to him, Ibn al-Biṭrīq shows his support for al-Nāṣir's religio-political authority and Imamophilic policy. Ibn al-Biṭrīq then situates himself as the servant of al-Nāṣir's *dawla* (*ʿabd dawlatihā*), namely his caliphate. While praising al-Nāṣir and his caliphate, Ibn al-Biṭrīq clearly states that he compiled the *ʿUmda* for the caliph. Following this allusion to al-Nāṣir, Ibn al-Biṭrīq cites the works of two poets in which ʿAbbās is presented as a member of the *ahl al-bayt*.[28] The two poets are al-Kumayt b. Zayd al-Asadī (d. 126/743), a Shiʿi but pro-Hāshimid poet, and Abū l-Aswad al-Duʾalī (d. 69/688), a pro-ʿAlid poet.[29] Given that Ibn al-Biṭrīq emphasizes these two poets were Shiʿi (*Shīʿat ʿAlī*), his intention was clearly to claim that Shiʿis, from the early period to Ibn al-Biṭrīq's time, agreed with the virtues of ʿAbbas and the ʿAbbasids.

It is known that the ʿAbbasids insisted on their membership in Muḥammad's family to bolster their legitimacy.[30] However, the normative Shiʿi position holds that the members of the *ahl al-bayt* are limited to the descendants of Fāṭima, a daughter of Muḥammad. Ibn al-Biṭrīq thus attempts to claim that Shiʿa as a whole also respected ʿAbbās and the ʿAbbasids as the *ahl al-bayt* by selectively citing the opinions and poems of Shiʿis that were regarded as outside the Shiʿi mainstream by his own time. Consequently, it is now clear that Ibn al-Biṭrīq had a political goal in compiling the *ʿUmda*, that is, to present the work to al-Nāṣir himself. And now, turning to the *sayyid* who requested Ibn al-Biṭrīq to compile ʿAlī's virtues, perhaps this *sayyid* is none other than al-Nāṣir himself. As Kohlberg points out, al-Nāṣir is said to have compile a *faḍāʾil* work on ʿAlī.[31] Although this work has not survived and its contents are unclear, it is possible that dedication of the *ʿUmda* sparked his interest in ʿAlī, or his *faḍāʾil* writing attracted Ibn al-Biṭrīq to the dedication.

It is well-known that caliph al-Nāṣir adopted a pro-Shiʿi policy. As mentioned above, he appointed Shiʿi *wazīr*s and demonstrated Imamophilia by restoring the monuments of the Imams located in Iraq. By taking a range of religious policies supporting Sunnism, Shiʿism, and Sufism, al-Nāṣir tried to reinforce the regained independence of the caliphate.[32] His sovereignty was a combination of various authorities: a caliph, a Sunni scholar transmitting Ibn Ḥanbal's *Musnad* by conferring *ijāza*,[33] a leader of social-sufistic organization,[34] the Mahdī,[35] and the supporter of the Shiʿi Imams. The respect for ʿAlī was of capital importance not only in his pro-Shiʿi policy, but also in the new social organization established by him.[36] Thus the Imamophilia was one link in his multilayered sovereignty.[37]

Ibn al-Biṭrīq's praise of al-Nāṣir and the ʿAbbasids suggests that he sought to respond to al-Nāṣir's interconfessional policy by writing the *ʿUmda*. Ibn al-Biṭrīq was not the only example of a Shiʿi scholar who reacted to al-Nāṣir. Another Twelver Shiʿi scholar who interacted with al-Nāṣir, Muḥammad b. Maʿadd al-Mūsawī (d. 620/1223), received an *ijāza* from him to transmit the *Musnad* of Ibn Ḥanbal and taught it to others in the mausoleum of Mūsā al-Kāẓim.[38] According to Ibn al-Ṭiqṭaqā, a Twelver Shiʿi historian and genealogist active in the late 13th and early 14th centuries, al-Nāṣir is also said to have asked Muḥammad b. Maʿadd to become his *wazīr*.[39] A student of Ibn al-Biṭrīq and prominent Twelver Shiʿi scholar of Ḥilla, Fikhār b. Maʿadd, was also a student of al-Nāṣir and transmitted traditions from the caliph.[40] These examples show that the compilation of the *ʿUmda* was one among a number of positive reactions by Iraqi Twelver Shiʿi scholars at that time.[41]

Exclusive Use of Sunni Sources

In the last section, we made clear that the *ʿUmda* was dedicated to al-Nāṣir. The next question is how Ibn al-Biṭrīq compiled the work to approve the interconfessional policy of the caliph. In the first half of the preface to the *ʿUmda*, Ibn al-Biṭrīq explains in detail his approach to the compilation. He thus lists the sources used in his work and emphasizes his intent to prove ʿAlī's leadership and virtues through authoritative Sunni sources while entirely excluding Shiʿi sources. This confirmation of ʿAlī's virtues from Sunni sources is the most remarkable feature of the work. Ibn al-Biṭrīq initially highlights the consensus between Sunnis and Shiʿis on ʿAlī's special position as Imam:

> Concerning the virtues of the Commander of the Faithful ʿAlī b. Abī Ṭālib – blessing of Allāh and peace be upon him – there are many differences of opinion among the Select and the Generality of the people (*al-Khāṣṣa wa-l-*

> *ʿĀmma*. i.e., Shiʿis and Sunnis), and they each have gone their own ways [. . .]. However, even if they [Shiʿis and Sunnis] disagree with each other over their belief in whether his Imamate was earlier or later, all believers in Islam have reached a consensus on his Imamate [itself] (*wa-in ikhtalafat ārāʾuhum fī l-iʿtiqād li-imāmatihi min taqdīm wa-taʾkhīr, maʿa anna sāʾir ahl al-Islām mujmaʿūn ʿalā al-qawl bi-imāmatihi*) [. . .]. The necessity [of his Imamate] comes from divine revelation, the designation by the Prophet, and the consensus of both enemies and supporters (*ijmāʿ min ʿaduww wa-walī*). [However,] As far as I see, most scholars, except those men protected by Allāh the Exalted, are absorbed in maintaining the things that their teachers left for them, namely, the works by the teachers on the studies of principles and derivative aspects [of the religion], while being satisfied with imitation and abandoning their duty to consider the matter on the basis of the two sources that are foundations of the divine guidance and right way (*mā waḍaʿahu lahum mashāyikhuhum min al-muṣannafīn fī l-uṣūl wa-l-furūʿ ikhlādan minhum ilā rāḥat al-taqlīd wa-iṭrāḥan li-waẓīfat al-naẓar fī mawḍiʿ al-dalīl min al-aṣlayn alladhayn humā sinkh uṣūl al-hudā wa-tasdīd*). Islām as a whole (*jamīʿ al-dīn*) is not based solely on deductive analogy or conjecture but is based on those two things, the Book of Allāh the Exalted and what is proved to be correct of the habitual practice of the Trustworthy Apostle (*laysa bi-mujarrad qiyās wa-lā takhmīn, bal huwa muʾasssas ʿalayhimā Kitāb Allāh taʿālā wa-mā ṣaḥḥa min sunnat al-Rasūl al-Amīn*).[42]

According to Ibn al-Biṭrīq, there was agreement on ʿAlī's special position between Sunnis and Shiʿis, despite various differences. However, a group of Sunnis deviated from this agreement under the influence of teachers who had expressed erroneous opinions and students who clung to their teachers' beliefs without taking adequate account of the Qurʾan and the *sunna* (practices of Muḥammad). Ibn al-Biṭrīq accepts that there was a difference of opinion on ʿAlī's Imamate between the two confessions and calls it "the belief in whether his Imamate was earlier or later." This clearly indicates the existence of a difference over whether ʿAlī's position was that of the first Imam, as in Shiʿi belief, or of the fourth Rightly Guided Caliph, as in Sunni belief. Ibn al-Biṭrīq minimizes the significance of this difference and asserts that, even if such a small difference remains, Sunnis ought to return to the essential agreement upon ʿAlī's virtues shared by Shiʿis, correcting the mistaken opinions proposed by previous Sunni scholars and relying directly on the Qurʾan and the *sunna.*

To prove interconfessional agreement on ʿAlī's leadership and virtues, Ibn al-Biṭrīq then lists seven Sunni works that present the words of Allāh and the sayings of Muḥammad: The two *Ṣaḥīḥ*s (Bukhārī and Muslim), *al-Jamʿ bayna al-Ṣaḥīḥayn* (the Synthesis of the Two *Ṣaḥīḥ*s) by al-Ḥumaydī (d. 488/1095), *al-Jamʿ bayna al-Ṣiḥāḥ* *al-sitta* (the Synthesis of the Six *Ṣaḥīḥ*s)[43] by Razīn b. Muʿāwiya al-ʿAbdarī (d. 524 or 535/1129 or 1140), the *Musnad* of Ibn Ḥanbal, the *Tafsīr* of al-Thaʿlabī, and the *Manāqib* on ʿAlī by Ibn al-Maghāzilī (d. 483/1090).[44] Ibn al-Biṭrīq declares that, to demonstrate ʿAlī's leadership and virtues, he will quote only these authoritative Sunni works, eschewing Shiʿi sources since his Sunni opponents will never deny the former and will never accept the latter.[45]

Among his Sunni sources, the two *Ṣaḥīḥ*s and the *Musnad* of Ibn Ḥanbal appear to have been quite well-known even among Shiʿis in Ibn al-Biṭrīq's time; al-Ḥumaydī's *al-Jamʿ* must also have been attractive to Ibn al-Biṭrīq because al-Ḥumaydī was a visitor to Baghdad and famous among Iraqi scholars.[46] Although al-ʿAbdarī was not so well-known at the time, Ibn al-Biṭrīq seems to have regarded him as noteworthy since his work was composed of hadiths from authoritative Sunni works.[47] Further, al-Thaʿlabī's *Tafsīr*, or *al-Kashf wa-l-bayān*, was a well-known Qurʾanic commentary in medieval Islam.[48] As Saleh noted, this commentary was quoted not only by Ibn al-Biṭrīq but also by Ḥillī scholars of subsequent generations.[49] Ibn al-Maghāzilī, the author of the *Manāqib* on ʿAlī, was a Shāfiʿī scholar from Wāṣit.[50]

In addition to these seven main sources, Ibn al-Biṭrīq states that he made limited use of the following ten works: *Gharīb al-ḥadīth* by Ibn Qutayba al-Dīnawarī (d. 276/889), *al-Maṣābīḥ* (*Maṣābīḥ al-sunna*) by al-Farrāʾ al-Baghawī (d. 510 or 516/1117 or 1122), *al-Firdaws* (*Firdaws al-akhbār*) by Shīrawayh b. Shahradār al-Daylamī (d. 509/1115), *al-Maghāzī* by Ibn Isḥāq (d. 150/767),[51] *al-Istīʿāb* (*al-Istīʿāb fī maʿrifat al-aṣḥāb*) by Yūsuf b. ʿAbd Allāh ibn ʿAbd al-Barr (d. 463/1071), *al-Sharīʿa* by al-Ājūrrī (d. 360/971), "*Kitāb Abī Zakariyyā b. Manda*" by Abū Zakariyyā b. ʿAbd al-Wahhāb ibn Manda (d. 511/1118), *al-Malāḥim* by Ibn al-Munādī (d. 336/947–48), *al-Tārīkh* of al-Ṭabarī (d. 310/923), and "*Tafsīr Muqātil*" by Muqātil b. Sulaymān (d. 150/767).[52] Again, none of these are Shiʿi sources.[53] Immediately after the preface, Ibn al-Biṭrīq presents his *isnād*s for these works in detail.[54]

Notably, despite highlighting the interconfessional agreement on ʿAlī's Imamate and depending exclusively on Sunni sources, Ibn al-Biṭrīq does not hesitate to use Shiʿi terminology. At the beginning of the preface, he includes "the Imams from his [i.e., Muḥammad's] family (*al-Aʾimma min ālihi*)" among those for whom he solicits God's blessing, though the identity of the Imams is never specified there.[55] Moreover, he uses the terms "enemy" (*ʿaduww*) and "opponent" (*mukhālif*) to allude to Sunnis.[56] To be clear, he does not apply "enemy" and "opponent" to Sunnis as a whole, but only to those who hold incorrect opinions about ʿAlī. Ibn al-Biṭrīq's usage indicates that there are "original" and "right" Sunnis in comparison to such "wrong" and "misguided" Sunnis, and the latter ought to accept what the former supports and Ibn al-Biṭrīq claims in the *ʿUmda* regarding ʿAlī's leadership and virtues.

The dates recorded in the *isnād*s show that Ibn al-Biṭrīq learned most of the relevant hadiths between 579/1183–84 and 585/1189. It signals his late start in studying with Sunni scholars.[57] Given that he was over eighty at the time of his death, he must have started studying with Sunni scholars when he was more than sixty years old. This late start implies that, in contrast to the later Ḥillī scholars Raḍī al-Dīn ʿAlī Ibn Ṭāwūs and al-ʿAllāma al-Ḥillī, it was uncommon among Ḥillī scholars at the time of Ibn al-Biṭrīq to study Sunni works under Sunni scholars.[58] The late start may also imply that after studying under Ibn Shahrāshūb, who resided in Iraq ca. 552–71/1157–75 and used various Sunni sources in his *faḍāʾil*, Ibn al-Biṭrīq imitated his teacher and began to study under Sunni scholars.

Interpretation of the Ghadīr Khumm Tradition

While avoiding a critical attitude toward Sunni doctrine, he carefully aims to validate the Shiʿi understanding. The most obvious part we can find this attitude is the part on the Ghadīr Khumm tradition, which is, for Shiʿis, the most important evidence for ʿAlī's direct succession to Muḥammad's leadership.[59] In the *ʿUmda*, Ibn al-Biṭrīq rarely presents interpretations for hadiths, restricting himself to mentioning similar ones repeatedly, implying his argument in the choice and repetition of hadith. However, the part on the Ghadīr Khumm tradition has an exceptionally long explanation. After repeating the relevant hadiths, Ibn al-Biṭrīq discusses the tradition at length, a discussion that provides an ideal example of how Ibn al-Biṭrīq uses Sunni texts to present his Shiʿi beliefs.

The tradition relates that, shortly before the death of Muḥammad, he said "for whomever I am his *mawlā*, ʿAlī is his *mawlā*" (*Man kuntu mawlāhu, fa-ʿAlī mawlāhu*), in front of the Companions. This speech became the primary basis for the Shiʿi theory of the Imamate and the designation of the Imam (*naṣṣ*).[60] For Shiʿis, the fact that the authoritative Sunni hadith collections include this tradition is definitive proof of its authenticity. Nonetheless, the Ghadīr Khumm tradition is ambiguous in its importance because of the equivocality of the Arabic word *mawlā*. One of the founders of Twelver Shiʿi doctrine, al-Shaykh al-Mufīd (d. 413/1022), wrote a short treatise on the interpretation of the tradition in which he attempted to arrive at a more precise meaning for the term *mawlā*. Al-Mufīd reported that *mawlā* had ten meanings in all, of which the most appropriate for the interpretation of the Ghadīr Khumm tradition was "the Imam, or the master to be obeyed (*al-imām al-sayyid al-muṭāʿ*), which means ʿAlī's Imamate.[61] This became the standard Shiʿi interpretation of the tradition.

After quoting the variants of the hadith, Ibn al-Biṭrīq presents the same ten meanings for *mawlā*, taking examples from usage in the Qurʾan. When he selects the most appropriate meaning for the tradition, he points out that the Prophet says "O people! Am I not closer (*awlā*) to your spirits than you are (*a lastu awlā minkum bi-anfusikum*)?" before the sentence mentioning *mawlā* and that this wording is almost consistent with the Qurʾanic verse 33: 6, "for them (the faithful), he (the Prophet) is closer than their spirits (*bihim awlā min anfusihim*)." Ibn al-Biṭrīq thus claims that the meaning of *awlā* in the saying of the Prophet is identical to that of *awlā* in the verse, and that the words *awlā* and *mawlā* in the tradition must be used in the same sense.[62] He holds that *mawlā* in this tradition means some capacity and position which the Prophet could grant to ʿAlī and states that only two of the ten meanings are suitable to this context: the closer/closest [to the faithful] (*al-awlā*) and the imam, or the master to be obeyed.[63] He states:

> Because what he [i.e., Muḥammad] meant [by using *mawlā*] does not correspond with any of those [eight] divisions [of meaning], we should know that his intention is what remains of them; that is obligation imposed on believers for his [i.e., Muḥammad's] sake and that is allowable to impose it [on believers] for the sake of whom he wants (*ʿalimnā anna murādahu mā baqiya minhā min-mā huwa wājib lahu ʿalā al-ʿibād wa-yaṣiḥḥu an yūjibahu li-man arāda*). [After all,] none remains but the last two divisions, that are the closer/closest [to the faithful] (*awlā*) and the master to be obeyed (*al-sayyid al-muṭāʿ*). Both are what [Muḥammad] meant, whatever different considerations we give to the topic. If [we supposed that] neither of the two was what he intended, or even either of them was not what he intended, his word would have no understandable meaning. [. . .] This [tradition] means that the Commander of the Faithful [ʿAlī] is the closer/closest [to the faithful] and the master to be obeyed [by them].[64]

Starting from the perspective that *mawlā* in this tradition denotes obligation, Ibn al-Biṭrīq selects the closer/closest and the master to be obeyed. He ultimately concludes that *mawlā* in this tradition signifies "the worthiness of the Imamate and the loyalty of the Muslim community" (*istiḥqāq al-imāma wa-l-walāʾ al-umma*),[65] a view almost consistent with the Shiʿi belief in ʿAlī's successorship to Muḥammad. Interestingly, he does not provide a positive reason for why *al-sayyid al-muṭāʿ* is the suitable meaning for the Ghadīr Khumm tradition. Rather, it seems that he quickly arrives at the answer, *awlā* and *al-sayyid al-muṭāʿ*, by a simple process of elimination that avoids the need to explain in detail the validity of the latter, which is favored by the Shiʿis.

Why does Ibn al-Biṭrīq select "the closer/closest," in addition to "the master to be obeyed" preferred by Shiʿis? Applying the former meaning in understanding the Ghadīr Khumm tradition is quite typical among Sunni *faḍāʾil* authors. Although those authors do not always interpret the tradition in their own words, citation of the tradition by them may be helpful in ascertaining how Sunnis reached that interpretation. The Sunni hadith collector and exegete of the Qurʾān, Ibn Mardawayh (d. 410/1020), wrote a *faḍāʾil* on ʿAlī in which he cited this tradition.[66] Although Ibn

Mardawayh does not present an interpretation of *mawlā* in his own words, his choice of which variant of the hadith to quote indicates how he understands the word. In the variant Ibn Mardawayh cites, reportedly transmitted from the Companion Riyāḥ b. al-Ḥārith, there is a hadith in which Arab cavalrymen tell ʿAlī what Muḥammad had said in Ghadīr Khumm. In this hadith, a soldier says to ʿAlī "He [i.e., Muḥammad] took your upper arm and said 'O people! Am I not closer (*awlā*) to the faithful than their spirits are?' Then we said, 'Yes, the messenger of Allāh.' He said, 'Truly Allāh is my *mawlā*, I am a *mawlā* of the faithful, and ʿAlī is a *mawlā* of whomever I am his *mawlā*.'"[67] In this hadith, it is apparent that *awlā* and *mawlā* are used with almost same meaning.

In another example, al-Muwaffaq b. Aḥmad al-Makkī al-Khwārazmī (d. 568/1172), nicknamed "Akhṭab Khwārazm" and known as the author of *Manāqib Abī Ḥanīfa*, also wrote a *faḍāʾil* on ʿAlī in which he cites the Ghadīr Khumm tradition.[68] In the chapter on ʿAlī's closeness to the Prophet and his position as *mawlā*, Akhṭab Khwārazm quotes the following hadith from Burayda al-Aslamī:

> When ʿAlī and I [i.e., Burayda] went to Yemen for war, I quarreled with him. Then I went to the Messenger of Allāh and I criticized ʿAlī. I saw his face went scarlet. He said "O Burayda! Am I not closer (*awlā*) to the faithful than their spirits?" I answered "Yes, the Messenger of Allāh." He said, "for whomever I am his *mawlā*, ʿAlī is his *mawlā*."[69]

This hadith likewise informs us that the meaning of *mawlā* could be understood through the meaning of *awlā*. After Ibn al-Biṭrīq, the well-known 13th century Sunni scholar and historian Sibṭ Ibn al-Jawzī (d. 654/1256) clearly states that the term *mawlā* in this tradition should be understood by the meaning of *awlā*.[70] In this opinion, he clearly follows in the footsteps of Ibn Mardawayh and Akhṭab Khwārazm. The examples of these Sunni *faḍāʾil* authors indicate that the meaning "the closer/closest" was preferred among Sunnis to the meaning "the master to be obeyed."

Thus, it was acceptable, if not required, among Sunni *faḍāʾil* authors to understand *mawlā* as it appears in this tradition to mean *awlā*. By interpreting *mawlā* as a special capacity and position passed down from the Prophet to ʿAlī and emphasizing the suitability of "closer/closest" and "master to be obeyed" in his interpretation, Ibn al-Biṭrīq justifies the Shiʿi understanding of the Ghadīr Khumm tradition. Nonetheless, he is silent on the significance of this tradition in connection with the "earlier or later" problem of ʿAlī's Imamate. Issues intimately connected to confessional identity, such as ʿAlī's immediate successorship to Muḥammad and the legitimacy of the caliphate of ʿAbū Bakr, are not addressed here. However, given that Ibn al-Biṭrīq examines this tradition and emphasizes the meaning of the master to be obeyed and ʿAlī's Imamate, his intention to justify Shiʿi belief is clear.

From ʿAlī to the Twelve Imams

Although Ibn al-Biṭrīq emphasizes the agreement of Sunnis and Shiʿis on ʿAlī's leadership and virtues in the preface to the *ʿUmda*, he does not focus on ʿAlī alone. After long discussions of ʿAlī, several chapters are devoted to the description of Fāṭima, ʿAlī's wife and Muḥammad's daughter, and Khadīja, Fāṭima's mother.[71] Ensuing chapters deal with Ḥasan and Ḥusayn (considered the second and third Imams by the Shiʿa),[72] Jaʿfar b. Abī Ṭālib (ʿAlī's brother),[73] Abū Ṭālib (ʿAlī's father),[74] "the twelve leaders,"[75] and the Mahdī.[76] I argue that the inclusion of these chapters in the *ʿUmda* represents Ibn al-Biṭrīq's attempt to present to his readers the important figures for Shiʿis, especially the Twelve Imams and the Mahdī.

Fāṭima, Ḥasan, and Ḥusayn hold a special status among ʿAlī's family because of the tradition of "the people of the cloak" (*ahl al-kisāʾ*: Muḥammad, ʿAlī, Fāṭima, Ḥasan, and Ḥusayn).[77] The inclusion of Fāṭima, Ḥasan, and Ḥusayn in a *faḍāʾil* on ʿAlī is therefore not exclusive to Shiʿi writing. For example, the *Manāqib* of Ibn al-Maghāzilī contains chapters on all three figures, in addition to that on Khadīja, following the book's main chapter on ʿAlī.[78] In short, Ibn al-Biṭrīq gradually expands his discussion from less controversial topics to those directly connected with Shiʿi doctrines.

From the short chapter on Abū Ṭālib, Ibn al-Biṭrīq enters into subjects considered disputable by Sunnis. In the chapter on Abū Ṭālib, his Islamic faith is highlighted,[79] reflecting Sunni suspicion of Abū Ṭālib's conversion to Islam, about which Shiʿis had no doubt. This dispute originated from the opposition between the ʿAbbasids and the Ṭālibids in the early ʿAbbasid period. To undermine esteem for the latter, the ʿAbbasids and their apologists claimed that ʿAbbās died as a Muslim, but his brother Abū Ṭālib died as a pagan.[80] Ignoring negative opinions, Ibn al-Biṭrīq uses Sunni materials to support the Shiʿi position.[81]

The following chapter concerns the twelve leaders, and Ibn al-Biṭrīq begins it with a tradition that the Prophet foretold the appearance of the twelve *amīr*s after his death.[82] Mention of the twelve leaders implies a belief in the Twelve Imams according to the ideas of Twelver Shiʿism. However, Ibn al-Biṭrīq never gives the leaders' names, nor does he refer to the twelve leaders as imams but as *khalīfa*s or *amīr*s. This clear avoidance of explicit reference to the Twelve Imams is a remarkable feature of the *ʿUmda*. Nonetheless, Ibn al-Biṭrīq occasionally inserts implicit references to the Twelve Imams into his discussion. He cites a few hadith that link the twelve leaders to the *ahl al-bayt*.[83] Moreover, at the end of the chapter he cites a tradition about the interpretation of the Qurʾanic verse 24: 35 from Ibn al-Maghāzilī. In this tradition, ʿAlī b. Jaʿfar, the son of the sixth Imam Jaʿfar al-Ṣādiq, asks "Abū l-Ḥasan" (probably his brother the seventh Imam Mūsā al-Kāẓim) the meaning of the verse. Abū l-Ḥasan says that "like a niche in which there is a lamp" (*ka-mishkāt fīhā miṣbāḥ*) in this verse refers to Fāṭima, Ḥasan, and Ḥusayn, while "even without being touched by fire. Light upon light" (*wa-law lam tamsashu nār nūr ʿalā nūr*) signifies that, from Faṭima's descendants, imams will appear one after another (*minhā imām baʿda imām*). Abū l-Ḥasan continues his interpretation by stating that "Allāh guides whoever He wills to His light" (*yahdī Allāh li-nūrihi man yashāʾu*) means that Allāh guides whoever He wills to our *walāya* (*yahdī Allāh li-walāyatinā man yashāʾu*).[84] Although the meaning of *walāya* is not explained in the text, Ibn al-Biṭrīq at least implies that it is almost equivalent to the Imamate. His quotation of this tradition is thus tantamount to claiming that the Imams are to appear from the Fāṭimids by divine guidance. It is beyond doubt that Ibn al-Biṭrīq indirectly indicates here that the twelve leaders were certainly the Twelve Imams of Shiʿism.

Finally, Ibn al-Biṭrīq turns to the Mahdī, whom Twelver Shiʿis generally identify with the twelfth of their Imams, Muḥammad b. al-Ḥasan. As in the previous chapter on the twelve leaders, Ibn al-Biṭrīq never mentions the Mahdī's personal name. It is striking that Ibn al-Biṭrīq, a Twelver Shiʿi author, avoids directly identifying the Mahdī, who embodied one of the most important doctrines for Twelver Shiʿis. This is all the more striking since al-Ḥilla, whence Ibn al-Biṭrīq hailed, was host to a tradition that Muḥammad b. al-Ḥasan would appear as the Mahdī in that city.[85] Citing a series of hadith, however, Ibn al-Biṭrīq gradually leads readers to understand who the Mahdī is and is not. First, several hadith that distinguish the Mahdī from ʿĪsā (Jesus) are presented.[86] Then, Ibn al-Biṭrīq quotes hadith which show that the Mahdī must be from the ʿAlids.[87] These points suggest that the very person the Twelver Shiʿis hold to be the Mahdī, that is, Muḥammad b. al-Ḥasan or the Hidden Imam al-Muntaẓar, must be a strong candidate for the Mahdī. On the other hand, this discussion seems unsuitable for al-Nāṣir's claim to the Mahdīship at the time.[88] Although the caliph is connected with the nature associated to the Imams and counted among the *ahl al-bayt*, Ibn al-Biṭrīq keeps distance from the idea inconsistent with the Shiʿi belief.

Ibn al-Biṭrīq begins the *ʿUmda* by emphasizing the agreement of Sunnis and Shiʿis on ʿAlī's virtues. Chapter by chapter, however, he guides his readers toward a belief in the legitimacy of the Twelve Imams, without directly expressing this belief or even writing the names of the relevant figures. This resonates with his approach to the Ghadīr Khumm tradition, in which he does not insist on reporting Shiʿi doctrines. As a result, the identity of the Imams, despite being a basic belief for Twelver Shiʿism, is not stated in the *ʿUmda*. However, by relating the Sunni traditions relevant to the Imams and the Mahdī, Ibn al-Biṭrīq reminds his readers of the Twelve Imams upheld by the Shiʿa and asserts their validity.

The *Mustadrak* and the *Khaṣāʾiṣ*

After the *ʿUmda*, Ibn al-Biṭrīq compiled two other *faḍāʾil*s on ʿAlī: the *Mustadrak* and the *Khaṣāʾiṣ*. However, their relationship to the *ʿUmda* and even the meaning of *mustadrak* (supplement) used as the title of the former remain unclear.

The *Mustadrak* has come down to us with no preface, and Ibn al-Biṭrīq's authorship is mentioned only at the end of the work.[89] The extant text of the *Mustadrak* begins with a quotation from Abū Nuʿaym al-Iṣfahānī (d. 430/1038), opening with the phrase "by the above-mentioned *isnād*" (*bi-l-isnād*).[90] This clearly indicates that the original text included one or more hadiths with a full *isnād* before this quotation. In the absence of the preface, the purpose of the compilation is not known from the author's own words, although it can be conjectured by reference to the quotations and the structure of the work.

In the *Mustadrak*, Ibn al-Biṭrīq again restricts himself to using Sunni sources, apart from his own *ʿUmda*.[91] He appears to have thought that quoting the *ʿUmda* would not be problematic because it only contained Sunni hadiths. With the exception of those drawn from the *ʿUmda*, most hadith used are quoted from five Sunni works in particular: *al-Maghāzī* by Ibn Isḥāq,[92] *Mā nazala min al-Qurʾān fī Amīr al-Muʾminīn ʿAlī b. Abī Ṭālib* and *Ḥilyat al-awliyāʾ* by Abū Nuʿaym al-Iṣfahānī,[93] *Faḍāʾil al-ṣaḥāba* (or, *Manāqib al-ṣahāba*) by Abū l-Muẓaffar al-Samʿānī (d. 489/1096),[94] and *Firdaws al-akhbār* by Shīrawayh b. Shahradār al-Daylamī.[95] These differ from the seven main sources used in the *ʿUmda*. It seems that Ibn al-Biṭrīq, maintaining his rule of using only Sunni materials, collected additional, and more detailed information from these new sources.

The structure of the *Mustadrak* parallels that of the *ʿUmda*. Ibn al-Biṭrīq spills much ink on ʿAlī,[96] but includes chapters on Fāṭima,[97] Khadīja,[98] and Ḥasan and Ḥusayn together.[99] After the chapter on Ḥasan and Ḥusayn and before the two chapters on the twelve leaders and the Mahdī,[100] a chapter on the fourth Imam al-Sajjād, the fifth Imam al-Bāqir, and the sixth Imam al-Ṣādiq, all absent in the *ʿUmda*, is added.[101] The inspiration for this addition appears to have been the *Ḥilyat al-awliyāʾ* by Abū Nuʿaym, which includes entries on these three Imams and describes them as admirable.[102] By quoting traditions from Abū Nuʿaym, the prominent Sunni hadith collector,[103] Ibn al-Biṭrīq convincingly presents that Sunnis agreed with the virtues of these Imams.[104] Given that Ibn al-Biṭrīq developed and expanded his topics using Sunni sources he had not used before, the *Mustadrak* was undoubtedly intended as a supplement to the *ʿUmda*.

The *Khaṣāʾiṣ*, as the phrase "*al-waḥy al-mubīn*" (the clear revelation) in its title shows, deals with Qurʾanic texts on ʿAlī. Ibn al-Biṭrīq here again relies exclusively on Sunni sources, all of which had appeared previously in the *ʿUmda* and the *Mustadrak*. As in the *ʿUmda*, he lists his *isnād*s after the preface.[105] Notably, Ibn al-Biṭrīq refers to the fact that he learned the text of Abū Nuʿaym from his own Twelver Shiʿi teacher, Ibn Shahrāshūb. In all three of Ibn al-Biṭrīq's works discussed here, this is likely the only point at which he reveals his Shiʿi connections. It is possible that Ibn al-Biṭrīq needed to present this *isnād* here as it was the shortest *isnād* from Abū Nuʿaym to him.[106] Unlike the *ʿUmda* and the *Mustadrak*, the *Khaṣāʾiṣ* includes many comments by Ibn al-Biṭrīq himself on the hadith and the interpretation of Qurʾanic verses. After each quotation, he begins his comments with the phrase "Yaḥyā b. al-Ḥasan [i.e., Ibn al-Biṭrīq] said 'Know (*iʿlam*) that [. . .]'." In this work, Ibn al-Biṭrīq introduces a new way of producing a compilation of *faḍāʾil*, which he did not use in the *ʿUmda* nor the *Mustadrak*.

Both the *Mustadrak* and the *Khaṣāʾiṣ* follow the *ʿUmda* in their exclusive use of Sunni sources and avoidance of any criticism of Sunnism. Ibn al-Biṭrīq's approach in the *ʿUmda* was carried on in the two supplemental works using new sources and methodology.

Conclusion

To explain ʿAlī's virtues in the *ʿUmda* and its supplemental works, Ibn al-Biṭrīq restricts himself to using Sunni materials exclusively, carefully making clear the kinds of sources he cited. This, however, does not mean that he only restates the Sunni understanding of ʿAlī. Instead, he ingeniously uses Sunni texts to conform to Shiʿi beliefs. In discussing the Ghadīr Khumm tradition, Abū Ṭālib, the Twelve Imams, and the Mahdī, Shiʿi ideas are presented indirectly under the cover of Sunni traditions. On the other hand, Ibn al-Biṭrīq consistently avoids either specifying what Shiʿi ideas exactly are or reproaching Sunni beliefs. His aim in these *faḍāʾil*s is to redefine Sunni beliefs as essentially harmonized with Shiʿi ones and to suggest that Sunnis who deny Shiʿism have already deviated from essential Sunni beliefs.

By promoting his interconfessional policy, al-Nāṣir li-Dīn Allāh sought to unite the various Islamic groups under his control and to establish a new social order based on his multilayered sovereignty which was rooted in the authority of ʿAlī and the Shiʿi Imams. However, this approach to Shiʿis and Shiʿi ideas sometimes provoked criticism and negative reaction from Sunnis.[107] The Iraqi Sunni historian Ibn al-Sāʿī (d. 674/1276) notes al-Nāṣir's Shiʿi tendency because of his rebuilding of the mausoleum of al-Kāẓim.[108] Conversely, the compilation of the *ʿUmda* should be considered a positive reaction by Iraqi Twelver Shiʿi scholars toward al-Nāṣir. Ibn al-Biṭrīq's aim in his *faḍāʾil*s, namely including the caliph among the *ahl al-bayt* and finding justification for Imamophilia in Sunni traditions, may have coincided with, or even been helpful in defending, al-Nāṣir's policy.

Some characteristics of the *ʿUmda* are, however, not always Ibn al-Biṭrīq's original ideas. Pierce, in his study of Ibn Shahrāshūb, briefly mentioned that Ibn

Shahrāṣhūb influenced Ibn al-Biṭrīq and later Twelver Shiʿi scholars from Ḥilla, such as Raḍī al-Dīn ʿAlī Ibn Ṭāwūs and al-ʿAllāma al-Ḥillī, though without elaborating concretely what this influence consisted of.[109] In the preface to *Manāqib Āl Abī Ṭālib*, Ibn Shahrāshūb also emphasizes that ʿAlī's Imamate can be confirmed by both the Sunni and Shiʿi traditions and lists the Sunni sources used in his work, presenting the *isnād*s through which he learned them.[110] This suggests the possibility that Ibn al-Biṭrīq engaged in a similar approach to compilation in the *ʿUmda*. However, there are remarkable differences between the two works.

First, compared to Ibn Shahrāshūb's use of both Sunni and Shiʿi sources, Ibn al-Biṭrīq avoids using Shiʿi sources altogether, as mentioned above. Second, Ibn al-Biṭrīq relies on several Sunni sources which his teacher did not use, for instance, *Manāqib ʿAlī b. Abī Ṭālib* by Ibn al-Maghāzilī and the two *Jamʿ*s, which are among his seven main sources.[111] It is likely that Ibn al-Biṭrīq limited his sources to more *ṣaḥīḥ*-based works and one Sunni *faḍāʾil* on ʿAlī. Third, the contents of the *ʿUmda* differ from the *Manāqib* of Ibn Shahrāshūb. While the latter deals with the Twelve Imams and devotes one chapter to each Imam, Ibn al-Biṭrīq focuses on ʿAlī and does not clarify who the Twelve Imams are. In so doing, he depends completely on Sunni sources and shows more clearly how authoritative Sunni sources agreed with ʿAlī's virtues and the appearance of the Twelve Imams. Finally, and most importantly, the praise for the ʿAbbasids and allusion to the ʿAbbasid caliph found in the *ʿUmda* are absent in the *Manāqib* of Ibn Shahrāshūb. These differences originate from the contrasting backgrounds of the works. The *Manāqib* of Ibn Shahrāshūb seems, as Pierce explains, to have been compiled as an apology for Shiʿism against Sunni opponents in Baghdad.[112] By contrast, the *ʿUmda* was written in the context of an ʿAbbasid caliph being indulgent toward the Shiʿa. The potential opponents of the *ʿUmda* were not Sunnis as whole, but those of them who reproached the Imamophilic policy of the caliph as heretical. From these points, we can find Ibn al-Biṭrīq's original methodology and purpose in the *ʿUmda*.

The relationship between Imamophilic Sunnis and Iraqi Twelver Shiʿi *faḍāʾil* authors persisted even after al-Nāṣir and Ibn al-Biṭrīq. From the 13th century, Imamophilic Sunnis appeared in various Islamic lands and engaged in more elaborate discussion about the Imams. The later ʿAbbasid caliphs also continued to indicate their respect for the Imams.[113] Utilizing the spread of Imamophilia, relying on various Sunni sources, avoiding direct criticism of Sunnism, and attaching importance to ʿAlī were all features shared in *faḍāʾil*s written by subsequent Iraqi Twelver Shiʿi scholars, such as *al-Yaqīn* by Raḍī al-Dīn ʿAlī Ibn Ṭāwūs, the *Kashf al-yaqīn* by al-ʿAllāma al-Ḥillī,[114] and the *Manhaj al-Shīʿa* by Jalāl al-Dīn.[115] ʿAlī b. ʿĪsā al-Irbilī, in his *faḍāʾil*, the *Kashf al-ghumma*, further extended these writing methods to the description of all Twelve Imams.[116] These authors, active in the ʿAbbasid, Ilkhanid, and Jalayrid periods, also compiled works for the rulers, or under the ruling authorities.[117] In short, Ibn al-Biṭrīq's strategic compilation of *faḍā'il* was replicated by later Iraqi Twelver Shi'i scholars. Further analysis of subsequent Iraqi Shi'i *faḍā'ils* in 13th to 14th centuries is needed to make clear how they strategically and continuously used knowledge on the Imams as power to approach the ruling authorities over the periods of several dynasties.

Notes

* This work was supported by JSPS KAKENHI Grant Numbers 21K20036 and 19H01317.

1 Marshall G. S. Hodgson, *The Venture of Islam: Conscience and History in a World Civilization* (Chicago: Chicago University Press, 1974), vol 2, 283–4; Angelika Hartmann, *An-Nāṣir li-Dīn Allāh: Politik, Religion, Kultur in der späten 'Abbāsidenzeit* (Berlin and New York: Walter de Gruyter, 1975), 166–7.

2 Ibn al-Biṭrīq al-Ḥillī, *'Umdat 'uyūn ṣiḥāḥ al-akhbār fī manāqib imām al-abrār*, ed. by Sa'īd 'Irfāniyān, 2 vols. (Qom: Maktabat al-'Allāma al-Majlisī, 2015). The *faḍā'il* (or, *manāqib/khaṣā'iṣ*) is an Islamic literary genre dealing with Qur'anic verses and traditions on the virtues and excellences of some person or thing. In addition to *faḍā'il* on the Shi'i Imams, for instance, *faḍā'il* on the Companions of the Prophet and on the Qur'ān are included in this genre. To avoid complication, this study uses the word "*faḍā'il*" or "*faḍā'il* work" in reference to relevant works on the Shi'i Imams.

3 Ibn al-Biṭrīq al-Ḥillī, *al-Mustadrak al-mukhtār fī manāqib waṣī al-mukhtār*, ed. by Sa'īd 'Irfāniyān (Qom: Maktabat al-'Allāma al-Majlisī, 2015).

4 Ibn al-Biṭrīq al-Ḥillī, *Kitāb Khaṣā'iṣ al-waḥy al-mubīn,* ed. by Muḥammad Bāqir al-Maḥmūdī (Qom: Dār al-Qur'ān al-karīm, 1996–97).

5 Walid A. Saleh, *The Formation of the Classical Tafsīr Tradition: The Qur'ān Commentary of al-Tha'labī (d. 427/1035)* (Leiden and Boston: Brill, 2004), 219.

6 Matthew Pierce, "Ibn Shahrāshūb and Shi'a Rhetorical Strategies in the 6th/12th Century," *Journal of Shi'a Islamic Studies* 5.4 (2012): 441–54.

7 Hassan Ansari and Sabine Schmidtke, "Between Aleppo and Ṣa'da: The Zaydī Reception of the Imāmī Scholar Ibn al-Biṭrīq al-Ḥillī," *Journal of Islamic Manuscripts* 4 (2013): 160–200.

8 Two other scholars among this generation are Ibn Idrīs al-Ḥillī (d. 598/1202) and Warrām b. Abī Firās (d. 605/1208), on whom see Heinz Halm, *Shi'ism*, 2nd ed. (New York: Columbia University Press, 2004), 64, and Etan Kohlberg, *A Medieval Muslim Scholar at Work: Ibn Ṭāwūs and His Library* (Leiden, New York and Köln: Brill, 1992), 3.

9 Woods proposed the term "confessional ambiguity" to explain the spread of loyalty to the 'Alids among Sunnis in 15th century West Asia. Pfeiffer used the term to discuss the interaction of political and religious situations during the Ilkhanids. Hirschler, by using the term "de-confessionalisation," considers why the Ashrafiyya, a Sunni-affiliated library in Ayyubid and Mamluk Syria, had various Shi'i works. Marlow also explains veneration of 'Alī among Sunnis in fourteenth-ceutury Iran by this term. "Imamophilia" and "Imamophilism," which refer more concretely to reverence for the Shi'i Imams by Sunnis, were first used by Melvin-Koushki in his analysis of the Sunni scholar, Ibn Turka (d. 835/1432). Even before Melvin-Koushki, during the second half of the 20th century researchers noted the Sunni scholars who praised the Twelve Imams of Twelver Shi'ism. Dānishpazhūh listed such Sunnis and called their piety "Twelver Sunnism" (*Tasannun-i Dawāzdah-Imāmī*), and Ja'fariyān developed this term and explored other examples. More recently, Masad dealt with Ibn Ṭalḥa (d. 652/1254), a Shāfi'ī scholar and author of *faḍā'il* on the Twelve Imams, and Dunietz focused on the Shāfi'ī scholar, Ḥusayn Maybudī (d. 910/1504), who praised 'Alī and the Twelve Imams in his work. See John E. Woods, *The Aqquyunlu: Clan, Confederation, Empire: A Study in 15th/9th Century Turko-Iranian Politics*,

revised and expanded ed. (Salt Lake City: The University of Utah Press, 1999), 1–23; Judith Pfeiffer, "Confessional Ambiguity vs. Confessional Polarization: Politics and Negotiation of Religious Boundaries in the Ilkhanate," in *Politics, Patronage and the Transmission of Knowledge in 13th–15th Century Tabriz*, ed. by Judith Pfeiffer (Leiden and Boston: Brill, 2014), 129–68; Konrad Hirschler, *Medieval Damascus: Plurality and Diversity in an Arabic Library, the Ashrafīya Library Catalogue* (Edinburg: Edinburg University Press, 2017), 102–32; Louise Marlow, "Translation of the Words of ʿAli b. Abi Ṭālib in Early Fourteenth-Century Iran: A Local Bilingual Network," *Iranian Studies* 53.5/6 (2020): 741–87; Matthew S. Melvin-Koushki, "The Quest for a Universal Science: The Occult Philosophy of Ṣāʾin al-Dīn Turka Iṣfahānī (1369–1432) and Intellectual Millenarianism in Early Timurid Iran," unpublished Ph.D. dissertation, Yale University, 2012; Muḥammad Taqī Dānishpazhūh, "(Intiqād-i kitāb) *Kashf al-ḥaqāyiq*," *Farhang-i Īrān-zamīn* 13 (1966): 299–310; Rasūl Jaʿfariyān, *Tārīkh-i Tashayyuʿ dar Īrān: Az āghāz tā qarn-i dahum-i Hijrī* (Tehran: Anṣāriyān, 1996–97), vol. 2, 725–32; Mohammad Ahmad Masad, "The Medieval Islamic Apocalyptic Tradition: Divination, Prophecy and the End of the 13th Century Eastern Mediterranean," unpublished Ph.D. dissertation, Washington University in St. Louis, 2008; Alexandra W. Dunietz, *The Cosmic Perils of Qadi Ḥusayn Maybudī in Fifteenth-Century Iran* (Leiden and Boston: Brill, 2016).

10 Ibn al-Shaʿʿār, *Qalāʾid al-jumān fī farāʾid shuʿarāʾ hādhā al-zamān*, ed. by Kāmil Salmān al-Jubūrī (Beirut: Dār al-kutub al-ʿilmiyya, 2005), vol. 7, 219–22.

11 Ibn Shahrāshūb was in Baghdad by 552/1157, then lived in Ḥilla from 567/1172 to 571/1175 (Pierce, "Ibn Shahrāshūb," 442).

12 Matthew Pierce, *Twelve Infallible Men: The Imams and the Making of Shiʿism* (Cambridge, MA and London: Harvard University Press, 2016).

13 Āghā Buzurg al-Ṭihrānī writes that, according to the *ʿUmdat al-ṭālib*, ʿImād al-Dīn was a teacher of Ibn al-Biṭrīq (Āghā Buzurg al-Ṭihrānī, *Ṭabaqāt aʿlām al-Shīʿa* [Beirut: Dār iḥyāʾ al-turāth al-ʿArabī, 2009], vol. 3, 337–8). However, I cannot verify this information.

14 Although Shādhān is said to have been active as late as the mid-13th century, this date is quite doubtful. According to the two *faḍāʾil*s ascribed to Shādhān, he learned traditions in 651/1253 and 652/1254 in Wāsiṭ (Shādhān b. Jibraʾīl al-Qummī, *al-Rawḍa fī faḍāʾil Amīr al-Muʾminīn ʿAlī b. Abī Ṭālib*, ed. by ʿAlī al-Shakarchī [Qom: Maktabat al-amīn, 2002–03], 21; Shādhān b. Jibraʾīl al-Qummī, *al-Faḍāʾil wa-mustadrakātuhā*, ed. by ʿAbd Allāh al-Ṣāliḥī al-Najafī [Karbalaʾ: al-ʿAtaba al-Ḥusayniyya, 2015], 302). However, these dates are long after the active period of his students, such as Muḥammad b. Jaʿfar al-Mashhadī (fl. 580/1185; transmitted from Shādhān in 571/1175–76) and Fikhār b. Maʿadd (Muḥammad b. Jaʿfar al-Mashhadī, *Iqrār al-ṣaḥāba bi-faḍāʾil imām al-hudā wa-l-qarāba, aw, Mā ittafaqa fīhi min al-akhbār fī faḍl al-aʾimma al-aṭhār*, ed. by Lajna min al-muḥaqqiqīn fī Maktabat al-ʿAllāma al-Majlisī [Qom: Maktabat al-ʿAllāma al-Majlisī, 2017–18), 59; Ghiyāth al-Dīn ʿAbd al-Karīm ibn Ṭāwūs, *Farḥat al-Gharī bi-ṣarḥat al-Gharī*, ed. by Thāmir Kāẓim al-Khafājī [Qom: Maktabat Āyatullāh Marʿashī Najafī, 2012], 375–6). In addition, among the younger generation, Fikhār's son ʿAbd al-Ḥamīd (d. 684/1285–86) and another Ḥillī scholar, ʿAbd al-Karīm ibn Ṭāwūs (d. 693/1294), learned traditions passed down by Shādhān via one intermediary, although they were present in Iraq in the mid-13th century (Ghiyāth al-Dīn ʿAbd al-Karīm ibn Ṭāwūs, *Farḥat al-Gharī*, 375; Ṣadr al-Dīn al-Ḥammūyī, *Farāʾid al-simṭayn fī faḍāʾil al-Murtaḍā wa-l-Batūl wa-l-sibṭayn wa-l-aʾimma min dhurriyyatihim*, ed. by Muḥammad-Bāqir al-Maḥmūdī [Beirut: Muʾassasat al-Maḥmūdī, 1978], vol. 1, 41, 49). It is thus likely that the two dates above are wrong and Shādhān was active mainly in the 12th century.

15 All these authors except Shādhān b. Jibraʾīl compiled *faḍāʾil*s on the Twelve Imams. Shādhān's works, the *Rawḍa* and the *Faḍāʾil* mainly deal with ʿAlī.

16 Ibn al-Biṭrīq, *al-ʿUmda*, vol. 1, 93.

17 Ansari and Schmidtke, "Between Aleppo and Ṣaʿda," 168.

18 Ibn al-Biṭrīq, *al-Mustadrak*, 135, 139, 146, 150, 154, 376.

19 Ibn al-Biṭrīq, *Khaṣāʾiṣ*, 50–1.

20 It is possible that the completion dates of the three works are not exactly in this order. From the date of an *isnād* in the *Khaṣāʾiṣ*, however, it is clear that this work was completed after 595/1199 (Ibn al-Biṭrīq, *Khaṣāʾiṣ*, 59).

21 Ansari and Schmidtke, "Between Aleppo and Ṣaʿda," 167–9.

22 Ibn al-Shaʿʿār, *Qalāʾid al-jumān*, vol. 7, 220.

23 For example, ibid., vol. 1, 193–4.

24 Ibn al-Biṭrīq, *al-ʿUmda*, vol. 1, 62.

25 Ibid., vol. 1, 68.

26 Ibid., vol. 1, 68–73. Ibn al-Biṭrīq cites al-Shaykh al-Ṭūsī's lost work, *Uns al-waḥīd.*

27 Ibid., vol. 1, 73.

28 Ibid., vol. 1, 73–5.

29 Al-Kumayt b. Zayd, one of "the Hāshimī Shiʿa" in early Islam, considered all the Hāshimids (e.g., the ʿAbbasids) as the family of Muḥammad (*āl Muḥammad*) and the *ahl al-bayt.* A Basran poet, al-Duʾalī wrote poems praising the Prophet's closest relatives and included ʿAbbās among them. See, Wilferd F. Madelung, "The "Hāshimiyyāt" of al-Kumayt and Hāshimī Shiʿism," *Studia Islamica* 70 (1989): 5–26, esp. 1–9, 17–8.

30 Cornelis van Arendonk and William A. Graham, "Sharīf," in *The Encyclopaedia of Islam, New Edition*, ed. by H. A. R. Gibb et al. (Leiden: Brill, 1960–2009), vol. 9, 331.

31 Kohlberg, *A Medieval Muslim Scholar at Work*, 155.

32 Erik S. Ohlander, *Sufism in an Age of Transition: ʿUmar al-Suhrawardī and the Rise of the Islamic Mystical Brotherhoods* (Leiden and Boston: Brill, 2008), 19–34.

33 Hartmann, *An-Nāṣir li-Dīn Allāh*, 211–2.

34 Ibid., 92–121.

35 Ibid., 121–2.

36 Al-Nāṣir reorganized the *futuwwa* groups (communal association based on moral behavior) under his control, and placed ʿAlī as the foundation of the *futuwwa* and al-Nāṣir himself as an emulator of ʿAlī (ibid., 101).

37 Recently, the sacred, combined and multi-layered rulership of Islamicate empire is discussed by scholars. Yılmaz discussed the mystical and apocalyptical aspects in Ottoman political thought. Melvin-Koushki also dealt with multilayered ideologies of the Safavid, Mughal and Ottoman empires. Brack treated the combination of Mongol and Islamic concepts and titles in the fusion of Mongol and Islamic elements in the Ilkhanate. Al-Nāṣir's interconfessional policy and his synthesis of various authorities, including the Mahdīship, can be considered an earlier example of those new types of Islamic rulership. See, Hüseyin Yılmaz, *Caliphate Redefined: The Mystical Turn in Ottoman Political Thought* (Princeton: Princeton University Press, 2018); Matthew S. Melvin-Koushki, "Early Modern Islamicate Empire: New Forms of Religiopolitical Legitimacy," in *The Wiley Blackwell History of Islam*, ed. by Armando Salvatore, Roberto Tottoli, and Babak Rahimi (Hoboken, NJ: Wiley Blackwell, 2018), 351–75; Jonathan Brack, "Theologies of Auspicious Kingship: The Islamization of Chinggisid Sacral Kingship in the Islamic World," *Comparative Studies in Society and History* 60.4 (2018): 1143–71.

38 Ibn al-Dubaythī, *Dhayl Tārīkh Madīnat al-Salām*, ed. by Bashshār ʿAwwād (Beirut: Dār al-gharb al-Islāmī, 2006), vol. 2, 132.

39 Ibn al-Ṭiqṭaqā, *al-Aṣīlī fī ansāb al-Ṭālibiyyīn*, ed. by al-Sayyid Mahdī al-Rajāʾī (Qom: Maktabat Āyat Allāh al-ʿUẓmā al-Marʿashī al-Najafī, 1997–98), 167.

40 Raḍī al-Dīn ʿAlī Ibn Ṭāwūs, *al-Yaqīn bi-ikhtiṣāṣ mawlānā ʿAlī bi-imrat al-muʾminīn, wa-yatlūhu, al-Taḥṣīn*, ed. by Muḥammad Bāqir al-Anṣārī and Muḥammad Ṣādiq al-Anṣārī (Beirut: Muʾassasat dār al-kitāb, 1992–93), 381–3. I would like to express my sincere gratitude to Kazuo Morimoto for providing me information about al-Nāṣir's relationship with Muḥammad b. Maʿadd and Fikhār b. Maʿadd.

41 The poet al-Fākhir b. ʿAlī al-Mūsawī (d. 620/1223–24) is another notable example whose details are recorded in Ibn al-Shaʿʿār's biographical dictionary and who composed a poem praising al-Nāṣir (Ibn al-Shaʿʿār, *Qalāʾid al-jumān*, vol. 4, 311–4). Although Ibn al-Shaʿʿār does not specify the poet's confessional identity, it is probable that he was a Shiʿi as he was born in Karkh of Baghdad, a quarter heavily populated by Shiʿa, and lived in al-Ḥilla.

42 Ibn al-Biṭrīq, *al-ʿUmda*, vol. 1, 61–2.

43 These "six *Ṣaḥīḥs*" do not correspond with the six most authoritative Sunni hadith collections: *al-Muwaṭṭaʾ* of Mālik b. Anas is included here, instead of the *Sunan* of Ibn Māja.

44 Ibn al-Biṭrīq, *al-ʿUmda*, 63.

45 Ibid., vol. 1, 64–5.

46 Ambrosio Huici Miranda, "Al-Ḥumaydī," in *The Encyclopaedia of Islam, New Edition.*

47 On al-ʿAbdarī, see Maribel Fierro "Razīn b. Muʿāwiya," in *The Encyclopaedia of Islam, New Edition*. For readers who did not recognize al-ʿAbdarī, Ibn al-Biṭrīq records not only the *isnād* from al-ʿAbdarī to himself, but also the *isnād*s from each author of the six *Ṣaḥīḥ*s to al-ʿAbdarī (Ibn al-Biṭrīq, *al-ʿUmda*, vol. 1, 96–100).

48 About this work, see Saleh, *The Formation of the Classical Tafsīr Tradition.*

49 Saleh presents Ibn al-Biṭrīq as the first Shiʿi scholar to use al-Thaʿlabī's *Tafsīr* (ibid., 218–20). But, as Pierce critically notes, the credit belongs to Ibn Shahrāshūb (Pierce, "Ibn Shahrāshūb," 449).

50 Ibn al-Maghāzilī, *Manāqib Amīr al-Muʾminīn ʿAlī b. Abī Ṭālib*, ed. by Abū ʿAbd al-Raḥmān Turkī b. ʿAbd Allāh al-Wādiʿī (Sanaa: Dār al-āthār, 2003), 17 (intro.); Shams al-Dīn al-Dhahabī, *Tārīkh al-Islām*, ed. by ʿUmar ʿAbd al-Salām Tadmurī (Beirut: Dār al-kitāb al-ʿArabī, 1987–99), vol. 33, 113; Ṣalāḥ al-Dīn al-Ṣafadī, *Kitāb Wāfī bi-l-wafayāt*, ed. by Aḥmad al-Arnāʾūṭ and Muṣṭafā Tidhkī (Beirut: Dār iḥyāʾ al-turāth al-ʿArabī, 2000), vol. 22, 85.

51 This work should be identified with *al-Siyar wa-l-maghāzī* (or, *al-Maghāzī wa-l-siyar*) by Ibn Isḥāq.

52 Ibn al-Biṭrīq, *al-ʿUmda*, vol. 1, 76–85.

53 It is worth mentioning that, in Shiʿi literary history, *al-ʿUmda* was not the first work to completely exclude Shiʿi sources. The much earlier *Miʾat manqaba* by Muḥammad b. Aḥmad ibn Shādhān al-Qummī (fl. 10th to early 11th centuries), a *faḍāʾil* on the Imams, consists of hadith transmitted only by Sunni scholars (Muḥammad b. Aḥmad ibn Shādhān al-Qummī, *Miʾat manqaba min manāqib Amīr al-Muʾminīn ʿAlī b. Abī Ṭālib wa-l-aʾimma min waladihi*, ed. by Nabīl Riḍā ʿAlwān [Qom: Muʾassasat Anṣāriyān, 2001]). Unlike the *ʿUmda*, Ibn Shādhān al-Qummī did not highlight the author's Shiʿi identity, instead leaving the divide between the two confessions ambiguous. Although the possible influence of *Miʾat manqaba* on Ibn al-Biṭrīq cannot be excluded, his methodology differs from Ibn Shādhān al-Qummī's.

54 Ibn al-Biṭrīq, *al-ʿUmda*, vol. 1, 89–96.

55 Ibid., vol. 1, 61.

56 Ibid., vol. 1, 62, 66. "*Mukhālif*" usually means Sunni(s) in Shiʿi texts (Devin Stewart, *Islamic Legal Orthodoxy: Twelver Shiite Responses to the Sunni Legal System* [Salt Lake City: The University of Utah Press, 1998], 53).

57 As an exception, one of the transmitters of Sunni tradition to Ibn al-Biṭrīq, Aḥmad al-Ṭāhir al-Ḥusaynī, died in 569/1173 (Ibn al-Dubaythī, *Dhayl Tārīkh Madīnat al-Salām*, vol. 2, 304–5). This means that Ibn al-Biṭrīq must have studied under him before that year.

58 On the Sunni teachers of Raḍī al-Dīn and al-ʿAllāma, see Kohlberg, *A Medieval Muslim Scholar at Work*, 7 and Sabine Schmidtke, *The Theology of al-ʿAllāma al-Ḥillī (d. 726/1325)* (Berlin: Klaus Schwarz Verlag, 1991), 15–22. Al-Jamil also discusses interconfessional religious life in 13th–14th century Baghdad. See, Tariq al-Jamil, "Cooperation and Contestation in Medieval Baghdad (656/1258–786/1384): Relationships between Shīʿī and Sunnī Scholars in the Madīnat al-Salām," unpublished Ph.D. dissertation, Princeton University, 2004.

59 Ibn al-Biṭrīq, *al-ʿUmda*, vol. 1, 306–14.

60 Moojan Momen, *An Introduction to Shiʿi Islam: The History and Doctrines of Twelver Shiʿism* (New Haven and London: Yale University Press, 1985), 15–6; Maria Massi Dakake, *The*

Charismatic Community: Shi'ite Identity in Early Islam (New York: State University of New York Press, 2007), 33–48; Najam Haider, *Shī'ī Islām: An Introduction* (New York: Cambridge University Press, 2014), 59–62; Jonathan A. C. Brown, *Hadith: Muhammad's Legacy in the Medieval and Modern World*, 2nd ed. (London: Oneworld Academic, 2018), 151–2.

61 Al-Shaykh al-Mufīd, *Aqsām al-mawlā fī l-lisān*, ed. by al-Shaykh Mahdī Najaf ([Qom]: al-Mu'tamar al-'ālamī li-alfiyyat al-Shaykh al-Mufīd, 1992–93), 34. The ten meanings that al-Mufīd enumerates are: *al-awlā* (the closer/closest), *mālik al-riqq* (owner of slave), *al-mu'taq* (manumitted slave), *al-mu'tiq* (manumitter of slave), *ibn al-'amm* (paternal cousin), *al-nāṣir* (supporter), *al-mutawallī* (the responsible), *al-ḥalīf* (ally), *al-jār* (neighbor), and *al-imām al-sayyid al-muṭā'* (the imam, or the master to be obeyed) (ibid., 27–9).

62 Ibn al-Biṭrīq, *al-'Umda*, vol. 1, 310–1.

63 Ibn al-Biṭrīq also uses the expression "the imam to be obeyed" (*al-imām al-muṭā'*) in the same sense as *al-sayyid al-muṭā'* (ibid., vol. 1, 310).

64 Ibid., vol. 1, 312–3.

65 Ibid., vol. 1, 314.

66 Ibn Mardawayh al-Iṣfahānī, *Manāqib 'Alī b. Abī Ṭālib wa-mā nazala min al-Qur'ān fī 'Alī*, ed. by 'Abd al-Razzāq Muḥammad Ḥusayn Ḥirz al-Dīn (Qom: Dār al-ḥadīth, 2001–02), 120–3.

67 Ibid., 122.

68 Al-Muwaffaq b. Aḥmad al-Makkī al-Khwārazmī, *al-Manāqib*, ed. by Mālik al-Maḥmūdī (Qom: Mu'assasat al-nashr al-Islāmī, 1990–91), 133–6.

69 Ibid., 134.

70 Sibṭ Ibn al-Jawzī, *Tadhkirat al-khawāṣṣ*, ed. by Muḥammad Ṣādiq Baḥr al-'Ulūm (Najaf: al-Maṭba' al-Ḥaydariyya, 1964), 30–4.

71 Ibn al-Biṭrīq, *al-'Umda*, vol. 2, 334–75.

72 Ibid., vol. 2, 378–419.

73 Ibid., vol. 2, 422–8.

74 Ibid., vol. 2, 432–8.

75 Ibid., vol. 2, 442–63.

76 Ibid., vol. 2, 466–514.

77 Momen, *An Introduction to Shi'i Islam*, 13–4; Haider, *Shī'ī Islām*, 36–7.

78 Ibn al-Maghāzilī, *Manāqib Amīr al-Mu'minīn 'Alī b. Abī Ṭālib*, 396–470. The 13th century Iraqi Twelver Shi'i scholar 'Alī b. 'Īsā al-Irbilī wrote in his *Kashf al-ghumma*, "About Amīr al-Mu'minīn [i.e., 'Alī], Ḥasan, and Ḥusayn, their virtues and merits are found in their [i.e., Sunni] books. So, it is enough [for evidence]." Al-Irbilī also notes that some Sunni scholars did not recognize the other Imams as special men ('Alī b. 'Īsā al-Irbilī, *Kashf al-ghumma fī ma'rifat al-a'imma*, ed. by 'Alī Āl Kawthar [Qom: al-Mujtama' al-'ālamī li-Ahl al-Bayt, 2012], vol. 1, 5–6).

79 Ibn al-Biṭrīq, *al-'Umda*, vol. 2, 438.

80 Fred M. Donner, "The Death of Abū Ṭālib," in *Love and Death in the Ancient Near East: Essays in Honor of Marvin H. Pope*, ed. by John M. Marks and Robert M. Good (Guilford, CT: Four Quarters, 1987), 237–45.

81 Ibn al-Biṭrīq's student, Fikhār b. Ma'add also defended Abū Ṭālib's faith in his *al-Ḥujja 'alā al-dhāhib ilā takfīr Abī Ṭālib*. Unlike Ibn al-Biṭrīq, Fikhār depended mainly on Shi'i sources and only rarely mentioned Sunni scholars, such as Ibn al-Jawzī (d. 597/1200) (Fikhār b. Ma'add al-Mūsawī, *Īmān Abī Ṭālib, al-ma'rūf bi-Kitāb al-Ḥujja 'alā al-dhāhib ilā takfīr Abī Ṭālib*, ed. by al-Sayyid Muḥammad Baḥr al-'Ulūm [Qom: Intishārāt Sayyid al-Shuhadā', 1989–90], 93).

82 Ibn al-Biṭrīq, *al-'Umda*, vol. 2, 442.

83 Ibid., vol. 2, 449–53, 456–7, 459–61.

84 Ibid., vol. 2, 462; Ibn al-Maghāzilī, *Manāqib Amīr al-Mu'minīn 'Alī b. Abī Ṭālib*, 382–3. Ibn al-Biṭrīq cites the same tradition in the discussion of 'Alī (Ibn al-Biṭrīq, *al-'Umda*, vol. 2, 287–8).

85 Generally, Samarra is better known as the location of the basement (*sardāb*) where the twelfth Imam al-Muntaẓar went into occultation. It is not clear when the Mahdī tradition of al-Ḥilla was

formed. Both Mustawfī (d. ca. 744/1344) and Ibn Baṭṭūṭa (d. 770 or 779/1368–69 or 1377) report this belief as widespread among the people of Ḥilla (Ḥamd Allāh Mustawfī Qazwīnī, *Nuzhat al-qulūb*, ed. by Mīr-Hāshim Muḥaddith [Tehran: Intishārāt-i Safīr Ardahāl, 2017–18], vol. 2, 780; Ibn Baṭṭūṭa, *Riḥlat Ibn Baṭṭūṭa, Tufḥat al-nuẓẓār fī gharā'ib al-amṣār wa-'ajā'ib al-asfār*, ed. by Muḥammad 'Abd al-Mun'im al-'Iryān and Muṣṭafā al-Qaṣṣāṣ [Beirut: Dār iḥyā' al-'ulūm, 1987], 229–31). Ibn Khaldūn (d. 808/1406) and al-Qalqashandī (d. 821/1418) report a belief that al-Muntaẓar went into the basement in al-Ḥilla, as if all Twelver Shi'a believed it (Ibn Khaldūn, *Tārīkh Ibn Khaldūn*, ed. by Khalīl Shaḥāda and Suhayl Zakkār [Beirut: Dār al-fikr, 2000–01], vol. 1, 249; al-Qalqashandī, *Ṣubḥ al-a'shā fī ṣinā'at al-inshā'* [Cairo: Wizārat al-thaqāfa wa-l-irshād al-qawmī, 1963], vol. 13, 229). This probably reflects the prosperity of al-Ḥilla as a Shi'i scholarly center. In 683/1284, a Ḥillī man, Abū Ṣāliḥ, announced himself to be "the deputy of the Lord of Our Time" (*nā'ib Ṣāḥib al-Zamān*) and gathered supporters (Ibn al-Fuwaṭī [attr.], *Kitāb al-ḥawādith*, ed. by Bashshār 'Awwād Ma'rūf and 'Imād 'Abd al-Salām Ra'ūf [Beirut: Dār al-gharb al-Islāmī, 1997], 475–6). Ṣāḥib al-Zamān is also a title of Muḥammad al-Muntaẓar. Abū Ṣāliḥ's proclamation might be related to the Mahdī tradition prevalent in Ḥilla.

86 For example, some hadiths relate that 'Īsā will pray behind the Mahdī when doomsday comes (Ibn al-Biṭrīq, al-*'Umda*, vol. 2, 477–8, 498).

87 Ibid., vol. 2, 489, 496–7, 500.

88 A court poet Sibṭ ibn al-Ta'āwīdhī (d. 584/1188) called al-Nāṣir "Mahdī" in his *qaṣīda*, regarding him as the renewer and perfector of Islam in the eschatological context (Hartmann, *An-Nāṣir li-Dīn Allāh*, 121–2).

89 Ibn al-Biṭrīq, *al-Mustadrak*, 433.

90 Ibid., 5.

91 Ibid., 135, 139, 146, 150, 154, 376.

92 Ibid., 99, 133–6, 139–41, 149, 151, *et passim.*

93 The text is clear on which of these two sources is being cited at any point. The references to Abū Nu'aym can be found at the following locations: ibid., 5, 7–13, 22, 24, 26–9, *et passim.*

94 Ibid., 77, 80, 82–4, 135, 138, *et passim.* Ibn al-Biṭrīq also refers to *al-Risāla al-Qiwāmiyya fī manāqib al-ṣaḥāba* (ibid., 93–5) as al-Sam'ānī's works in the *Mustadrak*. However, the relationship of this work to the *Faḍā'il al-ṣaḥāba* is unclear.

95 Ibid., 92, 117, 131, 137, 142–3, *et passim.*

96 Ibid., 5–254.

97 Ibid., 255–80.

98 Ibid., 281–7.

99 Ibid., 289–355.

100 Ibid., 375–7 and 379–89.

101 Ibid., 357–74.

102 Abū Nu'aym al-Iṣfahānī, *Ḥilyat al-awliyā' wa-ṭabaqāt al-aṣfiyā'*, ed. by Muṣṭafā 'Alī al-Qādir 'Aṭā (Beirut: Dār al-kutub al-'ilmiyya, 1997), vol. 3, 157–170, 211–24, 225–40.

103 Abū Nu'aym's strong Sunni identity is reflected in his refutation of Shi'ism, *Kitāb al-imāma wa-radd 'alā al-Rāfiḍa*. It is notable that he, in his *Ḥilya*, also mentions anti-Shi'i traditions attributed to these Imams, that al-Sajjād defended the three Rightly Guided Caliphs (i.e., Abū Bakr, 'Umar and 'Uthmān) from the criticism by Iraqi people, and al-Bāqir reproached the people who had denied Abū Bakr and 'Umar (ibid., vol. 3, 161, 216). In the *Mustadrak*, Ibn al-Biṭrīq ignores both traditions, undoubtedly because of its unsuitableness for his Shi'i belief.

104 Ibn al-Biṭrīq also added small chapters dealing with 'Abd al-Muṭṭalib (Ibn al-Biṭrīq, *al-Mustadrak*, 391–402), before that on Abū Ṭālib and after the chapter on the Mahdī (ibid., 402–33). His main source for both was *al-Maghāzī* by Ibn Isḥāq.

105 Ibn al-Biṭrīq, *Khaṣā'iṣ*, 55–61.

106 In addition to the *isnād* through Ibn Shahrāshūb, Ibn al-Biṭrīq refers to two other *isnād*s going back to Abū Nu'aym. In the latter *isnād*s, there are three or four transmitters between Ibn al-Biṭrīq

and Abū Nuʿaym, whereas there are only two transmitters between them in the *isnād* that passed through Ibn Shahrāshūb. I have not been able to identify the other two direct transmitters to Ibn al-Biṭrīq, ʿAlī b. al-Ḥusayn b. ʿAlī al-Mawṣilī and Muḥammad b. Aḥmad b. ʿUbayd al-Mawṣilī.

107 Hartmann, *An-Nāṣir li-Dīn Allāh*, 175–8.

108 Ibn al-Sāʿī, *Tārīkh al-khulafāʾ al-ʿAbbāsiyyīn*, ed. by ʿAbd al-Raḥīm Yūsuf al-Jamal (Cairo: Maktabat al-ādāb, 1993), 111.

109 Pierce, "Ibn Shahrāshūb," 451.

110 Ibn Shahrāshūb, *Manāqib Āl Abī Ṭālib*, ed. by Yūsuf al-Biqāʿī (Beirut: Dār al-aḍwāʾ, 1991), vol. 1, 13–32.

111 Among the ten additional sources, *Gharīb al-ḥadīth*, *al-Malāḥim*, *al-Sharīʿa*, *al-Istīʿāb*, and *al-Maṣābīḥ* are not used in *Manāqib ʿAlī b. Abī Ṭālib*.

112 Pierce, *Twelve Infallible Men*, 37–8.

113 Al-Ẓāhir (r. 1225–26) started to restore the mausoleums of al-Kāẓim and the next Imam Muḥammad al-Jawād (Ibn al-Ṭiqṭaqā, *al-Fakhrī fī l-ādāb al-sulṭāniyya wa-l-duwal al-Islāmiyya* [Beirut: Dār ṣādir, 1966], 329). Al-Mustanṣir (r. 1226–42) visited the former (Ibn al-Fuwaṭī [attr.], *Kitāb al-ḥawādith*, 124). This caliph restored the mausoleum of ʿAlī in Najaf, and the ones of ʿAlī al-Hādī and al-ʿAskarī (the tenth and eleventh Imams) in Samarra (Ghiyāth al-Dīn ʿAbd al-Karīm Ibn Ṭāwūs, *Farḥat al-Gharī*, 462; Ibn al-Fuwaṭī [attr.], *Kitāb al-ḥawādith*, 181–2). According to al-Irbilī, al-Mustanṣir visited the mausoleums of the latter two Imams (ʿAlī b. ʿĪsā al-Irbilī, *Kashf al-ghumma fī maʿrifat al-aʾimma*, vol. 4, 271). The last caliph, al-Mustaʿṣim (r. 1242–58), visited the mausoleum of al-Kāẓim (Ibn al-Fuwaṭī [attr.], *Kitāb al-ḥawādith*, 213) and, after destruction by floods, ordered its restoration (ibid., 277, 288).

114 Al-ʿAllāma al-Ḥillī, *Kashf al-yaqīn fī faḍāʾil Amīr al-Muʾminīn*, ed. by Ḥusayn al-Darkāhī (Tehran: Muʾassasat al-ṭabʿ wa-l-nashr, 1991).

115 Jalāl al-Dīn ʿAbd Allāh b. Sharafshāh al-Ḥusaynī (attr.), *Manhaj al-Shīʿa fī l-faḍāʾil waṣī khātam al-Sharīʿa*, ed. by al-Sayyid Hāshim al-Mīlānī ([Iran]: Nashr al-dalīl, 1999–2000).

116 Ryo Mizukami, "Strategical Quotation of Sunni Sources in the *Kashf al-Ghumma* by al-Irbilī: Describing Reverence for the Twelve Imams as Trans-sectarian Piety" (in Japanese), *Seinan-Ajia kenkyu* 91 (2020): 1–24.

117 Raḍī al-Dīn ʿAlī Ibn Ṭāwūs was close to the ʿAbbasid caliph al-Mustanṣir and, after the fall of Baghdad, he served the Ilkhanid ruler Hülegü (r. 1258–65) as *naqīb al-nuqabāʾ* (Rudolf Strothmann, *Die Zwölfer-Schiʿa: Zwei religionsgeschichtliche Charakterbilder aus der Mongolenzeit*, Leipzig: Otto Harrassowitz, 1926, repr. [Hildesheim and New York: Olms, 1975], 91–4; Kohlberg, *A Medieval Muslim Scholar at Work*, 5–9, 11–3). Al-Irbilī served the governor of Baghdad during the Ilkhanid period, ʿAlāʾ al-Dīn al-Juwaynī (d. 681/1283) (Rasūl Jaʿfariyān, *ʿAlī b. ʿĪsā Irbilī wa Kashf al-ghumma: Bargī az tārīkh-i Tashayyuʿ-i Dawāzdah-Imāmī* [Mashhad: Bunyād-i pazhūhish-hā-yi Islāmī-yi Āstān-i Quds-i Raḍawī, 1994–95], 15–20). Al-Juwaynī is not mentioned in the *Kashf al-ghumma*, probably because of his execution before the completion of the work. Al-ʿAllāma al-Ḥillī became a religious advisor to the Ilkhanid ruler Öljeitü (r. 1304–16) and dedicated the *Kashf al-yaqīn* to him (al-ʿAllāma al-Ḥillī, *Kashf al-yaqīn fī faḍāʾil Amīr al-Muʾminīn*, 2; Sabine Schmidtke, *The Theology of al-ʿAllāma al-Ḥillī*, 23–32). Jalāl al-Dīn dedicated the *Manhaj al-Shīʿa* to the Jalayrid ruler Shaykh Uways (r. 1356–74) (Jalāl al-Dīn ʿAbd Allāh b. Sharafshāh al-Ḥusaynī [attr.], *Manhaj al-Shīʿa*, 21–2).

Bibliography

Sources

Abū Nuʿaym al-Iṣfahānī. *Ḥilyat al-awliyāʾ wa-ṭabaqāt al-aṣfiyāʾ*. Ed. by Muṣṭafā ʿAlī al-Qādir ʿAṭā. 12 vols. Beirut: Dār al-kutub al-ʿilmiyya, 1997.

ʿAlī b. ʿĪsā al-Irbilī. *Kashf al-ghumma fī maʿrifat al-aʾimma*. Ed. by ʿAlī Āl Kawthar. 4 vols. Qom: al-Mujtamaʿ al-ʿālamī li-Ahl al-Bayt, 2012.

Al-ʿAllāma al-Ḥillī. *Kashf al-yaqīn fī faḍāʾil Amīr al-Muʾminīn*. Ed. by Ḥusayn al-Darkāhī. Tehran: Muʾassasat al-ṭabʿ wa-l-nashr, 1991.

Fikhār b. Maʿadd al-Mūsawī. *Īmān Abī Ṭālib, al-maʿrūf bi-Kitāb al-Ḥujja ʿalā al-dhāhib ilā takfīr Abī Ṭālib*. Ed. by al-Sayyid Muḥammad Baḥr al-ʿUlūm. Qom: Intishārāt Sayyid al-Shuhadāʾ, 1989–90.

Ghiyāth al-Dīn ʿAbd al-Karīm ibn Ṭāwūs. *Farḥat al-Gharī bi-ṣarḥat al-Gharī*. Ed. by Thāmir Kāẓim al-Khafājī. Qom: Maktabat Āyatullāh Marʿashī Najafī, 2012.

Ḥamd Allāh Mustawfī Qazwīnī. *Nuzhat al-qulūb*. Ed. by Mīr-Hāshim Muḥaddith. 2 vols. Tehran: Intishārāt-i Safīr Ardahāl, 2017–18.

Ibn Baṭṭūṭa. *Riḥlat Ibn Baṭṭūṭa, Tufḥat al-nuẓẓār fī gharāʾib al-amṣār wa-ʿajāʾib al-asfār*. Ed. by Muḥammad ʿAbd al-Munʿim al-ʿIryān and Muṣṭafā al-Qaṣṣāṣ. Beirut: Dār iḥyāʾ al-ʿulūm, 1987.

Ibn al-Biṭrīq al-Ḥillī. *Kitāb khaṣāʾiṣ al-waḥy al-mubīn*. Ed. by Muḥammad Bāqir al-Maḥmūdī. Qom: Dār al-Qurʾān al-karīm, 1996–97.

Ibn al-Biṭrīq al-Ḥillī. *Al-Mustadrak al-mukhtār fī manāqib waṣī al-mukhtār*. Ed. by Saʿīd ʿIrfāniyān. Qom: Maktabat al-ʿAllāma al-Majlisī, 2015.

Ibn al-Biṭrīq al-Ḥillī. *ʿUmdat ʿuyūn ṣiḥāḥ al-akhbār fī manāqib imām al-abrār*. Ed. by Saʿīd ʿIrfāniyān. 2 vols. Qom: Maktabat al-ʿAllāma al-Majlisī, 2015.

Ibn al-Dubaythī. *Dhayl Tārīkh Madīnat al-Salām*. Ed. by Bashshār ʿAwwād. 5 vols. Beirut: Dār al-gharb al-Islāmī, 2006.

Ibn al-Fuwaṭī (attr.). *Kitāb al-ḥawādith*. Ed. by Bashshār ʿAwwād Maʿrūf and ʿImād ʿAbd al-Salām Raʾūf. Beirut: Dār al-gharb al-Islāmī, 1997.

Ibn Khaldūn. *Tārīkh Ibn Khaldūn*. Ed. by Khalīl Shaḥāda and Suhayl Zakkār. 8 vols. Beirut: Dār al-fikr, 2000–01.

Ibn al-Maghāzilī. *Manāqib Amīr al-Muʾminīn ʿAlī b. Abī Ṭālib*. Ed. by Abū ʿAbd al-Raḥmān Turkī b. ʿAbd Allāh al-Wādiʿī. Sanaa: Dār al-āthār, 2003.

Ibn Mardawayh al-Iṣfahānī. *Manāqib ʿAlī b. Abī Ṭālib wa-mā nazala min al-Qurʾān fī ʿAlī*. Ed. by ʿAbd al-Razzāq Muḥammad Ḥusayn Ḥirz al-Dīn. Qom: Dār al-ḥadīth, 2001–02.

Ibn al-Sāʿī. *Tārīkh al-khulafāʾ al-ʿAbbāsīyīn*. Ed. by ʿAbd al-Raḥīm Yūsuf al-Jamal. Cairo: Maktabat al-ādāb, 1993.

Ibn al-Shaʿʿār. *Qalāʾid al-jumān fī farāʾid shuʿarāʾ hādhā al-zamān*. Ed. by Kāmil Salmān al-Jubūrī. 9 vols. Beirut: Dār al-kutub al-ʿilmiyya, 2005.

Ibn Shahrāshūb. *Manāqib Āl Abī Ṭālib*. Ed. by Yūsuf al-Biqāʿī. 5 vols. Beirut: Dār al-aḍwāʾ, 1991.

Ibn al-Ṭiqṭaqā. *Al-Aṣīlī fī ansāb al-Ṭālibiyyīn*. Ed. by al-Sayyid Mahdī al-Rajāʾī. Qom: Maktabat Āyat Allāh al-ʿUẓmā al-Marʿashī al-Najafī, 1997–98.

Jalāl al-Dīn ʿAbd Allāh b. Sharafshāh al-Ḥusaynī (attr.). *Manhaj al-Shīʿa fī l-faḍāʾil waṣī khātam al-Sharīʿa*. Ed. by al-Sayyid Hāshim al-Mīlānī. [Iran]: Nashr al-dalīl, 1999–2000.

Muḥammad b. Aḥmad ibn Shādhān al-Qummī. *Miʾat manqaba min manāqib Amīr al-Muʾminīn ʿAlī b. Abī Ṭālib wa-l-aʾimma min waladihi*. Ed. by Nabīl Riḍā ʿAlwān. Qom: Muʾassasat Anṣāriyān, 2001.

Muḥammad b. Jaʿfar al-Mashhadī. *Iqrār al-ṣaḥāba bi-faḍāʾil imām al-hudā wa-l-qarāba, aw, Mā ittafaqa fīhi min al-akhbār fī faḍl al-aʾimma al-aṭhār*. Ed. by Lajna min al-muḥaqqiqīn fī Maktabat al-ʿAllāma al-Majlisī. Qom: Maktabat al-ʿAllāma al-Majlisī, 2017–18.

Al-Muwaffaq b. Aḥmad al-Makkī al-Khwārazmī. *Al-Manāqib*. Ed. by Mālik al-Maḥmūdī. Qom: Muʾassasat al-nashr al-Islāmī, 1990–91.

Al-Qalqashandī. *Ṣubḥ al-aʿshā fī ṣināʿat al-inshāʾ*. 14 vols. Cairo: Wizārat al-thaqāfa wa-l-irshād al-qawmī, 1963.

Raḍī al-Dīn ʿAlī Ibn Ṭāwūs. *Al-Yaqīn bi-ikhtiṣāṣ mawlānā ʿAlī bi-imrat al-muʾminīn, wa-yatlūhu, al-taḥṣīn*. Ed. by Muḥammad Bāqir al-Anṣārī and Muḥammad Ṣādiq al-Anṣārī. Beirut: Muʾassasat dār al-kitāb, 1992–93.

Ṣadr al-Dīn al-Ḥammūyī. *Farāʾid al-simṭayn fī faḍāʾil al-Murtaḍā wa-l-Batūl wa-l-sibṭayn wa-l-aʾimma min dhurriyyatihim*. Ed. by Muḥammad-Bāqir al-Maḥmūdī. 2 vols. Beirut: Muʾassasat al-Maḥmūdī, 1978.

Ṣalāḥ al-Dīn al-Ṣafadī. *Kitāb Wāfī bi-l-wafayāt*. Ed. by Aḥmad al-Arnāʾūṭ and Muṣṭafā Tidhkī. 30 vols. Beirut: Dār iḥyāʾ al-turāth al-ʿArabī, 2000.

Shādhān b. Jibraʾīl al-Qummī. *Al-Faḍāʾil wa-mustadrakātuhā*. Ed. by ʿAbd Allāh al-Ṣāliḥī al-Najafī. Karbalaʾ: al-ʿAtaba al-Ḥusayniyya, 2015.

Shādhān b. Jibraʾīl al-Qummī. *Al-Rawḍa fī faḍāʾil Amīr al-Muʾminīn ʿAlī b. Abī Ṭālib*. Ed. by ʿAlī al-Shakarchī. Qom: Maktabat al-amīn, 2002–03.

Shams al-Dīn al-Dhahabī. *Tārīkh al-Islām*. Ed. by ʿUmar ʿAbd al-Salām Tadmurī. 55 vols. Beirut: Dār al-kitāb al-ʿArabī, 1987–99.

Al-Shaykh al-Mufīd. *Aqsām al-mawlā fī l-lisān*. Ed. by al-Shaykh Mahdī Najaf. [Qom]: al-Muʾtamar al-ʿālamī li-alfiyyat al-Shaykh al-Mufīd, 1992–93.

Sibṭ ibn al-Jawzī. *Tadhkirat al-khawāṣṣ*. Ed. by Muḥammad Ṣādiq Baḥr al-ʿUlūm. Najaf: al-Maṭbaʿa al-Ḥaydariyya, 1964.

Studies

Ansari, Hassan and Sabine Schmidtke. "Between Aleppo and Ṣaʿda: The Zaydī Reception of the Imāmī scholar Ibn al-Biṭrīq al-Ḥillī." *Journal of Islamic Manuscripts* 4 (2013): 160–200.

van Arendonk, Cornelis and William A. Graham. "Sharīf." In *The Encyclopaedia of Islam, New Edition*. Ed. by H. A. R. Gibb et al., 13 vols. Leiden: Brill, 1960–2009, vol. 9, 329–37.

Brack, Jonathan. "Theologies of Auspicious Kingship: The Islamization of Chinggisid Sacral Kingship in the Islamic World." *Comparative Studies in Society and History* 60.4 (2018): 1143–71.

Brown, Jonathan A. C. *Hadith: Muhammad's Legacy in the Medieval and Modern World*. 2nd ed. London: Oneworld Academic, 2018.

Dakake, Maria Massi. *The Charismatic Community: Shiʿite Identity in Early Islam*. New York: State University of New York Press, 2007.

Dānishpazhūh, Muḥammad Taqī. "(Intiqād-i kitāb) *Kashf al-ḥaqāyiq*." *Farhang-i Īrān-zamīn* 13 (1966): 299–310.

Donner, Fred M. "The Death of Abū Ṭālib." In *Love and Death in the Ancient Near East: Essays in Honor of Marvin H. Pope*. Ed. by John M. Marks and Robert M. Good. Guilford, CT: Four Quarters, 1987, 237–45.

Dunietz, Alexandra W. *The Cosmic Perils of Qadi Ḥusayn Maybudī in Fifteenth-Century Iran*. Leiden and Boston: Brill, 2016.

Fierro, Maribel. "Razīn b. Muʿāwiya." In *The Encyclopaedia of Islam, New Edition*. Ed. by H. A. R. Gibb et al., 13 vols. Leiden: Brill, 1960–2009, vol. 8, 479–80.

Haider, Najam. *Shīʿī Islām: An Introduction*. New York: Cambridge University Press, 2014.

Halm, Heinz. *Shiʿism*. 2nd ed. New York: Columbia University Press, 2004.

Hartmann, Angelika. *An-Nāṣir li-Dīn Allāh: Politik, Religion, Kultur in der späten ʿAbbāsidenzeit*. Berlin and New York: Walter de Gruyter, 1975.

Hirschler, Konrad. *Medieval Damascus: Plurality and Diversity in an Arabic Library, the Ashrafīya Library Catalogue*. Edinburg: Edinburg University Press, 2017.

Hodgson, Marshall G. S. *The Venture of Islam: Conscience and History in a World Civilization*. 3 vols. Chicago: Chicago University Press, 1974.

Jaʿfariyān, Rasūl. *ʿAlī b. ʿĪsā Irbilī wa Kashf al-ghumma: Bargī az tārīkh-i Tashayyuʿ-i Dawāzdah-Imāmī*. Mashhad: Bunyād-i pazhūhish-hā-yi Islāmī-yi Āstān-i Quds-i Raḍawī, 1994–95.

Jaʿfariyān, Rasūl. *Tārīkh-i Tashayyuʿ dar Īrān: Az āghāz tā qarn-i dahum-i Hijrī*. 2 vols. Tehran: Anṣāriyān, 1996–97.

Al-Jamil, Tariq. "Cooperation and Contestation in Medieval Baghdad (656/1258–786/1384): Relationships between Shīʿī and Sunnī Scholars in the Madīnat al-Salām." Unpublished Ph.D. dissertation, Princeton University, 2004.

Kohlberg, Etan. *A Medieval Muslim Scholar at Work: Ibn Ṭāwūs and His Library*. Leiden, New York and Köln: Brill, 1992.

Madelung, Wilferd F. "The 'Hāshimiyyāt' of al-Kumayt and Hāshimī Shiʿism." *Studia Islamica* 70 (1989): 5–26.

Marlow, Louise. "Translation of the Words of ʿAli b. Abi Ṭālib in Early Fourteenth-Century Iran: A Local Bilingual Network." *Iranian Studies* 53.5/6 (2020): 741–87.

Masad, Mohammad Ahmad. "The Medieval Islamic Apocalyptic Tradition: Divination, Prophecy and the End of the 13th Century Eastern Mediterranean." Unpublished Ph.D. dissertation, Washington University in St. Louis, 2008.

Melvin-Koushki, Matthew S. "The Quest for a Universal Science: The Occult Philosophy of Ṣāʾin al-Dīn Turka Iṣfahānī (1369–1432) and Intellectual Millenarianism in Early Timurid Iran." Unpublished Ph.D. dissertation, Yale University, 2012.

Melvin-Koushki, Matthew S. "Early Modern Islamicate Empire: New Forms of Religiopolitical Legitimacy." In *The Wiley Blackwell History of Islam*. Ed. by Armando Salvatore, Roberto Tottoli, and Babak Rahimi. Hoboken, NJ: Wiley Blackwell, 2018, 351–75.

Miranda, Ambrosio Huici. "Al-Ḥumaydī." In *The Encyclopaedia of Islam, New Edition*. Ed. by H. A. R. Gibb et al., 13 vols. Leiden: Brill, 1960–2009, vol. 3, 573–4.

Mizukami, Ryo. "Strategical Quotation of Sunni Sources in the *Kashf al-Ghumma* by al-Irbilī: Describing Reverence for the Twelve Imams as Trans-sectarian Piety" (in Japanese). *Seinan-Ajia kenkyu* 91 (2020): 1–24. (「イルビリー著『悲嘆の除去』におけるスンナ派文献の戦略的引用：超宗派的信仰として描かれる十二イマーム崇敬」『西南アジア研究』 91.)

Momen, Moojan. *An Introduction to Shiʿi Islam: The History and Doctrines of Twelver Shiʿism*. New Haven and London: Yale University Press, 1985.

Ohlander, Erik S. *Sufism in an Age of Transition: ʿUmar al-Suhrawardī and the Rise of the Islamic Mystical Brotherhoods*. Leiden and Boston: Brill, 2008.

Pfeiffer, Judith. "Confessional Ambiguity vs. Confessional Polarization: Politics and Negotiation of Religious Boundaries in the Ilkhanate." In *Politics, Patronage and the Transmission of Knowledge in 13th–15th Century Tabriz*. Ed. by Judith Pfeiffer. Leiden and Boston: Brill, 2014, 129–68.

Pierce, Matthew. "Ibn Shahrāshūb and Shiʿa Rhetorical Strategies in the 6th/12th Century." *Journal of Shiʿa Islamic Studies* 5.4 (2012): 441–54.

Pierce, Matthew. *Twelve Infallible Men: The Imams and the Making of Shiʿism*. Cambridge, MA and London: Harvard University Press, 2016.

Saleh, Walid A. *The Formation of the Classical Tafsīr Tradition: The Qurʾān Commentary of al-Thaʿlabī (d. 427/1035)*. Leiden and Boston: Brill, 2004.

Schmidtke, Sabine. *The Theology of al-ʿAllāma al-Ḥillī (d. 726/1325)*. Berlin: Klaus Schwarz Verlag, 1991.

Stewart, Devin. *Islamic Legal Orthodoxy: Twelver Shiite Responses to the Sunni Legal System*. Salt Lake City: The University of Utah Press, 1998.

Strothmann, Rudolf. *Die Zwölfer-Schi'a: Zwei religionsgeschichtliche Charakterbilder aus der Mongolenzeit*. Leipzig: Otto Harrassowitz, 1926. Repr., Hildesheim and New York: Olms, 1975.

Al-Ṭihrānī, Āghā Buzurg. *Ṭabaqāt aʿlām al-Shīʿa*. 17 vols. Beirut: Dār iḥyāʾ al-turāth al-ʿArabī, 2009.

Woods, John E. *The Aqquyunlu: Clan, Confederation, Empire: A Study in 15th/9th Century Turko-Iranian Politics*. Revised and expanded ed. Salt Lake City: The University of Utah Press, 1999.

Yılmaz, Hüseyin. *Caliphate Redefined: The Mystical Turn in Ottoman Political Thought*. Princeton: Princeton University Press, 2018.

8

A Ja'farid-Zaynabid Genealogy from Thirteenth-Century Egypt: '*Urbān* Uprising, Najafī Connection, and the Representation of the Twelve Imams

Kazuo Morimoto

Introduction

MS British Library Or. 1406 (hereafter Or. 1406) is a multi-text manuscript put together by 'Alī b. al-Qāsim al-Mūsawī al-Najafī, an expert on the genealogy of 'Alī b. Abī Ṭālib's kinfolk who flourished in the latter half of the fifteenth century CE. Al-Mūsawī al-Najafī, who operated in such regions as Iraq and Iran and was in all probability a Twelver Shi'i, copied texts in which he was interested into this "notebook."[1] This study discusses one of the texts copied into the manuscript, entitled the *Genealogy of the Prophet Muḥammad and the Ancestry of the Zaynabids and the Ḥusaynids* (*al-Shajara al-nabawiyya al-Muḥammadiyya wa-l-nisba al-Zaynabiyya wa-l-Ḥusayniyya*; hereafter the *Genealogy of the Tha'labids* in light of its intents and contents [explained below]). Although the *Genealogy of the Tha'labids* as copied into Or. 1406 is mentioned briefly in Charles Rieu's catalog description of Or. 1406 as well as in my own discussion of the manuscript published previously, no detailed study of the treatise has been conducted to date to the best of my knowledge.[2]

The author's name appearing on the first and the last pages of the *Genealogy of the Tha'labids* includes the *nisba* "al-Najafī." Repeated manifestations of special regard for the Twelve Imams, in addition, constitute a conspicuous feature of the treatise. The treatise, therefore, may at first glance look a Twelver Shi'i work written in Iraq. A closer examination of the text and investigation of sources external to it, however, reveal that the "Najafī" author is identifiable with one of the promotors of the practice of tomb visitation in Cairo (I use this toponym in the sense of metropolitan Cairo, not to refer narrowly to Fāṭimid Qāhira) previously known to scholarship who flourished in and around the middle of the thirteenth century. The figure in question, known by the appellation Ibn Ballūh (or Ibn Bulūla), was the author of at least one guidebook for tomb visitation and the custodian or an attendant of the shrine of al-Sayyida Sukayna, a well-known ʿAlid shrine in that metropolis. Additionally, an attempt at identifying the dedicatee of the treatise, the genealogy and virtues of whose lineage constitute the work's subject, leads to a resonant and interesting discovery. The treatise was written for Najm al-Dīn ʿAlī b. Ḥiṣn al-Dīn Thaʿlab al-Jaʿfarī al-Zaynabī (I will hereafter call the latter Ḥiṣn al-Dīn II) of the Banū Thaʿlab or the Thaʿlabids, that is to say, a son of the leader of the massive uprising of the *ʿUrbān* (Arab tribes) in Egypt that shook the central authorities in Cairo towards the middle of the thirteenth century.[3] It is, in addition, most likely that the treatise was written after Ḥiṣn al-Dīn II made manifest, possibly as early as in 647 AH/1250 CE, his disobedience to the central authorities in Cairo.

The *Genealogy of the Thaʿlabids*, with its clear manifestations of special regard for the Twelve Imams, reveals the hitherto unknown "Najafī" self-identification of Ibn Ballūh. Not only the fact that Ḥiṣn al-Dīn II had a son named Najm al-Dīn ʿAlī but any information about the son, including his connection to Ibn Ballūh "al-Najafī," are also what we learn for the first time from the treatise. But do these new findings point to Twelver Shiʿism of the promoter of tomb visitation in Cairo and the son of the leader of the *ʿUrbān* uprising in mid-thirteenth century Egypt? Does the *Genealogy of the Thaʿlabids* testify to the existence of a community of Twelver Shiʿis around the two figures in which they had no qualms in manifesting their Twelver Shiʿi beliefs? These are the main questions I will attempt to answer in the following pages.

As I showed elsewhere, pieces of evidence reveal the existence of an extensive network (or multiple networks plausibly related to one another) of Twelver Shiʿis centered on the confessional group's bases in Iraq from the early fourteenth century onwards. A wing of that network (or of one of those networks) extended westwards as far as to today's western Algeria. In a report by a figure who accompanied a group of people affiliated with that network in their travels from Tlemcen to Karbalāʾ, the group was met by the network's local members, who would meet the group in each town and supply it with provisions for its journey, even in the leg of the journey as distant from Iraq as Tlemcen to Tunis.[4] It would certainly make sense to link the Twelver Shiʿi identity of the author and the dedicatee of the *Genealogy of the Thaʿlabids*, if confirmed, to this previous finding and expand our knowledge about the Twelver Shiʿi network(s). Detection of a community of Twelver Shiʿis around the two figures, again if confirmed, could also be a meaningful addition to the current knowledge about the distribution of Twelver Shiʿi communities in Egypt in the thirteenth century, that is, to what we know about the declining communities in such locales as Aswān, Idfū, Isnā, Aṣfūn, Armant, and Qūṣ, high up the Nile Valley in Upper Egypt.[5]

The discussion in the following pages will show, however, that the matter is not so straightforward. Notably, the treatment of the Twelve Imams in the treatise, however conspicuously it manifests special regard for those figures, cannot be characterized as Twelver Shiʿi. Rather, evidence suggests that special regard for the Twelve Imams was presented as something that fell within the borders of Sunni Islam. The attempt at elucidating why Ibn Ballūh used the *nisba* "al-Najafī" will also not lead us to the most comfortable conclusion that he was from Najaf. Although he appears to have had a real connection with the scholarly circle of the Twelver Shiʿa whose important base was Najaf, it would appear more likely that he was from Egypt. How we should deal with these findings will be discussed in the conclusion. For now, we shall begin by confirming basic facts about the *Genealogy of the Thaʿlabids*.

The *Genealogy of the Thaʿlabids*: A Laudatory Genealogy

The *Genealogy of the Thaʿlabids* is copied into folios 30a–8b of Or. 1406, and no other manuscript of the work is known to be extant, to the best of my knowledge. The title of the work, mentioned above in the introduction, is stated towards the end of the preface, on folio 30a. The mentioned folios comprise five fragments of the work, seamlessly written one after another even without line breaks to indicate their beginnings and ends.[6] These fragments are copied out of the original order, but it is possible to reconstruct a text that can safely be considered almost continuous from the beginning to the end by reordering them on the basis of their contents and, in some cases, of the continuity of the sentences across their breaks.[7] The consolidated text thus reconstructed includes the opening *baslama* and continues down to what can reasonably be considered the end of the main text of the work.[8] The text of the *Genealogy of the Thaʿlabids* thus reconstructed can be divided into five sections in view of the subjects dealt therein:

> [Section I] The opening of the treatise, including the *basmala*, passages of invocation, and the preface (f. 30a, l. 5–f. 30a, l. 25). The first four lines of folio 30a are outside of the text per se of the treatise, although attributable to its author (details below).
>
> [Section II] This section presents the virtues of the lineal Jaʿfarid ancestors of the Thaʿlabids with minimal mention of their kinship relations. The figures dealt with in this section are Jaʿfar al-Ṭayyār, Jaʿfar's mother Fāṭima bt. Asad, Jaʿfar's wife Asmāʾ bt. ʿUmays, and ʿAbd Allāh al-Jawād, who was Jaʿfar's son from Asmāʾ. This section presents numerous Prophetic hadiths, and also anecdotal traditions and verses in the case of ʿAbd Allāh b. Jaʿfar, to highlight the virtues of the figures. The section occupies a space that amounts to between five and a half pages and a little less than six pages (f. 30a, l. 26–f. 31a, l. 11, f. 35b, l. 25–f. 37b, l. 10, f. 38a, ll. 1–30).

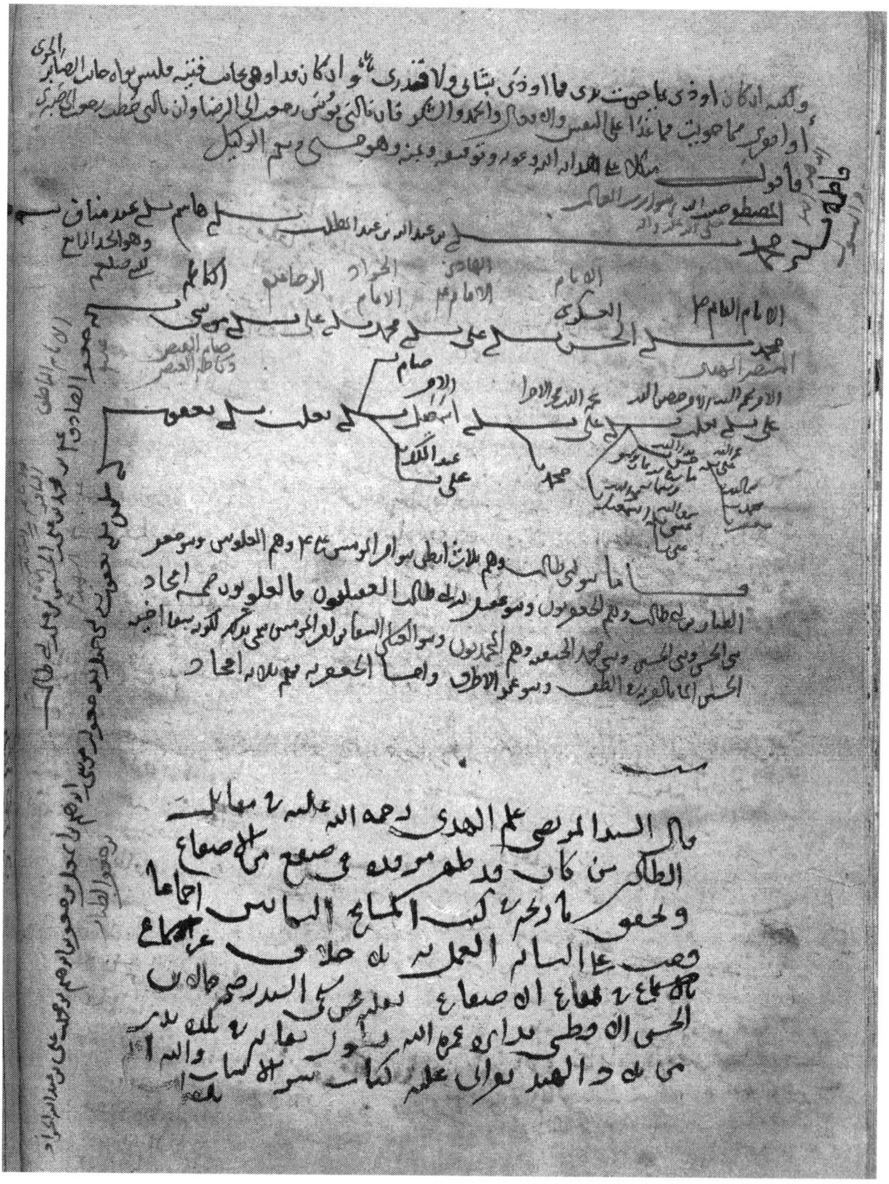

Figure 1: The Parallel Presentation of the Genealogies of the Prophet Muḥammad, the Twelve Imams, and the Thaʿlabids (Or. 1406, 32b). © British Library Board (Or. 1406, 32b).

[Section III] This section begins with a concise genealogy of the descendants of ʿAbd Allāh al-Jawād b. Jaʿfar with a focus on the line reaching down to the Thaʿlabids. The account of the genealogy includes verses praising the largesse of ʿAbd Allāh's son ʿAlī al-Zaynabī and ʿAlī's son Muḥammad and covers up to and including ʿAbd Allāh's fifth-generation descendant. Then the virtues of the dedicatee, ʿAbd Allāh's seventeenth-generation descendant Najm al-Dīn ʿAlī b. Ḥiṣn al-Dīn II, are enumerated at length. Numerous verses, including the author's own, are inserted in the course of the enumeration of Najm al-Dīn's virtues. This section occupies about four and a half pages (f. 38a, l. 30–f. 38b, l. 27 [i.e., the end of the page], f. 37b, ll. 10–29 [i.e., the end of the page], f. 31a, l. 11–f. 32a, l. 17).

[Section IV] The main content of this section is the genealogy of the Thaʿlabids presented in diagrammatic format and in parallel with two other genealogies – that of the Prophet Muḥammad and of the Twelve Imams respectively, also in (quasi-)diagrammatic format, on folio 32b (Figure 1). The genealogy of the Imams does not include the name of the second Imam al-Ḥasan and is in fact the genealogy of the Ḥusaynid Imams only. The author, however, refers to this genealogy as that of the Twelve Imams in the preface (30a). Only the beginning of the Prophet Muḥammad's genealogy is presented on folio 32b. I consider the presentation of the remainder of the genealogy, which is no longer presented in parallel with that of the Thaʿlabids, to form a separate section (Section V). The presentation of the three genealogical diagrams is preceded by a half-page introductory remark that includes an explanation of the contents of the diagrams. This section occupies one and a half pages from line 17 of folio 32a to the end of folio 32b. The content of this section explains why the treatise is entitled the *Genealogy of the Prophet Muḥammad and the Ancestry of the Zaynabids and the Ḥusaynids*. "The ancestry of the Zaynabids" refers to the genealogy of the Thaʿlabids, a lineage belonging to the Zaynabids, that is, the patrilineal descendants of ʿAlī al-Zaynabī, called so after ʿAlī's mother Zaynab bt. ʿAlī b. Abī Ṭālib. "The lineage" of the "Ḥusaynids," then, refers to the genealogy of the eleven Ḥusaynid Imams. This fact indicates that the presentation of the genealogy in this section, in spite of its insignificance in terms of length, was considered the core of the contents of this treatise by the author.

[Section V] As mentioned above, this section consists of the presentation of the remainder of the genealogy of the Prophet Muḥammad, that is, the continuation of what is presented on folio 32b, tracing it until it reaches back to Adam. The genealogy is presented in diagrammatic format down to folio 33b and in plain text thereafter. The portion in diagrammatic format traces back the Prophet Muḥammad's genealogy without mentioning collateral lines branching out of it. This portion often presents biographical information pertaining to the figures appearing in the genealogy, too. The portion in plain text, in contrast, often presents the genealogy of collateral lines and tends to provide less information about individual figures. The two portions thus have different textures. A comparison with *al-Muqaddima al-fāḍiliyya*, a genealogical compendium on the Arabs by Sharīf al-Dīn Muḥammad b. Asʿad al-Jawwānī (525/1131–588/1192–3) from twelfth-century Egypt, shows that the text of the portion in plain text consists basically of paragraphs and passages found in that previous work, in abridged form.[9] This section occupies a little less than six pages of Or. 1406 (from the beginning of f. 33a to f. 35b, l. 25).

In addition to the actual contents of the work, the author's description of the work in the preface shows that the *Genealogy of the Thaʿlabids* is a work that was composed in order to present and praise the ancestry and virtues of Najm al-Dīn and the Thaʿlabids. The author calls the work "an excellent gift on the subject of the root and branches of the [lofty] pedigree and genealogy of the Thaʿlabids, a Jaʿfarid and Zaynabid lineage" (*hadiya munīfa fī uṣūl aḥsāb banī Thaʿlab al-Jaʿfarī al-Zaynabī wa-fuṣūl ansābihim*; 30a). The inclusion of the lengthy presentation of the genealogy of the Prophet Muḥammad going back to Adam was also not irrelevant to the work's objective in the author's mind or claim. For, he characterizes the Prophet's genealogy as something that formed part of the "fortune" (*saʿāda*) of the dedicatee.[10] This characterization no doubt reflects the fact that the author considered the Thaʿlabids as part of the Prophet's kinfolk on account of their Hāshimid (Ṭālibid, to be precise) ancestry.

The name of the dedicatee and the first portion of his genealogy read as follows in the diagram of the Thaʿlabid genealogy on folio 32b: *al-amīr* Najm al-Dīn ʿAlī b. *al-amīr* Ḥiṣn al-Dīn Thaʿlab b. Najm al-Dīn Fakhr al-Umarāʾ ʿAlī b. *al-amīr* Ismāʿīl b. Thaʿlab (see Figure 1). As said above, this signifies that the dedicatee was not only a member of the Thaʿlabids, a patrilineal descent group named after Najm al-Dīn's great-great-grandfather (hereafter Ḥiṣn al-Dīn I as he had the same *laqab* as his great-grandson), but also a son of the leader of the *ʿUrbān* uprising in the middle of the thirteenth century.

The author's name is mentioned twice on the relevant folios of Or. 1406. The first mention is found at the top of folio 30a, where a statement explaining the work's contents and the author's name are presented immediately before the *basmala* that opens the work's text per se (see Figure 2). The relevant lines read:

> In the name of God, the Beneficent and the Merciful. // [This is] a book in which is presented the genealogy of the Prophet Muḥammad and the pedigree of the Jaʿfarids [and] the Ḥusaynids (*kitāb fīhi al-shajara al-nabawiyya al-Muḥammadiyya wa-l-nisba al-Jaʿfariyya al-Ḥusayniyya*), // by its author and drawer of the genealogical diagram (*muʾallifuhā wa-mushajjiruhā*), one who is in need of God the self-sufficient (*al-faqīr ilā Allāh al-ghanī*), Ibrāhīm b. Yaḥyā b. Muḥammad b. Mūsā al-Ḥusaynī the genealogist (*al-nassāba*) al-Najafī – May God forgive him (*ʿafā Allāh ʿanhu*) – // the/a servant of al-Sayyida Sukayna (*khādim al-Sayyida Sukayna*) – Peace be upon her –.[11]

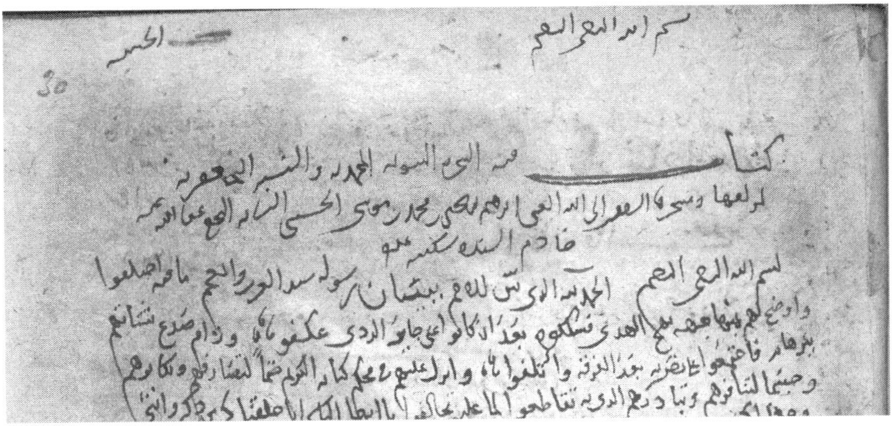

Figure 2: The Upper Part of Or. 1406, 30a, with a Concise Description of the Treatise's Subject and the Author's Name. © British Library Board (Or. 1406, 30a).

These lines are technically outside the text per se of the *Genealogy of the Thaʿlabids*. However, they are also safely attributable to the work's author on account of the use of the phrases "one who is in need of God the self-sufficient" and "May God forgive him." These are phrases that are conventionally used by an author to refer to himself. It would be quite unusual if a later copyist used them, especially in combination as found here, in relation to an original author. The attributability of the lines to the original author is also endorsed by the fact that no laudatory word or phrase is added to the author's name therein.

The second mention, found on folio 38b and this time in the work's text per se, reads:

> Thus says the author, writer, and drawer of the genealogical diagram of the work, Ibrāhīm b. Yaḥyā b. Muḥammad b. [sic] al-Ḥusaynī the genealogist (*al-nassāba*) al-Mashhadī al-Najafī.

The second mention thus reveals that the author of the *Genealogy of the Thaʿlabid*s was also a "Mashhadī." When put together, the two mentions make it clear that the author of the *Genealogy of the Thaʿlabids* was a Ḥusaynid genealogist named Ibrāhīm b. Yaḥyā b. Muḥammad b. Mūsā who styled himself as "al-Mashhadī al-Najafī" and that he characterized himself as "the/a servant of al-Sayyida Sukayna."

No mention of the date of composition is to be found in the *Genealogy of the Thaʿlabids* as it is preserved in Or. 1406.[12] The diagram presenting the genealogy of the Thaʿlabids in Section IV (32b), however, comprises a mention of the year 648/1250–51 as the one in which Ḥiṣn al-Dīn II's brother Badr al-Dīn died, probably a natural death (judging from the wording "he died" [*māta*]). Thus, the *Genealogy of the Thaʿlabids* was composed plausibly after that year. No *terminus ante quem* for the composition of the treatise can be set in a like manner. Ibrāhīm b. Yaḥyā, however, is known to have been operating as an established genealogist already in 626/1229, as will be discussed below. Therefore, the work was composed before about 1280 at the latest, based on the hypothesis that Ibrāhīm was about thirty (or twenty-five) years old in 626/1229 and lived until he was around eighty (or eighty-five).

The Dedicatee: Najm al-Dīn ʿAlī b. Ḥiṣn al-Dīn Thaʿlab II

The *ʿUrbān* uprising led by Ḥiṣn al-Dīn II is known to have been a major threat to the fledgling Mamluk regime. Ḥiṣn al-Dīn, launching the uprising at Dayrūṭ al-Sharīf (some 50 km down the Nile River from the city of Asyut) where he reportedly had a residence, succeeded in bringing a large part of Upper Egypt out of the control of Cairo.[13] The uprising also shook Lower Egypt, aggravating its threat to the authorities in Cairo. The precise development and timeline of Ḥiṣn al-Dīn II's actions as the leader of the uprising are difficult to reconstruct, given the faulty and biased records that the sources from the Mamluk period provide. Yet, the process, in two phases, can be reconstructed as follows.[14] The first phase began with Ḥiṣn al-Dīn's declaration of disobedience to the authorities in Cairo at Dayrūṭ al-Sharīf. His leadership was accepted not only by insurgents in Upper Egypt but by those in Lower Egypt. It is also recorded that Ḥiṣn al-Dīn was in communication with al-Nāṣir Yūsuf, the Ayyūbid ruler of Aleppo and Damascus (r. Aleppo 634/1236–658/1260, Damascus 648/1250–658/1260) who launched an abortive expedition to Egypt during the winter of 648/1250–51. This first phase ended in 651/1253 when Ḥiṣn al-Dīn was forced to go into hiding after his troops were routed at the decisive battle near Akhmīm in Upper Egypt by the expeditionary force that arrived from Cairo.[15] The expeditionary force was led by Fāris al-Dīn Aqṭāy and ʿIzz al-Dīn Afram, two leading figures among the Baḥrī mamluks. Fāris al-Dīn, the more powerful of the two and actually the leader of the Baḥrīs, went back to Cairo and ʿIzz al-Dīn stayed on in Upper Egypt.

The second phase began soon after the then sultan Aybak al-Turkmānī (r. 648/1250, 652/1254–655/1257) had Fāris al-Dīn Aqṭāy murdered in Cairo in 652/1254. Aybak's aim was to strike a decisive blow to the Baḥrī mamluks menacing his power by getting rid of their leader. This led ʿIzz al-Dīn Afram to launch a rebellion in Upper Egypt and to join forces with Ḥiṣn al-Dīn. The two leaders, however, could not resist the troops sent to crush their force in 653/1255. Having fled from Upper Egypt, and apparently after some subversive activities in Lower Egypt, Ḥiṣn al-Dīn was captured, imprisoned in Alexandria, and was finally executed by the order of Baybars in 658/1260.

Different opinions exist who exactly the "*ʿUrbān*" signified in Egypt in the periods encompassing the middle of the thirteenth century. The prevalent understanding among scholars until recently held that the term signified Arab nomadic pastoralists and, according to some, those former nomadic pastoralists who were at different stages of sedentarization. A recent thesis, submitted by Yossef Rapoport, holds that "*ʿUrbān*" consisted, at least mostly, of quite a large portion of the rural population of Egypt who, in the process of their conversion to Islam, came to imagine themselves as affiliated to Arab tribes, regardless of whether they were nomadic pastoralists or sedentary agriculturalists.[16] In any case, there is no doubt that the profiles of the leading figures of the Thaʿlabids contradict a (stereo)typical image of the leaders of the nomadic pastoralists. Najm al-Dīn's paternal great-grandfather Fakhr al-Dīn Ismāʿīl was the only person who could provide Cairo with wheat when the city was hit by a famine in 592/1195–96.[17] This would suggest that he controlled a considerable stretch of cultivated lands in the country side, plausibly, but not necessarily, in that part of the Nile Valley in Upper Egypt inhabited by the Jaʿāfira, the tribal group claiming descent from Jaʿfar al-Ṭayyār whose leadership the Thaʿlabids held.[18]

The geographical sphere of the Thaʿlabids' activities, in addition, was by no means limited to Upper Egypt. They notably had a basis also in Cairo and had a presence in the political scene of that metropolis. We know that Fakhr al-Dīn Ismāʿīl was "one of the generals of Egypt" (*aḥad umarāʾ Miṣr*) around the turn of the thirteenth century who served as the leader of the pilgrimage caravan (*amīr al-ḥājj*) in the year 592/1196.[19] An anecdote reporting how he came to establish a madrasa (named al-Madrasa al-Sharīfiyya) for the Shāfiʿī school of law in Cairo reveals that he was among the retinue of the Ayyubid Sultan al-ʿĀdil I (r. in Egypt 596/1200–615/1218).[20] Information is available concerning the properties Fakhr al-Dīn possessed in Cairo, too. In addition to the residence he converted into the mentioned madrasa, he possessed an orchard named the Bustān al-Sharīf Ibn Thaʿlab (75 *faddān*, i.e., ca. 3.2 ha) and a "development" (*munshaʾa*) named Munshaʾat Ibn Thaʿlab.[21] Fakhr al-Dīn's tomb, which he himself had completed a short while before his death in 613/1216, is also located in Cairo, in the vicinity of the mausoleum of al-Shāfiʿī.[22] That the family's presence in Cairo continued beyond the generation of Fakhr al-Dīn can be confirmed by the fact that his grandson Ḥiṣn al-Dīn II, that is, the very leader of the *ʿUrbān* uprising, sold the Bustān al-Sharīf Ibn Thaʿlab to the Sultan al-Ṣāliḥ II in Rajab 643/November–December 1245 for the price of 3,000 Egyptian dinars (*danānīr Miṣriyya*).[23]

We do not know exactly when the first phase of Ḥiṣn al-Dīn's subversive activities began. Claude Garcin, however, deems it possible that Ḥiṣn al-Dīn's declaration of the disobedience to the authorities in Cairo took place as early as shortly after the landing of the Seventh Crusade at Damietta in 647/1250.[24] The exact date of Ḥiṣn al-Dīn's fatal capture by the central authorities is also not recorded, although we know that it took place certainly after 653/1255, when ʿIzz al-Dīn Afram and Ḥiṣn al-Dīn were defeated in Upper Egypt, and probably before Aybak's assassination in 655/1257, since it is reported that it was by that Sultan that Ḥiṣn al-Dīn was entrapped and captured.[25]

The fate of Ḥiṣn al-Dīn's close of kins after the failure of the uprising is not recorded, either. The only relevant records related to the period of the uprising and the years immediately following it are that Ḥiṣn al-Dīn was hung together with a collateral patrilineal relative of his named *al-amīr* Jamāl al-Dawla Abū ʿAllāq Aḥmad (whose genealogy begins to overlap with that of Ḥiṣn al-Dīn's at his seventh-generation forefather) and that a son of Ḥiṣn al-Dīn's paternal granduncle was hung from the Zuwayla Gate of al-Qāhira earlier in 652/1254–55.[26] It is, however, certain that the Thaʿlabids were not annihilated. Ibn ʿAbd al-Ẓāhir (620/1223–692/1293) in his work on the topography of Cairo, *al-Rawḍa al-bahiyya al-zāhira*, states that the public bath named Ḥammām al-Kāmil was in the possession of the heirs of "al-Sharīf Ibn Thaʿlab" "at present."[27] Since it is known that Ibn ʿAbd al-Ẓāhir started the drafting of *al-Rawḍa al-bahiyya al-zāhira* only as late as in 647/1249–50 and the unicum manuscript of the work represents a recension that incorporates the information related to as late as the 680s/1280s, this "present" most likely pertains to the period after the suppression of the *ʿUrbān* uprising.[28] Likewise, al-Marqīzī in *al-Sulūk* reports that "al-Sharīf Ibn Thaʿlab" was one of those who, in 690/1291, helped the Vizier Ibn al-Salʿūs force out the Grand Qadi Taqī al-Dīn Ibn Bint al-Aʿazz from his numerous posts in a court intrigue. This Ibn Thaʿlab, in collaboration with the vizier and along with two other anonymous fellows, made false allegations against Ibn Bint al-Aʿazz in front of al-Ashraf Khalīl b. Qalāwūn (r. 689/1290–693/1293), which resulted in the dismissal of the grand qadi.[29] The survival of the Thaʿlabids through the *ʿUrbān* uprising can also be understood from the statement by Ibn ʿInaba (d. 828/1424), an Iraqi and Twelver Shiʿi expert on the genealogy of ʿAlī's kinfolk, that all of Ḥiṣn al-Dīn I's sons had continuing lines of descendants in Egypt at his time (*lahum jamīʿihim aʿqāb bi-Miṣr ilā al-ān*).[30] These pieces of information, however, do not necessarily point to the survival of the descendants of Ḥiṣn al-Dīn II who formed only a part of the Thaʿlabids.

If this is what the sources previously known to us confirmed about the Thaʿlabids, the very existence of Najm al-Dīn is something we learn for the first time thanks to the *Genealogy of the Thaʿlabids*. Najm al-Dīn ʿAlī shares his *laqab* and *ism* with his paternal grandfather ("Najm al-Dīn Fakhr al-ʿUmarāʾ ʿAlī" in the genealogical diagram on folio 32b) and it is therefore likely that he was the son of Ḥiṣn al-Dīn II's who was supposed to succeed, or had actually succeeded, to his father's leadership position when the *Genealogy of the Thaʿlabids* was composed.

Furthermore, the treatise suggests that Najm al-Dīn was a powerful figure with an elevated status at the time of its composition. The fact that Ibrāhīm b. Yaḥyā wrote the treatise (as well as another previous work, as will be discussed below) in Najm al-Dīn's name is not the only basis for this understanding. Ibrāhīm b. Yaḥyā lavishes Najm al-Dīn with a series of honorifics that is reminiscent of those known in relation to his forefathers: The Greatest *Sayyid*, *Sharīf*, the Most Special *Amīr*, Glory of the Tribes, Pride of the Sub-Tribes, Protection of the Muslims, Beauty and the Noble

One of the Lands, Pride and the High-Born One of the Caliphate, Prop of the Kings, Protection of the Refugee (*al-sayyid al-ajall al-sharīf al-amīr al-akhaṣṣ ʿizz al-qabāʾil fakhr al-ʿashāʾir ḥiṣn al-Muslimīn jamāl al-mamālik wa-ḥasībuhā fakhr al-khilāfa wa-nasībuhā ʿumdat al-mulūk ḥiṣn al-hārib*).[31] Although the use of honorifics does not vouch for accompanying substance, this series of honorifics, which implies both the leadership role among the *ʿUrbān* and the membership in the political regime headed nominally by the ʿAbbāsid caliph, shows that Najm al-Dīn at least posed himself as the heir to the previous heads of the Thaʿlabids such as Fakhr al-Dīn Ismāʿīl and Ḥiṣn al-Dīn Thaʿlabs.

Najm al-Dīn's power at the time of the treatise's composition can also be understood from the fact that Ibrāhīm b. Yaḥyā's lavish praises for Najm al-Dīn in Section III begin with references to Najm al-Dīn's patronage to mosques and shrines (*mashāhid*) which infer that Najm al-Dīn was known for building/repairing (*ʿimāra*) mosques and providing lighting to shrines by means of endowing those facilities with *waqf* incomes (31a). Ibrāhīm b. Yaḥyā, who, as we will see below, was linked to an ʿAlid shrine in Cairo, no doubt expected Najm al-Dīn to continue such patronage. The passage in question, in addition, indicates that Najm al-Dīn's sphere of activities included Cairo, just as those of his great-grandfather Fakhr al-Dīn Ismāʿīl and his father Ḥiṣn al-Dīn II did.

A question that remains open is whether the *Genealogy of the Thaʿlabids* shows Najm al-Dīn's survival through the *ʿUrbān* uprising and its immediate aftermath as well as his continued prominence afterwards. It is plausible that the treatise was composed in or after 648/1250–51, when the uprising may well have been under way. We, however, do not know if the composition took place during the uprising or after its suppression. It may, nonetheless, be useful to point out that the political situation within the Mamluk sultanate around the time of Ḥiṣn al-Dīn II's execution might not have been totally detrimental to the fate of Najm al-Dīn, provided that he was still alive at that time. Ḥiṣn al-Dīn, in the second phase of his uprising, sided with ʿIzz al-Dīn Afram, a prominent member of the Baḥrī mamluks, and fought against Aybak.[32] And it was by Aybak, the enemy of the Baḥrī mamluks, that Ḥiṣn al-Dīn was captured and imprisoned. It would therefore appear plausible that the Sultan Baybars, the leader of the Baḥrī mamluks at the time of Ḥiṣn al-Dīn's execution, would spare the life of the rebel's heir and let his line continue.[33] Possibly, "the heirs of al-Sharīf Ibn Thaʿlab" and "al-Sharīf Ibn Thaʿlab" alive in 690/1291, both mentioned in the sources from the Mamluk period, referred (partially in the case of the former?) to those who were linearly descended from Ḥiṣn al-Dīn II, and also from Najm al-Dīn.

The connection Najm al-Dīn had with Ibrāhīm b. Yaḥyā "al-Najafī" and the very fact that the latter composed for the former a work (in fact two works, as will be discussed below) that manifests special regard for the Twelve Imams are two other novel facts about the Thaʿlabids that we learn from the treatise. We, however, need to discuss who Ibrāhīm b. Yaḥyā al-Mashhadī al-Najafī was and how the Twelver Imams are treated in the *Genealogy of the Thaʿlabids* before trying to interpret those facts.

The Author: Ibrāhīm b. Yaḥyā al-Mashhadī al-Najafī, Ibn Ballūh

Clues available in the text let us identify the author of the *Genealogy of the Thaʿlabids*, Ibrāhīm b. Yaḥyā b. Muḥammad b. Mūsā al-Mashhadī al-Najafī, with a figure previously known to scholarship. Our author is identical with a figure best known by the name Ibn Ballūh (or Ibn Bulūla), a figure who has been noted by Yūsuf Rāġib in his studies on the practice of tomb visitation in Cairo and guidebooks for that practice.[34]

Ibn Ballūh appears in the guidebooks for tomb visitation composed in Mamluk Cairo in two different contexts. Firstly, he is mentioned as an "*al-sayyid al-sharīf*" whose tomb was found at the entrance of the ʿAlid shrine of al-Sayyida Sukayna along with that of his granddaughter Zaynab bt. al-Ḥasan.[35] Secondly, he is referred to as an expert on the Cairene shrines.[36] Ibn al-Zayyāt (d. 814/1412), one of the authors of those guidebooks, states that Ibn Ballūh was the author of a book on "the visitation of the [tombs and shrines of] the righteous people" (*ziyārat al-ṣāliḥīn*).[37] Ibn al-Zayyāt, in addition, cites Ibn Ballūh as one of the authorities who ensured the truth of al-Sayyida Nafīsa's burial in Cairo by enumerating numerous well-known figures who purportedly visited her tomb there.[38] The references in the guidebooks for tomb visitation also reveal that Ibn Ballūh's name was Abū Isḥāq Ibrāhīm b. Yaḥyā.[39]

Quotations from Ibn Ballūh's work by Ibn al-Zayyāt make it clear that the work dealt both with the shrines attributed to the members of ʿAlī's kinfolk and with those which were not. Ibn al-Zayyāt's locution, at the same time, shows that Ibn Ballūh was known primarily as an expert on the genealogy and history of the kinfolk of ʿAlī.[40] It is thus understood that Ibn Ballūh was a figure who was engaged in the promotion of the visitation to Cairene shrines at large while his primary expertise consisted in the genealogy and history of the kinfolk of ʿAlī. It is also known that he wrote a written attestation of the authenticity of genealogy for a descendant of Jaʿfar al-Ṭayyār on 27 Shawwāl 626/18 September 1229.[41] This reveals that Ibn Ballūh used his expertise as a genealogist not only when he discussed the shrines housing deceased people from the past but also when he dealt with his living contemporaries.

The year 626/1229 as the date of the mentioned written attestation as well as the fact that 17 Shawwāl 646/2 February 1249 is the reported death date of his granddaughter Zaynab bt. Ḥasan, also interred at the entrance of the shrine of al-Sayyida Sukayna, indicates that Ibn Ballūh was already active in the first half of the thirteenth century.[42] The source referring to Ibn Ballūh's written attestation also reveals that he used the *nisba* "al-Mashhadī" and he was known as a Qurʾān reciter (*al-muqri'*) in addition to as a genealogist (*al-nassāba*).[43] Maḥmūd Rabīʿ and Ḥasan Qāsim, the co-editors of the 1937 edition of the *Tuḥfat al-aḥbāb*, a guidebook for tomb visitation by al-Sakhāwī al-Ḥanafī (d. after 889/1484–85), attributed the *nisba* "al-Mashhadī" to Ibn Ballūh's "residence" (*iqāma*) at the shrine (*mashhad*) of al-Sayyida Sukayna.[44] Rabīʿ and Qāsim also noted that a mention of Ibn Ballūh was found in Ibn ʿInaba's *ʿUmdat al-ṭālib fī ansāb Āl Abī Ṭālib*.[45] In this compendium of the genealogy of ʿAlī's kinfolk, Ibn Ballūh's genealogy is presented as follows: Ibrāhīm b. Yaḥyā b. Muḥammad b. Mūsā b. Muḥammad b. Abī Tamīm b. Yaḥyā b. Ibrāhīm b. Mūsā al-Makḥūl b. Muḥammad b. Ismāʿīl b. Aḥmad b. Ismāʿīl b. Muḥammad b. Ismāʿīl b. Jaʿfar al-Ṣādiq. Ibn ʿInaba, in addition, notes that Ibrāhīm's *laqab* was Nūr al-Dīn and that "Ballūh" was the nickname of Ibrāhīm's father Yaḥyā.[46]

There is no doubt that the author of the *Genealogy of the Thaʿlabids* is none other than Ibn Ballūh. The author is an "*al-sayyid al-sharīf*" because of his Ḥusaynid descent, the descent he shared with Ibn Ballūh who, as Jaʿfar al-Ṣādiq's descendant, was also a Ḥusaynid. The author's genealogy going back to his great-grandfather coincides with Ibn Ballūh's as presented by Ibn ʿInaba. The author and Ibn Ballūh share not only an association with al-Sayyida Sukayna but also the *nisba* "al-Mashhadī."

It is Ibrāhīm b. Yaḥyā Ibn Ballūh's self-identification as a "Najafī" that we learn for the first time from the *Genealogy of the Thaʿlabids*. This self-identification is interesting not only because it might suggest a possible Iraqi Twelver Shiʿi connection of Najm al-Dīn and, by extension, the Thaʿlabids. Its interest also lies in the fact that it might suggest the participation, in the thirteenth century, of an Iraqi Twelver Shiʿi element, or an element connected to it, in the promotion of tomb visitation in Cairo, a practice for which the cult of the members of ʿAlī's kinfolk constituted an important factor. Although the promotion of the Cairene shrines commemorating members of ʿAlī's kinfolk by the Ismāʿīlī Fāṭimid dynasty has been well acknowledged, Twelver Shiʿi participation in the promotion of the practice of tomb visitation at large in the periods after the demise of the Fāṭimids, whether direct or indirect, has not been noted by relevant studies to the best of my knowledge.[47] Ibrāhīm b. Yaḥyā was not only an author who wrote in promotion of the practice of tomb visitation. He was also "the/a servant of al-Sayyida Sukayna" who was purportedly interred in the Cairene shrine attributed to that lady. Without doubt, he was the custodian or an attendant of the shrine.

Then, what kind of association with Najaf does this *nisba* signify and as what kind of place is Najaf referred to by this appellation? Ought we to see here evidence of Ibrāhīm b. Yaḥyā's Twelver Shiʿism or a claim to a connection with that confessional group? These questions will be tackled in the conclusion, after we have discussed the treatment of the Twelve Imams in the *Genealogy of the Thaʿlabids* in the next section. Whether or not we should regard the treatment as Twelver Shiʿi in nature will significantly affect our analysis. It is, however, useful to discuss at this point what several possible lines of interpretation can be.

First to be mentioned is the fact that two pieces of evidence suggest that Ibrāhīm b. Yaḥyā had a real connection with Najaf and the Twelver Shiʿi scholarly circle for whom Najaf was an important base. One is the very fact that the *Genealogy of the Thaʿlabids* is copied into Or. 1406. Al-Mūsawī al-Najafī, the genealogist who put Or. 1406 together, was a member of a lineage based at Najaf (the Banū Muḥsin) and it is most probable that he was from Najaf himself.[48] This background as well as the definite Twelver Shiʿi identify of his paternal uncle, with whom he evidently had a close relationship, leaves no reason to doubt al-Mūsawī al-Najafī's affiliation with the Twelver Shiʿi community.[49] We know that al-Mūsawī al-Najafī peregrinated widely through his career, not only in Iraq and the Iranian Plateau but even to the Deccan (presumably via the sea route), but there is no evidence to suggest his travelling westwards from Iraq.[50] Thus, al-Mūsawī al-Najafī probably came to know of the *Genealogy of the Thaʿlabids* in the Twelver Shiʿi or Twelver Shiʿi-centered scholarly environment in which he was operating in the aforementioned eastern regions, if not in Najaf itself.

The other fact suggesting Ibrāhīm b. Yaḥyā's real connection with Najaf is that Ibn ʿInaba recorded Ibrāhīm b. Yaḥyā's name and genealogy in his genealogical compendium, the *ʿUmdat al-ṭālib*. Ibn ʿInaba (d. 828/1425) was a Twelver Shiʿi genealogist from Ḥilla who, just like al-Mūsawī al-Najafī, operated in Iraq and the regions lying to the east of it.[51] Although confessional identity was never a criterion of inclusion or exclusion in a genealogical compendium such as the *ʿUmdat al-ṭālib*, the inclusion of the information about Ibrāhīm b. Yaḥyā in the work would suggest the circulation of the knowledge about him among the people affiliated to the Twelver Shiʿi or Twelver Shiʿi-centered scholarly circle closely linked to Najaf.[52]

Was Ibrāhīm b. Yaḥyā from Najaf, then? Although no evidence definitely denies the possibility, it appears more likely that he was not. The strongest basis for this judgment is a quotation from Ibrāhīm b. Yaḥyā (Ibn Ballūh) in Ibn al-Nāsikh's Cairene guidebook for tomb visitation (written towards the end of the thirteenth century) in which Ibrāhīm b. Yaḥyā cites his father as the source of a miracle tale attributed to al-Sayyida Nafīsa.[53] The transmission of such a tale that promotes the veneration of the most important (putative) ʿAlid woman interred in Cairo would suggest that Ibrāhīm b. Yaḥyā's father lived also in Cairo. The Egyptian origin of Ibrāhīm b. Yaḥyā, and his lineage more generally, is also suggested, albeit remotely, by what is written about the descendants of Ismāʿīl b. Jaʿfar al-Ṣādiq (Ibrāhīm b. Yaḥyā's fourteenth-generation ascendant) in several genealogical compendia.[54] Although the possibility remains that Ibrāhīm b. Yaḥyā's father or other close ascendant was from Najaf or, less likely, that Ibrāhīm b. Yaḥyā was concealing his Najafī origin in the statement cited by Ibn al-Nāsikh, the evidence suggests that Ibrāhīm b. Yaḥyā was from Egypt.

What does Ibrāhīm b. Yaḥyā's *nisba* "al-Najafī" mean? Two answers appear plausible at this point. One is that "al-Najafī" was intended to highlight Ibrāhīm

b. Yaḥyā's connection with Najaf as an important center of the Twelver Shiʿa as a confessional group and of the group's scholarly circle. We should, however, not forget that Najaf was a shrine city formed around the putative shrine of ʿAlī b. Abī Ṭālib, the veneration of whom was by no means confined to Twelver Shiʿa or Shiʿa more generally. The other plausible answer is that the use of the *nisba* was expected to highlight Ibrāhīm b. Yaḥyā's association with the putative shrine of ʿAlī b. Abī Ṭālib as a supra-confessional or even Sunni figure.[55] Such an association may well have helped him promote himself as an expert on genealogy and history of the kinfolk of ʿAlī. In this connection, it is worthwhile noting that the *nisba* "al-Mashhadī" may also have referred to the shrine in Najaf, instead of that of al-Sayyida Sukayna as surmised previously. It is also possible that it was expected to be taken in two different senses depending on the audiences, that is, as referring to Ibrāhīm b. Yaḥyā's link with the shrine of al-Sayyida Sukayna to some audiences and as indicating his connection with the shrine of ʿAlī b. Abī Ṭālib to others. The fact that his *nisba* "al-Najafī" is not recorded in the Cairene guidebooks for tomb visitation might indicate that the *nisba* was not used in the relevant milieu. Perhaps, the Twelver Shiʿi association of "al-Najafī," even when ʿAlī's supra-confessional facet was emphasized, was not something that would be totally lost in the larger environment in which Ibrāhīm b. Yaḥyā operated in Cairo.

The outstanding question is if the Najafī connection that we assume Ibrāhīm b. Yaḥyā really had also signifies his Twelver Shiʿism and whether he used the *nisba* "al-Najafī" in the *Genealogy of the Thaʿlabids* to imply that confessional identity. It is now necessary to discuss the treatment of the Twelve Imams in the *Genealogy of the Thaʿlabids* and determine whether that treatment can be considered Twelver Shiʿi or not.

Treatment of the Twelve Imams: A Sunni Representation

It is difficult for a reader of the *Genealogy of the Thaʿlabids* to miss the manifestations of special regard for the Twelve Imams therein. Especially visible and conspicuous is the parallel diagrammatic presentation of the genealogy of the Thaʿlabids with that of the Ḥusaynid Imams, in addition to that of the Prophet Muḥammad, in Section IV (Figure 1). Clearly with this special way of presentation in mind, Ibrāhīm b. Yaḥyā in the preface to the treatise writes that he will present the genealogy of the Thaʿlabids "as connected to the prop, that is, the stem of the genealogy [reaching back to Adam] of the Prophet Muḥammad the most glorious" (*murattabatan ʿalā ʿamūd al-nasab li-l-afkhar al-nabawī al-Muḥammadī*) and "as built upon the foundation, namely, the purest descent of the Twelve Imams" (*mabniyatan ʿalā mushayyad al-ḥasab al-aṭhar li-l-aʾimma al-ithnā-ʿashar*) (30a). Although it is not clear exactly what is meant by the phrases "as connected to" and "as built upon," this explanation leaves no doubt that an importance is attached to the Twelve Imams that is comparable to, if not equal to, the one attached to the Prophet. The parallel presentation of the genealogy of the Thaʿlabids with that of the Twelve Imams was thought to help highlight the loftiness of the Thaʿlabids' ancestry in the same manner that its parallel presentation with the genealogy of the Prophet did.

Also unmissable is a passage towards the end of the preface where Ibrāhīm b. Yaḥyā makes an excuse for not dealing with the virtues of the Twelve Imams in the work. Ibrāhīm b. Yaḥyā makes this excuse rather abruptly and with no apparent necessity. In addition, he cites as the reason for the omission, in addition to the topic's irrelevance to the work's subject, the fact that he previously authored a work entitled *The Luminous [Book/Treatise] on the Virtues of the Twelve Imams* (*al-Azhar fī manāqib al-aʾimma al-ithnā-ʿashar*) in the name of Najm al-Dīn (30a).

These features clearly show that Ibrāhīm b. Yaḥyā "al-Najafī" expressed special regard for the Twelve Imams as a group of special people in the original version of the *Genealogy of the Thaʿlabids*. But, should that special regard be considered *exclusively* Twelver Shiʿi? Questioning this is necessary since authors with clear self-identification as Sunnis also wrote works that manifested special regard for the Twelve Imams in the period the *Genealogy of the Thaʿlabids* was composed. The *Maṭālib al-saʾūl fī manāqib Āl al-Rasūl* by Kamāl al-Dīn Ibn Ṭalḥa al-Naṣībī al-Shāfiʿī (d. 652/1254), the *Tadhkirat al-khawāṣṣ min al-Umma bi-dhikr khaṣāʾiṣ al-aʾimma* by Sibṭ Ibn al-Jawzī (581/1185 or 582/1186–654/1256), and the *Kifāyat al-ṭālib fī manāqib ʿAlī b. Abī Ṭālib* with its sequel *al-Bayān fī akhbār ṣāḥib al-zamān* by al-Kanjī al-Shāfiʿī (d. 658/1260) are several better-known representatives of such works.[56] These Sunni authors in their respective works not only recognized the Twelve Imams as a group of twelve special people but clearly considered them to be *Imāms* (I will hereafter use "*Imām*" when I would like to make clear that what I mean is an Imam [signifying one of the twelve people recognized as the sole and successive infallible leaders of the Muslim Community after the Prophet Muḥammad by the Twelver Shiʿa] as perceived by the mentioned Sunni authors as one of the twelve special people; what an "*Imām*" exactly meant for each of them is beyond the scope of this study).[57]

The treatment of the Twelve Imams in the *Genealogy of the Thaʿlabids* cannot be considered as Twelver Shiʿi in nature but should be considered to be one that was, at the very least in its author's mind, within the borders of Sunni Islam. I argue this on the basis of both positive and passive evidence in the following pages. The references to the Twelve Imams in the *Genealogy of the Thaʿlabids* are by no means limited to the ones already mentioned. The remaining references to them will be presented below when I discuss pieces of passive evidence.

The positive evidence for the Sunni nature of the treatment of the Twelve Imams in the *Genealogy of the Thaʿlabids* lies in the fact that the treatise as a whole presents features that would render it a Sunni work. As can be expected from its subject, genealogy and virtues of a lineage with politico-military leadership, as well as from the above overview of its contents, the *Genealogy of the Thaʿlabids* is by no means a text that saliently displays a particular confessional orientation. Yet, two features attributable to Ibrāhīm b. Yaḥyā lead us to consider it a Sunni work, whatever his true understanding of his own confessional identity may have been.

One of those features is the way Ibrāhīm b. Yaḥyā presents the traditions he cites in Section II. As shown in Appendix, what Ibrāhīm b. Yaḥyā presents in Section II is, or originates from, a collection of traditions gathered by Yaḥyā b. al-Ḥasan al-ʿAqīqī (219/829–277/890–91), a Ḥusaynid expert on genealogy and history of ʿAlī's kinfolk who flourished in ninth-century Medina. What draws our attention here is the chain of transmission Ibrāhīm b. Yaḥyā presents at the beginning of the section. The chain of transmission, meant to show through what transmission path(s) Ibrāhīm b. Yaḥyā learned Yaḥyā b. al-Ḥasan's collection, conveys that the collection had been transmitted to him through generations of Sunni scholars (see Appendix).[58]

The other instance of a manifestation of confessional orientation (again true or pretended) attributable to Ibrāhīm b. Yaḥyā is the series of titles or nicknames with which Ibrāhīm b. Yaḥyā lavishes Najm al-Dīn. As discussed above, the series of appellations include the phrases "High-Born One of the Caliphate" and "Prop of the Kings." This is tantamount to admitting the Sunni political theory that underpinned the existing political establishment of the Ayyubids or the Mamluks, headed (nominally) by the ʿAbbasid Caliph.

These are the pieces of positive evidence for the non-Twelver Shiʿi and Sunni nature of the treatment of the Twelve Imams. They show that Ibrāhīm b. Yaḥyā wrote the *Genealogy of the Thaʿlabids* as a Sunni work, or at least in a way that would not lead a reader to recognize it as a work that manifests a non-Sunni or anti-Sunni stance. Having examined them, we shall now turn to the negative evidence, namely, the fact that no element of the treatment of the Twelve Imams in the treatise can be considered a clear or definitive sign of Twelver Shiʿism.

I begin by enumerating the features, paragraphs, and passages a reader of the *Genealogy of the Thaʿlabids* will note, in addition to the parallel presentation of the genealogies and Ibrāhīm b. Yaḥyā's excuse discussed above, as definite or possible manifestations of special regard for the Twelve Imams and as a possible indications of the text's Twelver Shiʿism. References to Fāṭima are also included in the enumeration, because of her status as one of the Fourteen Infallibles, along with the Prophet Muḥammad and the Twelve Imams, according to the Twelver Shiʿi dogma.

(1) The fact that the title "*al-imām*" or "*amīr al-muʾminīn*" is often attached to the name of an Imam (the latter only to the name of ʿAlī b. Abī Ṭālib). In addition, mentions of one or more of the Imams or of Fāṭima are followed by a *taṣliya* (an

optative soliciting God's blessing [i.e., *ṣalāt*, *ṣalawāt*] for the relevant figure[s]) four times in the text, although it is a *taslīm* (an optative soliciting "peace" [*salām*] for the relevant figure[s]) that is used in most of the cases where an optative is attached to the names of the relevant people.[59]

(2) The fact that the twelfth Imam is called "*al-imām*, the riser, the aider, and the divinely-guided" (*al-imām, al-qāʾim, al-muntaṣir, al-mahdī*) and the mention is followed by a *taṣliya* in abbreviation (*Ṣ-M*) in the genealogical diagram on folio 32b.

(3) The *taṣliya* for the Prophet Muḥammad and his kinfolk in the form "May God bless him and his kinfolk, the *imām*s who are the righteous people of the Muslim Community" (*ṣallā Allāh ʿalayhi wa-ālihi al-aʾimma ṣāliḥī al-Umma*), found in the preface to the work (30a). The "*imāms*" then are characterized as follows:

> Those who persevered, accomplished what they promised God to accomplish, took the lead in buckling down to endeavors in the *jihād*, and never stopped. [Those] to whom God promised empowerment on the earth while they promised fulfillment of the duties imposed upon them. [They are] those who never broke their promise [to God] while [God] also never broke His promise [to them].[60]

(4) The fact that five traditions out of the traditions (Prophetic or otherwise), anecdotes, and verses (hereafter only traditions for the sake of simplicity) cited in Section II that amount to forty-four in total are introduced by a chain of transmission that terminates with the name of an Imam or the names of Imams.[61] For example, the chain of transmission introducing the first tradition cited in the treatise (and Section II) terminates thus: "*al-imām* Jaʿfar al-Ṣādiq [transmitted] from his father *al-imām* Muḥammad al-Bāqir – *ʿ-L-S-M* [abbreviation for a *taslīm*] –. He [i.e., Muḥammad al-Bāqir] said that the Apostle of God – *Ṣ-L-ʿ-M* [abbreviation for a *taṣliya*] – said, [then the Prophet's utterance follows]" (*al-imām Jaʿfar al-Ṣādiq ʿan abīhi al-imām Muḥammad al-Bāqir ʿ-L-S-M qāla qāla Rasūl Allāh Ṣ-L-ʿ-M*).

(5) Other appearances of the names of one or more of the Imams and/or Fāṭima in contexts that definitely or possibly indicate special regard for them, namely:

  (a). The ones that take place in the main texts of the traditions cited in Section II, in which the figure's/figures' eminent position in the Muslim Community or among the Prophet's kinfolk is presupposed. A case in point is the tradition on folio 36b in which ʿAlī b. Abī Ṭālib's utterance concerning ʿAbd Allāh b. Jaʿfar's largesse is cited as evidence of that quality of the latter.[62]

  (b) The one where Yūshaʿ b. Nūn (Joshua) is depicted as a figure who shared the same status with ʿAlī b. Abī Ṭālib in terms of the "fact" that the miracle of the "return of the sun" (*radd al-shams*) took place for both of them (34b).[63]

  (c) The one where Shahzanān bt. Yazdjird as the mother of "*al-imām* ʿAlī Zayn al-ʿĀbidīn, the forebear of the Ḥusaynids" is mentioned in the course of the presentation of the Prophet Muḥammad's genealogy going back to Adam (35a).[64]

A quick comparison with the aforementioned works by the three Sunni authors shows that some of the items in this enumeration cannot be taken as a sign of Twelver Shiʿism because their parallels are found in those works. To begin with, the three Sunni authors invariably recognize the twelfth Imam's status as the Savior of the end times ([2]). The titles or nicknames attached to the twelfth Imam's name in their works parallel those found in the *Genealogy of the Thaʿlabids*, too. Ibn Ṭalḥa, for example, calls the twelfth Imam "the divinely-guided, the proof [of God on the earth], the righteous successor [of all prophets and their legatees], the awaited one" (*al-mahdī al-ḥujja al-khalaf al-ṣāliḥ al-muntaẓar*."[65] The belief in the "return of the sun" miracle ([5-b]) is also a feature that can be attested in the *Tadhkirat al-khawāṣṣ* and the *Kifāyat al-ṭālib*.[66] Al-Kanjī believes that Zayn al-ʿĀbidīn's mother was Shāh-zanān bt. Yazdjird ([5-c]) and counts the "fact" as God's dispensation to distinguish the line of the Imams, while Ibn Ṭalḥa and Sibṭ Ibn al-Jawzī refer to that name (Shahzanān in the *Maṭālib al-saʾūl*) as one of the candidates for the mother's name.[67]

The fact that as many as five traditions in Section II are accompanied by a chain of transmission terminating with the name of an Imam ([4]) draws our attention because it may indicate a special value attached to such traditions. Provided that that is indeed the case, however, the attachment of a special value to such traditions is embedded in the treatise's text in such a way that would not allow it to be considered a sign of Twelver Shiʿism. For, as said above, the treatise presents those traditions as parts of the collection Ibrāhīm b. Yaḥyā learned through a chain of Sunni transmitters (Appendix). The appearances of the Imams and Fāṭima in the main texts of several traditions in Section II in ways that presuppose their eminent positions in the Muslim Community or among the kinfolk of the Prophet ([5-a]) should be dealt with in the same manner.

The expression that equates the Prophet's kinfolk with the "*imām*s" found amid the invocations in the preface ([3]) appears rather excessive in its manifestation of special regard for those "*imām*s." A comparable expression, however, is found in Ibn Ṭalḥa's *Maṭālib al-saʾūl*.[68] In addition, the perceived excess might be due to the author's intention that the "*imām*s" here be understood to (also) signify the members of the Thaʿlabids. The characterization of the "*imām*s" quoted above that emphasizes their activism is not what we expect from a standard characterization of the Twelve Imams, while it tallies well with the situation of the Thaʿlabids, especially during the period they were fighting against the central authorities. Needless to say, as *sharīf*s belonging to the Ṭālibid branch of the Hāshimids, the members of the Thaʿlabids could be counted as members of the Prophet's family.

Less straightforward is the use of the titles and optatives expected typically in (Twelver) Shiʿi works in the *Genealogy of the Thaʿlabids* as preserved in Or. 1406 ([1]).[69] These are elements that are highly susceptible to modifications by later copyists in accordance with their own preferences.[70] At the same time, it is basically impossible to identify such modifications when we deal with a text preserved in a unicum copy, as they usually do not affect the context. Because of these, we cannot know which of the titles and optatives found in Or. 1406 are attributable to Ibrāhīm b. Yaḥyā and which others should be attributed to a later copyist, if not to al-Mūsawī al-Najafī, the compiler of Or. 1406.

All that said, I tentatively hypothesized that all the relevant uses of the titles and optatives were attributable to Ibrāhīm b. Yaḥyā and examined whether their parallels could be found in Sibṭ Ibn al-Jawzī's *Tadhkirat al-khawāṣṣ*. I only used the *Tadhkirat al-khawāṣṣ* as the target of comparison firstly because Taqī-zāda's edition of the work is the only one among the editions of the four works by the three Sunni authors that regularly notes textual variants among the manuscripts employed.[71] The second reason for the selection is that Taqī-zāda uses a manuscript allegedly copied from the author's original during the author's lifetime by a copyist who plausibly did not try to "Shiʿitize" the optatives found in the text.[72] These make the comparison with the *Tadhkirat al-khawāṣṣ* valuable.

The outcome of the comparison is as follows. The titles "*imām*" and "*amīr al-muʾminīn*" as well as the *taslīm* optative are attested abundantly in the said manuscript of the *Tadhkirat al-khawāṣṣ* as made accessible through Taqī-zāda's edition.[73] The use of *taṣliya* can also be attested, in the form "*ṣalawāt Allāh ʿalayhim ajmaʿīn*" and in relation to the "infallible *Imām*s" (*al-aʾimma al-maʿṣūmīn*), although that is admittedly the only instance found throughout the work.[74] This outcome allows us to safely conclude that the appearances of "*imām*," "*amīr al-muʾminīn*," and the *taslīm* in the *Genealogy of the Thaʿlabids*, even if we supposed that all of them originated from Ibrāhīm b. Yaḥyā's pen, would not make the treatise a Twelver Shiʿi work. It would also indicate that the appearances of the *taṣliya* optative in four places of the treatise should not be taken as a definitive evidence of the Twelver Shiʿi nature of Ibrāhīm b. Yaḥyā's text.[75] In addition, we need to take into consideration the unignorable possibility that (some of) those *taṣliya*s were added by a later copyist, when evaluating their value as evidence.[76]

Given these pieces of positive and negative evidence, it is appropriate to conclude that the treatment of the Twelve Imams in the *Genealogy of the Thaʿlabids* cannot be considered Twelver Shiʿi but should be regarded as one made from a Sunni position. No element of the representation allows us to definitely label it as Twelver Shiʿi while the treatise as a whole presents signs of the author's (true or pretended) Sunni standpoints. That is by no means to say that the Twelve Imams are treated in the treatise in a way that would be acceptable to all or most Sunni Muslims. The point here is that the treatment of the Twelve Imams in the *Genealogy of the Thaʿlabids cannot* be characterized as Twelver Shiʿi in spite of Ibrāhīm b. Yaḥyā's use of the *nisba* "al-Najafī" and the conspicuous manifestation of special regard for them in that treatise.

Conclusion

This study has brought to light that an author based in thirteenth-century Cairo who claimed to be a "Najafī" and apparently had a true connection with the Twelver Shiʿi scholarly circle linked closely to that shrine city wrote a treatise conspicuously manifesting special regard for the Twelve Imams. Notably, the treatise was written for a son of the figure who led the well-known *ʿUrbān* uprising that shook Egypt in the middle of the century. The author was one of the promotors of the practice of tomb visitation in Cairo, of which the reverence for or cult of the members of ʿAlī's kinfolk putatively interred in that metropolis constituted an important element. We started the discussion by asking whether the treatise testifies to the Twelver Shiʿi identity of the author and the patron as well as the existence of a community of co-confessionalists around them. These questions are relevant not only for elucidating the situation of the Twelver Shiʿa as a supra-regional confessional group but also for a better understanding of the Egyptian society in the thirteenth century, given the identities and standings of the two figures.

What are the answers we can give to the questions on the basis of the findings in the preceding sections? We cannot draw a definitive conclusion about whether the author, Ibrāhīm b. Yaḥyā or Ibn Ballūh, was Twelver Shiʿi. We cannot say that he was Twelver Shiʿi, because the *Genealogy of the Thaʿlabids*, the only known substantive source that preserves his own voice, fails to display a clear sign of Twelver Shiʿism. Rather, the text of the treatise suggests its Sunni nature. The same facts, however, do not allow us to conclude that he was *not* Twelver Shiʿi, either. It is conceivable that the treatise reflects his adaptation to the Sunni-dominated environment, if not total concealment of his own confessional identity. The case of *al-sayyid* Ibn ʿAbd al-Ḥamīd, an expert on the genealogy of ʿAlī's kinfolk who Ibn Baṭṭūṭa met at the court of Özbek Khan of the Golden Horde in the early 1340s is worth a mention here. Although he hailed from a well-known Twelver Shiʿi lineage in Najaf and clearly maintained communication with Iraqi centers of Twelver Shiʿism via a network of co-confessionalists, Ibn Baṭṭūṭa does not even hint at his Twelver Shiʿi identity. Apparently, Ibn ʿAbd al-Ḥamīd did not display the belief and practice of Twelver Shiʿism ostentatiously, given the religious atmosphere of the court headed by a khan who identified himself as a Sunni.[77]

The confessional identity of the dedicatee of the treatise, Najm al-Dīn ʿAlī b. Ḥiṣn al-Dīn II al-Jaʿfarī al-Zaynabī, remains as unclear. He certainly knew Ibn Ballūh's claim to be a Najafī, although Ibn Ballūh possibly made that claim only to certain audiences. He also shared with Ibn Ballūh special regard for the Twelve Imams, albeit not necessarily in the same sense. He may have been one of several things: a Sunni believing in Ibn Ballūh's Sunni identity; a Sunni not caring about Ibn Ballūh's confessional identity at all; a Sunni not minding or tolerating Ibn Ballūh's

Twelver Shiʿi identity; or a Twelver Shiʿi who, together with Ibn Ballūh, behaved properly, in a confessionally inconspicuous way, in a Sunni-dominated environment.[78] Given all the above, the question whether there existed a community of Twelver Shiʿis around Ibn Ballūh and Najm al-Dīn – and if such a community constituted a node in a network of Twelver Shiʿis as the one mentioned in the introduction – cannot be answered at the current stage of research.

The fact that we cannot give definitive answers to the questions posed at the beginning of this study, however, do not detract from the significance of the discoveries made here. Whatever the confessional identities of the two figures may have been, the discoveries are suggestive of (direct or indirect) connections they had with the Twelver Shiʿis centered in Iraq and calls for more attention to the role that Twelver Shiʿa, with its supra-regional network, may have played in the religious, social, and even political history of thirteenth-century Egypt.

A topic I have not been able to discuss properly in this study is the possible interrelation between the spread of special regard for the Twelve Imams as a whole among the Sunnis and the Sunni-Twelver Shiʿi interactions that we can assume to have taken place somewhere in or around the complex of interpersonal relationships that resulted in the compilation of the *Genealogy of the Thaʿlabids*. We cannot know whether the former was a cause for the latter or vice versa. It would nevertheless appear reasonable to see an interrelation between the two. I would like to close this study by noting that this observation may be meaningful for the much-desired efforts to elucidate the emergence and early phases of the spread of Sunni reverence for the Twelve Imams, a trend apparently observable from the twelfth century onwards and represented by the three Sunni authors already familiar to us from the last section. How we should assess the Twelver Shiʿi factor in the emergence and development of that trend constitutes an important line of future scholarly inquiry.[79]

Appendix

The fact that Ibrāhīm b. Yaḥyā used the traditions, anecdotes, and verses (hereafter only traditions for the sake of brevity) collected by Yaḥyā b. al-Ḥasan al-ʿAqīqī (219/829–277/890–91) that had been circulating among Sunni scholars at least for about a century and a half prior to his time is clear through an examination of the chains of transmission by which many of the traditions cited in Section II are accompanied.

Ibrāhīm b. Yaḥyā, in citing the first tradition, presents a chain of transmission that begins with the name of the figure from whom he heard the tradition and traces the transmission path via Yaḥyā b. al-Ḥasan to Muḥammad al-Bāqir (then the tradition per se reporting the Prophet's utterance is presented; 30a–b). The second tradition, however, is introduced only by the phrase "and by the above-mentioned chain of transmission" (*wa-bi-l-isnad al-muqaddam dhikruhu*; 30b). Then, for the third tradition, the phrase "and by the [same] chain of transmission, he said that Dāwūd b. al-Qāsim transmitted to him and said [. . .]" (*wa-bi-l-isnād qāla ḥaddathanā Dāwūd b. al-Qāsim qāla* [. . .]; underlines from the author) is used (30b). In like manner, Ibrāhīm b. Yaḥyā, in the rest of Section II, only mentions the names of several early transmitters at the most, indicating that the lineup of the later transmitters is the same as what he presented for the first tradition.

Ibrāhīm b. Yaḥyā does not mention anywhere in the text which of the figures appearing in the chain of transmission that precedes the first tradition is referred to as "he" and "him" in the transmission path of the third tradition (the latter of the quotations above) and those of the other relevant traditions. However, the identities of the figures whose names appear at the beginning of the chains of transmission attached to the relevant materials from the third tradition onwards (i.e., Dāwūd b. al-Qāsim in the case of the third tradition) and thus can, as a rule, be considered to be the figures who transmitted to "him" allow us to safely identify "him" with Yaḥyā b. al-Ḥasan.

Nineteen different figures appear in such positions.[80] It can be confirmed in sources other than the *Genealogy of the Thaʿlabids* that four of them (transmitting nine traditions altogether) transmitted to Yaḥyā b. al-Ḥasan at least one of the traditions they are depicted as having transmitted to "him" in the *Genealogy of the Thaʿlabids*.[81] Then, with regards five others (transmitting eleven traditions altogether), transmission of some other materials than those found in the *Genealogy of the Thaʿlabids* to Yaḥyā b. al-Ḥasan is confirmed.[82] Furthermore, the periods and places in which two others (transmitting four traditions altogether) lived (appear to) reasonably enable them to have had direct contact with and transmitted traditions to Yaḥyā.[83]

This examination allows us to safely conclude that Ibrāhīm b. Yaḥyā used a collection of traditions gathered to highlight the virtues of early Jaʿfarids (or a portion with the same objective of a larger collection) originally compiled by Yaḥyā b. al-Ḥasan.[84] What Ibrāhīm learned from the figure mentioned at the beginning of the first chain of transmission was not limited to the first tradition but was the collection as a whole. It is possible that Ibrāhīm b. Yaḥyā made his own selection from the collection. This, however, does not affect the conclusion that all the materials in Section II are presented as parts that together constitute a collection Ibrāhīm b. Yaḥyā learned through the transmission path(s) presented by the first chain of transmission.[85]

Now, the chain of transmission attached to the first tradition reads:

ما حدثني به (1)الشيخ الإمام العالم الفقيه الورع الفاضل جمال الدين أبو الحسن علي المظفر؟/الظفر؟ الحلبي بقراءتي عليه قال أخبرني (2)السيد الشريف العالم الفاضل النسابة محمد بن أسعد بن علي الحسيني الجواني نقيب النقباء سيد الأدباء قال أخبرني (3)الشيخ أبو عبد الله محمد بن إبراهيم بن ثابت المقرئ الفاضل قال حدثنا (4)الشيخ أبو الحسن علي بن الحسين بن عمر الموصلي المحدث قال أخبرني (5)الشيخ أبو الحسين عبد الكريم بن الحسين بن المحسن المكي المقرئ قال أخبرنا (6)الشريف أبو إبراهيم أحمد بن

القاسم بن ميمون بن حمزة العلوي الحسيني العبيدلي قال أخبرني (7)جدي الميمون بن حمزة العلوي بمصر
قراءة عليه قال أخبرنا (8)الشريف أبو القاسم جعفر بن محمد بن إبراهيم بن محمد بن عبيد الله بن الكاظم
قال حدثنا (9)الشريف النسابة أبو الحسين يحيى بن [الحسن بن] السيد جعفر بن عبد الله بن الحسين بن
علي بن الحسين بن علي بن ابي طالب علسم قال حدثني (*)عز الدين عبد الحميد قال أخبرني عن شيوخه
المتصلة إلى (10)عبد الجبار[68] بن سعيد عن (11)سليمان بن محمد عن (12)عمه عن (13)ابن جريج عن (14)
عطاء بن أبي رباح قال حدثنا (15)الإمام جعفر الصادق عن (16)أبيه الإمام محمد الباقر علسم قال: [. . .].

Regrettably, no biographical information about Jamāl al-Dīn Abū l-Ḥasan ʿAlī al-Muẓaffar/al-Ẓafar al-Ḥalabī ([1] in the chain of transmission), who transmitted the collection to Ibrāhīm b. Yaḥyā, has been available to me. However, the transmitter who passed down the collection to al-Ḥalabī was Sharīf al-Dīn Muḥammad b. Asʿad al-Jawwānī ([2]), known for his ostentatious antagonism against the Shiʿa.[87] Likewise, Abū ʿAbd Allāh Muḥammad b. Ibrāhīm b. Thābit ([3]), from whom al-Jawwānī heard the collection, and Abū l-Ḥasan ʿAlī b. al-Ḥusayn b. ʿUmar al-Mawṣilī ([4]), who transmitted the collection to Abū ʿAbd Allāh Muḥammad, were figures who are known to have operated and enjoyed general acceptance among the Sunnis in Egypt.[88] The chain of transmission, therefore, shows, or conveys the claim, that the materials presented in Section II are those which generations of Sunni scholars in Egypt deemed worth transmitting.[89]

This chain of transmission appears to also convey that Ibrāhīm b. Yaḥyā or al-Ḥalabī heard the first tradition or the collection of materials gathered by Yaḥyā b. al-Ḥasan from a figure named "ʿIzz al-Dīn ʿAbd al-Ḥamīd," too.[90] This figure may be identified with the Iraqi scholar ʿIzz al-Dīn ʿAbd al-Ḥamīd b. Ḥibat Allāh Ibn Abī l-Ḥadīd al-Madāʾinī (586/1192–655/1257 or 656/1258), the author of the famous commentary on the *Nahj al-balāgha*. If that is indeed the case, it will be counted as a highly important piece of information in considering Ibrāhīm b. Yaḥyā's activities and connections. No further investigation in this regard, however, is possible at the present. Here, it is only noted that the lineup of the traditions cited in the section of Ibn Abī l-Ḥadīd's commentary that deals with Jaʿfar al-Ṭayyār's martyrdom at Muʾta and his virtues does not correspond well with the lineup of traditions concerning Jaʿfar cited towards the beginning of Section II of the *Genealogy of the Thaʿlabids*.[91]

Given the limitation of space, other problems with this chain of transmission, such as the fact that ʿAṭāʾ b. Abī Rabāḥ is usually considered as a figure who transmitted traditions to and not from Jaʿfar al-Ṣādiq, will not be addressed here.[92]

Notes

* I would like to thank Professors Frédéric Bauden, Mimi Hanaoka, Takao Ito, and Rasūl Jaʿfariyān for their invaluable help in the preparation of this study. The research for this study was supported by JSPS Kakenhi Grants-in-Aid (19H01317 and 19H00564).

1 For Or. 1406, see my "The Notebook of a *Sayyid/Sharīf* Genealogist: MS. British Library Or. 1406," in *Scritti in onore di Biancamaria Scarcia Amoretti*, ed. by Daniela Bredi et al., 3 vols. (Rome: Dipartimento di Studi Orientali, Università di Roma "La Sapienza" and Edizioni Q, 2008), vol. 3, 823–6 and "An Enigmatic Genealogical Chart of the Timurids: A Testimony to the Dynasty's Claim to Yasavi-ʿAlid Legitimacy?" *Oriens* 44 (2016): 151–6. Twelver Shiʿism of al-Mūsawī al-Najafī can be deduced on the basis not only of his general background but also of the fact that his paternal uncle, with whom he evidently had a close relation, was certainly a Twelver Shiʿi scholar.

2 See Charles Rieu, *Supplement to the Catalogue of the Arabic Manuscripts in British Museum*, London, 1894, repr. (Hildesheim: Olms, 2000), 326–7; Morimoto, "The Notebook," 832–3. The present study corrects some observations I made in the latter. A facsimile edition of the treatise has been published, but with a one-page preface attributing the work wrongly to al-Mūsawī al-Najafī, the compiler of Or. 1406 (Ibrāhīm b. ʿAlī [sic], *al-Shajara al-Muḥammadiyya*, ed. by Muḥammad-Ḥusayn al-Ḥusaynī al-Jalālī [Chicago: The Open School, 2001–02]). I thank Ḥujjat al-Islām wa-l-Muslimīn ʿAlī Ṭabāṭabāʾī Yazdī for helping me access this facsimile edition.

3 Thaʿlab (and not Taghlib as in some sources and studies) is the way in which Ḥiṣn al-Dīn II's name must be read. The strongest basis for this reading is the fact that the name of Ḥiṣn al-Dīn's paternal grandfather Fakhr al-Dīn Ismāʿīl is carved clearly in the foundation inscription of his own tomb that he himself commissioned (completed in Rajab 613/October–November 1216) as follows: Fakhr al-Dīn [. . .] Abū [sic] Manṣūr Ismāʿīl b. [. . .] Ḥiṣn al-Dīn Thaʿlab b. Yaʿqūb b. Muslim b. Abī Jamīl al-Jaʿfarī al-Zaynabī (underline by the author). There is no doubt that Ḥiṣn al-Dīn II's name must be read in the same way as that of his great-grandfather (hereafter Ḥiṣn al-Dīn I). The name of the lineage of both Ḥiṣn al-Dīns, named after Ḥiṣn al-Dīn I, should also be read Banū Thaʿlab. See Max van Berchem, *Matériaux pour un corpus inscritionum arabicarum*, Première partie, *Egypte*, published as *Mémoires publiés par les membres de la Mission Archéologique Française au Caire*, Tome dix-neuvième (Paris: Ernest Leroux, 1903), 95 for the text of the inscription. An image of the inscription, in which the three dots above the first letter of the word Thaʿlab is clearly discernible, is accessible at the website *al-Qāhira al-Islāmiyya* (https://islamic.cultnat.org/Images/lg/AAAM_6550.jpg [accessed 17 April, 2022]).

4 Kazuo Morimoto, "Sayyid Ibn ʿAbd al-Ḥamīd: An Iraqi Shiʿi Genealogist at the Court of Özbek Khan," *Journal of the Economic and Social History of the Orient* 59 (2016): 678–9.

5 Devin J. Stewart, "Popular Shiism in Medieval Egypt: Vestiges of Islamic Sectarian Polemics in Egyptian Arabic," *Studia Islamica* 84 (1996): 57–61; Claude Garcin, *Un centre musulman de la Haute-Égypte médiévale: Qūṣ* ([Cairo]: Institut Français d'Archéologie Orientale du Caire, 1976), 309–12; Linda S. Northrup, "The Baḥrī Mamlūk Sultanate, 1250–1390," in *The Cambridge History of Egypt*, Vol. 1, *Islamic Egypt, 640–1517*, ed. by Carl Petry (Cambridge: Cambridge University Press, 1998), 265–6 (I thank Professor Frédéric Bauden for bringing the last reference to my attention). Stewart notes that the two most important sources he used were written by the authors from Idfū and Isnā respectively and that it is possible that "other pockets of Shiism existed in the other regions of Egypt" ("Popular Shiism," 61). For Twelver Shiʿi scholars who operated (also) in thirteenth-century Egypt while hiding their confessional identity, see Devin J. Stewart, *Islamic Legal Orthodoxy: Twelver Shiite Responses to the Sunni Legal System* (Salt Lake City: The University of Utah Press, 1998), 69–72. Activities of litterateurs and poets from Twelver Shiʿi centers in Iraq, above all Ḥilla, in Egypt during the period is a topic that awaits a serious attention. I thank Mr. Ryo Mizukami for bringing this question to my attention.

6 The five fragments occupy the following spaces, respectively: (1) f. 30a, l. 5–f. 31a, l. 11, (2) f. 31a, l. 11–f. 35b, l. 25, (3) f. 35b, l. 25–f. 37b, l. 10, (4) f. 37b, l. 10–f. 37b, l. 29, (5) f. 38a, l.

1–f. 38b, l. 27 (only the folio number [or the folio number and the line number as found here] will be given when referring to the *Genealogy of the Thaʿlabids* in this study). A pair of identical V-shaped symbols are written above line 10 of folio 37b and line 1 of folio 38a. They indicate the end of Fragment 3 and the beginning of Fragment 5, which are the two fragments that are continuous in their contents. No such signs are found at other fragment breaks.

7 The five fragments are to be reordered as follows: (1) → (3) → (5) → (4) → (2). The text is discontinued at the break between Fragments 1 and 3. The length of the lacuna is not known, but the texts preceding and following it invariably deal with the virtues of one and the same figure (Asmāʾ bt. ʿUmays). There might also be a lacuna at the break between Fragments 4 and 2, across which the presentation of the dedicatee's virtues is made.

8 That is to say, the consolidated text does not include the author's final remark which customarily announces the completion of the work, the date of the completion, and so on.

9 To be more precise, clear correspondence between the texts of the two works begins to be observed in the final portion of the genealogy presented in diagrammatic format (a notice attached to the name of Ilyās on folio 33b, corresponding to the text found on page 77 of al-Jawwānī, *al-Muqaddima al-fāḍiliyya*, ed. by Turkī b. Muṭlaq al-Qaddāḥ al-ʿUtaybī [Riyadh: Maṭābiʿ al-Ḥumaydī, 2006]). For al-Jawwānī, see my "Sharif al-Din al-Jawwani: A Talibid Genealogist from Twelfth-Century Egypt" (in Japanese), *Seinan Ajia kenkyū* 88 (2018): 1–19 and "al-Jawwānī," in *The Encyclopaedia of Islam Three*, ed. by Kate Fleet et al., pt. 2019.1 (Leiden and Boston: Brill, 2019), 101–2.

10 32a. To be exact, the author hereby explains the reason why the portion of the genealogy from ʿAdnān to Adam is not omitted in the work.

11 "//" signifies a line break. I take the second line (to be precise, "al-Ḥusayniyya" is written in the open space far above the line for no known reason; see Figure 2) to be a description of the content of the work, rather than its title. The mention of the work's title *al-Shajara al-nabawiyya al-Muḥammadiyya wa-l-nisba al-Zaynabiyya wa-l-Ḥusayniyya* towards the end of the preface is preceded by the phrase "I named this book of mine" (*naʿtu kitābī hādhā*) and shows that that should indeed be taken as the title.

12 See n. 8 above.

13 "Al-Sharīf" in today's toponym Dayrūṭ al-Sharīf is said to refer to the very Ḥiṣn al-Dīn II and thus the locale should have been known by other names such as Dharwat/Dharūt Sarabām in his days. For different names of the place and their etymology, see Richard Hartmann, "Politische Geographie des Mamlūkenreichs: Kapitel 5 und 6 des Staatshandbuchs Ibn Faḍlallāh al-ʿOmarī's," *Zeitschrift der Deutschen Morgenländischen Gesellschaft* 70 (1916): 482. I thank Professor Takao Ito for sharing this article with me.

14 The following account of the development of the uprising is based on Garcin, *Un centre musulman*, 183–9. Garcin synthesizes the accounts left behind by historians from the Mamluk period while the other relevant studies I have consulted only follow, as far as the general outline of the development is concerned, al-Maqrīzī's accounts, mainly in *al-Sulūk* and *al-Bayān wa-l-iʿrāb*, which Garcin (and A. H. Poliak before him) finds biased and faulty (Garcin, *Un centre musulman*, 184, n. 1, 188, n. 3). Those other studies include Youssef Rapoport, "Invisible Peasants, Marauding Nomads: Taxation, Tribalism, and Rebellion in Mamluk Egypt," *Mamlūk Studies Review* 8.2 (2004): 1, where Rapoport also enumerates relevant sources and studies in n. 1. See also Toshimichi Matsuda, "The Revolts of ʿurbān in Upper Egypt under the Baḥrī Mamlūks," *Tōyō gakuhō* 74 (1993): 72–3.

15 The account in al-Maqrīzī, *Kitāb al-Sulūk li-maʿrifat duwal al-mulūk*, vol. 1, pt. 2, ed. by Muḥammad Muṣṭafā Ziyāda (Cairo: Maṭbaʿat Dār al-Kutub al-Miṣriyya, 1936), 387 would suggest that the battle took place near Dayrūṭ, rather than Akhmīm.

16 See Rapoport, "Invisible Peasants" (literature review on 1–2) and idem, *Rural Economy and Tribal Society in Islamic Egypt: A Study of al-Nābulusī's* Village of the Fayyum (Trunhout: Brepols, 2018), 171–203 ("Chapter 7 Village and Tribe"; relevant literature review on 171–2).

See also Sarah Büssow-Schmitz, *Die Beduinen der Mamluken: Beduinen im politischen Leben Ägyptens im 8./14. Jahrhundert* (Wiesbaden: Ludwig Reichert Verlag, 2016), 3–5, 31–6.

17 Al-Maqrīzī, *Kitāb al-Sulūk*, vol. 1, pt. 1, ed. by Ziyāda, 2nd ed. (Cairo: Maṭbaʿat lajnat al-taʾlīf wa-l-tarjama wa-l-nashr, 1956), 130; Garcin, *Un centre musulman*, 185. Fakhr al-Dīn had the wheat transported to Cairo by his own river vessels and sold it at his own granaries (*bi-shuwanihi*). See also al-Maqrīzī, *Kitāb al-Sulūk*, vol. 1, pt. 1, 132.

18 According to al-Maqrīzī, the Jaʿāfira lived on both sides of the Nile between a point somewhat to the north of Manfalūṭ in the south and Samalūṭ (Samālūṭ) in the north as well as in some other places (*Bayān wa-l-iʿrāb ʿammā bi-arḍ Miṣr min al-Aʿrāb*, ed. by Ferdinand Wüstenfeld [Göttingen: Vandenhoeck und Ruprecht, 1847], 25). Dayrūṭ al-Sharīf, located some 30 km downstream from Manfalūṭ, falls within the range stated by al-Maqrīzī.

19 Al-Maqrīzī, *al-Mawāʿiẓ wa-l-iʿtibār fī dhikr al-khiṭaṭ wa-l-āthār*, ed. by Ayman Fuʾād Sayyid, 5 vols. in 6 pts. (London: Muʾassasat al-furqān li-l-turāth al-Islāmī, 2002–04), vol. 3, 393; idem, *Kitāb al-Sulūk*, vol. 1, pt. 1, 132, 134, 137–8, 139; Ibn ʿInaba, *ʿUmdat al-ṭālib fī ansāb Āl Abī Ṭālib*, ed. by Mahdī al-Rajāʾī (Qom: Maktabat al-Marʿashī al-Najafī, 2004), 55.

20 Ibn ʿAbd al-Zāhir, *al-Rawḍa al-bahiyya al-zāhira fī khiṭaṭ al-Muʿizziyya al-qāhira*, ed. by Ayman Fuʾād Sayyid (Cairo: Maktabat al-dār al-ʿArabiyya li-l-kitāb, 1996), 91–2; al-Maqrīzī, *al-Mawāʿiẓ wa-l-iʿtibār*, vol. 4, 481–4.

21 Al-Maqrīzī, *al-Mawāʿiẓ wa-l-iʿtibār*, vol. 3, 393–4. How this *munshaʾa* was utilized at Fakhr al-Dīn's own time cannot be known from al-Maqrīzī's account. For an account that indicates Fakhr al-Dīn's affluence (not necessarily in terms of his possessions in Cairo), see Ibn ʿAbd al-Ẓāhir, *al-Rawḍa al-bahiyya al-zāhira*, 24; al-Maqrīzī, *al-Mawāʿiẓ wa-l-iʿtibār*, vol. 3, 289–90.

22 See n. 3 above.

23 Al-Maqrīzī, *al-Mawāʿiẓ wa-l-iʿtibār*, vol. 3, 393. An assessment of whether the price is a fair one or otherwise is beyond the ability of the present author.

24 Garcin, *Un centre musulman*, 184. Garcin writes that the then Ayyubid central authorities in Cairo probably moved northwards part of the troops stationed in Upper Egypt to counter the Crusade, bringing about a favorable situation for discontents to launch a rebellion.

25 Al-Nuwayrī, *Nihāyat al-arab fī funūn al-adab*, ed. by Mufīd Qumayḥa et al., 34 vols. in 16 pts. (Beirut: Dār al-kutub al-ʿilmiyya, 2004), vol. 29, 282–3; al-Maqrīzī, *Kitāb al-Sulūk*, vol. 1, pt. 2, 388. The account in al-Qalqashandī, *Ṣubḥ al-aʿshā*, vol. 4 (Cairo: al-Maṭbaʿa al-amīriyya, 1914), 68, where Baybars is depicted as responsible not only for the execution but also for the capture, should not be made much of, as the account also reveals al-Qalqashandī's ignorance of the crucial events leading up to the capture.

26 Al-Maqrīzī, *al-Bayān wa-l-iʿrāb*, 23–4. Al-Nuwayrī reports that Fāris al-Dīn Aqṭāy brought back with him an unnamed "paternal cousin/paternal collateral relative" (*ibn ʿamm*) of Ḥiṣn al-Dīn from Upper Egypt and that the person was hung underneath the citadel of Cairo (*Nihāyat al-arab*, vol. 29, 276).

27 Ibn ʿAbd al-Zāhir, *al-Rawḍa al-bahiyya al-zāhira*, 101. Also, al-Maqrīzī, *al-Mawāʿiẓ wa-l-iʿtibār*, vol. 3, 262.

28 See Ibn ʿAbd al-Ẓāhir, *al-Rawḍa al-bahiyya al-zāhira*, 3–4 (editor's introduction) for the mentioned dates.

29 Al-Maqrīzī, *al-Kitāb al-Sulūk*, vol. 1, pt. 3, ed. by Ziyāda (Cairo: Maṭbaʿat lajnat al-taʾlīf wa-l-tarjama wa-l-nashr, 1939), 772. Earlier accounts of the same intrigue by al-Nuwayrī and Ibn al-Furāt do not include a mention of the slanderers' names (*Nihāyat al-arab*, vol. 31, 138; Ibn al-Furāt, *Taʾrīkh Ibn al-Furāt*, Vol. 8, *Sanat 683–696h.*, ed. by Qusṭanṭīn Zurayq and Najlā ʿIzz al-Dīn [Beirut: al-Maṭbaʿa al-Amīrkāniyya, 1939], vol. 8, 126).

30 Ibn ʿInaba, *ʿUmdat al-ṭālib*, 55. For Ibn ʿInaba, see my "Ibn ʿInaba," in *The Encyclopaedia of Islam Three*, ed. by Kate Fleet et al., pt. 2017.4 (Leiden and Boston: Brill, 2017), 135–7.

31 Cf. Fakhr al-Dīn: "*al-imām al-sharīf al-amīr al-ajall al-ṣadr al-kabīr al-isfahsalār al-mufaḍḍal al-mājid al-ṭāhir al-ḥasīb al-nasīb al-awḥad al-mujtabā (?) al-mukhtār al-amīr fakhr al-dīn*

ʿimād al-mulūk wa-l-salāṭīn ʿizz al-Islām wa-l-Muslimīn majd al-khilāfa sharaf al-umarāʾ ʿaḍud al-mulk rukn al-dawla wa-nāṣiruhā amīr al-ḥājj wa-l-Ḥaramayn dhū al-fakhrayn malik al-sharq nasīb amīr al-muʾminīn" (his cenotaph: Jean David Weil, *Calalogue general du Musée Arabe du Caire: Les bois à épigraphes jusqu'à l'époque mamlouke* [Cairo: Imprimerie de l'Institut Français d'Archéologie Orientale, 1931], 8); "*al-sharīf al-sayyid al-amīr al-ḥasīb al-nasīb fakhr al-dīn amīr al-ḥājj wa-l-Ḥaramayn dhū al-fakhrayn nasīb amīr al-muʾminīn*" (foundation inscription of his tomb: van Berchem, *Matériaux*, 95). Ḥiṣn al-Dīn I: "Ḥiṣn al-dawla majd al-ʿArab" (al-Maqrīzī, *Bayān wa-l-iʿrāb*, 22, 23), "Ḥiṣn al-dawla fakhr al-ʿArab" (al-Maqrīzī, *al-Mawāʿiẓ wa-l-iʿtibār*, vol. 4, 482).

32 See Garcin, *Un centre musulman*, 188, where he states "et cela en liaison avec les Bahrides réfugiés en Syrie."

33 See also A. N. Poliak's comment in "Les révoltes populaires en Égypte à l'époque des mamelouks et leurs causes économiques," *Revue des études islamiques* 8 (1934): 264: "Après la répression d'une révolte le gouvernement, la plupart du temps, s'efforçait de se concilier les cheiks et les émirs, leur concédant de nouveaux fiefs."

34 Yūsuf Rāġib, "Essai d'inventaire chronologique des guides à l'usage des pèlerins du Caire," *Revue des études islamiques* 41 (1973): 272; idem, "al-Sayyida Nafīsa, sa légende, son culte et son cimetière (suite et fin)," *Studia Islamica* 45 (1977): 28, n. 2. Rāġib calls the figure Ibn Bulūla while the spelling of the second word does not allow that reading. My reading "Ballūh" is more faithful to the spelling, but it has no particular basis. It could also be Billūh, Bullūh, or otherwise.

35 Ibn al-Nāsikh, *Miṣbāḥ al-dayājī wa-ghawth al-rājī wa-kahf al-lājī mimmā jamaʿa al-janāb al-Tājī*, MS Princeton University, Garrett 375Y, 5a; Ibn al-Zayyāt, *al-Kawākib al-sayyāra fī tartīb al-ziyāra fī l-Qarāfatayn al-Kubrā wa-l-Ṣughrā* (Miṣr: al-Maṭbaʿa al-amīriyya, 1907), 30–1; al-Sakhāwī al-Ḥanafī, *Tuḥfat al-aḥbāb wa-bughyat al-ṭullāb fī l-khiṭaṭ wa-l-mazārāt wa-l-tarājim wa-l-biqāʿ al-mubārakāt*, ed. by Abū Sahl Najāḥ ʿIwaḍ Ṣayyām (Cairo: Dār al-Muqaṭṭam, 2014), 70. The sentence referring to Ibn Ballūh's tomb in the earlier work by Ibn ʿUthmān, that is, *Murshid al-zuwwār ilā qubūr al-abrār al-musammā al-Durr al-munaẓẓam fī ziyārat al-Jabal al-Muqaṭṭam*, ed. by Muḥammad Fatḥī Abū Bakr (Cairo: al-Dār al-Miṣriyya al-Lubnāniyya, 1995), 155, is clearly a later interpolation as Ibn ʿUthmān died earlier than Ibn Ballūh in 615/1218–19 (Ibn Ballūh's period will be discussed below). The sentence in question also does not fit in well with the general context of the passages among which it is found. The relevant sentence in *al-Kawākib al-sayyāra* also appears to be a later interpolation as it also distorts the context therein. A note by the co-editors of the 1937 edition of the *Tuḥfat al-aḥbāb* may mean that the tombs of more of Ibn Ballūh's descendants (*ṭāʾifa min dhurriyyatihi wa-aḥfādihi*), including his son named al-Sayyid Ḥasan al-Mashhadī, were still extant in the mid-1930s (al-Sakhāwī al-Ḥanafī, *Tuḥfat al-aḥbāb*, ed. by Maḥmūd Rabīʿ and Ḥasan Qāsim [Cairo: M. al-ʿulūm wa-l-ādāb, 1937], 117, n. 1). None of those tombs, including Ibn Ballūh's own, is extant today according to "Shaykh Muḥammad," the custodian of al-Sayyida Sukayna complex (the mosque and the shrine). I thank Professor Junko Toriyama for visiting the complex and making inquiries for me on August 27, 2016.

36 Ibn al-Nāsikh, *Miṣbāḥ al-dayājī*, 6b, 34b; Ibn al-Zayyāt, 9, 34–5, 95, 158.

37 Ibn al-Zayyāt, *al-Kawākib al-sayyāra*, 4. Raġib, in "Essai," 272, suggests that Ibn Ballūh may have been the author of the *Murshid al-zuwwār ilā maʿrifat qubūr al-ṣaḥāba wa-ahl al-bayt al-abrār*, cited by al-Sakhāwī al-Ḥanafī in the *Tuḥfat al-aḥbāb*, ed. by Ṣayyām, 73.

38 Ibn al-Zayyāt, *al-Kawākib al-sayyāra*, 34–5; Rāġib, "al-Sayyida Nafīsa," 28, n. 2. The sentence in Ibn ʿUthmān, *Murshid al-zuwwār*, 177 which refers to Ibn Ballūh and Sharīf al-Dīn al-Jawwānī as the two important authorities who ensured the authenticity of al-Sayyida Nafīsa's tomb is clearly a later interpolation (see n. 35 above).

39 Ibn al-Zayyāt, *al-Kawākib al-sayyāra*, 30, 34; al-Sakhāwī al-Ḥanafī, *Tuḥfa*, ed. by Ṣayyām, 70.

40 Ibn al-Zayyāt, *al-Kawākib al-sayyāra*, 9, 34–5, 95, 158. In the last reference, Ibn al-Zayyāt, after stating that Ibn Ballūh mentioned the tomb of a certain woman, adds, "I do not know if she was

a *sharīfa* or not." Here, Ibn al-Zayyāt evidently presupposes that Ibn Ballūh tended to pay more attention to the members of ʿAlī's kinfolk.

41 Al-Udfuwī, *al-Ṭāliʿ al-saʿīd al-jāmiʿ asmāʾ nujabāʾ al-Ṣaʿīd*, ed. by Saʿd Muḥammad Ḥusayn (Cairo: al-Dār al-Miṣriyya li-l-taʾlīf wa-l-tarjama, 1966), 534. The genealogy of the Jaʿfarid separates from that of Najm al-Dīn ʿAlī at the generation of the grandson of Jaʿfar al-Ṭayyār. Al-Udfuwī also notes that the Jaʿfarid was reportedly a *qāḍī* in al-Qāhira. Murtaḍā al-Zabīdī (d. 1205/1791) also states that he saw a genealogy of the same Jaʿfarid in the handwriting of "*al-nassāba* Ibrāhīm b. Yaḥyā al-Mashhadī" (the *nisba* al-Mashhadī will be discussed below). Al-Zabīdī, however, mentions the year 626 as the year of the Jaʿfarid's birth, not as the date of the written attestation. Al-Zabīdī, *al-Rawḍ al-miʿṭār fī nasab al-sādat Āl Jaʿfar al-Ṭayyār*, ed. by ʿAbd Allāh Muḥammad al-Ḥusaynī (Kuwait: Dīwān al-ashrāf, 2012), 74.

42 See al-Sakhāwī al-Ḥanafī, ed. by Ṣayyām, 70 for the date of Zaynab's death.

43 See n. 41 above.

44 Al-Sakhāwī al-Ḥanafī, *Tuḥfat al-aḥbāb*, ed. by Rabīʿ and Qāsim, 117, n. 1. Rabīʿ and Qāsim do not cite the basis for their remark about Ibn Ballūh's residence in the shrine. Apparently, Rāġib simply followed the two co-editors when he also attributed Ibn Bulūla/Ballūh's *nisba* "al-Mashhadī" to Sukayna's shrine, although he referred to Ibn Ballūh's burial, instead of residence, therein ("Essai d'inventaire chronologique," 272).

45 Al-Sakhāwī al-Ḥanafī, *Tuḥfat al-aḥbāb*, ed. by Rabīʿ and Qāsim, 117, n. 1. Also, Rāġib, "Essai d'inventaire chronologique," 272, n. 6.

46 Ibn ʿInaba, *ʿUmdat al-ṭālib*, 294.

47 For the role of the Fāṭimids, see, e.g., Caroline Williams, "The Cult of ʿAlid Saints in the Fāṭimid Monuments of Cairo" ("Part I: The Mosque of al-Aqmar" and "Part II: Mausolea"), *Muqarnas* 1 (1983) and 3 (1985), in addition to Rāġib's works such as those cited in n. 34. Representative studies on the practice of tomb visitation in Cairo are Christopher S. Taylor, *In the Vicinity of the Righteous:* Ziyāra *and the Veneration of Muslim Saints in Late Medieval Egypt* (Leiden: Brill, 1999); Tetsuya Ohtoshi, *Ejiputo shisha no machi to seibo sankei: Musurimu to himusurimu no Ejiputo shakaishi* (*The City of the Dead in Egypt and the Visitation of the Holy Tombs: A Social History of Egypt beyond the Muslim–Non-Muslim Divide* [translation from the present author]) (in Japanese) (Tokyo: Yamakawa Shuppansha, 2018).

48 Morimoto, "The Notebook," 826.

49 See ibid., 826 for his uncle's role in the transmission of two well-known works on Twelver Shiʿi jurisprudence.

50 Morimoto, "An Enigmatic Genealogical Chart," 151–6. The name of the place al-Mūsawī al-Najafī visited in India, which I was not able to read in this previous article, later turned out to be بیدر, standing for Bīdar in the Deccan. I thank Professor Satoshi Ogura for suggesting the reading and sharing with me an attestation of the same spelling in a source from India. The note in which the toponym in question appears happens to be found on the very page where the diagram of the Thaʿlabids' genealogy is written and therefore can be read in Figure 1. The note is not a part of the *Genealogy of the Thaʿlabids*, however.

51 Morimoto, "Ibn ʿInaba."

52 Another piece of information that is worth noting here is the possible appearance of Ibn Abī l-Ḥadīd (586/1192–655/1257 or 656/1258), the author of the famous commentary on the *Nahj al-balāgha*, in the chain of transmission Ibrāhīm b. Yaḥyā presents at the beginning of Section II. If what is meant there is that Ibrāhīm b. Yaḥyā had direct contact with Ibn Abī l-Ḥadīd, it would most probably signify that he visited Iraq before he wrote the *Genealogy of the Thaʿlabids*. See Appendix for details.

53 Ibn al-Nāsikh, *Miṣbāj al-dayājī*, 6b.

54 A survey of a number of genealogical compendia, one on the Arabs as a whole and the rest specializing in ʿAlī's kinfolk, from the eleventh to the early fourteenth century yielded the following observations: (1) The latest lineal ascendant of Ibrāhīm b. Yaḥyā whose domicile

is noted in the genealogies is his ninth-generation ascendant, Muḥammad b. Ismāʿīl b. Aḥmad b. Ismāʿīl b. Muḥammad b. Ismāʿīl b. Jaʿfar al-Ṣādiq. Egypt and the Maghreb are the places that are mentioned as his domicile; (2) Genealogical compendia name Egypt as the representative domicile of the descendants of either the mentioned Muḥammad b. Ismāʿīl or his father Ismāʿīl. Although it is open to question to what extent these observations are relevant to considering the geographical background of Ibrāhīm b. Yaḥyā, they would suggest an Egyptian, rather than Iraqi, origin. Ibn Ḥazm, *Jamharat ansāb al-ʿArab*, ed. by ʿAbd al-Salām Muḥammad Hārūn, 5th ed. (Cairo: Dār al-maʿārif, 1982), 61 (Aḥmad, a brother of the ninth-generation ascendant Muḥammad died in "Miṣr" in 325/936–37); Fakhr al-Dīn al-Rāzī (attr.), *al-Shajara al-mubāraka fī ansāb al-Ṭālibiyya*, ed. by Mahdī al-Rajāʾī, 2nd ed. (Qom: Maktabat al-Marʿashī al-Najafī, 1998–99), 116 (the tenth-generation ascendant Ismāʿīl lived in "Miṣr" and the most of his descendants reside there); al-Marwazī al-Azwarqānī, *al-Fakhrī fī ansāb al-Ṭālibiyyīn*, ed. by Mahdī al-Rajāʾī (Qom: Maktabat al-Marʿashī al-Najafī, 1988–89), 24 (the ninth-generation ascendant Muḥammad lived in "Miṣr" and numerous descendants of his and of his two brothers are found there); Ibn al-Ṭiqṭaqā, *al-Aṣīlī*, xerox copy of a manuscript kept at the Kitābkhāna-ʾi Tārīkh-i Islām wa Īrān (Qom) under the call number 1-6-32, 64a and idem, *al-Aṣīlī fī ansāb al-Ṭālibiyyīn*, ed. by Mahdī al-Rajāʾī (Qom: Maktabat al-Marʿashī al-Najafī, 1997–98), 201 (the ninth-generation ascendant Muḥammad was a jurisprudent in the Maghreb); Ibn Muhannā al-ʿUbaydalī, *Tadhkirat al-ansāb*, MS Āstān-i Quds-i Raḍawī 3626, 70b (the same as in *al-Aṣīlī*).

55 It must, however, be noted that the truth of ʿAlī's burial in Najaf was never universally accepted by the Sunnis. See Rose Aslan, "From Body to Shrine: The Construction of Sacred Space at the Grave of ʿAlī ibn Abī Ṭālib in Najaf," Ph.D. dissertation, University of North Carolina at Chapel Hill, 2014, 112–84 (I have had no access to Khalid Sindawi, "The Grave of 'Ali b. Abi Talib: Different Views about Its Specific Location and the Locations of the Graves of Some Other Prophets Buried in It," *International Journal of Shi'i Studies* 1.2 [2003]: 37–74). Aslan's diachronic survey of relevant sources, however, leads her to note that "we can see a growing trend of hybrid scholars" (Aslan, *The Construction*, 176), that is, Sunni scholars with ʿAlid sympathies who also accept Shiʿi sources of information and thus, in this context, accept Najaf as the burial place of ʿAlī. Such "hybrid scholars" begin to appear in the thirteenth century in her survey. Aslan takes the concept of "hybrid scholars" from Mohammad Ahmad Masad's work cited in n. 79 below.

56 Ibn Ṭalḥa, *Maṭālib al-saʾūl fī manāqib Āl al-Rasūl*, ed. by ʿAbd al-ʿAzīz al-Ṭabāṭabāʾī (Beirut: Muʾassasat al-balāgh, 1999); Sibṭ Ibn al-Jawzī, *Tadhkirat al-khawāṣṣ min al-Umma bi-dhikr khaṣāʾiṣ al-aʾimma*, ed. by Ḥusayn Taqī-zāda, 2 vols. (Qom: Markaz al-ṭibāʿa wa-l-nashr li-l-Majmaʿ al-ʿĀlamī li-Ahl al-Bayt, 2005–06); al-Kanjī (al-Ganjī) al-Shāfiʿī, *Kifāyat al-ṭālib fī manāqib ʿAlī b. Abī Ṭālib*, ed. by Muḥammad-Hādī al-Amīnī, 3rd ed. (Tehran: Dār iḥyāʾ turāth Ahl al-Bayt, 1983–84). *Al-Bayān fī akhbār ṣāḥib al-zamān* is published in continuation to the *Kifāyat al-ṭālib* in the same volume.

57 The *Maṭālib al-saʾūl* is a work that presents the virtues of the Twelve Imams in twelve chapters. See p. 44 of the work for an explicit statement of Ibn Ṭalḥa's recognition of the Twelve Imams as the *Imāms* who number twelve, no more and no less. The *Tadhkirat al-khawāṣṣ*'s text deals with the virtues of ʿAlī and select members of his kinfolk not limited to the rest of the Twelve Imams (even Khadīja's virtues are dealt with). Sibṭ Ibn al-Jawzī, however, states in the preface that the work is meant to present the virtues of *Imāms* in as many chapters as their number (vol. 1, 102). The book is composed of twelve chapters, and the twelfth chapter "on the account of the *Imāms*" (*fī dhikr al-aʾimma*) comprises, in addition to an introductory section, nine sections each of which is dedicated to one of the Imams from the fourth to the twelfth (vol. 2, 373–519). Sibṭ Ibn al-Jawzī calls ʿAlī Zayn al-ʿĀbidīn "the father of the *Imāms*" (*abū l-aʾimma*), too (vol. 2, 382). The *Kifāyat al-ṭālib* is a work dedicated to ʿAlī's virtues, but it comprises a section that is dedicated to "the account of the *Imāms*" (*dhikr al-aʾimma*) in which the Imams from ʿAlī

Zayn al-ʿĀbidīn (the fourth; also called "*abū l-aʾimma al-abrār*" [439]) to Muḥammad b. al-Ḥasan (the twelfth) are dealt with (447–58). In both the *Tadhkirat al-khawāṣṣ* and the *Kifāyat al-ṭālib*, al-Ḥasan b. ʿAlī (the second) and al-Ḥusayn b. ʿAlī (the third) are deal with in separate sections before the rest of the Imams and are not called "*imām*" explicitly. They are, however, called "*amīr al-muʾminīn*" in the *Kifāyat al-ṭālib*, 413, 416. That Sibṭ Ibn al-Jawzī also regarded the two Imams as *Imāms* can be confirmed by the fact that he quotes a poem by al-Ḥaskafī (d. 551/1156–57 or 553/1158–59) in which the latter enumerates all the Twelve Imams to be his *Imāms* (*Tadhkirat al-khawāṣṣ*, vol. 2, 516–8).

58 Yaḥyā b. al-Ḥasan al-ʿAqīqī's confessional identity, which in itself constitutes a complicated question, is not relevant here.

59 The following shows how the titles and optatives (either *taṣliya* or *taslīm*) are used (*taṣliya*s and *taslīm*s are either spelled out or represented by an abbreviation). (I) In the portions other than the genealogical diagram on folio 32b: (1) *al-imām* and an optative: 30a, 30b (three instances), 36b (three instances), 38a; (2) *amīr al-muʾminīn* and an optative: 32b (but the relevant text may not be part of the treatise), 34b; (3) *al-imām* only: 35a; (4) *amīr al-muʾminīn* only: 30b; (5) an optative only: 30a, 30b (three instances), 31b, 36a (two instances, one of which being "*tazwīj ʿAlī Fāṭimata ʿalayhimā al-salām*), 38a; (6) mentions of one or more of the names of the Imams (along with Fāṭima's name in one case) without any title or optative: 30a, 30b, 36a (three instances, one of which being "*Fāṭima wa-ʿAlī*"), 37a, 38a (five instances), 38b. In all these, the instances in which the names of multiple relevant figures are mentioned in one place are counted as one. Fāṭima's name, when appearing alone, is accompanied by an optative twice on 36a and takes the form "(*al-sayyida*) Fāṭima bt. Rasūl Allāh–*Ṣ-L-ʿ-M* [abbreviation for a *taṣliya*]–" twice (36a, 38b; once with *al-sayyida* and once without). (II) In the genealogical diagram on 32b (see Figure 1): The following titles, nicknames, and optatives in abbreviations are found above and/or below the Imams' names: *al-imām*, *al-shahīd*, and a *taslīm* for al-Ḥusayn b. ʿAlī; *zayn al-ʿābidīn* and a *taslīm* for ʿAlī b. al-Ḥusayn; *al-imām*, *al-bāqir*, and a *taslīm* for Muḥammad b. ʿAlī; *al-imām*, *al-nāṭiq*, and a *taslīm* for Jaʿfar b. Muḥammad (also, *al-ṣādiq* and a *taslīm* ensue the name Jaʿfar on the main stem of the genealogy); *al-kāẓim*, *ṣāʾim al-qayẓ* (*al-qayḍ* in the text; I thank Professor Rasūl Jaʿfariyān for illuminating the correct reading to me), and *kāẓim al-ghayẓ* (*al-ghayḍ* in the text) for Mūsā b. Jaʿfar; *al-riḍā* and a *taslīm* for ʿAlī b. Mūsā; *al-imām*, *al-jawād* for Muḥammad b. ʿAlī; *al-imām*, *al-hādī*, and a *taslīm* for ʿAlī b. Muḥammad; *al-imām*, *al-ʿaskarī* for al-Ḥasan b. ʿAlī; *al-imām*, *al-qāʾim*, *al-muntaṣir*, *al-mahdī*, and a *taṣliya* for Muḥammad b. al-Ḥasan (as dealt with below in the main text). Among all these, the use of a *taṣliya* for the relevant figure(s) is attested as follows: once for the Twelve Imams as a whole (30a; spelled out; "*ṣalawāt Allāh ʿalayhim*"), once for the twelfth Imam (32b; in the genealogical diagram; in abbreviation; "*Ṣ-M*"), once for Fāṭima (36a; in abbreviation; "*Ṣ-L-ʿ-M*"), and once for ʿAlī (36b; spelled out; "*ṣalawāt Allāh ʿalayhi*").

60 *Alladhīna ṣabarū wa-awfaw bi-mā ʿāhadū Allāh ʿalayhi wa-sabaqū li-l-tashmīr fī l-ijtihād fī l-jihād wa-mā waqafū, wa-waʿadahum Allāh bi-l-tamkīn fī l-arḍ wa-waʿadū adāʾ mā ufturiḍa ʿalayhim min al-farḍ fa-mā akhlafū wa-lā ukhlifū.*

61 30b (two traditions about the Prophet's sayings, one tradition about the Prophet's deed, and one tradition reporting an Imam's utterance about the age at which Jaʿfar al-Ṭayyār died), 36b (a tradition reporting the Prophet's deed). On folio 36a is found a tradition reporting Asmāʾ bt. ʿUmays' preparation of Fāṭima's coffin that "ʿAlī b. al-Ḥusayn" transmitted from Ibn ʿAbbās.

62 The other appearances of this kind are found on folio 30b (Jaʿfar al-Ṭayyār participating with the Prophet and ʿAlī b. Abī Ṭālib in the allegedly first congregational prayer of Islam), 36a (ʿAlī b. Abī Ṭālib and Fāṭima bt. Muḥammad as the figures whose marriage offers an occasion on which the Prophet admits Asmāʾ bt. ʿUmays' virtues), 36a (Fāṭima appearing as a figure for whom Asmāʾ bt. ʿUmays made a coffin [what Asmāʾ did for Fāṭima is counted among her virtues]), 38a (ʿAlī b. Abī Ṭālib appearing in the dreams of ʿAbd Allāh b. Jaʿfar alongside the Prophet and Jaʿfar al-Ṭayyār to announce ʿAbd Allāh's death).

63 The "return of the sun" is a miracle attributed to the Prophet Muḥammad. Muḥammad purportedly made the sun move backward or pause its movement so that ʿAlī would be able to perform the afternoon prayer he was about to miss for good reason. The same or a comparable miracle to help Joshua is counted among the miracles of Moses or Joshua himself. See the references cited in n. 66 below for further details.

64 I do not consider the rest of the appearances of one or more of the Imams and/or Fāṭima in the *Genealogy of the Thaʿlabids* in need of consideration here. Those are: (1) the appearances as part of the genealogies or in the accounts of the kinship relations of their descendants or close of kins (30a [twice], 30b [twice], 38a, 38b [twice, one being Fāṭima's appearance]), (2) the appearance of ʿAlī b. Abī Ṭālib's name as that of the eponymous progenitor of the ʿAlids in an explanation of the genealogical structure of the Ṭālibids (32b; the relevant text may not be part of the treatise), (3) the appearance of ʿAlī b. Abī Ṭālib as the figure who washed Fāṭima's corpse with Asmāʾ bt. ʿUmays (36a; the act of washing the corpse is counted among Asmāʾ's virtues), (4) the appearance of ʿAlī b. Abī Ṭālib as the leader of the Muslim Community who accepted a landlord's petition through the mediation of ʿAbd Allāh b. Jaʿfar (37a; that ʿAbd Allāh acted as the mediator without asking for a remuneration is counted among his virtues), (5) the appearance of al-Ḥasan b. ʿAlī and al-Ḥusayn b. ʿAlī, along with ʿAbd Allāh b. al-ʿAbbās, as the people counted as "the generous among the Hāshimids" (*sukhāt Banī Hāshim*) besides ʿAbd Allāh b. Jaʿfar (38a), (6) the appearance of al-Ḥusayn b. ʿAlī as the figure with whom an early Jaʿfarid (ʿAwn b. Jaʿfar) was killed at Karbalāʾ (38a). The items from (3) to (5) take place in the texts of the traditions cited in Section II. A passage I have no clear idea how to deal with is the one where the saying "A man's religious belief never becomes perfect as long as he does not wish for his fellow what he wishes for himself" (*lā yakmulu īmān al-marʾ ḥattā yuḥibba li-akhīhi mā yuḥibbu li-nafsihi*) is attributed to a figure whose name is missing in Or. 1406 but the reference to whom is followed by a *taslīm* (i.e., "*qāla ʿalayhi al-salām*") (31b). This passage, about whose attributability to Ibrāhīm b. Yaḥyā there is no reason to doubt, appears to attribute the saying to an Imam (ʿAlī b. Abī Ṭālib?). I have, however, not been able to confirm a case in which the saying exactly in this wording is attributed to an Imam even in Twelver Shiʿi literature (I rely in this statement mostly on the website *Maktabat Madrasat al-Faqāha* [https://ar.lib.eshia.ir/ accessed July 1, 2022]).

65 For the recognition of the twelfth Imam's status as the Savior of the end times by the three Sunni authors, see Ibn Ṭalḥa, *Maṭālib al-saʾūl*, 311–21; Sibṭ Ibn al-Jawzī, *Tadhkirat al-khawāṣṣ*, vol. 2, 505–15; al-Kanjī, *Kifāyat al-ṭālib*, 458; idem, *al-Bayān fī akhbār ṣāḥib al-zamān*, 473–532; Wilferd Madelung, "al-Mahdī," in *The Encyclopaedia of Islam, New Edition*, ed. by H. A. R. Gibb et al., 13 vols. (Leiden: Brill, 1960–2009), vol. 5, 1236–7. The appellations Ibn Ṭalḥa uses are cited from *Maṭālib al-saʾūl*, 311. The phrases I added to the appellations for better comprehension reflect the usual Twelver Shiʿi understandings and might not accord with how Ibn Ṭalḥa understood those appellations.

66 Sibṭ Ibn al-Jawzī, *Tadhkirat al-khawāṣṣ*, vol. 1, 334–43; al-Kanjī, *Kifāyat al-ṭālib*, 381–8. An additional point with regards the treatment of the "return of the sun" miracle in the *Genealogy of the Thaʿlabids* is that the relevant passage displays a meaningful difference from a passage in al-Jawwānī's *al-Muqaddima al-fāḍiliyya* from which it derives (*al-Muqaddima al-fāḍliliyya*, 123). While the passage in *al-Muqaddima al-fāḍiliyya* allows the reading that Yūshaʿ is compared to ʿAlī in terms of their shared status as a legatee (*waṣī*) and a *fatā* (in the sense of a servant or younger companion) of a prophet (Mūsā and Muḥammad, respectively), the passage in the *Genealogy of the Thaʿlabids*, although still presenting Yūshaʿ as Mūsā's legatee and successor (*khalīfa*), compares the two figures only in terms of the occurrences of the same kind of miracle for both of them. In short, the passage in the *Genealogy of the Thaʿlabids* is a passage taken from a Sunni work that is modified in a way that makes it less reminiscent of a Twelver Shiʿi position. All the three Sunni authors count "legatee" (*waṣī*) among the appellations appropriate for ʿAlī, although their understandings of the term are evidently not the same (Ibn Ṭalḥa, *Maṭālib al-saʾūl*, 66; Sibt Ibn al-Jawzī, *Tadhkirat al-khawāṣṣ*, vol. 1, 123, 308; al-Kanjī, *Kifāyat al-ṭālib*, 260–2).

67 Al-Kanjī, *Kifāyat al-ṭālib*, 447; Ibn Ṭalḥa, *Maṭālib al-sa'ūl*, 267; Sibṭ Ibn al-Jawzī, *Tadhkirat al-khawāṣṣ*, vol. 2, 384.

68 Ibn Ṭalḥa, *Maṭālib al-sa'ūl*, 32. "*Fa-aḥsanumā naẓamathu aqlām al-afhām* [. . .] *ta'līf li-Āl al-Muṣṭfā a'immat al-hudā*."

69 For different attitudes taken by scholars and non-scholars of different confessional orientations towards the use of *taṣliya* and *taslīm* for people other than the Prophet Muḥammad, other prophets, and angels, see Ignaz Goldziher, "Ueber die Eulogien der Muhammadaner," *Zeitschrift der Deutschen Morgenländischen Gesellschaft*, 50 (1896): 97–128.

70 Goldziher cites interesting instances of such modifications in relation to the *taṣliya* and *taslīm* in "Ueber die Eulogien," 124–6. The attachment of the above-mentioned appellations and the *taṣliya* to the name of the twelfth Imam in the genealogical diagram on 32b, along with the attachment of comparable elements to names of the other relevant Imams therein (see n. 59 above), might also represent later additions or modifications, although it is certainly unlikely that Ibrāhīm b. Yaḥyā put down the Imams' names without any additional appellations in the diagram.

71 Taqī-zāda pays conscious attention to noting the variations in the use of optatives, too.

72 Sibṭ Ibn al-Jawzī, *Tadhkirat al-khawāṣṣ*, vol. 1, 58. The manuscript in question is the one numbered five and allocated the abbreviation *nūn* by Taqī-zāda. Taqī-zāda notes that *taṣliya*s in the manuscript do not include mention of the Prophet's kinfolk (*āl*), that is, they read "*ṣallā Allāh 'alayhi wa-sallama*" instead of "*ṣallā Allāh 'alayhi wa-ālihi* (or *wa-'alā ālihi*) *wa-sallama*."

73 The frequent appearances of "*imām*," "*amīr al-mu'minīn*," and the *taslīm* are also attested in the *Maṭālib al-sa'ūl*, *Kifāyat al-ṭālib*, and *al-Bayān fī akhbār ṣāḥib al-zamān* as represented by the respective editions used in this study.

74 Sibṭ Ibn al-Jawzī, *Tadhkirat al-khawāṣṣ*, vol. 1, 103, n. 10. The other instance of the use of *taṣliya* in relation to one or more of the Imams and/or Fāṭima noted by Taqī-zāda (vol. 2, 64, n. 3) is the use of "*ṣalawāt Allāh 'alayhi*" for the second Imam, in one manuscript with unclear provenance from the early seventeenth century.

75 Only the *Kifāyat al-ṭālib* among the three works by the two remaining Sunni authors, all represented by the respective editions used in this study, comprises instances of relevant use of the *taṣliya*: "*ṣalawāt Allāh 'alayhim*" for 'Alī, Fāṭima, al-Ḥasan, and al-Ḥusayn on page 96 and the same phrase for the group comprising 'Alī, Fāṭima, and 'Alī's children/descendants (*awlāduhu*) on page 202. Comparable uses are, however, attested in the contemporary work by the Sunni Ibn Khallikān, that is, *Wafayāt al-a'yān wa-anbā' abnā' al-zamān*, ed. by Iḥsān 'Abbās, 8 vols. (Beirut: Dār al-thaqāfa, n.d.), vol. 2, 65, 66 ("*ṣalawāt Allāh 'alayhā*" for Fāṭima in both places), to mention but a sample. It would appear that the *taṣliya* in nominal sentence is less prohibiting to be used for figures other than the prophets and angels than the one in verbal sentence (i.e., the one beginning with "*ṣallā Allāh*"). On another note, among five *taṣliya*s used for the Prophet Muḥammad and spelled out (i.e., not represented by an abbreviation that obliterates minor differences) in the *Genealogy of the Tha'labids* as represented in Or. 1406, three include mention of the Prophet's kinfolk (*āl*) and two do not (32b, 34a, 35b, 37a, 38a; the count does not include the *taṣliya* found in the invocations at the beginning of the treatise [30a] as a *taṣliya* in that position customarily includes such a mention regardless of the author's/copyists' orientation(s) and the one whose text is clipped after the first two words [33b]).

76 Worthy of note here is the mention of Fāṭima's name in the diagrammatic genealogy of the Prophet Muḥammad on folio 32b. Her name, clearly an addition to the original by al-Mūsawī al-Najafī himself (see Figure 1 for its location in the diagram), is accompanied by the same abbreviation to stand for a *taṣliya* as the one attached to the name of the twelfth Imam on the same page (namely, "*Ṣ-M*"; along with three nicknames). I did not include this mention in the enumeration in n. 59 above, as it clearly cannot be considered to be appearing in the text per se of the *Genealogy of the Tha'labids*.

77 Morimoto, "Sayyid Ibn 'Abd al-Ḥamīd," esp., 673–83.

78 It might be worth remembering here that Najm al-Dīn's great-grandfather Fakhr al-Dīn Ismāʿīl was no doubt Shāfiʿī in school of law, at least publicly, as shown by his founding a madrasa for its members. A typically improper behavior I have in mind when I refer to a proper behavior, of course, is to vilify the Companions of the Prophet, especially the first two caliphs.

79 The earliest written materials Muḥammad-Taqī Dānish-pazhūh and Rasūl Jaʿfariyān referred to as representing what they named "Twelver [or Twelve-Imami] Sunnis" (*Sunniyān-i Dawāzda-Imāmī*) and "Twelver [or Twelve-Imami] Sunnism" (*Tasannun-i Dawāzda-Imāmī*) respectively date from the twelfth century (Dānish-pazhūh, "Intiqād-i kitāb: *Kashf al-ḥaqāyiq*," *Farhang-i Īrān-Zamīn* 13 [1965–66]: 307–8; Jaʿfariyān, *Tārīkh-i Tashayyuʿ dar Īrān: Az āghāz tā pāyān-i qarn-i nuhum-i hijrī*, 2 vols. [Tehran: Nashr-i ʿilm, 2015–16], vol. 2, 1362–78). Mohammad Ahmad Masad in "The Medieval Islamic Apocalyptic Tradition: Divination, Prophecy and the End of Time in the 13th Century Eastern Mediterranean," Ph.D. dissertation, Washington University in Saint Louis, 2008 discusses the devotion to the Twelve Imams that such Sunni scholars as Ibn Ṭalḥa and al-Kanjī manifested in their works as a phenomenon deeply connected to their interest in apocalypse, divination, and occult sciences (see, esp., 95–166). Emphasizing the supra-confessional nature of such interest, Masad calls the relevant scholars " 'hybrid' Muslim scholars" (159) and scholars with "mixed Sunni-Shiʿi loyalties" (162). For a recent discussion of Ibn Ṭalḥa's *Maṭālib al-saʾūl*, in which the work is characterized to represent "the general intellectual tendency to the Shiʿitisation of Sunnism" (41), see Andrew C. S. Peacock "Politics, Religion and the Occult in the Works of Kamal al-Din Ibn Talha, a Vizier, *ʿAlim* and Author in Thirteenth-Century Syria," in *Syria in Crusader Times: Conflict and Coexistence*, ed. by Carole Hillenbrand (Edinburgh: Edinburgh University Press, 2020), 38–43. Stephennie Mulder, in a different vein, argues that a political aim to win over the strong Twelver Shiʿi community in Aleppo lay behind the *taṣliya*s for the Twelve Imams inscribed visibly at two ʿAlid shrines in that city under the patronage of the Ayyubid rulers al-Ẓāhir (r. 582/1186–613/1216) and al-ʿAzīz (r. 613/1216–634/1236) (*The Shrines of the ʿAlids in Medieval Syria: Sunnis, Shiʿis and the Architecture of Coexistence* [Edinburgh: Edinburgh University Press, 2014], 63–113). Except for in Mulder's thesis, why the Twelve Imams came to be singled out for special devotion among the numerous figures belonging to ʿAlī's kinfolk is not clearly explained.

80 Not all traditions are accompanied by a chain of transmission while some figures appear multiple times in relevant positions.

81 (1) Salma b. Musayyab (36a, 37b; cf. Abū l-Faraj al-Iṣfahānī, *Kitāb al-Aghānī*, ed. by Maktab Taḥqīq Dār Iḥyāʾ al-Turāth al-ʿArabī, 25 vols. in 13 pts. [Beirut: Dār iḥyāʾ al-turāth al-ʿArabī, 1994], vol. 12, 423), (2) al-Ḥusayn b. Muḥammad (38a; cf. al-Isfahānī, *al-Aghānī*, vol. 12, 426), (3) Bakr b. ʿAbd al-Wahhāb (30 b [two instances], 36a; cf. al-Ḥākim al-Naysābūrī, *al-Mustadrak ʿalā al-Ṣaḥīḥayn*, ed. by Muṣṭafā ʿAbd al-Qādir ʿĀṭā, 5 vols., 2nd ed. [Beirut: Dār al-kutub al-ʿilmiyya, 2002], vol. 3, 177), (4) Dāwūd b. al-Qāsim al-Jaʿfarī (30b [three instances]; cf. al-Shaykh al-Ṣadūq, *al-Khiṣāl*, ed. by ʿAlī Akbar al-Ghaffārī, 2 vols. [Qom: Muʾassasat al-nashr al-Islāmī, Jamāʿat al-Mudarrisīn, 1983], vol. 1, 76–7).

82 (5) al-Ḥasan b. ʿAlī al-Jalūdī (35b; see al-Iṣfahānī, *al-Aghānī*, vol. 12, 422), (6) Hārūn b. Mūsā al-Farwī (30b, 35b; see al-Mizzī, *Tahdhīb al-Kamāl fī asmāʾ al-rijāl*, ed. by Bashshār ʿAwwād Maʿrūf, 35 vols. [Beirut: Muʾassasat al-risāla, 1992], vol. 30, 115), (7) Zubayr b. Bakr (read Bakkār) (36b [three instances], 37a; see al-Iṣfahānī, *al-Aghānī*, vol. 9, 13 and cf. *op. cit.*, vol. 12, 423), (8) Abū l-Ḥasan Bakkār b. Aḥmad al-Azdī (36a; see al-Shaykh al-Mufīd, *al-Irshād fī maʿrifat ḥujaj Allāh ʿalā al-ʿibād*, ed. by Muʾassasat Āl al-Bayt li-iḥyāʾ al-turāth, 2 vols., 2nd ed. [Beirut: Muʾassasat Āl al-Bayt li-iḥyāʾ al-turāth, 2008], vol. 2, 171), (9) Ismāʿīl b. Yaʿqūb (36b; see al-Iṣfahānī, *al-Aghānī*, vol. 1, 204, 267).

83 (10) ʿAlī b. ʿAbd al-ʿAzīz (37a; see al-Dhahabī, *Siyar aʿlām al-nubalāʾ*, vol. 13, ed. by Shuʿayb al-Arnāʾūṭ and ʿAlī Abū Zayd, 9th ed. [Beirut: Muʾassasat al-risāla, 1993], 348–9 [al-Baghawī al-Makkī; 190s/805–15—286/899–900 or 287/900–01]), (11) Aḥmad b. ʿAbd Allāh (37a; transmitting the tradition therein from Naṣr b. Muzāḥim al-Minqarī [d. 212/827–28; see C. E.

Bosworth, "Naṣr b. Muzāḥim," in *The Encyclopaedia of Islam, New Edition*, ed. by H. A. R. Gibb et al., 13 vols. [Leiden: Brill, 1960–2009], vol. 7, 1015).

84 It is true that the periods of four others of the relevant figures (transmitting four traditions altogether) are (or appear to be) too early for them to have had direct contact with Yaḥyā b. al-Ḥasan: (12) Abū Uways al-Madanī (30b; see al-Mizzī, *Tahdhīb al-Kamāl*, vol. 15, 166–71 [d. 167/783–84]), (13) al-Aʿmash (36b; see al-Mizzī, *Tahdhīb al-Kamāl*, vol. 12, 76–91 [d. 148/765–66 or 147/764–65]), (14) Muḥammad b. Muslim (36a ["*wa-bi-l-isnād ʿan*]; see Ibn Abī l-Ḥadīd, *Sharḥ Nahj al-balāgha*, vol. 15, ed. by Muḥammad Abū l-Faḍl Ibrāhīm, 2nd ed. [[Cairo]: Dār iḥyāʾ al-kutub al-ʿArabiyya, ʿĪsā al-Bābī al-Ḥalabī, 1967], 71–3 [transmitting the same tradition as found in the *Genealogy of the Thaʿlabids* to al-Wāqidī [d. 207/822]), (15) Ḥafṣ b. Ghiyāth (36a; see al-Mizzī, *Tahdhīb al-Kamāl*, vol. 7. 56–70 [d. 194/809–10, 195/810–11, or 196/811–12]), (16) Muṣʿab b. ʿUthmān (38a; see al-Iṣfahānī, *al-Aghānī*, vol. 15, 6 [transmitting to al-Zubayr b. Bakkār, 172/788–89—256/870]). This, however, should be due to faulty presentation of the chains of transmission or loss of the relevant portions of the text in the transmission process. I have not been able to identify the remaining three figures: (17) Aḥmad b. ʿUthmān b. Aḥmad b. Yaḥyā (30b; transmitting from Yūsuf b. Yaʿqūb), (18) Ibrāhīm b. ʿAlī (30b; transmitting from his father who transmitted from Muḥammad b. Isḥāq [d. in or around 150/767]), and (19) al-Ḥasan b. ʿAlī (38a; "*wa-bi-l-isnād ḥaddathanā al-Ḥasan b. ʿAlī qāla ḥaddathanā Shurayḥ qāla ḥaddathanā Ismāʿīl b. Majd al-Dīn ʿan abīhi ʿan al-Shaʿbī*"; this chain of transmission is evidently corrupted).

85 It is beyond the scope of this study to make a precise comparison with other works, such as Ibn Funduq's *Lubāb al-ansāb*, where materials apparently deriving from the same collection are cited (ʿAlī b. Zayd al-Bayhaqī [Ibn Funduq], *Lubāb al-ansāb wa-l-alqāb wa-l-aʿqāb*, ed. by Mahdī al-Rajāʾī, in 2 pts. [Qom: Maktabat al-Marʿashī al-Najafī, 1989–90], 361–5]).

86 عبد الخير in the manuscript.

87 See the studies cited in n. 9 above.

88 For Abū ʿAbd Allāh Muḥammad b. Ibrāhīm b. Thābit, better known as Ibn al-Kīzānī (d. 562/1166–67), see Ibn Khallikān, *Wafayāt al-aʿyān*, vol. 4, 461–2; al-Ṣafadī, *al-Wāfī bi-l-wafayāt*, vol. 1, ed. by Helmut Ritter (Wiesbaden: Franz Steiner, 1962), 347–50; ʿAlī b. Yūsuf al-Qifṭī, *al-Muḥammadūn min al-shuʿarāʾ wa-ashʿāruhum*, ed. by Ḥasan Muʿammirī (Riyadh: Dār al-Yamāma li-l-baḥth wa-l-tarjama wa-l-nashr, [1970]), 111–3; al-ʿImād al-Iṣfahānī al-Kātib, *Kharīdat al-qaṣr wa-jarīdat al-ʿaṣr, qism shuʿarāʾ Miṣr*, ed. by Aḥmad Amīn, Shawqī Ḍayf and Iḥsān ʿAbbās, 2 vols., 1951, repr. (Cairo: Maṭbaʿat Dār al-Kutub wa-l-Wathāʾiq al-Qawmiyya, 2005), vol. 2, 18–40; al-Maqrīzī, *Kitāb al-Muqaffā al-kabīr*, ed. by Muḥammad al-Yaʿlāwī, 8 vols. (Beirut: Dār al-gharb al-Islāmī, 1991), vol. 5, 81–2; Ibn al-Nāsikh, *Miṣbāḥ al-dayājī*, 89b–90a; Ibn al-Zayyāt, *al-Kawākib al-sayyāra*, 303–4; al-Sakhāwī al-Ḥanafī, *Tuḥfat al-aḥbāb*, ed. by Ṣayyām, 302. Ibn al-Kīzānī held minority religious views (the pre-existence of human acts ["*afʿāl al-ʿibād qadīma*"] and anthropomorphism) and his corpse was exhumed, about twenty years after his death, from his original tomb near al-Shāfiʿī's mausoleum to be moved away to a new tomb. Although he did not enjoy universal acceptance in Sunni-dominated Egypt, he continued to be recorded as an outstanding Sufi, preacher, and poet and his new tomb continued to be visited. For the record of al-Jawwānī's transmission of al-Zubayr b. Bakkār's *Jamharat nasab Quraysh wa-akhbāruhā* from al-Kīzānī, see al-Jawwānī, *al-Muqaddima al-fāḍiliyya*, 14 (intro.). For Abū l-Ḥasan al-Mawṣilī, better known as Farrāʾ or Ibn Farrāʾ (433/1041–519/1125), see al-Silafī, *Muʿjam al-safar*, ed. by ʿAbd Allāh ʿUmar al-Bārūdī (Beirut: Dār al-fikr, 1993), 297–8 (al-Silafī studied al-Mālikī's *al-Mujālasa* under al-Mawṣilī); al-Dhahabī, *Siyar aʿlām al-nubalāʾ*, vol. 19, ed. by Shuʿayb Arnāʾūṭ, 11th ed. (Beirut: Muʾassasat al-risāla, 1996), 500–1.

89 A transmission path that is identical to the one shown by the portion of the chain of transmission from the figure (6) to Yaḥyā b. al-Ḥasan ([9]) is attached to an anecdote (also found in the *Genealogy of the Thaʿlabids* [37a]) cited in the biographical notice of ʿAbd Allāh b. Jaʿfar al-Ṭayyār as evidence of ʿAbd Allāh's largesse in Ibn ʿAsākir's *Taʾrīkh madīnat Dimashq* (ed. by ʿUmar b.

Gharāma al-ʿAmrawī, 80 vols. [Beirut: Dār al-fikr, 1995], vol. 27, 270). Ibn ʿAsākir apparently found no problem in citing a material transmitted through that path insomuch as such a subject was concerned. See also Ibn ʿAsākir, *Taʾrīkh madīnat Dimashq*, vol. 11, 373, vol. 70, 127; Abū Bakr al-Bayhaqī, *al-Jāmiʿ li-shuʿab al-īmān*, ed. by ʿAbd al-ʿAlī ʿAbd al-Ḥamīd Ḥāsid and Mukhtār Aḥmad al-Nadawī, 14 vols. (Riyadh: Maktabat al-rushd, 2003), vol. 3, 135. For information concerning the portion of the chain of transmission from (10) to (14), see Ibn Ḥajar al-ʿAsqalānī, *Lisān al-mīzān*, ed. by ʿAbd al-Fattāḥ Abū l-Ghudda, 10 vols. (Beirut: Maktab al-maṭbūʿāt al-Islāmiyya, 2002), vol. 5, 57–8; al-Dāraquṭnī, *Sunan al-Dāraquṭnī*, ed. by Shuʿayb al-Arnāʾūṭ et al., 6 vols. (Beirut: Muʾassasat al-risāla, 2004), vol. 5, 392; al-Mizzī, *Tahdhīb al-Kamāl*, vol. 5, 107, vol. 12, 51, vol. 18, 338, vol. 20, 74. I have not been able to confirm a record of the link between figures (12) and (13).

90 It is impossible that Yaḥyā b. al-Ḥasan in the ninth century would have transmitted anything from a figure with a *laqab* "X al-Dīn," as such titles came to be used much later.

91 Ibn Abī l-Ḥadīd, *Sharḥ Nahj al-balāgha*, vol. 15, 71–3. The first tradition in the *Genealogy of the Thaʿlabids* is presented on vol. 15, 72 on the authority of "Jaʿfar b. Muḥammad *ʿan abīhi*," that is, on the same authority as found in the *Genealogy of the Thaʿlabids* [30b], but with a different wording.

92 For ʿAṭāʾ b. Abī Rabāḥ (27?/647–48?–114/732–33, 115/733–34, or 117/735–36) and his relation with Jaʿfar al-Ṣādiq (80/699–700 or 83/702–03—148/765), see al-Mizzī, *Tahdhīb al-Kamāl*, vol. 20, 70, 73.

Bibliography

Aslan, Rose. "From Body to Shrine: The Construction of Sacred Space at the Grave of ʿAlī ibn Abī Ṭālib in Najaf." Ph.D. dissertation, University of North Carolina at Chapel Hill, 2014.

Al-Bayhaqī, Abū Bakr. *Al-Jāmiʿ li-shuʿab al-īmān*. Ed. by ʿAbd al-ʿAlī ʿAbd al-Ḥamīd Ḥāsid and Mukhtār Aḥmad al-Nadawī. 14 vols. Riyadh: Maktabat al-rushd, 2003.

Berchem, Max van. *Matériaux pour un corpus inscritionum arabicarum*, Première partie, *Egypte*, published as *Mémoires publiés par les membres de la Mission Archéologique Française au Caire*, Tome dix-neuvième. Paris: Ernest Leroux, 1903.

Bosworth, C. E. "Naṣr b. Muzāḥim." In *The Encyclopaedia of Islam, New Edition*. Ed. by H. A. R. Gibb et al. 13 vols. Leiden: Brill, 1960–2009, vol. 7, 1015.

Büssow-Schmitz, Sarah. *Die Beduinen der Mamluken: Beduinen im politischen Leben Ägyptens im 8./14. Jahrhundert.* Wiesbaden: Ludwig Reichert Verlag, 2016.

Garcin, Claude. *Un centre musulman de la Haute-Égypte médiévale: Qūṣ*. [Cairo]: Institut Français d'Archéologie Orientale du Caire, 1976.

Dānish-pazhūh, Muḥammad-Taqī. "Intiqād-i kitāb: *Kashf al-ḥaqāyiq*." *Farhang-i Īrān-Zamīn* 13 (1965–66): 298–310.

Al-Dāraquṭnī. *Sunan al-Dāraquṭnī*. Ed. by Shuʿayb al-Arnāʾūṭ et al. 6 vols. Beirut: Muʾassasat al-risāla, 2004.

Al-Dhahabī. *Siyar aʿlām al-nubalāʾ*, vol. 13. Ed. by Shuʿayb al-Arnāʾūṭ and ʿAlī Abū Zayd. 9th ed. Beirut: Muʾassasat al-risāla, 1993; vol. 19. Ed. by Shuʿayb Arnāʾūṭ. 11th ed. Beirut: Muʾassasat al-risāla, 1996.

Goldziher, Ignaz. "Ueber die Eulogien der Muhammadaner." *Zeitschrift der Deutschen Morgenländischen Gesellschaft*, 50 (1896): 97–128.

Al-Ḥākim al-Naysābūrī. *Al-Mustadrak ʿalā al-Ṣaḥīḥayn*. Ed. by Muṣṭafā ʿAbd al-Qādir ʿAṭā. 5 vols. 2nd ed. Beirut: Dār al-kutub al-ʿilmiyya, 2002.

Hartmann, Richard. "Politische Geographie des Mamlūkenreichs: Kapitel 5 und 6 des Staatshandbuchs Ibn Faḍlallāh al-'Omarī's." *Zeitschrift der Deutschen Morgenländischen Gesellschaft* 70 (1916): 1–40, 477–511.

Ibn ʿAbd al-Ẓāhir. *Al-Rawḍa al-bahiyya al-zāhira fī khiṭaṭ al-Muʿizziyya al-qāhira*. Ed. by Ayman Fuʾād Sayyid. Cairo: Maktabat al-dār al-ʿArabiyya li-l-kitāb, 1996.

Ibn Abī l-Ḥadīd. *Sharḥ Nahj al-balāgha*, vol. 15. Ed. by Muḥammad Abū l-Faḍl Ibrāhīm. 2nd ed. [Cairo]: Dār iḥyāʾ al-kutub al-ʿArabiyya, ʿĪsā al-Bābī al-Ḥalabī, 1967.

Ibn ʿAsākir. *Taʾrīkh madīnat Dimashq*. Ed. by ʿUmar b. Gharāma al-ʿAmrawī. 80 vols. Beirut: Dār al-fikr, 1995.

Ibn Funduq, ʿAlī b. Zayd al-Bayhaqī. *Lubāb al-ansāb wa-l-alqāb wa-l-aʿqāb*. Ed. by Mahdī al-Rajāʾī. In 2 pts. Qom: Maktabat al-Marʿashī al-Najafī, 1989–90.

Ibn al-Furāt. *Taʾrīkh Ibn al-Furāt*, Vol. 8, *Sanat 683–696h*. Ed. by Qusṭanṭīn Zurayq and Najlā ʿIzz al-Dīn. Beirut: al-Maṭbaʿa al-Amīrkāniyya, 1939.

Ibn Ḥajar al-ʿAsqalānī. *Lisān al-mīzān*. Ed. by ʿAbd al-Fattāḥ Abū l-Ghudda. 10 vols. Beirut: Maktab al-maṭbūʿāt al-Islāmiyya, 2002.

Ibn Ḥazm. *Jamharat ansāb al-ʿArab*. Ed. by ʿAbd al-Salām Muḥammad Hārūn. 5th ed. Cairo: Dār al-maʿārif, 1982.

Ibn ʿInaba. *ʿUmdat al-ṭālib fī ansāb Āl Abī Ṭālib*. Ed. by Mahdī al-Rajāʾī. Qom: Maktabat al-Marʿashī al-Najafī, 2004.

Ibn Khallikān. *Wafayāt al-aʿyān wa-anbāʾ abnāʾ al-zamān*. Ed. by Iḥsān ʿAbbās. 8 vols. Beirut: Dār al-thaqāfa, n.d.

Ibn al-Nāsikh. *Miṣbāḥ al-dayājī wa-ghawth al-rājī wa-kahf al-lājī mimmā jamaʿa al-janāb al-Tājī*. MS Princeton University, Garrett 375Y.

Ibn Ṭalḥa al-Naṣībī al-Shāfiʿī. *Maṭālib al-saʾūl fī manāqib Āl al-Rasūl*. Ed. by ʿAbd al-ʿAzīz al-Ṭabāṭabāʾī. Beirut: Muʾassasat al-balāgh, 1999.

Ibn al-Ṭiqṭaqā. *Al-Aṣīlī*. Xerox copy of a manuscript kept at the Kitābkhāna-ʾi Tārīkh-i Islām wa Īrān (Qom) under the call number 1-6-32; *Al-Aṣīlī fī ansāb al-Ṭālibiyyīn*. Ed. by Mahdī al-Rajāʾī. Qom: Maktabat al-Marʿashī al-Najafī, 1997–98.

Ibn ʿUthmān. *Murshid al-zuwwār ilā qubūr al-abrār al-musammā al-Durr al-munaẓẓam fī ziyārat al-Jabal al-Muqaṭṭam*. Ed. by Muḥammad Fatḥī Abū Bakr. Cairo: al-Dār al-Miṣriyya al-Lubnāniyya, 1995.

Ibn al-Zayyāt. *Al-Kawākib al-sayyāra fī tartīb al-ziyāra fī l-Qarāfatayn al-Kubrā wa-l-Ṣughrā*. Miṣr: al-Maṭbaʿa al-Amīriyya, 1907.

Ibrāhīm b. ʿAlī [sic]. *Al-Shajara al-Muḥammadiyya*. Ed. by Muḥammad-Ḥusayn al-Ḥusaynī al-Jalālī. Chicago: The Open School, 2001–02.

Al-ʿImād al-Iṣfahānī al-Kātib. *Kharīdat al-qaṣr wa-jarīdat fī l-ʿaṣr, qism shuʿarāʾ Miṣr*. Ed. by Aḥmad Amīn, Shawqī Ḍayf and Iḥsān ʿAbbās. 2 vols. 1951. Repr. Cairo: Maṭbaʿat Dār al-Kutub wa-l-Wathāʾiq al-Qawmiyya, 2005.

Al-Iṣfahānī, Abū l-Faraj. *Kitāb al-Aghānī*. Ed. by Maktab Taḥqīq Dār Iḥyāʾ al-Turāth al-ʿArabī. 25 vols. in 13 pts. Beirut: Dār iḥyāʾ al-turāth al-ʿArabī, 1994.

Jaʿfariyān, Rasūl. *Tārīkh-i Tashayyuʿ dar Īrān: Az āghāz tā pāyān-i qarn-i nuhum-i hijrī*. 2 vols. Tehran: Nashr-i ʿilm, 2015–16.

Al-Jawwānī. *Al-Muqaddima al-fāḍiliyya*. Ed. by Turkī b. Muṭlaq al-Qaddāḥ al-ʿUtaybī. Riyadh: Maṭābiʿ al-Ḥumaydī, 2006.

Al-Kanjī (al-Ganjī) al-Shāfiʿī. *Al-Bayān fī akhbār ṣāḥib al-zamān*. Published in continuation to al-Kanjī, *Kifāyat al-ṭālib*.

Al-Kanjī (al-Ganjī) al-Shāfiʿī. *Kifāyat al-ṭālib fī manāqib ʿAlī b. Abī Ṭālib*. Ed. by Muḥammad-Hādī al-Amīnī. 3rd ed. Tehran: Dār iḥyāʾ turāth Ahl al-Bayt, 1983–84.

Madelung, Wilferd. "al-Mahdī." In *The Encyclopaedia of Islam, New Edition*. Ed. by H. A. R. Gibb et al. 13 vols. Leiden: Brill, 1960–2009, vol. 5, 1230–8.

Al-Maqrīzī. *Al-Bayān wa-l-iʿrāb ʿammā bi-arḍ Miṣr min al-Aʿrāb*. Ed. by Ferdinand Wüstenfeld. Göttingen: Vandenhoeck und Ruprecht, 1847.

Al-Maqrīzī. *Al-Mawāʿiẓ wa-l-iʿtibār fī dhikr al-khiṭaṭ wa-l-āthār*. Ed. by Ayman Fuʾād Sayyid. 5 vols. in 6 pts. London: Muʾassasat al-furqān li-l-turāth al-Islāmī, 2002–04.

Al-Maqrīzī. *Kitāb al-Muqaffā al-kabīr*. Ed. by Muḥammad al-Yaʿlāwī. 8 vols. Beirut: Dār al-gharb al-Islāmī, 1991.

Al-Maqrīzī. *Kitāb al-Sulūk li-maʿrifat duwal al-mulūk*, vol. 1, pt. 1. Ed. by Muḥammad Muṣṭafā Ziyāda. 2nd ed. Cairo: Maṭbaʿat lajnat al-taʾlīf wa-l-tarjama wa-l-nashr, 1956; vol. 1, pt. 2. Ed. by Ziyāda. Cairo: Maṭbaʿat Dār al-Kutub al-Miṣriyya, 1936; vol. 1, pt. 3. Ed. by Ziyāda. Cairo: Maṭbaʿat lajnat al-taʾlīf wa-l-tarjama wa-l-nashr, 1939.

Al-Marwazī al-Azwarqānī. *Al-Fakhrī fī ansāb al-Ṭālibiyyīn*. Ed. by Mahdī al-Rajāʾī. Qom: Maktabat al-Marʿashī al-Najafī, 1988–89.

Masad, Mohammad Ahmad. "The Medieval Islamic Apocalyptic Tradition: Divination, Prophecy and the End of Time in the 13th Century Eastern Mediterranean." Ph.D. dissertation, Washington University in Saint Louis, 2008.

Matsuda, Toshimichi. "The Revolts of ʿurbān in Upper Egypt under the Baḥrī Mamlūks" (in Japanese). *Tōyō gakuhō* 74 (1993): 61–88.

Al-Mizzī. *Tahdhīb al-Kamāl fī asmāʾ al-rijāl*. Ed. by Bashshār ʿAwwād Maʿrūf. 35 vols. Beirut: Muʾassasat al-risāla, 1992.

Morimoto, Kazuo. "The Notebook of a *Sayyid/Sharīf* Genealogist: MS. British Library Or. 1406." In *Scritti in onore di Biancamaria Scarcia Amoretti*. Ed. by Daniela Bredi et al. 3 vols. Rome: Dipartimento di Studi Orientali, Università di Roma "La Sapienza" and Edizioni Q, 2008, vol. 3, 823–36.

Morimoto, Kazuo. "An Enigmatic Genealogical Chart of the Timurids: A Testimony to the Dynasty's Claim to Yasavi-ʿAlid Legitimacy?" *Oriens* 44 (2016): 145–78.

Morimoto, Kazuo. "Sayyid Ibn ʿAbd al-Ḥamīd: An Iraqi Shiʿi Genealogist at the Court of Özbek Khan." *Journal of the Economic and Social History of the Orient* 59 (2016): 661–94.

Morimoto, Kazuo. "Ibn ʿInaba." In *The Encyclopaedia of Islam Three*. Ed. by Kate Fleet et al., pt. 2017.4. Leiden and Boston: Brill, 2017, 135–7.

Morimoto, Kazuo. "Sharif al-Din al-Jawwani: A Talibid Genealogist from Twelfth-Century Egypt" (in Japanese). *Seinan Ajia kenkyū* 88 (2018): 1–19.

Morimoto, Kazuo. "Al-Jawwānī." In *The Encyclopaedia of Islam Three*. Ed. by Kate Fleet et al., pt. 2019.1. Leiden and Boston: Brill, 2019, 101–2.

Al-Mufīd, al-Shaykh. *Al-Irshād fī maʿrifat ḥujaj Allāh ʿalā al-ʿibād*. Ed. by Muʾassasat Āl al-Bayt li-Iḥyāʾ al-Turāth. 2 vols. 2nd ed. Beirut: Muʾassasat Āl al-Bayt li-iḥyāʾ al-turāth, 2008.

Mulder, Stephennie. *The Shrines of the ʿAlids in Medieval Syria: Sunnis, Shiʿis and the Architecture of Coexistence*. Edinburgh: Edinburgh University Press, 2014.

Northrup, Linda S. "The Baḥrī Mamlūk Sultanate, 1250–1390." In *The Cambridge History of Egypt*, Vol. 1, *Islamic Egypt, 640–1517*. Ed. by Carl Petry. Cambridge: Cambridge University Press, 1998, 242–89.

Al-Nuwayrī. *Nihāyat al-arab fī funūn al-adab*. Ed. by Mufīd Qumayḥa et al. 34 vols. in 16 pts. Beirut: Dār al-kutub al-ʿilmiyya, 2004.

Ohtoshi, Tetsuya. *Ejiputo shisha no machi to seibo sankei: Musurimu to himusurimu no Ejiputo shakaishi*. Tokyo: Yamakawa Shuppansha, 2018.

Peacock, Andrew C. S. "Politics, Religion and the Occult in the Works of Kamal al-Din Ibn Talha, a Vizier, *ʿAlim* and Author in Thirteenth-Century Syria." In *Syria in Crusader Times: Conflict and Coexistence*. Ed. by Carole Hillenbrand. Edinburgh: Edinburgh University Press, 2020, 34–60.

Poliak, A. N. "Les révoltes populaires en Égypte à l'époque des mamelouks et leurs causes économiques." *Revue des études islamiques* 8 (1934): 251–73.

Al-Qāhira al-Islāmiyya. https://islamic.cultnat.org/Images/lg/AAAM_6550.jpg. Accessed April 17, 2022.

Al-Qalqashandī. *Ṣubḥ al-aʿshā*, vol. 4. Cairo: al-Maṭbaʿa al-amīriyya, 1914.

Al-Qifṭī, ʿAlī b. Yūsuf. *Al-Muḥammadūn min al-shuʿarāʾ wa-ashʿāruhum*. Ed. by Ḥasan Muʿammirī. Riyadh: Dār al-Yamāma li-l-baḥth wa-l-tarjama wa-l-nashr, [1970].

Rāġib, Yūsuf. "Essai d'inventaire chronologique des guides à l'usage des pèlerins du Caire." *Revue des études islamiques* 41 (1973): 259–80.

Rāġib, Yūsuf. "Al-Sayyida Nafīsa, sa légende, son culte et son cimetière (suite et fin)." *Studia Islamica* 45 (1977): 27–55.

Rapoport, Youssef. "Invisible Peasants, Marauding Nomads: Taxation, Tribalism, and Rebellion in Mamluk Egypt." *Mamlūk Studies Review* 8.2 (2004): 1–22.

Rapoport, Youssef. *Rural Economy and Tribal Society in Islamic Egypt: A Study of al-Nābulusī's* Village of the Fayyum. Trunhout: Brepols, 2018.

Al-Rāzī, Fakhr al-Dīn (attr.). *Al-Shajara al-mubāraka fī ansāb al-Ṭālibiyya*. Ed. by Mahdī al-Rajāʾī. 2nd ed. Qom: Maktabat al-Marʿashī al-Najafī, 1998–99.

Rieu, Charles. *Supplement to the Catalogue of the Arabic Manuscripts in British Museum*. London, 1894. Repr. Hildesheim: Olms, 2000.

Al-Ṣadūq, al-Shaykh. *Al-Khiṣāl*. Ed. by ʿAlī Akbar al-Ghaffārī. 2 vols. Qom: Muʾassasat al-nashr al-Islāmī, Jamāʿat al-Mudarrisīn, 1983.

Al-Ṣafadī. *Al-Wāfī bi-l-wafayāt*, vol. 1. Ed. by Helmut Ritter. Wiesbaden: Franz Steiner, 1962.

Al-Sakhāwī al-Ḥanafī. *Tuḥfat al-aḥbāb wa-bughyat al-ṭullāb fī l-khiṭaṭ wa-l-mazārāt wa-l-tarājim wa-l-biqāʿ al-mubārakāt*. Ed. by Maḥmūd Rabīʿ and Ḥasan Qāsim. Cairo: M. al-ʿulūm wa-l-ādāb, 1937; Ed. by Abū Sahl Najāḥ ʿIwaḍ Ṣayyām. Cairo: Dār al-Muqaṭṭam, 2014.

Sibṭ Ibn al-Jawzī. *Tadhkirat al-khawāṣṣ al-Umma bi-dhikr khaṣāʾiṣ al-aʾimma*. Ed. by Ḥusayn Taqī-zāda. 2 vols. Qom: Markaz al-ṭibāʿa wa-l-nashr li-l-Majmaʿ al-ʿĀlamī li-Ahl al-Bayt, 2005–06.

Al-Silafī. *Muʿjam al-safar*. Ed. by ʿAbd Allāh ʿUmar al-Bārūdī. Beirut: Dār al-fikr, 1993.

Stewart, Devin J. "Popular Shiism in Medieval Egypt: Vestiges of Islamic Sectarian Polemics in Egyptian Arabic." *Studia Islamica* 84 (1996): 35–66.

Stewart, Devin J. *Islamic Legal Orthodoxy: Twelver Shiite Responses to the Sunni Legal System*. Salt Lake City: The University of Utah Press, 1998.

Taylor, Christopher S. *In the Vicinity of the Righteous:* Ziyāra *and the Veneration of Muslim Saints in Late Medieval Egypt*. Leiden: Brill, 1999.

Al-ʿUbaydalī, Ibn Muhannā. *Tadhkirat al-ansāb*. MS Āstān-i Quds-i Raḍawī 3626.

Al-Udfuwī. *Al-Ṭāliʿ al-saʿīd al-jāmiʿ asmāʾ nujabāʾ al-Ṣaʿīd*. Ed. by Saʿd Muḥammad Ḥusayn. Cairo: al-Dār al-Miṣriyya li-l-taʾlīf wa-l-tarjama, 1966.

Weil, Jean David. *Calalogue general du Musée Arabe du Caire: Les bois à épigraphes jusqu'à l'époque mamlouke*. Cairo: Imprimerie de l'Institut Français d'Archéologie Orientale, 1931.

Williams, Caroline. "The Cult of ʿAlid Saints in the Fāṭimid Monuments of Cairo, Part I: The Mosque of al-Aqmar." *Muqarnas* 1 (1983): 37–52.

Williams, Caroline. "The Cult of ʿAlid Saints in the Fāṭimid Monuments of Cairo, Part II: Mausolea." *Muqarnas* 3 (1985): 39–60.

Al-Zabīdī. *Al-Rawḍ al-miʿṭār fī nasab al-sādat Āl Jaʿfar al-Ṭayyār*. Ed. by ʿAbd Allāh Muḥammad al-Ḥusaynī. Kuwait: Dīwān al-ashrāf, 2012.

9

ʿIlm al-Siyāq and Bureaucrats in Safavid Iran

Nobuaki Kondo

Introduction

ʿIlm al-siyāq or *ʿilm al-ḥisāb* is a special knowledge of bookkeeping and financial affairs. This chapter discusses the relationship between knowledge and power in Safavid Iran. The general description of *siyāq* has already been provided by Mohammad Bagheri, and more recently, Brian Spooner and William L. Hanaway, but they explained *siyāq* as accounting, numerical notation, or numeracy.[1] Certainly, the *siyāq* notation (*raqam-i siyāq*) was a distinctive part of *ʿilm al-siyāq*. These numerals originated from numerals written in Arabic scripts, for example, *aḥad* (one) as د and *ʿašara* (ten) as عـــ . However, *ʿilm al-siyāq* contains more matters related to fiscal administration. There are still points to discuss on the history of *siyāq*, including the origin of the term *siyāq* and the difference between *siyāq* and *siyāqat*.

Contrarily, Walther Hinz worked on *siyāq* manuals from the Ilkhanid and Timurid period, including an edition of *Risāla-i Falakiyya*.[2] Recent publications by Ryoko Watabe also largely concern the Ilkhanid period.[3] These works focused mainly on fiscal administration and did not discuss the social background of *siyāq* as knowledge. In addition, the development of *siyāq* after the Ilkhanid period was not known in these studies.

Jean Aubin's article on the social background of Iranian notables in the early Safavid period is insightful. He noted that the fiscal technique (*ḥisāb*) was a factor that allowed Iranian notables to survive political changes during the advent of the Safavid state.[4] However, no researcher has elaborated on his idea afterwards. Moreover, *siyāq* manuals from Safavid Iran had been neglected for a long time, and no one had enough information on them until recently.

This study consists of four parts. The first part re-examines the history of *siyāq* and clarifies its position in the whole Islamicate sciences, using new sources. Second, a bookkeeping manual from Safavid Iran is examined and its discourse is analysed. This section shows how *siyāq* was recognised as knowledge during the Safavid period. The third part examines Safavid administration manuals, which relates to fiscal ledgers explained in the *siyāq* manual. The fourth part concerns the social context of *siyāq*, focusing on those who have mastered *siyāq* at that time. Presumably, *mustawfī*s – or accountants – mastered this knowledge, but other people could also have the same knowledge. This section examines how this knowledge affected their life histories. Overall, this study discusses how financial knowledge was related to political power in Safavid Iran.

History of *ʿIlm al-siyāq*

As mentioned, *ʿilm al-siyāq* or *ʿilm al-ḥisāb* concerns not only special numerals but also the entire Persian bookkeeping system. The most important feature of this system is the use of *madd*, a horizontal line, under which the accounting items are described. Under this system, a larger category, such as a total sum, came first with a longer *madd*; then, the next largest category was written under the second longer *madd*. In some cases, a ladder (*nardbān*) was used as a metaphor for this system, called a 'ladder step' (*nardbān-pāya*) in Persian.[5]

The *siyāq* manuals attempted to link *ʿilm al-siyāq* to ʿAlī b. Abī Ṭālib (d. 661). A short treatise on *siyāq*, compiled in Safavid Iran, tells the following story, which the author heard when he was a child.[6] In the early days of Islam, Muslims conducted many military expeditions and accumulated considerable booty. Prophet Muḥammad wanted to distribute it to Muslims. He ordered Abū Bakr to count the booty and show the data to him. However, Abū Bakr could not do so, and thus, the prophet gave this task to ʿUmar. He prepared a document (*siyāha*) on the number of camels that carried the booty and brought the document to the prophet; however, the total count of the booty was still unknown. Therefore, the task went to ʿAlī, who was the founder of *ʿilm-i siyāq*. He created a document on all the items of booty and showed it to the prophet, who distributed the booty using that document. Also, another Safavid work, Abū Isḥāq Kirmānī's *Ǧāmiʿ al-ḥisāb*, which will be disused below in detail, considered ʿAlī as the founder of *ʿilm al-ḥisāb*.

However, this story was not a Safavid invention: Šams al-Dīn Muḥammad Āmulī (d. after 1352–53) explained ʿAlī's reform of financial matters and called his new system *istīfā*.[7] Already in the 14th century, ʿAlī was linked to Islamicate bookkeeping, although we cannot say this for certain.

As a more probable theory, *siyāq* was believed to have been created during the reign of ʿAbd al-Malik b. Marwān, an Umayyad ruler (r. 685–705), when the Umayyads changed the language for fiscal administration from Greek or Middle

Persian to Arabic. The 14th-century historian and genealogist, Ibn al-Ṭiqṭaqā (d. 1310) only mentioned the secretary (*kātib*) of ʿAbd al-Malik b. Marwān as the founder.[8] An Ilkhanid historian and financial officer, Ḥamd Allāh Mustawfī (d. 1349) referred to ʿAbd al-Ḥamīd b. Yaḥyā (d. 750) as the creator of *siyāq* around 705. In his *Ẓafarnāma*, a historical work in poetic style, this is explained as a decision on the shape of notations and bookkeeping (*taʿīn-i ṣūrat-i ruqūm va siyāqat*).[9] However, this may not be correct because ʿAbd al-Ḥamīd b. Yaḥyā, who is known as the founder of Arabic epistolary style, served the last Umayyad caliph, Marwān b. Muḥammad (r. 744–50), as chief secretary.[10] ʿAbd al-Ḥamīd b. Yaḥyā's name was used here, probably because he was the master of Arabic epistles, which may indicate a close relationship between epistolary skills and *siyāq*.

Ibn al-Ṭiqṭaqā provided more stories on *siyāq*. His work concerned sayyids' genealogy, but he found the common techniques between genealogical science and *siyāq*, using *madd*. Moreover, he stated that there were two types of *siyāqat al-ḥisāb*. One was Arabic (*ʿarabiyya*), and the other was Persian (*ʿağamiyya*). As mentioned above, Arabic *siyāqat* was founded by the secretary of ʿAbd al-Malik b. Marwān, but the Persian version was created by Abū ʿAlī ibn Sīnā al-Buḫārī (Avicenna, d. 1037), when he supervised the chancery (al-*dīvān*).[11] We know that Avicenna was the *vazīr* of the Buwayhid ruler, Šams al-Dawla, in Hamadan in the years between 1014 and 1021;[12] however, we cannot assume that Persian was used in the Buwayhid fiscal administration in Hamadan. If the reference to Avicenna was also a legend, it is possible that *siyāq* scholars also used Avicenna's name to authorise their knowledge. Even so, the history of Persian *siyāq* was old enough for Ibn al-Ṭiqṭaqā to link it with Avicenna who lived more than two hundred years before.

Moreover, Ibn al-Ṭiqṭaqā's description obliges us to revise the history of *siyāq*. We understand that Persian *siyāq* emerged from ʿAbbasid practice, where we see a few surviving ʿAbbasid examples whose styles are similar to those of later Persian ones.[13] However, the origin of the term *siyāq* or *siyāqat* remains unclear, as Spooner and Hanaway state.[14] It is difficult to find suitable meanings related to accounting or bookkeeping for this word in Arabic dictionaries.[15] A 19th-century Persian dictionary claims that the word *siyāq* comes from its original meaning, 'to drive away' (*rāndan*), which meant accounting because, in accounting, people worked quickly with pens to save time.[16] However, this claim does not make much sense. This is one reason why one researcher claimed that its origin lies in the Iranian language.[17]

On the contrary, Bagheri claimed that the oldest usage of *siyāq* was found in Ibn al-Nadīm's *al-Fihrist* (c. 987).[18] However, Ibn al-Nadīm only mentioned 'religious, "*siyāq*" and other books' (*kutub al-diyāna wa-l-siyāq wa-ġayrihi*),[19] and the meaning of this '*siyāq*' is unclear. Moreover, an encyclopaedic work, al-Ḫwārizmī's *Mafātīḥ al-ʿulūm* (997), never mentioned the term *siyāq* or *siyāqat*, meaning that the term did not prevail in the late 10th century. Although the term *siyāq* or *siyāqat* was not used, the book contained some technical financial terms used in *siyāq* manuals such as *qānūn*, *awārağ*, *rūznāmağ* and *barāt* in Section 4 of Chapter 1, 'the art of writing (*kitāba*).'[20] In other words, the content of *siyāq* already existed without using the term *siyāq* or *siyāqat*. It is also important that al-Ḫwārizmī considered financial knowledge necessary for scribes.

Bagheri also cited Nāṣir Ḫusraw's travelogue, which mentioned *siyāq* twice in the event of year of 1046.[21] However, these two mentions of *siyāq* are from 19th century Tehran lithograph edition and not found in the earlier manuscripts.[22]

In this regard, Ibn al-Ṭiqṭaqā was the oldest source which clearly mentioned the expression, *siyāqat al-ḥisāb* (literally: 'financial method'). He also used the expression *ʿilm al-siyāqa wa-l-ḥisāb* (literally: knowledge on method and accounting). The origins of ʿArabic and Persian *siyāq* systems might date back to the Umayyad and the Buwayhid periods as he claimed but the financial term *siyāqat* came to be used around his lifetime, i.e. the Ilkhanid period.

The term *siyāqat* prevailed in the Ilkhanate. Ibn al-Ṭiqṭaqā emphasised in his work, *al-Faḫrī* (1302), that the Mongols had a special interest in the knowledge of bookkeeping and accounting, which was necessary for state administration as well as revenue and expenditure control.[23] Another encyclopaedic work, Āmulī's *Nafāʾis al-funūn* (1341–42) had a section on accounting (*ʿilm-i istīfā*) in the chapter on 'literary knowledge' (*ʿulūm-i adabī*), following the section on epistolography (*ʿilm-i inšā*).[24] He also wrote:

> The art of bookkeeping (*ṣanʿat-i ṣiyāqat*) is a select technique and a praiseworthy thing. The state's administration and control of the country always relate to it. [By this knowledge], a man of letters is respected and admired in front of the kings, and esteemed higher than other dignitaries and servants all the time.[25]

Here, *siyāqat* is considered as knowledge essential to statecraft.

Since Persian was an administrative language under the Ilkhanids, several Persian bookkeeping manuals were compiled during this period. Among them, four have been published: Tabrīzī's *Saʿādat-nāma* (1306–07) and *Qānūn-i saʿādat* (1306–11), Sarāvī's *Ǧāmiʿ al-ḥisāb* (c. 1340), and Māzandarānī's *Risāla-i Falakiyya dar ʿilm-i siyāqat* (1363).[26] An older manual, *al-Muršid fī l-ḥisāb* (1291–92), by al-Ḥasan b. ʿAlī, was recently investigated by various researchers.[27] According to Watabe, *al-Muršid* was the sole manual that reflected the Ilkhanid taxation system before Ghāzān Ḫān's reform (r. 1295–1304).[28]

On the other hand, the form *siyāq* (not *siyāqat*) became more apparent in the 15th century. The manuscript of another fiscal manual, titled *Šams al-siyāq*, compiled by ʿAlī Šīrāzī after 1428, probably in Herat, is preserved in the Süleymaniye Library in Istanbul.[29] A partial edition of the work by W. Hinz indicated that the term *siyāq* was used not only in the title but also in the text.[30] According to ʿUqaylī's *Āsar al-vuzarāʾ* from the late 15th century, a Timurid *vazīr* under Šāhruḫ, Ḫwāǧa Ġiyās al-Dīn Ḫwāfī made administrative reforms and introduced new ways of *siyāq*, financial ledgers (*daftar*), and the control of 'important things' (*zabt-i muhimmāt*).[31] Another Timurid historian, Ḫwāndamīr, used both *siyāqat* and *siyāq* as synonyms in his work, *Dastūr al-vuzarāʾ*, completed before 1510.[32] Conversely, another historian, Vāṣifī only used *siyāq* and did not mention *siyāqat* in his work *Badāyiʿ al-vaqāyiʿ* (after 1512).[33] Although no researcher explained the difference between *siyāq* and *siyāqat*, it can be said that the term *siyāq* was a new form of *siyāqat* because the art of Persian bookkeeping was mainly called *siyāq* from the Safavid period onwards.

This is also true for Central Asia and Mughal India,[34] where *siyāq* manuals were also produced.[35] On the other hand, the Ottoman usage of *siyāqat* (*siyakat*) may indicate that they adopted the Ilkhanid usage and kept it for centuries. We cannot find the same type of *siyāq* manuals from the Ottoman regions, which might indicate differences in the adaptation of Persian bookkeeping. *Siyāq* was part of Persianate culture and prevailed from the Ottoman Empire to the Mughal Empire and Central Asia.

This chapter shows how *siyāq* developed over time. Ibn al-Ṭiqṭaqā and Ḥamd Allāh Mustawfī recognised that the Arabic *siyāq* was founded around 705, during the reign of ʿAbd al-Malik b. Marwān. The Mongols had a special interest in *siyāq*, while the form *siyāq* emerged during the Timurid period. The authors mentioned ʿAlī b. Abī Ṭālib, ʿAbd al-Ḥamīd b. Yaḥyā and Avicenna, who might not have been the real founders of *siyāq*. However, the authors used these famous figures to add to *siyāq*'s value and establish it as a part of the Islamicate sciences.

As al-Ḫwārizmī and Āmulī indicated, *ʿilm al-siyāq* was related to literary knowledge but Ibn al-Ṭiqṭaqā found connection with genealogical science in terms of technique. *ʿIlm al-siyāq* found a place in the system of Islamicate sciences before the Safavid period.

Safavid *Siyāq* Manuals

Although researchers have paid attention to Ilkhanid and Timurid *siyāq* manuals, Safavid manuals have been ignored until quite recently. The recent publication of Kirmānī's *Ǧāmiʿ al-ḥisāb* is the first attempt to deal with Safavid *siyāq* manuals.[36]

The *Ǧāmiʿ al-ḥisāb*[37] is the most comprehensive *siyāq* manual from Safavid Iran. The author, Kirmānī, liked to acquire knowledge, even when he was a child. He went to scholars and studied various topics such as Arabic morphology and syntax, rhetoric, logic, and theology. He also learned poetical riddles and other required things.[38] One accountant discovered his arithmetic ability and told him to learn accounting (*ʿilm al-ḥisāb*). He did his best to master it.[39]

During the reign of Šāh Ṭahmāsb (1524–76), Kirmānī served Ḫwāǧa ʿAbd al-Rašīd Kirmānī, and later, his son Ḫwāǧa ʿAbd al-Qādir Kirmānī. They were from the notable Ḫwāǧa-hā family in Kerman who possessed huge property there.[40] *Ǧāmiʿ al-ḥisāb* records a *suyūrġāl* for Ḫwāǧa ʿAbd al-Rašīd, which mentions his income from six districts in Kerman.[41] His son, Ḫwāǧa ʿAbd al-Qādir, always urged Kirmānī to write a comprehensive treatise on accounting (*fann-i ḥisāb*).[42] ʿAbd al-Qādir came to the court of Šāh Ṭahmāsb by the order of the shah, serving as a *mušrif-i buyūtāt* (accountant of the royal supply department). He was considered a candidate for the office of the grand *vazīr*.[43] His master's position might be the reason why *Ǧāmiʿ al-ḥisāb* explains the ledgers for the royal *buyūtāt* in detail.

Section 13 of the introduction was written in 949 AH (1542–43).[44] Though we have no date for completion, it can be estimated as not much later than 951 AH (1544–45), the latest date mentioned in the work.[45] The author referred to four previous works that explored the *siyāq* accounting before him: *Baḥr al-siyāq* by Mawlānā Šaraf al-Dīn, *Šams al-siyāq* by Šams al-Dīn Muḥammad Ṣāḥib Dīvān Juvaynī (d. 1285), *Risāla-i taʿlīm-i siyāqat* by Sulaymān Šāh Kirmānī, and *Qavāʾid al-ḥisāb* by Muḥyī al-Dīn Kirmānī.[46] However, as these previous works were too long and too exaggerated, using odd metaphors and strange terms, one who wanted to learn bookkeeping could browse through the works but not master bookkeeping. Therefore, Kirmānī has compiled this work.[47]

The content of *Ǧāmiʿ al-ḥisāb* are as follows:

Foreword (Marʿašī manuscript: 1–32)

Introduction (*Muqaddima*) (33–123)

- Section 1: On honour and the value of this art and position of this knowledge
- Section 2: What kinds of people have the ability and skills for this important profession?
- Section 3: On the position of this knowledge and what it relates to
- Section 4: On the definition of accounting, its meaning, and what it belongs to
- Section 5: On the knowledge of fractions and numbers
- Section 6: On the number of *dīnār*s and *mann*s
- Section 7: On writing on the paper of ledgers (*daftar*), the length of *madd*s, and what belongs to them
- Section 8: On what a professional of this art should write everything and what relates to it
- Section 9: On individual sums (*tārīǧ*), distinctive marks (*ǧāʾiza*), and how to correct them
- Section 10: On supplements (*ḥašv*), total amount (*bāriz*), and what belongs to them
- Section 11: On the strikethrough line (*tarqīn*) and correction (*tartīq*)[48] which mean marks of deletion

Section 12: On what should be written first on the same line
Section 13: On various calendars and what relates to them
Section 14: On Arabic and Abjad numerals and what belongs to them
Section 15: On tax assessment (*qarār-e ǧamʿ*) and taxation rules (*qānūn*) of the God-protected provinces, harvest assessment (*rayʿ*) and conversion (*tasʿīr*) of agricultural products
Chapter 1: On daily records (*rūznāmača*) (123–35)
Chapter 2: On *tawǧīḥ* ledgers (135–55)
Section 1: On the meaning of *tawǧīh* and what it relates to
Section 2: On registering various documents such as *rūznāmača*s, *barāt*s, *taʿlīqa*s, copies (*musannā*), *sarḫaṭṭ*s, and what belong to them
Section 3: On how to write *tawǧīḥ* ledgers and what relates to them
Chapter 3: On *avāraǧa* ledgers (155–227)
Part 1: On various items of taxation (*abvāb al-māl*)
Part 2: On the receiver of deposits (*arbāb al-taḥāvīl*)
Chapter 4: On doubling, bisection, addition, subtraction, multiplication, division, and measurement (228–313)
Part 1 On whole numbers
Part 2: On calculations of fractions
Conclusion (313–366)
Part 1: On extractions of numbers, names, and others
Part 2: On various cases
Part 3: (no title)

The work has a foreword, a long introduction, four chapters, and a conclusion. In Section 2 of the introduction, Kirmānī explains the conditions to be a *mustawfī*: he must have a perfect pedigree and an authentic genealogy (*kamāl-i ḥasab va ṣiḥḥat-i nasab*). He must have so much knowledge of the sciences that he cannot learn more. He must distinguish Arabic expressions from Persian ones.[49] A *mustawfī* must place truth-speaking and accurate-writing at the centre of his occupation. In the fiscal account of his master under his supervision, if he finds anything that may lead to losses in his master's property, he should not accept such an account and avoid the losses. If his power and dignity increase, he must stay humble and maintain his ethics; he must not excessively blame his secretaries and officers.[50] Clearly, Kirmānī targeted those who wanted to become a *mustawfī* as readers of the work.

Section 5 of the introduction includes a description of *siyāq* notation. The Marʿašī manuscript spent only seven pages from a total of 366 on this topic.[51] It can be said that *siyāq* notation was only a small part of the knowledge that Kirmānī wanted to teach readers, although it was indispensable for the duties of *mustawfī*s.

Three of the four specific types of ledgers are *rūznāmača*, *tawǧīḥ*, and *avāraġa*. The most important feature of Kirmānī's work is the rich examples of the ledger styles, which have never been shown before.[52] Among them, the *rūznāmača* was a ledger on which accountants recorded financial transactions and related documents daily. Every solar year, the accountants created a new ledger. Unlike *tawǧīḥ*, *rūznāmača* was never chaptered.[53] The following is an example:[54]

هو

روزنامچه

حویجخانهٔ خاصهٔ شریفهٔ همایون

ایام

رمضان المبارک

فی الاحد

۱۵ منه

مصالح

شیلان

۷۹ من ۳/۴

برنج روغن نخود

۴۵ من ۱۸ من ۳/۴ ۵ من

پیاز نمک

۶ من ۵ من

صباح عشاء

۵۳ من ۲۶ من [۳/۴]

برنج روغن برنج روغن

۳۰ من ۱۵ من جهة شله پلاو جهة ایضاً

پیاز و زرد هریسه ۱۵ من ۳ من ۳/۴

پلاوه پلاو ۳ من نخود نمک

۱۵من ۱۵ من پیاز و ۲ من ۵ من

پلاو و خرما پیاز

۱۲ من ۵ من

پیاز و زرد

پلاو پلاو

۷ من ۳ من

۱/۲ ۳/۴

قیمه

۳/۴

نخود پیاز

۳ من ۵ من

تحویل

علی آقا حویجدار از بابت مالوجهات تمغاء دار السلطنهٔ تبریز بموجب پروانچه بتاریخ مذکور مضمون آنکه دولتمآب خواجه میریجان مبلغ ده تومان تبریزی جهة ضرورات حویجخانه معموره تحویل علی آقا حویجدار نماید که در خرج محاسبه او مجری است.

المقرر

۱۰ تومان

Text 1: An Example from a *Rūznāmača* Ledger in *Ǧāmi' al-ḥisāb* (Kirmānī, *Ǧāmi' al-ḥisāb*, 131)

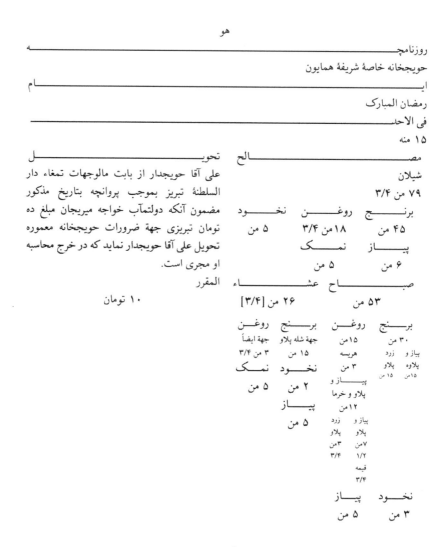

This record concerned the Royal kitchen (*ḥavīǧḫāna-i ḫāṣṣa-i šarīfa-i humāyūn*), and is dated Sunday, 15 Ramażān. It contained two transactions: one was a royal banquet in the morning and the night, which needed 79.75 *mann* foodstuffs and served pilaf and potage (*harīsa*). A reader may find this strange as it means that the shah had a banquet in the month of Ramażān, but the Marʿašī manuscript explained that the shah was travelling on the date and did not need to fast. The other transaction was a deposit. Ten *tumān*s from Tabriz's commercial tax (*tamġā*) were transferred to ʿAlī Āqā, *ḫavīġdār* (cook), as a deposit. ʿAlī Āqā was expected to purchase foodstuffs with this money. The *rūznāmača* ledger was already explained in the Ilkhanid *siyāq* manuals.[55]

The *tawǧīḥ* ledger concerned all the expenditures of the state, including salary payments, fees, rewards, *suyūrġāl*s, pensions, and so on. Maḥbūb Farīmānī's recent study provides numerous images from *tawǧīḥ* ledgers preserved in the Āstān-i Quds archives. She demonstrates that the examples cited in Kirmānī's work are identical with original ledgers in the archives in their form.[56] However, the study does not include any edited texts of the legers. It is worth bringing one example here:[57]

توجيهات

و مقررات و صورت احکام و پروانجات ممالک محروسه   سنهٔ بارس ئیل

مسعود الابتداء

محمود الانتها

توجيهات

تحصيلات

افتخار

الاعيان محمد آقا شيخ قورچی

سرخط

تاریخ ۲۰ شهر شعبان المعظم از مال وجهات دار
الامان کرمان بموجب پروانچهٔ اشرف فی تاریخ
المذکور مضمون آنکه ارباب و رعایاء دار الامان
کرمان مبلغ یکصد تومان از بابت مالوجهات سنهٔ
بارس ئیل در وجه تحصیل افتخار الاعظم محمد
آقا شیخ سامان و سرانجام نموده رسانند که خرج
مالوجهات ایشان محسوب و مجری ست
المقرر   ۱۰۰ تومان

سرخط

بتارخ ۲۷ شهر رمضان المبارک سنه ۹۴۹ از تمغای
دار السلطنهٔ تبریز بموجب پروانچهٔ اشرف فی التاریخ
مذکور مضمون آنکه دولتمآب سعادة نصابی خواجه
کمال الدین میریجان مبلغ دویست تومان تبریزی از
بابت مالوجهات و وجوهات تمغای دار السلطنه تبریز
در وجه تحصیل عمدة الاعیان محمد آقا شیخ قورچی
سامان نماید که بخرج او مجری و محسوب است
درین باب قدغن عظیم دانسته تقصیر نکند
المقرر   ۲۰۰ تومان

Text 2: An Example from a *Tawǧīḥ* Ledger in *Ǧāmiʿ al-ḥisāb* (Kirmānī, *Ǧāmiʿ al-ḥisāb*, 148)

Here, Muḥammad Āqā Šayḫ Qorčī received 300 *tumān*s: 100 *tumān*s came from the tax income from Kirman in the year of the Tiger, based on a royal edict (*parvānča*) dated 20 Šaʿbān, probably of 949 AH, while 200 *tumān*s came from the commercial tax (*tamġā*) from Tabriz, which was managed by Mīrījān, based on a royal edict dated 27 Ramażān 949 AH. In this ledger, expenditures were recorded along with the revenue sources. *Tawǧīḥ* ledgers emerged in the late Ilkhanid period after the financial reform of Ġāzān Ḫān.[58]

On the other hand, the *avāraǧa* ledger was originally created to show the balance of taxation in hand.[59] According to Watabe, the function of the *avāraǧa* ledger changed after Ġāzān Ḫān's reform; it was used to check expenditures from provincial tax income, and the records of issuing payment bills (*barāt*) were transferred to this ledger.[60] Kirmānī explains two types of the *avāraǧa* ledger: one is used for the clearance of tax income and expenditures, and the other maintains a record of tax income deposits (*taḥāvīl*). However, Kirmānī does not explain the first type extensively (just three pages in the Marʿašī manuscript), nor does he provide an example of the ledgers.

Instead, he describes the second type – the one for deposit receivers (*arbāb al-taḥāvīl*) – in detail, dedicating more than sixty pages to it in the Marʿašī manuscript and providing many examples. Here is one example:[61]

اوارجهٔ محاسبات و معاملات سرکار خاصه سنهٔ لوی ئیل
ارباب التحاویل والتحاصیل
التحاویـــل٣
اصناف‍ــــــــــــ
زرگ‍ــــــــــــــر

خواج‍ـــه
همایون شاه
مف‍ــردة
الاول عن تحویل جماعة
٤ تومان
حلاج‍ــــــــــــــــــــــــان حب‍ــــــــــــــــــــــــــازان
تبعهٔ خواجه سلطان محمود بتاریخ شهر ذی [قعده] تبعهٔ مولانا شاه برات فی التاریخ
سنهٔ ٩٤٩
٢ تومان ٢ تومان
صار من ذلک‍ــ
فی الصوغ جهة مکمل نمودن شبکه گردن بند معتبر بعمل خواجه همایون شاه مذکور
عدد ٣ تومان
٥٠ مثقالاً ٤٢٥٠ دینار
مص‍ــــــــــــــــــــــالح اج‍ــــــــــــــــــــــــــره
٣ تومان و غیره
١١٥٠ دینار ٣١٠٠ دینار
بهای طلا بهای انگشت بهای گل بوته اج‍ـــــــــــــره حق الیس‍ـــــــــــار
بقرار مثقال بقرار ١٠٠ مثقال؟
٣ تومان ١٠٠٠ دینار ١٥٠ دینار ٥٠ دینار مثقالان؟
٢٥٠٠ دینار المقرر
مثقال
٦٠٠ دینار
الق‍ــرار
از تتمة الاصل ٥٧٥٠ دینار
شبکه گردن بند معتبر
وضع من ذل‍ــک
تسلیم خادمان حرم فی تاریخ شهر ذیقعده
٥٧٥٠ دینار
شبکه گردن بند
عدد
٥٠ مثقالاً

Text 3: An Example from an *Avārağa* Ledger in *Ğāmiʿ al-ḥisāb* (Kirmānī, *Ğāmiʿ al-ḥisāb*, 171)

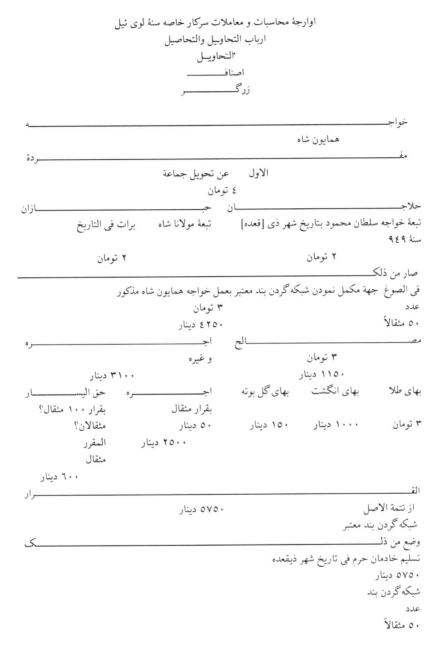

This record indicates the financial process of making a gold necklace with a net-shaped medal. The sovereign ordered a goldsmith (*zargar*), Ḫwāǧa Humāyūn Šāh, to make the necklace. Humāyūn received a total of four *tumāns* for this purpose, two *tumāns* each from the cotton dresser and baker. The necklace, with a weight of 50 *misqāl* (232 grams), cost three *tumāns* and 4,250 *dīnārs*, including gold bullion, the fee for a melting pot, wages, and so on. After completion, the necklace was delivered to the servants of the royal harem with a surplus of 5,750 *dīnārs*. These records covered the budget at the end of the transaction.

Kirmānī's work was compiled to record fiscal transactions in the ledgers. Chapter 4 and the conclusion concern arithmetic, but they comprise only 38 % of the total pages. *ʿIlm al-siyāq* contains arithmetic but focuses more on how to record it into the ledger.

Ledgers and Administration

Who in Safavid administration was involved in the ledgers that Kirmānī explained? Undoubtedly, they needed the *siyāq* technique. Although Kirmānī described the form of the ledgers, he did not state anything about their users. Some information can be found in the Safavid administrative manuals.

Rūznāmača

Rūznāmača simply means 'daily records', and this term could be used in the various departments of the Safavid administration. This is the reason why previous studies did not pay much attention to *rūznāmača*.[62] However, the Safavid administrative manuals mention mainly *the rūznāmača* of *buyūtāt*. According to the manuals, the *buyūtāt* accountant (*mušrif*) recorded daily income, expenditure, and balance of their department into the *rūznāmačas*.[63] Then, the *rūznāmača* was sent to *vazīr-i buyūtāt* who checked and endorsed it and to *nāẓir-i buyūtāt* (supervisor of the royal supply department), who place a seal on it. The *rūznāmača* was then preserved by *the mustawfī* of *arbāb al-taḥāvīl*, who adjusted the balance if necessary.[64]

Therefore, these officers needed knowledge of *rūznāmača* and *siyāq*. Specifically, the *mušrif* of the tailoring department must be an expert in *ʿilm-i siyāq* and writing (*navīsandagī*).[65] The *mušrifs* received both salaries and commission. For example, a *mušrif* in the saddle department (*zīnḫāna*) had a 20 *tumān* salary per year and one percent commission for registering a present to the shah (*pīškaš*) and 0.2 percent commission for registering a reward to the saddlers (*inʿām*).[66]

It is difficult to find an exact number for the *mušrifs* because sometimes one person held several *mušrif* posts at the same time. Chapter 8 of *Dastūr al-mulūk* mentioned 30 *mušrifs*, while the whole staff of *nāẓir-i buyūtāt* was counted as 84 people.[67]

Tawǧīh

The original meaning of *tawǧīh* came from 'to turn one's face,' which meant 'to assign a revenue source for paying expenditure' in *siyāq*.[68] The administration manuals mentioned two levels of *tawǧīh*: one in the central administration and the other in the local administration. In the centre, *ṣāḥib-tawǧīḥ* supervised all the state's expenditures, such as salaries, *tuyūls* and *suyūrġāls*, other than those of the *arbāb al-taḥāvīl* department.[69] His department (*sarkār-i tawǧīh*) received documents from the expenditure departments (*sarkārāt-i ḫarǧ*), checked them, and recorded them in the *tawǧīh* ledger.[70] A metaphor of miscellany (*ǧung*) was used for this ledger because it contained everything that one could imagine. *Ṣāḥib-tawǧīh* was the busiest position in the Safavid fiscal administration, and he had to be present at *daftarḫāna* every day.[71] He was supervised by a state accountant (*mustawfī al-mamālik*).[72] He received a 20 *tumān* salary and commission. For example, he received 11.25 *dīnārs* when he dealt with an amir's *tuyūl*, which valued one *tumān*.[73] His staff were nine clerks in the early period, increasing to up to 16 in the later period.[74]

In the local administration, the term *tawǧīh-nāmača* was used. This document was prepared for assigning expenditures to guilds and sealed by the city administrator (*kalāntar*) of Isfahan.[75] He had a secretary named *muḥaṣṣiṣ-i mamlakat*, who recorded fiscal transactions into his ledger for guilds, assigned expenditures among them, and prepared *tawǧīh-nāmača*.[76] The *kalāntar* of Isfahan, as well as the *kalāntar* of ʿAbbās-ābād and that of Julfa had the same duty.[77]

In addition, though administrative manuals do not mention it but Maḥbūb Farīmānī's recent study demonstrates that in *tawǧīḥ* ledgers were extensively used in the administration of the Imam Riżā shrine in Mashhad.[78]

Avāraǧa

As mentioned above, Kirmānī described two types of *avāraǧa* ledgers: one for tax and the other for *buyūtāt*. As *buyūtāt* was explained in relation to *rūznāmača*, here we discuss *avāraǧa* for tax. *Avāraǧa-navīses* were officers who recorded transactions in the *avāraǧa* ledger.[79] They belonged to the income department (*sarkār-i ǧamʿ*) and, except for *avāraǧa-navīs-i ḫāṣṣa*, were under the supervision of the state accountant.[80] There were six *avāraǧa-navīses*, and each had his own staff:[81]

Table 1: *Avāraġa-navīs*es in the Safavid Administration (based on Anṣārī, *Dastūr al-mulūk*, 67, 120–1, 150–3)

Office	Number of clerks (*muḥarrir*)
Avāraġa-navīs-i ʿIrāq (central Iran)	earlier 7 clerks, later 11 clerks
Avāraġa-navīs-i Fārs	earlier 3 clerks, later 5 clerks
Avāraġa-navīs-i Āẕarbāyīǧān	earlier 5 clerks, later 3 clerks
Avāraġa-navīs-i Ḫurāsān	earlier 5 clerks, later 7 clerks
Avāraġa-navīs-i ḫāṣṣa	2 clerks
Avāraġa-navīs-i maʿādin (mines)	2 clerks

The total number of clerks ranged from 22 to 30. In sum, 28–36 staff members worked in this department.

In total, those who worked at the *daftarḫāna* (*aṣḥāb-i daftarḫāna*) were 118 people, including the income department, the expenditure department and the *tawǧīh* department. Along with 84 *mušrif*s and others, possibly more than 200 bureaucrats learned *siyāq* and used it for their duties. There is no doubt *that siyāq* was an indispensable knowledge for Safavid bureaucrats.

ʿIlm al-siyāq in the Social Context

Although the administrative manuals indicate which officers were related to the ledgers, they do not give any personal names for who mastered *siyāq*. Thus, we must refer to other historical sources.

Two sources, Iskandar Beg's *Tārīḫ-i ʿālam-ārā-yi ʿAbbāsī* (1629), the well-known chronicle of Šāh ʿAbbās's reign, and Bāfqī's *Ǧāmiʿ-i Mufīdī* (1679), an account of Yazd's local history, give us some insight. The former mentions 10 people, and the latter refers to 13 who mastered *siyāq* at that time (see Table 2). We can assume that *siyāq* was a necessary skill, not only in the central government but also in the provinces. Comparing with the number of bureaucrats that worked at *daftarḫāna* and *buyūtāt*, the number of these samples is admittedly small; yet, they are nonetheless insightful.

Table 2: *Siyāq* Masters in Two Safavid Sources
(TAA: Iskandar Beg, GM: Bāfqī)

Name	Career Highlight	Source
Aḥmad Beg Nūr-i Kamāl Iṣfahānī	Grand *vazīr*	TAA, 160
Ḫwāğa Qāsim Naṭanzī	*Mustawfī al-mamālik*	TAA, 163
Abū Turāb Beg Naṭanzī	*Mustawfī-i māl*	TAA, 165
Ḫwāğa Muḥammad Amīn	*Avārağa-navīs*	TAA, 165
Āqā Šāh ʿAlī Iṣfahānī	*Mustawfī al-mamālik*	TAA, 531
Mīrzā Qivām al-Dīn Muḥammad Kafrānī Iṣfahānī	*Mustawfī al-mamālik*	TAA, 675
Adham Beg Urdūbādī	*Vazīr* of Tabrīz	TAA, 724–5
Abū Ṭurāb Beg Urdūbādī	*Vazīr* of Herat	TAA, 727
Abū Ṭālib Beg Urdūbādī	Grand *vazīr*	TAA,727
Mīrzā Hidāyat Allāh Maʿmūrī Iṣfahānī	*Vazīr-i baqāyā*	TAA, 163
Muʿizzā Šāhmīrā	*Kalāntar* of Yazd	GM, 99
Ḫwāğa Muḥammad Amīn Šūra-bīz Ḫurāsānī	*Vazīr* of Yazd	GM, 185
Ḫwāğa Šahābā Kirmānī	*Vazīr* of Yazd	GM, 186–7
Wağīh al-Dīn Qāḍī Afžal	*Mustawfī-i māl va maḥṣūl*	GM, 254
Tāğā Mīrzā Ḥasan Wāhib	*Vazīr* of Isfahan	GM, 255
Mīrzā Humāyūn	*Mustawfī* of Yazd	GM, 263
Ḫwāğa Quṭb al-Dīn Ḫusrawšāh Maybudī	*Mustawfī*	GM, 265–6
Šamsā Amīr Muḥammad Ṭāhir	*Nāẓir* of the crown property (*ḫāliṣa*) in Yazd	GM, 267–9
Muḥammad Mufīd Mustawfī Bāfqī	*Nāẓir* of waqf property in Yazd/ *Mīr sāmān* of a Mughal princess	GM, 268, 754–60, 814–5
Zaynā Amīr Sayyid ʿAliyā	*Mušrif-i kirkyarāq* in Yazd	GM, 269
Mīrzā Nūr al-Dahr Beg	*Sar-i laškarī* in the Golconda Kingdom	GM, 486–7
Ḫwāğa Pīr Aḥmad	*Vazīr* of a princess	GM, 487
Sayfā	*Zarkaš, darvīš*	GM, 510

Almost all of the above-mentioned individuals worked for the central and provincial governments. An exception was Sayfā Zarkaš, who first lived as a gold wire artisan (drawer) and then learned and mastered *ʿilm-i siyāq*. However, he was attracted to the Sufi path and became a disciple of a Sufi master in Isfahan. Even after his master's death, he lived as a hermit.[82] This case indicates that even an artisan had the opportunity to learn *siyāq*, although he did not utilise his knowledge professionally. Another exception was Mīrzā Nūr al-Dahr Beg, who acquired the art of *siyāq* and visited India to find a good position in 1669–70. He went first to Agra because his uncle served the Mughal Empire; however, he finally found positions, *ğamāʿat-dār* and *sar-laškarī,* in the Golconda Kingdom of Hyderabad, Deccan, India.[83] In addition, Bāfqī, the author of *Ğāmiʿ-i Mufīdī*, found a position in the Mughal empire and became *mīr sāmān* (*vazīr*) of a Mughal princess after spending years as a local financial officer of the Safavid state.[84] As the Deccan kingdoms and the Mughal Empire had adopted Persian bureaucracy, his knowledge of *siyāq* might have been useful there as well.

The sources include information on how these people learned about *siyāq*. Āqā Šāh ʿAlī Dawlat-ābādī Iṣfahānī, who was the state accountant (*mustawfī al-mamālik*) during the reign of Šāh ʿAbbas, was so good at *siyāq* that he was called the master accountant (*ustād al-muḥāsibīn*). In fact, a later state accountant, Mīrzā Qivām al-Dīn Muḥammad Kafrānī Iṣfahānī, became a disciple of Āqā Šāh ʿAlī in *siyāq*.[85] In Yazd, Šamsā Amīr Muḥammad Ṭāhir was famous for teaching *siyāq*. He learned *siyāq* from his grandfather during his childhood and served the local government as an accountant. He became the supervisor of royal property (*niẓārat-i ḫāliṣağāt*) in Yazd sometime after 1669–70. Those who mastered the *siyāq* in Yazd at that time, including the author, Bāfqī, learned it from him.[86] Ḫwāğa Quṭb al-Dīn Ḫusraw-Šāh, who was the tax assessor in Yazd during the reign of Šāh Ṭahmāsb, wrote a book named *Ḫulāṣat al-ḥisāb* for *siyāq* learning.[87]

In addition, the royal court and chancery were places for learning *siyāq*. Adham Beg Urdūbādī and his nephews, Abū Turāb Beg and Abū Ṭālib Beg, learned *siyāq* at the royal court (*urdū-yi humāyūn* or *urdū-yi muʿallā*) while Ḫwāğa Muḥammad Amīn Šūra-bīz studied *siyāq* at the royal chancery (*daftarḫāna-i humāyūn*) for a while.[88] At that time, there were various ways to learn *siyāq*. It was unlikely that they learned *siyāq* one-on-one or acquired *iğāza*s after mastering it. However, they could learn it not only in the royal chancery but also from a master in the province, or they could learn by themselves by reading a *siyāq* manual.

Naturally, those who mastered *siyāq* became accountants and other financial officers. Nine out of ten individuals who mastered *siyāq* in *Tārīḫ-i ʿālam-ārā* had at least once been a financial officer; three were state accountants (*mustawfī al-mamālik*), namely Ḫwāğa Qāsim Naṭanzī, Āqā Šāh ʿAlī, and Mīrzā Qivām al-Dīn Muḥammad. According to an administrative manual, state accountants were required to have perfect understanding of *ʿilm-i siyāq* and writing documents.[89] The list also includes an accountant for additional taxes (*mustawfī-i māl*),[90] an accountant for balance (*mustawfī-i baqāyā*), an *avārağa-navīs* of Azerbaijan and Shirvan, an accountant for a prince, and two provincial accountants for Herat and Mashhad. Moreover, six of the 13 individuals who learned *siyāq* were mentioned in the chapter on accountants in *Ğāmiʿ-i Mufīdī*, including two provincial accountants for Yazd and an accountant for additional taxes (*mustawfī-i māl va maḥṣūl*).[91] In addition, the author, whose autobiography is not included in the chapter of accountants, was also a *mustawfī* of waqf property in Yazd.[92]

However, their other careers were more interesting. Two of them assumed the office of the chief city administrator (*kalāntar*): Adham Beg was appointed to the office of Tabriz, while Muʿizzā Šāhmīrā held that of Yazd for 18 years.[93] The duty of *kalāntar* was not restricted to fiscal affairs, but, as discussed above, the knowledge of *siyāq* must have been useful for him because he was involved in the taxation of guilds.[94]

Another office occupied by *siyāq* masters was that of the provincial *vazīr*s. Mīrzā Qivām al-Dīn Muḥammad was the *vazīr* of Herat before he became the state accountant. Adham Beg was promoted from the *kalāntar* of Tabriz to the *vazīr* of the same city. His cousin, Abū Turāb Beg Urdūbādī, also became the *vazīr* of Herat after working for some years as an accountant there.[95] *Ǧāmiʿ-i Mufīdī* mentions two *vazīr*s of Yazd and one *vazīr* of Isfahan.[96] It also states that Ḫwāǧa Pīr Muḥammad was the *vazīr* of Princess Ṣafiyya Sulṭan Ḫānum, the daughter of Šāh Ismāʿīl II, which probably means he controlled the princess' property and financial matters.[97]

Moreover, two *siyāq* masters became *grand vazīr*s (*vazīr-i dīvān-i aʿlā*), which was the highest office in the Safavid bureaucracy. Aḥmad Beg Nūr-i Kamāl Iṣfahānī first served Husayn Ḫān Šāmlū, the governor of Herat, as his *vazīr*. He was appointed as the grand *vazīr* in 1532 and was dismissed from office in 1534–35.[98] According to Iskandar Beg, *inšā* writers and specialists of finance and *siyāq* applauded his expressions and clarity in writing.[99] The other was Abū Ṭālib Beg Urdūbādī. He first served as an accountant for Herat. When his father, Ḥātim Beg, the grand *vazīr*, was killed in battle in 1620, he was appointed as his successor. He remained in the office until 1629, the year when Šāh ʿAbbās passed away and then became the royal secretary (*vāqiʿ-navīs*).[100] Again, in 1632, he was appointed as the grand *vazīr* but was killed by Šāh Ṣafī in 1634.[101]

In addition, although Iskandar Beg did not mention their command over *siyāq*, three grand *vazīr*s had experienced the position of the state secretary before reaching the office of grand *vazīr*: Mīrzā Šukr Allāh Iṣfahānī (grand *vazīr* 1576–77), Mīrzā Muḥammad Kirmānī (1585–89), and the above-mentioned Ḥāṭim Beg Urdūbādī (1591–1620).[102] It can be assumed that they knew *siyāq*. According to an administrative manual, a grand *vazīr* controlled very difficult matters in writing, accounting, *ʿilm-i siyāq*, settling accounts, and correcting daily records. Every hour he had to reply to questions from every clerk concerning these matters and had to have sufficient knowledge on them.[103]

Ḫwāndamīr said, 'The main thing for performing *vazīr*'s duties is skills in financial affairs (*istīfāʾ*) and *siyāq*.'[104] In other words, *siyāq* was essential knowledge for *vazīr*s, and this gave an advantage to those who had mastered it to ascend the ladder of bureaucracy and obtain power.

Conclusion

ʿIlm al-siyāq was a practical knowledge of how to record fiscal transactions in ledgers. It included 'numerical notation and numeracy' or arithmetic but more concerned fiscal administration. Sometimes, it was also called art (*fann*) instead of knowledge (*ʿilm*). It began around 705, when the language of fiscal administration changed into Arabic, and was Persianised before the second half of the 11th century. The term *siyāq* or *siyāqat* probably came from the expression '*siyāqat al-ḥisāb*,' which was found in the work of Ibn al-Ṭiqṭaqā. It was highly developed under Mongol rule and was inherited by the Timurids and the Safavids.

It is remarkable that *siyāq* manuals try to explain it as science, although it had a practical aspect. They link *siyāq* with famous figures such as ʿAlī b. Abī Ṭālib, ʿAbd al-Ḥamīd b. Yaḥyā, and Avicenna as its founder. Islamicate encyclopaedic work considered *ʿIlm al-siyāq* to be related to the art of writing or literary knowledge. The *siyāq* manuals were compiled also in provinces such as Kerman and Yazd, though they did not survive to this day.

Ǧāmiʿ al-ḥisāb, the Safavid *siyāq* manual examined in this chapter, demonstrates how closely *siyāq* was related to fiscal administration. The greater part of the manual explains specific ledgers such as *rūznāmača*, *tawǧīḥ*, and *avāraǧa*. The manual indicates that not only salary payments for administrators and soldiers but also the order of necklaces for the harem women or foodstuff for a royal banquet were recorded in those ledgers. The clerks of the state chancery (*daftarḫāna*) and royal supply departments (*buyūtāt*), who totalled more than 200 people in the Safavid central administration, made entries in those ledgers. In addition, local officers, such as *kalāntar*, needed *siyāq* knowledge for allotting public expenditure to guilds.

The well-known Safavid chronicle, *Tārīḫ-i ʿālam-ārā-yi ʿAbbāsī*, and the Safavid local history of Yazd, *Ǧāmiʿ-i Mufīdī*, provide us with a short biography of 23 people who learned *siyāq* and excelled in it. They included two grand *vazīr*s, five local *vazīr*s, three state accountants, and various financial officers. As Ḫwāndamīr said, *ʿilm al-siyāq* was indispensable knowledge for the office of *vazīr*, and some figures used this knowledge to obtain power in state and local administration. Here, we can see an obvious connection between *siyāq* knowledge and political power.

ʿIlm al-siyāq continued to be highly regarded during the Qajar period. In fact, the Marʿašī manuscript of Kirmānī's *Ǧāmiʿ al-ḥisāb* was once possessed by Mīrzā Muḥammad Ismāʿīl Garkānī. He became a *mustawfī* after the Fatḥ ʿAlī Šāh period (1797–1834), as did his son Mīrzā Naṣr Allāh. His family was well known because of ʿAbd Allāh Mustawfī's memoir, which described their history in detail.[105] The first page of the manuscript contains a *waqf* deed for Muḥammad Ismāʿīl, dated 11 Šavvāl 1246 (25 March 1836); he made this manuscript a *waqf* on behalf of his future descendants.[106] Knowledge of fiscal administration was essential for their success, and they tried to keep this knowledge within the family. After 1910–11, the tradition of *siyāq* was abandoned due to modern financial reform.[107]

Notes

* The research for this study was supported by JSPS Kakenhi no. 17H02398. I would like to thank my colleagues from the *siyāq* project in Tokyo, which started in 2008: Yoichi Takamatsu, Ryoko Watabe, Naofumi Abe, and others for sharing their expertise on Persian bookkeeping.

1 M. Bagheri, "Siyāqat Accounting: Its Origin, History, and Principles," *Acta Orientalia* 51 (1998): 297–301; B. Spooner and W. L. Hanaway, "Siyaq: Numerical Notation and Numeracy in the Persianate World," in *The Oxford Handbook of the History of Mathematics*, ed. by E. Robson and J. Stedall (Oxford: Oxford University Press), 2009, 429–47.

2 W. Hinz, "Ein orientalisches Handelsunternehmen im 15. Jahrhundert," *Die Welt des Orients* 1 (1949): 313–40; idem, "Das Rechnungswesen orientalischer Reichsfinanzämter im Mittelalter," *Der Islam* 29 (1950), 1–29, 113–41; ʿAbd Allāh Māzandarānī, *Die Resālä-ye Falakiyyä des ʿAbdollāh ibn Moḥammad ibn Kiyā al-Māzandarānī: Ein persischer Leitfaden des staatlichen Rechnungswesens (um 1363)*, ed. by W. Hinz (Wiesbaden: Steiner, 1952).

3 R. Watabe, "Jusanseiki Mongoru shihaiki Iran no Perushiago zaimujutsu shinansho *Murshid fī al-ḥisāb*," in *Iranshiki bokijutsu no hatten to tenkai*, ed. by Yoichi Takamatsu (Tokyo: Toyo Bunko, 2011), 9–35; idem, "Census-Taking and the *Qubchūr* Taxation System in Ilkhanid Iran: An Analysis of the Census Book from the Late 13th Century Persian Accounting Manual *al-Murshid fi al-Ḥisāb*," *Memoirs of the Research Department of the Toyo Bunko* 73 (2015): 27–63; idem, "13–14 seiki Iruhanchoka Iran no chozei-seido: Bokijutsu shinansho-shiryo niyoru saikosei," in *Kinsei Isuramu-kokkashi kenkyu no genzai*, ed. by N. Kondo (Fuchu, Tokyo: ILCAA, 2015), 13–56.

4 J. Aubin, "Etudes safavides. I: Šāh Ismāʿīl et les notables de l'Iraq persan," *Journal of the Economic and Social History of the Orient* 2 (1959): 39.

5 Y. Takamatsu, "Joron," in *Iranshiki bokijutsu no hatten to tenkai*, ed. by Y. Takamatsu (Tokyo: Toyo Bunko, 2011), 2–3. Researchers in Turkey call it the Merdiban method, i.e., ladder method. See O. Güvemli et al., *Accounting Method Used by Ottomans for 500 Years: Stairs (Merdiban) Method* (Ankara: Maliye Bakanliği, 2008).

6 Muḥammad Mahdī b. Ḥāğğī Muḥammad Riżā, "Risāla dar ʿilm-i siyāq," MS no. 5379-2, Kitābḫāna-i Mağlis i Šūrā yi Islāmī, Tehran, ff. 24a–b. Since the author Muḥammad Mahdī was mentioned as the *vazīr* of the chief of the *ghulām* army (*vazīr-i sarkār-i ʿālīğāh qullar-āqāsī*), it is clear that the treatise was written in the later Safavid period.

7 Šams al-Dīn Muḥammad Āmulī, *Nafāʾis al-funūn fī ʿarāyis al-ʿuyūn*, ed. by Abū l-Ḥasan Šuʿarāʾī (Tehran: Islāmiyya, 2002–03), 302–3.

8 Ibn al-Ṭiqṭaqā, *al-Aṣīlī fī ansāb al-ṭālibiyyīn*, ed. by Sayyid Mahdī Rağāʾī (Qum: Marʿašī Najafī, 1997–98), 32. See also Ibn al-Ṭiqṭaqā, *al-Faḫrī fī l-ādāb al-sulṭāniyya wa-l-duwal al-Islāmiyya* (Beirut: Dār ṣādir, n.d.), 122. I thank Kazuo Morimoto for the former reference.

9 Ḥamd Allāh Mustawfī, *Ẓafar-nāma: Qism al-Islāmiyya*, ed. by Mahdī Madāyinī et. al., vol. 2 (Tehran: Pažūhišgāh-i ʿulūm-i insānī va muṭālaʿāt-i farhangī, 1991–92), 407–8. See also Ḥamd Allāh Mustawfī, *Tārīḫ-i guzīda*, ed. by ʿAbd al-Ḥusayn Navāʾī (Tehran: Amīr-i Kabīr, 1985–86), 277.

10 W. N. Brinner, "ʿAbd-al-Ḥamīd b. Yaḥyā," in *Encyclopædia Iranica*, ed. by Ehsan Yarshater (London and Boston: Routledge and Kegan Paul, 1982–), vol. 1, 111–2.

11 Ibn al-Ṭiqṭaqā, *al-Aṣīlī fī ansāb al-ṭālibiyyīn*, 34.

12 D. Gutas, "Avicenna ii. Biography," in *Encyclopædia Iranica*, vol. 3, 67–70.

13 A. von Kremer, "Ueber das Budget der Einnahmen unter der Regierung des Hârûn alraśîd nach einer neu aufgefundenen Urkunde," in *Verhandlungen des VII. internationalen Orientalisten-*

Congresses gehalten in Wien im Jahre 1886, semitische Section (Vienna: Alfred Bölder, 1888), Tafel 2 and 3; idem, "Ueber das Einnahmebudget des Abbasiden-Reiches vom Jahre 306 H. (918–919)," *Denkschriften der kaiserlichen Akademie der Wissenschaften. Philosophisch-historische Classe* 36 (1888): Tafel I–III.

14 Spooner and Hanaway, "Siyaq," 436.

15 An exception is Dozy, who explains the word *siyāqat* as "Semble avoir le sens de finances" and cites Ibn al-Ṭiqṭaqā's *al-Faḫrī*. R. Dozy, *Supplément aux dictionnaires arabes*, vol. 1 (Beirut: Librairie du Liban, 1991), 706–7.

16 Ġiyāṯ al-Dīn Muḥammad Rāmpūlī, *Ġiyāṯ al-luġāt*, ed. by M. Dabīr-e Siyāqī (Tehran: Kānūn-i ma'rifat, 1958), 584.

17 H. Rāhnamā, "Čand vāža-yi Īrānī: Siyāq, bāyrām, ḫurvarā," *Īrānšināsī* 7 (1995): 152–4.

18 Bagheri, "Siyaqat Accounting," 298–9.

19 Ibn al-Nadīm, *Kitāb al-Fihrist*, ed. by R. Tajaddud (Tehran: Marvī, 1971), 24.

20 Al-Ḫwārizmī, *Mafātīḥ al-'ulūm* (Beirut: Dār al-kitāb al-'Arabī, 1989), 81–2. See also C. E Bosworth, "Abū 'Abdallāh al-Khwārazmī on the Technical Terms of the Secretary's Art," *Journal of the Economic and Social History of the Orient* 12 (1969): 120–4. Also, al-Qalqašandī (d. 1418) mentioned *awārağ* and *rūznāmağ* but did not refer to *siyāq* or *siyāqat*, which means that the term *siyāq* or *siyāqat* was rarely used in Mamluk Egypt. Al-Qalqašandī, *Ṣubḥ al-a'šā fī ṣinā'at al-inšā'*, ed. by M. Ḥ. Šams al-Dīn (Beirut: Dār al-kutub al-'ilmiyya, 2012), vol. 13, 74, vol. 14, 131–2.

21 Bagheri, "Siyaqat Accounting," 299.

22 Nāṣir Ḫusraw, *Safarnāma*, ed. by Muḥammad Dabīr-i Siyāqī (Tehran: Zuvvār, 1991–92), 4.

23 Ibn al-Ṭiqṭaqā, *al-Faḫrī*, 19.

24 Āmulī, *Nafā'is al-funūn*, 302–38.

25 Ibid., 304.

26 Falak 'Alā Tabrīzī, *Die beiden persischen Leitfäden des Falak 'Alā-ye Tabrīzī über das staatliche Rechnungswesen im 14. Jahrhundert*, ed. by Mirkamal Nabipour (Göttingen: Georg-August-Universität zu Göttingen, 1973); 'Imād Sarāvī, *Das sogenannte Ǧāme'o'l-ḥesāb des 'Emad as-Sarāwī*, ed. by Nejat Göyünç (Berlin: EB Verlag, 2012); Māzandarānī, *Die Resālä-ye Falakiyyä*. The facsimile of the manuscript of *Risāla-i Falakiyya* preserved in the Mağlis Library in Tehran was also published along with its Japanese translation in *Bokijutsu ni kansuru Farakiya no ronsetsu*, ed. by Y. Takamatsu (Tokyo: Toyo Bunko, 2013), 73–111.

27 Watabe, "Perushiago zaimujutsu shinansho"; idem, "Census-Taking"; N. Īrānī, *Kuhantarīn farhangnāma-i Fārsī-i dāniš-i istīfā: Taṣḥīḥ va taḥlīl-i baḫš-i luġāt va musṭalaḥāt-i al-Muršid fī l-ḥisāb* (Tehran: Mīrāṯ-i maktūb, 2016).

28 Watabe, "Census-Taking," 38–40.

29 Hinz, "Ein orientalisches Handelsunternehmen," 313–40; M. Subtelny, *Timurids in Transition: Turko-Persian Politics and Acculturation in Medieval Iran* (Leiden: Brill, 2007), 80–2.

30 Hinz, "Ein orientalisches Handelsunternehmen," 316.

31 Sayf al-Dīn 'Uqaylī, *Āṯār al-vuzarā'*, ed. by M. H. Muḥaddiṯ (Tehran: Iṭṭilā'āt, 1985–86), 342; Subtelny, *Timurids*, 80.

32 Ġiyāṯ al-Dīn Ḫwāndamīr, *Dastūr al-vuzarā'*, ed. by S. Nafīsī (Tehran: Iqbāl, 1976–77), 90 (*dar fann-i siyāq va istīfā'*), 199 (*dar fann-i istīfā' va siyāqat*).

33 Vāṣifī (Zayn al-Dīn Maḥmūd), *Badāyi' al-vaqāyi'*, ed. A. N. Boldyrev (Tehran: Bunyād-i farhang-i Īrān, 1970–71), 5, 13, 244 (*'ilm-i siyāq*).

34 Mīr Sayyid Šarīf Rāqim Samarqandī, *Tārīḫ-i rāqim*, ed. by Ī. Afšār (Tehran: Mawqūfāt-i Duktur Mahmūd Afšār, 2001–02), 496–7 (*'ilm-i siyāq*); 'Abd al-Qādir Badāyunī, *Muntaḫab al-tavārīḫ*, ed. by A. A. Ṣāḥib, vol. 3 (Tehran: Anğuman-i āṯār va mafāḫir-i farhangī, 2001), 190 (*'ilm-i siyāq*), 192 (*fann-i siyāq*).

35 For examples, Mīrzā Badī' Dīvān, *Mağma' al-arqām*, ed. by A. B. Vildanova (Moscow: Nauka, 1981) (from 18th century Bukhara); Munšī Nandrām, *Siyāq-nāma* (Lucknow: Nawal Kishore, 1879) (from the late 17th century North India). I thank Naofumi Abe for providing a copy of *Siyāq-nāma* to me.

36 R. Watabe and N. Abe, "16-seiki Safavi-choki no Perushiago zaimu boki shinansho," *Journal of Asian and African Studies* 94 (2017): 383–485; Ġiyāṯ al-Dīn Abū Isḥāq Muḥammad Kirmānī, *Risāla'ī dar siyāq*, ed. by ʿAlī Rižā Nīkūnižād (Tehran: Nigāristān-i andīša), 2020. Watabe and Abe's contains the edition from chapter 7–15 of Kirmānī's introduction (*muqaddima*) and its Japanese translation. Nīkūnižād edited all the chapters, but he did not transcribe the *siyāq* parts of the text; instead, he inserted the facsimile of the parts in the Āstān-i Quds manuscript, which is the most readable but not the most accurate. An earlier article on the work is Aḥmad Gulčīn-maʿānī, "Risāla dar ʿilm-i siyāq," *Maǧalla-i Dāniškada-i Adabiyyāt* 12.4 (1965): 355–63.

37 This title is found in the front page of the Marʿašī manuscript, which is dated 1064 AH/1654 and the only manuscript with all the chapters. Abū Isḥāq Ġiyāṯ al-Dīn Muḥammad Kirmānī, *Ǧāmiʿ al-ḥisāb*, MS no. 8140, Marʿašī Naǧafī Library, Qum. I thank Dr. Sayyid Maḥmūd Marʿašī for access to this manuscript. Dirāyatī also uses the title *Ǧāmiʿ al-ḥisāb* to refer to Kirmānī's work. See, M. Dirāyatī, *Fihristgān-i nusḫa'hā-yi ḫaṭṭī-i Īrān*, 45 vols. (Tehran, Sāzmān-i asnād va kitābḫāna-i millī-i Ǧumhūrī-i Islāmī-i Īrān, 2012–15), vol. 9, 841–2.

38 Kirmānī, *Risāla'ī dar siyāq*, 33.

39 Ibid., 34–5.

40 Qāžī Aḥmad Qummī, *Ḫulāṣat al-tavarīḫ*, ed. by Iḥsān Išrāqī (Tehran: Dānišgāh-i Tihrān, 1980–84), 903; Iskandar Beg Turkmān, *Tārīḫ-i ʿālam-ārā-yi ʿAbbāsī*, ed. by Ī. Afšār (Tehran: Amīr-i Kabīr, 1971–72), 167.

41 Kirmānī, *Ǧāmiʿ al-ḥisāb*, 150. The record is dated 15 Ẕīqaʿda 949 AH (20 February 1543), but this date cannot be confirmed by other sources.

42 Kirmānī, *Risāla'ī dar siyāq*, 48.

43 Iskandar Beg, *Tārīḫ-i ʿālam-ārā*, 167. He returned to Kerman during the reign of Šāh Muḥammad Ḫudābanda, but he confronted Bektāš Ḫān Afšār, the governor, and was forced to escape to ʿAtabāt and Baghdad. Some researchers, including Watabe and Abe, believe that ʿAbd al-Qādir was the local *vazīr* of Kerman but there is no proof to confirm this (Watabe and Abe, "Zaimu boki shinansho," 388). His grandson, ʿAbd al-Rašīd, was appointed to the office of *kalāntar* of Kerman during the reign of Šāh ʿAbbās. See Fazli Beg Khuzani Isfahani, *A Chronicle of the Reign of Shah ʿAbbas*, ed. by K. Ghereghlou (Cambridge: Gibb Memorial Trust, 2015), vol. 2, 606–7; Mīr Muḥammad Saʿīd Mušīrī, *Taẕkira-i Ṣafaviyya-i Kirmān*, ed. by M. I. Bāstānī Pārīzī (Tehran: ʿIlm, 1990–91), 182, 205.

44 Kirmānī, *Risāla'ī dar siyāq*, 111.

45 Kirmānī, *Ǧāmiʿ al-ḥisāb*, 227, dated Muḥarram, 951 AH.

46 Kirmānī, *Risāla'ī dar siyāq*, 48. *Baḥr al-siyāq* was a comprehensive *siyāq* manual compiled at the court of Šāhruḫ (r. 1409–42) but now lost. ʿAlī Šīrāzī's *Šams al-siyāq* was its abridged version (Subtelny, *Timurids in Transition*, 80). Šams al-Dīn Muḥammad's *Šams al-siyāq* concerns laws of inheritance, using *siyāq* notation (Dirāyatī, *Fihristigān*, vol. 21, 155). Kirmānī may have intended to mention ʿAlī Šīrāzī's work with the same title. The details of two other works are unknown and probably lost, but it is insightful that such works were composed by the authors from Kerman.

47 Kirmānī, *Risāla'ī dar siyāq*, 48.

48 Here, I follow the reading by Watabe and Abe. Gulčīn-maʿānī and Nīknižād read as *tarsīf*, which does not make sense.

49 Kirmānī, *Risāla'ī dar siyāq*, 56.

50 Ibid., 58–9.

51 Kirmānī, *Ǧāmiʿ al-ḥisāb*, 51–7.

52 W. Floor only mentioned the names of the ledgers and included short, mostly inaccurate explanations of them, citing W. Hinz's article on Timurid *siyāq* manuals. See, W. Floor, *A Fiscal History of Iran in the Safavid and Qajar Periods 1500–1925* (New York: Bibliotheca Persia Press, 1998), 96, 511–2.

53 Kirmānī, *Risāla'ī dar siyāq*, 127.

54 Kirmānī, Ǧāmiʿ al-ḥisāb, 131.
55 Watabe, "13–14 seiki Iruhanchoka Iran no chozei-seido," 19.
56 I. Maḥbūb Farīmānī, Barrasī-i sāḫtār-i ẓāhirī va muḥtavāyī-yi dafātir-i tawǧīhāt dar ʿaṣr-i Ṣafavī (Tehran: Sāzmān-i asnād va kitābḫāna-'i millī, 2020–21).
57 Kirmānī, Ǧāmiʿ al-ḥisāb, 148.
58 Watabe, "13–14 seiki Iruhanchoka Iran no chozei-seido," 41–2.
59 Bosworth, "Abū ʿAbdallāh al-Khwārazmī," 119; Watabe, "13–14 seiki Iruhanchoka Iran no chozei-seido," 42–3.
60 Watabe, "13–14 seiki Iruhanchoka Iran no chozei-seido," 44.
61 Kirmānī, Ǧāmiʿ al-ḥisāb, 171.
62 Floor, *A Fiscal History*, 99.
63 Mīrzā Samīʿā, *Taẕkirat al-mulūk*, ed. by M. Dabīr-i Siyāqī (Tehran: Amīr Kabīr, 1989–90), 35; Mīrzā Mūḥammad Rafīʿ Anṣārī, *Dastūr al-mulūk*, ed. by N. Kondo (Tokyo: ILCAA, 2018), 159.
64 Anṣārī, *Dastūr al-mulūk*, 35, 125–6, 128, 159; Samīʿā, *Taẕkirat al-mulūk*, 10–1, 34; Yūsuf Raḥīmlū, ed., *Alqāb va mavāǧib-i dawra-i salāṭīn-i Ṣafaviyya* (Mashhad: Dānišgāh-i Firdawsī, 1993), 22, 65.
65 Raḥīmlū, ed., *Alqāb va mavāǧib*, 6.
66 Anṣārī, *Dastūr al-mulūk*, 165.
67 Ibid., 159–71, 220.
68 Compare with Floor's explanation: Floor, *A Fiscal History*, 532.
69 Anṣārī, *Dastūr al-mulūk*, 115; Samīʿā, *Taẕkirat al-mulūk*, 42; V. Minorsky, transl., *Tadhkirat al Mulūk: A Manual of Ṣafavid Administration* (Cambridge, E.J.W. Gibb Memorial Trust, 1980), 76–7, 143.
70 Anṣārī, *Dastūr al-mulūk*, 155–6.
71 Raḥīmlū, ed., *Alqāb va mavāǧib*, 58.
72 Samīʿā, *Taẕkirat al-mulūk*, 17.
73 Anṣārī, *Dastūr al-mulūk*, 116.
74 Ibid., 156.
75 Ibid., 88.
76 Ibid., 130, 133.
77 Ibid., 151.
78 Maḥbūb Farīmānī, *Dafātir-i tawǧīhāt*.
79 Anṣārī, *Dastūr al-mulūk*, 120; Samīʿā, *Taẕkirat al-mulūk*, 43–4; Raḥīmlū, ed., *Alqāb va mavāǧib*, 59–60; Minorsky, transl., *Tadhkirat al Mulūk*, 77–8.
80 Samīʿā, *Taẕkirat al-mulūk*, 17; Anṣārī, *Dastūr al-mulūk*, 67, 153–4.
81 Anṣārī, *Dastūr al-mulūk*, 67, 120–1, 150–3.
82 Mīrzā Muḥammad Mufīd Bāfqī, *Ǧāmiʿ-i Mufīdī*, ed. by Ī. Afšār, vol. 3 (Tehran: Asadī, 1961), 510.
83 Bāfqī, *Ǧāmiʿ-i Mufīdī*, 486–7.
84 Ibid., 754–60, 815.
85 Iskandar Beg, *Tārīḫ-i ʿālam-ārā*, 531, 675, 1092. W. Floor provided the list of *mustawfī al-mamālik*s, but it contained much confusion concerning Šāh ʿAbbās's reign and did not mention Āqā Šāh ʿAlī. W. Floor, *Safavid Government Institutions* (Costa Mesa, California: Mazda Publishers, 2001), 42–3. The accurate list can be found in Iskandar Beg, *Tārīḫ-i ʿālam-ārā*, 1092–3.
86 Bāfqī, *Ǧāmiʿ-i Mufīdī*, 267–9.
87 Ibid. 265–6. This work appears not to survive until today.
88 Iskandar Beg, *Tārīḫ-i ʿālam-ārā*, 725; Bāfqī, *Ǧāmiʿ-i Mufīdī*, 185.
89 Raḥīmlū, ed., *Alqāb va mavāǧib*, 47.
90 Iskandar Beg rephrased this term as *żābiṭa-navīs* and *mufrida-navīs*. Iskandar Beg, *Tārīḫ-i ʿālam-ārā*, 165.
91 Bāfqī, *Ǧāmiʿ-i Mufīdī*, 254–70.
92 Ibid., 752.

93 Iskandar Beg, *Tārīḫ-i ʿālam-ārā*, 725, 727; Bāfqī, *Ǧāmiʿ-i Mufīdī*, 99–100.
94 For his duty, see Anṣārī, *Dastūr al-mulūk*, 88–9.
95 Iskandar Beg, *Tārīḫ-i ʿālam-ārā*, 675, 725, 727.
96 Bāfqī, *Ǧāmiʿ-i Mufīdī*, 185, 187, 255.
97 Ibid., 487.
98 Qāżī Aḥmad Qummī, *Ḫulāṣat al-tavarīḫ*, 218, 236. Iskandar Beg erroneously states that Aḥmad Beg remained in the office of grand *vazīr* for six years.
99 Iskandar Beg, *Tārīḫ-i ʿālam-ārā*,160.
100 Iskandar Beg, *Tārīḫ-i ʿālam-ārā*, 807, 1091; Abū l-Mafāḫir Ḥusaynī Tafrišī, *Tārīḫ-i Šāh Ṣafī*, ed. by M. Bahrām-nižād (Tehran: Mīrāṯ-i maktūb, 2010), 25.
101 Muḥammad Maʿṣūm Iṣfahānī, *Ḫulāṣat al-siyar*, ed. by Ī. Afšār (Tehran: ʿIlmī, 1989), 127–8, 188.
102 Qāżī Aḥmad Qummī, *Ḫulāṣat al-tavarīḫ*, ed. by I. Išrāqī (Tehran: Dānišgāh-i Tihrān, 1980–84), 847; Iskandar Beg, *Tārīḫ-i ʿālam-ārā*, 206, 439.
103 Raḥīmlū, ed., *Alqāb va mavāǧib*, 5.
104 Ḫwāndamīr, *Dastūr al-vuzarāʾ*, 379.
105 ʿAbd Allāh Mustawfī, *Šarḥ-i zindigānī-i man yā tārīḫ-i iǧtimāʿī va idārī-i dawra-i Qāǧāriyya*, 3 vols. (Tehran: Zuvvār, 1981–82); Abdollah Mostofi, *The Administrative and Social History of the Qajar Period*, transl. by Nayer Mostofi-Glenn, 3 vols. (Costa Mesa, Cal., Mazda 1997).
106 Kirmānī, *Ǧāmiʿ al-ḥisāb*, 1v (this page is not numbered).
107 For the end of the *siyāq* tradition, see ʿI. Šayḫ al-Ḥukamāyī, "Saranjām-i siyāq-navīsī dar Īrān," *Tārīḫ-i Īrān* 15 (2014): 111–34.

Bibliography

Āmulī, Šams al-Dīn Muḥammad b. Maḥmūd. *Nafāʾis al-funūn fī ʿarāyis al-ʿuyūn*. Ed. by Abū l-Ḥasan Šuʿarāʾī. Tehran: Islāmiyya, 2002–03.

Anṣārī, Mīrzā Muḥammad Rafīʿ. *Dastūr al-mulūk*. Ed. by Nobuaki Kondo. Fuchu: ILCAA, 2018.

Aubin, J. "Etudes safavides. I. Šāh Ismāʿīl et les notables de l'Iraq persan." *Journal of the Economic and Social History of the Orient* 2.1 (1959): 37–81.

Badāyunī, ʿAbd al-Qādir. *Muntaḫab al-tavārīḫ*. Ed. by A. A. Ṣāḥib, vol. 3. Tehran: Anǧuman-i āṯār va mafāḫir-i farhangī, 2001.

Bāfqī, Mīrzā Muḥammad Mufīd. *Ǧāmiʿ-i Mufīdī*. Ed. by Īraǧ Afšār, vol. 3. Tehran: Asadī, 1961.

Bagheri, Mohammad. "Siyaqat Accounting: Its Origin, History, and Principles." *Acta Orientalia* 51 (1998): 297–301.

Bosworth, C. E. "Abū ʿAbdallāh al-Khwārazmī on the Technical Terms of the Secretary's Art." *Journal of the Economic and Social History of the Orient* 12 (1969): 113–64.

Brinner, W. N. "ʿAbd-al-Ḥamīd b. Yaḥyā." In *Encyclopædia Iranica*. Ed. by Ehsan Yarshater. London and Boston: Routledge and Kegan Paul, 1982–, vol. 1, 111–2.

Dirāyatī, Muṣṭafā, ed. *Fihristgān-i nusḫa'hā-yi ḫaṭṭī-i Īrān*. 45 vols. Tehran: Sāzmān-i asnād va kitābḫāna-i millī-i Ǧumhūrī-i Islāmī-i Īrān, 2012–15.

Dīvān, Mīrzā Badīʿ. *Maǧmaʿ al-arqām*. Ed. by A. B. Vildanova. Moscow: Nauka, 1981.

Dozy, R. *Supplément aux dictionnaires arabes*. 2 vols. Beirut: Librairie du Liban, 1991.

Floor, Willem. *A Fiscal History of Iran in the Safavid and Qajar Periods 1500–1925*. New York: Bibliotheca Persia Press, 1998.

Floor, Willem. *Safavid Government Institutions*. Costa Mesa, California: Mazda Publishers, 2001.

Gulčīn-maʿānī, Aḥmad. "Risāla dar ʿilm-i siyāq." *Maǧalla-i Dāniškada-i Adabiyyāt* 12.4 (1965): 355–63.

Gutas, D. "Avicenna ii. Biography." In *Encyclopædia Iranica*. Ed. by Ehsan Yarshater. London and Boston: Routledge and Kegan Paul, 1982–, vol. 3, 67–70.

Güvemli, Oktay et. al. *Accounting Method Used by Ottomans for 500 Years: Stairs (Merdiban) Method*. Ankara: Maliye Bakanliği, 2008.

Hinz, Walther. "Ein orientalisches Handelsunternehmen im 15. Jahrhundert." *Die Welt des Orients* 1 (1949): 313–40.

Hinz, Walther. "Das Rechnungswesen orientalischer Reichsfinanzämter im Mittelalter." *Der Islam* 29 (1950), 1–29, 113–41.

Ḫwāndamīr, Ġiyāṯ al-Dīn. *Dastūr al-vuzarāʾ*. Ed. by Saʿīd Nafīsī. Tehran: Iqbāl, 1976–77.

Al-Ḫwārizmī, Muḥammad b. Aḥmad. *Mafātīḥ al-ʿulūm*. Beirut: Dār al-kitāb al-ʿArabī. 1989.

Ibn al-Ṭiqṭaqā, Muḥammad b. ʿAlī. *Al-Faḫrī fī l-ādāb al-sulṭāniyya wa-l-duwal al-Islāmiyya*. Beirut: Dār ṣādir, n.d.

Ibn al-Ṭiqṭaqā, Muḥammad b. ʿAlī. *Al-Aṣīlī fī ansāb al-ṭālibiyyīn*. Ed. by Sayyid Mahdī Raǧāʾī. Qum: Kitābḫāna-yi Āyatullāh Marʿašī Najafī, 1997–98.

Īrānī, Nafīsa. *Kuhantarīn farhangnāma-i fārsī-i dāniš-i istīfā: Taṣḥīḥ va taḥlīl-i baḫš-i luġāt va musṭalaḥāt-i al-Muršid fī l-ḥisāb*. Tehran: Mīrāṯ-i maktūb, 2016.

Isfahani, Fazli Beg Khuzani. *A Chronicle of the Reign of Shah ʿAbbas*. Ed. by K. Ghereghlou. 2 vols. Cambridge: Gibb Memorial Trust, 2015.

Iṣfahānī, Muḥammad Maʿṣūm b. Ḫwāǧagī. *Ḫulāṣat al-siyar*. Ed. by Īraǧ Afšār. Tehran: ʿIlmī, 1989.

Iskandar Beg Turkmān. *Tārīḫ-i ʿālam-ārā-yi ʿAbbāsī*. Ed. by Īraǧ Afšār. Tehran: Amīr-i Kabīr, 1971–72.

Kirmānī, Abū Isḥāq Ġiyāṯ al-Dīn Muḥammad. *Ǧāmiʿ al-ḥisāb*. MS no. 8140, Marʿašī Naǧafī Library, Qum.

Kirmānī, Abū Isḥāq Ġiyāṯ al-Dīn Muḥammad. *Risālaʾī dar siyāq*. Ed. by ʿAlī Riżā Nīkūnižād. Tehran. Nigāristān-i Andīša, 2020.

Kremer, A. von. "Ueber das Budget der Einnahmen unter der Regierung des Hârûn alraśîd nach einer neu aufgefundenen Urkunde." In *Verhandlungen des VII. internationalen Orientalisten-Congresses gehalten in Wien im Jahre 1886, semitische Section*. Vienna: Alfred Bölder, 1888, 1–18.

Kremer, A. von. "Ueber das Einnahmebudget des Abbasiden-Reiches vom Jahre 306 H. (918-919)." *Denkschriften der kaiserlichen Akademie der Wissenschaften. Philosophisch-historische Classe* 36 (1888): 283–362.

Maḥbūb Farīmānī, Ilāh. *Barrasī-i sāḫtār-i ẓāhirī va muḥtavāyī-i dafātir-i tawǧīhāt dar ʿaṣr-i Ṣafavī*. Tehran: Sāzmān-i kitābḫāna va asnād-i millī-i Ǧumhūrī-i Islāmī-i Īrān, 2020–21.

Māzandarānī, Abd Allāh. *Die Resālä-ye Falakiyyä des ʿAbdollāh ibn Moḥammad ibn Kiyā al-Māzandarānī: Ein persischer Leitfaden des staatlichen Rechnungswesens (um 1363)*. Ed. by Walther Hinz. Wiesbaden: Steiner, 1952.

Minorsky, V., transl. *Tadhkirat al-Mulūk: A Manual of Ṣafavid Administration*. Cambridge: E.J.W. Gibb Memorial Trust, 1980.

Morimoto, Kazuo. "The Formation and Development of the Science of Talibid Genealogies in the 10th & 11th Century Middle East." *Oriente Moderno* n.s. 18 (1999): 541–70.

Mostofi, Abdollah. *The Administrative and Social History of the Qajar Period*. Transl. by Nayer Mostofi-Glenn. 3 vols. Costa Mesa, Cal.: Mazda, 1997.

Muḥammad Mahdī b. Ḥāǧǧī Muḥammad Riżā. *Risāla dar ʿilm-i siyāq*. MS no. 5379-2, Kitābḫāna-i Maǧlis-i Šūrā-yi Islāmī, Tehran.

Muširī, Mīr Muḥammad Saʿīd. *Tazkira-i Ṣafaviyya-i Kirmān*. Ed. by M. I. Bāstānī Pārīzī. Tehran: ʿIlm, 1990–91.

Mustawfī, ʿAbd Allāh. *Šarḥ-i zindigānī-i man yā tārīḫ-i iǧtimāʿī va idārī-i dawra-i Qāǧāriyya*. 3 vols. Tehran: Zuvvār, 1981–82.

Mustawfī, Ḥamd Allāh. *Tārīḫ-i guzīda*. Ed. by ʿAbd al-Ḥusayn Navāʾī. Tehran: Amīr-i Kabīr, 1960.

Mustawfī, Ḥamd Allāh. *Ẓafar-nāma: Qism al-Islāmiyya*. Ed. by Mahdī Madāyinī et al. Tehran: Pažūhišgāh-i ʿulūm-i insānī va muṭālaʿāt-i farhangī, 1991–92.

Nāṣir Ḫusraw. *Safarnāma*. Ed. by Muḥammad Dabīr-i Siyāqī. Tehran: Zuvvār, 1991–92.

Al-Qalqašandī, Aḥmad b. ʿAlī. *Ṣubḥ al-aʿšā fī ṣināʿat al-inšāʾ*. Ed. by Muḥammad Ḥusayn Šams al-Dīn, 15 vols. Beirut: Dār al-kutub al-ʿilmiyya, 2012.

Qummī, Qāżī Aḥmad. *Ḫulāṣat al-tavarīḫ*. Ed. by Iḥsān Išrāqī. Tehran: Dānišgāh-i Tihrān, 1980–84.

Raḥīmlū, Yūsuf, ed. *Alqāb va mavāǧib-i dawra-i salāṭīn-i Ṣafaviyya*. Mashhad: Dānišgāh-i Firdawsī, 1993.

Rāhnamā, Hūšang. "Čand vāža-yi Īrānī: Siyāq, bāyrām, ḫurvarā." *Īrānšināsī* 7 (1995): 152–7.

Rāmpūlī, Ġiyāṯ al-Dīn Muḥammad. *Ġiyāṯ al-luġāt*. Ed. by M. Dabīr-i Siyāqī. Tehran: Kānūn-i maʿrifat, 1958.

Samarqandī, Mīr Sayyid Šarīf Rāqim. *Tārīḫ-i rāqim*. Ed. by Īraǧ Afšār. Tehran: Mawqūfāt-i Duktur Mahmūd Afšār, 2001–02.

Samīʿā, Mīrzā. *Tazkirat al-mulūk*. Ed. by M. Dabīr-i Siyāqī. Tehran: Amīr Kabīr, 1989–90.

Sarāvī, ʿImād. *Das sogenannte Ǧāme'o'l-Ḥesāb des 'Emad as-Sarāwī: Ein Leitfaden des staatlichen Rechnungswesen von ca. 1340*. Ed. by Nejat Göyünç. Berlin: EB Verlag, 2012.

Šayḫ al-Ḥukamāyī, ʿImād al-Dīn. "Saranǧām-i siyāq-navīsī dar Īrān." *Tārīḫ-i Īrān* 15 (2014): 111–34.

Spooner, Brian and William L. Hanaway. 2009. "Siyaq: Numerical Notation and Numeracy in the Persianate World." In *The Oxford Handbook of the History of Mathematics*. Ed. by Eleanor Robson and Jacqueline Stedall. Oxford: Oxford University Press, 2009, 429–47.

Subtelny, Maria. *Timurids in Transition: Turko-Persian Politics and Acculturation in Medieval Iran*. Leiden and Boston: Brill, 2007.

Tabrīzī, Falak ʿAlā. *Die beiden persischen Leitfäden des Falak ʿAlā-ye Tabrīzī über das staatliche Rechnungswesen im 14. Jahrhundert*. Ed. by Mirkamal Nabipour. Göttingen: Georg-August-Universität zu Göttingen, 1973.

Tafrišī, Abū l-Mafāḫir Ḥusaynī. *Tārīḫ-i Šāh Ṣafī*. Ed. by Muḥsin Bahrām-nižād. Tehran: Mīrāṯ-i maktūb, 2010.

Takamatsu, Yoichi, ed. *Iranshiki bokijutsu no hatten to tenkai* イラン式簿記術の発展と展開. Tokyo: Toyo Bunko, 2011.

Takamatsu, Yoichi. "Joron 序論." In *Iranshiki bokijutsu no hatten to tenkai*. Ed. by Y. Takamatsu. Tokyo: Toyo Bunko, 2011, 1–7.

Takamatsu, Yoichi, ed. *Bokijutu ni kansuru Farakiya no ronsetsu* 簿記術に関するファラキーヤの論説. Tokyo: Toyo Bunko, 2013.

ʿUqaylī, Sayf al-Dīn. *Āṯār al-vuzarāʾ*. Ed. by Mīr Ǧalāl al-Dīn Muḥaddiṯ. Tehran: Iṭṭilāʿāt, 1985–86.

Vāṣifī, Zayn al-Dīn Maḥmūd. *Badāyiʿ al-vaqāyiʿ*. Ed. by A. N. Boldyrev. Tehran: Bunyād-i farhang-i Īrān, 1970–71.

Watabe, Ryoko. "Jusanseiki mongoru shihaiki Iran no Perushiago zaimujutsu shinansho *Murshid fī al-ḥisāb* 13 世紀モンゴル支配期イランのペルシア語財務術指南書 *Murshid fī al-ḥisāb*." In *Iranshiki bokijutsu no hatten to tenkai* イラン式簿記術の発展と展開. Ed. by Yoichi Takamatsu. Tokyo: Toyo Bunko, 2011, 9–35.

Watabe, Ryoko. "Census-Taking and the *Qubchūr* Taxation System in Ilkhanid Iran: An Analysis of the Census Book from the Late 13th Century Persian Accounting Manual *al-Murshid fi al-Ḥisāb*." *Memoirs of the Research Department of the Toyo Bunko* 73 (2015): 27–63.

Watabe, Ryoko. "13-14 seiki Iruhanchoka Iran no chozei-seido: Bokijutsu shinansho-shiryo niyoru saikosei 13-14 世紀イル・ハン朝下イランの徴税制度：簿記術指南書に基づく再構成." In *Kinsei Isuramu-kokkashi kenkyu no genzai* 近世イスラーム国家史研究の現在. Ed. by N. Kondo. Fuchu, Tokyo: ILCAA, 2015, 13–56.

Watabe, Ryoko and Naofumi Abe. "16-seiki Safavi-choki no Perushiago zaimu boki shinansho 16世紀サファヴィー朝期のペルシア語財務指南書." *Journal of Asia and African Studies* 94 (2017): 383–485.

10

Ma Dexin's Criticism of Saint Veneration: "Chinese"-Flavored Islam Formed by a Denominational Conflict

Tatsuya Nakanishi

Introduction

This chapter focuses on a famous Hui (Chinese-speaking) Muslim scholar Ma Dexin (d. 1874),[1] who lived in Yunnan, Southwest China, in the nineteenth century. Ma Dexin traveled through the Middle East between 1844 and 1848 and transmitted new Islamic knowledge back to China upon his return. He tried to reform beliefs and practices of the Hui into something consistent with an assumed "true" Islam from the Muslim heartland and simultaneously compatible with the Chinese milieu. The many ideas he brought back to China included critical views on the veneration of saints. One of these views objects to both blind adherence to Sufi masters and belief in their divine powers. These targets of objection were central tenets on which the Sufi orders gained power both among Hui Muslims and other Muslims. Ma Dexin preached in Yunnan, which was home to a modest number of followers of a Sufi order called the Jahriyya, who practiced saint veneration. Thus, Ma Dexin made adjustments and reinforcements to the relevant teachings from the Muslim heartland in keeping with the Sino-Islamic intellectual context of his time, thus intending to tempt Hui Muslims to accept views that discouraged saint-veneration. For example, he radicalized a negative opinion about the necessity of a Sufi master in his attacks against the Jahriyya.

In this chapter, I consider the ways in which Ma Dexin adapted critiques of saint veneration from the Islamic world to challenge the Jahriyya. Through this inquiry, I explore how an exotic theory from the Middle East became acceptable or even authentic knowledge among Hui Muslims,[2] and a powerful weapon in denominational disputes within their society, including that between Ma Dexin and Jahriyya.[3] I illuminate how

Chinese-influenced Islam was molded by a sectarian strife among Hui Muslims over policy to cope with a confrontation between Muslims and non-Muslims.

Previous studies have pointed out that the antagonism between Hui Muslims and non-Muslim Han Chinese people made the Hui reconcile with the Han and harmonize Islam with traditional Chinese thought.[4] My study expands on this conclusion by pointing out that conflicts among Hui Muslims also contributed to the formation of a mode of Islam that was distinctively Chinese.

This chapter also documents Ma Dexin's response to the changing historical circumstances by re-forging Chinese-oriented Islam. In his time, the intensification of antagonism between Hui Muslims and non-Muslim Han people dramatically endangered the survival of the Hui. During and after this period, new Islamic teachings and imported books were increasingly introduced to China from the West and South Asia by travelers as a result of the advances in transportation facilities and printing techniques. Previous studies have not sufficiently clarified the sophistication of the comprehension and expression of Islam by Chinese Muslim thinkers in keeping with such social and cultural transitions in China or similar shifts in the Islamic world.[5] By understanding the intellectual activities of Ma Dexin within their historical context, this study highlights an aspect of the dynamic struggles of Hui Muslims in observing Islam in China. This study presents the hitherto unknown impact of Middle Eastern Islamic trends on China and contributes to the depiction of the global history of Islamic thought.

Ma Dexin was the first person in China to condemn acutely the practice of saint veneration as blasphemous, because it assumes that a created being has divinity. His unfavorable comments on the belief that he alleged as polytheistic are found in his Chinese work *Essences of the Four Canons* (*Sidian Yaohui*),[6] which was published in 1859. He also discussed the topic more extensively in his Arabic work *Fixation of the Standard for Sufi Doctrines* (*Lixue Zhezhong*), published in 1867.[7] Working through these texts, I examine how Ma Dexin adapted foreign arguments to convince Hui Muslims of the erroneous practice of saint veneration and to prevent them from adhering to the Jahriyya.

Ma Dexin's Argument on Sufi Masters and Its Sources

Ma Dexin's Creative Discussion of Sufi Masters and the Oneness of Being

The *Essences of the Four Canons* suggests that Ma Dexin's castigation of impudent adherence to the Sufi master was triggered by admonishments from a certain Ismāʿīl, whom Ma Dexin met during his pilgrimage to Mecca. The *Fixation of the Standard for Sufi Doctrines* also repeats Ismāʿīl's lecture. However, the work not only skips his name for unknown reasons, but also radicalizes his precept based on the theory of the "Oneness of Being" (*waḥdat al-wujūd*). This section verifies this radicalization.

First, let us analyse the details of Ismāʿīl's teachings. According to the *Essences of the Four Canons*, Ma Dexin intended to look for a Sufi master (*shaiyihe<shaykh*) who might instruct him in the mystical stages of spiritual training (*daocheng<ṭarīqa*) and mystical union with God (*zhencheng<ḥaqīqa*). However, he gave up this intention after meeting Ismāʿīl, who said the following:

> Is the observance of the five pillars [of Islam] which contemporary people perform a false way? It is the five pillars that the Prophet and his pupils performed. It is the five pillars that the four eponyms of the Islamic law schools also performed. It is the five pillars that all classics carry. Is this not the true way? Although contemporary scholars and thousands of masses regard it as the [genuine] training, do only you regard it as an insignificant thing?
>
> A shallow person can merely perform [the five pillars] at a superficial level. A profound person can perform [the five pillars] at an essential level. The performance of a man of small caliber is trivial. That of a man of great caliber is significant. What everyone performs is nothing but the five pillars. Even though a Sufi master (*shaiyihe<shaykh*) has the brightness of the Sun, how useful is it to a blind man?
>
> What the heavenly mandate (*tianming*) prescribes [to a person as his fate] must be gained [by him] someday. Do not desire forcibly what is not prescribed [in the heavenly mandate]. Although everyone easily seeks the former, it is difficult for him to seek the latter. Even more, the performance of the five pillars is prescribed by God [to us]. We must fulfil it as our duty. The spiritual training and mystical union with God are not among the divine prescriptions, but supererogatory works we add by ourselves, the fulfilment of which is laudable, but we are not blamed for neglecting it. You should keep what God prescribes [as our fate and duty].[8]

Next, let us see Ma Dexin's argument on this point in the *Fixation of the Standard for Sufi Doctrines*. This work also insists that everyone must perform the *sharīʿa* because it is an obligation imposed on all people, whereas the *ṭarīqa* and *ḥaqīqa* can only be performed by spiritual elites.[9] This work refutes the notion that "Whoever participates in a circle [of disciples] (*dāʾira*) of a Sufi master (*murshid*) and is accepted by him becomes a friend of God (*walī*)," stating thus:[10]

> Being a friend of God (*walāya*) is being attracted (*jadhba*) by God Most High [to the rank close to Him]. It is [caused] by the mediation of a perfect friend

> of God, who is permitted by God to exert the influence (*taṣarruf*) [of such mediation], without any relation to a person whom human beings [by their own judgement] call "a friend of God."[11] The divine attraction, like the awe towards the prophecy and the divine favor, has no acquirement. Any bondman is unable to gain it either by his own action or being perfected by a friend of God who is his mentor (*walī murshid*). It is not compensated for anything, but rather it is a mercy God partially gives as a divine favor to bondmen towards whom God wishes to do so. If a bondman has a capacity (*qābiliyya*) for it, he thereby receives the attraction of God – Glory be to Him – [. . .]. The friend of God has a capacity to an extent that other people don't have. Anyone does not become a friend of God by many actions and trainings. The capacity is necessary [for being a friend of God]. Whoever has no preparedness (*istiʿdād*) for being a friend of God never becomes a friend of God. Even though he is nurtured under a perfect and true friend of God for one hundred years, he is nothing but like a blind man who stands under the sun without anything stopping its light from reaching him. Most people are ignorant about it. Thus, they rush to what is over their own efforts and abilities. When they hear that secrets (*mughayyabāt*) are disclosed to a person, he becomes one of the venerated persons (*mukarramīn*) for them.

Here, Ma Dexin states that whether someone can become a friend of God or not depends on divine attraction and his capacity and preparedness for it, but not on the instruction of his mentor. It is remarkable that Ma Dexin articulates that any Sufi master cannot, on his own initiative, lead anyone to friendship with God, or foster the religious perfection of a Muslim. Ma Dexin writes that divine attraction through which God draws someone into the group of His friends is caused "by the mediation of a perfect friend of God, who is permitted by God to exert the influence [of such mediation]." By this, he does not mean that the friend of God voluntarily introduces a stranger to God, but that God allows the established friend to mediate between Himself and a certain candidate for His friend that He has nominated in advance.[12] In proving the incompetence of the Sufi master, Ma Dexin uses the terms "capacity" and "preparedness." These terms also appear in the theory of the Oneness of Being as articulated by Ibn ʿArabī (d. 1240), who was also known as al-Shaykh al-Akbar ("the greatest *shaykh*") and whose teachings were elaborated on by his intellectual heirs, called Akbarians.

The idea of the Oneness of Being holds that God created all things by manifesting Himself. In this self-manifestation, God projects all His names, or His whole aspect, onto everything. However, each thing can only reflect a part of the divine names in accordance with its own capacity/preparedness for this divine self-projection. As a result, God manifests Himself as diverse created things, and each has a distinctive character according to its own capacity/preparedness. Only the perfect man (*insān kāmil*) has the capacity/preparedness to receive all the divine names. Only he can, by himself, mirror the entire aspect of God, which is disclosed by the universe (or the total of all other created things) as well.

What each thing will become and the extent to which it is capable/prepared are predestined by its own immutable entity (*ʿayn thābita*/ pl. *aʿyān thābita*), that is, the what-ness (*māhiyya*) of the individual thing eternally grasped by God's knowledge before His self-manifestation.[13] According to Ibn ʿArabī, in accordance with the immutable entity, God atemporally gives "the predetermination" (*qaḍā*) concerning each thing, which is named "the predestination" (*qadar*) when it is realized at the appointed time without any alternation from the state of the immutable entity.[14] From this perspective, only God has the ability to control whether a person can be His friend.[15] Thus, adhering to the teachings of a Sufi master and expecting to reach perfection through him amounts to attributing the divine ability to create things to a creature – in other words, saint veneration. Following the above citation, Ma Dexin reproaches masters who claim to assume divine power (*qudra ilāhiyya*) and make their disciples friends of God, exercise miracles, and intercede with Him in the next world, as well as their followers.[16]

Within the idea of the Oneness of Being, the above-cited passage declares that anyone without the proper capacity/preparedness cannot become a friend of God through a Sufi master's spiritual power. This argument is more radical in nullifying the efficiency of the Sufi master's spiritual guidance than the lecture of the Meccan Ismāʿīl in the *Essences of the Four Canons*. Whereas Ismāʿīl only stated that it is difficult to seek what is not prescribed in the heavenly mandate, Ma Dexin stated that this is impossible and somewhat heretical. Ismāʿīl was open to the possibility that a Sufi master may guide his disciples in a direction different from that which is determined by their predestination. However, the *Fixation of the Standard for Sufi Doctrines* rejected this possibility in accordance with the Oneness of Being.

Intellectual Trends in the Middle East in the Nineteenth Century

Ma Dexin radicalized the Meccan Ismāʿīl's teachings about Sufi masters' inability to counteract divine predestination. This radical interpretation seems to have originated with Ma Dexin. It does not, for example, appear to be an idea that he absorbed during his trip around the Middle East. In the Middle East, before the twentieth century, there were few scholars who negated the Sufi masters' capacity to cultivate disciples from the perspective of the Oneness of Being. This section provides some background for this idea and asserts the creativity of Ma Dexin's discussion.

According to El-Rouayheb, from the seventeenth century onward, Muslim scholars in the Arab world began to endorse seriously the concept of the Oneness of

Being.[17] Before the seventeenth century, Muslim scholars like Ibn Ḥajar al-Haytamī (d. 1567) and ʿAbd al-Wahhāb al-Shaʿrānī (d. 1565) defended Ibn ʿArabī's claims. However, they only offered feeble apologies for some of the more problematic theories he advanced in his *Bezels of Wisdom* (*Fuṣūṣ al-ḥikam*), including his ideas of the release from pain in the Fire,[18] the monotheistic belief of the Pharaoh,[19] and the Oneness of Being. These apologies included refusing the literal interpretation of his texts[20] and alleging that his "heretical" remarks had been falsified by another author.[21]

After the seventeenth century, some members of Sufi orders in Hijaz and Syria, such as Shaṭṭāriyya, Naqshbandiyya, and Khalwatiyya, overtly upheld Ibn ʿArabī's "extreme" ideas. For example, Ibrāhīm al-Kūrānī (d. 1690), a scholar who was active in Medina and affiliated with Shaṭṭāriyya and Naqshbandiyya, argued against Ibn Taymiyya's (d. 1326) notion which considered the Oneness of Being as a theory of incarnation (*ḥulūl*) and the identification of God with man (*ittiḥād*).[22] Al-Kūrānī and ʿAbd al-Ghanī al-Nābulusī (d. 1731), a Sufi master of Naqshbandiyya, refuted Saʿd al-Dīn al-Taftāzānī's (d. 1389–90) criticism of the identification of God with Being (*wujūd*) in the Oneness of Being.[23] Such prominent Middle Eastern defenders of the Oneness of Being had some interaction with these Sufi orders, and did not make light of Sufi masters. Al-Nābulusī, and Muḥammad b. ʿAbdullāh al-Khānī (d. 1862),[24] a Sufi master of Khālidiyya, even applied the Oneness of Being while justifying a Sufi master's qualifications for fostering his disciples.[25]

From the seventeenth century onwards, Muslim scholars in the Middle East started to re-evaluate the work of Ibn Taymiyya,[26] a strong opponent of Ibn ʿArabī. However, some of them vindicated al-Shaykh al-Akbar at the same time. This Taymiyyan trend evolved into a vehement objection to the accretions to original Islamic teachings, including innovative Sufi practices like saint veneration. However, we hardly find anyone in this period who questioned the Sufi masters' mentorship, even among Ibn Taymiyya's proponents.

For example, al-Kūrānī was a pioneer of Arab Muslim vindication of both Ibn Taymiyya and Ibn ʿArabī. He bridged the gap between theological doctrines of Ibn Taymiyya and al-Ashʿarī (d. 935–36) via the Oneness of Being.[27] Al-Kūrānī highlighted the necessity of discipleship under a Sufi master.[28] Abū l-Thanā Maḥmūd al-Alūsī (d. 1854), his son Khayr al-Dīn Nuʿmān al-Alūsī (d. 1899), and Jamāl al-Dīn al-Qāsimī (d. 1914), agreed with Ibn Taymiyya and simultaneously valued Ibn ʿArabī.[29] These Taymiyyan scholars were hostile to some Sufi practices, including unlawful and meaningless training, deviation from the *sharīʿa*, requests for Sufi master's intercession with God, and pilgrimages to tombs of Sufi masters.[30] However, these scholars paid homage to Sufis who maintained proper Sufism in conformity with *sharīʿa*.[31]

In the early twentieth century, ʿAbd al-Ḥamīd al-Zahrāwī (d. 1916), a supporter of Ibn Taymiyya, wrote an Arabic work titled the *Islamic Jurisprudence and Sufism* (*al-Fiqh wa-l-taṣawwuf*), in which he accused ascetic Sufis of idleness and departure from true Sufism. However, such an unconditional attack on Sufis was so exceptional that even Rashīd Riḍā (d. 1935), who also adopted Ibn Taymiyya's perspective, criticized al-Zahrāwī for his boldness.[32]

In line with this intellectual milieu, Ismāʿīl, whom Ma Dexin claimed to have met in Mecca, did not entirely discount the possibility that a Sufi master may transform his disciples into friends of God. Yang Guiping inferred that this Meccan scholar was an adherent of Wahhabism.[33] I am not sure whether this is correct. However, it is true that Muḥammad b. ʿAbd al-Wahhāb (d. 1791), the founder of Wahhabism, did not discuss Sufi training or the guidance of Sufi masters, whereas he strictly denounced saint veneration.[34]

Ma Dexin was apparently inspired to some extent by the Akbarian and Taymiyyan trends that arose in the Middle East after the seventeenth century. In his Arabic work, the *Secrets of Return* (*Asrār al-maʿād*), Ma Dexin copied Ibn ʿArabī's idea regarding the Fire and, in the same breath, seemingly mentioned Ibn Taymiyya's soteriology, which contradicts the Akbarian ideas of afterlife.[35] In addition, the *Fixation of the Standard for Sufi Doctrines* cites pre-seventeenth-century apologetics for al-Shaykh al-Akbar from Ibn Ḥajar al-Haytamī's *Meccan Gift as a Commentary on al-Hamziyya* (*al-Minaḥ al-Makkiyya fī sharḥ al-Hamziyya*) and ʿAlāʾ al-Dīn al-Ḥaskafī's (active in the mid-seventeenth century) *Selected Pearl* (*al-Durr al-mukhtār*). Here, Ma Dexin writes that al-Haytamī's *Gift* set forth that both Ibn ʿArabī and Ibn Fāriḍ were friends of God.[36] He also writes that "the *Selected Pearl* accounted that *Bezels of Wisdom* had various anti-*sharīʿa* remarks, some of which were fabrications of Jews attributed to the Shaykh."[37] The *Fixation of the Standard for Sufi Doctrines* repeats criticism of anti-Islamic practices of some false Sufis, which is reminiscent of Taymiyyan discourses.[38] The work rebukes not only people who pretended to have divine powers, as mentioned in the previous section,[39] but also those who boasted of their and their followers' exemption from *sharīʿa*.[40]

Ma Dexin did not share the Akbarian and Taymiyyan scholars' affirmative or indifferent attitudes toward Sufi masters' mentorship. This shows that his radicalization of Ismāʿīl's admonishments based on the Oneness of Being was not borrowed from foreign sources but was, instead, his own creation. We cannot confirm Ismāʿīl's original Arabic statements or whether he really existed. However, it is safe to say that Ma Dexin creatively formulated his own ideas of Sufi masters while he was likely influenced by the Middle Eastern Akbarian cosmology and Taymiyyan condemnation of saint veneration. In the next section, I explain how he derived his critique of saint veneration from the Chinese Islamic tradition.

The Chinese Islamic Tradition

Since before the nineteenth century, Hui Muslim scholars have espoused the theory of the Oneness of Being. One of the works on the theory, ʿAbd al-Raḥmān Jāmī's (d. 1492) *Rays of Flashes* (*Ashiʿʿat al-Lamaʿāt*) has been respected as an authoritative classic. In Chinese Islamic works written by Hui Muslim scholars, the Oneness of Being is harmonized with Chinese traditional religions (such as Confucianism, Buddhism, and Taoism) in order to adapt Islam to the Chinese religious context. Liu Zhi's (d. after 1724) *Nature and Principle in Islam* (*Tianfang Xingli*) is a typical example of these works. This section argues that the Hui Muslim academic tradition, and not the aforementioned Middle Eastern Akbarian and Taymiyyan trends, provided direct supporting evidence for Ma Dexin's assertion that the Sufi masters do not have the divine power they need to make their followers friends of God.

In the first half of the *Fixation of the Standard for Sufi Doctrines*,[41] Ma Dexin lays the foundation for his later discussion on Sufi masters with the following argument: the teaching of "monotheists" (*muwaḥḥidūn*) and "people of oneness" (*ahl al-waḥda*) – that is, the Oneness of Being – to begin with, rigorously distinguishes God from created things. In presenting this argument on the monotheistic character of the Oneness of Being, he refers to Chinese Islamic classics rather than recent works from the Middle East.

For example, citing the *Nature and Principle in Islam* under its Arabic title, *Kitāb silī al-Islām*, Ma Dexin clarifies that even the spirit attributed to God (*rūḥ iḍāfī*) – that is, the spirit of the perfect man, or the locus of the divine full manifestation – is not the same as God Himself.[42] There, he mentions the Chinese work of Liu Zhi as follows:[43]

> *Nature and Principle* (*silī*<*xingli*) *in Islam* (*Kitāb silī al-Islām*), the second volume (*daftar*), the fourth diagramming (*taṣwīr*), says as follows: the fourth stage of the self-manifestation of The Real <Glory to Him> is that of the mandate (*amr*), i.e., the spirit attributed to God (*al-rūḥ al-iḍāfī*). It is the first self-manifestation of the Being in the level of the individual thing. It belongs neither to the Substance, nor to the divine attribute and the divine deed. It is a self-manifestation in the level of the individual thing, to which the application of the divine name is wrong. The sixth volume, the second diagramming, says as follows: The level of the Substance is [that of] the absolute One. The level of the first spirit is [that of] the relative One. It is the beginning and end of numbers. From the phase of the divine reality, it is a created thing, while God is the Real. From the phase of the divine austere, it is a bondman, while God is the Lord. From the phase of the divine magnificence, it is a bubble, while God is the sea.[44]

Quoting a passage from the *Rays of Flashes*, Ma Dexin says, "Anyone who extinguishes himself in the Real is not Itself." Referring to the *Rays of Flashes*, he also writes, "Even though a human being reaches the stage of the perfection and the trace of his humanity disappears, it is so in his sight of the witness, but not in reality."[45]

This way, Ma Dexin separates the Oneness of Being from pantheism, or saint veneration, based on works that were considered authoritative classics among Hui Muslims. He reproaches people who, as a result of misunderstanding the Oneness of Being, advocated that "God incarnated Himself in the most excellent one in a certain age, who is the agent (*nāʾib*) and representation (*ṣūra*) of God."[46]

In short, Ma Dexin utilized Hui Muslim classics to prove that the idea of the Oneness of Being does not allow one to confuse created things with God, and to revere Sufi masters as owners of divine power to override predestination. He reinterpreted the idea of the Oneness of Being in the light of the Chinese Islamic tradition, and thus proceeded to radicalize critiques of saint veneration that originated in the Middle East.

The Background of Ma Dexin's Negative Views on Sufi Masters

Discord with the Jahriyya Order

Why did Ma Dexin's stance on the abilities and divinity of Sufi masters differ from those of Muslim scholars in the Middle East? This section explores several answers to this question other than the one provided above – that is, that he was encouraged to adopt a different stance by the Chinese Islamic tradition.

First, we should note how Ma Dexin and the Jahriyya order opposed each other on the Yunnan Muslim rebellion against the Qing dynasty (1856–74). The rebellion broke out because local Qing officials often took the side of the Han Chinese people while settling armed collisions between Hui Muslims and Han Chinese that escalated over time. In 1856, these officials approved or incited the latter to massacre the former in Kunming, Yunnan's capital, leading to a Muslim rebellion in response.[47]

During the rebellion, Ma Dexin led a rebel force from 1857 to 1862. In 1858, he temporarily surrendered. In 1862, he surrendered for good and swore allegiance to the Qing dynasty to restore the previous relatively peaceful relationship between Muslims and non-Muslims and secure the survival of the Hui. From then on, he cooperated with the Qing army to suppress the rebels. He seems to have thought that Hui Muslims should have stopped rebelling after the initial uprising, which demonstrated their rage against the Qing dynasty's injustices toward them and ensured their security. He probably believed that the Hui Muslims should have found a way to coexist with Han Chinese people, most of whom took the side of the Qing government, because the Hui were a minority who were unable to forcefully oppose the Han Chinese over the long term.[48]

During the same rebellion, Jahriyya followers in Yunnan fought against the Qing army. Even after Ma Dexin's withdrawal from the rebellion, they continued to resist the Qing army until their headquarters fell in 1871.[49] The Jahriyyas' behavior hindered Ma Dexin from peacefully settling the conflict between the Hui Muslims and the Han Chinese. It is not surprising that he argued against the divinity of Sufi masters in the *Fixation of the Standard for Sufi Doctrines*, which was published between the time of his defection to the Qing dynasty and the Jahriyyas' final defeat. It appears as though Ma Dexin may have tried to erode the authority of the Sufi masters and weaken the Jahriyya in order to calm the turmoil in Yunnan.

Ma Dexin doubtlessly felt antipathy toward the Jahriyya. According to an Arabic source that Ma Dexin's disciple Ma Lianyuan wrote, the former scholar criticized religious practices of the Jahriyya such as the recitation of "Oh, Shaykh" while slaughtering animals.[50] Ma Rulong, a former leader of the Yunnan Muslim rebellion who had surrendered to the Qing dynasty together with Ma Dexin, was also at odds with Ma Chenglin (or Ma Shenglin), the leader of the Yunnan Jahriyya. Émile Rocher, a French diplomat in Yunnan, seems to have attributed the antagonism to the point that Ma Rulong was a Muslim espousing a long-established Islamic teaching (*Mahometan de vieille date*), or affiliated with a traditional Muslim grope different from "a new sect" (*une secte nouvelle*) Ma Chenglin led.[51] This may have reflected Ma Dexin's critical view of the Jahriyya in religious matters, because Ma Rulong sincerely respected Ma Dexin as his mentor.[52]

Ma Dexin had already been critical of the Jahriyya since his first surrender to the Qing dynasty in 1858. In the next year, he published the *Essences of the Four Canons* with the support of Yunnan's local Qing officials. In this work, he writes:[53]

> *A Collection of Commentaries on the Ode* (*Gesuide jizhu*)[54] sets forth that the human society needs the president of the Sufi masters (*zongtong zhi shayyihe*) who is only one in every age, and, instead of the Prophet, leads people to return to God. The Sufi masters nowadays have such name but actually are not so.

This passage holds that the then Sufi masters did not deserve to be called "the president of the Sufi masters." However, in the *Essences of the Four Canons*, Ma Dexin did not divest the Sufi master of divine mentorship in principle, as he did later in the *Fixation of the Standard for Sufi Doctrines*. It was not until his final surrender to the Qing dynasty, or his irreversible split with the Jahriyya, that he advanced such a drastic argument against the Sufi masters.

Second, we should consider the traditional status of Sufi orders in China proper as follows: These orders exerted a strong influence over Hui Muslims in Northwest China since the seventeenth century but could not find the same support in other regions of China. In the seventeenth and eighteenth centuries, some Hui Muslims there also took pride in their isolation from Sufi orders.[55] The Chinese government was hardly concerned with the patronage of the Sufi masters which Middle Eastern political powers often willingly promoted.[56] Sufi orders in Qing China, unlike those in the Middle East, were vulnerable to criticism from opponents. The inferior position of Chinese Sufi orders facilitated Ma Dexin's open degradation of Sufi masters' credibility and ability. In short, Ma Dexin's negative views of Sufi masters were derived from his desire to foster cooperation between Muslims and non-Muslims and from the distinct vulnerability of Chinese Sufi orders.

Jahriyya Justifications of Sufi Masters' Abilities

Why did Ma Dexin deliberately cite Hui classics like the *Nature and Principle in Islam* and the *Rays of Flashes* in asserting the rigid monotheism of the idea of the Oneness of Being? This section argues that he may have done so in an attempt to counter Jahriyya scholars who espoused the same Chinese Islamic tradition, beyond making his preaching persuasive for Hui Muslims in general.

Jahriyya scholars thought that divinity can be found in Sufi masters entranced by their unification with God. This is evident in a Jahriyya hagiography titled *Trickling* (*Rashḥ*). This hagiography was written in Arabic and Persian by ʿAbd al-Qādir Guanliye during the reign of the Jiaqing Emperor (1796–1820). According to this hagiography, when Jahriyya founder Ma Mingxin trained in Yemen, he said, "Prostrate yourself to me! I am God, and I am the Prophet." Then, his master urged Ma Mingxin's servant to prostrate before Ma Mingxin.[57]

Two anecdotes in *Trickling* convey that the *Rays of Flashes* and Liu Zhi's works (such as the *Nature and Principle in Islam*) were respected among the Jahriyya. The first anecdote depicts a man who received a divine attraction (*majdhūb*) and immediately attained spiritual enlightenment when he attentively read the *Rays of Flashes*.[58] In the second one, Ma Mingxin declared that he was a friend of God after Liu Zhi had been a friend of God.[59]

The abovementioned report by Ma Lianyuan, that his teacher criticized religious practices of the Jahriyya, shows that Ma Dexin, to some extent, recognized the Jahriyyas' practices of saint veneration, and likely even esoteric ideas and authoritative books espoused among them such as those mentioned in *Trickling*. Therefore, it is highly possible that the *Fixation of the Standard for Sufi Doctrines* strategically cited the *Rays of Flashes* and *Nature and Principle in Islam* to refute the Jahriyya doctrine on the divinity of Sufi masters in ecstasies.

Ma Dexin may have intended to counter more sophisticated vindication of later Jahriyya scholars for saint veneration than that of ʿAbd al-Qādir Guanliye in *Trickling*. A hagiography of Jahriyya masters composed in the early twentieth century justifies the mentorship of Jahriyya leaders and their followers' veneration toward them via

Akbarian theory and the Hui classics. The hagiography in question was written in Arabic and titled *A Comparatively Short Treatise on the Spiritual Genealogy of the Jahriyya* (*Risāla aqṣariyya li-bayān al-silsila al-Jahriyya*) (*Treatise*). The author named Ma Xuezhi began writing this hagiography at the request of the seventh master of the Jahriyya, Ma Yuanzhang (d. 1920), long after Ma Dexin's death, and completed it in 1933. Statements on the Sufi masters in the *Fixation of the Standard for Sufi Doctrines* are more sharply contrastive with those in the *Treatise* than in *Trickling*. It tempts us to guess that Ma Dexin targeted something similar to Ma Xuezhi's apologetics for saint veneration.

The *Treatise* relates an anecdote that facilitates the worship of Jahriyya masters as perfect loci for divine self-manifestation, while illustrating that the Oneness of Being equates God with His full manifestations:[60]

> One day, the presence of the Khwāja (the fourth master of the Jahriyya, Ma Yide) <May God consecrate his secret!> together with religious fellows and travelers sat in a circle for *dhikr* (remembrance of God). Then, he stood up and started to dance and sing as follows. He put his right leg forward with his right hand at the first step, and then put his left leg forward with his left hand at the second step. He sang in a beautiful voice, while clicking his thumb and middle fingers. While doing so repeatedly, he turned round. At this time, he told secrets ordinary people cannot understand, and recited words even elites do not remember, like al-Ḥallāj <May God consecrate his secret!> said, "I am the Real," al-Shiblī <May God consecrate his secret!> said, "Is there anything except for me?" and Abū Yazīd al-Basṭāmī said "Glory to me! There is no God but me. Oh, my people! Obey me as my bondmen," and so on. Witnessing this state, Baqīyatullāh, i.e., Didawī (a man from Didao) <May God consecrate his secret!> prostrated himself. Other [participants in the circle of *dhikr*] followed that man, except for a grey hair man. As soon as the grey hair person supposed that it is not legitimate, he was struck by thunder, and became like a dead body. After the *dhikr* performance was finished, people left him to lose his senses. The next day, he recovered, and then went back home as a loser, while regretting the wretchedness of one who failed because of his ignorance.

This anecdote conveys that a Sufi master who unifies himself with God assumes divinity, and therefore veneration of such a master is legitimate. Ma Xuezhi backed up this claim by citing a passage from Ismāʿīl Ḥaqqī Bursawī's (d. 1725) Qurʾanic exegesis, *Spirit of Demonstration* (*Rūḥ al-bayān*),[61] which is a commentary on the verse 48: 10, "Allāh's hand is on their hands." There, based on the Oneness of Being, Bursawī states that al-Ḥallāj said "I am the Real," and other Sufi masters said similar things, in the same sense as it is said of the Prophet that he is "the place where the divine perfections appear, and the mirror that reflects His self-manifestations."[62] Bursawī articulates that the prophet to whom God entirely disclosed Himself manifested the divinity instead of the humanity in his inner part, and thus prostration to him is legitimate. These statements assert that the veneration of Sufi masters is legitimate as these masters, like the Prophet, fully reflect the self-projection of God.

Unlike Ma Dexin, Ma Xuezhi in the *Treatise* suggests that Sufi mentors can make their disciples full receptors of divine names – that is, make them friends of God:[63]

> Know. A word of His Holiness (the founder of the Jahriyya, Ma Mingxin, d. 1781) is as follows: "When the root letter is reversed, what is it?" And he said, "It signifies friends of God."[64] The following questions were asked: What is the root? What is the letter? How is it reversed? How do those who are reversed become friends of God? This feeble one <May God forgive him by means of the holiness (*ḥurma*) of friends of God!> says, while perceiving his misunderstanding, as follows: According to my opinion, which is not sufficient, the root letter is *alif*, and [each of] the [other] additional [letters] is a commentary [on the root, or the divine Substance] [. . .]. The reverse (*in'ikās*) denotes that a bondman travelling [on the Sufi path] approaches the Real firstly by instruction of the perfect mentor (*shaykh*), and secondly by his own various trainings and services of religious efforts in accordance with the divine order, "A bondman continues to approach Me by the supererogatory training (*nawāfil*) until I love him. When I love him, I am his ear, eye, and hand. He hears, sees, and beats by means of Me." Then, when the cover of individualizations (*ta'ayyunāt*) is removed from the mirror of his mind by the polish of inspiring *dhikr*, lights of Self-Manifestations from the root letter, or the Substance of Being called *alif*, are reflected (*in'akasat*) by the travelling bondman in accordance with the divine order, "If anyone approaches Me a palm, I approach him a palm; if one approaches Me a cubit, I approach him a cubit." The hadith ends here. This means that if anyone approaches by repentance and obedience, I approach him by mercy, prosperity, and aid. Bondmen who reflect [the divine self-manifestation] are friends of God.

Here, Ma Xuezhi interprets Ma Mingxin's maxim in line with the idea of the Oneness of Being. According to this interpretation, the reversal of "the root letter" denotes the full reflection of divine self-manifestation, that is – the reflector becomes a friend of God. Ma Xuezhi explains that the process of reversal or reflection comprises two stages, namely the approaches by means of supererogatory training (*qurb al-nawāfil*) and absolute duty (*qurb al-farā'iḍ*), which are explained in the *Rays of Flashes* as well.[65] The former (that is, the approach by means of the supererogatory training) entails human self-annihilation at the level of divine attributes. Through such annihilation, a human being approaches God via Sufi training and assumes divine attributes. The latter (that is, the approach by means of absolute duty) entails human self-annihilation at the level of divine substance. Through such annihilation, God approaches a human being such that His substance manifests in that person, and He behaves through that person. The above passage implicitly refers to the *Rays of Flashes* and insists that a practitioner can become a friend of God through the approach by means of absolute duty, but only after they have taken the approach by means of supererogatory training under the guidance of a Sufi master.

In other parts of his hagiography,[66] Ma Xuezhi describes how, when he studied the *Rays of Flashes*, his master Ma Yuanzhang interpreted both these approaches. Ma Yuanzhang taught that someone who approaches God by performing supererogatory training under his mentor's instruction can sometimes experience God approaching him. This suggests that the Sufi masters can have a hand in their disciples' attaining self-annihilation not only at the level of divine attributes but also at that of divine substance.

Ma Dexin's view ran counter to such an interpretation. In *Fixation of the Standard for Sufi Doctrines*, he emphasizes that the two ways to the unification of God and human beings, that is, "the approach by means of supererogatory trainings" and "the approach by means of absolute duty," are different both in terms of process and result.[67] Ma Dexin suggests that Sufi masters are not concerned with self-annihilation at the level of the divine substance.

It is not certain whether scholars of the Jahriyya before Ma Xuezhi maintained such elaborate teachings as he would advocate later, and whether Ma Dexin intended to refute those in particular. However, the adherents of the Jahriyya probably perceived the published criticisms of Ma Dexin as being against themselves. They reacted defensively in response to Ma Dexin's criticisms.[68] It may be possible to count Ma Xuezhi's insistence on the status and ability of the Sufi master among these defensive reactions. The significant clash between the arguments of *Fixation of the Standard for Sufi Doctrines* and *Treatise* about Sufi masters strongly indicates that the former was perceived as a grave menace by the adherents of the Jahriyya, including Ma Xuezhi.

Ma Dexin's negative statements on the veneration of saints and the significance of Sufi masters appear to take aim at the Jahriyya, who perceived divinity in enraptured Sufi masters and highly esteemed *Rays of Flashes* and the *Nature and Principle in Islam*. It is likely that Ma Dexin expected the prestige of these classics to increase the effect of his attacks on the Jahriyya. It is likely that his expectation was not wrong.

Conclusion

Ma Dexin went as far as to assert the unreliability of Sufi masters in mentorship for the spiritual travel based on the Oneness of Being, progressing beyond the scope of the discussions on the topic that originated in the Middle East. Ismāʿīl or the Akbarian and Taymiyyan trends likely inspired Ma Dexin to deny the ability of the Sufi master to make his disciple a friend of God. However, according to Ma Dexin's descriptions, Ismāʿīl showed neither sympathy for the idea of the Oneness of Being, nor any interest in undermining the status of Sufi masters. Prominent Middle Eastern proponents of the Akbarian and Taymiyyan ideas did not object to Sufi masters' tutorship before the twentieth century.

Ma Dexin did not merely repeat what he heard during his travels in the Middle East. He constructed a version of Islamic teachings that suited his requirements and the Chinese context of the time. Ma Dexin formed his own admonition against adhering to Sufi masters based on his interpretation of the classic Chinese Muslim texts to give himself an advantage in his confrontation with the Jahriyya. He intended to finish the Jahriyya's rebellion and construct a peaceful relationship between the Hui and Han people. Thus, his discussion about Sufi masters aimed to enhance the compatibility between Islam and China. In this adaptation of Islam in China, *Fixation of the Standard for Sufi Doctrines* did not call non-Islamic Chinese traditions into play and did not follow Hui Muslims' conventional strategy.

Ma Dexin creatively translated foreign teachings into such powerful counterarguments against his rivals that they surely regarded it as a great menace because of its accordance with the Sino-Islamic intellectual milieu. Thus, the dispute between Ma Dexin and the Jahriyya produced Chinese-specific Islamic knowledge.

Notes

* An earlier version of this study was published as Tatsuya Nakanishi, "19 seiki Unnan no Chūgoku Musurimu gakusha, Ba Tokushin no seija sūhai hihan" [Chinese Muslim Scholar Ma Dexin's Criticism of Saint Worship], *Tōhō gakuhō* (Kyōto) 94 (2019): 398–76. The research for this study was supported by JSPS Kakenhi Grants-in-Aid (21K00906, 20H05825, 19H01317, 17K03130, 16H01904).

1 For Ma Dexin, see Chang-Kuan Lin, "Three Eminent Chinese ʿUlamaʾ of Yunnan," *Journal of the Institute of Muslim Minority Affairs* 11.1 (1990): 100–17, esp. 103–8.

2 *Military Annals of Lanzhou* (*Lanzhou jilüe*) reports that Hui Muslims in China proper during the Qing period tended to consider the teachings and the books that disseminated in Xinjiang as being the most authentic. See Tōru Saguchi, *18–19 seiki higashi Torukisutan shakaishi kenkyū* [*The Social History of Eastern Turkistan in the 18th–19th Centuries*] (Tokyo: Yoshikawa Kōbunkan, 1963), 564; *Jinding Lanzhou jilüe*, ed. by Huaizhong Yang (Yinchuan: Ningxin Renmin Chubanshe, 1988), 254. However, Hui Muslims have neither always held that knowledge from the Islamic heartland was unimpeachably authentic nor accepted it blindly.

3 Tatsuya Nakanishi, Kazuo Morimoto, and Takashi Kuroiwa, "17–18 seiki kōtaiki no Chūgoku Kokōha Isurāmu: Kaihō Shusenchin no Arabiago hibun no kentō kara" [Islam of Old Practice (*guxing*) in China at the Turn of the 18th Century: From the Examination of an Arabic Inscription in Kaifeng and Zhuxianzhen], *Tōyō Bunka Kenkyūjo kiyō* 162 (2012): 55 (288)–120 (223) addresses a similar question: how did Hui Muslim scholars creatively apply Islamic jurisprudence books from Muslim heartlands in their own legal disputes in China?

4 For studies on the harmonization of Islam and traditional Chinese thought by Hui Muslims, see Tatsuya Nakanishi, "Chūgoku Isurāmu no kenkyū dōkō" [Trends of Studies on Islam in China], *Chūgoku shigaku* 26 (2016): 125–41; idem, "Ibunka kan no taiwa to kyōsei wo kangaeru: Chūgoku Musurimu kenkyū no kinnen no dōkō" [Considering the Dialogue and Symbiosis between Different Cultures: Recent Trends of Studies on Chinese-Speaking Muslims], *Shisō* (Iwanami Shoten) 1134 (2018): 116–26.

5 For example, Roberta Tontini, *Muslim Sanzijing: Shifts and Continuities in the Definition of Islam in China (1710–2010)* (Leiden and Boston: Brill, 2016), 113–55, elucidates how authors of the Muslim *Sanzijing* (three character classic) genre, including Ma Dexin, coped with shifts in and after Muslim rebellions in Yunnan and the North West during the second half of the nineteenth century. However, Tontini does not discuss their responses to intellectual trends in Muslim societies outside China. The same study concludes that a version of the Muslim *Sanzijing* co-authored by Ma Dexin and his disciple Ma Anli focuses on "spiritual growth and individual self-cultivation" rather than "aspects of sociopolitical relevance," or reflects "the less supportive attitude of Chinese Muslims vis-à-vis the cultural paradigms and the political authority structures under the Qing administration" at the time of the Yunnan Muslim rebellion. However, this conclusion is debatable because Ma Dexin was doubtlessly concerned with how to observe the Islamic law under the Qing rule. See Tatsuya Nakanishi, "Variations of 'Islamic Military Cosmopolitanism': The Survival Strategies of Hui Muslims during the Modern Period," in *Challenging Cosmopolitanism: Coercion, Mobility and Displacement in Islamic Asia*, ed. by R. Michael Feener and Joshua Gedacht (Edinburgh: Edinburgh University Press, 2018), 122–44, esp. 124–5.
Kristian Petersen, *Interpreting Islam in China: Pilgrimage, Scripture, & Language in the Han Kitab* (New York: Oxford University Press, 2018), 155–6, 197, et passim, argues that Ma Dexin intended to facilitate the Huis' "involvement in the global Muslim community" and "participating in global Islamic dialogues" as a result of "the growing interaction between Muslims throughout the world." However, this study does not concretely describe any intellectual interaction between the Huis and other Muslims outside China.

6 Strictly speaking, this work was written by Ma Dexin's disciple Ma Anli under the former's supervision. However, its basic idea was Ma Dexin's, although the Chinese expression was elaborated by Ma Anli.

7 Another of Ma Dexin's Arabic works, *Sincere Advice in Islam* (*Naṣīḥat al-Islām*) and its Chinese translation, *Admonition for Awakening People in the World* (*Xingshizhen*), also critique saint veneration. For more on Ma Dexin's negative opinion of saint veneration in *Essences of the Four Canons* and *Admonition for Awakening People in the World*, see Guiping Yang, *Ma Dexin sixiang yanjiu* [*Research on the Thought of Ma Dexin*] (Beijing: Zongjiao Wenhua Chubanshe, 2004), 188–92.

8 Ma Dexin, *Sidian Yaohui*, ed. by Yongchang Yang and Jizu Ma (Xinig: Qinghai Renming Chubanshe, 1988), 83.

9 [Ma Dexin], *Lixue Zhezhong*, n.p.: 1284 AH/1867, repr. in *Yunnan shaoshu minzu guji chenben jicheng*, vol. 48, ed. by Yunnan Shaoshu Minzu Guji Zhengli Chuban Guihua Bangongshi (Kunming: Yunnan Renmin Chubanshe, 2016), 65–130, esp. 17a–19a.

10 [Ma Dexin], *Lixue Zhezhong*, 19b–21b.

11 The expression "without any relation to a person whom human beings [by their own judgement] call "a friend of God" means that only God knows who His friends are. On this, see, for example, Najm al-Dīn Abū Bakr b. Muḥammad b. Shāhāwar b. Anūshirwān Rāzī maʿrūf ba-Dāya, *Mirṣād al-ʿibad*, ed. by Muḥammad Amīn Riyāḥī (Tehran: Bungāh-i tarjuma wa nashr-i kitāb, 1352 AHS/1973), 226, which cites the following *ḥadīth qudsī*: "My friends are under My domes. Only I recognize them." Ma Dexin cites this passage from this Persian work *Path of Bondmen* (*Mirṣād al-ʿibād*) in his Chinese work *Essences of the Four Canons*, where he calls the former work "*Classic for Exploration of the Origin in Travel on the Path*" (*Daoxing tuiyuan jing*). See Ma Dexin, *Sidian Yaohui*, 90–1.

12 "The mediation of a perfect friend of God" seems to indicate his instruction to his disciple by which the latter cannot deviate from but rather revert to his predestined course. As for this, we might be able to refer to Dāya, *Mirṣād*, 231 (Ma Dexin consulted this Persian work as mentioned above). According to it, Sufi masters guard their disciples from becoming haughty when the latter reaches a high spiritual station. Dāya expresses such guidance as "influences of a Sufi master's friendship with God which represent the Kindness of God" (*taṣarrufāt-i walāyat-i shaykh ki ṣūrat-i luṭf-i Ḥaqq ast*).

13 Jāmī's *Rays of flashes* (*Ashi''at al-Lama'āt*), an Akbarian work from which Hui Muslims, including Ma Dexin, traditionally understood the Oneness of Being, explains the concept of capacity/preparedness and the immutable entity as follows. Here, I have written the portions of Fakhr al-Dīn'Irāqī's (d. 1289) *Flashes* (*Lama'āt*), which *Rays of flashes* comments on, in bold: When *things* (*shu'ūn*) are discerned in divine Knowledge, their representations in the level of Knowledge, which are called 'the immutable entities,' assume the preparedness for appearing at the level of an individual being. [Each of the *things*, or the immutable entities,] has a different level of preparedness [. . .]. **The appearance of lights**, that is, lights of the Self-manifestation of God <Be exalted!>, **depends on an extent of preparedness**, that is, preparedness of a receptor of the Self-manifestation for [reflecting] the lights. **The overflow**, that is, the overflows composed of perceptions and intuitions accompanying the Self-manifestations, **depends on an extent of capability**, that is, preparedness of a receptor of the Self-manifestation for [containing] the overflows (Mawlānā Jāmī, *Ashi''at al-Lama'āt fī sharḥ al-Lama'āt*, in *Ganjīna-yi 'irfān: Ashi''at al-Lama'āt-i Jāmī, Sawāniḥ-i Ghazālī: Sharḥ-i dū bayt-i mathnawī, Maqṣad-i aqṣā, Zubdat al-ḥaqā'iq, muntakhab-i chahār 'unwān-i Kīmiyā-yi sa'ādat*, ed. by Ḥāmid Rabbānī [Tehran: Kitābkhāna-yi 'ilmiyya-yi Ḥāmidī, n.d.], 1–151, esp. 110–1). Ma Dexin also says, in *Fixation of the Standard for Sufi Doctrines*: 'When [a bondman] reaches the station of annihilation, his business is over. Afterwards, God has the right of disposal over the affair. God <Be exalted!> discloses Himself according to an extent to which [the bondman's] *thing* (*sha'n*) [in the divine Knowledge] requires.' See *Lixue zhezhong*, 12a.

14 Ma Dexin almost repeated exactly the idea of Ibn 'Arabī. See Tatsuya Nakanishi, "Ma Dexin and Ibn 'Arabī's Prospects regarding the Afterlife: A Chinese Expression of Sufism during the 19th Century," in *Islamic Studies and the Study of Sufism in Academia: Rethinking Methodologies*, ed. by Yasushi Tonaga and Chiaki Fujii (Kyoto: Kenan Rifai Center for Sufi Studies, Kyoto University, 2018), 151–70, esp. 163.

15 Sufis generally attribute novices' failure in mystical travel to their own incompetence but their success to the effective guidance of their masters, while implicitly taking for granted the divine arrangement behind it. For example, see Azīz Nasafī, *Maqṣad-i aqṣā*, in *Ganjīna-yi 'irfān*, 210–85, esp. 220–1. Although Ma Dexin was familiar with this Persian work *The Farthest Goal* (*Maqṣad-i aqṣā*) – his Chinese work *Ultimate Station of Travel* (*Daoxing jiujing*) is a Chinese translation of this Persian work – he contrastingly highlights the divine predestination, or predestined capacity of novices, as the cause of both their ends.

16 [Ma Dexin], *Lixue Zhezhong*, 21b–25b.

17 Khaled El-Rouayheb, *Islamic Intellectual History in the Seventeenth Century: Scholarly Currents in the Ottoman Empire and the Maghreb* (New York: Cambridge University Press, 2015), 249.

18 William C. Chittick, *Imaginal Worlds: Ibn al-'Arabī and the Problem of Religious Diversity* (Albany: State University of New York Press, 1994), 113–8; Nakanishi, "Ma Dexin and Ibn 'Arabī's Prospects," 157.

19 Carl Ernst, "Controversy over Ibn 'Arabī's *Fuṣūṣ*: The Faith of Pharoah," *Islamic Culture* 59 (1985): 259–66.

20 Basheer M. Nafi, "Salafism Revived: Nu'mān al-Alūsī and the Trial of Two Aḥmads," *Die Welt des Islams* 49 (2009): 49–97, esp. 68.

21 El-Rouayheb, *Islamic Intellectual History*, 240; Eliza Tasbihi, "Sufis versus Exoteric Ulama in Seventeenth-century Ottoman Turkey: The Debate on 'Pharaoh's Faith' in the Mevlevī and

Akbarian Sufī Traditions," in *Sufis and Their Opponents in the Persianate World*, ed. by Reza Tabandeh and Leonard Lewisohn (Irvine, Ca.: UCI, Jordan Center for Persian Studies, 2020), 167–203, esp. 200.

22 El-Rouayheb, *Islamic Intellectual History*, 277–85.

23 Ibid., 312–44.

24 Al-Khānī expounded teachings of his master Khālid al-Baghdādī (d. 1827) in light of the Oneness of Being. See Itzchak Weismann, *Taste of Modernity: Sufism, Salafiyya, and Arabism in Late Ottoman Damascus* (Leiden, Boston, Köln: Brill, 2001), 148.

25 Al-Nābulusī in his *Key of Coexistence* (*Miftāḥ al-ma'iyya*), as part of a comment on the absolute necessity of a mentor (*shaykh*) in Sufism, cites Ibn 'Arabī's theory, according to which everything/everyone can be a mentor, because each thing/person reflects a particular divine aspect, or its/his Lord (*Rabb*) corresponding to its/his servanthood (*'ibāda*). See 'Abd al-Ghanī al-Nābulusī, *Miftāḥ al-ma'iyya fī dastūr al-ṭarīqa al-Naqshbandiyya: Sharḥ Risālat Sayyidī al-Shaykh Tāj al-Dīn al-Naqshbandī raḍiya Allāh ta'ālā 'anhu wa-'uniya bihi fī ādāb al-ṭarīqa al-Naqshbandiyya*, ed. by Jūda Muḥammad Abū l-Yazīd al-Mahdī (Cairo: al-Dār al-Jūdiyya, 1429 AH/2008), 44–5. Al-Khānī in his work *Splendid Beauty* (*al-Bahja al-saniyya*) cites this passage of al-Nābulusī and says that this ubiquity of the mentor can be seen as the meaning of the proverb, 'there are as many paths to God as breaths of created things.' Al-Khānī writes based on Ibn Sulaymān's *Moist Garden on the Rules of the Way of the Naqshbandiyya and the Splendour of the Khālidiyya* (*al-Ḥadīqa al-nadiyya fī ādāb al-ṭārīqa al-Naqshbandiyya wa-l-bahja al-Khālidiyya*) as follows: 'All the paths are equal to each other in the point of leading to God <Be exalted!>, but different from each other in the point of nearness to God in leading and arriving. In reaching stations for recognizing Oneness, the most near and easy path for disciples is that of Naqshbandiyya <May God consecrate the secrets of the noble persons>.' In other words, al-Khānī insists that the Sufi masters of Naqshbandiyya can guide their disciples to God more easily than anyone or anything that Ibn 'Arabī qualified as a mentor. See Muḥammad b. 'Abdullāh al-Khānī al-Khālidī al-Naqshbandī al-Ḥanafī, *Kitāb al-Bahja al-saniyya fī ādāb al-ṭarīqa al-'āliyya al-Khālidiyya al-Naqshbandiyya, wa-yalīhi Irghām al-murīd fī sharḥ al-Naẓm al-'atīd li-tawassul al-murīd bi-rijāl al-ṭarīqa al-Naqshbandiyya al-Khālidiyya al-Ḍiyā'iyya qaddasa Allāhu asrārahum* (Istanbul: Hakîkat Kitâbevi, 2002), 8–10. As for Ibn Sulaymān and his *Moist Garden*, see Butrus Abu-Manneh, "Salafiyya and the Rise of the Khālidiyya in Baghdad in the Early Nineteenth Century," *Die Welt des Islams* 43.3 (2003): 349–72, esp. 367–71. Al-Khānī's *Splendid Beauty* was introduced to China at the latest in the early twentieth century, because it is cited in Zhanye's (d. 1924) *Manāqib*, an Arabic hagiography of the Jahriyya. See Florian Sobieroj, "Spiritual Practice in the Arabic Hagiography of the Chinese Ǧahrīya Sufi Order," *Zeitschrift der Deutschen Morgenländischen Gesellschaft* 169.1 (2019): 155–81, esp. 163.

26 Basheer M. Nafi, "Taṣawwuf and Reform in Pre-modern Islamic Culture: In Search of Ibrāhīm al-Kūrānī," *Die Welt des Islams* 42.3 (2002): 307–55, esp. 324, 329–34, 348–9, 353; Khaled El-Rouayheb, "From Ibn Ḥajar al-Haytamī (d. 1566) to Khayr al-Dīn al-Ālūsī (d. 1899): Changing Views of Ibn Taymiyya among Non-Ḥanbalī Sunni Scholars," in *Ibn Taymiyya and His Times*, ed. by Yossef Rapoport and Shahab Ahmed (Karachi: Oxford University Press, 2010), 269–318, esp. 300–11.

27 El-Rouayheb, *Islamic Intellectual History*, 283–4.

28 Ömer Yılmaz, *İbrahim Kûrânî: Hayatı, eserleri ve tasavvuf anlayışı* [*Ibrahim Kûrânî: Life, Works, and Understanding of Sufism*] (Istanbul: İnsan Yayınları, 2005), 418.

29 Abū l-Thanā criticized the idea of the Oneness of Being and prohibited people from reading Ibn 'Arabī's works. However, Abū l-Thanā believed in the sanctity of Ibn 'Arabī. See Basheer M. Nafi, "Abu al-Thana' al-Alusi: An Alim, Ottoman Mufti, and Exegete of the Qur'an," *International Journal of Middle East Studies* 34 (2002): 465–94, esp. 485. Abū l-Thanā favorably referred to Ibn Sawdakīn's tradition on Ibn 'Arabī's refusal of rational interpretation (*ta'wīl*) to vindicate

Aḥmad b. Ḥanbal explicitly and Ibn Taymiyya implicitly. See Shihāb al-Dīn al-Sayyid Maḥmūd Afandī al-Ālūsī al-Ḥusaynī, *Kitāb Gharā'ib al-ightirāb wa-nuzhat al-albāb* (Baghdad: Maṭbaʿat al-shābandar, 1327 AH/1909–10), 386. Khayr al-Dīn, like his father, prohibited people from reading Ibn ʿArabī's works. However, Khayr al-Dīn valued some arguments of Ibn ʿArabī, such as his rejection of the blind imitation of authoritative doctrines (*taqlīd*). See Itzchak Weismann, "The Naqshbandiyya-Khâlidiyya and the Salafî Challenge in Iraq," *Journal of the History of Sufism* 4 (2003–04): 229–40, esp. 231–2; Nafi, "Salafism Revived," 74–8. Al-Qāsimī stressed that the Oneness of Being is free from incarnation (*ḥulūl*) and the identification of God with human beings (*ittiḥād*). See Mun'im Sirry, "Jamāl al-Dīn al-Qāsimī and the Salafi Approach to Sufism," *Die Welt des Islams* 51 (2011): 75–108, esp. 86–95.

30 Nafi, "Salafism Revived," 82–5; David Dean Commins, *Islamic Reform: Politics and Social Change in Late Ottoman Syria* (New York and Oxford: Oxford University Press, 1990), 80–2.

31 Abū l-Thanā was affiliated with the Sufi order Khālidiyya, and even supported the practice of *rābiṭa* (connection) that Khālid al-Baghdādī (d. 1827), the founder of Khālidiyya, advocated (although in *rābiṭa* the disciple constantly pictures the figure of his mentor in his mind, Khālid required every member of Khālidiyya to imagine the figure of the founder). See Weismann, *Taste of Modernity*, 35–6, 117. Khayr al-Dīn was also affiliated with Khālidiyya (Nafi, "Salafism Revived," 56–7), although he questioned Khālid's *rābiṭa* (Weismann, *Taste of Modernity*, 113–4; idem, "The Naqshbandiyya-Khâlidiyya," 232). Al-Qāsimī critically described the Sufi masters as 'electric wires that generate spiritual madness and melancholy among the people.' See Sirry, "Jamāl al-Dīn al-Qāsimī," 83. However, al-Qāsimī continued to seek the advice of his initiator to Khālidiyya, Muḥammad al-Khānī (d. 1898), after his withdrawal from the Sufi order. See Weismann, *Taste of Modernity*, 277–8.

32 Commins, *Islamic Reform*, 58–9.

33 Yang, *Ma Dexin*, 186–7.

34 Esther Peskes, "The Wahhābiyya and Sufism in the Eighteenth Century," in *Islamic Mysticism Contested: Thirteen Centuries of Controversies and Polemics*, ed. by Frederick De Jong and Bernd Radtke (Leiden, Boston, and Köln: Brill, 1999), 145–61, esp. 150–1; Natana J. Delong-Bas, *Wahhabi Islam: From Revival and Reform to Global Jihad* (Oxford: Oxford University Press, 2004), 68–72, 83–4.

35 Ma Dexin, like Ibn Taymiyya, suggested that it was not only believers who are sinners but also infidels who will be purified by the Fire and find respite in the end from it. By contrast, Ibn ʿArabī argues that residents of the Fire abide there eternally in contentment with their otherworldly, final destination. See Nakanishi, "Ma Dexin and Ibn ʿArabī's Prospects," 156–8.

36 [Ma Dexin], *Lixue Zhezhong*, 26a–b; Aḥmad b. Muḥammad b. Hajar al-Haytamī, *al-Minaḥ al-Makkiyya fī sharḥ al-Hamziyya*, ed. by Bassām Muḥammad Bārūd (Abu Dhabi: al-Majmaʿ al-thaqāfī, 1998), vol. 3, 1469.

37 *Lixue Zhezhong*, 26a; Muḥammad Amīn al-shahīr bi-Ibn ʿĀbidīn, *Radd al-muḥtār ʿalā al-Durr al-mukhtār sharḥ Tanwīr al-abṣār fī fiqh madhhab al-Imām al-Aʿẓam Abī Ḥanīfa al-Nuʿmān* (n.p.: Shirka-yi ṣaḥāfiyya-yi ʿUthmāniyya, 1307 AH/1890), vol. 3, 406.

38 As for Taymiyyan agendas around Sufism, for example, see Abu-Manneh, "Salafiyya and the Rise of the Khālidiyya," 354–61; Butrus Abu-Manneh, "The Khālidiyya and the Salafiyya in Baghdad after Shaykh Khalid," *Journal of the History of Sufism* 5 (2007): 21–40, esp. 26–30; Mustapha Sheikh, "Taymiyyan *Taṣawwuf* Meets Ottoman Orthodoxy: Reformed Sufism in the Thought of Aḥmad al-Rūmī al-Āqḥiṣārī," *Muslim World* 108.1 (2018): 186–206; Nafi, "Salafism Revived," 82–5; Commins, *Islamic Reform*, 80–2; Delong-Bas, *Wahhabi Islam*, 68–72.

39 [Ma Dexin], *Lixue Zhezhong*, 25b, reads as follows:
We read articles mentioning miracles (*karāma*) of some Shaykhs, which state: They exterminated human characteristics from themselves, and ascribed the divine power to themselves; they perform anything as they want without conformity to God's permission; the divine attraction is caused by their hands; entering the Paradise or Fire is controlled by their desire. These statements

in the books are seemingly not sincere words. Rather, it is necessary for us to oppose to them in accordance with the standard measure of the *sharīʿa*.

The passage "Entering the Paradise or Fire is controlled by their desire" may be that which exaggerates the Sufis' claims to intercession (*shafāʿa*), which Taymiyyan scholars critically discussed. For example, Abū l-Thanā al-Alūsī, like Ibn Taymiyya, opposed "*tawassul* (seeking someone's help in the prayer) proper, that is, abjuring God through the mediating power of created beings" (*al-tawassul bi-l-dhāt wa-l-qasm ʿalā Allāh taʿālā bi-aḥad min khalqihi*), although the former scholar approved "asking for help from a person, making him an intercessor with God, in the sense of requesting him to pray to God by proxy" (*al-istighātha bi-makhlūq wa-jaʿluhu wasīlatan bi-maʿnā ṭalab al-duʿāʾ minhu*). See Nafi, "Salafism Revived," 83–4; Abū l-Faḍl Shihāb al-Dīn al-Sayyid Maḥmūd al-Ālūsī al-Baghdādī, *Rūḥ al-maʿānī fī tafsīr al-Qurʾān al-ʿaẓīm wa-l-sabʿ al-mathānī*, ed. by Sayyid ʿImrān (Cairo: Dār al-ḥadīth, 1426 AH/2005), vol. 6, 414–7. In the previously shown citation from *Fixation of the Standard for Sufi Doctrines*, Ma Dexin likewise appears to object to Sufis' boasting of their own power to exert influence on God and tempting ordinary people to invoke the same power. Ma Dexin did not negate the intercession of friends of God in the hereafter. An Arabic work of Ma Dexin, *Secrets of Return*, states that some people who are disobedient to God will be delivered by "the intercession of friends of God and pious people" (*shafāʿat awliyāʾ wa-muttaqīn*) as well as Muḥammad and other Prophets. See [Ma Dexin,] *Asrār al-maʿād* (n.p., n.d.), repr. in *Yunnan shaoshu minzu guji zhenben jicheng*, vol. 48, ed. by Yunnan Shaoshu Minzu Guji Zhengli Chuban Guihua Bangongshi (Kunming: Yunnan Renmin Chubanshe, 2016), 247–335, esp. 33b. This statement is not in contradiction to the view of Ibn Taymiyya. According to Ibn Taymiyya, "the only intercession that is acceptable to God is that which God Himself permits, such as His permission to the Prophet Muhammad, other prophets, and other righteous persons to intercede before God in the hereafter, especially for believers whose sins earn them a temporary place in Hell-Fire." See Jon Hoover, *Ibn Taymiyya* (London: Oneworld Academic, 2019), 69.

40 [Ma Dexin], *Lixue Zhezhong*, 20a–29a.

41 Ibid., 2a–17a.

42 Ibid., 7a–12a.

43 Ibid., 9b–10a.

44 'The second volume, the fourth diagramming' and 'The sixth volume, the second diagramming' respectively correspond to the first volume (*juan*), the fifth diagram (*tushuo*), and the fifth volume, the second diagram, of *Nature and Principle in Islam. Fixation of the Standard for Sufi Doctrines* seems to assign the appellation of the first volume to the main text (*benjing*) of *Nature and Principle in Islam*, which is followed by five volumes of diagrams. 'The second volume, the fourth diagramming' should be modified to 'the second volume, the fifth diagramming.' Both the first volume, the fifth diagram, and the fifth volume, the second diagram explain 'the mandate' (*daming*), 'the spirit attributed to God' (*jixing*), and the 'Muḥammadan spirit' (*zhisheng zhi xing*). See Sachiko Murata, William C. Chittick, and Weiming Tu (with a foreword by Seyyed Hossein Nasr), *The Sage Learning of Liu Zhi: Islamic Thought in Confucian Terms* (Cambridge and London: The Harvard University Asia Center for the Harvard-Yenching Institute, 2009), 212–9, 508–14.

45 [Ma Dexin], *Lixue Zhezhong*, 12a–13b. *Fixation of the Standard for Sufi Doctrines* presents 'Qūnawī's *Flashes* (*Lamaʿāt*)' as the source for this sentence. However, *Flashes* was not the work of Ṣadr al-Dīn Qūnawī (d. 1274), but instead the work of Fakhr al-Dīn ʿIrāqī (d. 1289), upon which Jāmī's *Rays of Flashes* is a commentary. This sentence may be based on the following passage from *Rays of Flashes* (Jāmī, *Ashiʿʿa*, 96–7):

Assume the Lover and the beloved, that is, possible thing and necessary being, as a circle, which is divided into two by a line, and in the appearance of which two arcs manifest. This remark means to compare the invisible and absolute He-ness to a circle, and the manifestation of possible thing and necessary being to the division of the circle into two arcs [. . .]. The line that either seems to be existent depending on the Real or is non-existent actually, that is, possible self-definitions differentiating possible thing from necessary being, is eliminated from the middle of possible thing and necessary being in their meeting, and [the line] disappears out of sight of the witness of traveler, although it does not actually vanish. Thus, the circle appears to be restored to an undivided one as it is originally, although it looks so in sight of the witness of traveler in fact.

46 [Ma Dexin], *Lixue Zhezhong*, 7b.

47 Shuhuai Wang, *Xiantong Yunnan huiming shibian* [*The Mohammedan Uprising in Yunnan 1856-1873*] (Taipei: Zhongyang Yanjiuyuan Jindaishi Yanjiusuo, 1968), 50–4, 99–105; David G. Atwill, *The Chinese Sultanate: Islam, Ethnicity and the Panthay Rebellion in Southwest China, 1856–1873* (Stanford, California: Stanford University Press 2005), 64–97.

48 Wang, *Xiantong*, 109–36.

49 Shōshi Chō (Chengzhi Zhang), *Junkyō no Chūgoku Isuramu: Shinpi shugi kyōdan Jafurīya no rekishi* [*Chinese Islam of Martyrdom: The History of the Mystical Order Jahriyya*], transl. by Hiroshi Umemura (Tokyo: Aki Shobō, 1993), 175–81; Jonathan N. Lipman, *Familiar Strangers: A History of Muslims in Northwest China* (Seattle and London: University of Washington Press, 1997), 179.

50 See Tatsuya Nakanishi, "After Criticism of Ma Dexin against Veneration of Saints: Rethinking Chinese Elaboration of Islam," *Kyoto Bulletin of Islamic Area Studies* 14 (2021): 138–61. I deeply thank Ms. Leila Chérif-Chebbi, an associate member of the Centre for Turkish Ottoman Balkan and Central Asia Studies (CETOBAC) at the École des hautes études en sciences sociales, Paris, for pointing out to me that the Arabic source mentions Ma Dexin's criticism against such religious practices.

51 See Émile Rocher, *La Province chinoise du Yün-nan* (Paris: Libraire de la société asiatique, 1880), vol. 2, 160, n. 1.

52 See Wang, *Xiantong*, 154.

53 Ma Dexin, *Sidian Yaohui*, 84.

54 *A Collection of Commentaries on the Ode* may be a commentary on al-Būṣīrī's *The Ode of the Mantle* (*Qaṣīdat al-burda*). Ma Dexin translated *The Ode of the Mantle* into Chinese with his disciple Ma Anli. Later, Ma Anli published *The Poetic Classic in Islam* (*Tianfang shijing*), where he added his commentary to the Chinese translation of *The Ode of the Mantle* based on commentaries of ʿUmar al-Kharbūtī (d. 1882) and Ibrāhīm al-Bājūrī (d. 1860), and a gloss of Abū Qāsim (unidentified). Any of the two commentaries and the gloss may be *A Collection of Commentaries on the Ode* cited here.

55 Tatsuya Nakanishi, "The Logic of Succession in the Case of Chinese Muslims during the Qing Period," *Orient* (*Reports of the Society for Near Eastern Studies in Japan*) 42 (2007): 55–70.

56 Nile Green, *Sufism: A Global History* (Chichester, West Sussex and Malden, MA: Wiley-Blackwell, 2012), 94–5, 126, 132–3.

57 Guanliye, *Reshiha'er*, transl. by Wanbao Yang, Xuekai Ma, Chengzhi Zhang (Beijing: Shenghuo Dushu Xinzhi Sanlian Shudian, 1993), 7.

58 Ibid., 68.

59 Ibid., 99.

60 Muḥammad Manṣūr Allāh Burhān al-Dīn, *Risāla aqṣariyya li-bayān al-silsila al-Jahriyya* (Lanzhou: n.p., 1352 AH/1933), 156; Mansu'er Ma Xuezhi, *Daotong Shizhuan*, transl. by Yi Ma, Shengjun Wang, Fuyin Ke, Wenxue Hai, 2 vols. (Xiji, Ningxia: Xijixian Beidasi, [1997] [vol. 1] and n.d. [vol. 2]), vol. 1, 137–8.

61 Ma Dexin also cited this exegesis in his work *Secrets of Return* ([Ma Dexin,] *Asrār*, 9a).

62 Ismāʿīl Ḥaqqī [Bursawī], *Kitāb Tafsīr al-Qur'ān al-musammā bi-Rūḥ al-bayān*, [Istanbul]: Maṭbaʿat al-ʿāmira, 1285 AH/1869, repr. ([Istanbul]: Maṭbaʿat al-Uthmāniyya, 1306 [AH]/1888–89?), vol. 4, 14–5.

63 Muḥammad Manṣūr, *Risāla aqṣariyya*, 52–3; Mansu'er, *Daotong Shizhuan*, vol. 1, 40–1.

64 This remark is found also in *Trickling*, one of the Jahriyya hagiographies mentioned above. See Guanliye, *Reshiha'er*, 16.

65 Jāmī, *Ashi‘‘a*, 15–6, reads as follows:

Short roads [to God] are religious actions and obedient services. On the one hand, they belong to the kind of supererogatory training. The Real <Be extolled and exalted!> does not require it of His bondmen. Rather, they by themselves practice it to approach God <Be exalted!>, and require it of themselves. In this practice and requirement, their existences are interposed, and hence the annihilation of the substance, in which the aspect of the creation is extinguished in that of the reality, does not occur. Rather, it brings the following result: His power, bodily parts, and limbs become the Real Itself in the meaning that the aspect of the reality becomes predominant over that of the creation so that the latter is overwhelmed and defeated. This is called 'the approach by means of supererogatory training.' In this approach, the travelling bondman is the actor conscious of it, and the Real <Be extolled and exalted!> is his instrument. The instruction about this stage is the following hadith: 'I am his hearing, his seeing, his tongue, his hand, and his leg. He hears by Me, sees by Me, talks by Me, strikes by Me, and walks by Me.' On the other hand, [short roads to God] belong to the kind of absolute duty. The Real <Be extolled and exalted!> requires actions and services from His bondmen. They practice it to take after what is ordered. In this practice and requirement, their existences are not interposed. The result is the annihilation of the substance of the traveler, in which the aspect of the creation is extinguished in that of the reality. This is called 'the approach by means of absolute duty.' In this approach, the presence of the Real <Be extolled!> is the actor conscious of it, and the traveler with his power, bodily parts, and limbs stands at the station of the instrument. The instruction about this stage is the following hadith: "Actually God says by the tongue of his prophet or bondmen, 'He listens to those who extol Him.'"

66 Muḥammad Manṣūr, *Risāla aqṣariyya*, 211–3; Mansu'er, *Daotong Shizhuan*, vol. 2, 36–8.

67 [Ma Dexin], *Lixue Zhezhong*, 30b–31a, reads as follows:

Likewise, some persons think that a traveler ascends from the approach by means of supererogatory training to the approach by means of absolute duty, then from the approach by means of absolute duty to the station of the convergence (*jam‘*). However, it is not correct. Rather, the approach by means of the absolute duty signifies that the divine attraction precedes the human travel. In other words, to begin with, the Real approaches the bondman. The instruction of it is His <Be extolled!> following remark: 'He loves them, and they love him.' The approach by means of supererogatory training signifies that the travel precedes the attraction. In other words, to begin with, the bondman approaches the Real. The instruction of it is His <Be extolled!> following remark: 'Oh you, remember me. We remember you.'

This emphasizes that the approach by means of absolute duty that God initiates is different from the approach by means of supererogatory training that human beings can handle. To explain the approach by means of absolute duty, Ma Xuezhi cited a Prophetic tradition highlighting the precedence of the human approach over the divine approach, while *Rays of Flashes* and Ma Dexin cited other traditions just focusing on God's initiative.

68 See Nakanishi, "After Criticism of Ma Dexin," 147–50.

Bibliography

Abu-Manneh, Butrus. "Salafiyya and the Rise of the Khālidiyya in Baghdad in the Early Nineteenth Century." *Die Welt des Islams* 43.3 (2003): 349–72.

Abu-Manneh, Butrus. "The Khālidiyya and the Salafiyya in Baghdad after Shaykh Khalid." *Journal of the History of Sufism* 5 (2007): 21–40.

Al-Ālūsī al-Ḥusaynī, Shihāb al-Dīn Abū l-Thanāʾ Maḥmūd. *Kitāb Gharāʾib al-ightirāb wa-nuzhat al-albāb*. Baghdad: Maṭbaʿat al-shābandar, 1327 AH/1909–10.

Al-Ālūsī al-Ḥusaynī, Shihāb al-Dīn Abū l-Thanāʾ Maḥmūd. *Rūḥ al-maʿānī fī tafsīr al-Qurʾān al-ʿaẓīm wa-l-sabʿ al-mathānī*. Ed. by Sayyid ʿImrān. 30 vols. Cairo: Dār al-ḥadīth, 1426 AH/2005.

Atwill, David G. *The Chinese Sultanate: Islam, Ethnicity and the Panthay Rebellion in Southwest China, 1856–1873*. Stanford, California: Stanford University Press 2005.

[Bursawī], Ismāʿīl Ḥaqqī. *Kitāb Tafsīr al-Qurʾān al-musammā bi-Rūḥ al-bayān*. 4 vols. [Istanbul]: Maṭbaʿat al-ʿāmira, 1285 AH/1869. Repr. [Istanbul]: Maṭbaʿat al-ʿUthmāniyya, 1306 [AH]/1888–89.

Chittick, William C. *Imaginal Worlds: Ibn al-ʿArabī and the Problem of Religious Diversity*. Albany: State University of New York Press, 1994.

Chō, Shōshi (Zhang, Chengzhi). *Junkyō no Chūgoku Isuramu: Shinpi shugi kyōdan Jafurīya no rekishi* [*Chinese Islam of Martyrdom: The History of the Mystical Order Jahriyya*]. Transl. by Hiroshi Umemura. Tokyo: Aki Shobō, 1993.

Commins, David Dean. *Islamic Reform: Politics and Social Change in Late Ottoman Syria*. New York and Oxford: Oxford University Press, 1990.

Dāya, Najm al-Dīn Abū Bakr b. Muḥammad b. Shāhāwar b. Anūshirwān Rāzī maʿrūf ba-. *Mirṣād al-ʿibād*. Ed. by Muḥammad Amīn Riyāḥī. Tehran: Bungāh-i tarjuma wa nashr-i kitāb, 1352 AHS/1973.

Delong-Bas, Natana J. *Wahhabi Islam: From Revival and Reform to Global Jihad*. Oxford: Oxford University Press, 2004.

El-Rouayheb, Khaled. "From Ibn Ḥajar al-Haytamī (d. 1566) to Khayr al-Dīn al-Ālūsī (d. 1899): Changing Views of Ibn Taymiyya among Non-Ḥanbalī Sunni Scholars." In *Ibn Taymiyya and His Times*. Ed. by Yossef Rapoport and Shahab Ahmed. Karachi: Oxford University Press, 2010, 269–318.

El-Rouayheb, Khaled. *Islamic Intellectual History in the Seventeenth Century: Scholarly Currents in the Ottoman Empire and the Maghreb*. New York: Cambridge University Press, 2015.

Ernst, Carl. "Controversy over Ibn ʿArabī's *Fuṣūṣ*: The Faith of Pharaoh." *Islamic Culture* 59 (1985): 259–66.

Green, Nile. *Sufism: A Global History*. Chichester, West Sussex and Malden, MA: Wiley-Blackwell, 2012.

Guanliye. *Reshiha'er*. Transl. by Wanbao Yang, Xuekai Ma, Chengzhi Zhang. Beijing: Shenghuo Dushu Xinzhi Sanlian Shudian, 1993.

Hoover, Jon. *Ibn Taymiyya*. London: Oneworld Academic, 2019.

Ibn ʿĀbidīn, Muḥammad Amīn al-shahīr bi-. *Radd al-muḥtār ʿalā al-Durr al-mukhtār sharḥ Tanwīr al-abṣār fī fiqh madhhab al-Imām al-Aʿẓam Abī Ḥanīfa al-Nuʿmān*. 6 vols. N.p.: Shirka-yi ṣaḥāfiyya-yi ʿUthmāniyya, 1307 AH/1890.

Ibn Ḥajar al-Haytamī, Aḥmad b. Muḥammad. *Al-Minaḥ al-Makkiyya fī sharḥ al-Hamziyya*. Ed. by Bassām Muḥammad Bārūd. 3 vols. Abu Dhabi: al-Majmaʿ al-thaqāfī, 1998.

Jāmī, Mawlānā. *Ashiʿʿat al-Lamaʿāt fī sharḥ al-Lamaʿāt*. In *Ganjīna-yi ʿirfān: Ashiʿʿat al-Lamaʿāt-i Jāmī, Sawāniḥ-i Ghazālī: Sharḥ-i dū bayt-i mathnawī, Maqṣad-i aqṣā, Zubdat al-ḥaqāʾiq, muntakhab-i chahār ʿunwān-i Kīmiyā-yi saʿādat*. Ed. by Ḥāmid Rabbānī. Tehrān: Kitābkhāna-yi ʿilmiyya-yi Ḥāmidī, n.d., 1–151.

Jinding Lanzhou jilüe. Ed. by Huaizhong Yang. Yinchuan: Ningxin Renmin Chubanshe, 1988.

Al-Khānī al-Khālidī al-Naqshbandī al-Ḥanafī, Muḥammad b. ʿAbdullāh. *Kitāb al-Bahja al-saniyya fī ādāb al-ṭarīqa al-ʿāliyya al-Khālidiyya al-Naqshbandiyya, wa-yalīhi Irghām al-murīd fī sharḥ al-Naẓm al-ʿatīd li-tawassul al-murīd bi-rijāl al-ṭarīqa al-Naqshbandiyya al-Khālidiyya al-Ḍiyāʾiyya qaddasa Allāhu asrārahum*. Istanbul: Hakîkat Kitâbevi, 2002.

Lin, Chang-Kuan. "Three Eminent Chinese ʿUlamaʾ of Yunnan." *Journal of the Institute of Muslim Minority Affairs* 11.1 (1990): 100–17.

Lipman, Jonathan N. *Familiar Strangers: A History of Muslims in Northwest China*. Seattle and London: University of Washington Press, 1997.

[Ma Dexin]. *Asrār al-maʿād*. N.p., n.d. Repr. In *Yunnan shaoshu minzu guji zhenben jicheng*, vol. 48. Ed. by Yunnan Shaoshu Minzu Guji Zhengli Chuban Guihua Bangongshi. Kunming: Yunnan Renmin Chubanshe, 2016, 247–335.

[Ma Dexin]. *Lixue Zhezhong*. N.p.: 1284 AH/1867. Repr. In *Yunnan shaoshu minzu guji chenben jicheng*, vol. 48. Ed. by Yunnan Shaoshu Minzu Guji Zhengli Chuban Guihua Bangongshi. Kunming: Yunnan Renmin Chubanshe, 2016, 65–130.

[Ma Dexin]. *Sidian Yaohui*. Ed. by Yongchang Yang and Jizu Ma. Xinig: Qinghai Renming Chubanshe, 1988.

Ma Xuezhi, Mansu'er. *Daotong Shizhuan*. Transl. by Yi Ma, Shengjun Wang, Fuyin Ke, Wenxue Hai. 2 vols. Xiji, Ningxia: Xijixian Beidasi, [1997] (vol. 1) and n.d. (vol. 2).

Muḥammad Manṣūr Allāh Burhān al-Dīn. *Risāla aqṣariyya li-bayān al-silsila al-Jahriyya*. Lanzhou, 1352 AH/1933.

Murata, Sachiko, William C. Chittick, and Weiming Tu (with a foreword by Seyyed Hossein Nasr). *The Sage Learning of Liu Zhi: Islamic Thought in Confucian Terms*. Cambridge and London: The Harvard University Asia Center for the Harvard-Yenching Institute, 2009.

Al-Nābulusī, ʿAbd al-Ghanī. *Miftāḥ al-maʿiyya fī dastūr al-ṭarīqa al-Naqshbandiyya: Sharḥ Risālat Sayyidī al-Shaykh Tāj al-Dīn al-Naqshbandī raḍiya Allāh taʿālā ʿanhu wa-ʿuniya bihi fī ādāb al-ṭarīqa al-Naqshbandiyya*. Ed. by Jūda Muḥammad Abū l-Yazīd al-Mahdī. Cairo: al-Dār al-Jūdiyya, 1429 AH/2008.

Nafi, Basheer M. "Abu al-Thana' al-Alusi: An Alim, Ottoman Mufti, and Exegete of the Qur'an." *International Journal of Middle East Studies* 34 (2002): 465–94.

Nafi, Basheer M. "Taṣawwuf and Reform in Pre-modern Islamic Culture: In Search of Ibrāhīm al-Kūrānī." *Die Welt des Islams* 42.3 (2002): 307–55.

Nafi, Basheer M. "Salafism Revived: Nuʿmān al-Alūsī and the Trial of Two Aḥmads." *Die Welt des Islams* 49 (2009): 49–97.

Nakanishi, Tatsuya. "The Logic of Succession in the Case of Chinese Muslims during the Qing Period." *Orient* (*Reports of the Society for Near Eastern Studies in Japan*) 42 (2007): 55–70.

Nakanishi, Tatsuya. "Chūgoku Isurāmu no kenkyū dōkō" [Trends of Studies on Islam in China]. *Chūgoku shigaku* 26 (2016): 125–41.

Nakanishi, Tatsuya. "Ibunka kan no taiwa to kyōsei wo kangaeru: Chūgoku Musurimu kenkyū no kinnen no dōkō" [Considering the Dialogue and Symbiosis between Different Cultures: Recent Trends of Studies on Chinese-Speaking Muslims]. *Shisō* (Iwanami Shoten) 1134 (2018): 116–26.

Nakanishi, Tatsuya. "Ma Dexin and Ibn ʿArabī's Prospects regarding the Afterlife: A Chinese Expression of Sufism during the 19th Century." In *Islamic Studies and the Study of Sufism in Academia: Rethinking Methodologies*. Ed. by Yasushi Tonaga and Chiaki Fujii. Kyoto: Kenan Rifai Center for Sufi Studies, Kyoto University, 2018, 151–70.

Nakanishi, Tatsuya. "Variations of 'Islamic Military Cosmopolitanism': The Survival Strategies of Hui Muslims during the Modern Period." In *Challenging Cosmopolitanism: Coercion, Mobility and Displacement in Islamic Asia*. Ed. by R. Michael Feener and Joshua Gedacht. Edinburgh: Edinburgh University Press, 2018, 122–44.

Nakanishi, Tatsuya. "19 seiki Unnan no Chūgoku Musurimu gakusha, Ba Tokushin no seija sūhai hihan" [Chinese Muslim Scholar Ma Dexin's Criticism of Saint Worship]. *Tōhō gakuhō* (Kyōto) 94 (2019): 398–76.

Nakanishi, Tatsuya. "After Criticism of Ma Dexin against Veneration of Saints: Rethinking Chinese Elaboration of Islam." *Kyoto Bulletin of Islamic Area Studies* 14 (2021): 138–61.

Nakanishi, Tatsuya, Kazuo Morimoto, and Takashi Kuroiwa. "17–18 seiki kōtaiki no Chūgoku Kokōha Isurāmu: Kaihō Shusenchin no Arabiago hibun no kentō kara" [Islam of Old Practice (*guxing*) in China at the Turn of the 18th Century: From the Examination of an Arabic Inscription in Kaifeng and Zhuxianzhen]. *Tōyō Bunka Kenkyūjo kiyō* 162 (2012): 55 (288)–120 (223).

Nasafī, Azīz. *Maqṣad-i aqṣā*. In *Ganjīna-yi ʿirfān: Ashiʿʿat al-Lamaʿāt-i Jāmī, Sawāniḥ-i Ghazālī: Sharḥ-i dū bayt-i mathnawī, Maqṣad-i aqṣā, Zubdat al-ḥaqāʾiq, muntakhab-i chahār ʿunwān-i Kīmiyā-yi saʿādat*. Ed. by Ḥāmid Rabbānī. Tehran: Kitābkhāna-yi ʿilmiyya-yi Ḥāmidī, n.d., 210–85.

Peskes, Esther. "The Wahhābiyya and Sufism in the Eighteenth Century." In *Islamic Mysticism Contested: Thirteen Centuries of Controversies and Polemics*. Ed. by Frederick De Jong and Bernd Radtke. Leiden, Boston, and Köln: Brill, 1999, 145–61.

Petersen, Kristian. *Interpreting Islam in China: Pilgrimage, Scripture, & Language in the Han Kitab*. New York: Oxford University Press, 2018.

Rocher, Émile. *La Province chinoise du Yün-nan*. 2 vols. Paris: Libraire de la société asiatique, 1879–80.

Saguchi, Tōru, *18–19 seiki higashi Torukisutan shakaishi kenkyū* [*The Social History of Eastern Turkistan in the 18th–19th Centuries*]. Tokyo: Yoshikawa Kōbunkan, 1963.

Sheikh, Mustapha. "Taymiyyan *Taṣawwuf* Meets Ottoman Orthodoxy: Reformed Sufism in the Thought of Aḥmad al-Rūmī al-Āqḥiṣārī." *Muslim World* 108.1 (2018): 186–206.

Sirry, Mun'im. "Jamāl al-Dīn al-Qāsimī and the Salafi Approach to Sufism." *Die Welt des Islams* 51 (2011): 75–108.

Sobieroj, Florian. "Spiritual Practice in the Arabic Hagiography of the Chinese Ǧahrīya Sufi Order." *Zeitschrift der Deutschen Morgenländischen Gesellschaft* 169.1 (2019): 155–81.

Tasbihi, Eliza. "Sufis versus Exoteric Ulama in Seventeenth-century Ottoman Turkey: The Debate on 'Pharaoh's Faith' in the Mevlevī and Akbarian Sufī Traditions." In *Sufis and Their Opponents in the Persianate World*. Ed. by Reza Tabandeh and Leonard Lewisohn. Irvine, Ca.: UCI, Jordan Center for Persian Studies, 2020, 167–203.

Tontini, Roberta. *Muslim Sanzijing: Shifts and Continuities in the Definition of Islam in China (1710–2010)*. Leiden and Boston: Brill, 2016.

Wang, Shuhuai. *Xiantong Yunnan huiming shibian* [*The Mohammedan Uprising in Yunnan 1856–1873*]. Taipei: Zhongyang Yanjiuyuan Jindaishi Yanjiusuo, 1968.

Weismann, Itzchak. *Taste of Modernity: Sufism, Salafiyya, and Arabism in Late Ottoman Damascus*. Leiden, Boston, Köln: Brill, 2001.

Weismann, Itzchak. "The Naqshbandiyya-Khâlidiyya and the Salafī Challenge in Iraq." *Journal of the History of Sufism* 4 (2003–04): 229–40.

Yang, Guiping. *Ma Dexin sixiang yanjiu* [*Research on the Thought of Ma Dexin*]. Beijing: Zongjiao Wenhua Chubanshe, 2004.

Yılmaz, Ömer. *İbrahim Kûrânî: Hayatı, eserleri ve tasavvuf anlayışı* [*Ibrahim Kûrânî: Life, Works, and Understanding of Sufism*]. Istanbul: İnsan Yayınları, 2005.

THE MAKING OF THE MODERN

11

The Politics of the *Bay'a* Ceremony in Modern Morocco

Nozomi Shiratani

Introduction

This chapter aims at explaining the roles of the *bay'a* (ceremony of allegiance) and the kings' *khuṭba*s (speeches and discourses) on the occasion of the Feast of the Throne in Morocco as political institutions to connect the king and people and to gain the people's support for the monarchy, showing that this traditional ritual contributes to the resilience of the Moroccan monarchy.

As a consequence of major political uprisings since 2010, known as the Arab Spring, the resilience of Arab monarchies, which have remained stable in contrast to most other Arab countries which are republics, has been recognized as a noteworthy phenomenon, and researchers have attempted to clarify the factors resulting in this situation.[1] The "rentier states theory"[2] and the "dynastic monarchy theory"[3] were significant for understanding the stability of the Arab monarchies, especially in the Gulf countries. However, the case of Morocco, which neither possesses enough "rents" to be distributed to the population nor can be governed by members of the royal family by dividing the state's responsible positions among them, shows that the resilience of monarchical regimes is still somewhat puzzling.

This chapter focuses on the religious rituals of *bay'a*. In the traditions of Islam, the *bay'a* normally refers to the act by which a certain number of persons recognize a person's authority.[4] Thus, the *bay'a* of a Caliph is the act by which one person is proclaimed and recognized as the head of the Muslim state.[5] In this sense, nominations of the head of some Arab countries, such as the Saudi kings, follow the traditional *bay'a* ceremony. However, in Morocco, the *bay'a* is an annual event indicating the "renewal of the contract (*tajdīd al-walā'*) between the king and people" on the occasion of the Feast of the Throne (*'Īd al-'Arsh*).[6] Many researchers have focused on the "unchanging" characteristics of *bay'a* and its traditions, such as the symbols in the ceremony, to explain the monarchy's legitimacy and the extent to which the Moroccan monarchy persists.[7] These studies have overlooked two important aspects. First, they missed the transitions in the role of *bayʿa* reflected in the venues of the ceremony because they have not paid attention to the kings' *khuṭba*s as part of the Feast of the Throne together with *bayʿa*. Second, they have mainly discussed how the regime has exploited religious symbols and rituals to maintain its stability, but the mechanism to gain people's support for the monarchy through their manipulation should also be discussed. Therefore, this study discusses the roles of the *bayʿa* and the kings' *khuṭba*s in the Feast of the Throne together and clarifies the mechanism whereby they connect the king and people and effect people's support for the monarchy.

Concretely, this study focuses on the transitions of (1) the venues of *bayʿa* and (2) the text of the king's *khuṭba*s on the Feast of the Throne since independence. These changes reflect the conditions and concerns faced by the regime. Therefore, through an analysis of these changes, it becomes clear how traditional and religious rituals have been institutionalized in the political system to promote the resilience of monarchical political authority.

Analytical Approach of This Study

In his study of national celebration in the Arab countries, Elie Podeh asserted that the national calendar tells the story of the nation, passed on from one generation to the next through holidays, and provides a reliable mirror of the core belief system of the nation.[8] Its analysis, therefore, takes us into the very inner mechanics of nation building and state formation. In the Arab countries, even with the introduction of Western inventions at the rituals such as coronation and accession days, some local Islamic tradition endured. One central ritual was the *bayʿa*, considered the only recognized, legal procedure that ensured the legitimacy of the nominated ruler. And in light of innovations in the political system, the *bayʿa* became a necessary ritual during this transitional period.[9] Even in the second half of the twentieth century, when the ceremony largely withered away and was replaced by secular state procedures – certain rulers in Iraq and Jordan attempted to revive the term, albeit in an adapted version – in their search for legitimacy.[10] Podeh interprets these situations as ones in which modern Arab rulers have used the *bayʿa* ritual to endow upon themselves what Eickelman and Piscatori term a "sacred authority."[11]

If we take a position to analyze the *bayʿa* in modern Morocco as the institution to show the legitimacy to rule and to receive public support for the monarchy, then the king's *khuṭba*s on the occasion of the Feast of the Throne must be analyzed as one body with the *bayʿa*. During the two-day ceremony, the king's *khuṭba*s are presented first as a reflection on the year, a confirmation of the issues that Morocco confronts at the time, and an announcement of newly started reforms under the leadership of the king. Representatives of the people will make a contract of allegiance, the *bayʿa*, after receiving and understanding the king's words. In short, through an analysis of not only the *bayʿa* but also the king's *khuṭba*s, we can clarify the effects of traditional rituals that monarchy expects.

How can we analyze the roles of these rituals and the ruler's statements? Wedeen used the concept of "symbolic power"[12] in her analysis of the continuation of authoritarianism in Syria under Ḥāfiẓ al-Asad (1971–2000) and the control and social oppression exerted by the authorities. The concept of "symbolic power," the power conveyed by the symbols, was helpful for Wedeen to clarify the mechanism of the phenomenon whereby Ḥāfiẓ al-Asad was idolized and worshiped by the people as well as the significance of the "politics of spectacle." She notes that the authorities had invested an enormous amount from the national budget in the relevant propaganda strategies, even though the image of al-Asad created by the authority was hackneyed and far from charismatic. Her hypothesis is that in newly independent nations like Syria whose borders were fixed regardless of the existing communities, people's sense of belonging is shifting closer to larger groups like Arabs or Muslims. The authority must thus tackle the difficult tasks of nation building and national integration at the same time, and they often make a perfunctory veneration for an individual of the dictator, the foundation of the nation.[13] In addition, for the authority, it is easier and more beneficial to establish a rule based on "obedience" than to make effort to acquire "legitimacy" from people. As part of these discussions, she analyzes the transition of the rhetoric adopted under the reign of al-Asad. The unconditional obedience that the Syrian authority demanded of the people involved the complete renunciation of their ego on the assumption that they "pretend to" admire the president, and so, fully denying their individuality and dignity, they will be politically powerless, an important element in maintaining autocracy.[14]

I will analyze the *bayʿa* and kings' *khuṭba*s in Morocco with reference to Wedeen's study on Syria. It has already been shown that the Moroccan monarchy has maintained its stability, so the mechanism of the manipulation of symbols and rhetoric used as political measures will be the focus of this study. First, I will explain the processes of emphasizing and positively installing traditional or religious legitimacies through institution-building simultaneously with the introduction of modern institutions such as the parliamentary system and party politics since independence. Next, the *bayʿa*, which is one of the most important rituals in Morocco, making people's allegiance to the kings visible, will be discussed. I will also focus on the process of that "renewal of allegiance" (*tajdīd al-walāʾ*),[15] a particularity of Morocco, which is politically institutionalized in combination with the kings' speeches, and then I shall analyze how the traditional rituals of the *bayʿa* and the king's *khuṭba*s have been politically exploited since independence and the roles they have played. Finally, I will emphasize that the *bayʿa* in combination with kings' *khuṭba*s is performed to encourage public mobilization and participation in Morocco.

Positive Measures to Install Religious Legitimacy through the Process of Institution-Building

Institution-Building Processes

Morocco was officially recognized as an independent state on March 2, 1956. Mohammed V, the first king of Morocco, returned to his homeland from Madagascar, ending two years of exile, on November 16, 1955, and his triumphant return advanced his independence movement. Immediately after independence, he intended to establish a constitutional monarchy even though his rivals, who had fought with him against France, answered in the negative. Mohammed V's idea was embodied in the organization of a constitutional convention through his *ẓahīr* (command) in 1960. This convention, composed of 78 persons appointed by the king, was entrusted with the task of establishing a constitution based on the most respected values of Islam and Moroccan tradition by the end of 1962.

Unfortunately, the king's committee was dissolved upon his death in 1961. His successor, Hassan II, did not follow the ways of his father and worked to establish a constitution by himself using his legal power to command through *ẓahīr*s. The first Moroccan constitution was finally promulgated, created by the king himself with the support of a small advisory group of *ulema* on December 7, 1962. In this constitution, modern institutions such as multi-party electoral systems and a bicameral legislature were included, yet traditional political institutions based on Islam like the privileges of sharifs (descendants of the Prophet Mohammed) were also incorporated. One of the aims of this constitution was to center all political powers in the king while allowing him to keep an eye on opposition groups. The 1962 constitution stated that Morocco is a "democratic and social country" (Art. 1) and that sovereignty rests with the people (Art. 24). At the same time, the document instituted hereditary monarchy (Art. 20) and specified that the nature of the state could not be subject to constitutional revision (Art. 108). The king was acknowledged as *amīr al-mu'minīn* (commander of the faithful), while his person was declared sacred and inviolable (Art. 23). Among other prerogatives, the monarch gained the power to nominate and dismiss the prime minister and ministers. The king also obtained the right to declare a state of emergency (Art. 35), which he used in 1965 to dismiss representative institutions.

Moroccan constitutions have been revised many times in numerous situations, but the kings' various titles and positions, particularly his highest position in religion, have not been the target of these thorough revisions. In his political and religious positions, the king has positively encouraged religious activities and practices,[16] but, at the same time, political parties based on religion and the exploitation of religion by political actors are prohibited. In other words, all political authority is centered around the king, who also holds absolute religious power.

Religious Legitimacy Supporting Royal Authority

It is believed that Sufism developed paralleling with the decline in the sultan's authority in Morocco before the colonization by Western Europe. Sufism-colored folk beliefs were also common in other Maghreb countries, but the combination of marabout[17] worship and sharif worship is considered unique to Morocco.[18]

Sufism and the worship of saints have long been deeply embedded in people's daily lives, leading them to apply to saints and Sufis to banish uneasiness and gain relief whenever the political or social situation becomes chaotic. These trends have given rise to a tremendous number of saints across societies. Some of these saints have tried to differentiate their authority from the others, and then their "sacred lineages" which could not be acquired through personal effort, were accentuated. These are the lineages of the sharifs. Their respected virtues are widely believed by Muslims of different orientations; however, in Morocco, a situation where sharifs have received special weight to perceive marabout worship in the context of various historical religious actors in society.

The political exploitation of the holy lineages arose during the Marinid period (1196–1465), because, unlike earlier dynasties, the Marinids were not based on a religious movement and had to find a different source of legitimacy to rule. In addition, oppositional actors such as Sufi groups were active at the time.[19] For these two reasons, the protection of sharifs was promoted by the sultans of the Marinids, even though they were not sharifs themselves, and succeeding dynasties followed this exploitation of the sharifs in politics. Since the early fifteenth century, Morocco has been ruled by two sharifian dynasties, namely the Saadi dynasty (1510–1659) and the present Alawis (1659–), whose ruling families are sharifs.

What kind of legitimacy do these lineages of sharifs possess? The concept of *baraka* (blessing/blessing power) must be understood here because sharifs inherited *baraka* through their lineages. During the kings' visits around the country, they put their fingers in the bowl of milk or kiss dates held out at the reception ceremony, and these touched elements were poured or sown on the ground in the belief that they bring fertility. Thus, sharifs claim sanctity for their own authority, and they are also respected as saints.[20] As long as religious spirit flows strongly in Moroccan society, the sharif will surely be entitled to a certain amount of differences.[21] These sacred lineages of the kings and their religious authorities are recognized widely in society, even by the largest, illegal Islamist organization, the "Movement of Justice and Charity."[22] At the same time, the Moroccan kings hold the title of *amīr al-muʾminīn* (commander of the faithful), indicating their responsibility for protecting Islam and faith. Then, the fact that the kings, as *amīr al-muʾminīn*, are also sharifs made their positions sacred and their political and religious authority "inviolable." Also, the title of *amīr al-muʾminīn* goes hand in hand with the concept of *bayʿa*, as will be discussed in the following paragraphs.[23]

Bay'a Ceremony in Morocco

History of the Bay'a *in Morocco*

Previous studies of *bay'a* in modern Morocco have mainly focused on the "unchanging" character of the *bay'a* and its traditions such as symbols contained in the ceremony to explain the monarchy's legitimacy and the extent to which it persisted in Moroccan monarchy.[24] Thus, only a few researchers have discussed changes in the ceremonies and the details of their structures. The *bay'a* began to be recorded in Morocco in the eighth century, but it is difficult to say that its function at that time is the same as it is at present. Thus, we must begin by examining the circumstances in 1934, the first year that the *bay'a* became an annual event, to understand its characteristic of the "renewal of allegiance."

Morocco was a protectorate of France and Spain from 1919 to 1956, but the political system ruled by the Alawi dynasty still functioned perfunctorily. However, rural regions had traditionally maintained their autonomy, and there was no political system that was accepted by all the layers of society from the top to the bottom. These cleavages between the cities and rural regions became a target of Western intervention. Under the French protectorate, sovereignty weakened completely, while the authority of rural notables grew. France fixed their eyes on the autonomy of rural regions and adopted the "Berber Dahir" (*al-Ẓahīr al-Barbarī*).[25] This *ẓahīr* changed the legal system in parts of Morocco where Amazigh (Berber) languages were primarily spoken, while the legal system in the rest of the country remained as it had before the French invasion. Even though the original intention of this *ẓahīr* was to "divide and rule" the country, it resulted in a booming nationalist movement in Morocco. Leaders of nationalist movements having a sense of impeding crisis for Berber *ẓahīr* carried out a grand celebration of the enthronement anniversary of Mohammed V through public media, such as the magazine *al-Maghrib* and the daily newspaper *L'action du people*.[26] These movements increased their mobilization through the media, and, in consequence, the ceremony of the *bay'a* was organized on the enthronement anniversary of 1934 and has been celebrated annually since then.

Basic Structure of Morocco's Bay'a *Ceremony*

The *bay'a* is the last event of the two-day ceremony of the Feast of the Throne. The date of the ceremony depends on the king's coronation; it was celebrated on March 3 during the rule of Hassan II, the last king, and on July 30 under King Mohammed VI. The Feast of the Throne ceremony is mainly composed of the following events:

- Reception for the guests (daytime of the 1st day)
- King's speech/*khuṭba* (the afternoon of the 1st day)

- The administration of an oath by new officers of different schools, the military, and civilian institutes (the morning of the 2nd day)
- *Bayʿa* ceremony (the afternoon of the 2nd day)

A series of these events are broadcast live on national TV and radio, as well as by satellite.[27] Daadaoui described the details and atmosphere of the *bayʿa* ceremony as follows:

> Around 5 pm, the grand gates of the palace open amidst royal fanfare. At the beginning of the royal procession stand dozens of *ʿabid* (descendants of slaves still at the service of the royal palace). After the *ʿabid*, six nonchosen and unmounted horses are led by other *ʿabid*. At the back of the procession, the king finally appears, riding a black Arabian horse. The king is the only one in the whole ceremony who is not on his feet. All participants are on the ground; even his brother and cousin by his side are on their feet. Wearing a white cape (*selham*) and djellaba, the king proceeds slowly under the shade of a green parasol, symbol of the three-century-old Alawi dynasty, to receive the renewal of allegiance. As the king proceeds on his horse, the dignitaries bow five times before the king and all at once appeal in chorus to the divine grace of the king. Subsequently, the *mokhazni* (servants of the royal palace) address the dignitaries and literally yell back the message of royal blessing "(May) our lord bless you and appeal for divine grace to be bestowed upon you." The process continues until all five thousand dignitaries have bowed before royal power. A spectacle one political official described as "a symbol of power that cement ties between king and people."[28]

Analysis of the *Bayʿa* and *Khuṭba*s: The Institutionalization of Religious Rituals

Venues of the Bayʿa *Ceremony*

Formal sessions for the offer of *bayʿa* were traditionally held in the centers of the different provinces.[29] The current *bayʿa* ceremony in Morocco also takes place not only in Rabat, the capital of the country, but also in palaces in cities all over the nation, such as Fès, Tangier, Tetouan, Marrakech, and Casablanca. What is noteworthy here is that the ceremony does not simply alternate among palaces but is the arbitrary choice of the king. People are not usually informed about the venue for the ceremony that year until one day prior. For example, people expected that the 2011 ceremony would be held in Rabat, the capital, because they thought that the king would not leave the capital during such a sensitive and crucial time because people might take to the streets in protest at any time.

Table 1: Venues of the *Bay'a* and Topics of the Kings' Speeches since Independence

	Year	#	Date	Venue	Topics of the King›s Speech			
					Monarchy Islam	Democracy Politics	Economy Development	Sahara
Mohammed V	1956	29	Nov. 18	Rabat	o			
	1957	30	Nov. 18	Rabat	o			
	1958	31	Nov. 18	Rabat	o			
	1959	32	Nov. 18	Rabat	o			
	1960	33	Nov. 18	Rabat	o			
Hassan II	1961		Mar. 4	Rabat	o			
	1962	1	Mar. 4	Rabat		o		
	1963	2	Mar. 4	Rabat		o		
	1964	3	Mar. 4	Rabat				o
	1965	4	Mar. 4	Marrakesh				
	1966	5	Mar. 4	Fes				
	1967	6	Mar. 4					
	1968	7	Mar. 4					
	1969	8	Mar. 4		o			
	1970	9	Mar. 4					
	1971	10	Mar. 4	Fes		o		
	1972	11	Mar. 4	Rabat	o	o		
	1973	12	Mar. 4	Fes			o	
	1974	13	Mar. 4	Fes	o			
	1975	14	Mar. 4	Rabat				o
	1976	15	Mar. 4	Fes				o
	1977	16	Mar. 4	Marrakesh	o			o
	1978	17	Mar. 4	Rabat				o
	1979	18	Mar. 4	Rabat				o
	1980	19	Mar. 4	Dakhla				o
	1981	20	Mar. 4	Rabat	o			o
	1982	21	Mar. 4	Marrakesh				o
	1983	22	Mar. 4	Fes			o	
	1984	23	Mar. 4	Casablanca				o
	1985	24	Mar. 4	Marrakesh	o			
	1986	25	Mar. 4	Marrakesh	o			
	1987	26	Mar. 4	Rabat	o			o
	1988	27	Mar. 4	Marrakesh		o		o

Hassan II	1989	28	Mar. 4	Marrakesh			o	
	1990	29	Mar. 4	Agadir	o			
	1991	30	Mar. 4	Rabat	o			
	1992	31	Mar. 4	Rabat		o		o
	1993	32	Mar. 4	Rabat		o	o	
	1994	33	Mar. 4	Rabat				o
	1995	34	Mar. 4	Rabat			o	
	1996	35	Mar. 4	Rabat		o		
	1997	36	Mar. 4	Rabat		o		
	1998	37	Mar. 4	Rabat		o		
Mohammed VI	1999		Jul. 23	Rabat		o		
	2000	1	Jul. 30	Rabat		o	o	
	2001	2	Jul. 30	Tetouan		o		
	2002	3	Jul. 30	Tetouan			o	
	2003	4	Jul. 30	Rabat	o			
	2004	5	Jul. 30	Tetouan	o		o	
	2005	6	Jul. 30	Tetouan			o	
	2006	7	Jul. 30	Rabat		o	o	
	2007	8	Jul. 30	Tetouan				o
	2008	9	Jul. 30	Fes		o		
	2009	10	Jul. 30	Tetouan			o	
	2010	11	Jul. 30	Tetouan			o	
	2011	12	Jul. 30	Tetouan		o		
	2012	13	Jul. 30	Rabat		o		
	2013	14	Jul. 30	Rabat			o	
	2014	15	Jul. 30	Rabat			o	
	2015	16	Jul. 30	Rabat			o	
	2016	17	Jul. 30	Tetouan		o	o	o
	2017	18	Jul. 30	Tetouan		o	o	
	2018	19	Jul. 30	Rabat		o	o	
	2019	20	Jul. 30	Tetouan	o		o	o
	2020	21	Jul. 30	N/A			o	
	2021	22	Jul. 30	N/A			o	o
	2022	23	Jul. 30	N/A		o	o	o

Sources: Ministère de la Communication (Direction de la Planification et de la Documentation), "Les discours et interviews du roi"; *Al-ʿAlam*; *Al-Anbāʾ*; *Le Matin*; *La Vigie marocaine.*

However, in the end, Tetouan, a northern city that had already been selected as the venue several years in a row, was again chosen as the venue.[30]

If we look at the list of venues since independence in 1956 (see Table 1), we find that city selection reflects the times. Under the rule of Mohammed V, the first king of Morocco, the capital was usually chosen as the venue. During the reign of Hassan II, palaces all over the country were selected for the ceremony. These are the characteristics of the selected sites under the reign of Hassan II (1961–99):

(a) As represented by the cities of Marrakech and Fès, symbolic cities of Moroccan historical dynasties were preferred for venues.
(b) He had a strong interest in the southern region.[31]

The latter point reflects the territorial conflict with Western Sahara at that time. In fact, in the year following Mauritania's abandonment of its possession of Western Sahara, the *bayʿa* ceremony took place in Dakhla, the first and the last time it was held in the region of Western Sahara in Moroccan history.

Since Mohammed VI ascended to the throne in 1999, the venue characteristics have changed dramatically. Other than the capital, Mohammed VI has only chosen Tetouan, a city in northern Morocco. Northern Morocco is a region that Hassan II had arbitrarily ignored because of its history of opposition during Spanish rule[32] and his strong interests in the South. Based on this attitude toward northern region through his reign, political interest among northern people is comparatively low, as demonstrated by the low voter turnout in elections.[33] Therefore, the present king's attitude toward the northern region can be understood as an attempt to pay greater attention to the ignored region and to co-opt the people's political support.

Topics of the King's Speeches

I now focus on the king's speeches, which are important elements of the ceremony of the Feast of the Throne, as they convey the conditions and concerns facing the regime at the time.

First, we must consider the protocol of the speeches. The topics vary each year, and five to seven topics are typically included in each speech. The speech begins with the most important topic at that time and ends with tributes to previous Moroccan kings and praise for the royal army and other security systems.

Successive kings have insisted in their speeches that the *bayʿa* is not a unilateral contract of allegiance from the people to the king but "the bilateral contract of allegiance" (*al-bayʿa al-mutabādila*)[34] between them. At the same time, they have also emphasized that this contract represents the eternal and inviolable connection and coexistence of the king with his people.

In addition to the "commander of the faithful," various titles are used to refer to the king in his speech, depending on the context. For example, the titles "guardian of the faith" and "guardian of the Muslim community" are commonly used when the identity of the Moroccan people, the importance of the Maliki tradition, and the understanding of true Islam are discussed. In contrast, when the King describes the socio-economic reforms that he is pursuing, he states his title as "the first servant of the people" (*khādimuk al-awwal)*[35] and "the king of all Moroccans" (*malik li-jamīʿ al-maghāriba*).[36] These titles promote the image of the king as a person who always considers his people his most important priority.

It is fixed protocol to discuss diplomacy and foreign policy in the latter half of the speech. In this section, the order in which foreign relationships are mentioned is understood as indicative of the priorities of Moroccan diplomacy. Relationships with Maghreb nations are mentioned first, accompanied by Western Sahara issues, then relationships with Arab countries and the Israeli-Palestinian issue are discussed next. Since the Arab Spring, relationships with Arab monarchies, especially the Gulf countries, have been mentioned separately from other Arab countries. In addition, the importance of Moroccan solidarity with Sub-Saharan countries and the leadership of Morocco in the African region are stressed using the term "South-South cooperation" (*al-taʿāun janūb-janūb*).[37] Not only EU countries but also Russia and China have often been mentioned in the context of economic cooperation in the last few years. [38]

The list of the topics of the king's speeches since independence in Table 1 presents a great variety of topics chosen to be included in the speeches over the years. The various topics of the kings' speeches thus reflect the times, as much as the ceremony venues do. In the first few years after independence, the monarchy itself as a political institution and Islam were discussed in the speeches. From the beginning of the 1970s until the 1990s, the Western Sahara issue was the focus. This can be explained by the unstable political situation,[39] clearly shown by the attempted *coups d'état* in 1971 and 1972. Hassan II tried to divert people's attention from this political instability through territorial arguments. According to some researchers, involvement in the Western Sahara issue and the Green March demonstration of 1975 increased the enthusiasm for Moroccan nationalism.[40] When the kings discussed Western Sahara, terms like the "autonomy (*al-ḥukm al-dhātī*) of Morocco/the monarchy,"[41] "Kingdom's territory (*ḥawza*),"[42] "national unity" (*waḥdat al-waṭan*),[43] and "territorial unity" (*waḥdat al-turābiyya*)[44] were frequently invoked as part of "Moroccan historical tradition" (*al-taqālīd al-tārīkhiyya al-magribiyya*), making the Western Sahara issue part of the "people's duty and reliability imposed on us" (e.g., *qaḍiyya kull al-maghāriba, wa-amāna fī aʿnāqinā jamīʿan*).[45]

From the 1980s to the beginning of the 1990s, topics about the history of the Moroccan monarchy and its religious legitimacy were often chosen. At the same time, as part of the political liberalization of the 1990s, the last king, Hassan II, preferred to discuss political reforms, democracy, elections, and constitutional amendments. After King Mohammed VI's accession to the throne, a trend in the main subjects included a focus on socio-economic problems and development. After the Arab Spring, implementation of the elections was announced in the king's speech on the occasion of the Feast of the Throne.[46]

The Roles of the Bayʿa *Ceremony: Focusing on the Mohammed VI Era*

The analysis to this point has clarified that the ceremony venues and the topics of the kings' speeches at the occasion of the *bayʿa* were selected depending on the situation. What kind of roles does the *bayʿa*, a traditional and religious ritual, play in the political system of modern Morocco? I will focus on the era of the present King Mohammed VI (1999–) and consider the roles of the *bayʿa*.

As discussed above, King Mohammed VI is strongly concerned with northern regions, traditionally understood as regions of rebellion or treason against the authority of the sultans. During the period when most of the land of Morocco was a French protectorate, its northern regions, with a 300 km coastline facing the Mediterranean Sea and including the Rif region, were under a Spanish protectorate.[47] Tribes who lived there, mainly speaking Tamazight (a Berber language), rebelled in 1921 in the "Rif War,"[48] demanding self-government, and they established the "Rif Kingdom," which was independent not only from the control of Spain but also from the authority of the Sultan for five years.[49]

Hassan II, who became the Supreme Commander of the royal army immediately after Morocco's independence, began to blame the opposition of the northern regions during the protectorate era and imposed a merciless oppression on Rif regions, mainly the city of Al Hoceima, resulting in numerous injuries and deaths.[50] It was said that no further visits to northern regions were made by Hassan II. However, at the end of his reign, because the territorial conflict of Western Sahara was tentatively resolved through a cease-fire, we can glimpse his attitude toward the northern regions changing once again. For example, he commanded that the "Agence pour la promotion et le développement du Nord" (APDN) be organized to promote socio-economic development in these regions.[51] It was also the first organization to aim for regional development in Morocco.[52]

Mohammed VI succeeded his father in 1999 and chose the northern regions and the Orient (northeastern part of the country) for his first official visit, making a tour of the major cities of these regions.[53] From the topics of the king's speeches, it is clear that King Mohammed VI regards solving the gap between cities and rural areas, regional development, and economic development as the most important issues, and has energetically implemented respective reforms. The measures taken for the development of the northern region in recent years have been remarkable. Mohammed VI has devoted great effort especially to the improvement of transportation networks. The coastal regions of northern Morocco are located between the complex coastline in the north and the steep Rif mountains in the south, and transportation networks in this area had long been behind the times and isolated from surrounding regions. Because of this geographical condition, this area could not make full use of its advantages, such as its geographical proximity to Spain (only 14 km away), and the lag in its socio-economic development had been a national problem. The first step launched under the king's order to solve this problem was to build a "Mediterranean Highway," running 507 km east to west, to connect the cities of Tangier and Saidia.[54] The railway between Taurirt and Nador was then laid in 2009, followed by the construction of a new airport in Al Hoceima.[55] In addition, Le port de Tangier MED was opened in Tangier, the third largest city in Morocco, to promote cooperation with the Mediterranean region and European countries.[56] The king's frequent visits and these drastic developments have been viewed favorably by the people in the northern region so far. King Mohammed VI added a new page to the history of the relationship between the king and those people, which had been regarded as discordant or indifferent, and succeeded in receiving high esteem and a good impression in the region.[57]

To choose these regions as the venue of the *bay'a* ceremony, one of the national events to which the Moroccan people attach great importance, gives northern people an image of the present king as taking care of these regions, unlike the last king, and a sense of security through the favor of the king. Furthermore, holding the *bay'a* ceremony means that people living in these regions are afforded the opportunity to see the king, the sovereign of the nation, directly with their own eyes, which they did not have before.[58] Moreover, the structure of the *bay'a*, which involves thousands of representatives of each region and political organization visiting and pledging allegiance to the king, serves to lead the people to reaffirm their feeling of national identity and as forming a part of the nation themselves. Consequently, the *bay'a* of the kings, mainly Mohammed VI, has not only served to raise their dignity through the traditional and religious symbols incorporated in the ceremony, but also played the role as a means for co-opting the people living in the region of the venue by impressing on them the king's interests and favor.[59] As a matter of fact, during the "Arab Spring" in 2011, even though people in northern region such as the cities of Tetouan and Al Hoceima took to the streets in protest, they demanded the reduction of the king's powers within the frame of the "monarchy," the dissolution of the parliament, and an eradication of corruption, the same as the demands of protests that arose in other cities.[60] In other words, there was no outcry against the existence of the king and the monarchy itself, even in northern cities, which have long been considered regions of rebellion or treason against the royal authority.

Conclusion

This chapter has shown that in Morocco, the legitimacy of the king based on Islam was adroitly incorporated within the frame of a modern nation through an institution-building process that promoted the resilience of the Moroccan monarchy. The background of this characteristic was the continuation of the dynastic rules in the region where Morocco is located and the traditional features of marabout worship and sharif worship, which created an environment that fostered people's loyalty to the kings.

In particular, the *bayʿa*, held as an annual event in which people show their allegiance directly to the king to convey the meaning of the "renewal of the contract between the king and people," serves to cement the national history of the long-lasting dynasty among the people and to reconfirm patriotism and the national identity. The full ceremony is broadcast live on national TV and radio, and the scene of thousands of national representatives forming a line to pledge their allegiance to the king constitutes the highlight of the ceremony. Traditional and religious symbols showing the national history are evident everywhere in the ceremony. According to Wedeen's discussion, they are "symbolic powers," one of the institutions that stabilize the Moroccan Monarchy.

At the same time, in her analysis of the symbols and rhetoric exploited by Ḥāfiẓ al-Asad, Wedeen emphasizes that the Syrian authority demanded of its people their "unconditional obedience" and "connivance," not their loyalty. Contrastingly, the rituals of the *bayʿa* in Morocco are wielded to stimulate public mobilization and participation positively because the present ceremony of the *bayʿa* reflects integration with a historical tradition in which religious legitimacy is emphasized as one with a grant of the authority and also favor of the king as *baraka* of sharif. For example, a king who wanders from place to place over the country for the *bayʿa* projects the figure, not of a powerful person forcing people's "unconditional obedience" and their "connivance," but of a generous and merciful king. The venues of the ceremony are chosen as the occasion may demand. The ceremony, repeated as the "renewal of allegiance" every year, is held with the intention of stimulating public mobilization and participation through the image of the king close to them. *Khuṭba*s, announced the day before the *bayʿa*, touch on various issues, mainly political or social, confronting the kingdom at that time, so that public mobilization and participation in the political system are conceived of in terms of the engagement in those concrete and familiar issues. *Khuṭba*s include various topics such as the diplomatic issues of Western Sahara and Palestine, domestic politics such as constitutional amendments and elections, and socio-economic problems such as poverty and regional developments. Thus, the issues are presented by the king's speeches and shared with the people to stimulate their mobilization and participation. The next day, representatives of the people show their approval of the king's call. In the feast of the throne, the relationship between the king and the people is represented as though it was a relationship between "master and disciple".[61]

In addition, it must be pointed out that the *bay'a* can be used as a political act contributing to the resilience of monarchical political authority. The establishment of a new constitution in 2011 was a good example. The "Arab Spring" presented Mohammed VI with the gravest difficulties he had faced since his enthronement. However, the various reforms promptly implemented by the king himself secured the people's favorable evaluation of the monarchy, as shown by their support for the amendment of the constitution. These amendments did not lead to many changes, as articles discussing the king's absolute power and inviolate character were not revised, even though some of his authority was reduced, such as the powers to appoint the prime minister and dismiss the parliament. Nevertheless, the amendments presented by the king were approved by the people at a level of 98.5 percent (72 percent voting rate). These referendum results show that the reforms under the direction of the king were successful. The *bay'a* ceremony was then held at the end of the constitutional reform and, in the *khuṭba*s therein, the king emphasized the democratic character of the new constitution and its support by an overwhelming majority.[62] Discussion of the king's authority has never been heard since then. In this process, the pseudo-master-disciples relationship between the king and the people was shown in duplicate by the referendum and the *bay'a*. Through the referendum, a modern and democratic institution, and the *bay'a*, a religious and traditional ritual, the king received the people's double approval, which then doubled his legitimacy.[63] This shows that the positive blending of modern political institutions and the symbols of Islam through the process of institution-building continues in these ways, and that the political resilience of Moroccan monarchy was proved in the critical phase of the "Arab Spring" that might have undermined the king's authority.

Notes

* This work was supported by JSPS KAKENHI Grants-in-Aid 16H07191 and 19H01317.

1 See for instance, Russell E. Lucas, Thomas Demmelhuber and Clausia Derichs, "Rethinking the Monarchy: Republic Gap in the Middle East," *Journal of Arabian Studies* 4.2 (2014): 161–2; Robert S. Snyder, "The Arab Uprising and the Persistence of Monarchy," *International Affairs* 91.5 (2015): 1027–45; Alfred Stepan, Juan J. Linz, and Juli F. Minoves, "Democratic Parliamentary Monarchies," *Journal of Democracy* 25.2 (2014): 35–51; Sean L. Yom and Gregory F. Gause III, "Resilient Royals: How Arab Monarchies Hang On," *Journal of Democracy* 23.4 (2012): 74–88.

2 Hazem Beblawi and Giacomo Luciani, *The Rentier State* (London and New York: Croom Helm, 1987). According to Schwarz, rents are defined as effortlessly accrued income streams, so rentier states can be seen as those whose economies are dependent on substantial external rents for state revenues. Beblawi and Luciani mentioned that rents incorporate only a fraction of society in the production of rents, while with the government acting as the principal recipient of the wealth, the majority engage in its distribution and utilization. Then, as Luciani and Hvidt stated,

rentier economies then become "allocation" states, distributing the rents they accrue, uninhibited by the need for taxation levied on productive economic sectors. See Rolf Schwarz, *War and State Building in the Middle East* (Gainesville, University Press Florida, 2012), 121; Beblawi and Luciani, *The Rentier State*, 385; Giacomo Luciani, "Allocation vs. Production States: A Theoretical Framework," in *The Arab State*, ed. by Giacomo Luciani (London: Routledge, 1990), 65–84; Martin Hvidt, "Economic and Institutional Reforms in the Arab Gulf Countries," *The Middle East Journal* 65.1 (2011): 89.

3 Michael Herb, *All in the Family: Absolution, Revolution, and Democracy in the Middle Eastern Monarchies* (Albany: State University of New York Press, 1999). According to Herb, in 1938 the ruling Al-Sabah family of Kuwait created a new form of government for the Persian Gulf. In that year, the Al-Sabah threw the merchants out of the Kuwaiti bureaucracy and replaced them with members of the royal family. The other Persian Gulf monarchies followed suit. In these types of regimes, which Herb calls "dynastic monarchies," the monarch typically installs members of the royal family as Prime Minister, Minister of the Interior, Minister of Foreign Affairs, and Minister of Defense. These and other positions in the bureaucracy are used by the monarch as consolation-prize bargaining chips to dole out to dissatisfied member of the royal family as a means of building consensus. As a result, these dynastic monarchies are much more stable than monarchies in which the monarch excludes the rest of the royal family from power.

4 E. Tyan, "Bayʿa," in *The Encyclopedia of Islam, New Edition*, ed. by H. A. R. Gibb et al., 13 vols. (Leiden: Brill, 1960–2009), vol. 1, 1113–4.

5 Ibid.

6 Mohamed Daadaoui, *Moroccan Monarchy and the Islamist Challenge: Maintaining Makhzen Power* (New York: Palgrave Macmillan, 2011), 83; Frédéric Rouvillois "Monarchie et consensus," in *L'exception marocaine*, ed. by Charles Saint-Prot and Frédéric Rouvillois (Paris: Ellipses, 2013), 45.

7 For instance, see Abdallah Laroui, *Les origins sociales et culturelles du nationalism marocain (1820–1912)* (Casablanca: Centre Culturel Arabe, 1993).

8 Elie Podeh, *The Politics of National Celebrations in the Arab Middle East* (New York: Cambridge University Press, 2011), 3.

9 Ibid., 287.

10 Ibid., 287.

11 Ibid., 287; Dale F. Eickelman and James Piscatori. *Muslim Politics* (Princeton: Princeton University Press, 1996), 57.

12 Lisa Wedeen, *Ambiguities of Domination: Politics, Rhetoric, and Symbols in Contemporary Syria* (Chicago and London: The University of Chicago Press, 1999).

13 Ibid., 15–7.

14 Ibid., 84.

15 Daadaoui, *Moroccan Monarchy and the Islamist Challenge*, 83.

16 For example, Mohammed VI positively encouraged such activities as the extermination of anti-Islamic actions, hosting symposiums and lectures related to Islam, the construction of mosques, and contributions to religious schools and madrasas. See Daadaoui, *Moroccan Monarchy and the Islamist Challenge*, 52.

17 A marabout is a Muslim religious leader and teacher in West Africa, and in the Maghreb often a scholar of the Qur'an, or religious teacher.

18 Henry Munson, Jr, *Religion and Power in Morocco* (New Haven: Yale University Press, 1993), 11–23.

19 John Waterbury, *The Commander of the Faithful: The Moroccan Political Elite: A Study in Segmented Politics* (London: Weidenfeld and Nicolson, 1970), 71.

20 Ibid., 144–5.

21 Ibid., 97.

22 Daadaoui, *Moroccan Monarchy and the Islamist Challenge*, 52.

23 For more information about Moroccan monarchy and its sharifism, see Mohsine Elahmadi, *La monarchie et l'Islam* (Casablanca: Ittisalat Salon, 2006); Waterbury, *The Commander of the Faithful*; Malika Zeghal, *Les islamistes marocains* (Paris: Le Fennec, 2005).

24 For example, see Daadaoui, *Moroccan Monarchy and the Islamist Challenge*; Muḥammad Ḍarīf, *al-Islām al-siyāsī fī l-Maghrib: Muqāraba wathā'iqiyya* (Casablanca: al-Majalla al-Maghribiyya li-ʿilm al-ijtimāʿ al-siyāsī, 1992); Abdellah Hammoudi, *Master and Disciple: The Cultural Foundation of Moroccan Authoritarianism* (Chicago: The University of Chicago Press, 1997).

25 The Berber Dahir (*ẓahīr*) was a decree issued by the French protectorate in Morocco on May 16, 1930. This *ẓahīr* changed the legal system in parts of Morocco where Amazigh languages were primarily spoken, while the legal system in the rest of the country remained the way it had been before the French invasion. Sultan Muhammad V signed the *ẓahīr* under no duress, though he was only 20 years old at the time. The new legal system in Amazigh communities would ostensibly be based on local Amazigh laws and customs rather than the authority of the sultan and Islamic Sharia, and it would be written in French. The French colonial authorities sought to facilitate their takeover of the Berber tribes' property under legal cover. For more information, see Susan G. Miller, *A History of Modern Morocco* (New York: Cambridge University Press, 2013).

26 *L'action du peuple* was the first francophone newspaper published by the Moroccan Nationalist Movement in the area under the control of the French Protectorate in Morocco. As the French authorities would not allow a nationalist publication in Arabic, it was published in French. Its founder and editor was Muḥammad b. al-Ḥassan al-Wazzānī. Its first issue was published in Fes on August 4, 1933, four months before the first Throne Day, which the newspaper promoted.

27 The events of ceremony have been broadcast live on national TV since 1962, when the first *bayʿa* of the last king Hassan II was held.

28 Daadaoui, *Moroccan Monarchy and the Islamist Challenge*, 57.

29 Tyan, "Bayʿa."

30 Nozomi Shiratani. *Kunshusei to minshushugi: Morokko no seiji to isuramu no gendai* (Tokyo: Fukyosha, 2015), 24.

31 Nozomi Shiratani. "Morokko osei no anteisei ni okeru baia (chusei no chikai) girei no yakuwari," in *Arabu kunshusei kokka no sonritsu kiban*, ed. by Hirotake Ishiguro (Chiba: IDE-JETRO, 2017), 122. The *bayʿa* had been held only in Rabat since 1989 because Hassan II chose not to travel long distances with age. Incidentally, he preferred to take a decorated convertible instead of the traditional procession on horseback at that time.

32 During the period when most of the land of Morocco was a French protectorate, its northern regions were under a Spanish protectorate. Tribes who lived there, mainly speaking Tamazight (a Berber language), rebelled in 1921 in the "Rif War," demanding self-government, and they established the "Rif Kingdom," which was independent not only from the control of Spain but also from the authority of the Sultan for five years.

33 For example, voting turnout of the legislative elections in 2011 was 45 percent at the national level but only 40 percent in the province of Taza-Al Hoceima-Taunat (the five constituencies), located in the Rif region.

34 *Al-ʿAlam*, July 31, 2013. For the reason why the *bayʿa* in Morocco is understood as "the bilateral contract of allegiance," see James N. Sater, *Civil Society and Political Change in Morocco* (New York: Routledge, 2007), 31.

35 *Al-ʿAlam*, July 31, 2012; July 31, 2015.

36 *Al-ʿAlam*, July 31, 2014.

37 *Al-ʿAlam*, July 31, 2000; July 31, 2005; July 31, 2009; July 31, 2012; July 31, 2014; July 31, 2015.

38 *Al-ʿAlam*, July 31, 2014; July 31, 2015.

39 The political sphere remained under control of an authoritarian regime that did not permit its liberation until 1990s when constitutions were revised, and leftists took governmental power for the first time.

40 For example, see Miller, *A History of Modern Morocco*, 180–4.
41 *Al-ʿAlam*, July 31, 2012; July 31, 2014; July 31, 2019.
42 *Al-ʿAlam*, July 31, 2019.
43 *Al-ʿAlam*, July 31, 2016.
44 *Al-ʿAlam*, July 31, 1999; July 31, 2000; July 31, 2008.
45 *Al-ʿAlam*, July 31, 2014.
46 *Al-ʿAlam*, July 31, 2011.
47 Western Sahara was also a Spanish protectorate.
48 The Rif War was an armed conflict fought from 1920 to 1926 between the colonial power of Spain (later joined by France) and the Berber tribes of the mountainous Rif region of Morocco.
49 For further information on the Rif War, see Germain Ayache, *Les origines de la Guerre du Rif* (Paris: Publications de la Sorbonne, 1981); Miller, *A History of Modern Morocco*, 104–11.
50 Rémy Leveau, *Le fellah marocain: Défenseur du trône* (Paris: Presses de la Fondation natinale des sciences politiques, 1985), 111.
51 Secrétariat général du gouvernement, *Bulletin officiel du Royaume du Maroc*, no. 4323 (1995).
52 For more information, see official website of APDN (www.apdn.ma/ [accessed August 24, 2022]).
53 *Jeune Afrique*, October 28, 2015.
54 *The Economist*, Oct 30,1999.
55 Moussa Hormat-Allah, *Le roi: Mohammed VI ou l'espoir d'une nation* (Rabat: Dar Nachr El Maârifa, 2005), 313.
56 Eva Sandberg and Seth Binder, *Mohammed VI's Strategies for Moroccan Economic Development* (Oxon and New York: Routledge, 2020), 57.
57 Hormat-Allah, *Le roi*, 313.
58 Shiratani, "Morokko osei no anteisei ni okeru baia (chusei no chikai) girei no yakuwari," 124.
59 Shiratani, "Morokko osei no anteisei ni okeru baia (chusei no chikai) girei no yakuwari," 124–5.
60 *Jeune Afrique*, February 21, 2011.
61 Hammoudi, *Master and Disciple*.
62 *Le Matin*, July 30, 2011.
63 Shiratani, *Kunshusei to minshushugi*, 27.

Bibliography

Ayache, Germain. *Les origines de la Guerre du Rif*. Paris: Publications de la Sorbonne, 1981.

Beblawi, Hazem and Giacomo Luciani. *The Rentier State*. London and New York: Croom Helm, 1987.

Daadaoui, Mohamed. *Moroccan Monarchy and the Islamist Challenge: Maintaining Makhzen Power*. New York: Palgrave Macmillan, 2011.

Ḍarīf, Muḥammad. *Al-Islām al-siyāsī fī l-Maghrib: Muqāraba wathāʾiqiyya*. Casablanca: al-Majalla al-Maghribiyya li-ʿilm al-ijtimāʿ al-siyāsī, 1992.

Eickelman, Dale F. and James Piscatori. *Muslim Politics*. Princeton: Princeton University Press, 1996.

Elahmadi, Mohsine. *La monarchie et l'Islam*. Casablanca: Ittisalat Salon, 2006.

Hammoudi, Abdellah. *Master and Disciple: The Cultural Foundation of Moroccan Authoritarianism*. Chicago: The University of Chicago Press, 1997.

Herb, Michael. *All in the Family: Absolution, Revolution, and Democracy in the Middle Eastern Monarchies*. Albany: State University of New York Press, 1999.

Hormat-Allah, Moussa. *Le roi: Mohammed VI ou l'espoir d'une nation*. Rabat: Dar Nachr El Maârifa, 2005.

Hvidt, Martin. "Economic and Institutional Reforms in the Arab Gulf Countries." *The Middle East Journal* 65.1 (2011): 85–102.

Laroui, Abdallah. *Les origines sociales et culturelles du nationalisme marocain (1820–1912)*. Casablanca: Centre Culturel Arabe, 1993.

Leveau, Rémy. *Le fellah marocain: Défenseur du trône*. Paris: Presses de la Fondation nationale des sciences politiques, 1985.

Lucas, Russell E., Thomas Demmelhuber and Clausia Derichs. "Rethinking the Monarchy: Republic Gap in the Middle East." *Journal of Arabian Studies* 4.2 (2014): 161–2.

Luciani, Giacomo. "Allocation vs. Production States: A Theoretical Framework." In *The Arab State*. Ed. by Giacomo Luciani. London: Routledge, 1990, 65–84.

Miller, Susan G. *A History of Modern Morocco*. New York: Cambridge University Press, 2013.

Munson, Henry Jr. *Religion and Power in Morocco*. New Haven: Yale University Press, 1993.

Podeh, Elie. *The Politics of National Celebrations in the Arab Middle East*. New York: Cambridge University Press, 2011.

Rouvillois, Frédéric. "Monarchie et consensus." In *L'exception marocaine*. Ed. by Charles Saint-Prot and Frédéric Rouvillois. Paris: Ellipses, 2013, 35–49.

Sandberg, Eva and Seth Binder. *Mohammed VI's Strategies for Moroccan Economic Development*. Oxon and New York: Routledge, 2020.

Sater, James N. *Civil Society and Political Change in Morocco*. New York: Routledge, 2007.

Schwarz, Rolf. *War and State Building in the Middle East*. Gainesville: University Press of Florida, 2012.

Secrétariat général du gouvernement. *Bulletin officiel du Royaume du Maroc*, no. 4323, 1995.

Shiratani, Nozomi. *Kunshusei to minshushugi: Morokko no seiji to isuramu no gendai*. Tokyo: Fukyosha, 2015.

Shiratani, Nozomi. "Morokko osei no anteisei ni okeru baia (chusei no chikai) girei no yakuwari." In *Arabu kunshusei kokka no sonritsu kiban*. Ed. by Hirotake Ishiguro. Chiba: IDE-JETRO, 2017, 109–30.

Snyder, Robert S. "The Arab Uprising and the Persistence of Monarchy." *International Affairs* 91.5 (2015): 1027–45.

Stepan, Alfred, Juan J. Linz, and Juli F. Minoves. "Democratic Parliamentary Monarchies." *Journal of Democracy* 25.2 (2014): 35–51.

Waterbury, John. *The Commander of the Faithful: The Moroccan Political Elite: A Study in Segmented Politics*. London: Weidenfeld and Nicolson, 1970.

Wedeen, Lisa. *Ambiguities of Domination: Politics, Rhetoric, and Symbols in Contemporary Syria*. Chicago and London: The University of Chicago Press, 1999.

Yom, Sean L. and Gregory F. Gause III. "Resilient Royals: How Arab Monarchies Hang On." *Journal of Democracy* 23.4 (2012): 74–88.

Zeghal, Malika. *Les islamistes marocains*. Paris: Le Fennec, 2005.

Website

Ministere de la Communication (Direction de la Planification et de la Documentation). "Les discours et interviews du roi." http://www.maroc.ma/ar/. Accessed November 30, 2021.

Newspapers

Al-ʿAlam (Casablanca)

Al-Anbāʾ (Casablanca)

Jeune Afrique (Paris)

Le Matin (Casablanca)

La Vigie marocaine (Casablanca)

12

The *Tawḥīd* of the Painting of God the Mother

William Gallois

Introduction

This chapter contends that understandings of Islamic art tend towards the impoverished in the modern age.[1] Such studies generally contrast the virtues of *classical* forms of culture, produced in a time before colonialism, with Muslim artists' need to respond to the west's revolutionary aesthetic power in the age of imperialism. These readings form one part of the complex of positions which cohere to generate a "normative" account of Islam. As Shahab Ahmed observed, this "Islam" often tended towards ahistoricism in its erasure of varieties of "being Islamic"; pincered into this position by complementary logics of Orientalism and defensive strategies designed to protect Islamic "orthodoxy."[2]

Mohammed ʿAbduh's famous 1904 CE *fatwā* on "Images and Statues, Their Benefits and Legality" lies absolutely central to this reductive culture.[3] Indeed, it was foundational in the sense that its authoritative legal and textual basis mapped out the contours of debates about art and its permissibility in the modern Islamic world.

As a judgement, it could be said to have been *colonial* in the sense that its premises were based upon western understandings of art and were remarkably incurious and unconversant with the variety of historic and contemporary modes of Islamic visual expression.

Had Mohammed ʿAbduh looked as carefully at the images which he would have encountered in Cairo, Beirut and Tunis as he did at pictures in Paris and Palermo, he might have perceived that artistic cultures were just as alive in the Islamic world as they were in the west in the late-nineteenth century. Those paintings may have been sited inside cafés, on the façades of houses or around the stalls of street vendors, rather than in museums or galleries, but there was no doubt that a vibrant artistic scene (in which figuration played a major part) was as much a feature of "Oriental" culture as it was in Europe.[4]

ʿAbduh could not "see" such work, for the spectacles through which he viewed art were those of the European, and there is ample evidence that westerners disdained the crude, primitive and tribal artistic traditions of the east (or at least they did until modernists such as Pablo Picasso, Paul Klee and Henri Matisse concluded that there were things worth borrowing from such naïve imagery).

In a backhanded fashion, the traditional Islamic arts of calligraphy, tiling and stucco were admired by Europeans, but they were also viewed as crafts rather than arts, as timeless rather than progressive forms, and as collective expressions rather than as signs of individual artistic genius.

Western scholars and "liberal Muslims" have always liked ʿAbduh's ruling because of its positive, commonsensical, contentions regarding the permissibility of art.[5] Citing Egyptian historians of art, Dina Ramadan notes in her brilliant critique of the *fatwā*, that ʿAbduh is portrayed as "a connoisseur of the arts, a lover of artistic creativity" and "one of the most enlightened men of the Muslim religion."[6]

His assertions were especially desirable because they framed time not in the sense of a divide between the *jāhiliyya* and the advent of Islam, but by positing the great difference between the time of Islam's arrival and that of the modern world. As ʿAbduh wrote:

> What is the legal judgement concerning these images in Islamic law [. . .]. Is it forbidden or permitted? [. . .] I would say to you that the painter has painted and that the benefit is unquestionable, undisputed. The idea of worship or the exaltation of pictures or statues has been wiped from people's minds.[7]

This *ijtihad* – or legal reasoning based upon historical context – acknowledged that early Islamic culture had been deeply aniconic, while suggesting that time could be seen to have influenced morality in two ways. The first was the progressive accumulation of the products of artistic practice across history, alongside their undeniable existence in the present; and the second, related, idea was that humans no longer lived in an era where they were at risk of being drawn into idol worship.

"It seems to me," ʿAbduh wrote, "that Islamic law is far from prohibiting one of the best tools for learning after it has been established that it is not a threat to religion."[8] "If you quote the hadith," he remarked, "'The most severely tortured people on Judgement Day will be the image makers,' [. . .] this hadith came during the days of paganism, [. . .when] people turned to images during that time for two reasons: the first was distraction [from God] and the second was to seek blessing from whichever of the righteous ones is being depicted. Religion detests the first of these reasons, and Islam came to wipe out the second."[9]

In the period between the lifetime of Prophet Mohammed and the present, however, other cultures had shown that images could be made for more benign reasons. ʿAbduh said no more as to why art constituted "one of the best tools for learning," seeming to think that this was self-evidently true if Europeans believed it to be the case.

After all, Muslims were rightly embarrassed that "The aptitude for preservation is not something we have inherited,"[10] and that if they wished to study manuscripts from their own tradition, these were as likely to be found in Cambridge as they were in Cairo.

This reflected a civilizational failing in Islamic culture, for "If you looked at the things religion obligates us to preserve, you would find that they are innumerable, and that we do not preserve any of them."[11] In contrast to the western mania for collecting and its institutional bases in the museum, the library, the archive and the university, ʿAbduh believed that Muslims ought to have felt shamed by their lack of interest in preserving accounts of their place in the human story.

ʿAbduh, however, also seemed to indicate that he had not yet discerned the precise role which pictures played in the building of this narrative – for he described the nations of the west's "preservation of images drawn upon paper or on cloth" as being based upon "a strange avidity."[12] Nonetheless, he advocated the mimicry of such practices, expressing a confidence that he and other Muslims would come to learn why the preservation of images was so valuable.

This was partly a strategic move to draw Muslims away from the many more questionable practices in which they engaged, especially "visiting the graves of saints" whom "they fear [. . .] as they fear God." People asked of them "what they fear God will not grant them," believing "that they [saints] are faster to respond to them than God Almighty," leading ʿAbduh to conclude that "There is no doubt that they are unable to reconcile these beliefs with belief in the unity of God."[13]

Such superstitious, pagan, and folk practices associated with particular localities (and especially with the lives of women) were far more dangerous to the integrity of Islam than the preservation of images, and it is intriguing that ʿAbduh's subconscious led him to connect art and popular belief in this way.[14] Critically, he alleged that the worship of saints drew Muslims away from the centrality of their faith and their belief in a singular God.

This evasion of *tawḥīd* – or divine oneness – replayed precisely the kind of *shirk*, or polytheism, which Islam had sought to eradicate in the world. Too many Muslims had failed to grasp the essential teaching of their faith, though we might wonder quite why ʿAbduh was so absolutely sure that there was "*no doubt* that they are unable to reconcile these beliefs with belief in the unity of God" (my italics).[15]

Argument

This chapter looks at one particular artwork from the era in which ʿAbduh wrote, so as to show that the practice of Islam was far more interesting and complex than ʿAbduh allowed, and that his binary understandings of morality deny the existence of richer Muslim understandings and practices of *tawḥīd*. Far from being "a threat to religion," the making of images can be seen to have constituted a defence of Islam and Muslims at a time when European colonial power was permeating almost every facet of indigenous life.

ʿAbduh's adaptive strategy in the face of western hegemony was a tactic which was well recorded for posterity, given its legal basis, its expression in print, and its association with learned pan-Islamic institutions such as al-Azhar. By contrast, painted expressions of resistance to empire created by ordinary believers have long since been forgotten because of their physical disappearance, their illegibility to later audiences, and their frequent association with institutions such as shrines, which were attacked by both reformist and traditionalist voices in the modern Islamic world.

Not only were images not "a threat to religion," but pictures can be shown to have saved religion from threats.

Figure 1: Detail from a Qayrawāni Fresco, c. 1881 CE[16]

The exemplary work discussed in this essay merits attention on a series of levels which tend to lie unconsidered in both studies of art (across all traditions) and analyses of Islamic culture (at all times).

Its depiction of God the Mother may seem provocative, but any such contemporary reaction is almost certainly grounded in considerations of art which depend on the vagueness of thinkers such as ʿAbduh. It can, as we will see, be proven that the picture was understood as deeply Islamic by its audience when it was made in around 1881 CE, and that its viewers operated with understandings of the theological and political potential of painting which reveal a vivid tradition of belief in the force of art.

The disregarding of this tradition is deeply gendered, for it has involved a forgetting of the place of women artists in Muslim culture, the erasure of sites of female sanctity, and the neglect of evidence pointing to feminine conceptions of the divine. As such, this chapter joins the work of scholars such as Farhad Daftary, Fatima Mernissi and Amina Wadud in setting out ways in which Muslims in the past often operated with more complex and nuanced understandings of gender than those which prevail in the world today.[17]

As ʿAbduh himself noted, the value of those histories lies insufficiently considered by Muslims in the modern world, leading to situations where moments of *gender troubling* (*pace* Judith Butler and Joseph Massad) are treated as isolated incidents lying outside the narrative coherence of the normative tradition, rather than as entry points into meditations on the nature of the tradition. Significantly, written texts are almost always accorded a generative place in the recounting of the story of Islam over time, whilst pictures are generally ignored.

Qayrawān

There can be no doubt that the site of the picture in question – Qayrawān – was a centre of "orthodoxy," with a distinct and important place in the history of Islamic civilisation. Founded by the Umayyads in the first century of Islam, the city was the earliest Muslim city founded in the Maghreb and the home of its first mosque – the Mosque of ʿUqba – which was also the first such building constructed with a minaret. Over the centuries, the sanctity of Qayrawān seemed unquestionable, not only for its place in Islamic history, but also owing to its university and other sites of learning, as well as its importance as a destination for pilgrimage. Like the Cairo of ʿAbduh's day, Qayrawān was a centre of Islamic life in which the preservation of traditions, law and orthodoxy were conjoined to an urban culture also rich in *zāwiya*s and public forms of art.

This heritage was well understood by Europeans when French troops occupied the city in 1881 CE. Although these invaders stressed the decrepitude of the city, and Islamic culture more generally, there was no doubt that they also perceived Qayrawān to be a site of historical significance.[18]

The capture of a site of such psychic and symbolic value was seen to mark something definitive in the conquest of north Africa, and this was celebrated in a unique legal arrangement in which westerners were encouraged to visit this emblematic town as a means of coming to understand the character of a defeated Other. Whereas non-Muslims were barred from entering mosques elsewhere in Tunisia, Morocco, and Algeria, they were encouraged to do so in Qayrawān, so that they might meditate on and speak of the fall of one civilization and the rise of another.

Le CONTROLEUR CIVIL de Kairouan autorise

MM.

au total 2 personnes, à visiter les Mosquées.

Kairouan, le 1907

Le Contrôleur Civil,

NOTA. — MM les Visiteurs sont priés d'éviter de marcher sur les Tapis des Mosquées.

Figure 2: Permit to Visit the Mosques of Qayrawān Issued by the French Colonial Authorities, 1907 CE[19]

The occupation of the city was therefore *absolute* in a sense which was qualitatively different to that of other urban centres in the region. While cafés, shops, markets, homes, bath-houses and shrines were all understood and experienced as islands of free life in oceans now ruled by unjust oppressors, mosques (and synagogues) undoubtedly stood at the apex of these spatial enclaves of independence.

By contrast, the very heart of Qayrawān had been captured, as well as the totality of its mosques, so it should perhaps not seem surprising that its inhabitants found ways to mark the body of the city so as to convey feelings of anguish, defiance and steadfastness.

Figure 3: Fading Mural Painted on a Qayrawāni Street Close to the Mosque of the ʿĪssāwā[20]

The distinctiveness of Qayrawān at this moment came in the fact that the whole of the town became a kind of gallery. Marks were made upon walls and surfaces around the town, such that its citizens' experience of circulating in space was constantly mediated through sets of sign systems which spoke incessantly to and with them about the experience of being in the city at that moment.

Although the life in Qayrawān before 1881 CE ought not to be thought of as having been perfect, its citizens had arguably inhabited a state of grace. Their world was not unchanging, yet it was grounded upon a singular, shared culture founded on notions of autonomy, community and justice. This singularity of Islamicate life (so-called for it also covered the lives of Jews and other minorities) could also be described as embodying oneness or *tawḥīd.* While its ethics were mainly local, it connected Qayrawān to the wider *umma* (and all humanity) through trans-Saharan trade networks and the web of Sufi nodes of learning and religious practice which lay across and beyond the Maghreb.

These connections were inherently international, or *un*-national, and, as such, they spoke to the origins of a city whose name derived from the Persian term "caravan" as it had travelled across the Arab world to reach the Maghreb. This flow of life in and out of Qayrawān was blocked and disrupted by the bordering realities of the imperial state, just as free circulation within the city was now subject to the norms of an occupying power.

Figure 4: Murals Painted in Whitewash around the Minaret of the Great Mosque, c. 1881–89[21]

Paintings

The only direct reference made to the murals of Qayrawān, amidst scores of texts which reflected on the decadence of the city, came in the reports of the archaeologist René Cagnat and the architect Henri Saladin. Writing in the popular journal *Le Tour du monde* in 1885, they described the "senseless whitewashing" which had sadly ruined the view of the Lalla Rihana gate into the Great Mosque, seen here in Saladin's sketch of the scene:

Figure 5: Le Tour du monde 1885[22]

By this they meant to indicate their distaste for what they considered to be a form of vandalism which "ruined" an architectural order which they had studied and described in their scholarship. It did not occur to them to think or ask why the exterior of the gate tower had been altered in this way, for its "senselessness" seemed obvious in this form of colonial logic.

For such men, the significance of Qayrawān lay in its past. For its heritage to be explicable, it was necessary that it should retain its original character and purity. A site which was quintessentially urban and urbane had now been sullied; thoughtlessly disfigured. Time intruded upon what ought to have been a timeless setting; the reality of historical change disrupting the myth of immutable heritage.

To European eyes, the painting of Bab Lalla Rihana also inverted what were assumed to be classical Islamic norms, for the spartan exteriors of the mosque were now decorated with symbols better suited to the interiors of buildings. It was almost as though the city had turned itself inside out, though a consideration of the radical nature of this reversal did not induce any self-consciousness as to its connection to the revolutionary quality of the European invasion of the city.

The fact that it was Bab Lalla Rihana which was the first site in Qayrawān to be painted in this novel fashion might also have occasioned some reflection, particularly given the fact that these giant murals wrapping their way around the Gate were composed within months of the arrival of French troops.

Intriguingly, photographic evidence reveals that in spite of the supposed crudity of the mural, Saladin's reproduction offered a remarkably poor reflection of the original, missing the distinctive curvature of the branches which came off the central root of the design, along with miscounting the number of these appendages. This mattered because it reflected a fundamental lack of interest in the specificity of the site and the painting, as well as a determination to see it only through predetermined lenses.

Figure 6: Untitled Photograph[23]

A more specific attendance to the Gate would have recognised its significance as the so-called "women's entrance" to the mosque, the fact that it was named after a woman saint, and the manner in which it was abutted by the *zāwiya* of Lalla Rihana (seen to the left of the gate in the image above).

Such shrines played important roles in everyday spiritual life, serving as places of prayer, imprecation and inspiration for the people of Qayrawān and others who would travel to "their" places of worship. Annual processes of whitewashing these structures were important occasions in which larger groups collectively recognised their responsibilities to the building and that which it signified. They were festivals of sanctity, joy, and commonalty shared by adherents from different places and backgrounds. They were also, almost certainly, the source of the lime wash which was used to paint the gate of the Mosque, formally and aesthetically connecting two forms of a unified religious life which often tended to be caricatured in binaries of folk/formal or magical/religious by Europeans.

Figure 7: Lalla Rihana Gate, The Great Mosque[24]

Critically, the traditional painting of such buildings, as well as the *avant-garde* extension of such painting onto the exterior of the Great Mosque, was undertaken by women. It deployed tropes from the image world of women and sacred signs which were "owned" or "entrusted" to them (whilst decorated goods produced commercially were often made and sold by men).[25] These signs redeployed *idiomata* which had traditionally been found in house decoration, tattoos, pottery, jewellery and other realms of female aesthetic production, magnifying and generalising their presence in the world through their new attachment to sites of collective value.

While this amuletic iconic tradition and its gendered art of protection had generally sought to manage hazards associated with childbirth, infertility, infidelity, sickness and travel, such risks had traditionally been associated with the lives of individuals and family units.[26] In such circumstances, it made sense that art should attach itself closely to the body and the home; in contrast to the emergency of empire where pervasive and all-encompassing threats to life and to modes of being affected whole societies. There, all the world needed to be made a home and places of safety made through painting.

Just as traditional "signs of belonging" – symbols branded upon livestock or camels, inscribed upon houses, etched on the body, stitched onto fabrics and clothes – identified the particular within the universal across the Maghreb, walls in towns were now painted as a means of expressing the unity of a collectivity before God. That which was good and beautiful and testament to relations between God and man needed strengthening, and, as the traditional creators of sanctity, it was primarily the responsibility of women to design and make such public art. The frescoes of Bab Lalla Rihana thus brought together the visual traditions of amuletic inscription upon the walls, gates, and doors of the home, with mobile forms of art expressed in clothing, manuscripts and talismans which travelled with believers in the world.

Figure 8: General View of the Great Mosque[27]

The proportional increase in the size of such paintings, as compared with the scale of their antecedents before 1881, was a function of the magnitude of a city as compared with that of a house or a body. They needed to be signs which were unmissable to the inhabitants of Qayrawān as they walked around the town.

If their abstraction was read as a form of primitivism by Europeans, for local peoples it was surely viewed as a point of connection with the principles of Islamic art, along with the anonymous character of their production and the frequency with which artworks were produced by collectives rather than individuals.

While there was something profoundly unusual about the way in which the exterior of a holy building needed to be painted to be protected in the world, the inner principles which underpinned this shift in outward appearance lay quite in line with prevailing aesthetic norms. For such art to have "worked," and for it to have lain *in situ* for decades, it was surely necessary for it to have been legible to the population of the town.

This decipherability, however, stood in stark contrast to the absolute inability of Europeans to read such signs in a manner which generated meaning, *and*, critically, later generations of Tunisians, who have preserved no memory of the painting of Qayrawān in stories of the town or histories of the journey from freedom to tyranny and from oppression to independence.

Figure 9: Ghostly Remnants of the Painting of Bab Lalla Rihanna Still Visible in the 1970s; Now Utterly Erased[28]

Such amnesia, especially as it relates to visual cultures, is arguably a by-product of the move to the nation as the primary mode of spatial organisation in the Islamic world, as opposed to the formerly prevailing combination of the local and the universal.[29]

Mystery, therefore, now prevails in memories of the paintings of Qayrawān, for in spite of the existence of an extensive *visual archaeological* record, it seems hard to speak about signs whose meanings were apparently commonly understood, yet which now seem unintelligible just two or three generations later.

Figure 10: View of Paintings around the Minaret of the Great Mosque, c. 1930 CE[30]

Looking, for instance, at the eastern face of the minaret of the Great Mosque, are we able to see the marking of the sun rising from the fabric of the building? As dawn broke, illuminating the minaret, did it light a painting which spoke of the true purpose of the Mosque at a time when it had become museum open to all of the peoples of the world? Did painting act as a complement or prompt for the dawn prayer, *Fajr*, speaking of the capacity of art to describe the rhythms and temporality of Muslim life?

Its hemispherical form would appear to have depicted the sun in the process of rising, while its ascension seemed to come from the body of the Mosque itself. In a world materially and politically turned upside down, the image provided a reminder of eternal values and a reaffirmation of the strength of the place of worship in protecting and instilling such goods. The mural, like its counterparts, was visible to believers from afar, in the way that minarets are always embodied an idea of architecture as an accompaniment to faithful life.

Such an interpretation also leads us to a parallel set of images on the western side of the minaret in which forms of language could be seen to sink into the structure of the mosque as the sun set for the Maghrib prayer:

Figure 11: Exterior of the Great Mosque[31]

While we cannot know exactly what these signs *meant* and what they connoted to local audiences who were semiotically attuned in ways which we are not, it seems very likely that these were also marks which referenced the deep human past of the Maghreb. They appear to have expressed notions of "us" and "ours," with reference to a community of believers from the land, through the use of shapes which are familiar from Tifinagh or ancient Lybic inscriptions, which themselves drew upon a series of earlier Mediterranean scripts.

There is abundant evidence that such sign systems were still common several millennia later in the Saharan world and while alphabets might no longer have fully tallied with living languages as they were spoken, individual letters still retained real force in the world. This was particularly true of those shapes which had migrated into later forms of Berber and Tuareg scripts, which is germane in this instance since the markings which we see on the minaret are clearly related to designs which were commonly found on Berber pottery, carpets and clothing.

The letters from the Tamazight alphabet which were described were especially significant since they appear to connote the letter "Z" (also known as "yaz" or "aza"), which was itself the name which was given to the language and the culture of which it spoke. The word "Tifinagh" combines Tuareg terms denoting "discovery" (*itif*) and "our" (*nnegh*) and what is happening on the side of the mosque would appear to enact a similar form of linguistic game or play.[32] The letter "Z" was likely to have been read as expressing the notion of the *Amazigh* as the archetypal "free man" in a pointedly political fashion at this moment in the history of the city.

Qayrawān had been governed by many different rulers and empires across time, but never before had the very being of free life been called into question. How change would be effected so as to right the order of the world was answered partly by the spirit of steadfastness which these images conveyed, but also through their dialogue with the other designs which wrapped their way around the minaret.[33]

These paintings which were conjoined to the building also referred to traditions of submerged letters in Islam. This Qur'anic custom was grounded in the belief that the Holy Book contained only a fraction of the things which can begin to be said and that the reservoir of ink[34] which it would be necessary to possess so as to say all things was beyond man (or beyond his normal ken).[35] It also referenced the idea of *walbatinu* – or that which lies hidden – which lay central to Muslim, and especially African Sufi, spirituality, and ideas of secrecy and the sacred were of paramount importance in both traditional Islamic and sub-Saharan African art.[36]

Just at that moment when the urban order of Qayrawān was disrupted by imperialism, art therefore possessed the capacity to induce a sense of being in space and time which linked immediate experiences in the world to unseen structures beyond the direct human apperception of things.

Figure 12: Tifinagh Sign[37]

Figure 13: Tifinagh Sign[38]

Figure 14: A Selection of Tifinagh Signs Painted around Qayrawān.[39]

Just as the Islamic city was protected by linguistic signs which connoted the earliest forms of human culture in the Maghreb – predating the arrival of Arabic as a sacred alphabet by centuries or even millennia – there exists abdundant evidence that the painters of Qayrawān also represented God in ancient fashions.[40]

Such an idea, let alone the reality of its practice, lies strikingly distant from the parameters of Mohammed ʿAbduh's discussion of art and its permissibility as an Islamic practice at this same moment. Yet it is ʿAbduh ideas which have become canonical, rather than the scores of paintings and popular forms of representation which Muslims made across north Africa at this time when their religion lay threatened. Their work merits remembrance and attention, not least since the bounds within which it operated lay so far from understandings of art which have come to be seen as normative in the Islamic world.

God the Mother

The artists of Qayrawān depicted not only the cast of saints, animals and Prophets which were mainstays of Maghrebi visual culture, but they also painted God. Furthermore, they painted Her in the form in which she had been depicted thousands of years before in Carthage and across the eastern Mediterranean world, in the form of the Phoenician goddess Tanit.[41]

Figure 15: Painting of Tanit Flanked by Two Vegetal Forms, with the ʿĪssāwā Mosque in the Background.[42]

If we wish to dignify the lives and works of the people of Qayrawān in the late-nineteenth century, it is imperative that we see such speech acts as being deeply Islamic, and as forms of defence of the singularity of the One God's love for her people across all time and space.[44]

Figure 16: Tanit Depicted on a Second-Century BCE Punic Stele, Found Close to Constantine, in What Is Today Algeria.[43]

Since the world began with God, and not with the advent of Islam, earlier cultures' representations of the divine were not necessarily evidence of *shirk* or polytheism, but could instead be viewed as authentic expressions of faith. Artistically representing God in this fashion hundreds of years later therefore spoke to the endurance of God and humans' love of God across time.

In the beginning there was only God, which we see described in perhaps the greatest of all of the Qayrawāni works of art: a mural sequence painted along the side of a warehouse which looked towards Bab Lalla Rihanna, as the picture below reveals in its revelation of the dialogue of visual forms taking place around the Great Mosque.

Figure 17: Figures on Wall of the Exterior of the Great Mosque[45]

Read from right to left, this frieze consisted of four chief forms, akin to the ideograms and symbols painted around the city, but here conjoined in ways which encourage our eyes and our minds to move across the whole so as to make sense of, and to be affected by, its singular force.

This notion of the work's oneness is also conveyed through the manner in which the fabric of the building onto which it is painted forms a part of the work of art. The designs of the second character reach not only into the frame of the door, but then reappear on its far side, developing the idea that the art is a part of the home and the home is a part of the art. Its charge traverses the door in a way which is quite foreseeable given the important roles which we know that entrances played in African Islamic visual culture.[46] Indeed, once that entry is perceived as a part of the work, its oneness can be seen to be made up of five elements, together making *khamsa* or the protective sign of five.[47]

While this essay does not aim to decrypt one of the greatest of Islamic works of art in the modern era, it is vital to see that this story of love and protection began with God, and with the Deity presented as Tanit.

She was known from tombs, homes and amulets, always associated with moments of great import and with an ideal of protection. She stands facing the city so as to protect not just her home but the lives of those around her. She is a cipher crossing time and space, aided by the talismanic power of her "magic square" (the four spheres painted around the core of her body)[48] and by the manner in which she is conjoined to speech in the shape of the Tifinagh symbol to her left. She holds language and is grasped by it, expressing notions of the sanctity of holy texts which would have been widely understood, yet were clearly unusual in this articulation. Tifinagh as an idiom, women as spiritual beings, art as a form of expression, are all therefore described as quintessentially Islamic in quite orthodox ways, no matter how unorthodox they may seem to outsiders (in Qayrawān and the world, then and now).[49]

She provided shelter and security through her ancient form, standing as the First Figure, initiating language and a complex narrative enjoined in symbolic forms which spoke of the triumph of goodness and the destruction of evil in the world.

The fact that this work begins with her image only enhances the idea that this might also be read as a form of self portrait. If it is objected that it looks nothing like self portraits in any other artistic tradition, one might observe that it perhaps drew on understandings of the self which were unlike those found in other cultures. Its anonymity, its reproducibility and its collectivity implied a sense of selfhood which we might also be interested in reconstructing or recuperating from Qayrawān.[50] Intriguingly, and almost uniquely in terms of mural painting, not only in Qayrawān but across the region, we are almost able to glimpse the artist of this piece at work, sitting in a tent at the edge of the piece, perhaps preparing her materials or sheltering from the midday sun.

The declarative intent of the piece comes from the mind of one woman and although her conception of selfhood may have been communal and expansive, there is a sense that this art needed to possess some form of individual agency for its power to be activated in the world.[51] Her people, this town and her God guided her hand as she painted, but it was also true that the citizens of Qayrawān and their Creator needed her spiritual sustenance, here manifested in brushstrokes upon a building. Painting can be seen to be a prayerful act; an expression of enduring love.

If such ideas of the self can be imagined to speak of hybrid and unified identities across time and space, there is a natural logic to the notion that no real divide existed between the artist and God at the moment of creation. The painter did not arrogate to themselves a sense of divinity, but worked in the tradition of thinkers such as Bāyazid Basṭāmī or Ḥusayn b. Mansūr al-Hallāj, who famously said "There is nothing wrapped in my turban but God" and, more contentiously, *Anā al-Ḥaqq* "I am The Truth."[52]

A painting which began with God could then take its audience back to a moment before Islam, whilst performing as a present-tense assurance of the future return of justice to the world. Art mimicked the divine lordship of time, but in a specific gendered form which stressed God's female qualities.

If imperialism was a project in which men seized a set of moral powers which were not theirs to take, what better means of contesting this order than through an articulation of the eternal love and force of the feminine divine? As Audre Lorde would later remark, "The Master's Tools Will Never Dismantle the Master's House," suggesting that hegemons could only be countered by other logics, and not by attempting to assert control using the language, ideas and ethics of a dominating power.[53]

Signs which seemed utterly meaningless to the Master, were pregnant with meaning for the work's true audience. That which the European saw as primitive, was a cipher capable of communicating a sense of infinite power and care across time and space. At a time when Muslims were forced to endure lives characterised by injustice, what better reminder of the everlasting nature of the divine than through a painterly reminder of "God before God": the Absolute as she had been represented by earlier peoples who had walked upon this same land and who had expressed their faith in the Deity in this manner?

Figure 18: Evidence of the Fading Presence of the Qayrawāni Mural, c. 1920 CE[54]

The *Qayrawān Mural* was far grander than those found on the houses of the women of the mountains and the deserts who had fled to the city of as a place of safety. It serves as one of the chief forms of evidence we possess for a broad culture of public art produced by women in the Maghreb which had as its purpose the extension of forms of aesthetic protection of the home and the body to cities and to the wider body politic of Islamicate Africa. As was the case elsewhere, this work was only saved for posterity through its accidental capture as incidental backdrops to the colonial photographic record. The art itself dematerialized over time, as it had always been designed to do, for it was intended to play a distinct role at a particular moment. It undermined the bases of the new European order of the world by stressing the enduring worth of a culture, recasting values in novel ways just as their decline was predicted and promoted by invaders.

The copy or the reflection was placed in full view of all in the public sphere, described in an idiom of great simplicity and abstraction which could be understood by all. The very bases of language, shape and the human capacity to manipulate forms in the world were conveyed in a manner which reminded the observant of God whose name was ٱلْمُصَوِّرُ, al-Muṣawwir,[55] the Fashioner. Deriving from the triliteral root *ṣād-waw-rāʾ*, God was revealed in language as the creator who had formed, made, and pictured the world, so it made great sense that art which did the will of God should seek to mirror such ideas in its appearance. A just God adorned and prepared the world, so a just art might do the same.

Lucky as we are to possess photographic records of such works, we can only guess at how they were received by their audiences. The longevity of the pictures' presence in Qayrawān does seem to make it possible to say that the images were a constant presence and backdrop to life for most of the colonial period. They became an integral part of life, owned and authored not just by those who had originally applied paint to walls, but to those who repaired and added to them over time, as well as those who glanced, glimpsed or meditated on them.

Although the paintings seem unusual additions both to the history of art and the long story of Muslims' reflections on the morality of image-making, the work which they undertook in the everyday lives of believers can be seen as lying much more central to lived traditions of Islam. Such are the web of daily experiences and interactions which Sajjad Rizvi characterises as a life of "Qurʾanicity":

> Discerning and perceiving the beauty of the Qurʾan is not simply an act of textual reception but of aesthetic perception of life imbued with 'Qurʾanicity'; appreciation of that art does require cultural literacy such that someone who is functionally illiterate recognises the calligraphic tokens, the melodies and intonation of recitation, the motifs in the plastic arts, and the signatures and citations in music.[56]

In other words, these images which filled the spaces of life of culturally-literate Qayrawānis, served as ambient reminders of the constant presence of God in lives "imbued with Qur'anicity."

They were not "masterpieces," but "*tuḥfa*," the Arabic word which is used in the modern world as a translation of this western term, yet which looks backwards in its etymology to its classical linguistic origins in *hadith* and Shi'i Alawi texts where it connoted ideas of "the gift." This gift originated in the divine, but was made manifest in the world by men, or, in this instance, by women, who established a "*matḥaf*" (or museum) across the city which worked to re-establish an order of rightness in the world. Their art was given to fellow believers as an expression of hope, a description of desires, a statement of the capacity of the work of humans to enjoin a conversation with God, and a physical manifestation of presence which spoke of that which was impermanent and that which would be in the world forever.

Conclusion

As Dina Ramadan observes, Mohammed 'Abduh's formative *fatwā* possessed a narrow conception of art and its place in human life, stressing the value of culture only insofar as it offered an accurate record of things and times; "flattening [. . .] [artworks] into a means of documentation emptied of any kind of aesthetic worth."[57]

Such misconceptions matter because in the modern era, the views of thinkers like 'Abduh have framed the so-called "image debate" in Islam. As positions such as his have been cast as existing at the permissive or liberal end of a spectrum of approaches to art, this has had the deleterious effect of somehow casting iconophilic parts of the Muslim world (such as Senegal, much of the Balkans, Iran, India and Tunisia) as non-normative or errant in their approaches. Meanwhile, the analysis of individual works such as the Qayrawāni mural, west African reverse paintings on glass, Persian miniatures, Dervish *tekke* decorations or signs painted around the tombs of saints, invariably reveal cultural forms whose devotional performances often combine ideas of great complexity in ways which are understood by, and which resonate with, broad publics.[58]

The one distinct work of art which 'Abduh mentioned in his *fatwā* was a canvas by Raphael whose value was made plain in the huge price which western institutions were willing to pay for such pieces.

It is surely a tragedy that 'Abduh was so lost in European understandings of art that he ascribed to the notion that the market connoted aesthetic worth through money value. He lived in a time when thousands of ordinary believers filled their lives and those of their neighbours with images which instead spoke of a quite different set of values which came not from men and their avarice, but from God. Cities, towns, and existence itself could be lived aesthetically and the museum was not a cloistered bourgeois playground, but the very canvas of material life which surrounded everyday being in places such as Qayrawān.

In his *fatwā*, ʿAbduh lauds not just western painting, but also pre-Islamic poetry, for its preservation of human culture for future generations, yet he misses the preservative effect of art in his own present. This work found visual means of saving the very bases of life, belief, community and a relationship with God which ʿAbduh sought to find at the heart of Islam. Art did not need to accurately depict life, for it possessed the far greater and more important task of accompanying and preserving the good life in states where Muslims lived as conquered subjects.

Above all else, art was predicated on the communication of the idea of *tawḥīd* or the oneness of God and the universal truth of this idea across all time. The aesthetic manifestation of this idea in the 1880s and '90s may have appeared novel, revolutionary or strange, but the times in which Muslims lived were far from normal. The majority of their lands had been conquered by rulers who brought evil into the world; not because they were not Muslims, but because their sense of cultural superiority exceeded their capacity for ethical reflection, or any desire they possessed to see Others as equal and different forms of humanity.

Many more such works and voices await rediscovery, and when a larger corpus of works are considered, it seems likely that our understandings of both Islamic culture and the history of art may change. When these works were painted, prevailing notions of culture in both the Islamic world and the west presumed that art was professionally made, that it was a product invested with financial value, that it was a permanent form, that its value was intimately related to ideas of finesse and skill, and that it was most likely to have been made by men. In the Islamic world, it was unlikely to be signed, but it might well have been seen to be the work of an individual author, and, as the structures of western museums, galleries and publishing were exported globally, this assignation of individual provenance only grew in importance.

The paintings of Qayrawān, by contrast, were truly anonymous and wholly collective in their conjoined sense of authorship and reception. They lay outside, in public places, never sleeping; always in close contact with the people of the city. Like their audience, they needed air to breathe and were in contact with the sky, the stars, the sun, the moon and all that such signs in nature connoted in describing sacred ideas of time and life.

This art which sought to protect and preserve was largely ignored and disdained by rulers in the colonial era, and only began to be comprehensively erased in the postcolonial period in the name of a return to a prelapsarian state. The desire to reanimate culture and modes of life which had been repressed by Europeans was quite understandable, but the recreation of totemic sites such as the Great Mosque of Qayrawān tended to be undertaken in ways which created a frozen portrayal of culture which mirrored westerners' description of the timeless, retarded character of Islam. The complexities and beauties of a faith which sustained and was sustained by shrines dedicated to holy women, encrusted to the very side of the mosque, was no longer remembered, whilst the aesthetic work of those women, which protected the mosque and the town, was utterly forgotten.[59]

What *is* remembered, and therefore becomes, *the* history of art in Tunisia are nineteenth-century pioneers of the kinds of western fine art which can hang for posterity in the gallery or museum, alongside their twentieth-century complements, modernist paintings and sculptures which aped the work of European avant-gardes, but which are now taken to speak of multiple modernisms and transnational varieties of modernity. Meanwhile, modes of normative experience and expression which only came to be seen to be aberrant when Islamic moral reasoning absorbed the lessons of the colonial Master, now lie forgotten, as does the role which thinkers such as Mohammed ʿAbduh played in such processes.

Rather than taking ʿAbduh at his word in comparing art in the Islamic world in 1904 CE. with paintings hanging on the walls of palaces in Palermo, perhaps now is the moment when we return to look at the pictures which Muslims themselves were making in their responses to empire and in defence of Islam.

In Qayrawān, we encounter a form of public art which expressed the genius of Islamic synthesis in its combination of Black African forms (ranging from linguistic sign systems which were thousands of years-old through to Magic Squares which still travelled around the world of the Sahara)[60] with Phoenician and Carthaginian sacred iconographies. Such combinations spoke not of the irruption of the ancient into the modern world, but of art's capacity to embody and convey that which had always been there: God's Oneness. Pictures were enactments of *tawḥīd* in the sense that they afforded access to a sense of being in time, in which believing viewers found themselves placed in a state of singular grace; in which the constant love of God the Mother was known for them and for all time.

Notes

1 This essay refuses the terms "modern," "modernity" and "modernism," contending that critiques of their west-centricity (*pace* Jalal al-e Ahmad) ought to have led to their abandonment as universal, naturalised categories. The neologism "modern" disrupts the constellation of assumptions which underpin occidental understandings of the world, but it also writes the Kaʿba into understandings of time and change, arguing not just for the cultural specificity of Islamicate history, but also for another genealogy of civilizational meaning.

2 Shahab Ahmed, *What Is Islam? The Importance of Being Islamic* (Princeton: Princeton University Press, 2015).

3 The foundational place of ʿAbduh's text can be seen in its prominent placement in Anneka Lenssen, Sarah Rogers and Nada Shabout, eds., *Modern Art in the Arab World: Primary Documents* (Durham, N.C.: Duke University Press, 2018), 42–5; Dina Ramadan, "'One of the

Best Tools for Learning': Rethinking the Role of 'Abduh's Fatwa in Egyptian Art History," in *A Companion to Modern African Art*, ed. by Gitti Salami and Monica Blackmun Visonà (New York: John Wiley, 2013), 137–53.

4 One of the few texts to include a serious consideration of nineteenth century indigenous painterly forms in the nineteenth century can be found in Marion Vidal-Bué, *L'Algérie des peintres: 1830–1960* (Paris: Paris-Méditerranée, 2005).

5 Key works which helpfully problematize questions surrounding the exchange of modernism in the Arab-Islamic world include Sussan Babaie, "Voices of Authority: Locating the 'Modern' in 'Islamic' Arts," *Getty Research Journal* 3 (2011): 133–49; Mary Vogl, "Algerian Painters as Pioneers of Modernism," in *A Companion to Modern African Art*, 195–217; Finbarr Barry Flood, "Picasso the Muslim: Or, How the Bilderverbot Became Modern (Part 1)," *Res. Anthropology and Aesthetics* 67/68 (2017): 42–60; and Nada M. Shabout, "The Arabic Connection in Articulating North African Modernity in Art," *South Atlantic Quarterly* 109.3 (2010): 529–43. See also Alex Dika Seggerman, *Modernism on the Nile: Art in Egypt between the Islamic and the Contemporary* (Chapel Hill: University of North Carolina Press, 2019); Brahim Ben Hossain Alaoui and Marie-Odile Briot, eds., *Croisement de signes* (Paris: Institut du Monde Arabe, 1989); Hamid Keshmirshekan, "Neo-Traditionalism and Modern Iranian Painting: The "Saqqa-khaneh" School in the 1960s," *Iranian Studies* 38.4 (2005): 607–30; and two works by Christiane Gruber: *The Praiseworthy One: The Prophet Muhammad in Islamic Texts and Images* (Bloomington: Indiana University Press, 2019) and *The Image Debate: Figural Representations in Islam and across the World* (London: Gingko, 2019).

6 Ramadan, "'One of the Best Tools for Learning,'" 138. And see Ramadan's brilliant analysis of the language of 'Abduh's article and that which it avoided in terms of thinking about the unspoken concepts of *fann* (art) and *al-funūn al-jamīla* (fine arts) (ibid., 144–5).

7 Ibid., 43.

8 Ibid., 43.

9 Ibid., 43.

10 Ibid., 44.

11 Ibid., 44.

12 Ibid., 42.

13 Ibid., 43–4.

14 The quotation marks used here are mine and not those of 'Abduh.

15 The saints whom he mentions had, after all, led lives of great devotion to God and few would have been associated with anything besides the promotion of a pretty clear form of monotheism, often stressing the "secondary" or "ancillary" character of the sanctity of their shrine, their personage or their practices. 'Abduh's ignorance as to how religion was practiced in *zāwiya*s was reflective of the broader limits of his worldview and a contextualism which ultimately sought to find truth in written texts which were somehow able to conjure a normative core for the faith.

16 Detail of *Vue générale de la Grande Mosquée (extérieur)*, LL, c. 1905, photographic postcard. Original card and digital copy held in Fond d'Imagerie Décoloniale Africaine, University of Exeter (hereafter IDA), IDA1.

17 Fatima Mernissi, *The Forgotten Queens of Islam* (Oxford: Oxford University Press, 2003) and *Women's Memory and Islamic Rebellion* (London: Zed, 1996); Farhad Daftary, "Sayyida Hurra: The Ismaili Sulayhid Queen of Yemen," in *Women in the Medieval Islamic World: Power, Patronage and Piety*, ed. by Gavin R. G. Hambly (New York: St. Martin's Press, 1998), 117–30; Amina Wadud, *Qur'an and Woman: Rereading the Sacred Text from a Woman's Perspective* (Oxford: Oxford University Press, 1999).

18 See, amongst many others, René Fage, *Vers les steppes et les oasis, Algérie-Tunisie* (Paris: Hachette, 1906); Paul-Henri-Benjamin Estournelles de Constant, *La politique française en Tunisie: Le protectorat et ses origines (1854–1891)* (Paris: Librairie Plon, 1891); Paul Fagault, *Tunis et Kairouan* (Paris: Librairie algérienne et coloniale, 1889).

19 *Permis de visiter les mosquées*, publisher unknown, 1905. IDA1475.

20 Untitled photograph, photographer unknown, c. 1900. IDA5634.

21 *Kairouan: La Grande Mosquée*, F. Soler (Tunis), c. 1900, photographic postcard. IDA3681.

22 *Le Tour du monde*, 1272 (1885): 326. "[Lalla Réjane] Un badigeonnage inintelligent a malheureusement dénaturé l'aspect de ce monument."

23 Untitled photograph, photographer unknown, 1923. IDA2678.

24 *Porte Lalla Rihana, Grande Mosquée*, LL, photographer unknown, photographic postcard, c. 1910. IDA5681.

25 A. Bayram, "La naissance à Tunis dans les milieux de la bourgeoisie traditionnelle," *Cahier des Arts et Traditions Populaires* 4 (1971): 7–16, esp. 11 and Habib Chabbi, "Esthétique, ornementation et croyances," *Cahiers des Arts et Traditions Populaires* 9 (1987): 7–44, esp. 7; Jean Mazel, *Énigmes du Maroc*, nouvelle éd. (Paris: Robert Laffont, 1971), 191 and Mohand Abouda, *Axxam, Maisons Kabyles: Espaces et fresques murales* (Goussainville: M. Abouda, 1985).

26 This essay treats "amuletic" and "apotropaic" as being synonymous, preferring the simplicity of the former. See also Francesca Leoni, ed., *Power and Protection: Islamic Art and the Supernatural* (Oxford: Ashmolean Museum, 2016).

27 Detail of *Vue générale de la Grande Mosquée (extérieur)*, LL, c. 1905, photographic postcard. IDA1.

28 *Kairouan – La Grande Mosquée*, Société Tunisienne de Diffusion, c. 1985, photographic postcard. IDA3561.

29 See also William Gallois, "The Destruction of the Islamic State of Being, Its Replacement in the Being of the State," *Settler Colonial Studies* 8.2 (2018): 131–51.

30 *Kairouan: Minarett der Moschee Sidi Okba*, publisher and date unknown, but probably c. 1932, photographic postcard. IDA4563.

31 *Extérieur de la Grande Mosquée de Kairouan*, Photo Garrigues (Tunis), c. 1885, glass-plate photograph. IDA45.

32 Lahcen Oulhaj, *Grammaire du tamazight: Eléments pour une standardisation* (Rabat: Centre Tarik ibn Zyad pour les études et la recherche, 2000), 16, argues that the word *tifinagh* derives from a Tuareg pun meaning *itif* ("discovery") *nnegh* ("our") i.e., *our discovery*. See also J.B. Moreau, *Les grands symboles méditerranéens dans la poterie algérienne* (Algiers: Société Nationale d'Édition et de Diffusion, 1976).

33 Lisa Bernasek, *Artistry of the Everyday: Beauty and Craftsmanship in Berber Art* (Cambridge, Mass.: Peabody Museum Press, 2008), 62. Jean Gabus, *Au Sahara: Arts et symboles* (Neuchâtel: Éditions de la Baconnière, 1958), 317. Dominique Casajus, "Études & Essais: Écritures ordinaires en pays touareg," *L'Homme: Revue française d'anthropologie* 201 (2012): 31–54. And see also Jean-Jacques Glassner, "Dominique Casajus, *L'Alphabet touareg*," *Gradhiva* [en ligne] 25 (2017) at https://journals.openedition.org/gradhiva/3346 (accessed September 15, 2022). See also the negative colonial judgment on "tiffinar" made by M.H. Lelong, *Le Sahara aux cent visages* (Paris: Éditions Alsatia, 1948), 97: "le tiffinar, écriture étrange qui procède indifferemment dans tous les sens. Elle existait seulement à l'état de graffiti."

34 I am indebted to Bruce Lawrence for introducing me to the idea that there might be another seven oceans of ink from which new scriptures could be written, and that secret ayatollahs might exist in such concealèd places.

35 Could it even have been the case that a subtler form of play was at work, which relied on the ability of local people to grasp the difference between ancient Lybic and more modern Tifinagh scripts, for the modern X form which seems to be begun here was in fact only made up of the old W mark in the ancient language?

36 Mary H. Nooter, ed., *Secrecy: African Art That Conceals and Reveals* (Munich and New York: The Museum for African Art and Prestel, 1993).

37 Untitled photograph, photographer unknown, 1924. IDA56324.

38 *Kairouan, Route de Gafsa*, LL, photographer unknown, c. 1900, photographic postcard. IDA8752.

39 Untitled and anonymous glass-plate photograph, c. 1890. IDA3573.

40 In thinking about these paintings, it seems important to recognise that which they are not, in the sense that they are generally exclude all that is not depicted in Islamic art on the basis that there exist certain unrepresentable perfections.

41 See F.O. Hvidberg-Hansen, *La Déesse TNT: Une étude sur la religion canaanéo-punique*, 2 vols. (Copenhagen: G.E.C. Gads Forlag, 1979) and its discussions of Tanit's derivation from the Canaanite goddesses Aṯirat, Anat and Aṯtarté, as well as Gilbert Picard, *Carthage* (London: Elek, 1964), noting especially the discussion (84) of a shift c. 450 BCE when Tanit rises to become the virtual queen of the city and this revives archaic Aegean representations of a silhouetted triangular circle female figure.

Intriguingly, similar processes which connect the "deep time" of the ancient past with periods up until the present can be observed in cities such as Palmyra, where popular memories associated with Phoenician heritage are kept alive, in part, through the common experience of living amongst the remains of earlier cultures. The gendered quality of this "living across time" is also apparent in its people's affection for Zenobia and their pride in a longstanding association with female political and religious power. Like Qayrawān, Palmyra is also a major node in transnational networks of trade and ideas, perhaps suggesting a linkage between popular conceptions of complex, cosmopolitan temporality, and identity with such centres.

42 Untitled photograph, photographer unknown, c. 1900. IDA56324.

43 Carthaginian stele, author's photograph, Constantine Museum, Algeria.

44 References to Tanit need not necessarily be seen to be theological (in their invocation of the gods of a superseded polytheistic culture), but as cultural references to the synthetic genius of Islam and the philosophical question which instead asks, "How is Tanit not God or a worthy representation of the oneness of God?" Tanit and her force had been at work in Africa for millennia, so why could she not be seen as a local expression of the eternal qualities of God? Her female gender made sense in a culture in which the aesthetic expression of divine love was universally accepted to be the preserve of women. Tanit's association with the power of the moon also established an affinity not only with Islamic temporality but, quite specifically, with lunar and solar murals which had been painted around the minaret of the Great Mosque.

45 Detail of *Kairouan – Vue générale de la Grande Mosquée (extérieur)*, LL, c. 1925, photographic postcard. IDA 2.

46 See, for instance, Salima Naji, *Portes du sud marocain* (Aix-en-Provence: Edisud, 2003).

47 Significantly, seeing here explicitly invokes the mind's ability to count and to reason as well as the brain's function in processing visual information provided by the eyes. This is the art of apperception in which the five fingers of a hand come to be seen as a singular form. See also Punic representations of the hand of God (Picard, *Carthage*, 37 and 42) as well as depictions of the deity as a pillar, linking to the Arab stress on the verticality of the letter *alif* as a sign of God.

48 See Edward Westermarck, *Pagan Survivals in Mohammedan Civilisation: Lectures on the Traces of Pagan Beliefs, Customs, Folklore, Practices and Rituals Surviving in the Popular Religion and Magic of Islamic Peoples* (Amsterdam: Philo Press, 1933), 30.

49 There is no space here in which more fully to explore the aesthetics of a mode of representation which might be called *abstract realism*; in the sense in which the recognisable depiction of the human form is nonetheless wholly abstracted as an archetype.

50 Given that need his image world lies undescribed in literatures from the time, one can only speculate as to who was responsible for such erasures. It could plausibly have been the owners of properties, it might have been the traditional civic authorities of the town or it may have been the colonial authorities. It is the latter group which seems the likeliest, for if the authorities responsible for the Great Mosque allowed its walls, gates and minaret to be painted, it seems implausible that they would not tolerate similar graffiti around the city, while for similar reasons, it also seems unlikely that the community of believers in the town would object to such forms of visual expression on exterior street walls, which were after all generally considered to be common forms of property.

51 In the language of contemporary art history, the pictures achieved what they wanted. See W.J.T. Mitchell, *What Do Pictures Want?* (Chicago: University of Chicago Press, 2005) and Christopher Pinney, *The Paintings of the Gods: The Printed Image and Political Struggle in India* (Oxford: Oxford University Press, 2004).

52 A. Schimmel, "Ana'l-Ḥaqq," in *Encyclopædia Iranica*, ed. by Ehsan Yarshater (London and Boston: Routledge and Kegan Paul, 1982–), vol. 1, fasc. 9, 1001–2, available online at http://www.iranicaonline.org/articles/anal-haqq-i-am-the-truth-the-most-famous-of-the-sufi-sathiyat-ecstatic-utterances-or-paradoxes (accessed December 30, 2018).

53 Audre Lorde, "The Master's Tools Will Never Dismantle the Master's House," in idem, *Sister Outsider: Essays and Speeches* (Berkeley: Crossing Press, 2007 [1984]), 110–4.

54 Detail of *Vue générale de la Grande Mosquée (extérieur)*, LL, c. 1905, photographic postcard.

55 See Qur'an 59: 24, "He is Allah, the Creator, the Inventor, the Fashioner; to Him belong the best names. Whatever is in the heavens and earth is exalting Him. And He is the Exalted in Might, the Wise." And see also *Study Qur'an Project Root List*: http://www.studyquran.co.uk/PRLonline.htm (accessed September 15, 2022).

56 Sajjad Rizvi, "Reversing the Gaze? Or Decolonizing the Study of the Qur'an," *Method & Theory in the Study of Religion* 33 (2021): 132.

57 Ramadan, "'One of the Best Tools for Learning,'" 148.

58 See, for example, See Michael Barry's *Figurative Art in Medieval Islam and the Riddle of Bihzād of Herāt (1465–1535)* (Paris: Flammarion, 2004) and Mohamed Masmoudi, *La Peinture sous verre en Tunisie* (Tunis: Cérès Productions, 1972). Both are works of colossal importance and richness, the former for the depth of its analytic knitting of close readings of artworks to Sufi theology, and the latter as an exemplary documentation of indigenous arts.

59 Ridha Moumni, ed., *L'Éveil d'une nation* (Tunis: Officina Libraria, 2016).

60 René Bravmann, *Islam and Tribal Art in West Africa* (Cambridge: Cambridge University Press, 1974); Labelle Prussin, *Hatumere: Islamic Design in West Africa* (Berkeley: University of California Press, 1986); Allen Roberts and Mary Nooter Roberts, *A Saint in the City: Sufi Arts of Urban Senegal* (Los Angeles: UCLA Fowler Museum, 2003).

Bibliography

Abouda, Mohand. *Axxam, Maisons Kabyles: Espaces et fresques murals*. Goussainville: M. Abouda, 1985.

Ahmed, Shahab. *What Is Islam? The Importance of Being Islamic*. Princeton: Princeton University Press, 2015.

Alaoui, Brahim Ben Hossain and Marie-Odile Briot, eds. *Croisement de signes*. Paris: Institut du Monde Arabe, 1989.

Babaie, Sussan. "Voices of Authority: Locating the 'Modern' in 'Islamic' Arts." *Getty Research Journal* 3 (2011): 133–49.

Barry, Michael. *Figurative Art in Medieval Islam and the Riddle of Bihzād of Herāt (1465–1535)*. Paris: Flammarion, 2004.

Bayram, A. "La naissance à Tunis dans les milieux de la bourgeoisie traditionnelle." *Cahier des Arts et Traditions Populaires* 4 (1971): 7–16.

Bernasek, Lisa. *Artistry of the Everyday: Beauty and Craftsmanship in Berber Art*. Cambridge, Mass.: Peabody Museum Press, 2008.

Bravmann, René. *Islam and Tribal Art in West Africa*. Cambridge: Cambridge University Press, 1974.

Casajus, Dominique. "Études & Essais: Écritures ordinaires en pays touareg." *L'Homme: Revue française d'anthropologie* 201 (2012): 31–54.

Chabbi, Habib. "Esthétique, ornementation et croyances." *Cahiers des Arts et Traditions Populaires* 9 (1987): 7–44.

Daftary, Farhad. "Sayyida Hurra: The Ismaili Sulayhid Queen of Yemen." In *Women in the Medieval Islamic World: Power, Patronage and Piety*. Ed. by Gavin R. G. Hambly. New York: St. Martin's Press, 1998, 117–30.

Estournelles de Constant, Paul-Henri-Benjamin. *La politique française en Tunisie: Le protectorat et ses origines (1854–1891)*. Paris: Librairie Plon, 1891.

Fagault, Paul. *Tunis et Kairouan*. Paris: Librairie algérienne et coloniale, 1889.

Fage, René. *Vers les steppes et les oasis, Algérie-Tunisie*. Paris: Hachette, 1906.

Flood, Finbarr Barry. "Picasso the Muslim: Or, How the Bilderverbot Became Modern (Part 1)." *Res. Anthropology and Aesthetics* 67/68 (2017): 42–60.

Gabus, Jean. *Au Sahara: Arts et symboles*. Neuchâtel: Éditions de la Baconnière, 1958.

Gallois, William. "The Destruction of the Islamic State of Being, Its Replacement in the Being of the State." *Settler Colonial Studies* 8.2 (2018): 131–51.

Glassner, Jean-Jacques. "Dominique Casajus, *L'Alphabet touareg*." *Gradhiva* [en ligne] 25 (2017) at https://journals.openedition.org/gradhiva/3346 Accessed September 15, 2022.

Gruber, Christiane. *The Image Debate: Figural Representations in Islam and across the World*. London: Gingko, 2019.

Gruber, Christiane. *The Praiseworthy One: The Prophet Muhammad in Islamic Texts and Images*. Bloomington: Indiana University Press, 2019.

Hvidberg-Hansen, F.O. *La Déesse TNT: Une étude sur la religion canaanéo-punique*. 2 vols. Copenhagen: G.E.C. Gads Forlag, 1979.

Keshmirshekan, Hamid. "Neo-Traditionalism and Modern Iranian Painting: The 'Saqqa-khaneh' School in the 1960s." *Iranian Studies* 38.4 (2005): 607–30.

Lelong, M.H. *Le Sahara aux cent visages*. Paris: Éditions Alsatia, 1948.

Lenssen, Anneka, Sarah Rogers and Nada Shabout, eds. *Modern Art in the Arab World: Primary Documents*. Durham, N.C.: Duke University Press, 2018.

Leoni, Francesca, ed. *Power and Protection: Islamic Art and the Supernatural*. Oxford: Ashmolean Museum, 2016.

Lorde, Audre. "The Master's Tools Will Never Dismantle the Master's House." In idem, *Sister Outsider: Essays and Speeches*. Berkeley: Crossing Press, 2007 [1984].

Masmoudi, Mohamed. *La Peinture sous verre en Tunisie*. Tunis: Cérès Productions, 1972.

Mazel, Jean. Énigmes du Maroc. Nouvelle éd. Paris: Robert Laffont, 1971.

Mernissi, Fatima. *Women's Memory and Islamic Rebellion*. London: Zed, 1996.

Mernissi, Fatima. *The Forgotten Queens of Islam*. Oxford: Oxford University Press, 2003.

Mitchell, W.J.T. *What Do Pictures Want?* Chicago: University of Chicago Press, 2005.

Moreau, J.B. *Les grands symboles méditerranéens dans la poterie algérienne*. Algiers: Société Nationale d'Édition et de Diffusion, 1976.

Moumni, Ridha, ed. *L'Éveil d'une nation*. Tunis: Officina Libraria, 2016.

Naji, Salima. *Portes du sud marocain*. Aix-en-Provence: Edisud, 2003.

Nooter, Mary H., ed. *Secrecy: African Art That Conceals and Reveals*. Munich and New York: The Museum for African Art and Prestel, 1993.

Oulhaj, Lahcen. *Grammaire du tamazight: Eléments pour une standardisation*. Rabat: Centre Tarik ibn Zyad pour les études et la recherche, 2000.

Picard, Gilbert. *Carthage*. London: Elek, 1964.

Pinney, Christopher. *The Paintings of the Gods: The Printed Image and Political Struggle in India*. Oxford: Oxford University Press, 2004.

Prussin, Labelle. *Hatumere: Islamic Design in West Africa*. Berkeley: University of California Press, 1986.

Ramadan, Dina. "'One of the Best Tools for Learning': Rethinking the Role of ʿAbduh's Fatwa in Egyptian Art History." In *A Companion to Modern African Art*. Ed. by Gitti Salami and Monica Blackmun Visonà. New York: John Wiley, 2013, 137–53.

Rizvi, Sajjad. "Reversing the Gaze? Or Decolonizing the Study of the Qurʾan." *Method & Theory in the Study of Religion* 33 (2021): 122–38.

Roberts, Allen and Mary Nooter Roberts. *A Saint in the City: Sufi Arts of Urban Senegal*. Los Angeles: UCLA Fowler Museum of Cultural History, 2003.

Schimmel, Annemarie. "Anaʾl-Ḥaqq." In *Encyclopædia Iranica*. Ed. by Ehsan Yarshater. London and Boston: Routledge and Kegan Paul, 1982–, vol. 1, fasc. 9, 1001–2. Available online at http://www.iranicaonline.org/articles/anal-haqq-i-am-the-truth-the-most-famous-of-the-sufi-sathiyat-ecstatic-utterances-or-paradoxes Accessed December 30, 2018.

Seggerman, Alex Dika. *Modernism on the Nile: Art in Egypt between the Islamic and the Contemporary*. Chapel Hill: University of North Carolina Press, 2019.

Shabout, Nada M. "The Arabic Connection in Articulating North African Modernity in Art." *South Atlantic Quarterly* 109.3 (2010): 529–43.

Vidal-Bué, Marion. *L'Algérie des peintres: 1830–1960*. Paris: Paris-Méditerranée, 2005.

Vogl, Mary. "Algerian Painters as Pioneers of Modernism." In *A Companion to Modern African Art*. Ed. by Gitti Salami and Monica Blackmun Visonà. New York: John Wiley, 2013, 195–217.

Wadud, Amina. *Qur'an and Woman: Rereading the Sacred Text from a Woman's Perspective. Oxford: Oxford University Press, 1999.*

Westermarck, Edward. *Pagan Survivals in Mohammedan Civilisation: Lectures on the Traces of Pagan Beliefs, Customs, Folklore, Practices and Rituals Surviving in the Popular Religion and Magic of Islamic Peoples*. Amsterdam: Philo Press, 1933.

Study Qurʾan Project Root List: http://www.studyquran.co.uk/PRLonline.htm Accessed 15 September 2022

13

Teaching Iranian History: Narrative Style and Messages

Keiko Sakurai

Introduction

Since 1963, when the Pahlavi government introduced a policy requiring the exclusive use of state-designated textbooks at all school levels in both the public and private sectors, every student receiving Iran's compulsory education has studied the story of their national history. Though the history described in school textbooks was continuously revised, the underlying policy of using them to teach the official history has remained unchanged since the policy was implemented. For this reason, the textbooks have served as extensions of state media that disseminate the official ideologies.[1]

Existing studies on Iranian textbooks, especially those focused on teaching history, have highlighted the relationship between history and nationalism. They have analyzed how and what sort of "national history" or "national collective memory" has been constructed and how this has changed or remained the same from the Pahlavi dynasty up to the existing Islamic Republic of Iran.[2] Based on the idea that the nation is constructed and imagined,[3] the formation of national identities was analyzed as the process of defining "us" while excluding "others."[4] The issues are who defines our attributes in order to construct the "nation" and what attributes have been given to the nation.[5] The popular arguments revolve around the selection of historical events, the accuracy of historical facts, the validity of the explanations of events' causes and consequences, the evaluation of past events and the role of historical figures, and the underlying ideology that shapes the storyline.

In contrast to existing studies, this chapter attempts to identify dominant repeated patterns of explaining the historical transition from the ancient to the present, rather than analyzing historical event selection and the way each one has been evaluated or depicted in the textbooks. This method was adopted based on the assumption that textbooks shape students' fundamental modes of thinking about how the history of

Iran has been shaped or how it should be. This fundamental mode of thinking may have endured, even if students have forgotten the historical details. Hence, this chapter attempts to highlight the dominant patterns of explaining the historical transition in the social studies textbooks used in the first secondary school cycle, which is where students spend their last three years of compulsory education.

Review of the History Textbooks

Beginning in 1963, Iran has had an eight-year compulsory education system composed of a five-year primary cycle (*dabestān*) and a three-year guidance cycle (*doure-ye rāhnamā'ī-ye taḥṣīlī*).[6] As the gross primary school enrollment ratio has dramatically improved alongside a decrease in the number of school-age children over the last few decades, Iran's Ministry of Education extended primary school from five to six years, and the three-year guidance cycle became the three-year first cycle of secondary education (*doure-ye avval-e motavasseṭe*). These changes arose after the Education Reform Act of 2012; as an overall result, compulsory education was extended from eight to nine years. New textbooks for the first secondary education cycle have been published since the 1392–93/2013–14 academic year.[7]

Under the eight-year compulsory education system, one of the sections of the fourth and fifth grade social studies textbook was dedicated to history. Subsequently, in the three-year guidance cycle, history was taught as an independent subject. However, under the new education system, Iran's history is only presented to seventh, eighth, and ninth grade secondary school students as one of three social studies sections, including civics and geography. In primary school, historical information is provided when students study Iran's culture, society, and geography. This dramatically reduced the amount of historical information that is taught in compulsory education. In the second cycle of secondary education, history is taught only to students majoring in humanities. For this reason, the history taught in the first cycle of secondary education is the first and only instance of history instruction for all Iranian pupils since 2013. Based on this fact, this chapter analyzes the history presented in social studies textbooks published in 1396–97/2017–18 for use in Grades 7, 8, and 9 during the first cycle of secondary education.[8]

The Grade 7 social studies textbook dedicates four chapters to history. It teaches the history of ancient Iran until the end of the Sassanid dynasty. Similarly, the Grade 8 social studies textbook teaches about the rise of Islam on the Arabian Peninsula, Islam's entrance into Iran, and the dynastic changes from the Umayyads to the Timurids. The Grade 9 social studies textbook covers the Safavid dynasty up to Āyatollāh Khāmene'ī's inauguration as supreme leader of the Islamic Republic of Iran.

The history presented in the social studies textbooks is divided into two periods: the pre-Islamic era and the Islamic era (7th: 121). The former refers to the history of Iran before the rise of Islam, and the latter begins with the fall of the Sassanid dynasty and Islam's entrance into Iran (7th: 107). The history that appears in the social studies textbooks is presented as the official history of Iran, though the boundaries demarcating "Iran" have changed with the expansion and contraction of the historical dynasties' territories.

The history in the textbooks also includes the history of the Prophets of the monotheistic religions who lived outside Iran such as Noah, Abraham, Joseph, Moses, and Jesus. It also includes the early history of Islam such as its birth on the Arabian Peninsula and the martyrdom of Ḥosein, one of the Prophet's grandsons and the third Imām of the Shiʿites at Karbala in present-day Iraq. Though none are generally considered Iranians, they are mobilized to shape Iran's national history. These characteristics indicate that the history presented in the textbooks is composed of historical elements that are essential to justify the Islamic Republic ruled by the Shiʿite clergy.

Method of Analysis

The study focuses on sentences in the history sections of the social studies textbooks published in 1396–97/2017–18 for use in Grades 7, 8, and 9. All of the sentences – except the boxed explanations, questions, captions, and the explanations of each chapter's purpose – were read, and the sentences that narrate historical events impacting Iran, Iranians, and the Shiʿites were chosen. Sentences that only provide historical information with no particular evaluation were excluded from the analysis. The chosen sentences were classified into groups based on their subject matter. This analysis yielded three observations. First, various past events introduced in the textbooks can be reduced to three major subject matters, which can be further divided into subgroups. Second, the dominant pattern of the historical descriptions in the textbooks is the contrast between positive and negative situations and struggles against the latter. Finally, regardless of the political situation, Iranians' contributions to culture and science are introduced as proof of their greatness as a people.

Analysis of the Textbooks (1): The Fight against Oppressors and the Established

The first recurrent subject is the fight against oppressors. This subject can be further divided into four subgroups: good versus oppressive rulers, the established versus the deprived, resistance to oppressive rulers, and ʿulama's leadership during resistance.

Good versus Oppressive Rulers

The textbooks contrast good leaders with oppressive ones and explain the qualities of each. For example, Deioces, the ruler of the Media, is presented as a good ruler. He was popular among all of the tribes because of his "good behavior (*khosh raftārī*) and justice-seeking (*ʿadālat-khahī*) nature" (7th: 116). King Cyrus of the Achaemenid Empire was a "wise (*kheradmand*) king" who treated the people of the conquered lands "with softness and justice" (*bā narmī va ʿadālat*) (7th: 119). Karīm Khān, the founder of the Zand dynasty, treated people "gently and kindly" (*bā molāyemat va mehrbānī*). He "prevented internal insecurity and riots by peaceful means (*shīve-hā-ye mosālematāmīz*)" (9th: 73). During his reign, he created "relative stability" (*s̱ābet va ārāmesh-e nesbī*), which resulted in an improved socioeconomic situation (9th: 74). These sentences teach that "good behavior," "justness," "wisdom" "softness," "gentleness," and "kindness" are the essential traits of a good ruler and that a good ruler can maintain stability through "peaceful means." Though having a good ruler is important for peace, stability, and a better economic situation, the textbooks only provide minimal examples of good rulers.

In contrast to the scarcity of examples of good rulers, Iranian history textbooks abound with autocrats who ruled Iran from ancient times until the end of the Pahlavi dynasty. Terms such as "oppression" (*ẕolm va setam*) and "despotism" (*estebdād*) are frequently used. The first autocrat introduced in seventh grade history are the rulers of ancient civilizations such as Elam, Mesopotamia, and the Nile Valley. Despite these civilizations' prosperity, "poor conditions dominated people's lives and social relations" (7th: 112), as the rulers lived a "dissolute life" (*khosh-goẕarānī*) in "magnificent palaces and greatly oppressed people" (7th: 112).

The Grade 7 textbook also highlights the oppressive nature of the "monarchy" (7th: 123). Kings had "absolute power and absolute authority (*qodrat-e moṭlaq va farmānravāʾī-ye moṭlaq*) over administrative, military, and religious affairs" (7th: 123). "The commands of the kings were a law that should be implemented throughout the country, and nobody should disobey them" (7th: 123). "The hereditary system" (*ḥokūmat-e mourūs̱ī*; 7th: 123), another essential characteristic of the monarchy, is portrayed as problematic. Typically, the throne is passed from father to son, but sometimes, "disagreement over the succession of throne led to the killing of people, war and bloodshed" (7th: 123).

Furthermore, the textbook points out that "heavy court expenses were covered by taxing people" (7th: 124). Most of the kings "accumulated wealth and ignored people's well-being, and oppressed them" (7th: 123), though very rarely, there was a king who tried to impart justice (7th: 124). The textbook's historical examples of the rulers of ancient Iran teach students the fundamental nature of monarchy – which was overthrown in the 1979 Revolution – and instill in them a dichotomous world view of the oppressor and the oppressed.

Iranians' conversion to Islam opened a new chapter of Iranian history, but it did not improve their political situation for two reasons: Arab rulers' oppression of Iranians and Shiʿites. The textbook links Iranians with the Shiʿites by explaining that Iranians were attracted by the Prophet's and Shiʿite Imāms' morality. For instance, Salmān Farsī, the first Iranian convert, was "one of the faithful companions of Imām ʿAlī" (8th: 68). During his reign, Imām ʿAlī never considered Arabs to possess "superiority and privilege" (*bartarī va emtiyāzī*) over non-Arabs (8th: 68). Imām Reżā, his sister Fāṭeme and brother Shāh-e Cherāgh, and the children of Imāms in Iran did much to draw Iranians' attention to Islam (8th: 68). Although the majority of Iranians embrace Shiʿism only after Esmāʿīl Ṣafavī officialized it in the early sixteenth century, the textbooks always equate Iranians with Shiʿites because their narratives are written from the contemporary perspective.

The Umayyads "ignored religious commands," and "the nobles and heads of the Arab tribes ruled over major parts of Iran" with "violence and oppression" (*khoshūnat va ẓolm*; 8th: 66). Contrary to the teaching of the Qurʾan, the Umayyads believed that the "the Arab is superior and nobler (*bartar va sharīftar*) than other ethnic groups" and that "non-Arab ethnic groups, including Iranians, were humiliated and insulted (*taḥqīr va touhīn*)" (8th: 66). Iranians endured prolonged suffering under the Abbasid caliphs, who were as oppressive as the Umayyad caliphs; moreover, "the Shiʿite Imāms were imprisoned on the grounds that they fought against oppression and were martyred" (8th: 66). In contrast to the Umayyads, the Abbasids appointed Iranians to important positions. Nevertheless, many met a bitter fate. For instance, Abū Muslim al-Khorāsānī was killed in a cowardly manner (8th: 66). The Abbasids are also condemned as despotic, and similar to the Umayyads, "the Abbasids also lived luxurious lives in palaces" (8th: 66). The Abbasid caliphs imprisoned and killed the Barmakiān, a famous Iranian family whose members had assumed important positions under Abbasid rule (8th: 67).

The sultans of the Seljuk dynasty "ruled tyrannically (*bā ẓolm va khodkāmegī*) and punished (*mojāzāt*) their opponents severely" (8th: 84). They had "a luxurious (*por-tajammolī*) life and owned a lot of property and wealth (*amlāk va s̱arvat*)" (8th: 84). While the textbook used in Grade 9 portrays the formation of the Safavid dynasty positively, it does not neglect to touch upon its negative aspects; for example, "The Safavid kings ruled the country with despotism (*bā estebdād*), and all the state officials and soldiers subordinated to the Shāh's command" (9th: 61).

The list of oppressive rulers continues into the Qajar dynasty. Unlike most of the oppressive rulers, Moẓaffar al-Dīn Shāh was "a soft and weak (*narmkhū va nātavān*) ruler." Due to his weakness, "the abuses and oppression (*sūʾestefāde va setamgarī*) of government officials and the interference of foreigners (*dekhālat-e bīgānegān*) in the state affairs continued" during his reign, increasing the people's "anger and dissatisfaction" (*khashm va nārežāyatī*; 9th: 87). Moḥammad ʿAlī Shāh was another "tyrannical king" (*pādshāhī mostabed*) of the Qajar dynasty (9th: 89). With Russia's support, as well as that of "domestic tyrants" (*mostabeddān-e dākhelī*), he destroyed the new constitutional government, bombarded and dissolved parliament, and restored the "despotic monarchy" (*neẓām-e pādshāhī-ye estebdādī*; 9th: 89).

The severe condemnation of Pahlavi despotism is intended to justify the Islamic Republic that toppled the Pahlavi monarchy. For this reason, the textbook dedicates many pages to describing the Pahlavi regime's oppressive nature. For instance, it is stated that from the beginning of his reign, Reżа Shāh turned to "despotism and dictatorship" (*estebdād va dīktātorī*; 9th: 94). During his reign, neither the Council of Ministers nor parliament had much autonomy or independence, and they were subject to the Shāh's orders (9th: 94). Reżа Shāh's government prohibited independent parties and newspapers by "force and violence" (*zūr va khoshūnat*); he reigned over society by creating an "atmosphere of suffocation, fear, and suppression" (*fażā-ye khafaqān, tars va sarkūb*; 9th: 94). Those who opposed the Pahlavi regime were fated to face "exile, imprisonment, torture and execution" (*tab'īd, zendān, shekanje va e'dām*; 9th: 94).

In the textbook, Moḥammad Reżа Shāh, Pahlavi II, is harshly criticized, and many examples are given to describe his repressive policies against oppositional groups and demonstrators. After the coup of 1953, Moḥammad Reżа Shāh became "a tyrant and oppressor" (*mostabed va setamgar*) and overtly ignored the principles of the constitution (9th: 97). He established the State Security and Intelligence Organization (SAVAK) to suppress opposition, and once again, "an atmosphere of fear and repression (*fażā-ye tars va khafaqān*) dominated Iran" (9th: 97). Moḥammad Reżа Shāh's regime "ordered its agents to shoot down the demonstrators and suppress the uprising" (9th: 101). The Pahlavi regime seemed to be at the peak of its power in the first half of the year 1356/1977, and "the Shāh suppressed most of his opponents" (9th: 103). "The Pahlavi regime ignored the rights of the people and constitutional principles" (9th: 103). "Despotism and suppression" (*estebdād va sarkūb*) were the other factors that provoked Iranians' "anger and hatred" (*khashm va nefrat*) toward the regime (9th: 103). The newspapers also had no freedom to criticize the king and government officials (9th: 104). The SAVAK and military officers "suppressed oppositionists with all kinds of torture and many dissidents were sentenced to death, imprisonment, and exile" (9th: 104). People were angry about the Pahlavi regimes' "embezzlement and plunder (*ḥeif-o-meil va ghārat*) of the nation's wealth and capital" (9th: 104). On Black Friday, September 8, 1978, regime officials ruthlessly killed and injured many demonstrators (9th: 105).

In addition to their tyrannical rule, the textbook condemns the Pahlavi monarchs' oppressive policies aimed at weakening Islam. The results of the many policies Reżа Shāh introduced under the pretext of socioeconomic progress were a "weakening of religious values and the spread of non-Iranian culture (*farhang-e gheir-e Īrānī*)"

(9th: 94). Reża Shāh ordered that "the veil be taken from Iranian women's heads by force" (9th: 94). Muḥammad Reża Pahlavi abolished "the condition of being Muslim" for those who stood or were eligible for election. He also abolished "the oath of the Qur'an" for those who were elected (9th: 100). These changes were a clear assault on the "religious identity of Iran's Islamic society" (9th: 100). The Iranian people were dissatisfied with the king and his policies because the Pahlavi government "did not pay attention to Islamic culture and values," and its cultural activities – especially via radio, television, and cinema – aimed at "weakening Islamic culture" (9th: 103).

Though the textbooks contrast oppressive rulers with good ones, the narratives teach students that the majority of the monarchs who ruled Iran were dictatorial, oppressive, exploitative, discriminative, corrupt, unjust, and anti-Islamic. The textbooks' thorough criticism of monarchy justifies its overthrow via the Islamic Revolution.

The Established versus the Deprived

In the Grade 7 textbook, the subsection titled "Social inequality" (*nābarābarī-ye ejtemāʿī*) focuses on social stratification during the Sassanid period. Critical descriptions of the Zoroastrian class society help to enhance the legitimacy of the clerical rule of the Islamic Republic. For this reason, the textbook repeatedly portrays Sassanid society as discriminative, oppressive, and exploitative.

The people were displeased with Sassanid rule because of "the class system (*neẓām-e ṭabaqātī*), injustice (*bī-ʿadālatī-ha*) and social discriminations (*tabʿīż-ha-ye ejtemāʿī*) and heavy taxes (*māliyāt-ha-ye sangīn*)" (8th: 64). The class system was the result of "the concentration of power and wealth" (*tamarkoz-e qodrat va s̱arvat*) in the hands of the kings, princes, and other government officials (7th: 134). "The class divisions (*ekhtelāfāt-e ṭabaqātī*) peaked in the Sassanian period," and its society was "discriminatory" (*tabʿīżāmīz*), as it was divided into "the upper-class people" and "the common people" (7th: 134).

The textbook uses this dichotomous framework to explain each group's characteristics. The upper class is comprised of "a king and princes, Zoroastrian clerics, military commanders and secretaries," and "they owned plenty of land and wealth but were exempted from taxes," in addition to possessing many "rights and privileges" (*ḥoqūq va emtiyāz*) (7th: 134).

A luxurious life was another mark of privilege. For instance, the ancient kings and princes enjoyed extremely luxurious, dissolute lives in their palaces (7th: 135). Khosrou Parvīz's crown was made of pure gold and decorated with pearls as big as sparrow eggs. He also had a chess set made of rubies and emeralds, and his emperor's seat was made of ivory and featured a gold and silver handrail (7th: 135). In the textbooks, the rulers' opulent lives are criticized in clear contrast to that of Imām ʿAlī, who was "a good role model for others with a very simple life, far from luxury" (8th: 58).

The common people were craftsmen, traders, farmers, and livestock keepers, and they were deprived of many rights, which made it difficult for them to receive an education; they were also burdened with heavy taxes (7th: 134). In ancient Iran, although farmers comprised the majority and engaged in important economic activities, they were deprived of many "social rights" (7th: 134). Moreover, farmers formed "the infantry corps in wars," and if they ran away from a war, they were severely punished (7th: 134).

The Zoroastrian priests legitimatized ancient Iran's class divisions; one could not move from one class to the other, and those from the deprived class could not marry anyone from the upper class (7th: 134–5). Clothing and housing differed based on social class. Craftsmen and farmers could not live in areas populated by upper-class people; even the Zoroastrian fire temples were separated by social class (7th: 135).

In ancient Iran, taxes were governments' main source of income, and farmers paid the majority of the taxes. In addition to the ordinary tax, a per capita tax was collected exclusively from the common people (7th: 141). Tax officials were oppressive, and they urged people to pay more than what was expected (7th: 141). Taxes were collected to fill the treasury in order to cover war expenses; sustain the lifestyles of the kings, princes, and courtiers, including financing palace construction; pay government employees' salaries; and build and maintain fire temples, caravans, qanats, and dams (7th: 141).

Through detailed descriptions of the social inequality that prevailed under the Sassanids, the textbooks teach about the social rift between the establishment (the exploiters) and the people (the exploited), and how the Zoroastrian priests benefited from the class system. These explanations are aimed not only at justifying the Iranian people's acceptance of Islam as a religion of equality, but also at justifying the current Islam-based governance.

Resistance to Oppressive Rulers

The most important message the textbooks deliver teaches about resistance as a means of challenging oppressors. The Grade 7 textbook refers to Prophets such as Noah, Abraham, Joseph, Moses, and Jesus. Although these Prophets lived outside contemporary Iran, they are introduced as exemplary models of fighting against "the oppressive rulers" (*ḥākemān-e setamgar*) of their time (7th: 112). The Prophets warned people that God would destroy "the wicked and the oppressors" (*badkārān va setamgarān*), and they also demanded that people stay away from "sins (*gonāhān*), practice good deeds (*raftār-e nīkū*), and refrain from obeying the oppressors (*ẓālemān*)" (7th: 112).

The textbook introduces many episodes related to how Prophet Moḥammad strived to propagate God's message in Mecca and fought against his enemies to defend the Islamic community. Similarly, the struggle of Imām Ḥosein and his companions against the "oppressive and corrupt government" (*ḥokūmat-e setamgar va fāsed*) of Yazīd, the second caliph of the Umayyads, is explained in detail, although they are not Iranians (8th: 60).

As previously mentioned, the Umayyad dynasty is described as one of the worst and most tyrannical that ruled over Iranians, and the textbook highlights Iranians' fight against the Umayyads. In fact, while suffering under the ethnocentric Umayyads' oppressive rule, Iranians took every opportunity to fight against them (8th: 66). Iranians were instrumental in many of the "uprisings and rebellions" (*qiyām-hā va shūresh-hā*) against the Umayyads (8th: 66). When Mukhtār Ṯaqafī rebelled against the Umayyads to avenge Imām Ḥosein's murder, Iranians enthusiastically joined the fight in support of Mukhtār (8th: 66).

Iranian Muslims (*Īrāniyān-e Mosalmān*), especially from Khorasan, accepted the Abbasids' invitation to join an uprising against the Umayyads (8th: 66). The Sarbedarān uprising was one of the most important resistances to "oppression and oppressors" (*ẓolm va ẓālemān*) after the collapse of the Ilkhanid dynasty (8th: 95). The inhabitants of Bashtin village, who were plagued by the "greed and arrogance" (*ziyādekhāhī va gostākhī*) of the Mongolian officials in Khorasan, rose up and punished them (8th: 96). Their uprising expanded rapidly, and they achieved victory over the Mongols in Khorasan (8th: 96). The Sarbedarān government supported Shiʿism (8th: 96).

During the Qajar period, leaders, inspired by their Western experiences, introduced new ideas and reforms to combat corruption and autocracy. Amīr Kabīr initiated extensive reforms for the "renovation and efficiency of government organizations, and the fight against administrative and economic corruptions (*mafāsed*)" (9th: 79). Famous intellectuals, who were often educated in Europe and Dār al-Fonūn, tried to familiarize people with "the merits of the constitutional government and the disadvantages of the despotic government (*ḥokūmat-e estebdādī*)" (9th: 87).

The Grade 9 textbook elaborates on a series of oppositional movements against the Pahlavi monarchy as the climax of the resistance. Those who were duty-bound to fight against the tyrannical Shāh are referred to as "Iranian Muslims," "revolutionary people" (*mardom-e enqelābī*), and "demonstrators" (*taẓāhorkonandegān*) (9th: 101, 105).

The 15 Khordad uprising of 1342/1963 was put down with gunfire and violence, and this oppressive response amplified the revolutionaries' "anger and hatred" (*khashm va nefratī*) for the Shāh and his government agents, and strengthened the people's incentive to fight until they overthrew the Pahlavi regime (9th: 101). People held demonstrations to express their opposition to the referendum on the six principles (9th: 101). Imām Khomeinī's arrest caused "anger and mass protests among Iran's Muslim people" in various cities (9th: 101). In addition to the followers of Imām Khomeinī, other groups also participated in the fight against the Pahlavi regime (9th: 103).

On January 9, 1978, people protested the publication of an offensive newspaper article against Shāh's opponents (9th: 104). The people's street protests continued in 1979, and as time went by, more people joined the demonstrations and called for the end of the Shāh's regime (9th: 105). Finally, as a result of the Iranian people's struggle, the Shāh was forced to flee the country on January 16, 1979 (9th: 105).

The ʿUlama's Leadership amidst Resistance

The textbook emphasizes the ʿulama's leadership as the key to successful resistance, as ʿulama (*rūḥāniyūn*) are respected and trusted in Iranian society. They led the people's protests during the Qajar period. For instance, during the tobacco movement, Āyatollāh Mīrzā Ḥasan Shīrāzī, a Shiʿite *marjaʿ al-taqlīd* in Samarra, declared tobacco use to be religiously prohibited in support of the movement (9th: 82). The movement's victory strengthened the people's self-confidence and their "spirit of resistance" (*rūḥiyye-ye moqāvemat va mobāreze*; 9th: 82).

The textbook highlights the ʿulama's leadership during the constitutional revolution in the early twentieth century and emphasizes that the teachings of Islam and Shiʿism call people to fight against oppression and strive for the establishment of justice (9th: 86). It also mentions that the Muslim people of Iran learned from Imām Ḥosein's uprising and the Karbala incident and were therefore always ready to stand against oppression and injustice (9th: 86).

During the constitutional revolution, two famous ʿulama in Tehran, Āyatollāh Ṭabāṭabāʾī and Āyatollāh Behbahānī, formed a society of "freedom seekers" (*āzādī khāhān*) to seek changes for the benefit of the people (9th: 87). A group of ʿulama led by Āyatollāh Ṭabāṭabāʾī moved from Tehran to Ray and sought refuge at the holy shrine of ʿAbd al-ʿAzīm as a sign of protest (9th: 88).

The ʿulama's leadership, especially that of Imām Khomeinī, was paramount in the anti-Shāh movement, which resulted in the 1979 Revolution. The textbook reads, "The most prominent figure of the opposition was the brave scholar, Āyatollāh Sayyid Ruhollāh Khomeinī" (9th: 100).

Imām Khomeinī urged people not to participate in the referendum on the six principles of the White Revolution (9th: 101). He reminded them that silence in the face of an oppressive government (*ḥokūmat-e setamgar*) helps the enemies of Islam (9th: 101). Imām Khomeinī continued to fight in exile and invited people to fight the Shāh and Israel (9th: 102). The ʿulama, academics, students, and bazaar merchants continued to fight even after the movement's leader was exiled. They regarded their role as Imām Khomeinī's followers and participants in the struggle to be religious duty and a dictate of divine law (9th: 103).

Āyatollāh Moṭahharī and Dr. ʿAlī Sharīʿatī introduced "revolutionary Islam" (*Eslām-e enqelābī*) to young people (9th: 103). As the leader of the revolution, Imām

Khomeinī prevented the revolution from stagnating or deviating from its path (9th: 105). The Islamic Revolution of Iran had religious characteristics (9th: 106). This revolution successfully eliminated the country's dependence on foreigners and secured the rights of the nation within the framework of Islamic law and values, under the slogan of independence, freedom, and the Islamic Republic (9th: 106).

Finally, the textbook teaches that "faith and belief in Islam" (*īmān va e'teqād be Eslām*), "the unity and endurance of the nation" (*vaḥdat va esteqāmat-e mellat*), and "Imām Khomeinī's decisive and conscious leadership" (*rahbarī-ye qāṭe' va hūshyārāne-ye Imām Khomeinī*) were three factors that contributed to the success of the Islamic Revolution (9th: 106). The textbook concludes that Imām Khomeinī struggled for the "eminence of Islam and pride of Islamic Iran" (*ta'ālī-ye Eslām va sarbolandī-ye Īrān-e Eslāmī*; 9th: 111).

Analysis of the Textbooks (2): The Fight for National Integration and Independence

Integrated versus Disintegrated Iran

Across all rulers, the textbooks describe the combination of territorial integration and a powerful central government positively, as it brings stability, security, and prosperity. A good example is the description of the Safavids. Esmā'īl Ṣafavī's conquest of Iran is described positively, as he officialized Shi'ite Islam, defeated enemies, and dominated Iran. As a result, the government became "integrated and strong" (*yek-pārche va nīrūmand*; 9th: 59). The Safavid government placed "all the Iranian ethnic groups" (*hame-ye aqvām-e Īrānī*) under its control, which made Iran "more united and integrated" (*hambastegī va etteḥād-e bīshtar*; 9th: 59). The Safavids fought with "foreign enemies" (*doshmanān-e khārejī*) to defend "Iran's geographical integration" (*yek-pārchegī-ye joghrāfīyā'ī-ye Īrān*; 9th: 59). A powerful government's achievement of territorial integrity was key in upsetting enemies; for instance, the Ottoman sultan was unhappy with "the formation of the powerful Shi'ite Safavid dynasty" (9th: 59).

The textbook emphasizes that during the Safavid period, "a powerful central government (*ḥokūmat-e markazī-ye qodrat-mandī*) was created" (9th: 61), and thanks to the existence of "a strong central government" (*ḥokūmat-e markazī-ye nīrūmand*) and the establishment of "order and security" (*neẓām va amniyat*) throughout the country, "the appropriate conditions for the prosperity of socio-economic life were established" (9th: 64).

Another example is Āghā Moḥammad Khān's establishment of the Qajar government, under which Iran regained its territorial integrity (*yek-pārchegī-ye sarzamīn-e khod*) and established "a relatively strong central government" (9th: 74).

Dynastic collapse and internal division are two significant causes of the disintegration and weakening of the central government. Across all rulers, the textbooks portray weak, disintegrated governments negatively. For instance, the political confusion during the last days of the Sasanian Empire was due to Khosrou's refusal to accept the Prophet's invitation to Islam (8th: 64). "The commanders' insurrections" (*shūresh-ha-ye farmāndehān*) and interference in politics weakened military strength and contributed to the Sasanian Empire's decline (8th: 64). This state of internal confusion and weakness caused the Sassanid dynasty's military defeat and facilitated the Arab Muslims' conquest of Iran (8th: 64). It is worth noting that while the Sassanid kings are described as oppressive, and it is stated that the people were unhappy with the class system developed under the Sassanid dynasty, the internal disputes and the Sassanids' military defeat by the Muslim Arab forces are described in a negative light.

The weakening of the Abbasid Caliphate is attributed to "the formation of governments in various parts of Iran" and the division of the vast territory (8th: 68). After the collapse of the Ilkhanids, who had brought about a politically integrated and united Iran, the nation was again consumed by "chaos, riots, wars, murder, and looting" (*harj-o-marj, āshūb, jang, va qatl-o-ghārat-hā*; 8th: 94–5). Iran faced political disunity as local leaders competed with each other (8th: 95).

Before the rise of the Safavids, Iran was divided, with "no single, powerful government" (*ḥokūmat-e vāḥed va qodrat-mandī*; 9th: 58). The cities and villages lacked "security and tranquility" (*amniyat va ārāmesh*) and Iran's neighboring countries, such as the Ottoman Empire and the Uzbeks, were seeking to expand their territories (9th: 58). After Shāh Abbas' death, the government's affairs were disrupted, and the country fell into chaos. Under these circumstances, Solṭān Ḥosein Ṣafavī could not even quash a small rebel group, and the rebel leader took control of the capital and parts of Iran (9th: 60).

In the wake of the Afghan domination of Isfahan, Iran was "divided" (*tajziye va tafraqe*; 9th:72). However, the Afghans did not have the power to rule across Iran, which gave rise to pretenders in every corner of the country. Although Nāder Shāh founded the Afsharid dynasty, he was obliged to keep fighting foreigners and quelling internal riots. Though he tried to make Iran a powerful, integrated country, "successive disobedience and insurrections" (*nāfarmānī-hā va shūresh-hā-ye payāpey*) made him suspicious of his commanders, and he reacted with brutality. Eventually, Nādir Shāh was killed by his commanders, and Iran was again divided amidst "fighting between the regional and tribal leaders" (9th: 72).

World War I caused "instability and turmoil" (*bīs̱obātī va āshoftegī*), and because of the occupying forces and military conflicts, the central government became "weak and helpless" (*żaʿf va darmāndegī*) and lost control of state affairs. "Disobedience to and defiance (*nāfarmānī va sarpīchī*) of the government decree" proliferated, and "people's security and comfort" (*amniyat va āsāyesh-e mardom*) disappeared (9th: 91). In these years, "Iranians suffered great disasters such as famine, poverty, hunger and the spread of contagious diseases, and many people died" (9th: 91). After the oil industry was nationalized, "a dispute" (*ekhtelāf*) emerged between the movement's leaders and supporters, and internal conflict deepened. As a result, "unity and solidarity (*etteḥād va hamdelī*) turned into division and hostility (*tafraqe va doshmanī*)" (9th: 97).

Even after the success of the Islamic Revolution, Iran faced internal conflicts, in which political figures in Imām Khomeinī's regime, as well as his close friends, were martyred; furthermore, Āyatollāh ʿAlī Khāmeneʾī was seriously injured by "terrorist acts" (*eqdām-hā-ye terorīstī*) (9th: 109). Though the textbooks provide various examples of internal conflict and division from ancient times to the present day, their mode of explanation is simple and dichotomous. A strong government brings about national unity, but such a government is, in many cases, tyrannical. However, the textbooks avoid discussing the issue of whether tyranny is inevitable to achieve national integration.

Independence versus Foreign Invasion and Occupation

Positive experiences with foreign countries are limited; one of only a few examples is the territorial expansion that Iran experienced in the pre-Islamic era. For instance, during Cyrus' and then Darius' time, the Achaemid Empire's geographic territory covered the major countries of that day and was considered to be "the first world empire" (7th: 119). Another case is the great territorial expansion that occurred under the reign of Shāpūr I of the Sassanids (7th: 121).

Except for a few examples pertaining to the ancient Iranian empire, which ruled vast territories, Iranian history is characterized by bitter experiences of being invaded and occupied by external forces. An early example is Alexander's defeat of the Achaemenid army and conquest of Iran, which involved the burning of many Iranian cities, including Persepolis (7th: 120). Iran then fell into Seleucus' hands (7th: 120).

The textbook describes the Mongol invasion as one of the most disastrous events in Iran's history. Using negatively connotated language, the textbook states, for example, that "the terrifying invasion (*hojūm-e houlnāk*) of Chingīz was one of the catastrophes (*fajāyeʿ*) of Irania history" (8th: 94). Many Iranians were killed, captured or displaced. "Fear" (*tars va vaḥshat*) spread throughout the country, and people preferred to sequester themselves from society (8th: 94). Chingīz's armies destroyed many cities and villages, and caused extensive damage to agricultural fields and qanats. They destroyed mosques, schools, and libraries, and also burned books (8th: 94). Teymūr attacked Iran and caused significant damage to the Iranian people, many of whom died or had their property looted (8th: 96).

The nature of international relations changed with the rise of the Western colonial powers. In this new international environment, Iran fell victim to the British-Russian rivalry in the nineteenth and twentieth centuries. The textbook details these two colonial powers' political influence on Iran.

Russia and the Ottomans occupied parts of northern and western Iran (9th: 72). After ten years of war, Russia won and imposed the Treaty of Golestan on Iran (9th: 75). Iran fought again with Russia, and the Treaty of Turkmenchay – which was even more detrimental than the Treaty of Golestan – was imposed on Iran. Accordingly, Russia captured the Iranian lands north of the Aras River (9th: 75–6). The Qajar government was forced to agree to Afghanistan's separation from Iran as well as the eastern part of Sistan and Baluchestan (9th: 77). Furthermore, some islands in the Persian Gulf were occupied and converted into British military bases (9th: 77). Britain and Russia divided Iran under the 1907 Anglo-Russian Convention. Subsequently, Russia intervened in Iran's domestic affairs and prevented both the government and parliament from regulating the national chaos (9th: 90). Russian troops entered Iranian territory, killed some constitutionalists in Tabriz, and bombarded the Imām Reżā Shrine in Mashhad (9th: 90). Britain, Russia, and the Ottomans ignored Iran's neutral stance in World War I and brought their troops into the country, turning some areas of the nation into a battlefield where Russian and British forces fought the Ottoman forces (9th: 91).

The end of World War I did not change the situation. While the new Soviet government was busy with domestic issues, Britain used this situation to "affirm its influence and domination (*nofūẕ va solṭe*)" in Iran (9th: 92). During World War II, although Iran declared neutrality, the Allies occupied the land to exploit Iran's strategic geographical position and resources (9th: 95). Iran was "occupied by the aliens" (*eshghāl-e bīgānegān*) until the end of the war (9th: 94).

In addition to direct foreign invasion and occupation, Iran has been tormented since the nineteenth century under first Russia's, then Britain's, and finally, the United States' political and economic domination. During Naser al-Din Shāh's reign, Russia and Britain acquired "economic privileges" (*emtyāz-hā-ye eqteṣādī*) in Iran, which caused a lot of damage (9th: 81). Large foreign trading companies imported European goods with little or no customs fees attached (9th: 81). "The weakness and incompetence of the Qajar government" was the main cause of "the foreign domination (*tasalloṭ-e bīgānegān*) of the economic resources" (9th: 86). Under the Anglo-Persian Agreement of 1919, the Iranian Military and Financial Affairs Office was placed under the British military's and financial experts' control. However, after failing to implement the Anglo-Persian Agreement, Britain sought to pursue its goals through a coup in Iran. They eventually chose a commander from among the Cossack forces, Reżā Khān, and the pro-British politician Sayyed Żiā᾿ al-Dīn Ṭabāṭabā᾿ī as political instruments in the coup (9th: 92).

The Pahlavi dynasty was thus born of British political ambition and intervention – which led to further British intervention. The privilege of exploiting Iran's oil resources was given to the British during the time of Moẓaffar al-Dīn Shāh; Reżā Shāh revoked this privilege, but eventually returned it to Britain (9th: 96).

World War II caused considerable "damage" (*khesārat va āsīb*) to Iran's economy and society, and the Iranian people faced severe food shortage; consequentially, many died of hunger and malnutrition (9th: 95). Although the British influence in Iran declined as a result of Iran's nationalization of its oil industry, American influence increased. The textbook attributes the failure of the nationalization of the oil industry to the movement's leaders, as each became "a captive of ambition" (*asīr-e jāhṭalabī*) and "political selfishness" (*khodkhāhī-ye siyāsī*), and collectively, they failed to prevent "internal disputes" (*ekhtelāfāt-e darūnī*). As a result, the people's "unity and sympathy" toward the movement transformed into "division and hostility" (*tafreqe va doshmanī*). The British and US governments exploited this condition to overthrow Dr. Moṣaddeq's government via a coup (9th: 97). After the success of the August 2nd coup, Iran's oil was again placed under the "control of foreigners" (*ekhtiyār-e bīgānegān*) and the United States' "influence and domination" (*nofūẕ va solṭe*) over the country gradually increased (9th: 97).

The United States advised the Shāh to make social and economic changes in order to discourage popular uprisings and preserve the Pahlavi regime (9th: 100). The United States forced the Iranian government to grant US military officers' judicial immunity (9th: 102). The Pahlavi government's "political dependency on the foreigners" (*vābastegī-ye siyāsī be bīgānegān*) and "the influence and interference of the foreign countries" (*nofūẕ va dakhālat-e keshvar-hā-ye khārejī*), especially the United States, intensified the people's dissatisfaction (9th: 103).

Hence, the Islamic Revolution aimed to end the country's dependence on foreigners and secure national rights within the framework of Islamic laws and values (9th: 106). Contrary to the people's expectations, "hegemonic and tyrannical governments" (*doulat-hā-ye solṭegar va zūrgū*), led by the United States, launched extensive efforts to derail and destroy the newly established Islamic Republic (9th: 108). During the first years of the Islamic Revolution, "internal counter-revolutionary groups" (*gorūh-hā-ye żedd-e enqelāb-e dākhelī*), supported by the revolution's foreign enemies, began creating instability in parts of the country – especially in the border regions – with the intention to launch a civil war (9th: 109). At the beginning of the revolution, the US embassy in Iran became the center of support for the counter-revolutionary groups (9th: 110). While Iran was involved in a massive internal rebellion, foreign enemies of the Islamic Revolution imposed war on the Iranian nation (9th: 110). Ṣaddām, the head of the Ba'athist government of Iraq, started a war against Iran and occupied "the soil of our homeland" (*khāk-e mīhan-e mā*; 9th: 110).

The textbook's frequent references to foreign enemies and the negative consequences of foreign occupation, domination, invasion, intervention, influence, and exploitation are intended to instill a sense of caution toward foreign countries. The textbook also emphasizes the dangers of weak, incompetent government, rulers' dependency on foreign countries, and internal division, all of which could lead to foreign domination and exploitation.

Resistance to Foreign Invasion and Liberation from Foreign Domination

The textbook teaches that Iran's rulers and people have constantly strived to resist foreign aggression, defend Iran's independence, and liberate Iran from foreign domination. Seventh-graders are taught that Iran has always been exposed to enemy invasion due to its geographic location. For this reason, the governments of ancient Iran created robust and well-equipped corps and military to defend Iran's borders (7th: 127). The Media gradually strengthened, overcame their enemies, and founded a powerful government in Iran (7th: 116). King Cyrus of the Achaemenid dynasty occupied Babylonia and Lydia, and expanded Iran's territory from the Persian Gulf to the Mediterranean Sea (7th: 119). Arshak, head of one of the Parthian tribes, united the Parthians with "other Iranian tribes" (*dīgar aqvām-e Īrānī*) to confront the Seleucids. By exploiting the disputes within the Seleucid Empire, he was able to liberate parts of Iran (7th: 121). The Arsacids fended off the Roman army's powerful attacks and "never let the foreigners dominate our homeland again" (7th: 121).

During the Safavid period, the Ottomans occupied Tabriz, but the resistance and struggle of the people forced them to retreat (9th: 59). Tahmāsp's victories over enemies such as the Uzbeks and the Ottomans allowed him to "consolidate" (*taṯbīt va taḥkīm*) the Safavid regime (9th: 59). The Uzbeks and the Ottomans remained enemies, but King Abbās I defeated them (9th: 59).

With the rise of the European colonial powers, the government's function of confronting foreign enemies declined, while the people's contribution to protecting the country increased. For instance, the Qajar's military and political defeats at the hands of Russia and Britain drew Iranians' attention to the European countries' scientific and industrial progress. Accordingly, some politicians, scholars, and ʿulama looked for a solution to remedy Iran's backward status and work toward the preservation of independence and development (9th: 78). Crown Prince ʿAbbās Mīrzā of Fatḥ ʿAlī Shāh, who also served as the commander of the Iranian army, was aware that Iran's defeat was attributable to the country's lack of advanced military knowledge and equipment. Therefore, he sent people to Europe to study science and technology (9th: 78).

In foreign policy, Amīr Kabīr paid special attention to "the preservation of the country's independence" and sough to reduce "Russia's and Britain's influence and interferences" in Iran (9th: 79). Iran's Muslim people were aware that transferring economic privileges to Russia and Britain would give foreigners more control over Iran's wealth and market resources. Rather than remaining silent, people openly opposed some of the concessions (9th: 81).

The tobacco movement was "the first serious movement by the Iranian people" (*nokhostīn ḥarakat-e jeddī-ye mardom-e Īrān*). It aimed to emancipate them from the "foreign influence and domination" and stand against "domestic oppression" (*setam-e dākhelī*; 9th: 82). The tobacco movement's success, followed by the assassination of Nāṣer al-Dīn Shāh, doubled the people's will to fight "despotism and foreign domination" (*estebdād va solṭe-ye khārejī*; 9th: 87). Britain, Russia, and the Ottomans ignored Iran's neutral stance at the beginning of World War I. Therefore, in some parts of Iran, "popular forces, especially brave tribes" stood against the British "occupation forces" (*qovā-ye eshghālgar*; 9th: 91).

The people's fight continued up to the time of the nationalization of the oil industry in 1951. Britain's efforts to prevent this action failed because of the "people's unity and solidarity with the leaders" (*vaḥdat-e mellat va hamdelī-ye rahbarān-e nahżat*; 9th: 96).

The Islamic Revolution did not end the fight against foreign enemies. The student followers of the Imām's Line announced that they would release their hostages if the United States handed over the Shāh and committed to refrain from interfering in Iran's internal affairs (9th: 110). The "imposed war" (*jang-e taḥmīlī*) with Iraq eventually ended after eight years of "the people's resistance and warriors' sacrifices" (*pāydārī-ye mellat va īs̱ār-e razmandegān*; 9th: 110).

The ʿUlama's Leadership in Fighting Foreign Enemies

On many occasions, such as the tobacco movement, the 1919 Anglo-Iranian Agreement, the nationalization of the oil industry, and the White Revolution, the ʿulama's leadership is described positively, and many ʿulama are mentioned by name. The emphasis on the ʿulama's leadership in fighting foreign enemies is particularly important, given that the current regime, led by Āyatollāh Khāmeneʾī, is facing pressure from the United States and its allies.

The tobacco movement was one of the broadest social movements in protest to the transfer of economic concessions to foreigners. In support of the protest against the tobacco concession that was given to Talbot, Āyatollāh Mīrzā Ḥasan Shīrāzī, the Shiʿite *marjaʿ al-taqlīd* in Samarra, declared the use of tobacco is "religiously unlawful" (*ḥarām*; 9th: 82). Many "activists and freedom seekers" (*mobārez va āzādīkhāh*), such as Āyatollāh Modarres and Sheikh Moḥammad Khiyābānī, opposed the 1919 Anglo-Iranian Agreement (9th: 92). During the nationalization of the oil industry, Āyatollāh Kāshānī played a leading role, as did Dr. Moṣaddeq (9th: 96).

Imām Khomeinī condemned the Shāh for his "oppression, cooperation with Israel and dependence on the United States" (*setamgarī, hamkārī bā Esrāʾīl va vābastegī be Āmrīkā*; 9th: 101). Imām Khomeinī and other fighting ʿulama (*ʿolamā-ye mobārez*) were aware that implementing the six principles of the White Revolution would strengthen "American domination" (*solṭe-ye Āmrīkā*) over Iran and increase Iran's "political and economic dependence" (*vābastegī-ye siyāsī va eqteṣādī*) on foreign countries. Imām Khomeinī therefore urged people not to participate in the referendum on the six principles (9th: 101). He asserted that granting Americans judicial immunity would be detrimental to Iran's independence, and he strongly criticized the Shāh for his dependence on the United States (9th: 102). Though the textbook does not refer to the present day, these statements support the anti-American and anti-Israeli line of the Islamic Republic's clerical rule.

Analysis of the Textbooks (3): Iranians' Greatness

Contributions to Culture and Science

In contrast to Iran's political history, which is overwhelmed by bitter experiences under oppressive kings, foreign invasions, and domination, Iran's cultural history is full of glories and greatness in both the pre- and Islamic periods. Interestingly, on the one hand, the Grade 7 textbook criticizes the religions of pre-Islamic Iran with the following statements: "Instead of worshiping one single God, people worshiped the sun and the moon or idols and they were astray (*gomrāh*)" (7th: 112) and "Ethics, behavior, law, as well as regulations that people followed, were full of ignorance, deviation, superstition, and oppression (*jahl, gomrāhī, khorāfāt, va ẓolm-o-setam*)" (7th: 112). However, the textbook also admires "ancient Iranian civilization" (*tamaddon-e kohan-e Īrān*) as a "great civilization" (*tamaddon-e bozorgī*) (7th: 110, 111) that embodied "glory" (*shokūh va ʿaẓamat*; 7th: 150).

The word "progress" (*pīshraft*) is also used to praise ancient Iranians. For instance, the ancient Iranians made significant scientific and technological developments (7th: 152). They were advanced in astronomy, and they created the world's most unique calendar (7th: 152). The Iranians also developed medicine, and the ancient architectures demonstrate "Iranians' progress" (*pīshraft-e Īrāniyān*) in that area of knowledge (7th: 153). The textbooks teach that Iranians were "the first" in many fields; for example, they were "the first human civilizations" (*nokhostīn tamaddon-hā-ye basharī*; 7th: 108) and "the first universal empire" (*nokhostīn emperātūrī-ye jahānī*; 7th: 119). Furthermore, the Iranian plateau was one of the first areas where agriculture and animal husbandry began (7th: 137). Iranians seem to have been the first to divide the land into different districts (7th: 126). Moreover, Iranians were among the first to design and wear trousers (7th: 146). Researchers have claimed that the ancient Iranians invented the game polo (7th: 147).

The textbook's praise of pre-Islamic civilization as great on the one hand and its criticism of pre-Islamic religion on the other hand give students the impression that civilization and religion are unrelated. However, the Grade 8 textbook presents an opposite idea by describing Iranians' conversion to Islam as a driving force for their advancements in various fields. "After Iranians became Muslims, they began working in various fields of political, scientific, cultural and economic affairs and contributed to the progress and prosperity of Iranian Islamic culture and civilization (*farhang va tamaddon-e Īrānī-Eslāmī*)" (8th: 62). After converting to Islam, Iranians mobilized their abilities and talents to advance and expand Islamic culture and civilization (8th: 72). The Iranian Muslims were pioneers in the establishment and expansion of the Islamic sciences and humanities, as well as experimental sciences and the arts, including literature (8th: 73).

The Iranian dynasties, especially the Samanids and the Buyids, played a significant role in the prosperity of "Iranian-Islamic culture and civilization." Most of these dynastic rulers were interested in science and literature, and they greatly valued and respected scholars in these knowledge areas; in fact, the capitals of these dynasties were centers of knowledge (8th: 73). The most prominent Muslim scholars in the various science fields during the golden age of Iranian-Islamic culture and civilization were predominantly Iranian (8th: 73) The textbook used in Grade 8 refers to the contributions of "Iranian Muslim thinkers" (*andīshmandān-e Mosalmān-e Īrānī*), "Iranian religious scholars" (*ʿālemān-e Īrānī*), and "Iranian Muslim scholars" (*dāneshmandān-e Mosalmān-e Īrānī*) in the fields of Islamic sciences, commentary on the Qurʾan, philosophy, history, geography, and music. Iranians even contributed to the development of Arabic language and literature, syntax rules, and Arabic grammar (8th: 73). Iranian writers and translators translated books about the ancient kings and heroes of Iran, as well as a book containing advice and rules of government, from the Pahlavi language to Arabic (8th: 73).

Iran's architecture and Islamic era art represent the continuation of Iran's ancient architecture, and mosques and shrines are one of the manifestations of "Iranian-Islamic architecture" (8th: 75). After the arrival of Islam in Iran, Arabic became the administrative language. However, during the Saffarid and the Samanid era, Persian literature, such as that from Rūdakī and Ferdousī, also flourished (8th: 75).

The frequently used terms "Iranian-Islamic" and "Iranian Muslim" allude to Iranian pride, and these terms teach students that as the inheritors of a great cultural civilization that existed before the conversion to Islam, Iranians occupy a special place among Muslims.

Iranians have also contributed to governance. For instance, the Seljuks were desert people who were not familiar with urban life, and they used Iranian ministers to govern their vast territory (8th: 85). Iranian ministers thus played an important role in Seljuk government, leading to growth in various fields (8th: 85).

During the Safavid period, Iranians once again revealed their talents and abilities in science, culture, and art (9th: 67). The textbook dedicates three subsections, namely "Industrial prosperity" (*shekūfāʾī-ye ṣanʿat*), "Flourishing trade" (*rounaq-e tejārat*), and "Science and cultural prosperity" (*shekūfāʾī-ye ʿelmī va farhangī*) (9th: 65–9), to elaborating on Iranians' achievements.

European tourists' testimonies, such as that of renowned traveler Jean Chardin, have shown that Iranian farmers' lives compared favorably to those of farmers in the fertile regions of Europe during the Safavid period (9th: 64). The textbook also includes European tourists' observations about the safety of Iran's roads and the road police officers' ethical behavior toward travelers (9th: 66).

The textbook emphasizes that Iranians demonstrated their greatness through their contributions to culture and science, even before their conversion to Islam. This is consistent with the testimony of Dr. ʿAbbās Partovī Moqaddam, one of the members of the Supervisory Council of Planning and Writing (*Shūrā-ye Neẓārat bar Barnāmerīzī va Taʾlīf*), who was in charge of preparing the textbook. In a session on the role of history teaching in textbooks, he stated that "Throughout history, we have repeatedly experienced political ruptures, but we have never experienced cultural divisions. With this in mind, the new history textbook team defined the Islamic period as how Iranians who converted to Islam tried not to forget their identity and historical past. For this reason, the new history textbook team depicted how Iranians who converted to Islam tried to remember their identity and historical past."[9] The following description reflects Dr. Moqaddam's testimony: During the Safavid period, in addition to Nourūz and other ancient festivals, people celebrated Islamic festivals such as ʿEid al-Qorbān, ʿEid al-Fiṭr, and ʿEid al-Ghadīr. These celebrations and ceremonies increased people's "empathy and solidarity" (*hamdelī va hambastgī*; 9th: 69).

Conclusion: Narrative Style and Messages

As discussed so far, the historical narratives in the textbooks are dominated by dichotomous explanations such as good versus oppressive rulers, integrated versus disintegrated, independence versus foreign invasion and occupation, Islamic versus anti-Islamic, and Shiʿite versus anti-Shiʿite.[10] In all of these binaries, the former term is described as positive and desirable, while the latter is portrayed as negative and undesirable; the criterion that separates the former from the latter is whether or not it is in the interest of Iran, Iranians, Shiʿites, and the ʿulama.

Complex, diverse, and rich historical facts are evaluated through the lens of the current regime; that is, they are dominated by a dualistic good and evil worldview and have been reduced into a single story of struggle and resistance against domestic and foreign oppressors and exploiters. An overwhelming number of stories about oppressive rulers, as well as foreign and domestic enemies, teach students that from ancient times up to the present, Iranians have been doomed to keep fighting unjust un-Islamic rulers and resisting foreign intervention and domination. Although some rulers protected the country from foreign invasion, liberated occupied territory, and brought temporary peace, the Iranian people have been repeatedly ruled by dictators and have never enjoyed enduring peace – even after the Islamic Revolution. Balancing a history of hardship, the textbook gives students a sense of pride in being Iranian by emphasizing that Iranians have consistently made significant contributions to culture and science across all regimes, from pre-Islamic ancient times to the present.

The chronological transformation is explained solely based on the rise and fall of dynasties. The history of culture, science and technology are all presented as the evidence of Iranians' greatness, while contributions from those who the present regime sees as enemies or as insignificant are ignored – including women.[11] In short, through dualistic explanations, the textbooks impart the Islamic Republic's fundamental mission: to resist tyrannical rule, fight Iran's domestic and foreign enemies, and accept the ʿulama's leadership.[12]

Notes

1 Keiko Sakurai, *Kakumei Iran no kyokasho media: Isramu to nashonarizumu no sokoku* [*Textbook as a Media of Revolutionary Iran: Conflict between Islam and Nationalism*] (Tokyo: Iwanami Publisher, 1999), 47, 61–4.

2 Mostafa Vaziri, *Iran as Imagined Nation: The Construction of National Identity* (New York: Paragon House, 1989), 78–91. Haggay Ram, "The Immemorial Iranian Nation? School Textbooks and Historical Memory in Post-Revolutionary Iran," *Nations and Nationalism* 6.1 (2000): 67–90. Keiko Sakurai, "Creating an Image of Community through Textbooks in Iran," *Annals of Japan Association for Middle East Studies* 9 (1994): 143–64; Farzin Vejdani, *Making History in Iran: Education, Nationalism, and Print Culture* (California: Stanford University Press, 2014).

3 Benedict Anderson, *Imagined Communities: Reflections on the Origin and Spread of Nationalism* (London: Verso, 2016), 6.

4 Golnar Mehran, "The Presentation of the 'Self' and the 'Other' in Postrevolutionary Iranian School Textbooks," in *Iran and the Surrounding World: Interactions in Culture and Cultural Politics*, ed. by Nikki R. Keddie and Rudolph P. Matthee (Seattle: University of Washington Press, 2002), 232–49.

5 Saeed Paivandi, *Discrimination and Intolerance in Iran's Textbooks* (Washington: Freedom House, 2008), 1–80. Maryam Soltan Zadeh, "History Education and the Construction of National Identity in Iran," PhD dissertation, Florida International University, 2012, 1–311 (https://core.ac.uk/download/pdf/46952066.pdf [accessed September 12, 2022]).

6 Sakurai, *Kakumei Iran no kyokasho media*, 61.

7 The new education system has been introduced since the 2013/14 academic year. *Iranian Students' News Agency*, Khordad 7, 1392 (May 28, 2013), "ʿAnāvīn-e doure-hā va pāye-hā-ye taḥṣīlī-ye madāres taghīr kard" [The Titles of the Cycles and Grades Were Changed] (https://www.isna.ir/news/92030704056/ [accessed September 13, 2022]).

8 Vezārat-e Āmūzesh va Parvaresh, Sāzmān-e Pazhūhesh va Barnāmerīzī-ye Āmūzeshī [Ministry of Education, Institute of Educational Research and Planning], *Moṭāleʿāt-e ejtemāʿī (madanī,*

joghrāfiyā, tārīkh) [Social Studies (Civics, Geography, History)], pāye-ye haftom, doure-ye avval-e motavassete, sāl-e taḥṣīlī 1396–97 [7th grade, first cycle of secondary education, academic year 1396–97/2017–18] (hereafter 7th).
Vezārat-e Āmūzesh va Parvaresh, Sāzmān-e Pazhūhesh va Barnāmerīzī-ye Āmūzeshī [Ministry of Education, Institute of Educational Research and Planning], *Moṭāleʿāt-e ejtemāʿī (madanī, joghrāfiyā, tārīkh)* [Social Studies (civics, geography, history)], pāye-ye hashtom, doure-ye avval-e motavassete, sāl-e taḥṣīlī 1396–97 [8th grade, first cycle of secondary education, academic year 1396–97 (2017–18)] (hereafter 8th).
Vezārat-e Āmūzesh va Parvaresh, Sāzmān-e Pazhūhesh va Barnāmerīzī-ye Āmūzeshī [Ministry of Education, Institute of Educational Research and Planning], *Moṭāleʿāt-e ejtemāʿī (madanī, joghrāfiyā, tārīkh)* [Social Studies (civics, geography, history)], pāye-ye nohom, doure-ye avval-e motavassete, sāl-e taḥṣīlī 1396–97 [9th grade, first cycle of secondary education, academic year 1396–97 (2017–18)] (hereafter 9th).

9 *Amordadnews*, Khordad 9, 1398 (May 30, 2019), (https://amordadnews.com/11474/ [accessed May 25, 2019]).

10 Golnar Mehran analyzed the textbooks of social studies, Persian and religious studies published in postrevolutionary Iran and contended that "a content analysis of primary-school books points to clear demarcation lines based on Iranian/non-Iranian, Muslim/non-Muslim, good/evil, friend/enemy, and male/female dichotomies." Mehran, "The Presentation of the 'Self' and the 'Other'," 232.

11 From ancient times to the present day, only two women are mentioned by name; one is Khadīja, a wife of the Prophet Moḥammad, and the other is Somaiye, a wife of Yāser, an early companion of the prophet. Interestingly, neither of them is Iranian (8th: 49, 51).

12 The importance of resistance is well expressed in the words of Khāmeneʾī, which reads "If a society and country are devoid of the spirit of being prepared to stand up against evil and to show resistance on the path of the truth, that society will be ruined." *Khamenei.IR*, "A Society Devoid of the Spirit of Resistance on the Path of the Truth, Will be Ruined," December 16, 2019, (http://english.khamenei.ir/news/7277/A-society-devoid-of-the-spirit-of-resistance-on-the-path-of-the [accessed January 13, 2020]).

Bibliography

Published Sources

Anderson, Benedict. *Imagined Communities: Reflections on the Origin and Spread of Nationalism*. London: Verso, 2016.

Mehran, Golnar. "The Presentation of the 'Self' and the 'Other' in Postrevolutionary Iranian School Textbooks." In *Iran and the Surrounding World: Interactions in Culture and Cultural Politics*. Ed. by Nikki R. Keddie and Rudolph P. Matthee. Seattle: University of Washington Press, 2002, 232–49.

Paivandi, Saeed. *Discrimination and Intolerance in Iran's Textbooks*. Washington: Freedom House, 2008.

Ram, Haggay. "The Immemorial Iranian Nation? School Textbooks and Historical Memory in Post-Revolutionary Iran." *Nations and Nationalism* 6.1 (2000): 67–90.

Sakurai, Keiko. "Creating an Image of Community through Textbooks in Iran." *Annals of Japan Association for Middle East Studies* 9 (1994): 143–64.

Sakurai, Keiko. *Kakumei Iran no kyokasho media, Isramu to nashonarizumu no sokoku* [*Textbook as a Media of Revolutionary Iran: Conflict between Islam and Nationalism*]. Tokyo: Iwanami Publisher, 1999.

Soltan Zadeh, Maryam. "History Education and the Construction of National Identity in Iran," PhD dissertation, Florida International University, 2012. https://core.ac.uk/download/pdf/46952066.pdf. Accessed September 12, 2022.

Vaziri, Mostafa. *Iran as Imagined Nation: The Construction of National Identity*. New York: Paragon House, 1989.

Vejdani, Farzin. *Making History in Iran: Education, Nationalism, and Print Culture*. California: Stanford University Press, 2014.

Vezārat-e Āmūzesh va Parvaresh, Sāzmān-e Pazhūhesh va Barnāmerīzī-ye Āmūzeshī [Ministry of Education, Institute of Educational Research and Planning], *Moṭāleʿāt-e ejtemāʿī (madanī, joghrāfīyā, tārīkh)* [Social Studies (Civics, Geography, History)], pāye-ye haftom, doure-ye avval-e motavasseṭe, sāl-e taḥṣīlī 1396–97 [7th grade, first cycle of secondary education, academic year 1396–97/2017–18].

Vezārat-e Āmūzesh va Parvaresh, Sāzmān-e Pazhūhesh va Barnāmerīzī-ye Āmūzeshī [Ministry of Education, Institute of Educational Research and Planning], *Moṭāleʿāt-e ejtemāʿī (madanī, joghrāfīyā, tārīkh)* [Social Studies (Civics, Geography, History)], pāye-ye hashtom, doure-ye avval-e motavasseṭe, sāl-e taḥṣīlī 1396–97 [8th grade, first cycle of secondary education, academic year 1396–97/2017–18].

Vezārat-e Āmūzesh va Parvaresh, Sāzmān-e Pazhūhesh va Barnāmerīzī-ye Āmūzeshī [Ministry of Education, Institute of Educational Research and Planning], *Moṭāleʿāt-e ejtemāʿī (madanī, joghrāfīyā, tārīkh)* [Social Studies (Civics, Geography, History)], pāye-ye nohom, doure-ye avval-e motavasseṭe, sāl-e taḥṣīlī 1396–97 [9th grade, first cycle of secondary education, academic year 1396–97/2017–18].

Internet Sources

Amordadnews, Khordad 9, 1398 (May 30, 2019), https://amordadnews.com/11474. Accessed September 13, 2022.

Iranian Students' News Agency, Khordad 7,1392 (May 28, 2013), "ʿAnāvīn-e doure-hā va pāye-hā-ye taḥṣīlī-ye madāres taghīr kard" [The Titles of the Courses and the Educational Grade of the Schools Were Changed], https://www.isna.ir/news/92030704056. Accessed September 13, 2022.

Khamenei.IR, "A Society Devoid of the Spirit of Resistance on the Path of the Truth, Will be Ruined," December 16, 2019, http://english.khamenei.ir/news/7277. Accessed January 13, 2020.

14

Inscribing "God's Words" in Japan: Connecting the Past to the Present through the Translations of the Qur'an

Emi Goto

Introduction

Islam was introduced in Japan in the later decades of the nineteenth century, and the earliest conversions were thus reported in 1891. However, despite over 130 years of existence, the Muslim population in Japan is limited to less than 0.2% of the total population.[1] Nevertheless, there has always been a certain interest in Islam among intellectuals and the general public; thus, various publications on Islam have emerged.[2] The Qur'an, the sacred text of the Muslim religion has attracted the attention of the Japanese people who wish to understand Islam and Muslims. Since its original language, Arabic, was foreign to Japanese readers, translation played an important role in disseminating the Qur'an's contents. Over the last 100 years, at least eleven complete Japanese translations of the Qur'an have been published. This chapter elaborates on how the publications of the Japanese translations of the Qur'an introduced "God's words" to people in Japan through its various translations.

Several studies have discussed the translations of the Qur'an. Azuma[3] and Krämer[4] introduced and compared the major works and discussed the influences of terms and concepts that originated from other religions in Japan, especially Buddhism, whereas Haggag's linguistic studies[5] have compared expression styles used in the translations. Further, Morimoto[6] and Goto[7] traced the historical development of the Japanese translations of the Qur'an. From these studies, we understand that these translations have been a product of the translator's academic zeal, high value on the Muslim faith, and above all, their attempt to introduce the Qur'an, the most respected text for Muslims, to Japanese readers. Words, expressions, putting commas or periods, or any other literal expressions in the translational works were thus, the result of thoughtful choices of each translator.

The interpretive methods employed by the Japanese translators, however, need further examination. While the translations of the Qur'an by Muslims are usually referred to as *tafsīr* (Qur'anic commentary) and have been compared and analyzed within the Islamic tradition and variations, Japanese translations are more complex since some translations by non-Muslim scholars are also well-circulated and appreciated, especially among the non-Muslim readers. This chapter focuses on two major works published in the latter half of the twentieth century: *The Koran* by Toshihiko Izutsu (1914–93) and *The Holy Qur'an* by Ryoichi Mita (1892–1983), as one is a non-Muslim translation and the other a Muslim one. Izutsu's works, published in 1957–58 and revised in 1964, were known as the first complete translation of the Arabic sources, and has been gaining authority, among academics and general readers, as a reliable translation by a non-Muslim scholar. Muslim scholar Mita's pioneering translation, published in 1972, became the basis of the Japan Muslim Association (JMA)'s official Qur'an translation.

This study compares these works by asking the following questions: What were the goals of the translators; what were the ways and means employed by the translators to accomplish their ends; and what were the differences in the resulting translations? This chapter argues that these translations shared the common aim of connecting the past, or what the early Muslims had, to present readers. The difference rests, however, in their focus of the "past," and therefore, bringing forth two completely different inscriptions of "God's words" in the Japanese language.

Translations of the Qur'an: A Brief History

The Qur'an was originally written in Arabic, and many Muslims insist that translated works cannot be truly considered as the Qur'an.[8] Believers usually recite the verses only in Arabic, during their prayers and other rituals, regardless of their native and learned languages. Despite this emphasis on the use of Arabic as the language of religion, translations have ensured that non-Arabic Muslims understand the meaning of the Qur'an. Some verses were said to be translated into Persian and other languages as early as during the Prophet Muhammad's time.[9] The earliest existing translation of the Qur'an is a Persian translation of a *tafsīr* dating to the tenth century.[10] In the nineteenth century, Muslims of Central, South, and Southeast Asia, China, and Africa began to translate the Qur'an into their local languages.[11]

Translations were undertaken not only by the Muslim followers, but also by non-believers interacting with Muslims. A Latin translation by Robert of Ketton, an English Christian, in 1143, was the first such work in a European language. Several centuries later, Italian (1547), German (1616, translated from Italian), Dutch (1641, translated from German), French (1647, translated from Arabic), and English (1648, translated from French) translations emerged.[12] From the nineteenth century, Christian missionaries, Hindu and Jewish religious scholars, and Orientalists began translating the Qur'an into other languages.[13] While some non-Muslim translators openly expressed prejudice against Islam, many conducted their translations with academic sincerity while referring to classical Arabic literature, including mediaeval *tafsīr*s.[14]

In Japan, information on Islam was introduced, albeit fragmentarily, with a geography book published in 1713, authored by Hakuseki Arai (1657–1725).[15] More detailed information became available 150 years later during the Meiji era. The end of the nineteenth century saw the publishing of several biographies of the Prophet Muhammad, and the earliest wave of Islamic conversions in Japan. Shotaro Noda (1868–1904), a newspaper journalist who had visited the Ottoman Empire, was reported to be the first convert, in 1891.[16] Other Japanese people who worked among Muslims in Asian countries followed suit in the early 1900s.[17]

The first translation of the Qur'an, *Koran kyo* [*The Koran Scripture*], a two-volume-book, was compiled by Ken'ichi Sakamoto, a historian and writer, who also published biographies of the Prophet Mohammad in 1899 and 1923, and *World History* in 1903.[18] The translation was part of the *Sekai seiten zenshu* [*Complete Collection of Holy Scriptures of the World*]. The second work, *Sei koran kyo (Isuramu kyoten)* [*The Holy Koran: The Scripture of Islam*], was translated by Goro Takahashi (1856–1935) and Amado Ariga (1868–1946). Takahashi was a linguist and translator with experience in translating the Bible, and Ariga, whose birth name was Bunpachiro, was one of the earliest converts to Islam. Ariga held strong religious enthusiasm, with regards to the publication as part of his missionary activities. The main reference for these pioneering works was the Orientalist English translations.

The three translations that followed were works of non-Muslim scholars. These works shared common characteristics of deep and sincere commitment to the study of Islam, wealth of knowledge, and humility of their position and work. For example, Shumei Okawa (1886–1957), a scholar of Islam who published *Koran* [*The Koran*] in 1950, also authored an introductory book, *Kaikyo gairon* [*Introduction to Islam*], in 1942). Further, in the introduction to *The Koran*, Okawa elaborated on his longtime commitment to complete the translation of the Qur'an as follows:

> Needless to say, I have no qualifications as a translator [of the Qur'an] because I am not a believer of Islam, and my knowledge of Arabic is feeble. However, my deep interest in Islam was intrigued while I studied various religions at the university. I continued my study on Islam, though intermittently, and have now learned to feel the spirit of the Qur'an, for all that I may not be able to understand its whole and best teachings. While in Matsuzawa hospital [a mental

> healthcare hospital he was admitted to], I had enough time to open the Qur'an and to attempt translations and annotations for my own pleasure. I began my work in the early spring of 1946 and completed it by the early winter of 1948. Thus, it took two years to complete. I have referred to various translations in Chinese, English, French, and German. I will be satisfied if this translation and annotation becomes a cue to urge a perfect Japanese translation of the Qur'an in the future.[19]

Okawa associated translating the Qur'an with the religious, ethical, and social lives of Muslims; thus, he believed that only "faithful believers in Islam who have a thorough knowledge of Arabic and are well versed in Japanese" may be able to work on it.[20] Despite this belief, Okawa's zest to study Islam led him to accomplish a difficult and complicated task.

A similar humble tone towards translating the Qur'an was found in the writings of Toshihiko Izutsu. In the postscript for the revised edition, he referred to the difficulty of using exegetical works written by Muslim scholars:

> Since every word in the Qur'an came from Allah himself, it was a sacred obligation for believers to seek His Will by discovering the exact meanings of the words. Scholars staked their lives for their interpretations [. . .]. Ironically, however, the result of seeking only the genuine meaning brought about numerous interpretations [. . .]. Most words have been interpreted differently [among the scholars], and sometimes in contradicting ways. It is usual for one term to be interpreted with five or six different meanings. Translation may change with the choice of reference by a translator, as it is very difficult to decide which is the correct meaning. Therefore, the impact of the translator's personal subjective sense of value is inevitable in translational work.[21]

According to Izutsu, interpretations of the Qur'anic passages thus varied, even among Muslim scholars. As a translator himself, it was inevitable that he would have to choose one of the meanings that had been presented while translating each passage.

After Izutsu's translation, *Koran* [*The Koran*] (1970) was edited by Katsuji Fujimoto (1921–2000), who specialized in Islamic history. It was translated by Kosai Ban (1918–2012), an Arabic philologist, and Osamu Ikeda (1933–), a scholar of Arabic literature. The work was part of the *Sekai no meicho* [*Great Books of the World*] series, targeting Japanese youth, and thus uses simple, easy-to-understand expressions.[22]

A Muslim scholar's pioneering translation was *Nichia taiyaku chukai sei kuran* [*The Holy Qur'an: Bilingual Japanese-Arabic Version and Annotations*] compiled by Ryoichi Mita. He served as the second president of the JMA, and a revision of his work was later published as the JMA editions of the Qu'ran. Since Mita's work, translations by Muslim translators have flourished. *Sei kuruan* [*The Holy Qurʾan*] (1988) by Atsushi Kobayashi (1931–) was produced by a publisher affiliated with the Ahamadiyya Muslim Community, which has been active in Japan since 1935. *Nichia taiyaku Kuruan, yakukai to seito ju dokusho chukai* [*The Qurʾan: Bilingual Japanese-Arabic Version with Annotations on the Texts and the Ten Orthodox Recitations*] (2011, 2014) was edited by Ko Nakata (1960–), a Muslim scholar who has written books and articles on Islamic political thoughts and the *fiqh* (Islamic law) in Japanese. Two translators, Kaori Nakata (1961–2008), the first female translator for Japanese translation, and Kazuki Shimomura (1975–), were both Muslim scholars who specialized in Islamic studies. An article by Yohei Matsuyama (1984–), titled "Seito ju dokusho chukai" [Annotations on the Texts and the Ten Orthodox Recitations] was attached to the translation. Tatsuichi Sawada (1964–), translator of *Sei kuruan nihongo yaku* [*The Holy Qurʾan: Japanese Translation*] (2013), completed his religious studies in Iran. His work is known to be the Shiʿi translation, published in Japanese. Recently, two new editions by Muslim scholars were published: *Kuruan, yasashii wayaku* [*The Qurʾan in Easy Japanese*] (2019), translated by Makoto Mizutani (1948–), who edited the ten-volume series *Shinko sosho* [*On Islamic Faith*], and *Sei kuruan nichia taiyaku chukai* [*The Holy Qurʾan: Bilingual Japanese-Arabic Version with Annotations*] (2019) by Saeed Sato, which was printed in King Fahd Complex in Medina, Saudi Araiba.

Below is a list of these Japanese translations of the Qurʾan, with the basic information of the publications, whether it has a parallel Arabic text along with the translations, main references mentioned, and translator's commentaries in various forms.

In the following sections, a detailed analysis will be conducted on Izutsu's works (List: 4) and Mita's works (List: 6). This selection was made for three reasons: First, these are regarded as the pioneering works of the original Arabic text of the Qurʾan. Second, both have translators' commentaries in abundance, through which their intentions and efforts are expressed. Third, they make a good contrast, while Izutsu is a well-known non-Muslim scholar on Islam whose translations are circulated widely among non-Muslim majority readers, Mita is a Muslim scholar whose translations became the official text used by the Muslim association in Japan. The comparative analysis of these contemporary translations exhibits a few facets of the available knowledge of Islam in Japan.

Table 1: List of Japanese Translations of the Qur'an

	Name of Translator(s) Title of the Book Publication Data	Presence of Arabic Text	Main References Mentioned	Translators' commentaries
1	Ken'ichi Sakamoto *Koran kyo* [*The Koran Scripture*] 2 vols. Tokyo: Sekai Seiten Zenshu Kankokai, 1920. Vols. 14 and 15 of the *Complete Collection of Holy Scriptures of the World.*	None	Arabic Qur'an and English translations by George Sale (1734), John Meadows Rodwell (1861), and Edward Henry Palmer (1880).	Introductory notes for each chapter and translator's footnotes (located at the end of each volume), "Postscript."
2	Goro Takahashi and Amado Ariga *Sei koran kyo (Isuramu kyoten)* [*The Holy Koran: The Scripture of Islam*] Tokyo: Sei Korankyo Kankokai, 1938.	None	None (probably Rodwell's English translation)	None
3	Shumei Okawa *Koran* [*The Koran*] Tokyo: Iwasaki Shoten, 1950.	None	Arabic Qur'an with 'various translations' (Chinese, English, French, and German)	"Introduction," "On the Qur'an," introductory notes for each chapter and translator's footnotes.
4	Toshihiko Izutsu *Koran* [*The Koran*] 3 vols. Tokyo: Iwanami Shoten, 1957–58 (first edition), 1964 (revised edition).	None	Arabic Qur'an (Flügel edition), Commentary of al-Bayḍāwī.	"A prefatory note," "Commentary" at the end of each volume, For revised edition, "Introduction for the Revised Edition," and "Postscript for the Revised Edition of the Koran."
5	Katsuji Fujimoto (general editor), Kosai Ban and Osamu Ikeda (translators) *Koran* [*The Koran*] Tokyo: Chuokoronsha, 1970. Vol. 15 of the *Great Books of the World.*	None	Arabic Qur'an (standard Egyptian edition)	"Koran and Islamic Thought," translator's footnotes, "Chronicle."
6	Ryoichi Mita *Nichia taiyaku chukai sei kuran* [*The Holy Qur'an: Bilingual Japanese-Arabic Version and Annotations*] Tokyo: Nichiyaku Kuran Kankokai, 1972. Revised by the Japan	Inserted	Arabic Qur'an (Karachi edition [1972] and Cairo Azhar edition [1982]), lectures by Abdul Rashid al-Shad, and Arabic-English parallel texts	"A Prefatory Note," "On Translator's Note for the Holy Qur'an," introductory notes for each chapter and translator's footnotes.

	Muslim Association as *Nichia taiyaku chukai sei kuruan* [*The Holy Qur'an: Bilingual Japanese-Arabic Version and Annotations*] Tokyo: Japan Muslim Association, 1982, 1996 (revised edition).		by Mawlana Abdul Majid and A. Yusuf Ali.	For revised editions, "On the Revised Edition," "Procedure for the Revision."
7	Mohammad Owais Atsushi Kobayashi *Sei kuruan* [*The Holy Qur'an*] London and Nagoya: Islam International Publications, 1988.	Inserted	None	"Introduction," translator's footnotes.
8	Ko Nakata (translation supervisor), Kaori Nakata and Kazuki Shimomura (translators) *Yakukai kuruan* [*Qur'an: Translation and Annotations*] Tokyo: Reimei Isuramu Gakujutsu Bunka Shinkokai, 2011. Revised as Idem. *Nichia taiyaku kuruan* [*The Qur'an: Bilingual Japanese-Arabic Version with Annotations*] Tokyo: Sakuhinsha, 2014.	Inserted	Arabic Qur'an (King Fahd Complex edition and Cairo Azhar edition), *Tafsīr* of al-Jalālayn, classical sources, and modern *tafsīr*s	Preface, "Introduction," introductory notes for each chapter and translator's footnotes, Yohei Matsuyama "Seito ju dokusho chukai" [Annotations on the Texts and the Ten Orthodox Recitations].
9	Tatsuichi Sawada *Sei kuruan nihongo yaku* [*The Holy Qur'an: Japanese Translation*] Qum: The Center for Translation of the Qur'ān, 2013.	Inserted	Arabic Qur'an, Shi'i *tafsīr*s, and Ryoichi Mita's translation	"A Prefatory Note."
10	Makoto Mizutani (general translator) and Kyoichiro Sugimoto (supplement) *Kuruan: Yasashii wayaku* [*The Qur'an in Easy Japanese*] Tokyo: Kokusho Kankokai, 2019.	None	Arabic Qur'an, *Tafsīr* of al-Rāzī, and the *Arabic-English Dictionary of Qur'anic Usage* of Badawi and Abdel Haleem	Preface, compliments and recommendation, introductory notes for each chapter and translator's footnotes, "Appendix."
11	Saeed Sato *Sei kuruan* [*The Holy Qur'an*] Medina: King Fahd Complex for the Printing of the Holy Quran, 2019.	Inserted	Arabic Qur'an (King Fahd Complex edition), *Tafsīr* of Muyassar, classical sources, and modern *tafsīr*s	"On Translation of the Meaning of the Qur'an," "Translator's Notes," and Translator's footnotes.

Connecting the Past to the Present

Reviving the Moments of the Revelation: The Koran by Toshihiko Izutsu

Toshihiko Izutsu[23] was a leading Islamic studies scholar in post-war Japan. He began work on the translation of the Qurʾan around 1950, while in his thirties, upon the request of an editor of the Iwanami Book Library.[24] It took him eight years to complete the first edition of his translation, a small three-volume book published in 1957 (Volume 1) and 1958 (Volumes 2 and 3). A revised edition was published in 1964, and several reprints, as well as new editions, have been issued since.[25]

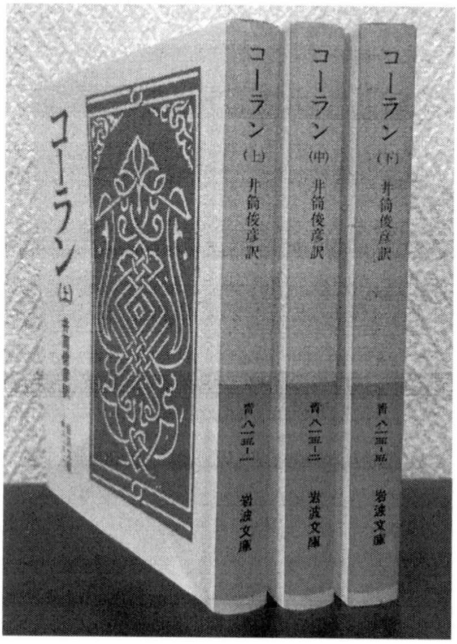

Figure 1: *The Koran* (1964) by Toshihiko Izutsu

In his first edition, Izutsu wrote that the Qurʾan is the *root* of the widespread Islamic religion, which "holds a few hundred million believers in the region from Western to Southeast Asia"[26]; the sacred text "commands all the respect of the believers in the most enthusiastic ways, prescribes various aspects of their lives, and becomes a living source for their ideas and emotions."[27] He also noted a surge of interest in the Qurʾan's contents among Japanese readers of various fields.[28] Thus, Izutsu embarked on his translation work to satisfy Japanese readers' curiosity.

In the prefatory note, Izutsu explained that he used Flügel's edition of the Qurʾan as his original text and referenced the medieval *tafsīr* of al-Bayḍāwī (d. 1286). According to Izutsu, Flügel's edition, published in 1841, was "the first academic text," and Flügel "was one of the greatest scholars of Europe during that time,"[29] whereas al-Bayḍāwī was a "scholar of the Qur'an during the thirteenth century and his interpretation has been paid utmost respect in Sunni Islam."[30] While placing value on al-Bayḍāwī's *tafsīr*, Izutsu noted that it had certain faults according to modern academic standards. Arabic philology had made significant progress since the nineteenth century. Thus, while working on his translation, Izutsu adopted some methodologies of Arabic studies in Europe.[31]

Izutsu's translation was peculiar in its colloquial expressions. While working on the translation, he considered the use of literary language or colloquial language and arrived at the conclusion that because the Qur'an is "a monologue of the God,"[32] speaking directly to Muhammad on various issues, colloquial expressions seem more appropriate. He thus elaborates:

> My ultimate wish, while translating this sacred text called *Koran* in a colloquial style, before anything else, was to present it as a living human document for the wider general readers [. . .]. Of course, the *Koran* is, for 300 million believers around the world, the absolute truth, words of God, and the most sacred text of all the scriptures. For us nonbelievers, this sacred text is a precious document of the ancient East. It may have the value of a unique human document that arouses interest and empathy in our hearts.[33]

While admitting that the Qur'an is a "sacred text" for Muslims, he called it, from the point of view of the "nonbelievers," a valuable "human document." He was presenting it, to the Japanese readers, as historical material.

The main reason for Izutsu to publish revised edition was to modify the style of language used. He realized that because of the plain colloquial language that he employed, "the distinguished peculiarity of the original text, the beauty and the religiosity, was altered." He then took on the challenge to "revive it [the language of the Qur'an] in Japanese by coming closer to the spirit of the original text and gaining a better understanding of it."[34]

From these words, one may infer that Izutsu saw the Qur'an as a kind of historical document, and he tried to work on a translation that revived the earliest days of Islam. Adopting a colloquial style was one such means to bring back the days and the experience of Muhammad and his contemporaries. The *Tafsīr* of al-Bayḍāwī, which Izutsu mainly referred to, was a "condensed and amended edition" of *tafsīr* written by al-Zamakhsharī (1075–1144), a scholar of Arabic linguistic sciences.[35] One may imagine that Izutsu chose al-Bayḍāwī's *tafsīr* along with the European Arabic scholarship because they had a philological approach to the Qur'an; these works aimed to seek the "original" meaning of the Qur'an as it had appeared during the time of revelation, by analyzing Arabic grammar, vocabulary, and rhetorical expressions. In sum, it can be said that Izutsu attempted translating the Qur'an to revive the moments of the revelation, into Japanese.[36]

Relating the Revelation to Contemporary Lives: The Holy Qur'an by Ryoichi Mita

Mita encountered Islam in China, where he had been living since 1916 and worked for the South Manchurian Railroad Company.[37] According to an account, during the first years of his stay the "cleanness in the lives of Chinese Muslims and their loyalty towards the religion" deeply impressed him.[38] He thus converted from Buddhism to Islam in 1941 at a mosque in Beijing, when he was 49 years old. In 1945, Mita returned to Japan. He joined the newly established JMA in 1952. During the 1950s and the 1960s, he engaged in Muslim missionary activities in cooperation with Tablighi Jamaat among the Japanese Muslim community. Mita became the second president of JMA in 1960 at the age of 68, retaining the position for only two years. He then set out to work on his translation of the Qur'an, which he completed in 1972 at the age of 80.

Mita's translation differed from Izutsu's in several ways. First, his version had Arabic-Japanese parallel texts,[39] where the original Arabic version was taken from the Karachi edition of the Qur'an. The Karachi edition "was popular among non-Arab people, especially in Eastern nations, since it had detailed explanatory notes for recitation."[40] The Arabic-Japanese parallel text style with detailed phonetic signs was intended for the ease of the practicing Muslims in Japan who were not entirely familiar with the Arabic language; thus with the help of the texts and signs, they could recite it more easily.

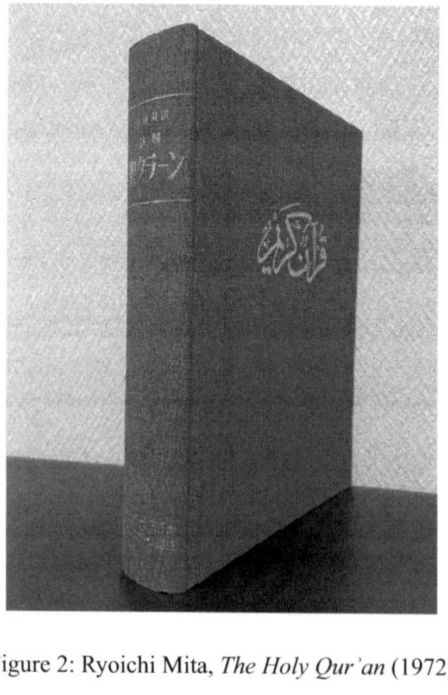

Figure 2: Ryoichi Mita, *The Holy Qur'an* (1972)

Second, Mita's version had translator commentaries in which the historical and local context of the revelations were explained. In its introductory note, Mita stressed that the Qur'an is "the eternal words of Allah" that "six hundred million devoted men and women of all ages recite every morning and night."[41] He admitted that it was impossible to translate "the natural flavor" of the original text, which was written in nuanced, beautiful, and powerful Arabic[42] and that understanding the messages is not easy, especially for novice Japanese readers. Under the title "To the readers who read the Qur'an for the first time," he wrote:

> [While reading the Qur'an you may experience] feelings of doubts about high-tension situations and local customs at the time of the revelation. Though it is important to consider these issues, we wish you to leave the things you find hard to understand and read the whole of the Qur'an, to understand its basic tenets and spirituality. If you are caught up by preconceptions, superficial matters, or some of the expressions, you might increase your misunderstanding.[43]

Mita asserted that it was impossible to understand the background information of the revelation of dogmas peculiar to the Islamic faith only through reading the Qur'an. Thus, he invited the readers to refer to the introductory notes for each chapter and footnotes for each page, "along with contemplation to deepen the understanding."[44]

Third, both versions relied on different references. Mita listed contemporary Muslim works instead of medieval *tafsīr* or works by European scholars. The sources comprised lectures from a Pakistani shaikh, Abdul Rashid al-Shad; two English translations by Muslim intellectuals from the Indian subcontinent, Mawlana Abdul Majid Daryabadi (1892–1977) and Abdullah Yusuf Ali (1872–1953); as well as "various translations in and outside of Japan."[45] Moreover, he consulted religious authorities in Mecca, where he had stayed between 1963 and 1965, and established an international revision committee who were tasked with checking the entire translation.[46]

Fourth, Mita's version had a different attitude toward the Qur'an compared to Izutsu's. Summarized at the beginning of the work, in a preface by the Team for Publishing Japanese Translation of the Qur'an, it reads:

> Qur'an is the absolute truth, containing the words of God, and the only sacred text for Islam. It does not favor one view or one race; it provides a straight path to be shared by all mankind of all ages, on every issue in day-to-day life, concretely, supportive, and lively, on the basis of the belief in one God [. . .].[47]

It declared not only that the Qur'an contains the words of God but also that it is directed toward believers of all ages.

Changes in the Interpretations

The differences between Mita's and Izutsu's translations of the Qur'an have certain results that need consideration. Examples are taken from the fourth chapter of the Qur'an, the Women's Chapter, in which various verses on male-female relationships in the family and society are detailed. While in Izutsu's work, the chapter's first sentence (*basmala*) immediately follows the chapter's title, Mita's version includes an introductory note which begins with the following words:

> This chapter is called the Women's Chapter because there are many revelations related to women. [. . .] Most were revealed after the battle of Uhud, in which 74 people were killed. These revelations were related to the issues faced by the community: the marriage of widows, divorce, inheritance, and protection of orphans. It should be noted that these revelations were originally meant to be temporary measures, however, became Islamic law governing the everyday lives of Muslims.[48]

In verse 4: 3, which approves of polygamous marriages (i.e., "If you fear that you shall not be able to deal justly with the orphans, marry women of your choice – two, or three, or four. But if you fear that you shall not be able to deal justly, then only one, or that which your right hands possess [. . .]"), Mita adds two footnotes, in the first clause ("If you [. . .]") and in the second clause ("marry women [. . .]"). The first note explains the terms and expressions of the sentence, saying, "That means, when women of solitude are under your protection, you may violate their profits and rights over their property and the marriage." The second note provides background information and commentary on the misunderstanding of this verse:

> After the battle of Uhd, in which 74 soldiers out of 700 were killed, giving aid to orphans and widows became the most difficult task for the society of the time. This was the situation in which the verse was revealed; it is regrettable that the two conditions mentioned in the verse that are attached to polygamy in Islam are now ignored. It is obvious from the expressions of this verse that the spirit of Islam is monogamy; the reality in Muslim societies is also generally monogamous.[49]

Compared to Izutsu's version, in which only some words are supplemented in parentheses (e.g., "If you think that you shall not be able to deal justly with the orphans [by yourself], marry women you like [. . .]"), Mita's version gives much more information; for Japanese readers who are not familiar with Islam's early history, Mita's notes try to establish the context of the revelation and provide hints on how it affects contemporary Muslim lives.

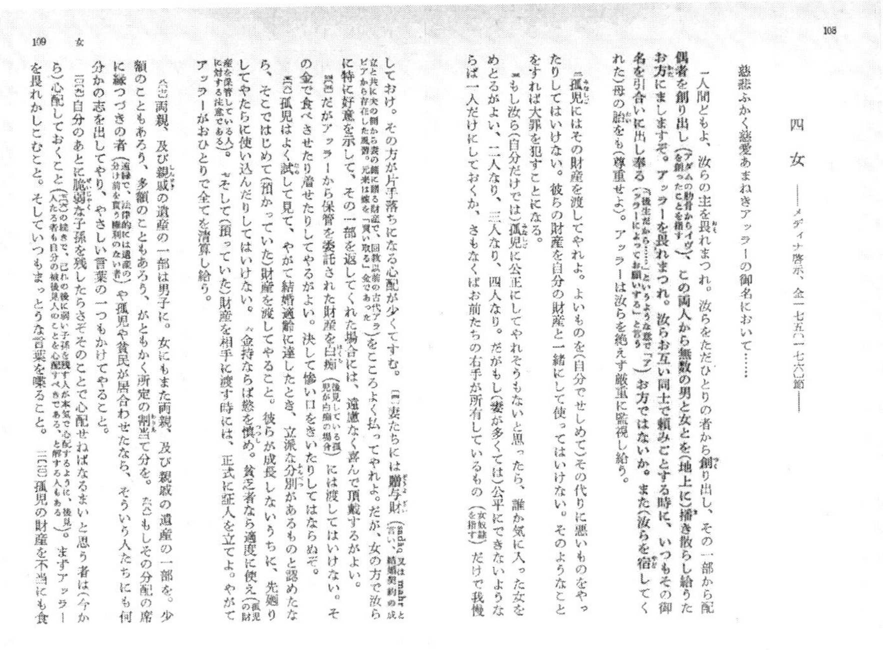

108

四　女　——メディナ啓示、全一七五〔一七六〕節——

慈悲ふかく慈愛あまねきアッラーの御名において……

一人間どもよ、汝らの主を畏れまつれ。汝らをただひとりの者から創り出し、その一部から配偶者を創り出し（アダムの肋骨からイヴを創ったことを指す）、この両人から無数の男と女とを（地上に）播き散らし給うたお方にましますぞ。アッラーを畏れまつれ。汝らお互い同士で頼みごとする時に、いつもその御名を引合いに出し奉る（「後生だから……」というような意で「アッラーによってお願いする」と言う）お方ではないか。また（汝らを宿してくれた）母の胎をも（尊重せよ）。アッラーは汝らを絶えず厳重に監視し給う。

二孤児にはその財産を渡してやれよ。よいものを（自分でせしめて）その代りに悪いものをやったりしてはいけない。彼らの財産を自分の財産と一緒にして使ってはいけない。そのようなことをすれば大罪を犯すことになる。

三もし汝ら（自分だけでは）孤児に公正にしてやれそうもないと思ったら、誰か気に入った女をめとるがよい、二人なり、三人なり、四人なり。だがもし（妻が多くては）公平にできないようならば一人だけにしておくか、さもなくばお前たちの右手が所有しているもの（女奴隷を指す）だけで我慢しておけ。その方が片手落ちになる心配が少くてすむ。四妻たちには贈与財（saduq 又は mahr 婚姻契約の成立と共に夫の側から妻の側に贈る財産で、回教以前の古代アラビアから存在した風習。元来は嫁を「買い取る」金であった）をこころよく払ってやれよ。だが、女の方で汝らに特に好意を示して、その一部を返してくれた場合には、遠慮なく喜んで頂戴するがよい。

五だがアッラーから保管を委託された財産を白痴（後見している孤児が白痴の場合）には渡してはいけない。その金で食べさせたり着せたりしてやるがよい。決して惨い口をきいたりしてはならぬぞ。

六孤児はよく試して見て、やがて結婚適齢に達したとき、立派な分別があるものと認めたなら、そこではじめて（預かっていた）財産を渡してやること。彼らが成長しないうちに、先廻りしてやたらに使い込んだりしてはいけない。金持ならば慾を慎め。貧乏者なら適度に使え（孤児の財産を保管している人に対する注意である）。そして（預っていた）財産を相手に渡す時には、正式に証人を立てよ。やがてアッラーがおひとりで全てを清算し給う。

八〔七〕両親、及び親戚の遺産の一部は男子に。女にもまた両親、及び親戚の遺産の一部を。少額のこともあろう、多額のこともあろう、がともかく所定の割当て分を。九〔八〕もしその分配の席に縁つづきの者（遠縁で、法律的には遺産の分け前を貰う権利のない者）や孤児や貧民が居合わせたなら、そういう人たちにも何分かの志を出してやり、やさしい言葉の一つもかけてやること。

一〇〔九〕自分のあとに脆弱な子孫を残したらさぞそのことで心配せねばなるまいと思う者は（今から）心配しておくこと（一〇〔八〕の続きで、己れの後に弱い子孫を残す人が本気で心配するように、後見人たる者も自分の被後見人のことを心配すべきである、と解する人もある）。まずアッラーを畏れかしこむこと。そしていつもまっとうな言葉を喋ること。一一〔一〇〕孤児の財産を不当にも食

109　女

Figure 3: The First Pages of Chapter 4 in Izutsu's Version

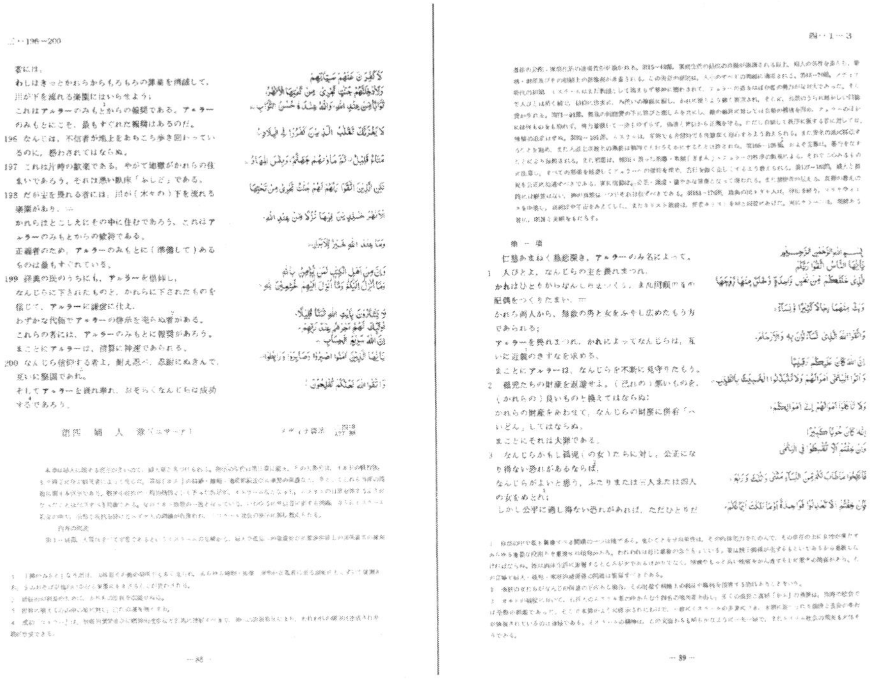

Figure 4: The First Pages of Chapter 4 in Mita's Version

Another example is the translation of verse 4: 34, which (purposely retains some Arabic terms) reads, "Men are *qawwāmūn* over women, with what Allah *faḍḍala* to one of them over the other, and with what they spend from their property." The meanings and implications of this verse are understood differently because of the terms *qawwām* (singular of *qawwāmūn*) and *faḍḍala*. *Qawwām* may mean "manager," "director," "superintendent," "caretaker," "keeper," "custodian," or "guardian," and *faḍḍala* can mean third person singular past of "to prefer," "to like better," or "to give preference over, before, or above."[50] Selecting one over another can dramatically change the sentence's overall meaning, and in the modern period, this has given rise to controversy among Muslims about the significance of the phrase.[51]

The Japanese translations by Izutsu and Mita are as follows:

> ***The Koran*** **by Izutsu (1964)**
>
> Men should be above women because Allah made them superior (over women) from the beginning and because they spend their money (for the necessities of life).[52]
>
> アッラーはもともと男と(女)との間には優劣をおつけになったのだし、また(生活に必要な)金は男が出すのだから、この点で男の方が女の上に立つべきもの。
>
> ***The Holy Qur'an*** **by Mita (1972)**
>
> Men are protectors of women (or the heads of families) because Allah gave them more strength than the other and because they spend their properties (to maintain).[53]
>
> 男は女の擁護者(家長)である。それはアルラーが、一を他よりも強くなされ、かれらが己れの資財から(扶養するため)、費やすゆえである。

As noted above, Izutsu's translation was made in reference to a *tafsīr* of the thirteenth-century scholar al-Bayḍāwī, according to which men's rule over women was justified by what was naturally bestowed on them by God and by the sums they spent on dowries or marriage maintenance.[54] This sense of male superiority over women was shared by most medieval *tafsīr*s.[55] Izutsu's translation reproduced this in modern Japanese.

For the translation of this verse, Mita most probably referred to an English translation by Abdullah Yusuf Ali, first published in Lahore in the 1930s. Ali's translation aimed to reflect the thoughts and experiences of his contemporaries.[56] In this work, the first sentence of verse 4: 34 reads, "Men are the protectors and maintainers of women, because Allah has given the one more (strength) than the other, and because they support them from their means."[57] This modern translation has attempted to remove the expressions of male superiority over women.[58] It should be pointed out that though Mita referred to Abdul Majid's work while translating the text and consulted Yusuf Ali's work for commentary, as he indicated in the introductory note, he did not follow this general rule when he translated this verse. Abdul Majid's translation reads, "Men are overseers over women, by reason of that wherewith Allah has made one of them excel over another, and by reason of what they spend of their riches"[59]; the nuance is closer to the medieval interpretations that suggested male superiority over women. The fact that Mita's translation shared almost the same wording as Ali's and not that of Abdul Majid suggests that Mita, who referred to both, deliberately dismissed Abdul Majid's interpretation and followed Ali's while compiling his Japanese version of the Qur'an. Therefore, it expressed a completely different understanding of the male-female relationship in the Qur'an from that of preceding translations by Izutsu; at the same time, it may better reflect the growing sense of gender justice that was observed in Japanese society in the 1960s and the early 1970s.[60]

Mita's Successors: Japan Muslim Association

If we broaden our analysis to the later versions of Mita's translation, we may find more forces of change in the interpretations. Mita published *The Holy Qur'an: Japanese Version and Annotations* with the JMA in 1973, following his original edition. As the title suggests, it was a Japanese version without the original Arabic text. While editing this version, Mita made minor revisions to Japanese expressions.[61] In 1982, the JMA published a new edition of Mita's translation with a title: *Nichia taiyaku chukai sei kuruan* [*The Holy Qur'an: Bilingual Japanese-Arabic Version and Annotations*]. The Arabic text was replaced with text from the Cairo edition of the Qur'an as certain passages were found to be incomplete in the earlier version which used Karachi edition. The translation was also reviewed by Mita, the original translator. The re-translation was done by a team composed of the members of the JMA, "who studied Arabic and Islamic sciences in Egypt and Saudi Arabia," and other Japanese scholars. The fluency of Japanese was stressed upon in this revision. The team composed Japanese sentences that both younger and older people could easily read, to promote a better understanding of Islam in Japan.[62]

With occasional revisions, the JMA version has been updated to reflect changes in the interpretive currents, which makes it stand apart from Izutsu's work. An example is found in the verse 4: 1. The first two sentences of Izutsu's translation and that of the latest version of the JMA are as follows:

The Koran **by Izutsu (1964)**

O mankind, fear thy Lord. He is the one who created thee from a single person, created the mate from a part of the person (indicating the creation of Eve from Adam's limb), from them twain scattered the countless men and women (on the land).[63]

人間どもよ、汝らの主を畏れまつれ。汝らをただひとりの者から創り出し、その一部から配偶者を創り出し（アダムの肋骨からイヴを創ったことを指す）、この両人から無数の男と女とを（地上に）撒き散らし給うたお方にましますぞ。

The Holy Qur'an **by JMA (revised version of 1996)**

O mankind, fear your Lord. He created you from a single soul, also created a mate from it, and from them twain propagated the countless men and women.[64]

人びとよ、あなたがたの主を畏れなさい。かれはひとつの魂からあなたがたを創り、またその魂から配偶者を創り、両人から、無数の男と女を増やし広められた方であられる。

The first half of the second sentence, where we find the difference, may be translated from the original Arabic text while purposely retaining some Arabic terms as follows: "[W]ho created you from a single *nafs*, also created a mate from it." Izutsu chose "a single person" for the translation of *nafs and* composed his translation as "one who created thee from a single person, created the mate from a part of the person." He added a supplemented sentence in parentheses following al-Bayḍāwī and other medieval scholars' interpretations that God created Adam and used his rib to create Eve.[65]

In the original JMA version published in 1982, the translation was rather similar to Izutsu's, suggesting that Adam was created first, and a mate was created using a part of him.

The Holy Qur'an **by JMA (first edition of 1982)**

O mankind, fear your Lord. He created you from a single person (Adam), also created a mate from (a part of) the person, and from them twain propagated the countless men and women.[66]

人びとよ、あなたがたの主を畏れなさい。かれは一人の者（アーダム）からあなたがたを創り、またその者（の一部）から配偶者を創り、両人から、無数の男と女を増やし広められた方であられる。

The second sentence has been revised in the JMA's 1996 edition. The equivalent term for Arabic *nafs* became the "soul"; thus the nuance of the sentence was changed to be more gender neutral: "He created you from a single soul, also created a mate from it." It may be suggested that this revision was backed by the interpretations that emphasized gender equality during the latter half of the twentieth century, contending that men and women were created from one soul, one origin, and thus being equal and complementary.[67]

From this last example, we may say that, while Izutsu's work has retained its form since 1964, Mita's translation, which was succeeded by that of the JMA members' editions, had its contents revised even after his demise.

Conclusion

Izutsu positioned the Qur᾿an as a historical document and hoped to describe the moment of revelation through his Japanese translation. In other words, his goal was to revive the experiences of the Arab Prophet in the seventh century using contemporary Japanese language. He referred to achievements that shared the same goal, that of a medieval *tafsīr* and the European scholarship of Arabic studies. For Mita, the Qur᾿an was "the eternal words of Allah" that is directed to humankind of all ages, and on every issue in day-to-day life. He related it to his own life and that of his fellow Muslims. He connected the seventh-century revelation that was passed down from the Arab Prophet to the lives and experiences of twentieth-century Japanese Muslims by providing contextual information on the revelation, by adopting contemporary references and choosing interpretations that may reflect the values of the day. It was succeeded by the JMA versions and developed even after his demise.[68]

These works shared the common aim of connecting the past, or the experiences of the early Muslims, to the present readers. However, the difference was in their focus of the "past"; while Izutsu tried to revive the moments of the revelation through his translation, Mita and the succeeding JMA members made efforts to relate the contents and meanings of the revelation to the lives of contemporary readers. As a result, it brought forth two completely different inscriptions of the "God's words" in the Japanese language.

Since the publication of Mita's work, various translations by Japanese Muslims have appeared. Inserting Arabic text, using modern and contemporary references, and adding commentaries have become standard features of these later translations of the Qur᾿an. The variation of references, explanations in the translators' notes, and the resulting translations suggest a highly complex path to connect the past to the present.

Notes

* This research was supported by the funding from the Institute for Advanced Studies on Asia, University of Tokyo (2019–2020).

1 For the estimation of Muslim population in Japan, see Hirofumi Tanada, "Sekai to nihon no musurimu jinko 2018" [Estimate of Muslim Population in the World and Japan, 2018], *Waseda Journal of Human Sciences* 32.2 (2019): 253–62.

2 Titles may be retrieved via search engines such as "Bibliographical Database of Islamic and Middle East Studies in Japan 1868–2015" (http://search.tbias.jp/en/books) and "Bibliographical Database of Middle East Studies in Japan" (http://www.james1985.org/database/database-e.html).

3 Ryusin Azuma, *Nihon no bukkyo to isuramu* [*Japanese Buddhism and Islam*] (Tokyo: Shunjusha, 2002).

4 Hans Martin Krämer, "Pan-Asianism's Religious Undercurrents: The Reception of Islam and Translation of the Qur'ān in Twentieth-Century Japan," *The Journal of Asian Studies* 73.3 (2014): 619–40.

5 Rana Haggag, "Koe no bunka to honyaku riron: Tekusuto to shite no kuruan to sono honyaku wo megutte" [Culture of Voices and Translation Theory: On the Qur'an as a Text, and Its Translation], PhD thesis, Hitotsubashi University, 2015; ibid, "Translating 'Islam' into Japanese: Concerning the Japanese Version of the Qur'an and Its Translation Strategy," *Hitotsubashi Journal of Arts and Sciences* 60 (2019): 39–49.

6 Takeo Morimoto, "Sei kuran nichiyaku no rekishi" [A History of the Japanese Translations of the Holy Qur'an], *Assalām* 6 (1976): 18–23, 7 (1977): 20–5, 9 (1977): 50–7, 10 (1978): 54–6.

7 Emi Goto, "Nihon ni okeru kuruan honyaku no tenkai" [Development of the Translation of the Qur'an in Japan], *Kuruan nyumon* [*Introduction to the Qur'an*] (Tokyo: Sakuhinsha, 2018), 125–73.

8 On the Muslim discourse on translation, see Abdullah Saeed, *The Qur'an: An Introduction* (London and New York: Routledge, 2008), 126–9.

9 On the translation of the Qur'an in general, I refer to Ekmeleddin İhsanoğlu, ed., *World Bibliography of Translations of the Meanings of the Holy Qur'an: Printed Translations, 1515–1980* (Istanbul: Research Centre for Islamic History, Art and Culture, 1986); Craig Alan Volker, "On Translating the Holy Qur'ān," *The Annals of Gifu Shotoku Gakuen University* 44 (2005): 19–25; Hartmut Bobzin, "Translations of the Qur'ān," in *Encyclopaedia of the Qur'ān* (Leiden: Brill, 2006), vol. 5, 340–58; Saeed, *The Qur'an: An Introduction*; and Bruce B. Lawrence, *The Koran in English* (Princeton and Oxford: Princeton University Press, 2017).

10 Bobzin, "Translations," 341.

11 This is said to have been done as a reaction to the influx of Western (Christian) ideas and cultures, which may have threatened the faith of Muslims who were not familiar with the Arabic language (Bobzin, "Translations," 341; Volker, "On Translating," 21).

12 İhsanoğlu, *World Bibliography*, xxxv–vi.

13 Volker, "On Translating," 22.

14 Consulting medieval *tafsīr* was a customary practice among translators of the Qur'an since the first translation into Latin by Robert of Ketton. See for example, Lawrence, *The Koran in English*.

15 His book *Sairan-igen* was completed in 1713 and supplemented in 1725. On the Japanese encounter to Islam and its knowledge, see Hideaki Sugita, *Nihon jin no chuto hakken: Gyakuenkinho no naka no hikaku bunkashi* [*The Japanese Discovery of the Middle East: A Comparative Cultural History in Mutual Perspectives*] (Tokyo: University of Tokyo Press, 1995).

16 Nobuo Misawa and Göknur Akçadağ, "The First Japanese Muslim, Shotaro NODA (1868–1904)," *Annals of Japan Association for Middle East Studies* 23.1 (2007): 85–109.

17 Sugita, *The Japanese Discovery*, 152–3.

18 On the history of Qur'anic translations in Japan, see Morimoto, "A History of the Japanese Translations"; Krämer, "Pan-Asianism's Religious Undercurrents"; and Goto, "Development of the Translation."

19 Shumei Okawa, transl., *Koran* [*The Koran*] (Tokyo: Iwasaki Shoten, 1950), 4.

20 Ibid., 3.
21 Toshihiko Izutsu, transl., *Koran* [*The Koran*], revised ed. (Tokyo: Iwanami Shoten, 1964), vol. 3, 338–9.
22 Morimoto, "A History of the Japanese Translations," *Assalām*, 9: 51–2.
23 Specializing in philosophy, linguistics, and Islamic studies, Izutsu was a former professor at Keio University. His main works in Japanese language include *Arabia shiso-shi: Kaikyo shingaku to kaikyo tetsugaku* [*History of Arabian Thoughts: Islamic Theology and Islamic Philosophy*] (Tokyo: Hakubunkan, 1941); *Arabia go nyumon* [*Introduction to Arabic Language*] (Tokyo: Keio Shuppansha, 1950); *Mahometto* [*Mahommed*] (Tokyo: Kobundo, 1952); *Koran* [*The Koran*] (Tokyo: Iwanami Shoten, 1957–58, 64), and in English, *The Structure of the Ethical Terms in the Koran: A Study in Semantics* (Tokyo: Keio Institute of Philological Studies, 1959); *God and Man in the Koran: Semantics of the Koranic Weltanschauung* (Tokyo: Keio Institute of Philological Studies, 1964); and *The Concept of Belief in Islamic Theology: A Semantic Analysis of Īmān and Islām* (Tokyo: Keio Institute of Philological Studies, 1965).
24 The library widely circulated the paperback series published by Iwanami Shoten, a major publishing house in Japan.
25 The latest of the Iwanami Book Library at the time of writing is the 74th printing of vol. 1 (2020) and the 62nd and 61st printings of volumes 2 and 3, respectively (2019). A large-print version was published in 2004 by the same library. Chuokoronsha, another major publishing house, published a one-volume edition as part of a collection of Izutsu's writings (Toshihiko Izutsu, transl., *Koran* [*The Koran*], Izutsu Toshihiko chosakushu [Collection of Works by Toshihiko Izutsu], vol. 7 (Tokyo: Chuokoronsha, 1992)). His complete works have also been published by Keio University Press since 2013.
26 Toshihiko Izutsu, transl., *Koran* [*The Koran*] (Tokyo: Iwanami Shoten, 1957), vol. 1, 305.
27 Ibid., 305.
28 Ibid., 305.
29 Ibid., 3.
30 Ibid., 4.
31 Ibid., 4.
32 Ibid., 314.
33 Izutsu, *The Koran* (1958), vol. 3, 345.
34 Izutsu, *The Koran*, revised ed., (1964), vol. 3, 337.
35 Cf. J. Robson, "al-Bayḍāwī," in *The Encyclopaedia of Islam, New Edition*, ed. by H. A. R. Gibb et al. (Leiden: Brill, 1960–2009), vol. 1, 1129. Izutsu referred to the connection between al-Zamakhsharī and al Bayḍāwī in the prefatory note (Izutsu, *The Koran* [1957], vol. 1, 4).
36 In a supplement to the Chuokoronsha edition of Izutsu's *The Koran*, Kojiro Nakamura, a scholar of Islamic studies, pointed out that "the aim of Izutsu was to revive Muhammad as a human with a heartbeat, not as [an image] understood through the tradition and dogma of Islam. [For Izutsu,] the Qur'an was a record, and its translation should be done in the ways and styles necessitated for the purpose." Thus, philological approaches and the colloquial style in expressions were naturally selected by Izutsu (Kojiro Nakamura, "Koran to honyaku" [Koran and Its Translation], in *Furoku: Izutsu Toshihiko chosakushu*, 7, *Koran* [*Appendix of Collection of Works by Toshihiko Izutsu, The Koran*] (Tokyo: Chuokoronsha, 1992), vol. 7, 4.
37 On Mita's biography, with reference to Morimoto, "A History of the Japanese Translations," *Assalām* 9: 52–57 and Hiroshi Suzuki (Ahmad), " 'Nihon musurimu kyokai' rekidai kaicho retsuden" [The Biographies of the Presidents of "Japan Muslim Association"], in *Isuramu to nihonjin* [*Islam and Japanese*], ed. by Kasuke Iimori (Tokyo: Kokusho Kankokai, 2011), 159–64.
38 Morimoto, "A History of the Japanese Translations," *Assalām* 9: 53.
39 Although previous complete translations had no Arabic texts, one partial translation in an academic journal, *Kaikyoken* [*Muslim World*], published between 1938 and 1944, had Arabic texts along with Japanese translations.

40 Ryoichi Mita, transl., *Nichia taiyaku chukai sei kuran* [*The Holy Qur'an: Bilingual Japanese-Arabic Version and Annotations*] (Tokyo: Nichiyaku Kuran Kankokai, 1972), vii.
41 Ibid., iii.
42 Ibid., vi.
43 Ibid., iv.
44 Ibid., iv.
45 Ibid., vi.
46 Ibid., vi.
47 Ibid., ii.
48 Ibid., 88.
49 Ibid., 89.
50 Hans Wehr, *A Dictionary of Modern Written Arabic*, ed. by J. Milton Cowan (Beirut: Librairie du Liban, 1980).
51 Regarding the controversy of the verse's interpretation, see, for example, Saeed, *The Qur'an: An Introduction*, 129–33; Ayesha S. Chaudhry, *Domestic Violence and the Islamic Tradition* (Oxford: Oxford University Press, 2013), 40 ff.; Lawrence, *The Koran in English,* 100–3; Emi Goto, "Kuruan to jenda: Danjo no arikata to yakuwari wo chushin ni" [Qur'an and Gender: On the Male-Female Relationship], in *Kuruan nyumon* [*Introduction to the Qur'an*], ed. by Yohei Matsuyama (Tokyo: Sakuhinsha, 2018), 389–413; and Asma Afsaruddin, "Women and the Qur'an," in *The Oxford Handbook of Qur'anic Studies*, ed. by Mustafa Shah and Muhammad Abdel Haleem (Oxford: Oxford University Press, 2020), 527–37.
52 Izutsu, *The Koran* (1964), vol. 1, 115.
53 Mita, *The Holy Qur'an* (1972), 95–6.
54 Nāṣir al-Dīn Abū l-Khayr ʿAbd Allāh ibn ʿUmar al-Bayḍāwī, *Anwār al-tanzīl wa-asrār al-ta'wīl* (Cairo: Muṣṭafā al-Bābī al-Ḥalabī wa-awlāduhu bi-Miṣr, 1968), vol. 1, 217–8.
55 See the references in the note 51.
56 Abdullah Yusuf Ali, *The Holy Qur'ān: English Translation with Original Arabic Text* (New Delhi: Kitab Bhavan, 2000), vi.
57 Ibid., 92.
58 Lawrence called Yousef Ali's translation of this verse the "high-water mark for an inclusive reading" (Lawrence, *The Koran in English,* 100–1).
59 Mawlana Abd al-Majid Daryabadi, *Translation and Commentary of the Holy Qur'an* (Lucknow: Academy of Islamic Research and Publications, 2007), vol. 1, 325.
60 For the feminist movements against the gender discriminations in Japan during the period, see Vera Mackie, *Feminism in Modern Japan: Citizenship, Embodiment and Sexuality* (Cambridge: Cambridge University Press, 2003) and Barbara Molony, Janet Theiss, and Hyaeweol Choi, *Gender in Modern East Asia: China, Korea, Japan, An Integrated History* (Boulder: Westview Press, 2016).
61 Mita reviewed, for example, some of the supplementary explanations he added in the main text in parentheses, removing the symbols of parentheses, or removing the whole supplementations.
62 Japan Muslim Association, ed., *Nichia taiyaku chukai sei kuruan* [*The Holy Qur'an: Bilingual Japanese Arabic Version and Annotations*] (Tokyo: Japan Muslim Association, 1982), iii.
63 Izutsu, *The Koran* (1964), vol. 1, 108.
64 Japan Muslim Association, ed., *Nichia taiyaku chukai sei kuruan* [*The Holy Qur'an: Bilingual Japanese Arabic Version and Annotations*] (Tokyo: Japan Muslim Association, 1996), 92.
65 On the traditional and the contemporary interpretations of verse 4: 1, see Reiko Okawa, "Interpretation of *Ḥawwā'* (Eve) in Contemporary Egypt: *Tafsīr* (Interpretation of the Qur'ān) of Muḥammad Mitwallī al-Shaʿrāwī and Muḥammad Sayyid Ṭanṭāwī," in *Orient* 56 (2021): 5–24.
66 JMA, *The Holy Qur'an* (1982), 92.
67 Sayyid Qutb, an Egyptian intellectual who wrote a modern commentary, was one of the Muslim thinkers that introduced the idea. See Sayyid Quṭb, *Fī ẓilāl al-Qur'ān* (Cairo: Dār al-shurūq,

1972), vol. 1, 574; Sayyid Quṭb, *In the Shade of the Qur'ān*, transl. and ed. by Adil Salahi and Ashur Shamis, vol. 3 (Markfield: Islamic Foundation, 2001), 24–5.

68 The differences of goals and methodologies between Izutsu and Mita bear a parallel to the difference between the analytical concepts of "textualism" and "contextualism" proposed by Abdullah Saeed for Muslim interpretation of the Qur'an. While the textualists scholars draw on linguistic analysis and "believe that the language of the Qur'an has concrete, unchanging references, and therefore the meaning that a Qur'anic verse had upon its revelation still holds for the contemporary context," the contextualist scholars employ social or historical analysis and perceive that a meaning of particular Qur'anic verse evolves, and "is dependent upon the socio-historical, cultural and linguistic contexts of the text" (Saeed, *The Qur'an: An Introduction*, 220–1).

Bibliography

Afsaruddin, Asma. "Women and the Qur'an." In *The Oxford Handbook of Qur'anic Studies*. Ed. by Mustafa Shah and Muhammad Abdel Haleem. Oxford: Oxford University Press, 2020, 527–37.

Ali, Abdullah Yusuf. *The Holy Qur'ān: English Translation with Original Arabic Text*. New Delhi: Kitab Bhavan, 2000 (first edition 1934).

Azuma, Ryusin. *Nihon no bukkyo to isuramu* [*Japanese Buddhism and Islam*]. Tokyo: Shunjusha, 2002.

Al-Bayḍāwī, Nāṣir al-Dīn Abū l-Khayr ʿAbd Allāh ibn ʿUmar. *Anwār al-tanzīl wa-asrār al-taʾwīl*. 2 vols. Cairo: Muṣṭafā al-Bābī al-Ḥalabī wa-awlāduhu bi-Miṣr, 1968.

Bobzin, Hartmut. "Translations of the Qur'an." In *Encyclopaedia of the Qur'ān*. Ed. by Jane Dammen McAuliffe. 6 vols. Leiden: Brill, 2006, vol. 5, 340–58.

Chaudhry, Ayesha S. *Domestic Violence and the Islamic Tradition*. Oxford: Oxford University Press, 2013.

Daryabadi, Mawlana Abd al-Majid. *Translation and Commentary of the Holy Qur'an*. 4 vols. Lucknow: Academy of Islamic Research and Publications, 2007.

Fujimoto, Katsuji, general ed., Kosai Ban and Osamu Ikeda, transl. *Koran* [*The Koran*]. Great Books of the World Series, vol. 15. Tokyo: Chuokoronsha, 1970.

Goto, Emi. "Nihon ni okeru kuruan honyaku no tenkai" [Development of the Translation of the Qur'an in Japan]. In *Kuruan nyumon* [*Introduction to the Qur'an*]. Ed. by Yohei Matsuyama. Tokyo: Sakuhinsha, 2018, 125–73.

Goto, Emi. "Kuruan to jenda: Danjo no arikata to yakuwari wo chushin ni" [Qur'an and Gender: On the Male-Female Relationship]. In *Kuruan nyumon* [*Introduction to the Qur'an*]. Ed. by Yohei Matsuyama. Tokyo: Sakuhinsha, 2018, 389–413.

Haggag, Rana. "Koe no bunka to honyaku riron: Tekusuto toshite no kuruan to sono honyaku wo megutte" [Culture of Voices and Translation Theory: On the Qur'an as a Text, and Its Translation]. PhD thesis, Hitotsubashi University, 2015.

Haggag, Rana. "Translating 'Islam' into Japanese: Concerning the Japanese Version of the Qurʾan and Its Translation Strategy." *Hitotsubashi Journal of Arts and Sciences* 60 (2019): 39–49.

İhsanoğlu, Ekmeleddin, ed. *World Bibliography of Translations of the Meanings of the Holy Qurʾan: Printed Translations, 1515–1980*. Prepared by İsmet Binark and Halit Eren. Istanbul: Research Centre for Islamic History, Art and Culture, 1986.

Izutsu, Toshihiko, transl. *Koran* [*The Koran*]. 3 vols. Tokyo: Iwanami Shoten, 1957–58.

Izutsu, Toshihiko. *Koran* [*The Koran*]. Revised ed. 3 vols. Tokyo: Iwanami Shoten, 1964.

Izutsu, Toshihiko. *Koran* [*The Koran*]. Izutsu Toshihiko Chosakushu [Collection of Works by Toshihiko Izutsu], vol. 7. Tokyo: Chuokoronsha, 1992.

Japan Muslim Association, ed. *Nichia taiyaku chukai sei kuruan* [*The Holy Qurʾan: Bilingual Japanese-Arabic Version and Annotations*]. Tokyo: Japan Muslim Association, 1982.

Japan Muslim Association. *Nichia taiyaku chukai sei kuruan* [*The Holy Qurʾan: Bilingual Japanese-Arabic Version and Annotations*]. Tokyo: Japan Muslim Association, 1996 (revised ed.).

Kobayashi, Mohammad Owais Atsushi, transl. *Sei kuruan* [*The Holy Qurʾān*]. London and Nagoya: Islam International Publications, 1988.

Krämer, Hans Martin. "Pan-Asianism's Religious Undercurrents: The Reception of Islam and Translation of the Qur'ān in Twentieth-Century Japan." *The Journal of Asian Studies* 73.3 (2014): 619–40.

Lawrence, Bruce B. *The Koran in English: A Biography*. Princeton and Oxford: Princeton University Press, 2017.

Mackie, Vera. *Feminism in Modern Japan: Citizenship, Embodiment and Sexuality*. Cambridge: Cambridge University Press, 2003.

Misawa, Nobuo and Göknur Akçadağ. "The First Japanese Muslim, Shotaro NODA (1868–1904)." *Annals of Japan Association for Middle East Studies* 23.1 (2007): 85–109.

Mita, Ryoichi, transl. *Nichia taiyaku chukai sei kuran* [*The Holy Qurʾan: Bilingual Japanese-Arabic Version and Annotations*]. Tokyo: Nichiyaku Kuran Kankokai, 1972.

Mita, Ryoichi. *Nichiyaku chukai sei kuran* [*The Holy Qurʾan: Japanese Version and Annotations*]. Tokyo: Nichiyaku Kuran Kankokai, 1973.

Mizutani, Makoto, transl., and Kyoichiro Sugimoto, supplement. *Kuruan, yasashii wayaku* [*The Qurʾan in Easy Japanese*]. Tokyo: Kokusho Kankokai, 2019.

Molony, Barbara, Janet Theiss, and Hyaeweol Choi. *Gender in Modern East Asia: China, Korea, Japan, An Integrated History*. Boulder: Westview Press, 2016.

Morimoto, Takeo. "Sei kuran nichiyaku no rekishi" [A History of the Japanese Translations of the Holy Qurʾan]. *Assalām* 6 (1976): 18–23, 7 (1977): 20–5, 9 (1977): 50–7, 10 (1978): 54–6.

Nakamura, Kojiro. "Koran to honyaku" [Koran and Its Translation]. In *Furoku: Izutsu Toshihiko chosakushu*, 7, *Koran* [*Appendix of Collection of Works by Toshihiko Izutsu,* Vol. 7, *Koran*]. Tokyo: Chuokoronsha, 1992, 1–5.

Nakata, Ko, transl. supervisor, Kaori Nakata and Kazuki Shimomura, transl., Yohei Matsuyama, annotations on the ten orthodox recitations. *Yakukai kuruan, Kuruan seito ju dokusho no imi to kino* [*The Qur'an: Translation and Annotations, The Meanings and Functions of Ten Orthodox Recitations*]. Tokyo: Reimei Isuramu Gakujutsu Bunka Shinkokai, 2011.

Nakata, Ko, transl. supervisor, Kaori Nakata and Kazuki Shimomura, transl., Yohei Matsuyama, annotations on the ten orthodox recitations. *Nichia taiyaku Kuruan, yakukai to seito ju dokusho chukai* [*The Qur'an: Bilingual Japanese-Arabic Version with Annotations on the Texts and the Ten Orthodox Recitations*], Tokyo: Sakuhinsha, 2014.

Okawa, Reiko. "Interpretation of *Ḥawwā'* (Eve) in Contemporary Egypt: *Tafsīr* (Interpretation of the Qur'ān) of Muḥammad Mitwallī al-Shaʿrāwī and Muḥammad Sayyid Ṭanṭāwī." *Orient* 56 (2021): 5–24.

Okawa, Shumei, transl. *Koran* [*The Koran*]. Tokyo: Iwasaki Shoten, 1950.

Quṭb, Sayyid. *Fī ẓilāl al-Qur'ān*. 6 vols. Cairo: Dār al-shurūq, 1972.

Quṭb, Sayyid. *In the Shade of the Qur'ān.* Transl. and ed. by Adil Salahi and Ashur Shamis. 18 vols. Markfield: Islamic Foundation, 2001.

Robson, J. "Al-Bayḍāwī." In *The Encyclopaedia of Islam, New Edition*. Ed. by H. A. R. Gibb et al., 13 vols. Leiden: Brill, 1960–2009, vol. 1, 1129.

Saeed, Abdullah. *The Qur'an: An Introduction*. London and New York: Routledge, 2008.

Sakamoto, Ken'ichi. *Koran kyo* [*The Koran Scripture*]. 2 vols. Complete Collection of Holy Scriptures of the World, vols. 14 and 15. Tokyo: Sekai Seiten Zenshu Kanko Kai, 1920.

Sato, Saeed, transl. *Sei kuruan nichia taiyaku chukai* [*The Holy Qur'an: Bilingual Japanese-Arabic Version with Annotations*]. Medina: King Fahd Complex for the Printing of the Holy Quran, 2019.

Sawada, Tatsuichi, transl. *Sei kuruan nihongo yaku* [*The Holy Qur'an: Japanese Translation*]. Qum: The Center for Translation of the Qur'ān, 2013.

Sugita, Hideaki. *Nihon jin no chuto hakken: Gyakuenkinho no naka no hikaku bunkashi* [*The Japanese Discovery of the Middle East: A Comparative Cultural History in Mutual Perspectives*]. Tokyo: University of Tokyo Press, 1995.

Suzuki, Hiroshi (Ahmad). " 'Nihon musurimu kyokai' rekidai kaicho retsuden" [The Biographies of the Presidents of "Japan Muslim Association"]. In *Isuramu to nihonjin* [*Islam and Japanese*]. Ed. by Kasuke Iimori. Tokyo: Kokusho Kankokai, 2011, 155–86.

Takahashi, Goro and Amado Ariga, transl. *Sei koran kyo (Isuramu kyoten)* [*The Holy Koran: The Scripture of Islam*]. Tokyo: Sei Korankyo Kankokai, 1938.

Tanada, Hirofumi. "Sekai to nihon no musurimu jinko 2018" [Estimate of Muslim Population in the World and Japan, 2018]. *Waseda Journal of Human Sciences* 32.2 (2019): 253–62.

Volker, Craig Alan. "On Translating the Holy Qur'ān." *The Annals of Gifu Shotoku Gakuen University* 44 (2005): 19–25.

Wehr, Hans. *A Dictionary of Modern Written Arabic.* Ed. by J. Milton Cowan. Beirut: Librairie du Liban, 1980 (first edition 1961).

Postscript

Shigeru Kamada

The present volume is a collection of research studies in the field of Islamic Studies prepared by fourteen contributors belonging to two groups, one connected with Exeter University in the United Kingdom and the other those affiliated with various universities in Japan. The joint efforts of Professors Kazuo Morimoto and Sajjad Rizvi, the editors of the present work, realized this valuable and significant collection. It is a great pleasure and somewhat a wonder for me to find that Japanese scholars specializing in Islamic and Islamicate studies occupy the majority of contributors in this learned production.

Islamic Studies in Japan started in the first half of the twentieth century and was financially supported by Japan's colonial project in a similar way as occurred in colonialist Europe. However, Imperial Japan's defeat in World War II stopped its further development along a colonialist path. Research institutions were abolished and amassed research materials were broken up. A limited number of Japanese Islamicists who survived wartime had to start over from scratch. Toshihiko Izutsu (1914–93) is an internationally known specialist of Islamic thought, as well as being a philosopher of the "Oriental Philosophy" as he himself claimed to be. He started his academic career during the Wartime, survived the confusion of the Japanese defeat, and continued his studies both at home and abroad to become a globally recognized scholar. Izutsu's case is probably a happy exception.

Half a century ago when I began my research in Islamic Studies, our university library had no meaningful collection of Arabic texts or research monographs on Islamic subjects. We had to choose our research topics from the limited number of texts available to us. We had no choice to initiate research solely based on our personal research interest since we could not enter upon our studies without any relevant texts. In those early days we were very far from our current condition in which we have easy access to almost any classical text or many journal articles through the Internet. It is truly a wonder for me that so many Japanese scholars are actively working in a global setting as evidenced in this present volume.

The fourteen studies included here appear not to be collected or organized from a unified perspective, rather their authors treat a variety of subjects which they themselves now find most interesting. Most of these scholars may belong to a younger generation and live in this world of modernity, whatever sense this has; thus behind their preferred research topic or the method utilized I apprehend an awareness of the problem reflecting the contemporary world situation. Our present age wherein we act and think is characterized by plurality and a confusion of values. Humans seek ways to their goals in this confused situation. This observation may be generally applicable across the global scene, and the Muslim world may not be any exception.

The modern trend of pluralism or confusion of values affects *how* we understand "Islam." The answer may not be uniform or single, but it is certainly important to understand the potential of Islam as widely as possible by investigating the past heritage Muslims left in differing areas. A mode of thinking overshadowed by a major trajectory of thought for a long time yet secretly maintained within a minor group, may possibly function well in the contemporary society. Such cases should be included in the Islamic heritage, on the basis of which one may hope could contribute to the future viability of Islam. To know Islam through its manifold intellectual and spiritual developments, some manifest others hidden, inevitably leads us to appreciate the richness of Islam, from which we may seek clues to solve our contemporary dilemmas or even to realize Islam in a form appropriate for this present age. The meaning of investigations into the abundant Islamic intellectual tradition must be found in our efforts to explore new realities and ideas Muslims produced within their own cultural surroundings.

Scholars of the early unfolding of Islam in the West have often been criticized for implicit Eurocentrism in their approach. Humans wedded to their own value systems cannot easily accept another way of thinking or moral judgment beyond their own inherited tradition. Religious or intellectual achievements in a certain civilization, however, must primarily be observed in its own cultural context. This is not an easy task, yet we should carry out this task to reach a better understanding of our research objects. The "decolonization of knowledge" which one of the editors Sajjad Rizvi mentions in his contribution may be rephrased in the context of Islamic Studies as understanding Islam within its own authentic frame of reference, not in the prevailing framework of the Euro-American mindset (or any other non-Islamic civilization). Rizvi quotes passages from the introduction of Mullā Ṣadrā's *magnus opus* – from them we savour a flavour really different from European philosophy. We should understand Ṣadrā's thought as an integrated or unified mode of wisdom, not merely as a mixture of philosophy *and* religion. So the most desirable way of research seeks to understand Islam in its own cultural context, rather than observing various phenomena in Islam from a non-Islamic (mostly Euro-American) perspective. We have already piled up an enormous amount of knowledge about Islam and Muslim civilization. But there are still more manuscripts and research data no one has used in his/her study, and even more creative approaches to such data which no one has yet imagined in previous studies.

It is no simple task for present day Islamicists to conduct their study of Islam and its civilization in its own authentic cultural context since we are dealing with such a diversity of issues regarding materials and approaches. In such circumstances surrounding Islamic Studies the contributors to this volume bravely chose their research topics and carried out work. The chapters brought together here cover a wide range of topics in the development of thought and history in Islamic societies in the wider sense, and embrace a variety of approaches. Some contributors discuss specific topics of Islam in relation to previous civilizations, which tint Islam in the selected area with a characteristic shade of color. Some make efforts to present an integral image of a chosen thinker whose works have been studied individually but not viewed in their totality, or whose specific text shows only scattered images without much coherency. Yet others conduct their original investigation from fresh points of view in little studied areas. These respective studies aim to elucidate particular problems that have not yet been fully studied. I am confident that this volume must be an important and meaningful step to renew our understanding of Islam and its history and cultures, given that the topics treated here display both the geographical extent and spiritual depths of Islamic civilization.

Among many possible ways the most suitable path for Muslims must be to know thoroughly their own traditional heritage and to apply the acquired legacy of wisdom to the contemporary problems they are now facing. Non-Muslim Islamicists are driven not only by their intellectual curiosity but may also be moved by the strong quest for the true meaning of Islamic wisdom in order to orient their research objects within the cultural context of Islam and thereby indirectly uncover clues for solving their own dilemmas. Treasures buried in the varied marvels of Islamic experience are precious for all humans on our globe. Whether we embrace the particular standpoint of Muslims or do not, it has a cardinal importance for us to make efforts to understand Islam in its totality, including both its manifest and hidden interior aspects.

While we acknowledge the various forms of Islam visible to sight, which are in a sense accumulated forms of judgments made by past generations of Muslim intellectuals, these are not enough to solve all problems that humans, whether Muslims or not, now face. Some insights and judgments have disappeared long ago and lie hidden in the documents sleeping on a shelf in an archive. Certain findings may be well known in a particular cultural arena in Muslim lands, but unknown in other Muslim societies. It may be an important task for Islamicists to make common knowledge and available to all what remains obscured in oblivion, or what no-one today except certain persons in a confined area are aware of.

In the past fifty years our research situation in the field of Islamic Studies has changed so much in Japan as noted above. Human communication on a global scale becomes much easier and rapidly activated especially through the medium of Zoom, which enabled us to convene in 2021 “A Joint Exeter-Tokyo Seminar,” forming the basis of the present volume. Zoom is certainly a convenient and efficient tool of communication, but it cannot fully realize communication in the depth of humanity that integrates body, soul, and spirit. Learning in the Humanities should cover all these human dimensions, and therefore those who work in a confined area of humanities should at least have a keen interest in the totality of human experience. I sincerely hope that such true communication will be realized among the scholars who participated in this project, as implied in the words of a Sage of ancient China, "Is it not delightful to have friends coming from distant quarters?" (*Confucian Analects*, transl. by James Legge, I, 2)

About the Contributors

William Gallois is Professor of the History of the Mediterranean Islamic World at the University of Exeter. His monographic publications include *A History of Violence in the Early Algerian Colony* (2014), *Time, Religion and History* (2008) and *The Amuletic City* (forthcoming 2024).

Emi Goto is Assistant Professor at the Research Institute for Languages and Cultures of Asia and Africa at Tokyo University of Foreign Studies. Her research interests include the intellectual history of contemporary Islam, Qurʾanic studies, and women and gender.

Shigeru Kamada is Emeritus Professor of the University of Tokyo. His research interest covers Islamic mystical philosophy, Shiʿa thought, hermeneutical study of the Qurʾan and hadith, and comparative religion.

Nobuaki Kondo is Professor in Iranian History at Research Institute for Languages and Cultures of Asia and Africa, Tokyo University of Foreign Studies. His research interests include Safavid and Qajar history, Persian documents, shariʿa courts and Islamic law, Islamicate diplomacy and international law, and Persianate culture.

István T. Kristó-nagy is Senior Lecturer in Arabic and Islamic Studies at the University of Exeter. He has published on Islamic social and intellectual history, political and religious thought, advice literature and art. His approach is comparative and interdisciplinary, investigating biological, psychological, and social patterns lying behind political and religious ideas expressed in literary and artworks.

Ryo Mizukami is JSPS Postdoctoral Fellow at the Research Institute for Languages and Cultures of Asia and Africa, Tokyo University of Foreign Studies. His research interests include Sunni-Shiʿi relationship, trans-sectarian reverence for the Twelve Imams, and *faḍāʾil* literature concerning the Twelve Imams in the Medieval Islamic lands.

Kazuo Morimoto is Professor in Islamic and Iranian History at the Institute for Advanced Studies on Asia, University of Tokyo. His research interests cover *sayyids* and *sharīfs* in Muslim societies, Shiʿism, Islamicate historiography (with special reference to genealogy), Persianate studies, and medieval Iranian history.

Tatsuya Nakanishi is Associate Professor at the Institute for Research in Humanities, Kyoto University. His research interests include the intellectual history of Hui Muslims (Chinese-speaking Muslims), especially with respect to their relations with non-Muslim Chinese communities and their reception of Islamic thought from beyond China.

Ian Richard Netton is Emeritus Professor of Islamic Studies at the University of Exeter. He is the author or editor of 23 books and numerous articles and essays. His main research interests include Islamic philosophy and theology, Sufism, comparative religion, semiotics, and anthropology with a particular focus on ritual. He is also the Series Editor for the Routledge Culture and Civilisation in the Middle East Series, the Routledge Sufi Series, and the Edinburgh History of the Islamic Empires Series.

Hisashi Obuchi is a PhD Student in Islamic Studies at Albert-Ludwigs-Universität Freiburg. Supervised by Professor Nadja Germann, he is writing his dissertation on Zayn al-Dīn al-Kaššī (d. before 1228), who is best known as a student of Faḫr al-Dīn al-Rāzī (d. 1210), with a focus on moral philosophy.

Sajjad Rizvi is Professor of Islamic Intellectual History at the University of Exeter. A specialist in philosophical traditions of the Islamic East, he is currently writing a book on contemporary philosophy in the Muslim world.

Keiko Sakurai is Professor at the School of International Liberal Studies, Waseda University. She specializes in comparative sociology and has conducted research on social and educational changes in contemporary Iran and surrounding regions.

Mohammed Sanad obtained his PhD from the University of Exeter. His research focuses on classical Arabic literary criticism and linguistics.

Emily Selove is Senior Lecturer in Medieval Arabic Language and Literature at the University of Exeter, where she is also the head of the Centre for Magic and Esotericism. She is currently translating and co-editing Sirāj al-Dīn al-Sakkākī's *Kitāb al-Shāmil* (Book of the Complete) and writing a book about donkeys titled *The Donkey King: Asinine Symbology in Ancient and Medieval Magic.*

Nozomi Shiratani is Associate Professor in Moroccan politics and Maghreb studies at the Faculty of Foreign Studies, Aichi Prefectural University. Her interests include political systems in MENA region, especially monarchies, Islamist movements, politics of Maghreb countries.

Tetsuro Sumida is a PhD Student at the Graduate School of Letters, Kyoto University. The theme of his PhD dissertation is the intellectual dimension of the religio-political history of Iran in the post-Mongol period, especially the works by the self-claimed *Mahdī*s, such as Sayyid Muḥammad al-Mushaʿshaʿ, Faḍlullah Astarābādī and Muḥammad Nūrbakhsh.